Population Biology

Population Biology

Gerald D. Elseth
Bradley University

Kandy D. Baumgardner
Eastern Illinois University

D. VAN NOSTRAND COMPANY
NEW YORK CINCINNATI TORONTO LONDON MELBOURNE

D. Van Nostrand Company Regional Offices:
New York   Cincinnati

D. Van Nostrand Company International Offices:
London   Toronto   Melbourne

Library of Congress Catalog Card Number: 79-92238
ISBN: 0-442-26235-3

Published by D. Van Nostrand Company
135 West 50th Street, New York, N.Y.   10020

10   9   8   7   6   5   4   3   2   1

Preface

Population Biology is intended for advanced undergraduate and graduate students. Familiarity with the basic principles of integral and differential calculus is assumed, and a knowledge of elementary probability and statistics is helpful. The first two chapters present basic concepts of mathematical modeling and emphasize their use in modeling biological phenomena. The need for precise models of biological systems and the methods by which such models can be formulated mathematically are stressed. The emphasis throughout the text is on model building and testing. For those needing a review of basic operations of calculus, matrix algebra, or statistical testing, we include such material in the Appendix.

Since the approach taken in the text emphasizes the theoretical basis of population biology, problem solving is considered to be of utmost importance if the student expects to obtain an in-depth understanding of the material. We have, therefore, made every effort to include an ample number of problems of varied degree of difficulty at the end of each chapter. The problems are divided into two groups. Immediately following each chapter is a section containing worked example problems designed to illustrate and amplify basic theory and to demonstrate the development of alternative models. A double line sets off example problems which are considered to be rather difficult for the less advanced students. The example problems are organized into subsections designated by the corresponding text headings. It is our belief that the instructor should encourage students to consult these problems immediately upon completion of each major section in the chapter. This will help students grasp the underlying meaning of the theory before they advance to new material. The example problems are an integral part of each chapter and are separated from the body of the text only to avoid disrupting the continuity of reading.

v

In addition to the solved example problems, graded sets of supplementary problems are also furnished which provide necessary repetition of basic principles. These problem exercises are designed to test the reader's comprehension of the subject material and to challenge the ability of the student to apply the information learned to new situations. The answers to these exercises can be found at the end of the book.

We have given a balanced coverage of the concepts of population genetics and population ecology along with their relationship to the modern theory of evolution. More material is presented than is normally covered in a one-semester course, giving instructors with varied backgrounds and interests a chance to pick and choose. Basic principles of population genetics, population ecology, and evolution are integrated into a single text, but in a fashion such that the component parts can be dissected out for individual course needs. The subject matter is organized into four major parts, each being sufficiently complete and containing enough cross references to make different ordering of topics meaningful. The first part, Chapters 1 and 2, presents fundamental information on the development and application of simple mathematical models in population biology. Some instructors may choose not to cover this topic in lecture, but rather treat the section as an appendix. The second part, Chapters 3–6, covers material normally discussed in a course on population genetics. Chapter 3 presents an overview of population genetics early in the text, giving students a general understanding of the goals and methods of this area of study before pursuing the subject in greater detail. It also serves to introduce students to the fundamentals of gene transmission and processes affecting genic variability. Instructors interested in conveying only the most basic principles of population genetics, because of the complexity of the material or because of time limitations, may find it best to omit part or all of Chapters 5 and 6. Chapters 7–11 form a third part that focuses on problems generally regarded as ecological in nature. The chapters proceed from a description of single species populations to a discussion of interspecies relations and community structure. Although the emphasis is on theory, extensive laboratory and field data are presented that lend support to certain models. Instructors wishing to shorten the coverage of population ecology may do so by omitting discussions on species diversity. Finally, the last three chapters comprise a fourth part dealing specifically with evolutionary processes. The treatment of natural selection in Chapter 12 combines concepts of genetics and ecology. Taking full advantage of this material therefore requires previous coverage of Chapters 3, 4, and 8 and parts of Chapters 10 and 11. Certain sections of Chapter 12, such as that on multiple locus systems, can be omitted without loss of continuity.

We would like to acknowledge the valuable comments and criticisms of John Boyer, Union College; Brian Bradley, University of Maryland, Baltimore County; Philip Hedrick, University of Kansas; and Alan Stiven, University of North Carolina, Chapel Hill, who read all or parts of the manuscript during its development. We are also indebted to the highly talented staff of D. Van Nostrand for their excellent suggestions and encouragement.

Contents

Part Two   Genetics of Populations

3.   Population Genetics: An Overview   72

4.   Random Mating and Genetic Equilibrium   109

5.   Components of Variation and Resemblance   141

6.   Inbreeding and Assortative Mating   174

Part Three   Ecology of Populations

Part Four   Evolution of Populations

Introduction

A population is a collective group of organisms of a single species which occupies a particular space at a particular time. Populations, like the individuals that compose them, possess structure and have a life history in that they grow, differentiate, and respond to environmental changes. In addition to the properties which are common to all living systems, populations possess attributes that are unique to groups or aggregates of individuals. For example, density, birth and death rates, and age and spatial distribution are meaningful only in reference to populations and are usefully described in mathematical terms. The properties of populations, particularly those not shared with their component organisms, make up the subject matter of population biology.

The study of populations is inevitably related to that of evolutionary biology. This develops from the fact that populations are the fundamental units of adaptive change. An individual cannot evolve since it has a finite lifespan and a fixed genetic makeup at birth. A population, on the other hand, can maintain itself over long periods of time and can change in genetic composition from one generation to the next. The long-term sequence of changes in the hereditary characteristics of a population is the genetic process of evolution.

Because of its scope and the level of complexity of its unit of study, population biology incorporates elements of a number of different subject areas, including demography, ethology, and systematics. However, its deepest roots lie in two major disciplines: population genetics and population ecology. The first of these, population genetics, deals with the origin and maintenance of variation and the evolutionary consequences of genetic change. Much of the theoretical basis of population genetics was established in the 1920s and early 1930s by the work of three men: R. A. Fisher, J. B. S. Haldane, and Sewall

Wright. After laying the groundwork, in this area, these men continued to dominate the field for several years during which a substantial body of theory developed, far in advance of field observations. Their theoretical work, along with the experimental studies of S. S. Chetverikov, Theodosius Dobzhansky, E. B. Ford, and others, helped to establish the modern or neo-Darwinian synthesis of evolution. The theory as it now stands consists largely of deductions which can be made on the basis of Mendelian laws of gene transmisson. Populations are viewed in terms of genes rather than individuals and evolution in terms of changes in gene frequencies. The evolutionary changes in the frequency of genes are assumed to be directed primarily by the process of natural selection and caused, to a lesser extent, by chance events. On the other hand, the genetic variation which provides the raw materials on which selection can act is believed to originate by mutation and then introduced to neighboring groups by migrational gene flow. Thus, to a large degree, evolution can be pictured as a weeding process in which the fate of new mutant genes is determined by their ability to increase in number through natural selection and to spread to all breeding units of the population.

Population ecology, the second major area of investigation, is the study of the relationships between a population and its environment (biotic and physical) that determine its size and internal organization. Again, the study is of factors affecting spatial and temporal patterns, but in this case the focus is on number of individuals, rather than frequencies of genes, as influenced by dispersal, reproductive rates, age-structure, regulatory mechanisms, and interspecies relationships. Unlike population genetics, which started as a theoretical discipline, population ecology has its roots in natural history. Nonetheless, several theoretical papers of note were published during its early infancy. Perhaps the first theoretical contribution was made by Thomas Malthus in 1798. By comparing the geometric nature of the increase in the number of individuals in the human population over time with a postulated linear increase in food supply, he predicted that reproduction must eventually be checked by the availability of food. Hence, growth cannot proceed indefinitely at a geometric rate. Numerous other articles were subsequently published, including the important theoretical contributions to population dynamics by P. F. Verhulst, A. J. Lotka, V. Volterra, and G. F. Gause. Until recently, however, theory has not received the attention or respect in ecology that it has in the area of genetics. This is largely due to the lack of a theoretical framework comparable to that served in genetics by Mendel's laws of inheritance. Nevertheless, the past twenty years has seen a kindling of interest in the theoretical approach, especially as it relates to evolutionary ecology. This rise in popularity can be attributed in part to the work of one man, Robert MacArthur, who dealt with a broad spectrum of problems ranging from the evolution of optimal strategies of resource allocation among competing populations to the evolution of species abundance and diversity.

Historically, scientists interested in population problems have specialized in either genetics or ecology. The overall effect has been two more-or-less separate schools concentrating their efforts on a common unit of study. Over the years, their methods of approach have grown apart. On the one hand, ecologists have tended to disregard the problems of genetic heterogeneity while geneticists, on the other hand, have ignored the complications of age distribution and fluctuating environments. Additionally, ecologists have concentrated on short-term changes in population density and distribution in response to the biotic environment, whereas geneticists have dealt more with long-term responses of gene frequencies to the physical environment. This trend has started to reverse, since there is now increasing evidence to suggest that ecological time and evolutionary time are commensurate, thus indicating a need for geneticists and ecologists to pool their talents and deal with the problems of age and genetic and environmental heterogeneity simultaneously.

Despite the experimental and theoretical advances that have been made in recent years, the questions confronting a population biologist are many. What are the mechanisms of adaptation? What is the relationship between genotype and phenotype in a changing environment? What is the extent of genetic variation in populations and how is this variation maintained? What is its evolutionary significance? How much of this variation is functional, that is, used to diversity within a habitat or expand into different habitats? How does a population change through time? How do populations adapt to fluctuating and uncertain environments? What factors are involved in the regulation of population size? What variables have a stabilizing effect and which have a destabilizing influence on populations? What relations, if any, exist between stability and complexity? What limits the ability of populations to overcome the biotic controls on spatial distribution and density by means of adaptation? How are species integrated into communities? What are the factors that determine species abundance and diversity? These are just some of the important problems of immediate concern in population biology and represent a few of the questions dealt with in this book. In a general sense, population biologists are proceeding to answer these questions along three interrelated paths: the collection and analysis of field data, the performance of laboratory experiments, and the construction of mathematical models. The first approach usually involves making careful observations and then establishing correlations on the basis of collected data. This is of primary importance since the ultimate concern is what happens in nature (i.e., the field). The second approach involves simplifying nature by developing systems which are of manageable size and complexity In laboratory research, relationships are discovered by conducting experiments under conditions more strictly controlled than those present in nature. Such experiments can employ both genetic and ecological factors as variables and are usually performed by holding all other extraneous (uninteresting) variables constant. Finally, the use of mathematical models permits one to formulate and solve problems by means of mathematical reasoning. Such models can take on many different forms ranging from simple, "explanatory" models, which serve to sharpen our understanding about the processes operating in nature, to complex, "predictive" models, which attempt to describe the future behavior of populations and have obvious practical applications. It is this latter approach, in particular the development of explanatory models, which is emphasized throughout the following chapters.

Part One

Mathematical Models: Applications and Implications

1

Mathematical Models
in Population Biology

Many students find the subject matter of population biology extremely interesting but have difficulty with the basic mathematical concepts in the area. This is largely due to a lack of experience in applying mathematics to biological problems. As is frequently the case, students are asked to take courses in statistics and even calculus and are seldom given the opportunity to apply these analytical skills to anything more demanding than working through the calculations of a chi-square test. Even when mathematical concepts are presented in various textbooks or courses in biology, they are often treated from a purely descriptive viewpoint. Consequently, the student rarely gets to see the entire logical development of a model from its basic set of assumptions. Without this needed experience, many students develop the attitude that mathematical modeling is a pastime of a few which is of little use to practicing biologists. This is far from the truth. At its simplest level, mathematical reasoning helps to clarify relations even when the end result is nothing more than a crude approximation. At its best, mathematical modeling can open up a whole new area to scientific investigation. At the present time, an extensive body of literature is developing in the area of theoretical biology; much of it concerns concepts in population biology. But without some background and experience in the development of mathematical models, much of this theory will remain unintelligible to and neglected by the majority of biology students. It is with this problem in mind that this and the following chapters are written.

We begin with a brief description of the nature and development of mathematical models. This is followed by some concepts and a few tricks in the development of models which can be used to describe population dynamics.

2

It is assumed that students have a good understanding of basic algebraic operations and have been introduced to the most elementary concepts of calculus.

THE NATURE AND DEVELOPMENT OF MATHEMATICAL MODELS

A model is any abstract representation of a real situation which may be formulated verbally, graphically, or in terms of a mathematical equation. All three types are helpful in science since a better understanding of any system is always gained through a knowledge of relationships, whether they be expressed in qualitative or quantitative form. In population biology, however, preference is usually given to mathematical models. This is largely due to their usefulness in developing and testing hypotheses. First of all, a mathematical model is an exact method of representing the individual properties of a system and their various relationships. This exactitude permits predictions to be made with a degree of precision that can never be equaled by mere verbalization. Moreover, the precision gained from an exact set of relationships lends the model to a more clear-cut test by means of experimental and observational data. In fact, at times it is difficult to know what experiment to do without first mathematically exploring the consequences of alternative ideas. This is often the case when more than one hypothesis can explain a given set of observations. An experimental test might then depend on exact relational differences between the various hypotheses that can only be made obvious by the construction of mathematical models. In brief, a mathematical model makes relationships more apparent, predictions more precise, and hypotheses more subject to well-defined experimental tests.

The first step in formulating a mathematical model is to identify those factors which are believed to be acting in the process under study. This usually takes the form of identifying the important dependent and independent variables. The purpose here is to eliminate unimportant details that could make an ensuing analysis unnecessarily complex. One then makes rational idealizations about the process in order to gain a precise mental image of how the component parts of the system might be behaving. This is facilitated in many cases by representing the real situation by means of a simplified diagram which includes all essential features of the process. Once the system is clearly defined, further simplifying assumptions are often made in order to arrive at specific quantitative relations. The end result of this procedure is one or more equations in which the real quantities and processes are replaced by symbols and mathematical operations.

A rather simple biological example of this scheme is illustrated by an analysis of the growth of a laboratory population of bacteria. In this case, growth is measured by the increase in number of viable cells. Therefore, the dependent variable (i.e., the variable to be measured) is cell number. Since reproduction is by fission, each cell will divide and give rise to two daughter cells. Each daughter cell, in turn, divides to yield two new cells, and this process of successive doublings continues with time. Thus, time of measurement is a suitable independent variable.

With the variables defined, the problem now is finding their exact relationship. This is simplified by visualizing the growth of an inoculum of N_o cells in terms of the following sequence of division cycles:

Population Doublings:	0	1	2	3	$\ldots\ldots$	n
Cell Number:	N_o	$2N_o$	$4N_o$	$8N_o$	$\ldots\ldots$	2^nN_o
Time:	0 ———————————— $\int$ $\int \rightarrow t$					

Thus we see that the number of cells present in the population is a geometric function of the number of doublings, or in symbolic form, 2^nN_o.

Now, to arrive at the final expression, we make two simplifying assumptions: (1) factors such as the concentration of nutrients, the space available for growth, and temperature and oxygen level all remain essentially constant during the time of measurement; and (2) there is no initial time lag in beginning the growth process (i.e., all N_o cells are actively growing at time 0). These assumptions mean that a doubling in cell number occurs at regular time intervals. Defining T_d as a constant equal to this time required for doubling, we can then express the number of doublings as $n = t/T_d$. Substituting this into our previous expression, we get $N_t = N_o2^{t/T_d}$, where N_t is the number of cells at time t. This model enables us to predict population size at any time once T_d is known.

Once a model is developed, its validity can be tested by comparing its predictions with observation. Often some disagreement is found, particularly if this is the initial attempt at modeling the process being studied. This requires a reanalysis of the idealizations and assumptions made in its development. Changes in these conditions result in a changed model and thus, automatically, in new information about previously unknown or unappreciated factors involved in the process. When agreement appears to have been found between prediction and observation, then tentative acceptance of the model is justified. We then have a method for representing, explaining, and predicting the phenomenon under investigation, and we are developing an understanding of the process involved.

In applying the understanding gained from such a procedure, we must always keep in mind that a model is an approximation and is good only in light of the assumptions made in its derivation. A certain model may be too restrictive to apply to a wide range of similar phenomena occurring under different conditions. However, a model is not static; it should be continually modified and broadened in attempts to make it more general. The goal of model-building is to derive a model capable of describing a specific situation with a great deal of precision, yet one that is generalized enough to predict the consequences of the process under a wide range of conditions.

There are usually several mathematical relations that one can choose from in order to describe a particular situation. Many predict similar outcomes. Therefore, the proper choice depends to a large extent on the experience and knowledge of the investigator. Futhermore, the mathematical relations used to describe a biological situation can be developed in either deterministic or stochastic form. *Deterministic models* are those which are developed under the assumption that events can be predicted with absolute certainty. Such models actually describe the theoretical average about which any real population is assumed to vary. They are, therefore, reasonable approximations when applied to large populations where random fluctuations (sampling variation) can be ignored. *Stochastic models*, on the other hand, are probabilistic models which incorporate the concepts of random processes and uncertainty. Due to their indeterminate nature, we will postpone any further consideration of stochastic models until after a discussion of probability theory in the next chapter.

The types of mathematical models used throughout the remainder of this text were chosen from several relations which appear to describe the biological processes with reasonable precision. The criterion for choice of form was primarily to unify the concepts discussed. The particular models used are, for the most part, simple enough to allow students to manipulate the relations for themselves, yet general enough to provide biologically useful information.

DETERMINISTIC MODELS AS APPLIED TO POPULATION DYNAMICS

Possibly the simplest way of describing a change in one or more properties of a population is by way of a deterministic model. Such models are usually developed in the form of either difference or differential equations. A *difference equation* would describe the change in a variable such as population size or gene frequency during certain fixed intervals of time. Such equations are appropriate for describing populations which reproduce in discrete nonoverlapping generations and for those populations with overlapping generations but having fixed breeding seasons. They can also be applied to populations of continuous breeders as long as a census is taken at regular intervals (e.g., once a year). A *differential equation*, in turn, would describe changes within a population as a continuous function of time. When applied to variables such as population size or gene frequency, differential equations are generally most suitable for large populations of continuous breeders. As we shall see in the remaining sections of this chapter, however, the distinctions between difference and differential equations are not always clear and they are, in fact, readily interchangeable under a variety of conditions.

First order linear equations.   The simplest mathematical expression that can be used as a deterministic model is a first order linear equation. For discrete time-dependent processes, the appropriate model would be the first order linear difference equation given for the general case as

$$\Delta x_t = ax_t + b \qquad (1.1)$$

where x_t is some time-dependent variable and a and b are constants. In this expression, $\Delta x_t = x_{t+1} - x_t$ and represents the change in x between two successive time intervals t and $t + 1$. In words, a first order linear difference equation is an expression in which the change in a variable x during a single time interval is directly proportional to the value of x at the start of that interval. It is useful in modeling many time-dependent processes in population genetics such as mutation and migration and for describing exponential growth of populations.

A solution for x_t in terms of t can be obtained by first expressing equation (1.1) in terms of a recurrence relation. Adding x_t to both sides of the expression, we obtain

$$x_{t+1} = (1 + a)\, x_t + b \qquad (1.2)$$

If we designate x_t as x_e when $\Delta x_t = 0$, we see that $x_e = -b/a$. Replacing b with $-ax_e$ and subtracting x_e from both sides, (1.2) becomes

$$x_{t+1} - x_e = (1 + a)\,(x_t - x_e)$$

Thus, if we describe the development of x over time by the sequence of numbers $x_o, x_1, x_2, \ldots, x_{t-1}, x_t$ and assume that the values of a and x_e remain constant during successive time intervals, it becomes apparent that

$$x_1 - x_e = (1 + a)\,(x_o - x_e)$$
$$x_2 - x_e = (1 + a)\,(x_1 - x_e) = (1 + a)^2\,(x_o - x_e)$$
$$x_3 - x_e = (1 + a)\,(x_2 - x_e) = (1 + a)^3\,(x_o - x_e)$$

Extending this pattern to time t, we then get

$$x_t - x_e = (1 + a)^t\,(x_o - x_e) \qquad \text{or} \qquad x_t + b/a = (1 + a)^t\,(x_o + b/a) \qquad (1.3)$$

in which x is related to time in an exponential manner.

There are some specific cases of (1.3) which have special importance to population biology and, therefore, need to be analyzed in greater detail. For instance, if the proportionality constant, a, is positive ($a > 0$) and the value of b is equal to zero, we then have the classic exponential growth equation

$$x_t = (1 + a)^t x_o$$

On the other hand, if $-1 < a < 0$ and x_e is some positive value, (1.3) describes a case where the difference between x and x_e will gradually diminish such that x will approach x_e as an asymptote. We can then regard x_e as a stable equilibrium point. However, when $a < -1$, the approach to x_e is oscillatory in nature; the oscillations being damped when $-2 < a < -1$ and increasing in amplitude

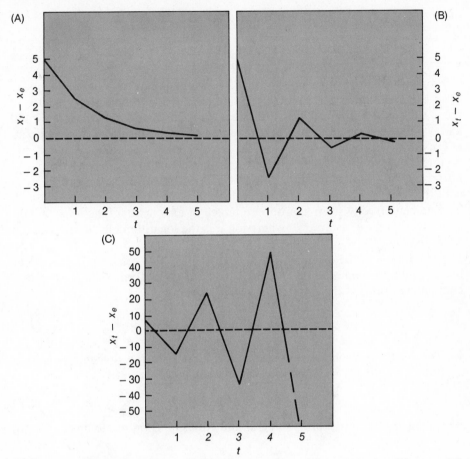

Figure 1.1   Plots of equation (1.3) for different values of the constant a. (A) a = −0.5; (B) a = −1.5; (C) a = −2.5.

when $a < -2$. These examples are illustrated in Figure 1.1 by plots of equation (1.3) for different values of a. Observe that when a is a large negative value, the equilibrium at x_e is no longer stable and x will continue to diverge from this value.

When the value of a is small in comparison to one, equation (1.3) can be modified further by approximating $(1 + a)^t$ as e^{at}, e being the base of natural logarithms. The value of e is approximately equal to 2.718 and is defined as the limit

$$e = \lim_{a \to 0} (1 + a)^{1/a}$$

Thus, under conditions of small a, equation (1.3) becomes approximately

$$x_t - x_e = (1 + a)^t (x_o - x_e)$$
$$= [(1 + a)^{1/a}]^{at} (x_o - x_e)$$
$$= e^{at}(x_o - x_e)$$

For a numerical example, suppose that a bacterial population increases in size at an exponential rate such that $x_t = (1 + a)^t x_o \simeq x_o e^{at}$ where x_o is the size at the start of incubation and x_t is the size after t minutes of growth. If $x_o = 100$ and $a = 0.01$ per minute, what is the size of the population after, say, five hours of growth? To answer this question, let $t = (5)(60) = 300$ minutes. Hence, the product $(a)(t) = (0.01)(300) = 3$ and x_t will be equal to $(100)(e^3)$ or, approximately, 2,000. For the benefit of those who have not worked to any great extent with the base of natural logarithms, values of e^z (z being some variable) can be obtained directly from appropriate tables of exponential functions or indirectly by writing e^z as $10^{(\log e)z}$ where log e is the logarithm of e to the base 10 equal to about 0.434.

In addition to the discrete models that we have just considered, first order linear equations can also be expressed in differential form. The appropriate continuous analog is the differential equation

$$dx/dt = ax + b \tag{1.4}$$

where dx/dt is the derivative of x with respect to time, t. To find a solution, we approach the problem in a manner analogous to the preceding discrete situation by letting $x = x_e = -b/a$ when $dx/dt = 0$. We get

$$dx/dt = a(x - x_e) \tag{1.5}$$

Rewriting (1.5) in terms of its integral and choosing appropriate limits, we get

$$\int_{x_o}^{x_t} \frac{dx}{x - x_e} = a \int_0^t dt$$

which yields upon integration (see Appendix II)

$$\ln[(x_t - x_o)/(x_o - x_e)] = at \qquad \text{or} \qquad x_t - x_e = e^{at}(x_o - x_e) \tag{1.6}$$

where the symbol ln stands for the logarithm to the base e (ln x = 2.303 log x). The latter equation was written in this way in order to illustrate that it is the same as the approximate solution obtained for the preceding difference model in which we assumed small values of a. Thus, as long as the constant of proportionality, a, in a first order linear equation is small (on the order of 0.01 or less), difference and differential equations predict basically the same results. Note that the first order linear differential equation, in contrast to a difference equation, will never predict an oscillatory approach to an equilibrium condition, regardless of the value of a. Its approach to the limiting asymptote must always be gradual and smooth.

First order nonlinear equations.   In addition to the first order linear equations which, as we have observed, give rise to exponential solutions, there are also a few first order nonlinear equations which are of importance in population biology, particularly in describing the growth of populations when limited by food or space. One that is frequently used in this regard is a difference equation of the form

$$\Delta x_t = (a - bx_{t+1})x_t = \frac{ax_t - bx_t^2}{1 + bx_t} \tag{1.7}$$

where, again, a and b are constants. In this equation, $\Delta x_t = 0$ at two different values of x_t: $x_t = 0$ and $x_t = x_e = a/b$. Considering only the latter, nontrivial case and making this substitution for x_e, we obtain

$$\Delta x_t = \frac{ax_t(1 - x_t/x_e)}{1 + ax_t/x_e} \tag{1.8}$$

As a biological example, suppose that a population reproduces in discrete, nonoverlapping generations and that Δx_t in (1.8) describes the increase in population size during generation t. Since Δx_t is positive for all values of x_t between 0 and x_e and is negative for all values of x_t greater than x_e, the population must increase in size when it is below x_e and decrease in size when above it. Hence, the parameter x_e must represent an equilibrium level to which the size of a population will tend to approach as a consequence of growth. This is shown more clearly in Figure 1.2A in terms of a plot of Δx_t versus x_t. Note that Δx_t does not increase linearly with x_t but, instead, reaches a maximum, at intermediate values of x_t and then continues to decline in a curvilinear manner, eventually cutting the x_t axis at the value x_e. The value of x_t when Δx_t is maximum (x_{max}) can be obtained by taking the derivative of this equation with respect to x_t and setting it equal to zero. The derivative becomes

$$d(\Delta x_t)/dx_t = (a - 2ax_t/x_e - a^2x_t^2/x_e^2)/(1 + ax_t/x_e)^2$$

which, when set equal to zero and solved for $x_t = x_{max}$, gives rise to

$$x_{max} = (x_e/a)[(1 + a)^{1/2} - 1]$$

This describes a positively skewed curve with the maximum displaced towards the origin. Note, however, that if the constant a is very small in value such that the denominator in the derivative can be taken as unity and the a-squared term in the numerator can be ignored in comparison with the other terms, then $d(\Delta x_t)/dx_t = a - 2ax_t/x_e$. The resulting curve is symmetrical above $\Delta x_t = 0$ with a maximum occurring at $\frac{1}{2}x_e$.

A solution to equation (1.8) can be found by first writing it in the form of a recurrence relation. By adding x_t to both sides, we obtain

$$x_{t+1} = \frac{(1 + a)x_t}{1 + ax_t/x_e} \tag{1.9}$$

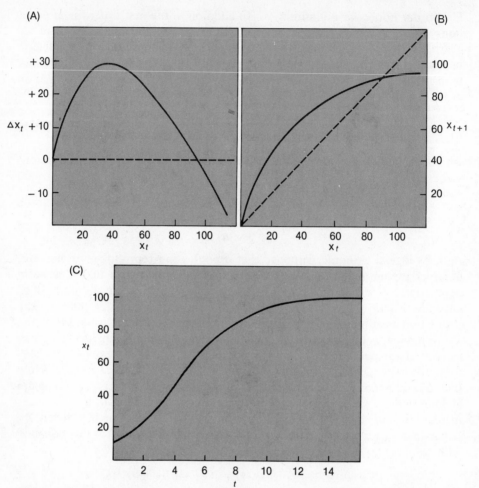

Figure 1.2. Changes predicted by equations (1.8), curve (A); (1.9), curve (B); and (1.10), curve (C). Observe that an equilibrium is established without oscillations. It is assumed that a = 2 in the first two plots and a = 0.65 in the last case.

This relation is pictured in Figure 1.2B in terms of a plot of x_{t+1} versus x_t. The exact form of this relationship is commonly referred to as a rectangular hyperbola in which the dependent variable x_{t+1} gradually approaches a maximum value of $(1 + a)x_e/a$, in this case, when x_t is increased indefinitely.

Now, if we rewrite (1.9) as $x_{t+1}/(x_{t+1} - x_e) = (1 + a)x_t/(x_t - x_e)$, we can then find a general solution as follows:

$$\frac{x_1}{x_1 - x_e} = (1 + a)\,\frac{x_o}{x_o - x_e}$$

$$\frac{x_2}{x_2 - x_e} = (1 + a)\frac{x_1}{x_1 - x_e} = (1 + a)^2\frac{x_0}{x_0 - x_e}$$

$$\frac{x_3}{x_3 - x_e} = (1 + a)\frac{x_2}{x_2 - x_e} = (1 + a)^3\frac{x_0}{x_0 - x_e}$$

Continuing this process up to generation t, we obtain

$$\frac{x_t}{x_t - x_e} = (1 + a)^t\frac{x_0}{x_0 - x_e}$$

or, when solved for x_t,

$$x_t = \frac{x_e x_0(1 + a)^t}{(x_e - x_0) + x_0(1 + a)^t} \tag{1.10}$$

This expression is plotted as x_t versus t in Figure 1.2C. As the graph illustrates, equation (1.10) predicts an S-shaped curve similar in outline to the sigmoid growth curve observed for a number of different species. We do not mean to imply that this is the only relationship which gives rise to a S-shaped curve; many do. However, this is one expression which is frequently used to model such growth patterns.

When the value of a is small, $(1 + a)^t$ in equation (1.10) can be approximated as e^{at}. This yields upon rearrangement

$$x_t = \frac{x_e}{1 + \dfrac{(x_e - x_0)}{x_0}e^{-at}} \tag{1.11}$$

This expression is usually simpler to work with than is (1.10) due to the ease with which e^{-at} can be computed from appropriate tables.

While arriving at the preceding solutions, we have assumed that the parameter, a, possesses some value other than zero. When $a = 0$, we must apply a different approach in order to obtain a solution. To show this, we shall rewrite (1.7) as a recurrence relation in which $a = 0$. This yields

$$x_{t+1} = \frac{x_t}{1 + bx_t} \tag{1.12}$$

This general form of recurrence relation is frequently encountered in population genetics when describing the effects of assortative mating (Chapter 6) and in certain selection models (Chapter 12). We can obtain a general solution as follows:

$$x_1 = \frac{x_0}{1 + bx_0}$$

$$x_2 = \frac{x_1}{1 + bx_1} = \frac{x_o/(1 + bx_o)}{1 + bx_o/(1 + bx_o)} = \frac{x_o}{1 + 2bx_o}$$

$$x_3 = \frac{x_2}{1 + bx_2} = \frac{x_o/(1 + 2bx_o)}{1 + bx_o/(1 + 2bx_o)} = \frac{x_o}{1 + 3bx_o}$$

Extending this approach to the end of time interval t, we have

$$x_t = \frac{x_o}{1 + tbx_o} \tag{1.13}$$

Thus, when $a = 0$, x_t will decrease with time in a curvilinear manner. By taking the reciprocal of the above equation, we see that it can also be written as $1/x_t = bt + 1/x_o$. In this case, a plot of $1/x_t$ versus t should yield a straight line. This fact has been used to distinguish equation (1.13) from a host of other relationships which predict similar curvilinear reductions in the dependent variable.

So far in this section, we have only been concerned with the nonlinear difference model given in general form by equation (1.7). The continuous analog of this expression would be the differential equation

$$dx/dt = ax - bx^2$$
$$= ax(1 - x/x_e) \tag{1.14}$$

where $x_e = a/b$. This differential equation was introduced into population dynamics as a model for the growth of populations in a limited environment by Verhulst in 1838. It has since become known to population biologists as the logistic model for population growth. This expression can be solved by first writing it as

$$\int_{x_o}^{x_t} \frac{x_e dx}{x(x_e - x)} = a \int_0^t dt$$

Now, integrating over these limits, we get (see Appendix II)

$$\ln\left[\frac{x_t(x_e - x_o)}{x_o(x_e - x_t)}\right] = at \quad \text{or} \quad x_t = \frac{x_e}{1 + \dfrac{(x_e - x_o)}{x_o} e^{-at}}$$

Note that, when solved for x_t, the expression is the same as equation (1.11). Again we see an example of where discrete and continuous models, though slightly different in their starting form, predict basically the same results. As one might gather from this and previous examples, the choice of whether a discrete or a continuous model should be used can be somewhat arbitrary, especially when an investigator is only concerned with obtaining an approximate solution. In fact, theoretical biologists quite often attempt to describe the dynamics of seasonal breeding populations with the aid of differential equations such as the logistic model. This is not because they fail to understand the biology of the situation; they are quite aware of it. The investigator feels that what he gains in convenience from using a simpler form of mathematical equation more than compensates for the obvious loss in accuracy. This, of course, is a highly subjective matter which is open to criticism.

The case where $a = 0$ also has a continuous analog. It is the differential equation

$$dx/dt = -bx^2 \tag{1.15}$$

This expression has been used quite extensively in the past to describe survivorship in populations in which individuals are competing for food or space. If x is the size of the population at some moment in time, the equation states that the rate of reduction in the number of survivors is directly proportional to the number of competitive encounters between them, expressed by the square of the existing size (x^2). This is usually a reasonable first approximation.

Equation (1.15) can be solved by writing it as

$$\int_{x_o}^{x_t} \frac{-dx}{x^2} = b \int_0^t dt$$

Integration will then yield (see Appendix II)

$$1/x_t - 1/x_o = bt \qquad \text{or} \qquad x_t = \frac{x_o}{1 + tbx_o}$$

Note that this solution is the same as the discrete analog expressed by equation (1.13).

Second order linear equations.   The last examples of the types of expressions used as deterministic models in population biology that we shall consider are the second order linear equations. In the discrete case, such models can be exemplified in terms of a finite difference equation of the form

$$\Delta^2 x_t = a\Delta x_t - bx_t \tag{1.16}$$

where $\Delta^2 x_t = \Delta x_{t+1} - \Delta x_t = (x_{t+2} - x_{t+1}) - (x_{t+1} - x_t) = x_{t+2} - 2x_{t+1} + x_t$. Hence, (1.16) would correspond to the recurrence relation

$$x_{t+2} - 2x_{t+1} + x_t = ax_{t+1} - ax_t - bx_t$$

which, after collecting like terms, becomes

$$x_{t+2} = (2 + a)x_{t+1} - (1 + a + b)x_t \tag{1.17}$$

This model might arise in population dynamics when the size of a population is not only dependent on the size of its parental generation (x_{t+1}) but also on the size of its grandparental generation (x_t). Such might be the case for an annually reproducing population of herbivores in which the reproductive potential depends on the amount of vegetation consumed. If the population temporarily disrupts its range through overgrazing, the reproductive potential of the parents might depend on the amount consumed, and thus on the population size, in the previous year.

Solutions to (1.17) can be found by first writing the equation as

$$x_{t+2} - Bx_{t+1} + Cx_t = 0$$

where $B = 2 + a$ and $C = 1 + a + b$. Now assume a solution of the form $x_t = k\lambda^t$ as encountered for first order linear equations. Upon making this substitution into our recurrence relation, we obtain

$$k\lambda^{t+2} - kB\lambda^{t+1} + kC\lambda^t = \lambda^2 - B\lambda + C = 0$$

This is a quadratic equation with two roots

$$\lambda_1 = \frac{1}{2}B + \frac{1}{2}\sqrt{B^2 - 4C} = \frac{1}{2}(2 + a) + \frac{1}{2}\sqrt{a^2 - 4b}$$

and

$$\lambda_2 = \frac{1}{2}B - \frac{1}{2}\sqrt{B^2 - 4C} = \frac{1}{2}(2 + a) - \frac{1}{2}\sqrt{a^2 - 4b}$$

If $B^2 - 4C > 0$ (or $a^2 - 4b > 0$), both roots are real. Hence, the general solution can be expressed as a linear combination of the two basic solutions $k_1\lambda_1^t$ and $k_2\lambda_2^t$ as follows:

$$x_t = k_1\lambda_1^t + k_2\lambda_2^t \tag{1.18}$$

A simple proof of this expression is given in Appendix III. In this general solution, the values of the constants k_1 and k_2 are chosen to fit initial conditions and can, therefore, be determined from knowledge of x_o and x_1. For instance, when $t = 0$, $x_o = k_1 + k_2$; whereas, when $t = 1$, $x_1 = k_1\lambda_1 + k_2\lambda_2$. Solving for k_1 and k_2, we then get

$$k_1 = (x_1 - x_o\lambda_2)/(\lambda_1 - \lambda_2) \quad \text{and} \quad k_2 = (\lambda_1 x_o - x_1)/(\lambda_1 - \lambda_2)$$

For a numerical example, suppose that an annual population grows according to the relation $x_{t+2} = 5x_{t+1} - 4x_t$ where t, $t + 1$, and $t + 2$ are consecutive years. We can then calculate λ_1 and λ_2 as follows: $\lambda_1 = \frac{1}{2}(5) + \frac{1}{2}\sqrt{25 - 16} = 4$ and $\lambda_2 = \frac{1}{2}(5) - \frac{1}{2}\sqrt{25 - 16} = 1$. Hence, $x_t = k_1(4)^t + k_2$. To obtain values for k_1 and k_2, say that the population was measured during the first two years and found to be $x_o = 2$ and $x_1 = 8$. Substituting the required values into the pair of expressions for k_1 and k_2, we determine that $k_1 = 2$ and $k_2 = 0$. Thus we see that the solution for this specific example can be given as $x_t = 2^{2t+1}$.

In contrast to the above case, if $B^2 - 4C < 0$ (or $a^2 - 4b < 0$), λ_1 and λ_2 are complex numbers. The general solution then becomes (see Appendix III)

$$x_t = (C)^{\frac{1}{2}t} [k_1\cos(\theta t) + k_2\sin(\theta t)] \tag{1.19}$$

where θ is the angle for which the cosine is $B/2\sqrt{C}$, symbolized as $\theta = \cos^{-1}(B/2\sqrt{C})$. This expression predicts an oscillatory change in the value of x_t. Note that when $C < 1$, the oscillations are damped; whereas values of $C > 1$ lead to oscillations of increasing amplitude. The special case in which $C = 1$ is illustrated in terms of a numerical example where a population is assumed to grow according to the recurrence relation $x_{t+2} = \sqrt{3}\, x_{t+1} - x_t$. In this case, the roots are complex and, since $B = \sqrt{3}$ and $C = 1$, the value of $\theta = \cos^{-1}(\sqrt{3}/2) = \pi/6$ in radian measure. If we also assume for the purpose of solving this problem that $x_o = 2$ and $x_1 = 2\sqrt{3}$, we then get $k_1 = 2$ and $k_2 = [2\sqrt{3} - 2\cos(\pi/6)]/\sin(\pi/6) = 2\sqrt{3}$. Hence, our specific solution becomes $x_t = 2\cos(\pi t/6) + 2\sin(\pi t/6)$. We would, therefore, expect to observe periodic changes in the size of this population with a constant average amplitude of oscillation.

Having described the solutions for second order difference equations, we can now extend this approach to the solution of differential equations of the same order. The simplest form of a second order linear differential equation can be expressed as

$$d^2x/dt^2 = a\,dx/dt - bx \tag{1.20}$$

where $d^2x/dt^2 = d(dx/dt)/dt$ and is the second derivative of x with respect to time, t. As one might expect from the way the differential equation is written, we can approach a solution in a manner analogous to that taken with its discrete analog. First, we assume a solution of the form $x = ke^{\lambda t}$ which is similar to the solution of a first order differential equation. Since $dx/dt = \lambda k e^{\lambda t}$ and $d^2x/dt^2 = \lambda^2 k e^{\lambda t}$, their substitution into equation (1.20) yields

$$\lambda^2 k e^{\lambda t} - a\lambda k e^{\lambda t} + bk e^{\lambda t} = \lambda^2 - a\lambda + b = 0$$

Again we have a quadratic equation with two roots:

$$\lambda_1 = \frac{1}{2}a + \frac{1}{2}\sqrt{a^2 - 4b} \quad\text{and}\quad \lambda_2 = \frac{1}{2}a - \frac{1}{2}\sqrt{a^2 - 4b}$$

Thus, if $a^2 - 4b > 0$, both roots are real and we can express the general solution as

$$x_t = k_1 e^{\lambda_1 t} + k_2 e^{\lambda_2 t} \tag{1.21}$$

On the other hand, when $a^2 - 4b < 0$, both roots are complex. Using logic similar to that applied in the discrete case, the general solution can then be written in the following form:

$$x_t = e^{\frac{1}{2}at}[k_1\cos(\theta t) + k_2\sin(\theta t)] \tag{1.22}$$

where $\theta = \frac{1}{2}\sqrt{4b - a^2}$. Thus, we see that oscillations will develop. They are damped when $a < 0$ and will increase in amplitude when $a > 0$. When $a = 0$, the exponential term drops out and oscillations are expected to occur with constant amplitude. This latter case corresponds to the differential equation $d^2x/dt^2 = -bx$ which is the basic expression for a harmonic oscillator.

NUMERICAL SOLUTIONS AND LINEAR APPROXIMATIONS

Although the emphasis in the foregoing sections has been placed on finding solutions to linear equations, a number of the models which are currently being used in an attempt to realistically describe natural populations are not linear and, furthermore, many cannot be solved analytically. Even with these complications, such equations still serve as useful models for predictive purposes. With the coming of age of computers, one is no longer restricted to the use of simple mathematical equations for which tabulated solutions exist. Numerical solutions can be obtained for almost any equation with the aid of a digital computer. Even without access to a computer, it is quite often desirable and comparatively simple to obtain an approximate solution by applying an iterative procedure with nothing more than a pocket calculator. An example is the growth equation expressed by the following recurrence relation:

$$x_{t+1} = 300(1 - e^{-0.01x_t})$$

Although this equation does not have a tabulated solution in which x can be expressed as a simple function of time, an approximate numerical solution can be obtained by substituting different values of x_t and calculating what happens. For example, if the initial population were $x_o = 50$, our values would appear as follows:

t	0	1	2	3	4	5
x_t	50	118	208	262	278	281
x_{t+1}	118	208	262	278	281	282

The relationship described by this set of numbers is seen more clearly in the graph in Figure 1.3. Note that the numerical solution of x versus t describes an S-shaped growth curve somewhat similar in overall appearance to that described by the logistic equation. The major difference lies in the fact that the inflection point for the data in Figure 1.3 falls closer to the initial value than that expected for logistic growth.

Another way in which a solution can be found for a complex nonlinear equation is by first converting the expression to a linear form. Although a solution can usually be found for the linear form of the equation, it is normally an approximation which only holds for small values of x. For example, suppose that an equation contains the exponential function e^{ax} in which a is a constant. This function can be written in the form of an infinite series as

$$e^{ax} = 1 + ax + \frac{(ax)^2}{2!} + \ldots + \frac{(ax)^n}{n!} + \ldots$$

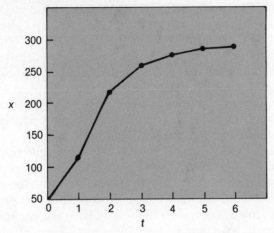

Figure 1.3.   A plot of the recurrence relation $x_{t+1} = 300\,(1 - e^{-0.01\,x_t})$ over 6 generations.

Thus if ax is small, on the order of 0.01 or less, the terms in which x is raised to powers of 2 or greater can be reasonably ignored when compared with x. Hence. for small values of ax, we can approximate e^{ax} as $1 + ax$. This approximation quite often simplifies the mathematics considerably.

A similar approximation which can be used under basically the same conditions is one involving an expression of the form $(1 + x)^n$. In this case, we employ the binomial expansion as follows:

$$(1 + x)^n = 1 + nx + \frac{n(n-1)}{2!}x^2 + \frac{n(n-1)(n-2)}{3!}x^3 + \dots$$

Again, if x is small, we can ignore the terms with higher powers of x and approximate $(1 + x)^n$ as $1 + nx$ under these conditions.

Yet another linear approximation which is frequently made in similar situations is one in which $-\ln(1 - x)$ is taken as being equal to x. The basis for this approximation can be shown by expressing $-\ln(1 - x)$ in terms of the integral

$$-\ln(1 - x) = \int (1 - x)^{-1}\, dx$$
$$= \int (1 + x + x^2 + \dots)\, dx$$

in which $(1 - x)^{-1}$ is expanded according to the binomial theorem. Integrating term by term, we get the infinite series

$$-\ln(1 - x) = x + \frac{x^2}{2} + \frac{x^3}{3} + \dots$$

which is essentially equal to x when x is small.

THE STABILITY OF AN EQUILIBRIUM

When constructing deterministic population models, it is often necessary to test for the stability of equilibrium points. Such equilibria are said to be stable if populations, when perturbed, return to their equilibrium values. It is sometimes convenient to think of a stable equilibrium as a point of attraction and an unstable equilibrium as a point of repulsion. This is shown graphically by the plots in Figure 1.4. Graph (a) represents a plot of one particular relationship between the values of x (population size, gene frequency, etc.) in two successive unit time intervals, t and $t + 1$. In this example, the equilibrium line for which $x_{t+1} = x_t$ is plotted as a 45° diagonal. Thus all values of x_{t+1} above the line correspond to positive values of Δx_t. The reverse is true for points below the equilibrium line. This is also indicated by a corresponding plot of Δx_t versus x_t in graph (b). In this latter case, however, all potential equilibrium values fall on the line $\Delta x_t = 0$. Two equilibrium points are shown in this example. The first, $\hat{x}_1$, is unstable since perturbations cause x_{t+1} to continue to move away from the point in either one direction or another. In contrast, the second, $\hat{x}_2$, is an attracting fixed point. In this case, departures from $\hat{x}_2$ result in the eventual return of x_{t+1} to this value. These results are extended to a more complex x_{t+1} versus x_t relationship in Figure 1.5. Note that whenever the equilibrium line is approached from above, the resulting equilibrium is potentially stable; whereas, if approached from below, an unstable situation develops. As a consequence of this, successive equilibrium points will always alternate with regard to their ability to attract or repel the variable x. Thus if the initial point is attracting, the remaining points will alternate as repelling—attracting—repelling—attracting and so on.

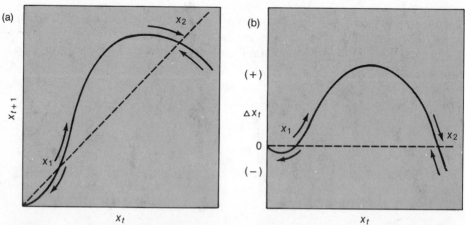

Figure 1.4. Plots of a relationship between values of x in two successive unit time intervals showing two equilibrium points, x_1 and x_2. The arrows show the direction the population will take given departures from the equilibrium values.

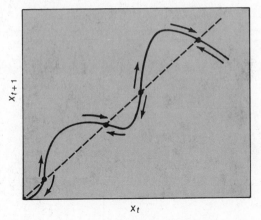

Figure 1.5.   A plot of x_{t+1} versus x_t showing four equilibrium points which alternate with regard to potential stability.

Time delays and stability.   If a time lag is incorporated into a mathematical model, as in the case of a linear difference equation where the time delay is exactly one unit interval, there is a tendency for a variable to overcompensate when disturbed and overshoot the equilibrium point. When this happens, the return to equilibrium may be achieved through damped oscillations rather than monotonically through exponential damping. Furthermore, if the tendency to oscillate is sufficiently great so that the disturbance will amplify itself, instability can arise at what would normally be regarded as a stable or attracting point through oscillations of increasing amplitude. This tendency of a system to oscillate can be measured in terms of its *characteristic return time*, T_R, which gives an estimate of the time required for a population to return to its equilibrium value following a disturbance. To arrive at a relationship for T_R, consider a population variable x described by the following difference equation:

$$\Delta x_t = a - bx_t$$

in which b is the regression coefficient (i.e., slope) of a plot of Δx_t versus x_t and where the equilibrium value of x is $x_e = a/b$. By letting $a = bx_e$, we can write

$$b = (x_t - x_{t+1})/(x_t - x_e)$$

Hence,

$$x_{t+1} - x_e = (1 - b)(x_t - x_e)$$

Now suppose that the population is disturbed from the equilibrium, x_e, to a point x_t. Two possible paths by which a return to equilibrium is achieved are shown in Figure 1.6. It is apparent from the geometric relations which are shown that the difference $(t + T_R) - t$ is to $(t + 1) - t$ as $x_t - x_e$ is to $x_t - x_{t+1}$. Thus,

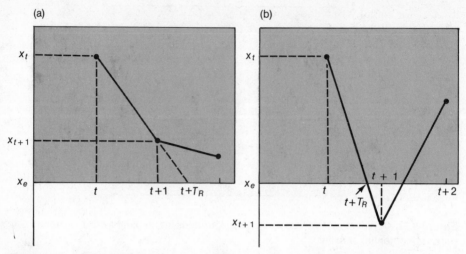

Figure 1.6. Two possible paths by which a return to equilibrium is achieved showing the relationship between the characteristic return time (T_R) and the generation time. Graph (a) shows an approach to equilibrium when the value of b is less than unity while graph (b) shows an approach when b is greater than unity. (Adapted from R. M. May et al., 1974. J. Anim. Ecol. 43: 747.)

$$T_R = (x_t - x_e)/(x_t - x_{t+1}) \qquad (1.23)$$

By comparing this relationship to that given for b, we get

$$T_R = 1/b$$

and

$$x_{t+1} - x_e = (1 - 1/T_R)\,(x_o - x_e)$$

The conditions required for stability in this case are summarized in Table 1.1. Observe that when $T_R < 0$, x_e is a repelling fixed point since, once disturbed, the value of x will continue to diverge from this point through exponential growth or decay. On the other hand, x_e is an attracting point when $T_R > 0$. It is important to note, however, that oscillations do occur when $T_R < 1$, becoming divergent for values of $T_R < \frac{1}{2}$. Thus, we see that if the characteristic return

TABLE 1.1.   Stability criteria for the linear difference model.

Range of b	Range of T_R	Stability
$b < 0$	$T_R < 0$	Unstable; divergent exponential
$0 < b < 1$	$T_R > 1$	Stable; convergent exponential
$1 < b < 2$	$\frac{1}{2} < T_R < 1$	Stable; convergent oscillation
$b > 2$	$T_R < \frac{1}{2}$	Unstable; divergent oscillation

time is too small when compared to the normal time delay in the system (one generation in this case), even an attracting point will be unstable.

The concept of a characteristic return time can also be applied to a differential equation. To do so, let $a = \alpha \, \Delta t$ and $b = \beta \, \Delta t$. Substituting into the difference equation $\Delta x_t = a - bx_t$ and expressing the derivative of x with respect to t as $dx/dt = \lim_{\Delta t \to 0} (\Delta x_t / \Delta t)$, we then get

$$dx/dt = \alpha - \beta x$$

The characteristic return time can now be redefined in a more general way as $T_R = 1/\beta$ which will equal $1/b$ only when $\Delta t = 1$. Observe that for a linear differential equation in which Δt approaches zero and there is no added time lag, an attracting fixed point can only be approached through exponential damping since any value of β other than zero must now be larger than the normal time delay in the system.

Local versus global stability.   So far, the discussion on the stability of an equilibrium has been confined to the analysis of local (or neighborhood) stability. A local stability analysis of this sort involves determining the results of very small perturbations from the equilibrium value. By investigating the behavior of populations in the vicinity of the equilibrium point, one can demarcate the parameter values that result in exponential and oscillatory damping from those that lead to divergent oscillations. These two regions of parameter space (i.e., regions of stability and instability) are divided by a line of neutral stability in which the system continues to oscillate at an amplitude determined by the extent of the initial disturbance.

In addition to analyzing the local stability of an equilibrium situation, it is also possible to determine its stability with respect to large amplitude disturbances; that is, its global stability. For linear equations, as we have seen, a local stability analysis also describes the global stability of the system since the resulting departures from the equilibrium point also hold for large perturbations. This is not the case, however, for nonlinear equations. To illustrate, consider the difference equation

$$\Delta x_t = (b - cx_t)x_t \tag{1.24}$$

which has been used to model the growth of populations with discrete, non-overlapping generations (Maynard Smith, 1968). The recurrence form of this equation (i.e., $x_{t+1} = (1 + b)x_t - cx_t^2$) is plotted as x_{t+1} versus x_t in Figure 1.7. Note that the curve has a critical point, $dx_{t+1}/dx_t = 0$, at intermediate values of x_t. If the critical point is to the left of x_e, as shown in this example, the curve can pass through the equilibrium point with a negative slope. This implies that the function contains a sufficient time lag to produce an overshoot of the equilibrium value and result in oscillations.

A local stability analysis can be performed on this function by restricting

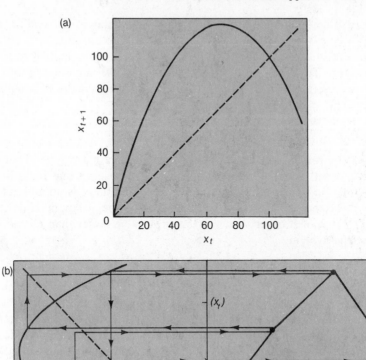

Figure 1.7. (a) Plot of the recurrence form of equation (1.24) as x_{t+1} versus x_t. (b) Analysis of the time course from graph (a).

considerations to only small departures from equilibrium. We can then approximate the relationship between x_{t+1} and x_t by a straight line drawn tangent to the curve at the point of intersection with the 45° diagonal (Figure 1.8). The equation of this line can be given as

$$x_{t+1} - x_e = (dx_{t+1}/dx_t)_{x_e} (x_t - x_e)$$

where $(dx_{t+1}/dx_t)_{x_e}$ is the slope of the x_{t+1} versus x_t curve at $x_t = x_e$. Differentiating equation (1.24) and replacing x_t with x_e, we get

$$(dx_{t+1}/dx_t)_{x_e} = 1 + b - 2cx_e = 1 - b$$

Thus, as before, the tendency to oscillate can be predicted from the value of b or from the characteristic return time $T_R = 1/b$.

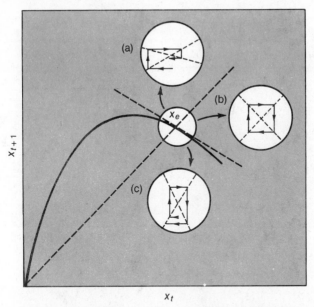

Figure 1.8.   A representative plot of x_{t+1} versus x_t showing a straight-line approximation. For small displacements about the equilibrium level, the proposed relationship can be expressed in the form of a linear equation. The inserts show possible trajectories depending on the slope of the tangent to the curve at the point x_e. (a) a slope less than 2, convergent oscillations; (b) a slope equal to 2, oscillations of equal amplitude; (c) a slope greater than 2, divergent oscillations.

Although a neighborhood analysis provides a useful first approximation as to the stability of nonlinear systems, a more complete or global analysis is needed when oscillations are predicted having increasing amplitudes ($b > 2$, $T_R < \frac{1}{2}$). The behavior of nonlinear difference equations in this region of parameter space has been described by May and Oster (1976). They have shown that for many nonlinear models, such oscillations are in fact bounded above and below by finite and positive maximum and minimum values. To illustrate, reconsider the effects of increasing the value of b on the dynamical behavior of equation (1.24). This is shown graphically in Figure 1.9 in terms of different plots of x_{t+2} versus x_t. Note that at low values of b, only one equilibrium point exists and this is the value $x_{t+2} = x_t = x_e$. As b increases, however, the original fixed point becomes unstable and bifurcates into two new attracting fixed points. These new points now become the boundaries of a 2-point cycle (Figure 1.10). This dynamical behavior has been termed a stable limit cycle since, if disturbed, the system will return to the same periodic trajectory. Such behavior is in contrast with the oscillations expected for neutral stability (i.e., $b = 2$) which, like in the case of a "frictionless pendulum," do not experience any attracting or retarding force and simply increase in amplitude when subjected to an additional disturbance.

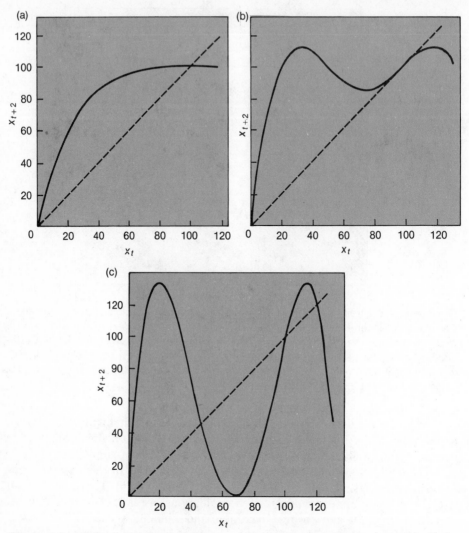

Figure 1.9. Plots of equation (1.24) as x_{t+2} versus x_t for increasing values of b. As the value of b increases, the stable point in graph (a) bifurcates into two new points. Graph (a) $b = 1, c = 0.01$; graph (b) $b = 2, c = 0.02$; graph (c) $b = 3, c = 0.03$.

If the value of b is increased still further, the two new points gradually become unstable, each again forming two additional attracting fixed points. This is illustrated by the plot of x_{t+4} versus x_t in Figure 1.11. Once the second bifurcation takes place, the system will begin to demonstrate a stable 4-point limit cycle. This bifurcation process will continue to occur as long as the value of b increases, producing stable limit cycles with points of 8, 16, 32, 64, etc. The various points of transition are summarized in Table 1.2. Note that the system enters a chaotic regime once $b > 2.57$. Beyond this limit there are an

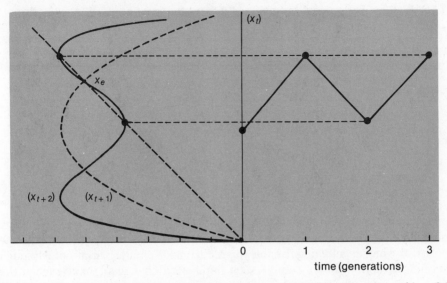

Figure 1.10. Plots of x_{t+1} and x_{t+2} versus x_t for equation (1.24) with values of $b = 2.2$ and $c = 0.022$. The single point x_e bifurcates into two new attracting points (x_{t+2} curve) which serve as the boundaries for a 2-point cycle.

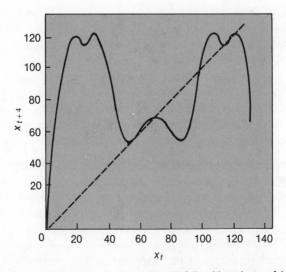

Figure 1.11. Plot of x_{t+4} versus x_t for equation (1.24) with values of $b = 2.5$ and $c = 0.025$. Each stable point in Figure 1.10 bifurcates into two new points, resulting in four attracting points which serve as the boundaries for a 4-point cycle.

TABLE 1.2.   Dynamical behavior of a population described by equation (1.24).

Population dynamics	Value of b
Stable equilibrium point	$0 < b < 2.000$
Stable limit cycles	
2-point cycle	$2.000 < b < 2.449$
4-point cycle	$2.449 < b < 2.544$
8-, 16-, 32-, etc. point cycles	$2.544 < b < 2.570$
Chaotic behavior	$b > 2.570$
(Seemingly aperiodic behavior)	

*Adapted from May, 1976

infinite number of periodic points as well as an uncounted number of starting points for which the cycle pattern never repeats. This consequently leads to behavior which is indistinguishable in practice from chance variation. Although seemingly random in trajectory, such population changes cannot exceed the maximum and minimum values predicted by the difference equation. If the function has a peak to the left of the replacement line, the upper bound or maximum value of x (x_{max}) will be the value of x_{t+1} at the critical point ($dx_{t+1}/dx_t = 0$). The minimum value (x_{min}), on the other hand, will occur in the cycle immediately following x_{max}. In the case of equation (1.24), for example, the maximum and minimum values are $x_{max} = (1 + b)x_c - cx_c^2$ and $x_{min} = (1 + b)x_{max} - cx_{max}^2$ where $x_c = (1/2b)(1 + b)x_e$ and is the value of x_t at the critical point.

The range of dynamical behavior exhibited by the finite difference model (1.24) is illustrated by means of the series of plots in Figure 1.12. Note that the dynamics in the chaotic regime depend on the initial value of x and cannot be predicted simply from the magnitude of b. This means that, even though the equation is deterministic, the exact relationship between x_{t+1} and x_t can never be reconstructed from experimental data except under identical starting conditions. Similar, though not identical, patterns of dynamical behavior are shown by other nonlinear models and will be discussed in later sections of the text.

Stability of multicomponent systems.   Models are often constructed in population biology which include two or more interacting components (e.g., genotypes, populations, species). To adequately describe such a system, two or more equations must be written indicating how the components affect their own behavior and interact with each other.

Consider, for example, two species populations of sizes x and y involved in a symbiotic relationship. If this interaction is essential for the continued existence of both species, each population will increase in the presence of the other species and decline in its absence. A possible, though highly simplified,

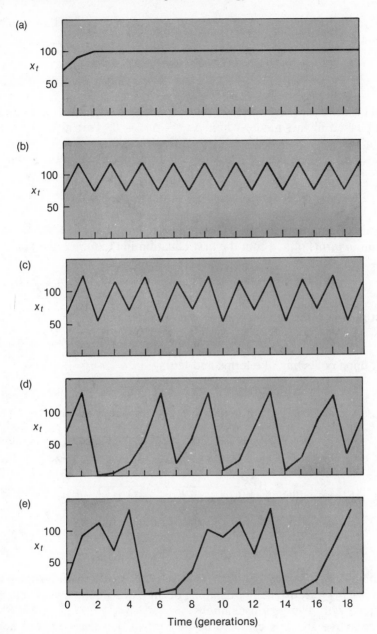

Figure 1.12. Range of time-dependent behavior exhibited by equation (1.24). (a) $b = 1$, $c = 0.01$, stable equilibrium; (b) $b = 2.2$, $c = 0.022$, 2-point cycle; (c) $b = 2.5$, $c = 0.025$, 4-point cycle; (d) $b = 3.0$, $c = 0.03$, $x_o = 70$, chaotic regime; (e) $b = 3.0$, $c = 0.03$, $x_o = 30$, chaotic regime.

model for this behavior is given by the following set of linear difference equations:

$$\Delta x_t = -ax_t + by_t$$
$$\Delta y_t = a'x_t - b'y_t$$

(1.25)

for which the ratios a/b and a'/b' are assumed to be equal. An equilibrium is established in this model when $\Delta x_t = \Delta y_t = 0$. This gives $x_e = (b/a)y_e = (b'/a')y_e$.

To analyze the stability of this system, rewrite the difference equations as

$$x_{t+1} = (1 - a)x_t + by_t$$
$$y_{t+1} = (1 - b')y_t + a'x_t$$

(1.26)

This pair of equations can be solved by deriving a second order difference equation in terms of x. From the first equation in (1.26), we see that

$$y_t = (1/b)x_{t+1} - [(1-a)/b]x_t \quad \text{and}$$

$$y_{t+1} = (1/b)x_{t+2} - [(1-a)/b]x_{t+1}$$

Substituting into the second equation in (1.26), we have

$$x_{t+2} - (1-a)x_{t+1} = (1-b')x_{t+1} - (1-a)(1-b')x_t + a'bx_t$$

which, upon collecting like terms and letting $ab' - a'b = 0$, yields

$$x_{t+2} - (2 - a - b')x_{t+1} + (1 - a - b')x_t = 0$$

This is a second order linear equation for which the roots are

$$\lambda_1 = \frac{1}{2}(2 - a - b') + \frac{1}{2}\sqrt{(2 - a - b')^2 - 4(1 - a - b')} = 1$$

and

$$\lambda_2 = \frac{1}{2}(2 - a - b') - \frac{1}{2}\sqrt{(2 - a - b')^2 - 4(1 - a - b')} = 1 - (a + b')$$

The general solution then becomes

$$x_t = k_1 + k_2[1 - (a + b')]^t$$

(1.27)

It is, therefore, apparent that if $0 < (a + b') < 1$, exponential damping occurs; if $1 < (a + b') < 2$, oscillatory damping occurs; and if $(a + b') > 2$, the system is unstable with divergent oscillations.

The above analysis can also be performed on related sets of nonlinear equations when suitable linear approximations are made. Since these simplifying procedures include ignoring departures from equilibrium that are raised to powers of 2 or greater, the results of such an analysis can only apply to the behavior of the system in the vicinity of the equilibrium point. Numerous examples will be presented in later chapters of the text.

SOLVED EXAMPLE PROBLEMS

Deterministic Models

1. The difference between the variable x and the equilibrium value x_e is observed to change by a factor of -0.5 in each successive time interval. Describe the approach of x to x_e.

    solution   From the information given, we can write the following equation: $x_{t+1} - x_e = (-0.5)(x_t - x_e)$ for which the solution is $x_t - x_e = (-0.5)^t (x_o - x_e)$. By comparing with equation (1.3), we see that $1 + a = -0.5$, giving $a = -1.5$. Since $-2 < a < -1$, x will approach x_e through damped oscillations.

2. When Norway rats invade a new warehouse where living conditions are ideal, they multiply at the rapid rate of 0.015 individuals gained per rat per day. Assume 100 rats to be in the starting population. (a) Write a difference equation describing population growth. (b) Write a differential equation describing population growth. (c) What will be the population size after 1 year assuming growth continues in this manner?

    solution   (a) $\Delta x_t = 0.015 x_t$; (b) $dx/dt = 0.015x$; (c) Since a is small in value, we may use the solution to either the difference or the differential equation. Substituting into $x_t = x_o e^{at} = (100)e^{(5.468)\,(1)}$, we obtain $x_t = 23{,}700$ rats.

3. It is often convenient to express a variable relative to its equilibrium value by letting $x_t/x_e = p_t$. Using this notation, show that the difference equation (1.7) implies that the ratio p_t/q_t, where $q_t = 1 - p_t$, will increase by a factor $1 + a$ times the ratio p_{t-1}/q_{t-1} in each succeeding time interval.

    solution   Since (1.9) is an alternative form of equation (1.7), we can write the reduced form of this expression as $x_{t+1}/x_e = ((1 + a)x_t/x_e)/(1 + ax_t/x_e)$ or $p_{t+1} = (1 + a)p_t/(1 + ap_t)$. Multiplying through by $1 + ap_t$ and subtracting $p_t p_{t+1}$ from both sides, we get $p_{t+1} - p_t p_{t+1} + ap_t p_{t+1} = (1 + a)p_t - p_t p_{t+1}$ or $p_{t+1}(1 - p_t) = (1 + a)p_t(1 - p_{t+1})$. Thus, by changing subscripts, we can write $p_t/q_t = (1 + a)p_{t-1}/q_{t-1}$.

4. Suppose that we start with a mixture of two cell types, A and B, which decline exponentially in abundance as a result of mortality according to the expressions $x_{A,t} = x_{A,o}e^{-at}$ and $x_{B,t} = x_{B,o}e^{-bt}$. Show that the proportion of type A in the mixture will change with time in a sigmoid (or logistic) fashion.

    solution   Let $p_t = x_{A,t}/x_t$ and $1 - p_t = x_{B,t}/x_t$ where $x_t = x_{A,t} + x_{B,t}$. We can, therefore, write $p_t/(1 - p_t) = (e^{-at}/e^{-bt})p_o/(1 - p_o)$. Solving for p_t, we get $p_t = p_o/[p_o + (1 - p_o)e^{-(a-b)t}]$ which is of the same form as equation (1.11).

5. Show that a plot of dx/dt versus x in equation (1.14) yields a curve with a single maximum at $x = \tfrac{1}{2}x_e$.

    solution   To evaluate the maximum value, we take the first derivative and set it equal to zero. We get $d(dx/dt)/dx = a - 2bx = 0$. This yields $x = a/2b = \frac{1}{2}x_e$.

6. Suppose that the number of survivors in a population decreases according to the differential equation $dx/dt = - bx^2$. Show that the time required for the number of survivors to decrease to one-half their initial value is $t = 1/bx_o$.

   solution   Let $x_t = \frac{1}{2}x_o$. The integrated form of the above equation can then be written as $\frac{1}{2}x_o = x_o/(1 + tbx_o)$ or $1 + tbx_o = 2$. Thus, solving for t, we get $t = 1/bx_o$.

7. A population increases in size in such a way that the change in generation $t + 1$ is twice that of the preceding generation. Describe the process as a difference equation and solve for x_t, given the initial conditions are $x_o = 4$ and $x_1 = 8$.

   solution   Since $\Delta x_{t+1} = 2\Delta x_t$, then $x_{t+2} - x_{t+1} = 2(x_{t+1} - x_t)$ and the difference equation is of the second order: $x_{t+2} - 3x_{t+1} + 2x_t = 0$. The roots are $\lambda_1 = 2$, $\lambda_2 = 1$ so that the solution is $x_t = k_1 2^t + k_2$. Using the initial conditions, we find that $k_1 = 4$ and $k_2 = 0$ and, therefore, $x_t = 4(2)^t = 2^{2+t}$.

8. A certain population increases according to the relationship $x_{t+2} = 4x_{t+1} - 5x_t$. Show that such a large effect on the mortality of a generation by individuals two generations back results in oscillations of population size from one generation to the next.

   solution   Rewrite the expression as $x_{t+2} - 4x_{t+1} + 5x_t = 0$ where $B = - 4$ and $C = 5$. Since $B^2 - 4C < 0$, the roots are complex numbers. Hence the solution is $x_t = (5)^{\frac{1}{2}t}[k_1\cos(\theta t) + k_2\sin(\theta t)]$ and oscillations will occur with increasing amplitude.

9. The differential equation $d^2x/dt^2 = - bx$ describes a conservative (or neutral) oscillation (i.e., an oscillation like that of a frictionless pendulum in which the amplitude is constant and is determined by initial conditions). Comment on the stability of such a system and its potential usefulness as a model in biology.

   solution   The oscillation described by this relationship is constant only as long as conditions do not change. If the system is perturbed in any way, it will oscillate with a different amplitude determined by the extent of the disturbance. The relationship is also structurally unstable in that, even the smallest arbitrary change in the equation (e.g., $d^2x/dt^2 = - bx + cdx/dt$) will cause the behavior to change to either a convergent or divergent oscillation. It is, therefore, unrealistic as a model for biological systems which are almost certain to experience some alteration due to changes in environmental conditions.

Numerical Solutions and Linear Approximations

10. Show that the equation $y = Y(1 - e^{-ax})$ can be expressed approximately as $y = aYx$ for small values of ax.

solution One can apply either one of the following approaches: (a) Write e^{-ax} in terms of its infinite series as $1 - ax + (ax)^2/2! - \ldots$. Thus, for small values of ax, $y = Y[1 - (1 - ax)] = aYx$. (b) Rearrange the terms of the equation to yield $-\ln(1 - y/Y) = ax$. Since ax is small in value, y will be much less than its maximum value Y. Hence, $-\ln(1 - y/Y) = y/Y$ and $y = aYx$.

The Stability of an Equilibrium

11. Evaluate T_R and analyze the consequences of small departures from equilibrium for the nonlinear difference equation $x_{t+1} = ax_t/(1 + cx_t^n)$.
     solution First, let $x_{t+1} = x_t = x_e$. We find that $x_e^n = (a - 1)/c$. Second, evaluate the slope when $x_t = x_e$. We get

$$(dx_{t+1}/dx_t)_{x_e} = [a(1 + cx_e^n) - acnx_e^n]/(1 + cx_e^n)^2 = 1 - n(a - 1)/a.$$

Hence, $T_R = 1/b = a/n(a - 1)$. Applying the stability criteria in Table 1.1, it can be shown that for small displacements from equilibrium:

$$a/n(a - 1) > 1: \text{exponential damping}$$

$$\frac{1}{2} < a/n(a - 1) < 1: \text{oscillatory damping}$$

$$a/n(a - 1) < \frac{1}{2}: \text{divergent oscillations}$$

PROBLEM EXERCISES

1. A bacterial population grows according to the expression $x_t = (1 + a)^t x_o$, increasing from 10^3 to 10^6 cells in 200 minutes. (a) What is the value of the proportionality constant, a? (b) What is the doubling time of the population?

2. The radioisotope ^{32}P exponentially decays at the rate of 50% every 14 days. What fraction of the initial amount will remain at the end of two months?

3. At birth, animal A weighs 40 kg and animal B weighs 60 kg. Each grows by increasing its weight by 10% each month. (a) By what factor will the weights differ after n months? (b) What will be the weight difference after n months?

4. One of the models of population growth that includes a fixed upper limit to the size of the population, based on a fixed amount (B) of resources for growth, states that the rate of change in number with time is proportional to the amount of resources remaining for use. Write this relationship as a differential equation and solve for x_t.

5. Compare the equation for growth in the preceding problem with equation (1.14). Write an equation for dx/dt as a logistic function of $B - x$.

6. Suppose that a symbiotic relationship can be modeled by the following pair of differential equations: $dx/dt = -x + y$ and $dy/dt = x - y$. Solve the equations in terms of x and analyze the equilibrium stability of the system.

7. The human zygote undergoes six mitotic division cycles during the first 96 hours following fertilization. (a) At this time, how many cells will be present? (b) What is the average cell-doubling time during this period?

8. A young animal grows by increasing its weight by 10% each month, where the weight at birth is 30 kg. Assuming no initial lag, what will be the total percent increase in weight after four months?

9. A population increases in size during a favorable year by 25%, but it decreases by 10% during the next year. What is the net percent change over the 2 year time period?

10. A population of English sparrows increases by 20% each year due to birth and death processes under optimum conditions. An additional source of mortality, due to physical factors, such as windstorms, claims 30 sparrows per year. If the starting population size is 200, what will be the population size after 5 years?

11. Suppose that under crowded conditions the number of survivors in a species of insect declines as $x_t = 10^3/(1 + 3t)$ where t is expressed in days. How many days are required to reduce x_t to one-tenth its initial value?

12. Consider an irreversible chemical reaction between compounds A and B to produce compound C, where $1A + 1B \rightarrow 1C$. Let a_o and b_o be the initial concentrations of A and B and let c_t be the concentration of C at time t. Now, write a nonlinear differential equation describing the rate of increase in compound C in terms of a_o, b_o, and c_t.

13. Let dx/dt and dy/dt be two measures of the growth of an organism (e.g., x = length of tail and y = length of body, or x = weight of body and y = height of body). The relative growth rates can then be given as dx/xdt and dy/ydt. The allometric law of growth states that the relative growth rates of different parts of a body are proportional, i.e., that $dy/ydt = kdx/xdt$ where $k > 0$. Note that the relationship between the relative rates is not affected by the particular type of function describing either growth rate. Solve this differential equation for y.

14. Determine the general solutions of the following linear equations.

a) $\Delta x_t + 2x_t = 4$ e) $dx/dt + 2x = 4$
b) $\Delta^2 x_t + 3\Delta x_t = 0$ f) $d^2x/dt^2 + 3dx/dt = 0$
c) $\Delta^2 x_t + 3\Delta x_t + 3x_t = 0$ g) $d^2x/dt^2 + 3dx/dt + 3x = 0$
d) $\Delta^2 x_t + 3\Delta x_t + 5x_t = 0$ h) $d^2x/dt^2 + 3dx/dt + 5x = 0$

15. Determine the general solutions of the following pairs of linear equations and comment on the stability of each system.

   a) $\Delta x_t = -x_t + 2y_t$
      $\Delta y_t = 2x_t - 4y_t$

   b) $\Delta x_t = x_t - 2y_t$
      $\Delta y_t = -2x_t + 4y_t$

   c) $dx/dt = -x + 2y$
      $dy/dt = 2x - 4y$

   d) $dx/dt = x - \frac{1}{2}y$
      $dy/dt = -\frac{1}{2}x + \frac{1}{4}y$

2

Probability Theory
and Stochastic Models

Many of the fundamental processes of importance to population biology can be investigated more fully with the development of stochastic models. As pointed out in the preceding chapter, stochastic models are probabilistic models in which chance mechanisms are incorporated. Thus, a stochastic model of population growth would attempt to give the probability that the population has attained a size equal to say, x after some time interval t. This is in contrast to a deterministic model of the same process which would disregard sampling variation and random environmental fluctuations and predict a size of exactly x at time t. Because of the importance of probabilistic concepts in stochastic modeling, what follows is a brief introduction to the mathematics of probability. The treatment is not meant to be complete in any way but is limited to those concepts which are useful later in the text. Furthermore, no attempt is made at mathematical rigor. Hopefully, by keeping the number of mathematical proofs and mathematical formalism to a minimum, the following discussion will be comprehensible to a reader who has only been introduced to the fundamental laws of probability and to the basic concepts of differential and integral calculus. Nonetheless, the reader will find that a good knowledge of certain mathematical topics is essential. These include logarithms, general functional notation, and exponential and power functions.

RANDOM VARIABLES

It is a common experience in science that when experiments are performed repeatedly under controlled conditions, they do not give rise exactly to the same result but tend to vary in outcome due to chance. For instance, when the number of mutant cells is measured in a series of "identical" bacterial cultures, some cultures are observed to contain no mutants of a specified type, while others may possess 1, 2, 3, etc. mutants depending on the time the bacteria in each culture are permitted to grow. In this example, as with most repeated experiments in science, the results are summarized by way of a series of numbers. Consequently, the variability in experimental results is expressed by the variation in the numbers observed. We refer to these variable quantities as random variables. Thus, we can think of random variables as the results of repeated observations which are affected by some chance mechanism.

Random variables tend to fall into two categories: discrete and continuous. Discrete random variables are those which take on at most a countable number of possible values. For instance, the number of mutant cells observed in a series of bacterial cultures is a discrete variable since the observed values represent a limited and thus countable series of positive integers. On the other hand, continuous random variables are those whose set of possible values is uncountable. Common examples of quantities which are customarily treated as continuous variables are length, area, volume, and time. These quantities tend to vary along some continuous scale of measurement. Thus, if it were possible to measure these quantities to an infinite number of decimal places, they could take on an infinite array of possible values within any specified interval, since regardless of what two limits are chosen on the scale of measurement, there is always a potentially infinite number of values between them. Obviously, such accuracy can never be achieved in the real world, and because of the inherent limitations in any measuring device, all measured quantities are basically discrete. Nevertheless, the concept of a continuous random variable is a useful abstraction which provides great mathematical simplification in many real problems.

As would be expected, discrete and continuous random variables require different mathematical methods for their description and analysis. First consider the case of discrete variables. Assume for present purposes that x is a random variable which can take on values $x_1, x_2, x_3, \ldots, x_N$. Let x_i represent the value associated with class i, i being one of N classes, that is $i = 1, 2, 3, \ldots, N$. We can now define the *probability mass function*, $p(x_i)$, as the probability that x assumes a value x_i. Stated symbolically,

$$p(x_i) = P(x = x_i)$$

Since x must assume a value associated with one of the N classes, the sum of $p(x_i)$ over all N classes must equal one. We have

$$\sum_{i=1}^{N} p(x_i) = 1$$

Our symbol definitions also permit us to define the *cumulative distribution function*, $F(x)$, as the probability that x takes on a value that will be less than or equal to some value, say x_k. Thus,

$$F(x) = P(x \leqslant x_k) = \sum_{i=1}^{k} p(x_i)$$

For example, if a set of values 0, 1, and 2 occur with probabilities $\frac{1}{4}$, $\frac{1}{2}$, and $\frac{1}{4}$, respectively, the probability that the observed value is less than or equal to one is then $F(x) = P(x \leqslant 1) = P(x = 0) + P(x = 1) = 1/4 + 1/2 = 3/4$.

Now consider the case of continuous random variables. As in the previous situation, let x represent the random variable. In contrast, however, assume that x varies along some continuous scale of measurement and can take on any one of a potentially infinite array of values between the limits a and b. Since there are now a potentially infinite number of possible values for x, then if all can occur with equal likelihood, the probability of selecting any one particular value of x would be $1/\infty = 0$. Obviously, defining a probability mass function in this case would be inappropriate. To get around this problem, we define the *probability density function*, $f(x)$, such that $f(x)dx$ is the probability that the observed value of x is within some small interval $x \pm \frac{1}{2}dx$. We are thus defining the probability that x is approximately equal to or "close" to some specific value. Since x must assume some value within its entire range from a to b, the integral of $f(x)$ over these limits must equal one. In symbolic form,

$$\int_{a}^{b} f(x)dx = 1$$

Again letting $F(x)$ represent the cumulative distribution function [i.e., the probability that x assumes a value less than or equal to x_k (where $a < x_k < b$)], its relation to $f(x)$ can be expressed by the integral

$$F(x) = \int_{a}^{x_k} f(x)\, dx$$

Note that $f(x)$ can be obtained by simply differentiating $F(x)$ with respect to x. Thus, if the cumulative distribution function were given by $F(x) = 1 - e^{-ax}$ where a is a constant, then $f(x) = dF(x)/dx = ae^{-ax}$.

DESCRIPTIVE PROPERTIES OF DISTRIBUTIONS

When the possible values of a random variable are represented in tabular or graphical form along with a corresponding probability for each value or range of values, we refer to this profile of the random variable as a *probability distribution*. We can think of a probability distribution as a plot of $p(x)$ versus x in the discrete case or as a plot of $f(x)$ versus x when x is a continuous variable. This is illustrated by plots of a symmetrical curve known as the normal probability distribution and a roughly similar discrete distribution in Figure 2.1A. For a comparison, the cumulative distribution functions which correspond to these distributions are plotted in Figure 2.1B.

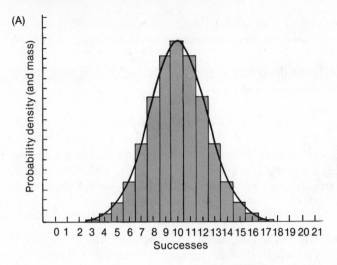

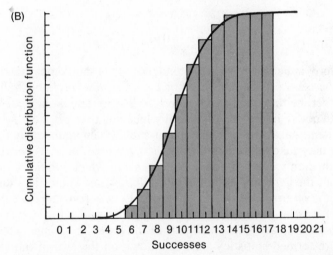

Figure 2.1. Plots of symmetrical continuous and discrete distributions. (A) Probability density and probability mass functions. (B) The corresponding cumulative distribution functions.

Measures of central tendency.   Every probability distribution can be described by a number of different parameters. One of the most useful in positioning a distribution along the x coordinate is the *mean* (or arithmetic average). The mean, which we shall designate as either m or $E(x)$, is the expected value of a random variable. For a discrete distribution in which x can take on N possible values, the mean is defined as

$$E(x) = \sum_{i=1}^{N} x_i \, p(x_i) \tag{2.1}$$

Thus, if x can take on values 0, 1, and 2 with probabilities $\frac{1}{4}, \frac{1}{2}$, and $\frac{1}{4}$, respectively, the expected value for this distribution would be $E(x) = (0)\frac{1}{4} + (1)\frac{1}{2} + (2)\frac{1}{4} = 1$.

A continuous distribution, on the other hand, will have an expected value given by the integral

$$E(x) = \int_a^b xf(x)dx \tag{2.2}$$

where a and b are the limits of the distribution. For a numerical example, suppose that we have a uniform distribution for which the density function is $f(x) = 1$ over the range $0 \leqslant x \leqslant 1$. Applying our definition of the mean, we get $E(x) = \int_0^1 x(1)\,dx = \frac{1}{2}x^2]_0^1 = \frac{1}{2}$ which one would intuitively expect.

We can also define the mean as a constant which satisfies the condition that the sum (or integral) of all departures from this value will equal zero. In symbolic form,

$$\sum_{i=1}^N (x_i - m)p(x_i) = 0$$

It is, therefore, a measure of central tendency. This should not imply that $E(x)$ is always the centrally located value or even the most probable value for that matter. In fact, neither can be true when the distribution is skewed. Moreover, $E(x)$ should not be interpreted as literally meaning that it is the value expected in any particular measurement. Indeed, it should be noted that, in the discrete case, $E(x)$ may take on values that are not possible for x. Nevertheless, the mean or expected value is a convenient measure which provides useful information about the general location of centrally located values in a distribution.

Since it is often impossible or impractical to observe an entire population, especially if it is large, we generally estimate the theoretical parameters of a distribution on the basis of a small part of the group or sample. These sample estimates are termed statistics and, depending on the size of the sample, are subject to experimental error. The statistic which gives the most reliable estimate of $E(x)$ is the *sample mean*, designated $\bar{x}$. The sample mean can be computed by using the following formula:

$$\bar{x} = \frac{1}{n} \sum_{i=1}^n x_i \tag{2.3}$$

where x_1, x_2, etc. are the measured values of x and n is the number of measurements (i.e., the sample size). Thus, if a set of three measurements yielded values 4, 6, and 8, the sample mean would then be $\bar{x} = (4 + 6 + 8)/3 = 6$. From the law of large numbers, we know that when the sample size increases, the sample mean becomes a better and better estimate of the true average. Thus, when the number n of trials is large, $\bar{x}$ can be taken as being approximately equal to m.

At times, the variable of interest is a derived quantity which varies in such a way that its arithmetic mean is not the best measure of its "average" value. In such cases, other measures of central tendency can be developed from the mathematical relationships which are assumed to exist. One such measure is the *geometric mean*, $\bar{x}_G$, defined as the nth root of the product (Π) of n values of x. Symbolically,

$$\bar{x}_G = \left[\prod_{i=1}^{n} x_i \right]^{1/n} \quad \text{or} \quad \log \bar{x}_G = \frac{1}{n} \sum_{i=1}^{n} \log x_i \qquad (2.4)$$

Observe that when the geometric mean is expressed in terms of its logarithm, its form is equivalent to the arithmetic mean. One situation in which the geometric mean is used is in computing the average growth per generation of a population. For example, suppose that the size of a population (N) changes in each generation (t) according to the following recurrence relation:

$$N_t = x_{t-1} N_{t-1} = x_{t-1} x_{t-2} N_{t-2} = x_{t-1} x_{t-2} \ldots x_o N_o$$

where x represents the ratio of population sizes in succeeding generations (e.g., $x_{t-1} = N_t/N_{t-1}$). If x is assumed to vary from generation to generation, then

$$N_t = N_o \prod_{i=0}^{t-1} x_i = N_o (x_G)^t$$

To illustrate numerically, say that a population increases in size by factors of 2, 3, and 4 in three successive generations. Since the geometric mean of these three values is $\bar{x}_G = (2 \cdot 3 \cdot 4)^{1/3} = 2.89$ (approximately), the population would then be growing as though it were increasing in a truly exponential manner by a factor of 2.89 in each generation.

Another measure of central tendency which is commonly used in population biology is the harmonic mean, $\bar{x}_H$, defined as the reciprocal of the arithmetic average of the reciprocal values of x. Symbolically,

$$1/\bar{x}_H = \frac{1}{n} \sum_{i=1}^{n} 1/x_i \qquad (2.5)$$

One situation in which the harmonic mean is used is in calculating average velocities. Since the concept of the harmonic mean is rather difficult, we shall use a numerical example which is familiar to all of the readers but is not related to population biology in any way. Suppose that you drove a car across your state and back again. Now say that you drove 90 mph in one direction (without being apprehended by the police) and 10 mph during the return trip. What is your "average" rate of speed? One's initial reaction is to say 50 mph; however, the correct average in this case is the harmonic mean. To illustrate, we shall generalize, and assume that the car was driven n times across the state for a total distance of nd. If we let t_i be the driving time during the ith trial, then the average velocity is $nd/(t_1 + t_2 + \ldots + t_n)$. Designating $x_i = d/t_i$ as the velocity in the ith trial, we obtain

$$(t_1 + t_2 + \ldots + t_n)/nd = \frac{1}{n} \sum_{i=1}^{n} 1/x_i = 1/\bar{x}_H$$

The answer to our problem is then $\bar{x}_H = 2(900/100) = 18$ mph. As you can see, your initial reaction can at times be quite misleading.

Measures of variation.   Unlike the mean which is a measure of central tendency, the *variance*, designated either as $V(x)$ or σ^2, is a measure of variation. In a sense, the variance measures the dispersion of values about the mean. The theoretical variance of a distribution is defined as the expected value of $(x - m)^2$ where m is the mean. For a discrete distribution, the variance can be expressed as the sum of the squared-deviations from the mean, or symbolically,

$$V(x) = \sum_{i=1}^{N} (x_i - m)^2 \, p(x_i) \qquad (2.6)$$

and, for a continuous distribution, as the integral

$$V(x) = \int_{a}^{b} (x - m)^2 f(x)\,dx \qquad (2.7)$$

Due to the $(x - m)^2$ term in both formulae, the units associated with the variance will be the square of the units of x and m.

It is often more convenient to express $V(x)$ as the mean of the squared value of x minus the square of the mean. The mathematical basis for this conversion can be illustrated by expanding the $(x - m)^2$ term in $V(x)$. For a discrete random variable, we get

$$V(x) = E(x - m)^2 = E(x^2) - E(2mx) + E(m^2)$$

$$= \Sigma\, x_i^2\, p(x_i) - 2m\,\Sigma\, x_i\, p(x_i) + m^2\, \Sigma\, p(x_i)$$

Since $\Sigma\, x_i\, p(x_i) = m$ and $\Sigma\, p(x_i) = 1$, it is evident that

$$V(x) = E(x^2) - m^2 \qquad (2.8)$$

where $E(x^2) = \Sigma x_i^2\, p(x_i)$ in the discrete case. For a numerical example, say that x is a discrete variable which can take on values 0, 1, and 2 with probabilities of $\frac{1}{4}, \frac{1}{2}$, and $\frac{1}{4}$, respectively. Since $E(x) = 1$, as we found in a previous calculation, $V(x) = (0)^2\,\frac{1}{4} + (1)^2\,\frac{1}{2} + (2)^2\,\frac{1}{4} - (1)^2 = \frac{1}{2}$.

As one would expect, equation (2.8) can also be applied to a continuous random variable. In this case $E(x^2) = \int x^2 f(x)\,dx$. To illustrate the computation of the variance given a continuous distribution, say that x varies uniformly between 0 and 1 with $f(x) = 1$. Since it has been shown earlier that $E(x) = \frac{1}{2}$ in this case, the variance can then be computed through integration

as $V(x) = \int_{0}^{1} x^2(1)\,dx - (\frac{1}{2})^2 = x^3/3 \Big]_{0}^{1} - \frac{1}{4} = 1/12$.

It should be apparent from the preceding paragraphs that the expected value notation can be a real time-saving device when deriving relationships which involve the mean and variance. In this regard, it is worth mentioning one other useful property of expected values. This property can be expressed in terms of the following theorem: "The variance of a constant times a variable is equal to the constant-squared times the variance of the variable." For a simple proof, let $y = Ax + B$ be a linear function of x in which A and B are constants. Since $E(y) = E(Ax + B) = A \Sigma x_i p(x_i) + B \Sigma p(x_i) = AE(x) + B$, assuming x can be treated as a discrete variable, then, if we let $m_y = E(y)$ and $m_x = E(x)$, $V(y)$ becomes

$$V(y) = E(y - m_y)^2 = E[(Ax + B) - (Am_x + B)]^2$$

$$= \Sigma (Ax_i - Am_x)^2 p(x_i) = A^2 \Sigma (x_i - m_x)^2 p(x_i)$$

$$= A^2 V(x)$$

One interesting application of the aforementioned theorem occurs in the derivation of the variance of the sample mean, $V(\bar{x})$. Assuming that the sample consists of n independent measurements, then $V(\Sigma x) = nV(x)$. Hence,

$$V(\bar{x}) = E(\bar{x} - m)^2 = V(\Sigma x/n) = (1/n)^2 V(\Sigma x) = V(x)/n \qquad (2.9)$$

Thus, we see that the variance of the sample mean will decrease inversely with the sample size, n. This accounts for the desirability of basing your estimates on large samples.

As in the case of the mean, the theoretical variance of a distribution can be estimated from sample data by way of a *sample variance*, designated, in this case, as s^2. Ideally, the sample variance should be expressed as $\Sigma (x - m)^2/n$ where m is the population mean and n is, again, the sample size. Unfortunately, m is rarely known. Consequently, sample estimates of the variance are usually computed from equations in which $\bar{x}$ is substituted for m. This introduces another source of variability and requires that the equation for the sample estimate be modified in form. To illustrate, suppose that we let $s^2 = V(x)$ where $V(x)$ is now the expected variance for a finite sample. Then,

$$s^2 = E(x - m)^2 = E[(x - \bar{x}) + (\bar{x} - m)]^2$$

$$= E(x - \bar{x})^2 + 2(\bar{x} - m)E(x - \bar{x}) + E(\bar{x} - m)^2$$

Since we can express $E(x - \bar{x})^2$ as $\Sigma(x_i - \bar{x})^2/n$ for a sample of size n and, since $E(x - \bar{x}) = 0$ and $E(\bar{x} - m)^2 = V(x) = s^2/n$, we then have $s^2 = \Sigma(x_i - \bar{x})^2/n + s^2/n$. Solving for s^2, we get

$$s^2 = \frac{1}{n-1} \sum_{i=1}^{n} (x_i - \bar{x})^2 \qquad (2.10)$$

Thus, for the same set of values which were used earlier for the sample mean, the sample variance would be $s^2 = [(4 - 6)^2 + (6 - 6)^2 + (8 - 6)^2]/2 = 4$.

Yet another measure of variation is the *standard deviation* designated σ (or *s* for the sample estimate). As the symbols imply, the standard deviation is the square-root of the variance and can, therefore, take on both positive and negative values. The standard deviation is particularly useful when working with quantities which are assumed to follow a normal probability distribution. In this case, $m + \sigma$ and $m - \sigma$ represent the inflection points of the curve (see Figure 2.2). Hence, the amount of spread in the distribution will depend directly on the magnitude of σ.

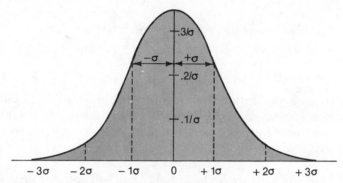

Figure 2.2.   The relationship of the standard deviation to a normal distribution with a mean of zero.

DISCRETE PROBABILITY DISTRIBUTIONS

Many of the models that will be presented in this text are developed with reasoning based on the mathematics of probability. Therefore, the reader will find it useful to first become familiar with the probability models commonly used in population biology. What follows are three of the most frequently occurring models, along with some common variations, which describe distributions of discrete random variables.

Bernoulli and binomial distributions.   Suppose there are only two mutually exclusive possible outcomes for a given trial which we will label success and failure. Let $x = 1$ for a success and $x = 0$ for a failure and let us represent the probabilities of success and failure by the symbols p and q, respectively. The random variable x is then said to have a Bernoulli distribution described by the following probability model:

$$
\begin{array}{ccc}
x: & 0 & 1 \\
p(x): & q & p
\end{array}
$$

where $p + q = 1$. For example, the birth of a single child can be treated as a trial in which the sex of the child is a Bernoulli random variable. In this case, the sex of the child can be either male or female with approximately equal likelihood. Thus, if we let $x = 0$ if the child is male and $x = 1$ if the child is female, we can represent the chance that the child is a girl by p and the chance that the child is a boy by $q = 1 - p$ where $p = q = \frac{1}{2}$.

The expected value and variance of x for the Bernoulli distribution can be obtained by applying the symbol definitions for $E(x)$ and $V(x)$. We get

$$E(x) = (0)q + (1)p = p$$

$$V(x) = (0 - p)^2 q + (1 - p)^2 p = pq(p + q) = pq$$

As long as successive trials are independent in a statistical sense, the Bernoulli distribution can be readily extended to predict the number of successes in any number of trials. Thus, we find that if the probability of an event occurring in a single trial is p and of not occurring is $1 - p = q$, the probability that the event occurs exactly x times out of n independent trials is

$$p(x) = \binom{n}{x} p^x q^{n-x} \tag{2.11}$$

where $\binom{n}{x}$ is a short-hand way of expressing the combinational formula given as $n!/x!(n - x)!$. Equation (2.11) represents the $x + 1$ term of the binomial expansion $(p + q)^n$ and has been appropriately termed the *binomial distribution*. One can derive the binomial formula by merely observing that for independent events, the probability that any one particular sequence of, x successes in n total trials is $p^x q^{n-x}$, and since any possible sequence would be regarded as a successful outcome, the number of ways of getting x successes in n total trials is $n!/x!(n - x)!$. Multiplying the two expressions yields the binomial formula. For a numerical example, we can ask what is the probability, in a family of four children, that 2 are girls and 2 are boys? The answer to this question can be obtained by letting p equal the chance that any child is a girl ($p = \frac{1}{2}$) and q be the chance that a child is a boy ($q = \frac{1}{2}$). Since there are $4!/2!2! = 6$ ways of getting 2 girls and 2 boys in any order of birth, the probability of $x = 2$ girls and $n - x = 2$ boys in a family of $n = 4$ children is then

$$\binom{4}{2} \left(\frac{1}{2}\right)^2 \left(\frac{1}{2}\right)^2 = (6) \left(\frac{1}{2}\right)^4 = 3/8$$

Since the binomial distribution is merely an extension of the Bernoulli distribution to n independent trials, $E(x)$ (i.e., the expected number of successes in n trials) and $V(x)$ for the binomial distribution can be expressed as

$$E(x) = np \qquad \text{and} \qquad V(x) = npq \tag{2.12}$$

It is important to note that if the number of occurrences is binomially distributed, then the proportion of occurrences (x/n) must also have a binomial distribution. Thus, the mean or expected proportion of successes out of n total trials is

$$E(x/n) = E(x)/n = p \qquad (2.13)$$

and, by applying a previously described theorem for the computation of variances, the variance of this proportion becomes

$$V(x/n) = (1/n)^2 V(x) = pq/n \qquad (2.14)$$

Note that as n increases, the variance of x/n decreases. Hence, one expects a greater clustering of values about the mean when n is large.

Poisson distribution.   If p is very small but n is large so that np is not negligible, then the binomial distribution can be closely approximated by the *Poisson distribution* defined by the equation

$$p(x) = \frac{(np)^x}{x!} e^{-np} \qquad (2.15)$$

where e is the base of natural logarithms. The above formula can be derived directly from the binomial distribution. This is shown by first rewriting the binomial formula as follows:

$$p(x) = \frac{(n)(n-1)(n-2)\ldots(n-x+1)}{x!} p^x (1-p)^{n-x}$$

When n is very large such that $n - x$ is essentially equal to n, $p(x)$ can be written approximately as

$$p(x) = \frac{(np)^x}{x!}(1-p)^n = \frac{(np)^x}{x!}\left[(1-p)^{-1/p}\right]^{-np}$$

which for small values of p (or more precisely for values of p approaching zero), yields equation (2.15).

One useful property of the Poisson distribution resides in the equivalence of its variance and mean. Since p is very small, $np(1-p)$ can be taken as being essentially equal to np. Hence,

$$V(x) = np = E(x)$$

Although the Poisson probability function is frequently derived as an approximation to other probability distributions, it is also important for its own sake. One useful feature of the Poisson probability formula is that it describes the distribution of events or things which occur at random along some continuous scale of measurement as in time or space. The Poisson distribution is then the counting distribution for a stochastic point process termed the *Poisson process*. For example, consider the distribution of bacterial cells in space within a liquid culture medium. We might ask for the probability that a volume v is empty (i.e., that it contains no bacterial cells). In this case, it is reasonable to assume that bacteria are dispersed at random. Consequently, we proceed as follows. First, choose a volume element dv which is so small that the chance of it containing more than one cell is negligible. The probability that our volume element dv contains one cell is then $P(1,dv) = mdv$ where m is the average number of cells per unit volume. The probability of zero cells in a volume element dv is thus $P(0,dv) = 1 - mdv$. We now ask for the probability of zero cells in a volume element $v + dv$ which we designate as $P(0,v + dv)$. Since occurrences in the volume elements v and dv are assumed to be independent, we can express the probability as

$$P(0,v + dv) = P(0,v)P(0,dv) = P(0,v)(1 - mdv)$$

where $P(0,v)$ is the probability of zero cells in v. Rearranging, we get

$$\frac{P(0,v + dv) - P(0,v)}{dv} = \frac{dP(0,v)}{dv} = -mP(0,v)$$

Since the probability of zero cells in zero volume is one, integration of the above equation over the limits of 0 and v for volume yields

$$P(0,v) = e^{-mv}$$

which is the $p(0)$ term of the Poisson distribution for unit volume. Applying logic similar to that used in the preceding analysis, one can show that the probability of a volume v containing exactly k cells is

$$P(k,v) = \frac{(mv)^k}{k!} e^{-mv}$$

Since the Poisson distribution is used so frequently in theoretical biology, it is of interest to examine a few of its properties which are helpful in making calculations.

1. The probability of zero occurrences or successes ($x = 0$) is $p(0) = e^{-m}$. Thus, the mean (m) can be estimated directly from experimentally determined values of $p(0)$ as $m = -\ln p(0) = 2.303 \log p(0)$.
2. The sum of all values of $p(x)$ must equal one. Hence, the probability of one or more successes can be written as $1 - e^{-m}$.
3. When m is small (on the order of 0.01 or less), $p(0)$ can be expressed approximately as $1 - m$. This can be shown by writing e^{-m} in terms of its infinite series.
4. Values of e^{-m} (or e^m) can often be approximated when m is greater than 0.01 by taking the sum of a finite number of terms of the infinite series. This is illustrated by letting the absolute value of the exponent equal unity and adding the first six terms. We get

$$\exp(1) = e \simeq 1 + 1 + \tfrac{1}{2} + \tfrac{1}{6} + \tfrac{1}{24} + \tfrac{1}{120} = 2.7168$$

which is a reasonable approximation of the value of e. Better estimates can be obtained by including more terms in the summation.

Negative binomial and geometric distributions.   Consider again a sequence of independent trials in which the probability of a certain event (a success) occurring in a single trial is p and the probability of its not occurring is q. If the sampling process is continued until the kth success occurs, then the probability that exactly x failures will occur before the kth success occurs, is a *negative binomial* probability

$$p(x) = \binom{x + k - 1}{k - 1} p^k q^x \tag{2.16}$$

in which case the number of trials is $n = x + k$. Note that the number of independent trials required to obtain the kth success is a random variable. Hence, the probability that the kth success occurs at the end of n trials is

$$p(n) = \binom{n - 1}{k - 1} p^k q^{n-k} \tag{2.17}$$

The negative binomial distribution gets its name from the fact that it can be defined in terms of the expansion of the negative binomial expression $(Q - P)^{-x}$ where $Q - P = 1$ and $P = q/p$. This is analogous to the definition of the binomial distribution in terms of the (positive) binomial expression $(p + q)^n$ where $p + q = 1$.

The negative binomial formula can be derived by noting that in the first $x + k - 1$ independent trials, the probability of a particular sequence of x failures and $k - 1$ successes is $p^{k-1}q^x$. Since any arrangement of x failures and $k - 1$ successes satisfies the desired outcome during the first $n + k - 1$ trials, the total number of ways in which these successes and failures can be ordered is $(x + k - 1)!/x!(k - 1)!$. Now, the probability that a success will occur in the $(x + k)$th trial is p. Therefore, the total probability is the product of these terms

$$p(x) = \frac{(x + k - 1)!}{x!(k - 1)!} (p^{k-1})(q^x)(p) = \binom{x + k - 1}{k - 1} p^k q^x$$

For a numerical example, suppose that a couple wants exactly 2 boys and will stop having children once the second boy is born. What is the probability that this couple will have 4 children? In this case, $n = 4$, $k = 2$, and $p = q = \frac{1}{2}$. Thus,

$$p(n = 4) = \binom{3}{1} \left(\frac{1}{2}\right)^2 \left(\frac{1}{2}\right)^2 = \frac{3}{16}$$

It can be shown that the mean and variance of the variable x in the negative binomial distribution are

$$E(x) = kq/p \qquad \text{and} \qquad V(x) = kq/p^2 \tag{2.18}$$

while the mean and variance of the variable $n = x + k$ (the waiting time distribution) are

$$E(x + k) = E(x) + k = k/p, \text{ and}$$

$$V(x + k) = V(x) = kq/p^2 \tag{2.19}$$

Thus the variances are the same for both cases.

It is often useful to express the probability mass function of the negative binomial distribution and the variance of this distribution in terms of the mean of x. Since $m = k(1 - p)/p$, we see that $p = k/(k + m)$ and $q = m/(k + m)$ since $p + q = 1$. Using these expressions, we obtain

$$p(x) = \binom{x + k - 1}{k - 1} \left[\frac{k}{k + m} \right]^k \left[\frac{m}{k + m} \right]^x$$

$$= \binom{x + k - 1}{k - 1} (m/k)^x (1 + m/k)^{-(x+k)}$$

and

$$V(x) = m + m^2/k$$

These equations can be used to illustrate the relationship existing between the negative binomial and Poisson distributions. To do so, assume that q is very small and k is large such that k is much greater than x. The negative binomial function can then be written approximately as

$$p(x) = \frac{(k)(k + 1) \ldots (k + x - 1)}{x!} (m/k)^x (1 + m/k)^{-k}$$

$$= \frac{k^x}{x!} (m/k)^x [(1 + m/k)^{k/m}]^{-m}$$

which for large values of k yields approximately

$$p(x) = \frac{m^x}{x!} e^{-m}$$

with

$$V(x) = m$$

In the special case where $k = 1$, the distribution can be written as either

$$p(x) = pq^x \qquad \text{or} \qquad p(n) = pq^{n-1} \tag{2.20}$$

where $n = x + 1$. Both expressions constitute a term in a geometric progression $p(1 + q + q^2 + \ldots + q^n)$ in which the sum (as n approaches infinity) is equal to one. Because of these special features, the probability mass functions given by (2.20) constitute what is known as the *geometric distribution*. As a numerical example of this important distribution, suppose that a couple decides to continue having children until a boy is born and will then stop. What is the expected family size? Letting p equal the probability that any one child is a boy, the mean in this case is given by (2.19) when $k = 1$. Thus, the expected number of children will be $E(x + 1) = E(n) = 1/p = 2$ since $p = \frac{1}{2}$.

Distinguishing discrete distributions.   Having described some of the more important discrete distributions, it would be useful to indicate one obvious and distinguishable difference between them. The most readily apparent distinction among the three types of distribution is the value of the ratio of variance to mean. This is less than one for the binomial, equal to one for the Poisson, and greater than one for the negative binomial distribution. Regardless of the sampling variation, the value of (sample variance)/(sample mean) is usually a good guide as to which of these types of distribution is to be used, given that one is to be used. Such a comparison is illustrated in Figure 2.3.

CONTINUOUS PROBABILITY DISTRIBUTIONS

In addition to discrete distributions, a variety of continuous probability distributions are also frequently used as probability models in population biology. What follows is a brief description of three important probability functions, along with certain variations, which are applied later in the text.

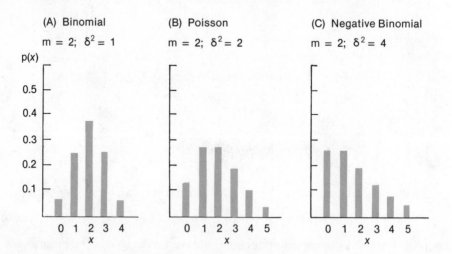

Figure 2.3.   Discrete probability distributions. The value of $E(x)$ is 2, whereas, values of the variance are 1, 2, and 4 for the binomial, Poisson, and negative binomial distributions, respectively. In the last two cases, the variable x can take on values from zero to infinity. Its restriction to 5 is done solely for convenience.

Gamma and exponential distributions.   One distribution of a continuous variable which is frequently applied is the *gamma distribution* defined by the probability density function

$$f(x) = \frac{a(ax)^{k-1}}{\Gamma(k)} e^{-ax} \tag{2.21}$$

for $x > 0$. In this expression a and k are positive numbers and $\Gamma(k)$ is the *gamma function* defined by the integral

$$\Gamma(k) = a^k \int_0^\infty x^{k-1} e^{-ax} dx \tag{2.22}$$

Values of the gamma function have been tabulated and are provided in textbooks of probability theory. When k is an integer, it can be shown, through repeated integration by parts, that

$$\Gamma(k) = (k-1)\,\Gamma(k-1) = (k-1)\,(k-2)\,\Gamma(k-2) = (k-1)!$$

For example, $\Gamma(4) = 3! = 6$. The gamma function is thus commonly referred to as the factorial function.

The mean of the gamma distribution is

$$E(x) = k/a \tag{2.23}$$

and the variance of the variable x is

$$V(x) = k/a^2 \tag{2.24}$$

These relations permit the estimation of a and k from experimentally determined values of the sample mean and sample variance. By substituting these statistics into the preceding relationships for their corresponding population parameters, we get the estimates

$$a = \overline{x}/s^2 \quad \text{and} \quad k = \overline{x}^2/s^2$$

The probability density function of the gamma distribution with $a = 1$ is plotted for various values of k in Figure 2.4. Observe that the distribution is skewed, although this skewness becomes less pronounced at higher values of k.

One useful feature of the gamma distribution is its relationship to the Poisson counting process. An example of this relation is illustrated by the random dispersal of bacterial cells. Recall from an earlier discussion that the probability of a volume v containing exactly k randomly dispersed bacterial cells can be expressed by means of the Poisson formula. Reconsider this problem but from a different point of view. Let v_k represent the random volume with exactly k cells. Now, what is the probability that v_k is in the interval v to $v + dv$? Since occurrences in v and dv are independent, we can express the probability as

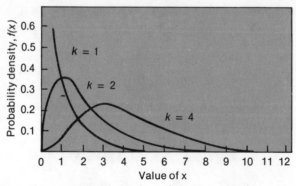

Figure 2.4. Graphs of probability density function of the gamma distribution for $a = 1$ and $k = 1, 2,$ and 4.

$$P(v < v_k \leqslant v + dv) = P(k - 1, v)\, P(1, dv)$$

where $P(k - 1, v)$ is the probability that volume v contains exactly $k - 1$ cells and $P(1, dv)$ is the probability that an additional volume dv contains one cell. Since $P(k - 1, v) = (mv)^{k-1}e^{-mv}/(k - 1)!$, where m is the average number of cells per unit volume, and $P(1, dv) = mdv$, the expression becomes

$$P(v < v_k \leqslant v + dv) = \frac{(mv)^{k-1}}{(k - 1)!}\, e^{-mv}\, (mdv)$$

Thus, the probability density function of v_k is

$$f(v_k) = \frac{m(mv)^{k-1}}{\Gamma(k)}\, e^{-mv}$$

which is the density function of the gamma distribution.

The special case $k = 1$ has been used so frequently as a probability model that it warrants its own name as the *exponential distribution*. The probability density function of the exponential distribution is obtained by letting $k = 1$ in the gamma density function. We get

$$f(x) = ae^{-ax} \tag{2.25}$$

for $x > 0$. Since the exponential distribution is but a special case of the gamma distribution, the mean and variance are

$$E(x) = 1/a \quad \text{and} \quad V(x) = 1/a^2 \tag{2.26}$$

The exponential distribution is one of the most frequently used probability models in population biology. Part of its success can be attributed to the fact that the exponential function describes the distribution of the time interval between successive random events. To illustrate one example where this is useful in population biology, consider a pure death process occurring within a specified population. Suppose that each individual of this population has a constant probability of dying per time interval dt. Designate this probability as $P(dt) = adt$ in which a is a constant. If we then let N be the number in the population at some time t, the decrease in population size during time interval dt can be expressed as

$$- dN = P(dt)N = aNdt$$

If we designate by zero the time at which we begin observing the process, the equation will integrate to yield $N = N_o e^{-at}$ where N_o is the number at time zero. The fraction of individuals surviving, $G(t)$, (i.e., the probability that an individual survivies for at least time t) is then

$$G(t) = N/N_o = e^{-at}$$

Similarly, the probability that a particular individual dies by time t will be the cumulative distribution function

$$F(t) = 1 - G(t) = 1 - e^{-at}$$

Note that if lifetimes follow an exponential distribution, a plot of $\ln G(t)$ versus t will yield a straight line with a slope of $- a$.

In addition to serving as a useful model by itself, the exponential distribution can also be used in the process of constructing models of more complex situations. For example, actual survivorship data often reveal that the ratio of survivors to deaths, $G(t)/F(t)$, is greater than $e^{-at}/(1 - e^{-at})$ as would be the case if lifetimes were truly exponential. One possible explanation for this result might be that the joint occurrence of several malfunctions (not just one as implied by the exponential model) is required to produce damage which is severe enough to cause the death of an organism. One way to model this situation is to let

$$G(t)/F(t) = \frac{be^{-at}}{(1 - e^{-at})}$$

where b is some constant greater than one. Letting $F(t) = 1 - G(t)$ and then solving for $G(t)$, the surviving fraction becomes

$$G(t) = b/(b + e^{at} - 1) \qquad (2.27)$$

This is commonly referred to as the *logistic model* for survivorship. Observe that when $b = 1$, $G(t) = e^{-at}$, which is the survivorship value expected for an exponential model. Note also that when t is large such that e^{at} is much greater than $b - 1$, $G(t)$ becomes be^{-at}. Thus, in the limiting case where t is large, a plot of $\ln G(t)$ versus t will again yield a straight line with a slope equal to $- a$ and an extrapolated intercept of $\ln b$. This overall pattern is illustrated graphically by the series of plots in Figure 2.5.

Beta distribution.   Quite often it is necessary to construct a model in which the continuous variable is a fractional number with all possible values occurring

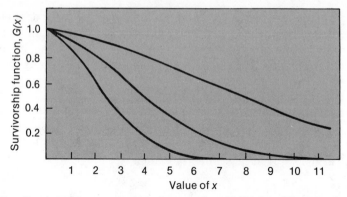

Figure 2.5. Survivorship curves given by equation (2.27) for different values of a.

in the range from 0 to 1. This is particularly true in areas of population genetics where the primary concern is with changes in proportions of individuals or genes rather than total numbers. A useful distribution in this regard is the *beta distribution* defined by the probability density function

$$f(x) = \frac{1}{B(a,b)} (x)^{a-1} (1 - x)^{b-1} \tag{2.28}$$

for $0 < x < 1$. In this expression, a and b are constants and $B(a,b)$ is the *beta function* which is given by the relationship

$$B(a,b) = \frac{\Gamma(a)\,\Gamma(b)}{\Gamma(a + b)} \tag{2.29}$$

For example, $B(3,4) = 2!3!/6! = \dfrac{1}{60}$.

Plots of the beta distribution are shown in Figure 2.6. Observe that a variety of shapes are possible depending on the values of a and b. When both a and b are greater than one, the distribution is peaked with a single modal value. When a and b are both less than one, the distribution becomes U-shaped in appearance. Finally, when both a and b are equal to one, the distribution is flat and all values of x are equally probable.

The mean of the beta distribution can be given as

$$m = E(x) = a/(a + b) \tag{2.30}$$

and the variance of the variable x is

$$V(x) = ab/(a + b)^2 (a + b + 1) = m(1 - m)/(a + b + 1) \tag{2.31}$$

We can, therefore, use the sample mean and sample variance for the purpose of estimating the parameters, a and b. This is shown by solving (2.30) and (2.31) for a and b and substituting $\bar{x}$ and s^2 for the theoretical mean and variance. We get

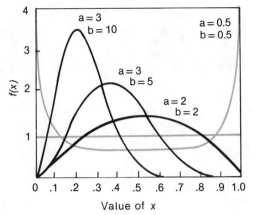

Figure 2.6. Graphs of the probability density function of the beta distribution for different values of a and b. The plot of $f(x) = 1$ is when $a = b = 1$.

$$a = \bar{x}\left[\frac{\bar{x}(1-\bar{x})}{s^2} - 1\right] \quad \text{and} \quad b = (1-\bar{x})\left[\frac{\bar{x}(1-\bar{x})}{s^2} - 1\right]$$

Normal and lognormal distributions.   The normal probability density function is undoubtedly the most frequently used of all probability distributions. Its frequent use is due in part to the fact that the normal distribution often occurs in many real situations and in part to the precision with which it can be used to approximate a large number of distributions. The density function for the normal random variable is defined by the following equation:

$$f(x) = \frac{1}{\sigma\sqrt{2\pi}} e^{-(x-m)^2/2\sigma^2} \tag{2.32}$$

in which m and σ^2 are the mean and variance, respectively. This equation describes a symmetric, bell-shaped curve, as pictured earlier in Figure 2.1A. It has a maximum value of $f(x)$ at the mode where $x = m$ and has two points of inflection occurring at $m \pm \sigma$. In a graph of the normal curve, the frequencies included within the intervals $m \pm \sigma$, $m \pm 2\sigma$, and $m \pm 3\sigma$ are equal respectively to 0.6827, 0.9545, and 0.9973, of the total, which is one.

Even if the normal random variable never occurred in practice, the normal distribution function would still be one of the most important of all probability laws because of its role in the *central limit theorem*. The central limit theorem asserts that when the sum or average of a large number n of independent and identically distributed random variables $x_1 + x_2 + \ldots + x_n$ is being considered, the distribution of this sum (or average) is approximately the normal distribution. This permits one to use the normal density function as an approximation to other distributions in the limiting case when n is large. For example, consider the sum of n Bernoulli trials each with probabilities of success and failure equal to p and q, respectively. Since the probability that x of n trials are successes

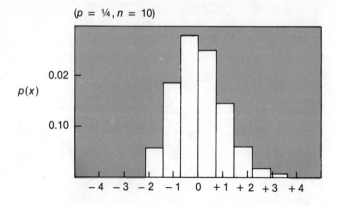

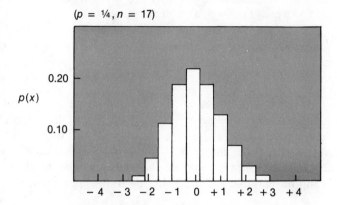

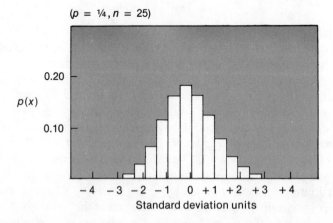

Figure 2.7. The central limit theorem as shown in terms of the approach of a binomial distribution to that of a normal distribution.

is given exactly by the binomial probability mass function, the central limit theorem asserts that the normal curve will become a better and better fit to the binomial distribution as n gets large. This is illustrated graphically in Figure 2.7 for different values of n. Note that as n increases, there are more classes within the same range with smaller differences between them. Ultimately, $p(x)$ for the binomial distribution becomes essentially equal to the normal density function having a mean np and a variance npq.

An argument similar to that given in the central limit theorem can also be made for product of a large number of random variables. For instance, if $x = (y_1)(y_2) \ldots (y_n)$ is the product of a number of positive independent random variables such that $\log x = \log y_1 + \log y_2 + \ldots + \log y_n$, the distribution of $\log x$ will tend to a normal distribution when n becomes large. The variable x, on the other hand, will tend to a *lognormal distribution* defined by the density function

$$f(x) = \frac{1}{x\delta\sqrt{2\pi}}\, e^{-(\log x - u)^2/2\delta^2} \tag{2.33}$$

where the parameters u and δ^2 define the distribution. A plot of the lognormal distribution is shown in Figure 2.8. Unlike the distribution of $\log x$ which is normal (symmetrical) in appearance, the distribution of x is highly skewed towards low values of x.

The mean and variance of the lognormal distribution can be shown to be

$$E(x) = e^{u+\frac{1}{2}\delta^2} \qquad \text{and} \qquad V(x) = e^{2u+\delta^2}(e^{\delta^2} - 1)$$

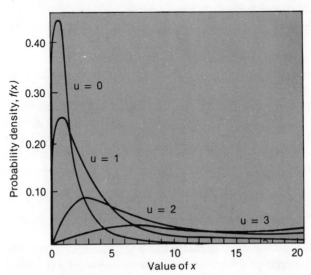

Figure 2.8. Graphs of the probability density function of the lognormal distribution for $\delta = 1$ and $u = 0, 1, 2,$ and 3.

JOINT AND COMPOUND DISTRIBUTIONS

Thus far, we have concerned ourselves with distributions of only single random variables. Such distributions are appropriate when there is reason to believe that only one variable quantity such as population size or gene frequency is of major importance in determining the outcome of some natural or experimental situation. Quite often, however, more than one variable factor actually influences the outcome of the event in question. If such is the case, it may be desirable to determine the probability distribution which includes all the variables of interest. In order to illustrate those methods which are commonly used in developing more complex probability models, what follows are some examples that have direct application in population biology theory.

Joint probability functions.   In order to deal with the joint occurrence of two (or more) random variables, we define a joint probability mass function, $p(x,y)$, which is the probability that two discrete variables take on values x_i and y_i. We can define a joint probability density function, $f(x,y)$, for continuous random variables in a similar manner. The joint probability functions are related to the individual probability functions of the variables by

$$p(x) = \sum_y p(x,y) \quad \text{and} \quad f(x) = \int_y f(x,y)dy$$

where both the summation and integration are carried out over all possible values of y.

Joint probability functions can be easy to work with when the variables are statistically independent. When variables are independent, the joint probability function can be computed as the product of their individual probability functions. Thus, in the discrete case $p(x,y) = p(x)p(y)$, while in the continuous case $f(x,y) = f(x)f(y)$. One interesting example is the diffusion of particles in two-dimensional space. This might be visualized as occurring by random movements on an (x,y) plane. According to statistical theory, such particle displacements can be described in both the x and y directions by means of a normal probability function having a mean displacement of zero and a variance of σ^2. Since each displacement can occur in any direction with equal likelihood, successive displacements must then be independent. Thus, the joint probability function becomes

$$f(x,y) = f(x)f(y) = (1/\sigma\sqrt{2\pi})e^{-x^2/2\sigma^2} (1/\sigma\sqrt{2\pi}) e^{-y^2/2\sigma^2}$$
$$= (1/2\pi\sigma^2)e^{-(x^2 + y^2)/2\sigma^2}$$

The above density function is plotted in Figure 2.9. Observe that we now get a three-dimensional surface with a maximum value of $f(x,y)$ at the origin.

Another joint probability function which is particularly useful for computing a wide range of probabilities is that of the *multinomial distribution*. The mul-

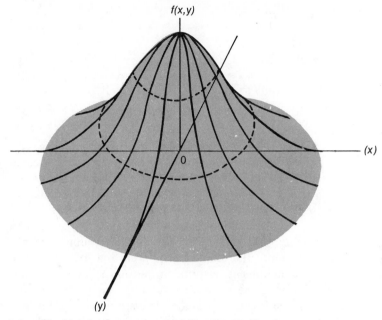

Figure 2.9.   The bivariate normal probability density function.

tinomial distribution function is merely an extension of the binomial probability law which states that if there are k different kinds of objects or things in a very large population with proportions $p_1, p_2, \ldots, p_k$, the probability of selecting x_1 objects of type 1, x_2 of type 2, $\ldots, x_k$ of type k in a random sample of size n is then

$$p(x_1, x_2, \ldots, x_k) = \frac{n!}{x_1! x_2! \ldots x_k!} p_1^{x_1} p_2^{x_2} \ldots p_k^{x_k} \qquad (2.34)$$

This is the probability mass function for the multinomial distribution in which $x_1 + x_2 + \ldots + x_k = n$.

Distributions of sums of variables.   Suppose z is the sum of two random variables x and y (i.e., $z = x + y$). The mean value of z, m_z, is then the sum $m_z = m_x + m_y$ where m_x and m_y are the respective means of x and y. The variance, in turn, will be

$$V(z) = V(x) + V(y) + 2C(x,y) \qquad (2.35)$$

In this expression, $C(x,y)$ represents the *covariance* of x and y defined as the expected value of the cross-product $(x - m_x)(y - m_y)$ (i.e., $C(x,y) = E(x - m_x)(y - m_y)$). For a simple proof of (2.35), let n be the size of the population under study and assume that x and y are discrete variables. Then,

$$V(z) = \frac{1}{n}\Sigma(z - m_z)^2 = \frac{1}{n}\Sigma[(x - m_x) + (y - m_y)]^2$$

$$= \frac{1}{n}\Sigma(x - m_x)^2 + \frac{1}{n}\Sigma(y - m_y)^2 + \frac{2}{n}\Sigma(x - m_x)(y - m_y)$$

$$= V(x) + V(y) + 2C(x,y)$$

since $C(x,y) = \frac{1}{n}\Sigma(x - m_x)(y - m_y)$ when x and y are discrete.

The covariance is a measure of the degree to which x and y are co-related. For example, if x and y are independent (unrelated) variables, their joint tendency to deviate from their expected values in the same direction is as great as their tendency to deviate in opposite directions. In the first case, $(x - m_x)$ and $(y - m_y)$ are either both positive or both negative in value. Hence, the product $(x - m_x)(y - m_y)$ will be greater than zero. In the second case, one deviation will be negative and the other positive, thus yielding a product which is less than zero. It should, therefore, be apparent that by computing $E(x - m_x)(y - m_y)$, positive and negative terms in the sum will tend to cancel since both are equally likely and the value of $C(x,y)$ will equal zero. Thus, for independent random variables, the variance of a sum is simply the sum of the variances. In contrast, when x and y are directly or positively related, $C(x,y) > 0$; whereas, when x and y are inversely or negatively related, $C(x,y) < 0$. Knowledge of the covariance of co-related variables is, therefore, required to calculate the variance of their sum.

Although the covariance is a useful measure of the co-relatedness of variables, it does have one major drawback and that is its sensitivity to the scale of measurement used. Thus, for example, the absolute value of $C(x,y)$ for co-related variables will be greater if the variables are measured in units of, say, millimeters than if measured in meters. This can obviously lead to misinterpretations about the degree to which the variables are related. In order to get around this problem, statisticians have defined another measure of the strength of correlation between two variables termed the *correlation coefficient*, $r_{x,y}$. It is expressed by the following ratio:

$$r_{x,y} = C(x,y)/\sqrt{V(x)V(y)} \tag{2.36}$$

Unlike the covariance, the correlation coefficient is dimensionless. Moreover, it can only range in value from -1 to $+1$. The correlation coefficient is equal to $+1$ when there is perfect positive correlation; it equals -1 for perfect negative correlation; and it is zero when the variables are uncorrelated (i.e., independent). A number of different possibilities are illustrated in Figure 2.10.

The correlation coefficient can also be directly related to the slope of a line, $b_{y,x}$ (also termed the *regression coefficient*). This is illustrated as follows: Let $y = bx + a$ so that $m_y = bm_x + a$. Subtracting the second expression from the first yields $y - m_y = b(x - m_x)$. Now multiply both sides by $x - m_x$ and

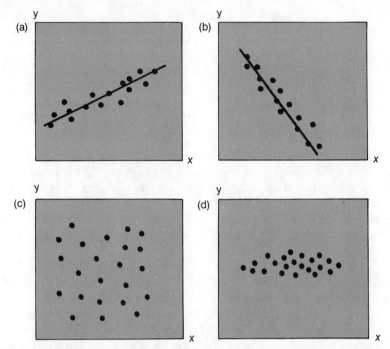

Figure 2.10.   Graphical data showing (a) positive linear correlation, (b) negative linear correlation, and (c) and (d) no correlation. The plots show the location of points (x,y) on a rectangular coordinate system.

take expected values. This yields $E(x - m_x)(y - m_y) = bE(x - m_x)^2$. Since the first expected value is the covariance of x and y and the second is the variance of x, the slope can then be expressed as

$$b_{y,x} = C(x,y)/V(x) = r_{x,y}\sqrt{V(y)/V(x)} \qquad (2.37)$$

The subscripts are added simply to indicate which variables are involved.

It is often important to be able to determine the distribution of the sum of two variables, $x + y$, from their individual distributions when x and y are independent. To illustrate the approach which is generally taken, let x and y be independent Poisson variables with expected values m_x and m_y. We ask for the probability that $x + y$ is some value, say n, and designate this as $P(x + y = n)$. Since any union of events $(x = k, y = n - k)$ for $0 < k < n$ can give rise to $x + y = n$, we can calculate the probability as the sum

$$P(x + y = n) = \sum_{k=0}^{n} P(x = k, y = n - k)$$

$$= \sum_{k=0}^{n} P(x = k)P(y = n - k)$$

$$= \sum_{k=0}^{n} \frac{m_x^k}{k!} e^{-m_x} \cdot \frac{m_y^{n-k}}{(n-k)!} e^{-m_y}$$

$$= \frac{e^{-(m_x+m_y)}}{n!} \sum_{k=0}^{n} \frac{n!}{k!(n-k)!} (m_x)^k (m_y)^{n-k}$$

$$= \frac{(m_x + m_y)^n}{n!} e^{-(m_x+m_y)}$$

Thus, we see that the sum of two independent Poisson variables will also have a Poisson distribution with an expected value $m_x + m_y$. Some other special cases which are of importance are as follows: (1) the sum of two binomial random variables has a binomial distribution; (2) the sum of two normal random variables has a normal distribution; (3) the sum of two gamma random variables has a gamma distribution; (4) the sum of two exponential random variables has a gamma distribution.

Mixed probability distributions.   When attempting to model a complex situation, one frequently encounters two or more variable quantities which vary according to different probability distributions. One interesting example involves compounding a binomial with a Poisson distribution. Suppose that the number of migrants entering a new habitat is Poisson distributed with a mean number of m per season. If each migrant has a constant probability, p, of becoming established in the new area, what is the chance that exactly x migrants become established during a particular season? To answer this question, let

$$p(x \backslash n) = \binom{n}{x} p^x (1 - p)^{n-x}$$

be the conditional probability that x migrants become established in the area, given n migrants to begin with. Since $p(n)$ is Poisson distributed, we can calculate $p(x)$ as follows:

$$p(x) = \sum_{n=x}^{\infty} (P(x \backslash n) p(n)) = \sum_{n-x=0}^{\infty} \binom{n}{x} p^x (1 - p)^{n-x} \cdot \frac{m^n}{n!} e^{-m}$$

$$= \frac{(mp)^x}{x!} e^{-m} \sum_{n-x=0}^{\infty} \frac{(m(1 - p))^{n-x}}{(n - x)!} = \frac{(mp)^x}{x!} e^{-m} e^{-m(1-p)}$$

$$= \frac{(mp)^x}{x!} e^{-mp}$$

In words, if binomial and Poisson distributions are mixed, the resultant distribution is Poisson.

     A second mixture of distributions which is extremely important in certain aspects of population ecology theory is one involving a Poisson combined with a gamma distribution. To illustrate, consider the previous example again in which migrants enter a given area at a Poisson rate. Now, suppose that due to environmental heterogeneity the average rate, m, varies from season to season. Because of the wide range of situations which can be described with the gamma function, it is customary to assume that variation in m can be approximated by some gamma distribution with a density function

$$f(m) = \frac{a^k m^{k-1}}{\Gamma(k)} e^{-am}$$

In other words, it is assumed that m is a random gamma variable. Since the conditional probability of x migrants entering an area, given a specified value of m, $p(x\backslash m)$, is a Poisson function, we can then compute $p(x)$ as

$$p(x) = \int_0^\infty p(x\backslash m) f(m) dm = \int_0^\infty \frac{m^x}{x!} e^{-m} \cdot \frac{m^{k-1} a^k}{\Gamma(k)} e^{-am} \, dm$$

$$= \frac{a^k}{x! \, \Gamma(k)} \int_0^\infty m^{k+x-1} e^{-m(1+a)} \, dm$$

This would appear to be a very complex integral, yet it has a rather simple solution. Recall that the gamma function can be expressed as

$$\Gamma(n) = u^n \int_0^\infty m^{n-1} e^{-um} \, dm$$

Letting $n = k + x$ and $u = 1 + a$, we see that the terms within the integral of $p(x)$ are simply $\Gamma(k + x)/(1 + a)^{k+x}$. By making this substitution, we get

$$p(x) = \frac{\Gamma(k+x)}{x! \, \Gamma(k)} \left[\frac{a}{1+a} \right]^k \left[\frac{1}{1+a} \right]^x$$

This is the probability mass function of the negative binomial distribution having a mean of k/a and a variance of $k/a + k/a^2$. The negative binomial function has been used extensively to model situations in which events, because of environmental conditions or due to the intrinsic nature of the organisms themselves, do not precisely follow a random Poisson pattern.

MONTE CARLO TECHNIQUES

When applying a stochastic model to different aspects of population dynamics, it is customary to treat the process as though it were a game of chance; hence, the reference to a name that is synonymous with gambling. The procedure is rather straightforward, though laborious and time-consuming when large numbers of calculations have to be made. One simply computes the value expected of the probability distribution involved and then modifies this outcome in such a way as to simulate chance deviations from the expected value. To illustrate this procedure when applied to random events within a population, consider a "pure" death process occurring within a cohort (group of individuals born at the same time). If we designate the time of birth as time zero and assume that all individuals have a constant probability of dying within each time interval dt, the probability that an individual survives to at least time t is then an exponential function

$$p = e^{-ut}$$

where u is a constant. Therefore, the probability that exactly N out of the initial number (N_o) will survive to at least time t is the binomial probability

$$p(N,t) = \binom{N_o}{N} p^N (1 - p)^{N_o - N} = \binom{N_o}{N} (e^{-ut})^N (1 - e^{-ut})^{N_o - N}$$

If N_o is reasonably large (greater than or equal to 15 as a general rule of thumb), $p(N,t)$ can be approximated by a normal density function having the same expected value

$$E(N) = N_o e^{-ut}$$

and variance

$$V(N) = N_o e^{-ut}(1 - e^{-ut})$$

Observe that the expected value is simply the deterministic model of this death process. In other words, the deterministic model only describes the expected value about which the population will tend to vary.

   To arrive at a series of possible values for N over time, we compute $E(N)$ at discrete time intervals $1, 2, \ldots, t - 1, t$. We are, therefore, approximating a continuous time process with one that is discrete. We then evaluate the standard deviation ($\sqrt{V(N)}$) for each time and multiply its value by a randomly chosen number from a table of random normal deviates. Finally, we add the above products to their corresponding values of $E(N)$. For a numerical example, let $u = 0.20$ and suppose that the number at the beginning of the first time interval, N_o, equals 200. The expected (or deterministic) value at the end of this interval will be $E(N) = (200)e^{-0.2} = 163.74$. Now say that we select a value from a table of random normal deviates (Beyer, 1968) and obtain $+0.906$. After calculating the standard deviation as $\sqrt{V(N)} = [(200)e^{-0.2}(1 - e^{-0.2})]^{1/2} = 5.448$, the stochastic value (i.e., value that might occur as a result of random variation) can then be computed as $163.74 + (0.906)(5.448) = 168.68$. If this process is continued for the next unit time interval, now using 168.68 as N_o, we might get 143.99 for the stochastic value as opposed to 138.09 for $E(N)$. Two results obtained when employing this procedure over several successive unit intervals are shown in Figure 2.11. Note that, as a consequence of sampling error, each trial tends to be different. Thus, each represents one possible stochastic path taken by the population about that expected from deterministic predictions.

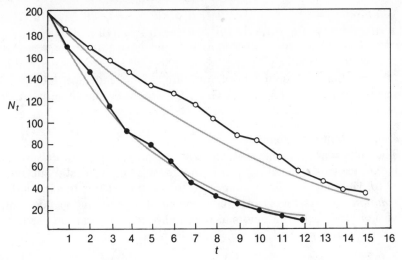

Figure 2.11.   A stochastic model of a pure death process. Open symbols, $u = 0.1$, closed symbols, $u = 0.2$.

SOLVED EXAMPLE PROBLEMS

Descriptive Properties of Distributions

1. Find (a) the arithmetic mean, (b) the geometric mean, and (c) the harmonic mean of the numbers 2, 6, 7, 7, 9, 12, 14, and 20.

   solution   (a) $\bar{x} = (2 + 6 + 7 + 7 + 9 + 12 + 14 + 20)/8 = 9.62$. (b) log $\bar{x}_G = (\log 2 + \log 6 + \log 7 + \log 7 + \log 12 + \log 14 + \log 20)/8 = (0.301 + 0.778 + 0.845 + 0.954 + 1.079 + 1.146 + 1.301)/8 = 0.906$. Thus, $\bar{x}_G = 8.05$. (c) $1/\bar{x}_H = (\frac{1}{2} + \frac{1}{6} + \frac{1}{7} + \frac{1}{7} + \frac{1}{9} + \frac{1}{12} + \frac{1}{14} + \frac{1}{20})/8 = 1.268/8 = 0.158$. Therefore, $\bar{x}_H = 6.31$.

   A comparison of these values illustrates the fact that for a series of positive numbers which are not all equal, the arithmetic mean will be greater than the geometric mean which, in turn, is greater than the harmonic mean.

2. It is readily apparent that the effect of a deviation of, say, 1 gram in a measurement of 10 grams is considerably different than that of 1 gram in a measurement of 100 grams. For this reason, the standard deviation is not particularly useful for comparing variability when units are different. A better measure in this regard is the coefficient of variation (CV). This is a measure of the relative variation about the mean defined by σ/m (or the ratio of sample estimates $s/\bar{x}$). To provide a numerical example, calculate the value of the coefficient of variation for the following numbers: 2, 6, 7, 9, 10, 12, 14, 20.

solution $\bar{x} = (2 + 6 + 7 + 9 + 10 + 12 + 14 + 20)/8 = 10$; $s^2 = [(2 - 10)^2 + (6 - 10)^2 + (7 - 10)^2 + (9 - 10)^2 + (10 - 10)^2 + (12 - 10)^2 + (14 - 10)^2 + (20 - 10)^2]/7 = 30$; thus, $s = 5.48$ and $CV = 5.48/10 = 0.548$ or 54.8%.

Observe that the coefficient of variation is independent of the units used in the calculation of $\bar{x}$ and s. Thus, CV would be the same whether the numbers were, say, 0.1 as great or 10 times greater.

Discrete Probability Distributions

3. The empirical probability of survival of a certain type of cell for time t is 0.4. (a) Out of 6 cells, what is the chance that at least 4 survive time t? (b) How many cells are expected to survive for this time period?
    solution   (a) Assuming that the survival of a cell is independent of that of any other cell, the binomial probability function can be used, where $n = 6$, $x \geqslant 4$, $p = 0.4$, and $q = 0.6$. Hence,

$$p(x \geqslant 4) = \sum_{i = 4}^{6} p(x_i) = \binom{6}{4}(0.4)^4(0.6)^2 + \binom{6}{5}(0.4)^5(0.6) + (0.4)^6$$

$$= 0.1382 + 0.0369 + 0.0041 = 0.1792$$

Hence, the chance that at least 4 cells survive is approximately 18%. (b) For the binomial distribution, $E(x) = np$. Thus, $E(x) = 6(0.4) = 2.4$, or roughly 2 cells on the average.

4. Studies on bacterial populations have shown that mutation is a random process with all cells of a population having a very small but equal chance of experiencing a specific kind of mutation event such as in the development of penicillin resistance. An experiment was performed in which several cultures were each inoculated with one thousand nonmutant cells which were allowed to grow for several generations. At the end of this period of growth, the cultures were checked for the presence of mutant cells. Of 100 cultures examined, 85 contained one or more mutants. How many mutations, on the average, have occurred in each culture during the period of growth?
    solution   First, it is important to recognize that the specified characteristics of mutation (very small but equal chance of occurrence) and the large number of opportunities for mutation (large number of cells in each culture) satisfy the requirements of the Poisson distribution. Therefore, the fraction of culture tubes with exactly x mutations (note: mutations, not mutant cells) can be estimated by equation (2.15) in which $np = m$ is now the average number of mutations per culture. Since a mutant cell must initially arise by mutation, the fraction of tubes with one or more mutations is $1 - e^{-m} = \frac{85}{100} = 0.85$. Hence, the fraction with no mutations is $p(0) = e^{-m} = 1 - 0.85 = 0.15$. We can now estimate m as $m = -\ln(0.15) = 1.9$. Note that once m is known, it is possible to estimate the fraction of cultures with any specified number of mutations.

5. To estimate the size of a fish population, x of the fish are captured, tagged, and returned to the pond, where there are no subsequent effects of the tagging. Independent repeats are then made of the random sampling of single fish from the pond, with success being a tagged fish. Ignoring any problems of capture prone animals, derive an expression from which N, the population size, can be estimated from the recapture data.

    solution Let n = number of samplings required to obtain the kth tagged fish; thus n = the number of trials necessary to obtain the kth success and n is a negative binomial variable. Therefore, $E(n) = k/p = kN/x$ and $N = xE(n)/k$. The value of $E(n)$ can be experimentally determined by repeating the successive random sampling procedure several times and calculating the mean value of n.

6. The empirical probability of survival of a certain type of cell for time t is 0.4 independent of any other cell. An investigator studying these cells needs one cell to survive time t in order to complete an experiment. How many cells should he start with in order to be at least 90% sure of finishing the experiment?

    solution The geometric is the appropriate distribution here, where the first success can occur on or prior to the nth trial. Thus, we want to solve for i in the expression $p(n = i) = \sum_{n=1}^{i} p(n) \geq 0.9$, where $p(n) = pq^{n-1}$.

    We simply add successive $p(n)$ terms until the value of the summation equals or exceeds 0.9: $p(n = 1) + p(n = 2) + p(n = 3) + \ldots + p(n = i) \geq 0.9$ which becomes $0.4 + 0.4(0.6) + 0.4(0.6)^2 + \ldots + 0.4(0.6)^{i-1} \geq 0.9$. This expression can be solved directly; however, recognition of the terms as forming a geometric series greatly facilitates calculations. The terms represent a series of the form $a + ar + ar^2 + \ldots + ar^{i-1}$, where $a = 0.4$ and $r = 0.6$. The sum of this series can be shown to be $a(1 - r^i)/(1 - r)$. Therefore, $0.4(1 - 0.6^i)/(1 - 0.6) \geq 0.9$, and solving for i, we obtain $(0.6)^i \leq 0.1$ or $i = 5$. The experiment should be started with 5 cells in order to be 90% certain that one survives.

Continuous Probability Distributions

7. Suppose that the lifetime distribution for a particular insect species is modeled as a gamma density function with an average lifespan of $\bar{x} = 21$ days and a variance of $s^2 = 18$ days^2. What is the modal value of the lifespan (x) for this distribution?

    solution We begin by determining the value of x when $f(x)$ is maximum. To simplify mathematical considerations, we note that, since $\Gamma(k)$ is constant, the form of the distribution may be studied by merely plotting the function $y = a^k x^{k-1} e^{-ax}$. Taking the derivative of this function and setting it equal to zero, we obtain

    $$dy/dx = (k-1)a^k x^{k-2} e^{-ax} - a^{k+1} x^{k-1} e^{-ax} = k - 1 - ax = 0$$

Hence, the modal value (x_m) is $(k-1)/a$. But, from the relationships of a and k to $\bar{x}$ and s^2, we see that $x_m = (\bar{x}^2 - s^2)/\bar{x}$. Therefore, $x_m = (21^2 - 18)/21 = 20$ days, approximately.

8. Suppose that the frequencies of two genotypes vary from place to place according to a beta distribution. It is observed that in most localities both genotypes occur at the same relative frequency. Show that this is to be expected when the parameters of the beta distribution, a and b, are equal and greater than unity.

   solution Since $B(a, b)$ is constant, the form of this function can be given by a plot of $y = x^{a-1}(1 - x)^{b-1}$. Taking the derivative of this expression and setting it equal to zero, we obtain

   $$dy/dx = 0 = (a-1)x^{a-2}(1 - x)^{b-1} - (b-1)x^{a-1}(1 - x)^{b-2}$$

   $$= (a-1)(1 - x) - (b-1)x$$

   which gives $x_m = (a-1)/(a + b - 2)$. Thus, we see that when $x_m = \frac{1}{2}$, $a + b - 2 = 2a - 2$ or $a = b$ and the distribution becomes symmetrical. It should be apparent that x_m constitutes a maximum only when both a and b are greater than unity.

9. Show that the normal distribution has a mode at $x = m$ and inflection points at $x = m \pm \sigma$.

   solution Note that the form of this distribution is given by a plot of $y = e^{-\frac{1}{2}(x-m)^2/\sigma^2}$. Setting the first derivative equal to zero, we get

   $$dy/dx = - (1/\sigma^2)(x - m)e^{-\frac{1}{2}(x-m)^2/\sigma^2} = 0$$

   This yields $x = m$ as the modal value. Proceeding in the same way with the second derivative, we obtain

   $$d^2y/dx^2 = - (1/\sigma^2)e^{-\frac{1}{2}(x-m)^2/\sigma^2} + (1/\sigma^2)^2(x - m)^2 e^{-\frac{1}{2}(x-m)^2/\sigma^2} = 0$$

   Hence, $x = m + \sigma$ and $x = m - \sigma$ are the inflection points.

10. The lognormal distribution is one of the most frequently encountered nonnormal distributions in biology. For example, in ecology, such variables as the number of individuals per species, the number of parasites per host, and the number of people sick with different diseases quite often follow this distribution (Williams, 1964). Several other examples will be described later in the text. One distinguishing feature of the lognormal distribution is the direct relationship between the standard deviation and the mean of x. Using the formulas for these parameters, show why this relationship exists and indicate how u and δ^2 can be evaluated from sample estimates of $E(x)$ and $V(x)$.

    solution Since $E(x) = e^{u + \frac{1}{2}\delta^2}$ and $V(x) = e^{2u + \delta^2}(e^{\delta^2} - 1)$, the variance can be written as $V(x) = [E(x)]^2(e^{\delta^2} - 1)$. Therefore, $\sqrt{V(x)} = E(x)(e^{\delta^2} - 1)^{1/2}$. Thus, by dividing $\sqrt{V(x)}$ by $E(x)$, we see that the direct relationship expected between the standard deviation and the mean makes the coefficient of variation independent of u and dependent only on δ^2. Note that δ^2 can, therefore, be estimated as $\ln(1 + s^2/\bar{x}^2)$, and u as $\ln \bar{x} - \frac{1}{2}\delta^2$.

Joint and Compound Distributions

11. Humans can be classified according to four blood types A, B, AB, and O. Given that the frequencies of these blood types in a certain population are 0.30, 0.16, 0.04, and 0.50, respectively, what is the probability that, if five individuals are selected at random, two will be type A, one type AB, and two type O?

    solution The appropriate distribution here is the multinomial. Thus, if we let x_1, x_2, and x_3 be the numbers of A, AB, and O individuals in our sample, then

    $$p(x_1 = 2, x_2 = 1, x_3 = 2) = \frac{5!}{2!1!2!}(0.30)^2(0.04)(0.50)^2 = 0.027$$

12. Show, with the aid of expected value notation, that the covariance, $C(x,y)$, is equal to $E(x)(y) - E(x)E(y)$.

    solution
    $$C(x,y) = E[(x - m_x)(y - m_y)]$$
    $$= E[xy - m_x y - m_y x + m_x m_y]$$
    $$= E(x)(y) - m_x E(y) - m_y E(x) + m_x m_y$$
    $$= E(x)(y) - m_x m_y = E(x)(y) - E(x)E(y)$$

    where, in the case of a discrete variable, $E(x)(y) = \Sigma(x)(y)p(x,y)$.

13. Since the correlation coefficient is defined as $r = C(x,y)/\sqrt{V(x)V(y)}$, it is possible to express this parameter in terms of the following formula:

    $$r = \Sigma(x - \bar{x})(y - \bar{y})/\sqrt{\Sigma(x - \bar{x})^2 \, \Sigma(y - \bar{y})^2}$$

    Using this expression, calculate r for the following sets of numbers:

    $$x = 1 \quad 2 \quad 3 \quad 4 \quad 5 \quad 6 \quad 7 \quad 8$$
    $$y = 2 \quad 6 \quad 7 \quad 9 \quad 10 \quad 12 \quad 14 \quad 20$$

    solution

x	y	$(x - \bar{x})$	$(y - \bar{y})$	$(x - \bar{x})^2$	$(y - \bar{y})^2$	$(x - \bar{x})(y - \bar{y})$
1	2	−3.5	−8	12.25	64	28
2	6	−2.5	−4	6.25	16	10
3	7	−1.5	−3	2.25	9	4.5
4	9	−0.5	−1	0.25	1	0.5
5	10	0.5	0	0.25	0	0
6	12	1.5	2	2.25	4	3
7	14	2.5	4	6.25	16	10
8	20	3.5	10	12.25	100	35

$$r = 91/(6.48)(14.49) = 0.969$$

We can, therefore, conclude that there is very good positive correlation between the variables x and y.

14. When analyzing the sources of variability, it is often useful to treat a population as though it were subdivided into a number of groups of varying proportions. It is then possible to express the total variance, $V(x)$, in terms of two components, $\overline{V}(x)$ and $V(\bar{x})$, where $\overline{V}(x)$ is the average variance of all groups (within-group variance, V_w) and $V(\bar{x})$ is the variance of group means (between-group variance, V_B). As their names imply, $\overline{V}(x)$ measures the variation in some attribute within the groups of a subdivided population while $V(\bar{x})$ measures the amount of divergence in group measurements. Using the appropriate symbol definitions for $\overline{V}(x)$ and $V(\bar{x})$, show that the total variance is the sum of the within-group and between-group components.

solution　Let m_j and $V(x_j)$ be the mean and variance of the jth group where $m_j = \sum_i x_i p_i$ and $V(x_j) = \sum_i x_i^2 p_i - m_j^2$. The symbol $\sum_i$ represents the sum of all classes within the jth group. The mean and variance of the total population can then be written as $m = \sum_j m_j p_j$ and

$$V(x) = \sum_j \left(\sum_i x_i^2 p_i \right) p_j - m^2.$$ The symbol $\sum_j$ is the sum of all groups.

The within-group and between-group components will, in turn, be

$$\overline{V}(x) = \sum_j V(x_j) p_j$$

$$= \sum_j \left(\sum_i x_i^2 p_i - m_j^2 \right) p_j \quad \text{and} \quad V(\bar{x}) = \sum_j m_j p_j - m^2$$

Thus,

$$\overline{V}(x) + V(\bar{x}) = \sum_j \left(\sum_i x_i^2 p_i \right) p_j - \sum_j m_j^2 p_j + \sum_j m_j^2 p_j - m^2 = V(x)$$

PROBLEM EXERCISES

1. A nursery man wants to prepare flats of a particular type of plant, guaranteeing his customers 100 plants per flat. He knows that there is a 90% chance of germination per seed for this plant. Assume that growth conditions are such that individual seeds do not influence each other's germination. (a) What is the number of plants expected per flat if he uses 100 seeds for each? (b) How many seeds should he plant per flat to have confidence in his guarantee?

2. A liquid culture contains bacteria at a mean density of 3/ml. Ten 1 ml tubes are filled with the liquid. (a) Calculate the probability that all 10 test tubes will show bacterial growth. (b) How many tubes should receive 4 or more cells?

3. Suppose the probability that an atom of radioactive material will disintegrate by time t is given by $1 - e^{-at}$, where a is a constant depending on the specific isotope used. (a) Find the function describing the length of life of such an atom. (b) If half of the atoms deteriorate in 1,000 time units, what is the chance that the life of an individual atom exceeds 2,000 time units? (c) What is the expected lifetime of an atom of this material?

4. Assume that the height of adult females in a population is normally distributed with a mean of 175 cm and a variance of 64 cm². (a) What fraction of the population is expected to have a height in the range of 159–191 cm? (b) What proportion should be taller than 191 cm?

5. Show that Poisson probabilities increase and then decrease, as long as m is greater than 1, with increasing values of x. Also determine which value(s) of x has (have) maximum probability. (Hint: consider the ratio of neighboring probabilities.)

6. Show that the mean and variance of the difference between two independent random variables $(x - y)$ can be expressed as $m_x - m_y$ and $V(x) + V(y)$, respectively.

7. Suppose that a couple desires exactly 2 boys and will stop having children once this goal is attained. What is the probability that they will have at least 4 children?

8. Weather records for a certain county show that on the average, 3 out of 30 days in November receive precipitation. (a) Assuming each day's weather is not influenced by that of any other day, find the chance that next November will be dryer than average. (b) Give a reason why one might not be justified in using the binomial distribution for this situation.

9. Work problem 8(a) using the Poisson distribution as an approximation. Why do your answers differ somewhat?

10. Consider a random mutation process where the average mutation rate per gene is 10^{-4} per generation and 4 particular loci must independently undergo mutation to cause a phenotypic effect. What is the probability that the mutant phenotype will not occur for at least 10^4 generations? (Hint: consider the distribution of time intervals between successive random events.)

11. In baseball's World Series, the series is concluded when one team has won 4 games. Denote the probability of team A winning any single game as p, and assume that p remains constant throughout the series. What are

the odds of the series ending in 4, 5, 6, and 7 games if (a) $p = 0.5$, and (b) $p = \frac{2}{3}$.

12. Consider a predator that has a 30% chance of success in catching a certain prey. If hunting trials are independent of one another, (a) what is the expected number of catches in 12 trials? (b) How many attempts will the predator need to be at least 95% sure of capturing a prey?

13. The following data were obtained on the length of sparrow wings at various times after hatching:

Age (days):	3.0	4.0	5.0	6.0	8.0	9.0	10.0	11.0	12.0
Wing length (cm):	1.4	1.5	2.2	2.4	3.1	3.2	3.2	3.9	4.1

Age (days):	14.0	15.0	16.0	17.0
Wing length (cm):	4.7	4.5	5.2	5.0

(a) Calculate the correlation coefficient for these two variables.
(b) Is there significant correlation between age and wing length?

14. The number of bacteria surviving exposure to 200 kv X-rays for varying lengths of time was measured in an experiment with the marine bacterium *Achromobacter fischeri* (Lorenz and Henshaw, 1941, Radiology 36: 471–481). The data are given below:

Length of exposure to X-radiation (min)	Number of surviving bacteria (10^{-2}; average of 11 replicas)
7.5	32.72
15.0	15.62
30.0	6.25
45.0	2.66
60.0	0.94
75.0	0.31
90.0	0.19

(a) Using graphical methods, determine if the death of a cell is due to a "single-hit" of X-rays (an exponential varying lifetime).
(b) What is the mean lifetime per irradiated cell?

15. For the data given in the preceding problem, calculate the regression coefficient and write the equation of the linear function relating x and y.

Part Two

Genetics of Populations

3

Population Genetics: An Overview

Having described some of the mathematical methods used in the study and description of population phenomena, we are now in a position to consider some of the basic principles of population biology. A good place to start is with a general description of the genetic characteristics of populations. These characteristics, which are collectively referred to as the genetic structure of a population, include the kinds and frequencies of genes and genotypes and the way in which individuals select their mates. Of particular interest to population geneticists are those factors which can either change or conserve this genetic structure. Among these are the elemental forces of evolution, such as selection and mutation, which function in the continuing adaptation of populations to new and changing environments.

In this chapter, we shall consider many of the basic concepts of population genetics along with a few of their applications. Special emphasis will be placed on the fundamental principles of gene transmission and on those processes which tend to promote or to erode genetic variability. We shall defer more detailed descriptions of many of these topics to later chapters.

TRANSMISSION OF GENES IN POPULATIONS

One important axiom of population genetics states that, with the possible exception of monozygotic twins, no two individuals in a sexually reproducing population are identical in all their characteristics. Thus, phenotypic differences are expected in even the smallest populations that are studied. To a large degree, the basis for this enormous potential for genetic variation lies in the segregation of alleles and the assortment of different allelic pairs during meiosis. This can be illustrated by some rather simple but convincing arithmetic calculations. Suppose, for example, that at each of 1,000 gene loci there are two alleles. Since there are three diploid genotypes possible at each locus, the total number of genotypes which could theoretically occur when all loci are included is then 3^{1000}, a value obviously greater than the existing size of any real population. This potential becomes even more staggering when considered over time, since the meiotic process continues to break up existing gene combinations and produce new and different genotypes in each succeeding generation.

Due to the potential variety and transitory existence of genotypes, any attempt at describing the transmission of genes and their distribution among the progeny becomes almost hopelessly complex unless an effort is made to reduce the problem to its simplest terms. One simplification that can be made is to view a population as a potentially large assemblage of genes, or *gene pool*, rather than merely as a collection of individual organisms. Reproduction occurring in each generation can then be regarded as a sampling process in which a finite number of genes in the form of gametes is drawn from the parental gene pool and combined in different ways to form the genotypes of the progeny. The progeny, in turn, contribute their genes to form the pool of the next generation. As a consequence, the genetic composition of each population will depend on the kinds and frequencies of genes in the sample drawn from the pool of the previous generation.

A second and more obvious simplification is to consider the problem in terms of a single gene locus rather than considering all the different loci that contribute to the whole genotype. Only by restricting our attention to the events at one or just a few gene loci is it possible to discover their underlying principles.

In order to depict the sampling process in more explicit terms, consider the case of a single autosomal locus with two alleles B and b which are distributed within a diploid population as follows:

	Genes		Genotypes		
	B	b	BB	Bb	bb
Frequencies:	p	q	P	H	Q

Since only two alleles are being considered, $p + q = 1$ and $P + H + Q = 1$. If the alleles segregate normally during meiosis, their frequencies among the gametes of this population can be related to the frequencies of the existing parental genotypes in the following manner:

$$p = P + \tfrac{1}{2} H$$
$$q = Q + \tfrac{1}{2} H$$

$$(3.1)$$

The factor H is multiplied by $\tfrac{1}{2}$ in both equations since one-half of the gametes of the heterozygotes (Bb) carry the B gene and the other half carry its allele, b. These equations permit us to calculate p and q if we know P, H, and Q.

Thus, if a population consists of 10% BB, 20% Bb, and 70% bb, then $p = 0.1 + \frac{1}{2}(0.2) = 0.2$ and $q = 1-p = 0.8$. The reverse is not necessarily true; we cannot calculate P, H, and Q from values of p and q unless more is known about the mating system of the population.

In biparental populations, both sexes must contribute an equal number of gametes to the next generation regardless of sex ratio. Therefore, if p_m and q_m are the frequencies of B and b among the males and p_f and q_f are the corresponding frequencies among the females, the effective frequencies of B and b in the gene pool as a whole can then be expressed as

$$p = \tfrac{1}{2}(p_m + p_f)$$
$$q = \tfrac{1}{2}(q_m + q_f)$$

(3.2)

Thus if $p_m = p_f$ (and $q_m = q_f$), gene frequencies can be evaluated from genotype frequencies by way of (3.1) without regard to the sex of the individuals. On the other hand, if gene frequencies should differ within the two sexes, (p_m, q_m) and (p_f, q_f) have to be evaluated separately before one can calculate p and q. For a numerical example, suppose that males consist of 10% BB, 20% Bb, and 70% bb and females are 70% BB, 20% Bb, and 10% bb. Then, $p_m = 0.1 + \frac{1}{2}(0.2) = 0.2$ and $p_f = 0.7 + \frac{1}{2}(0.2) = 0.8$. Hence, the effective frequencies of B and b in the gene pool are then $p = \frac{1}{2}(0.2 + 0.8) = 0.5$ and $q = 1-p = 0.5$.

Now, suppose that a sample of $2N$ gametes is drawn from the parental gene pool to form the progeny population consisting of N individuals. Since the sample is finite in size, gene frequencies will be subject to sampling variation in the next generation. For a sample of size $2N$ (since we are assuming a diploid population of N individuals), gene frequencies among the progeny, p_1 and q_1, can have any one of $2N + 1$ possible values. These values can be designated as

$$0, 1/2N, 2/2N, 3/2N, \ldots, x/2N, \ldots, (2N-1)/2N, 1$$

If the $2N$ gametes constitute a random sample, the probability that the sample contains exactly x B genes (i.e., the probability that $p_1 = x/2N$) is then

$$p(x) = \binom{2N}{x} p^x q^{2N-x}$$

(3.3)

where p and q are again the frequencies of genes B and b in the parental gene pool. Since the sum of the frequencies of the two alleles must add up to one, (3.3) is also the probability that $q_1 = 1 - x/2N$.

When $2N \geq 15$, which is usually the case, the binomial formula in (3.3) can be approximated by a normal density function with the standardized variable given by $z = (x - 2Np)/\sqrt{2Npq}$. In this approximation, $2Np$ is the mean and $2Npq$ is the variance of the variable x. For a numerical example, suppose that a population of 50 progeny is formed from a parental generation in which $p = q = \frac{1}{2}$. Within what range of values is p_1 expected to fall in about 68.3% of such cases? Since 0.683 is the probability that the value (x) of B genes received by the progeny is within one standard-deviation unit of the mean (assuming a normal distribution), the number x is then expected to lie in the range $2Np \pm \sqrt{2Npq} = 50 \pm 5$. Dividing through by $2N = 100$, we get the corresponding range of values for p_1 which is 0.5 ± 0.05 or between 0.45 and 0.55.

A solution to the preceding problem can be obtained more directly by employing the mean and the variance of the ratio $x/2N$ rather than of x. Since x is binomially distributed, p_1 (or $x/2N$) will also have a binomial distribution for which the mean and variance are

$$\bar{p} = E(p_1) = p \quad \text{and} \quad V_p = V(p_1) = pq/2N \tag{3.4}$$

Thus, for $2N \geqslant 15$, the distribution is essentially normal and the probabilities of p_1 falling within the intervals $p \pm \sqrt{V_p}$, $p \pm 2\sqrt{V_p}$, and $p \pm 3\sqrt{V_p}$ are 0.683, 0.954, and 0.997, respectively. Note that when N becomes sufficiently large (i.e., when N is 100,000 or greater as a general rule of thumb), the variance is essentially zero and gene frequencies will tend to remain the same from one generation to the next.

The variance given in (3.4) only applies to uniparental populations and to biparental populations in which there are equal numbers of both sexes. The equation can be modified, however, to take unequal sex ratios into account. To do so, consider the formation of a population consisting of N_m males and N_f females for which $N_m + N_f = N$. Since males are formed from a sample of $2N_m$ and females from a sample of size $2N_f$, the variance of p_m and p_f are then

$$V_{p_m} = pq/2N_m \quad \text{and} \quad V_{p_f} = pq/2N_f$$

Since $p = \frac{1}{2}(p_m + p_f)$, we see that

$$V_p = \frac{1}{4}(V_{p_m} + V_{p_f})$$

which upon substitution and rearrangement becomes

$$V_p = pq(1/8N_m + 1/8N_f) \tag{3.5}$$

Note by comparison with the corresponding equation in (3.4) that a large disparity in sex ratio can greatly increase the sampling variance. For example, if $N_m = 1$ and $N_f = 9$, assuming $p = q = \frac{1}{2}$, the variance predicted by (3.5) is 5/144. If, on the other hand, $N_m = N_f = 5$, the variance with equal numbers of males and females becomes 5/400; a reduction in variance by almost three-fold. Observe that when $N_m = N_f = \frac{1}{2}N$, the variance given by (3.5) reduces to the variance equation (3.4) as it should.

CHANGES IN GENE FREQUENCY

Random drift.   Since the variance of allelic frequencies is inversely related to the existing size of a population, one would expect to observe random or stochastic fluctuations in p and q in small populations. These stochastic fluctuations have been termed random genetic drift (or simply genetic drift) since the measured values of p and q in small populations tend to drift about in a random fashion during successive generations. An example of these changes is illustrated in Figure 3.1 in which some small experimental populations of the same species are started with the same gene frequency and maintained with equal numbers for several generations.

If only a single population is followed, it is convenient to express the effect of drift in terms of the difference $\delta p = p_1 - p$ in which δp denotes the indeterminate change in gene frequency per generation due to sampling variation. Although the exact magnitude and direction of change can never be known with absolute certainty, the probability that δp is some value, say $x/2N - p$, is the same as the probability that p_1 equals $x/2N$ and is given by the binomial formula in (3.3). Since the distribution of δp, like that of p_1, is binomial, the mean and variance of δp are then

$$\overline{\delta p} = E(p_1 - p) = E(p_1) - p = 0$$

and

$$V_{\delta p} = V(p_1 - p) = V(p_1) = pq/2N$$

Unlike numerous other examples of equilibria which are presented in this text, gene frequencies in our present model conform to a case of neutral stability and, once disturbed, do not show any tendency to return to a particular set of values. Therefore, one potential consequence of drift is the gradual divergence of gene frequencies within a series of independent populations. Suppose, for example, that we follow several experimental populations of equal size and with the same initial gene frequencies for a number of generations. The results

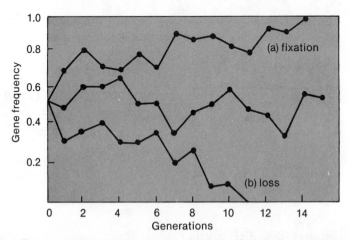

Figure 3.1.   Random drift in the frequency of a gene in three hypothetical isolates of equal size and starting gene frequency. The ultimate outcome is homozygosity due to random fixation (a) or loss (b) of the gene.

expected for a few specified intervals, when $p = q = \frac{1}{2}$ initially, are plotted in Figure 3.2. Observe that sampling variation gives rise at first to a gene frequency distribution that is essentially binomial in character. As this dispersive process continues, however, each population within a given class of the distribution is subjected to still further gene frequency change. This continued compounding of sampling variation ultimately produces a flat (or nearly flat) distribution in which all but the terminal classes ($p = 0$ and $p = 1$) are approximately equal in frequency. Once this phase is reached, the uniform distribution for the subterminal classes decreases at a constant rate. Mathematically, this stochastic process is known as an absorbing Markov chain in which the terminal gene frequency classes serve as absorbing barriers. A comparable analogy is the gradual spreading of a pile of dry sand when a trough of this sand is subjected to periodic agitation (Falconer, 1960). In this analogy, the spreading motion is

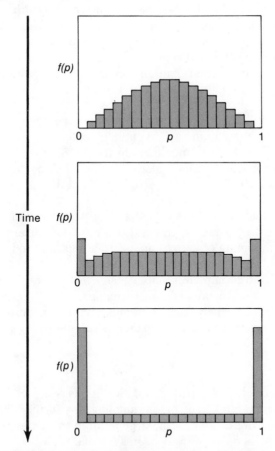

Figure 3.2.   The change in gene frequencies in a series of isolated subpopulations due to genetic drift. Once the distribution is flat, a fraction 1/2N of all groups undergo fixation and loss in each generation.

obviously an ultimate consequence of the movements of individual sand grains just as the spreading of the gene frequency distribution in Figure 3.2 is a result of random changes in gene frequencies within the individual populations. Furthermore, the increase in the terminal gene frequency classes might be likened to the time-dependent loss of sand at the edges of the trough, thus resulting in a gradual reduction in the depth of the remaining pile of sand.

The gradual build-up in the terminal gene frequency classes serves to point out a second major consequence of drift and this is the reduction in genetic variability within small populations due to the random fixation and loss of genes. We see from equation (3.3) that the probability of the B allele being lost in a single generation, $p(x = 0)$, is $(1 - p)^{2N}$ while its chance of fixation, $p(x=2N)$, is p^{2N}. Therefore, a gene has its greatest probability of being lost when p is small while its chances of fixation increase as p approaches one. Once a gene is fixed (or lost), gene frequencies can no longer vary within the population since all of its members are of identical genotype with respect to that locus.

If a gene is not fixed or lost in the first generation, it is exposed again to sampling error during the next reproductive cycle. This continues until every population will have reached fixation for one allele or the other. Since the fixation process is completely random, all of the $2N$ genes at this locus have an equal chance of being fixed. This means that if we consider a series of identical populations to begin with, each with gene frequencies p and q, a fraction p of these populations will eventually undergo fixation for the B gene while a' fraction q will experience fixation for the alternative allele. Once all populations have reached homozygosity for one allele or the other, the mean gene frequency will be $E(p) = (1)p + (0)q = p$ and the variance of p becomes $V_p = (1 - p)^2 p + (0 - p)^2 q = q^2 p + p^2 q = pq$. As is apparent from these calculations, the mean value of p, being equal to the initial value, stays the same throughout the spreading process, while the variance of p continues to increase from a minimum of zero at time-zero in this case to a maximum value of pq.

The approach to complete homozygosity through drift can be shown in more explicit terms by means of a mathematical model relating the variance of p to the number of generations of sampling variation. In order to arrive at this expression, say that after $t - 1$ generations, the mean and variance of p are

$$\bar{p} = \Sigma p_i f_i \quad \text{and} \quad V_{p,t-1} = \Sigma p_i^2 f_i - p^2$$

where f_i is the frequency of the ith population in this series. Since the spreading effect is due solely to random errors in sampling, any further dispersion in gene frequencies occurring during the next generation must then be measured in terms of the mean sampling variance. In symbolic terms, we have

$$\Delta V_{p,t} = \Sigma V_{\delta p_i} f_i = \Sigma p_i(1 - p_i) f_i / 2N$$

where $\Delta V_{p,t} = V_{p,t} - V_{p,t-1}$ and represents the increase in the variance from generation $t - 1$ to generation t. From the mean and variance of p in generation $t - 1$, we see that $\Sigma\, p_i f_i - \Sigma\, p_i^2 f_i = \Sigma\, p_i (1 - p_i) f_i = p(1 - p) - V_{p,t-1}$. Hence, the change in variance becomes

$$\Delta V_{p,t} = (1/2N)(pq - V_{p,t-1})$$

To arrive at a recurrence relation which can be readily solved, add $V_{p,t-1} - pq$ to both sides of the preceding expression. This yields

$$V_{p,t} - pq = (1 - 1/2N)(V_{p,t-1} - pq) = pq(1 - 1/2N)^t$$

which states that the difference between the variance and its equilibrial value decreases by a factor of $(1 - 1/2N)$ in each generation due to sampling. This result is of importance in describing the rate of decay of genetic variability once a flat gene frequency distribution is formed. At this period of decay, the variance of p for the subterminal classes will remain constant since the form of their distribution stays the same. Therefore, the only factor contributing to the overall increase in variance during this phase is the rise in the terminal classes due to gene fixation and loss. This means that a fraction $1/2N$ of all populations undergo fixation and loss per generation during this final period of decay. Since the distribution of remaining unfixed loci is flat, fixation and loss should be equally probable. Hence, at this final phase, fixation and loss should each proceed at a relative rate of $1/4N$ per generation.

Since $1/2N$ is usually quite small, $(1 - 1/2N)^t$ can be approximated as $e^{-t/2N}$. Making this substitution into the preceding expression and solving for the variance, we get the desired relationship:

$$V_{p,t} = pq\left(1 - e^{-t/2N}\right) \tag{3.6}$$

Note that as t increases, $e^{-t/2N}$ must approach zero. Consequently, the variance will increase monotonically to its maximum value pq. Once this value is reached, all populations will be homozygous with a fraction p consisting of only BB individuals and a fraction q made up of only homozygous recessives.

Equation (3.6) is useful in describing the effect of population size on the approach to homozygosity. This effect is shown in its simplest form by solving for the time required to increase the variance to one-half its maximum value (i.e., to $\frac{1}{2}pq$). Letting $t_{1/2} = t$ when $V_{p,t} = \frac{1}{2}pq$, equation (3.6) becomes

$$\frac{1}{2} = 1 - e^{-t1/2/2N} \text{ or } e^{-t1/2/2N} = \frac{1}{2}$$

Solving for $t_{\frac{1}{2}}$, we get

$$t_{1/2} = 2N(\ln 2) = 1.39N$$

Thus, an increase in N will tend to slow the approach by the same order of magnitude.

The effect of population size on the approach to homozygosity is also shown in Figure 3.3 by a plot of equation (3.6) for different values of N. It

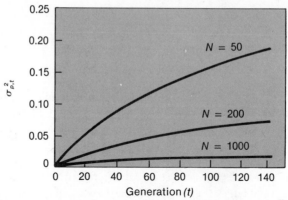

Figure 3.3. Effect of population size on the rate of divergence due to genetic drift. It is assumed that each series of isolated populations starts with a gene frequency of $p = 0.5$.

is assumed once again that all populations begin with a gene frequency of $p = \frac{1}{2}$. Consequently, once fixation and loss have occurred in all groups, the maximum variance will be 0.25.

Selection.   In order to arrive at the preceding equations, it was necessary to assume that gametes are sampled at random from the parental gene pool during each and every generation. If sampling is to be random, all individuals must have the same opportunity of contributing genes to the next generation. Although this serves as a useful first approximation, genotypes under natural conditions quite often express differences in survival and fertility, thus leading to a situation which corresponds to a biased sampling of genes. For example, if the reproductive rate of a particular genotype is greater than the average rate for the population as a whole, the contribution of this genotype to the next generation must be greater than that predicted on the basis of its frequency alone. In this case, the gene frequencies among the gametes which are actually sampled will differ from the frequencies calculated by the set of equations given by (3.1) where equal weight is awarded to each genotypic class. This differential contribution of genes by genotypes to succeeding generations constitutes the generally accepted definition of selection.

   To illustrate one important effect of selection, suppose that due to reproductive inequalities on the part of the genotypes, gene B has a $1 + s$ greater chance of being transmitted to the next generation than does its allele, b. Here, s represents the selective advantage conferred by the B gene on its bearers. Now if we assume a large population so that we can ignore sampling variation, then after one generation of selection, the ratio of p to q will be

$$p_1/(1 - p_1) = (1 + s)\, p/(1 - p)$$

   If the value of s remains constant over several generations, the p to q ratio can then be expressed in terms of a more general recurrence relation

$$p_t/(1 - p_t) = (1 + s)p_{t-1}/(1 - p_{t-1}) = (1 + s)^t p_o/(1 - p_o)$$

where t and $t - 1$ are successive generations and p_o is the frequency of gene B when $t = 0$.

Since s is usually a small fraction, $(1 + s)^t$ can be written approximately as e^{st}. Making this substitution and solving for p_t, we get

$$p_t = \frac{p_o}{p_o + (1 - p_o)e^{-st}} \qquad (3.7)$$

A plot of (3.7) is shown in Figure 3.4. Note that the greatest rate of increase in the frequency of B occurs when $p = \frac{1}{2}$. The rate is extremely slow, however, when p is close to zero or to one. When taken to its logical conclusion, continued reproductive inequalities of this sort will result in the eventual fixation of gene B, coupled with the elimination of its less adapted allele.

THE ORIGIN OF GENETIC VARIATION

Although there is a tendency for random drift and natural selection to reduce genetic variability within populations through the fixation and loss of genes, there are various processes which normally counteract these effects and thus ensure the maintenance of variation. One such process is mutation. Broadly defined, a mutation is any heritable change in the genetic material. As such, mutations constitute the mechanism by which new alleles of a gene are formed and thereby serve as the ultimate source of genetic variability.

Kinds of mutation.   Mutations are often classified according to the size of the mutational alteration. When classified in this way, mutations can be regarded

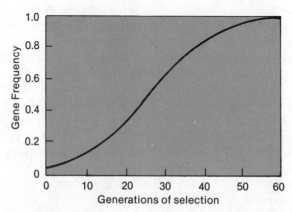

Figure 3.4.   Change in the frequency of an allele as a consequence of selection. The selection intensity is assumed to be $s = 0.1$. Note that the greatest rate of change occurs at intermediate gene frequencies.

as either (1) *point mutations* (intragenic mutations) or (2) *chromosome aber-rations* (extragenic mutations).

Point mutations occur through changes at the nucleotide level of DNA. They include addition-deletion mutations, which occur by the gain or loss of a DNA segment; and substitution mutations, proceeding through an exchange of one base pair for another. Nucleotide substitutions, in turn, may involve *transitions*, in which a purine replaces another purine or a pyrimidine another pyrimidine; or *transversions*, where purines replace pyrimidines and vice versa. One molecular mechanism which is thought to give rise to transitions is that of a *tautomeric shift*, shown in Figure 3.5. In this mechanism, proton migration leads to the formation of a rare isomeric form in a purine or pyrimidine having altered base-pairing properties. Thus, in the case of adenine, for example, the common amino ($-NH_2$) form is replaced by the rare imino ($=NH$) form which now participates in complementary hydrogen bonding with cytosine. When such modified bases occur in the template strand, DNA replication can give rise to a copy error, replacing one base pair with another in one of the daughter molecules.

Such nucleotide changes, be they base-pair replacements, gains, or losses, will give rise to altered codons and, through transcription and translation, may produce changes in the amino acid sequence in the polypeptide chain coded for by the gene. A few of the possible changes are pictured in Figure 3.6. Note that nucleotide additions and deletions will produce shifts in the reading frame of a gene (frame-shift mutations), thus leading in almost every case to the production of a protein which is so altered structurally that it can no longer perform its normal function. On the other hand, base substitutions do not always give rise to amino acid replacements (commonly referred to as missense mutations). Due to codon degeneracy (synonymy of codons), single-base replacements in the third position of a codon quite often lead to silent mutations in which the triplet codes for the same amino acid. Moreover, nonsense mutations can occur yielding codons which cause the premature termination of polypeptide synthesis. An example of how silent, missense, and nonsense mutations might all occur at the same codon is shown in Figure 3.7.

The recent experimental elucidation of the genetic code has made it possible to estimate the fraction of all single-base substitutions which give rise to detectable changes in polypeptides. Such calculations start with the assumption that each of the three nucleotides within a codon can be exchanged for any one of three others with equal likelihood. This is a rather crude first approximation since studies by Benzer (1955) and others have tended to indicate that the frequency of substitution is not the same for all DNA bases. Nevertheless, making this assumption and considering only the 61 codons that specify amino acids, there are then $3 \times 3 \times 61 = 549$ possible nucleotide substitutions. Upon listing these various possibilities, one finds with the aid of the genetic code (Figure 3.8) that 134 out of 549 (or 24.4%) of these nucleotide substitutions result in silent mutations: 23 out of 549 (or 4.2%) give rise to nonsense mutations;

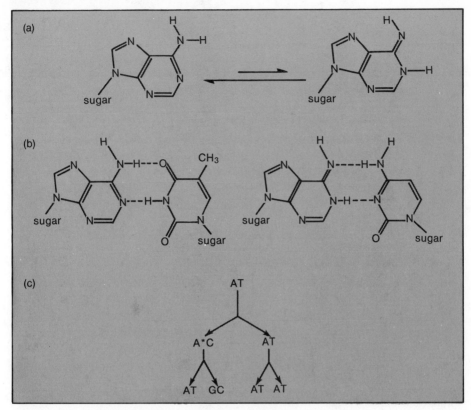

Figure 3.5.   The occurrence of a gene mutation by nucleotide substitution. In (a) adenine undergoes a tautomeric shift, changing from the usual amino form (left) to its rare imino derivative (right). The electronic rearrangement results in changed pairing properties, shown in (b). Normally adenine is complementary to thymine (left); the hydrogen bonding properties of the imino form, however, allow adenine to pair with cytosine (right). The overall result (c) is the substitution of a GC pair for an AT pair.

Wild type:	ATG	TTC	CGG	GAG	
	(tyr)	(lys)	(ala)	(leu)	
Substitution:	ATG	CTC	CGG	GAG	
	(tyr)	(glu)	(ala)	(leu)	
Deletion:	ATG	TCC	GGG	AG–	
	(tyr)	(arg)	(pro)	—	
Addition:	ATG	TAT	CCG	GGA	G–
	(tyr)	(ile)	(gly)	(pro)	—

Figure 3.6.   Basic mutational alterations in DNA. The base sequence is shown in terms of codons while the amino acid which is coded for by each codon is shown below.

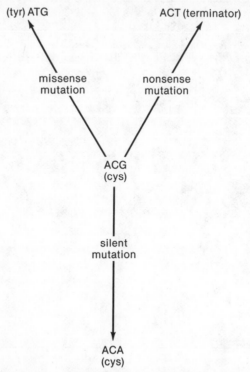

Figure 3.7. Amino acid (or other) changes resulting from different substitution-type mutations in the DNA codon ACG.

| First position | Second position (read across) | | | | Third position |
(read down)	A	G	T	C	(read down)
	phe	ser	tyr	cys	A
	phe	ser	tyr	cys	G
A	leu	ser	stop	stop	T
	leu	ser	stop	trp	C
	leu	pro	his	arg	A
	leu	pro	his	arg	G
G	leu	pro	gln	arg	T
	leu	pro	gln	arg	C
	ile	thr	asn	ser	A
	ile	thr	asn	ser	G
T	ile	thr	lys	arg	T
	met	thr	lys	arg	C
	val	ala	asp	gly	A
	val	ala	asp	gly	G
C	val	ala	glu	gly	T
	val	ala	glu	gly	C

Figure 3.8. The genetic dictionary of DNA base codons and the amino acids for which they code. The three stop code words serve as terminators of polypeptide synthesis, while TAC (met) specifies the initiation of translation.

and 392 out of 549 (or 71.4%) are missense mutations. A comparison of these expected frequencies with those actually observed in proteins tends to show that they are reasonable approximations for vertebrate species (Kimura, 1968) in which the guanine-cytosine content of DNA is relatively constant, ranging only from 40 to 44%. Since amino acid replacements are usually detected experimentally by electrophoretic techniques (e.g., acrylamide-gel electrophoresis), estimates of mutational differences in proteins are usually biased towards those which involve changes in electrostatic charge. Assuming that at the pH commonly used for electrophoresis, lysine and arginine are the only positively charged amino acids and aspartic and glutamic acids are the only ones with a net negative charge, Nei and Chakraborty (1973) have calculated that the fraction of amino acid replacements which give rise to a charge change in proteins is roughly in the range of 0.25 to 0.3. Thus, only about one-fourth to one-third of all mutational differences in proteins can be detected on the basis of charge alone.

In contrast to point mutations, chromosome aberrations involve the breakage and structural rearrangement of whole chromosomes. Such structural alterations are often large enough to be detected with the aid of a light microscope and include deficiencies (loss of a segment), duplications (repeat of a segment), inversions (reversal of a segment), and translocations (transfer of a segment to a different chromosome). The major classes and possible origins of chromosome aberrations are shown in Figure 3.9. Many of these structural alterations are known to cause a distinct phenotypic effect as a consequence of the relocation of chromosomal material. Such phenotypic changes arising as a result of the altered position of genes are termed position effects. Chromosome aberrations are also associated with changes in viability and fertility. For example, deletions are usually lethal when homozygous, while individuals that are heterozygous for reciprocal translocations generally show a marked reduction in fertility due to the production of unbalanced gametes (i.e., gametes with deficiencies and duplications). The chromosomal basis for semisterility of translocation heterozygotes is shown in Figure 3.10. As pictured in the illustration, synapsis in translocation heterozygotes occurs through the formation of a cross configuration involving all four chromosomes. Therefore, the only way that functional gametes can be produced is by the meiotic translocation figure forming a "figure-eight" during the two-by-two disjunction of chromosomes.

Chromosome aberrations have undoubtedly played an important role in evolution. Duplications and deletions are important since they represent possible mechanisms for the gain and loss of genetic material. For example, studies by Bachmann, Goin, and Goin (1974) have shown that the amount of DNA in the cells of many teleost, anuran, and placental species conforms to a lognormal random variable. These results indicate that changes in DNA content have occurred through many small independent additions and deletions rather than by way of changes in whole chromosome sets. Duplications are also responsible for a wide diversity of related gene functions (e.g., genes coding for hemoglobins in vertebrates). This is due to the fact that once a duplication has occurred,

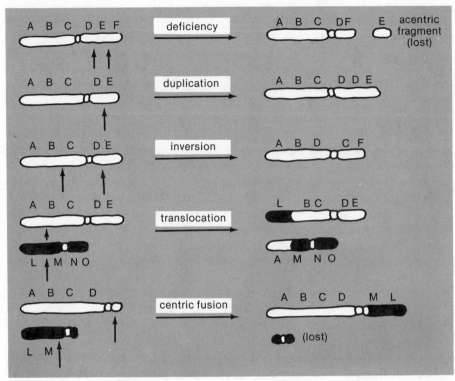

Figure 3.9. Five basic types of chromosome aberrations. Normal chromosomes are pictured on the left and altered chromosomes on the right. The arrows indicate possible breakage points required for the structural rearrangement.

duplicate genes will tend to diverge in character independently of each other since only one need retain its original function.

Inversions and translocations, on the other hand, allow for the rearrangement of genes, resulting in the formation of new linkage groups. In addition, whole arm translocations, such as those involving the fusion of two acrocentric chromosomes (called centric fusions), can be responsible for a reduction in chromosome number. For example, fusions of this type have been shown to be responsible for the reduction in the haploid chromosome number in several species of the genus *Drosophila* from a primitive number of six (Sturtevant and Novitski, 1941).

The process of inversion has also played an important part in the evolutionary development of several species by its role as a crossover suppressor. That is, recombinants for genes within an inverted segment do not appear among the offspring of inversion heterozygotes. Crossing over does occur but gametes carrying crossover products are nonfunctional due to large deletions of chromosomal material. This is shown in Figure 3.11. Genes within an inverted segment are thus held together in the form of a "super gene" and inherited in

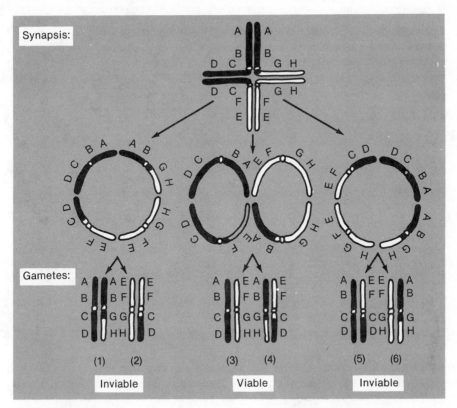

Figure 3.10.   Synapsis and gamete formation in translocation heterozygotes. The majority of all gametes produced are inviable due to large deficiencies.

the same way as alleles. This then represents an important mechanism by which favorable combinations of genes can be assured of joint inheritance without being split up through crossing over into new and possibly less adaptive genotypes.

Rate of mutation.   Mutations occur spontaneously under natural conditions. Such spontaneous mutations are rare, however, with newly mutated genes at any given locus usually occurring in less than 1 in every 1,000 gametes. They are also random events. By random in this case we mean that they are not directed by the environment in which they occur; that is to say, they are not produced as an adaptive response to environmental conditions. Instead, all mutations regardless of type can occur in any generation—some of these may, by chance, be preadaptive.

The probability with which mutations occur is generally expressed in the form of a relative rate termed the *mutation rate*. For present purposes, it is useful to define the mutation rate as the probability that a specified type of mutation occurs per gamete per generation. To clarify our definition, suppose

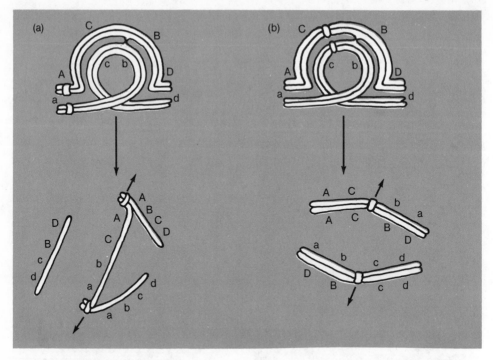

Figure 3.11. The results of crossing over within an inversion loop of an inversion heterozygote. In (a) the centromere is outside the inversion, whereas in (b) the centromere lies within the inversion. In either case, the crossover products are nonfunctional due to large deficiencies.

that some parental population consisting of only BB individuals contributes $2N$ gametes to the formation of the next generation. If gene B mutates at a rate u during this generation interval, the expected number of mutant genes in the gamete sample is then $2Nu$. This is not the number which might actually occur, however. Since mutations are exceedingly rare events and occur independently in time, the probability that exactly x mutant genes are present in the sample can be expressed approximately by the Poisson formula:

$$p(x) = \frac{(2Nu)^x}{x!}\, e^{-2Nu} \tag{3.8}$$

This equation permits one to estimate the number of mutant genes in a finite population once N and u are known, or to design experiments in which u can be determined from measured values of $p(x)$ and N.

Although mutation rates tend to vary with the gene and the organism, those probabilities which can be estimated experimentally range in order of magnitude from about 10^{-9} to 10^{-4} per generation with values between 10^{-5} and 10^{-6} being most common. Some examples of mutation rates observed in various organisms

TABLE 3.1.   Mutation rates at specific loci for various organisms

Organism	Trait	Mutation Rate* (per gamete per generation)
Escherichia coli**	Phage T1 resistance	3×10^{-8}
	Arginine independence	4×10^{-9}
Neurospora crassa**	Adenine independence	4×10^{-8}
	Inositol independence	8×10^{-8}
Zea mays	Shrunken (Sh)	1×10^{-6}
	Purple (Pr)	1×10^{-5}
Drosophila melanogaster	Yellow body	1×10^{-4}
	Ebony body	2×10^{-5}
Mus musculus	Brown coat	4×10^{-6}
	Albino coat	1×10^{-5}
Homo sapiens	Huntington's chorea	1×10^{-6}
	Retinoblastoma	1×10^{-5}

*Estimates derived from a variety of sources including Glass and Ritterhoff (1956), Stadler (1942), Schlager and Dickie (1967), and Neel (1962).
**Mutation rates were measured on a per cell per generation basis.

are shown in Table 3.1. It should be stressed that the rate evaluated for a particular mutational change is not always constant but can be altered significantly by both environmental and genetic causes. It is known, for example, that mutations can be induced by the treatment of organisms with ionizing radiation, ultraviolet light, and various chemical mutagens. These treatments tend to increase the mutability of all genes in direct proportion to their dosage. It has also been shown that the presence of mutator genes can alter the rates of mutation in a variety of organisms. For example, genes which produce defective repair and replicative enzymes in the bacterium *Escherichia coli* can increase the frequency of mutants by as much as 100,000 fold (Cox, 1976). Similar, though less spectacular, effects have been observed in *Drosophila* (Green, 1973). Since mutation rates are under genetic control, it seems reasonable to suppose that optimal values have evolved; or, if not optimal, at least minimal, as a consequence of selection. Mathematical models have been developed which suggest that optimal mutation rates have been struck in asexual organisms between mutational load and the biochemical cost of proofreading for replicative errors (Leigh, 1973). When such models are applied to sexual organisms, however, they suggest that segregation of advantageous mutant genes from the mutator genes which cause them results in the elimination of mutator genes and the reduction of mutation rates to minimal values.

Kinetics of mutation.   The time-dependent effects of recurrent mutation on gene frequency can be shown by considering a large population in which a normal (nonmutant) gene designated B mutates at a rate u to its mutant allelic form, b. We can show this symbolically as

Mutation: $B \xrightarrow{\quad u \quad} b$
Gene frequency: p q

As a consequence of mutation occurring in the parental gene pool, the frequency of the normal allele will be reduced in the first generation by an amount equal to u times the frequency at which B occurs. Therefore, the frequency of the nonmutant gene in generation 1 can be expressed as

$$p_1 = p - up = p(1 - u)$$

and the change in gene frequency during a single generation becomes

$$\Delta p = p_1 - p = - up$$

If mutation continues to occur with the same relative rate, the frequency of the B allele must continue to decline by the factor $1 - u$ in each generation. The value of p can then be expressed in terms of the general recurrence relation

$$p_t = (1 - u)p_{t-1} = (1 - u)^t p_o$$

Because u is such a small quantity, $(1 - u)^t$ is essentially equal to e^{-ut}. Thus, p_t can be written as

$$p_t = p_o e^{-ut} \tag{3.10}$$

in which p_o is the frequency when $t = 0$. As this equation clearly shows, the limiting frequencies of the nonmutant and mutant genes are $p = 0$ and $q = 1$. Therefore, the nonmutant gene will eventually be eliminated from the population.

Although our model predicts a gradual replacement of one gene by another through recurrent mutation, due to the rarity of this process, the time required for a significant change in gene frequency is extremely long. For example, suppose that $u = 10^{-5}$, $p_o = 0.9$, and $p_t = 0.3$. The time required to achieve this change in gene frequency can be obtained by solving (3.10) for t and replacing the symbols with our numerical quantities. We get

$$t = (1/u)\ln(p_o/p_t) = (10^5)\ln(0.9/0.3) = 1.099 \times 10^5 \text{ generations}$$

Note that t is dependent on the reciprocal of the mutation rate. Consequently, a reduction in u will cause an increase in the value of t by the same order of magnitude.

Reversibility of mutation.   Mutations do not always occur in one direction only. Once the mutant allele is formed, it may also have a measurable chance of reverting back to the normal or nonmutant state. The reversibility of the process can be represented as follows:

Mutation: $B \underset{v}{\overset{u}{\rightleftharpoons}} b$
Gene frequency: p q

where v is the reverse mutation rate (b to B). In general, reverse mutation rates tend to be lower than forward mutation rates by a factor of 10 or so. This is due to the much greater variety of nucleotide alterations that can modify or destroy gene function than the possible changes in coding that can produce a particular reversion of a mutant gene.

Due to the reversible nature of the mutation process, the frequency of the B gene will not only decrease due to forward mutation but will also increase in each generation as a result of reverse mutation. We can, therefore, write

$$p_1 = p - up + vq = v + (1-u-v)p$$

Hence, the change in gene frequency becomes

$$\Delta p = vq - up$$

Since forward and reverse mutations have opposing effects on gene frequencies, an equilibrium will be established when $\Delta p = 0$. When this occurs, the frequencies of the two alleles can be expressed by the following formulae:

$$\hat{p} = v/(u + v) \qquad \text{and} \qquad \hat{q} = u/(u + v) \tag{3.11}$$

Thus, once mutational equilibrium has been achieved, gene frequencies are determined solely by forward and reverse mutation rates.

The attainment of a stable equilibrium situation can be seen more clearly by writing the frequency of gene B in terms of the recurrence relation

$$p_t = v + (1 - u - v)p_{t-1}$$

Substituting $(u + v)\hat{p}$ for v and subtracting $\hat{p}$ from both sides, the expression becomes

$$
\begin{aligned}
p_t - \hat{p} &= (u + v)\hat{p} - \hat{p} + (1 - u - v)p_{t-1} \\
&= (1 - u - v)(p_{t-1} - \hat{p}) \\
&= (1 - u - v)^t(p_o - \hat{p})
\end{aligned}
$$

Since u and v are both small quantities, $(1 - u - v)^t$ can be approximated by $e^{-(u+v)t}$. Making this substitution and solving for p_t, we get

$$p_t = \hat{p} + (p_o - \hat{p})e^{-(u+v)t} \tag{3.12}$$

Note that if t is large and $p_o < \hat{p}$, p_t will increase monotonically to its equilibrium value. On the other hand, when $p_o > \hat{p}$, p_t decreases monotonically to $\hat{p}$. Thus, equilibrium is eventually approached from either direction.

Fate of individual mutations.   The deterministic models that we have developed for selection and mutation do not take sampling variation into account and, therefore, only apply to large populations when the frequencies of mutant genes are not close to zero or to one. In small populations, random fluctuations in gene frequency may result in the fixation or loss of mutant genes within a few generations. Chance is also an important ingredient in large populations when mutant genes occur in small numbers. In such instances, mutant genes may be lost through chance events before being replenished. This is particularly true of mutations like many kinds of chromosome aberrations, which are so rare as to be virtually unique. Such mutations have little permanent effect on populations due to their small chance of survival.

Assume, for example, that a mutation occurs in a population of size N. Once formed, the newly arising mutant gene will then comprise a proportion of $1/2N$ of all genes at its locus. Now suppose that the population produces N progeny in the next generation (generation 1). If the gametes from which the progeny are formed constitute a random sample, the probability that a particular gamete carries the mutant gene must then be $1/2N$ and $1 - 1/2N$ that it does not. Therefore, the probability that the gene is absent from all $2N$ gametes and thus eliminated in one generation is $(1 - 1/2N)^{2N}$. If N is large, the probability of elimination becomes

$$[(1 - 1/2N)^{-2N}]^{-1} \simeq e^{-1} = 0.3679$$

The probability that the gene survives is then $1 - 0.3679 = 0.6321$.

Now, assume that the members of generation 1 reproduce, again leaving N offspring. Since the conditional probability that a gamete carries the mutant gene, given that the gene survives the first generation, is $1/2N$, the total chance that the mutant gene is carried by any one particular gamete is now reduced to $0.6321/2N$. Hence, the probability that the gene is absent from all $2N$ gametes and eliminated after two generations will then be

$$(1 - 0.6321/2N)^{2N} \simeq e^{-0.6321} = 0.5315$$

These calculations can be summarized in symbolic form by observing that our method of approach will always yield the recurrence relation

$$l_{t+1} = e^{-(1-l_t)} \tag{3.13}$$

where l_t and l_{t+1} are the probabilities that the mutant gene is lost in t and $t + 1$ generations from the time of the initial mutation. Note in Table 3.2 that the probability of loss increases in each generation, gradually approaching a limiting value of one. Thus, unless mutant genes continue to arise through recurrent mutation, they will ultimately experience extinction.

Equation (3.13) only applies to selectively neutral genes that do not confer any reproductive advantage or disadvantage on their carriers. Single advantageous mutations, on the other hand, do have a chance of survival, although the probability is usually small. To illustrate, consider a mutant gene which increases the reproductive rate of its bearer by a factor of $1 + s$ times that of other genotypes. The probability that this mutant gene is absent in the next generation will then be $(1 - (1 + s)/2N)^{2N} = e^{-(1+s)}$ for large N. After two generations, the probability of elimination increases to $l_2 = e^{-(1+s)(1-l_1)}$. Hence, in general, we can write

$$l_{t+1} = e^{-(1+s)(1-l_t)} \tag{3.14}$$

TABLE 3.2   Probabilities of survival of a selectively-neutral mutant gene.

	PROBABILITY	
Generation (t)	Extinction (l_t)	Survival $(1 - l_t)$
1	0.3679	0.6321
2	0.5315	0.4685
4	0.6879	0.3121
8	0.8110	0.1890
16	0.8934	0.1066
32	0.9428	0.0572
64	0.9702	0.0298
128	0.9848	0.0152
Limit	1.0000	0.0000

The limiting conditions in this case can be evaluated by letting $1 - l_t = 1 - l_{t+1} = y$ be the ultimate chance of survival. Taking logarithms, we get

$$- \ln(1 - y) = (1 + s)y$$

The term $- \ln(1 - y)$ can now be expressed in the form of its series $y + y^2/2 + y^3/3 + \ldots$ Solving for s, we obtain

$$s = y/2 + y^2/3 + \ldots$$

If y is small, the terms raised to powers of 2 or greater can be ignored and the ultimate chance of survival can be given approximately as

$$y = 2s \tag{3.15}$$

For example, with a 1% reproductive advantage ($s = 0.01$), the gene will have a 2% chance of ultimate survival and a 98% chance of eventual loss. Clearly, most mutations with a small or even moderate beneficial effect on reproductive success are eliminated by chance shortly after they arise.

Thus far, the discussion of mutation has been confined to very large populations of constant size. In finite (small) populations, genes can escape accidental loss, even when neutral or somewhat deterimental in character, and eventually reach fixation through random drift. For example, consider a selectively neutral gene mutation occurring in a population of size N. When subjected to sampling variation, a neutral mutant gene must have the same chance as any nonmutant gene at its locus of ultimately being present in the homozygous condition in all N members of the population. The probability that a selectively neutral mutation will be eventually fixed in the population must then be equal to its initial frequency. Hence,

$$y = 1/2N \tag{3.16}$$

The probability of eventual loss is then $1 - y = 1 - 1/2N$. Since the probabilities are inversely proportional to N, its chances of fixation are greater in small populations. As pointed out earlier, the probability of eventual loss will approach unity in very large populations.

Population geneticists including Fisher (1930), Wright (1931), and Kimura (1964) have extended the theory of gene fixation in small populations to include favorable mutations. Kimura has found that, in the case of a semidominant gene, the probability of ultimate fixation (y) for a beneficial gene mutation is

$$y = (1 - e^{-2N_e s/N})/(1 - e^{-4N_e s}) \qquad (3.17)$$

where N and N_e are, respectively, the actual and effective population sizes (for N_e, see Chapter 13). When progeny number per individual varies according to a Poisson distribution, $N_e = N$. Under these conditions and when s is small, (3.17) becomes approximately

$$y = 2s/(1 - e^{-4Ns}) \qquad (3.18)$$

regardless of the value of N. Thus, if N is very small, e^{-4Ns} is essentially equal to $1 - 4Ns$ and y becomes $1/2N$ as in (3.16). The mutation will then behave as though it were selectively neutral in character. If N is very large such that the denominator is essentially equal to one, y reduces to $2s$ which is the value obtained earlier for a very large population. We see that if populations are small enough, even beneficial mutations are fixed in populations solely due to sampling error.

Gene flow.   In addition to mutation, the introduction of new genes into a population may also be accomplished through occasional matings with migrants, usually from contiguous populations. When migration is recurrent, it results in a flow of genes into the gene pool of a recipient population and can then be measured in terms of a *migration rate* (M). The migration rate can be defined as the proportion of new migrants (or new genes) which enter a population per generation. As defined, the value of M depends not only on the amount of dispersal but also on the probability of gene exchange once the migrants are present in the recipient population.

To illustrate the genetic consequences of recurrent migration, or gene flow as it is frequently called, consider a population with initial gene frequencies p_o and q_o which experiences immigration from a neighboring population with gene frequencies p_m and q_m. Assume that after one generation, a fraction m of the recipient population is migrant and $1 - M$ native. The gene frequency of the recipient population after one generation of migration is then simply the average frequency among migrants and natives. Thus,

$$p_1 = Mp_m + (1 - M)p_o = p_o - M(p_o - p_m)$$

Therefore, the change in gene frequency after one generation is

$$\Delta p = - M(p_o - p_m)$$

Note that the change in gene frequency per generation depends not only on M

but also on the difference in gene frequencies between natives and migrants $(p_o - p_m)$. Hence, after one generation this difference is reduced to

$$p_1 - p_m = p_o - M(p_o - p_m) - p_m = (1 - M)(p_o - p_m)$$

If migration continues to occur with the same relative rate, this difference is further reduced by the factor $1 - M$ in each additional generation. Therefore, the difference existing after t generations will be

$$p_t - p_m = (p_o - p_m)(1 - M)^t \tag{3.19}$$

assuming p_m is constant. Since $(1 - M)^t$ approaches zero as t gets large, the gene frequency in the recipient population must eventually equal p_m.

As the preceding expressions show, the effects of migration and mutation are basically similar in that both can be described by linear first-order difference equations. Thus, when both are important in altering gene frequencies, the net change per generation can be expressed as the sum

$$\Delta p = v(1 - p) - up - M(p - p_m)$$
$$= -(u + v + M)(p - \hat{p}) \tag{3.20}$$

where $\hat{p} = (Mp_m + v)/(u + v + M)$ is the value of p when $\Delta p = 0$. In populations which are not isolated in a geographic or ecological sense, M is usually much larger than $u + v$ and the effects of mutation on gene frequencies can then be neglected when mutation and migration are considered jointly.

LONG-TERM EVOLUTIONARY CHANGES

Considerable knowledge has been gained in recent years concerning long-term evolutionary changes by comparing the DNA, RNA, and proteins of distantly related organisms. Comparative studies of this type have revealed evolutionary trends, thereby leading to an understanding of the molecular mechanisms responsible for evolution. Ultimately, such work should make possible the construction of detailed evolutionary histories for many species. What follows is a brief description of the results of some of these studies, starting with a discussion of their theoretical basis.

Rate of gene substitution.   All genes are under recurrent mutation pressure. But, to have importance in evolution, a mutation must spread throughout the breeding population and ultimately reach fixation. At the molecular level, evolution can be viewed as occurring through a series of replacements of nucleotide sequences in DNA. Each sequence would originate from a mutation event, usually by way of a substitution of one base pair for another. This process is pictured in Figure 3.12 in terms of some changes which extend over time in the sequence of base pairs within a hypothetical gene. Since an average gene might

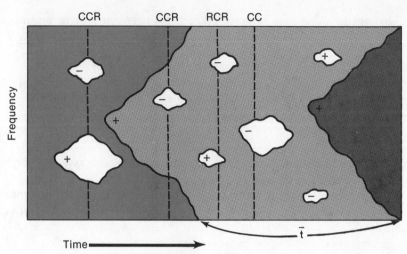

CCR   CCR   RCR   CC

Frequency

Time

$\bar{t}$

Figure 3.12. A diagrammatic representation of the extinction and multiplication of single-site mutations over evolutionary time. At any point in time, the population might be polymorphic for a different combination of rare and common alleles (CCR, RCR, CC, etc.). The symbol $\bar{t}$ represents the average time required for gene substitution, while + and − signs indicate whether the mutations have slight positive or negative effects on survival and fertility.

consist of from 500 to 1,500 nucleotide pairs, the number of mutational possibilities is usually quite large. In addition, many of these mutational events are likely to be indistinguishable by normal procedures. For example, some amino acid substitutions may have no detectable effect on the catalytic activity of an enzyme. Such selectively neutral mutations would not normally be distinguished from wild type. Other variations in amino acid sequence may affect the phenotype similarly in the way in which they enhance or reduce enzyme activity and thus be regarded as the same mutation. Most mutations are, therefore, polyallelic when considered at the nucleotide level and, as a consequence, the mutation rate of classical genetics is the sum of the rates of nucleotide substitutions which affect the phenotype in a similar manner.

In order to arrive at a suitable model for the above situation, we shall first consider a single base pair which can only give rise to selectively neutral mutations should substitutions occur. Let k be the rate of base substitution per gamete per generation at this nucleotide site. Since the mutation rate at a single base pair is very small (on the order of 10^{-9} per round of DNA duplication), the average rate of base substitution ($2Nk$) will tend to be much less than one and we can safely ignore the possibility of more than one mutation arising at a given nucleotide site during the course of any generation. As shown in equation (3.16), each mutation when considered separately has a $1/2N$ chance of eventual survival. Thus, if we assume independence, the average rate of neutral gene substitution becomes

$$(2Nk)\,(1/2N) = k \tag{3.21}$$

when only one mutable site is considered. If we extend our treatment to all, say m, nucleotide sites within a gene which can potentially give rise to a neutral mutation, the average rate of gene substitution will then be $\sum\limits_{i=1}^{m} k_i = u$. Hence, for neutral mutations, the average number fixed per generation is dependent only on mutation rates.

If only a single generation is considered, equation (3.21) can be regarded as the probability of neutral gene substitution per mutable (nucleotide) site. It can also be used to approximate the probability of gene substitution when extended over time by writing (3.21) as the product kt, where t is the time expressed in generations. When t gets large, however, multiple substitutions become quite probable for a single site. Hence, kt starts to depart significantly from the true probability when t gets large and can actually become greater than one when extended through evolutionary time. We can bypass this difficulty if we assume that base substitutions at a particular site occur randomly in time. Successive neutral gene substitutions can then be approximated as a Poisson process. Therefore, we can express the probability that exactly x neutral mutations are fixed at this site over a period of t generations as

$$p(x) = \frac{(kt)^x}{x!}\, e^{-kt} \tag{3.22}$$

Since t is now an exponential random variable, the average time between successive gene substitutions is $\bar{t} = 1/k$.

Kimura and Ohta (1971a) have also derived expressions for the average time in generations to neutral extinction ($\bar{t}_o$) and to neutral gene fixation ($\bar{t}_1$) from the generation of a single mutant's origin. They are, approximately,

$$\bar{t}_o = 2N_e \ln(2N)/N \qquad \text{and} \qquad \bar{t}_1 = 4N_e \tag{3.23}$$

Thus, the length of time to fixation exceeds that to loss by the factor $2N/\ln(2N)$.

The preceding logic can also be applied to beneficial mutations. As in the previous case, the average rate of mutation at a given nucleotide site is $2Nk$. If $4Ns$ in equation (3.18) is sufficiently large so that the ultimate chance of survival of a given base substitution is $2s$, the average rate of favorable gene substitution can be given approximately as

$$(2Nk)(2s) = 4Nks \tag{3.24}$$

Furthermore, if there are m such sites undergoing base substitution, each with a selective advantage equal to s, the average rate of gene substitution becomes $4Ns \sum\limits_{i=1}^{m} k_i = 4Nsu$. For a numerical example, say that the mutation rate of a given gene (u) is 2.5×10^{-5} per generation and that each mutation has a selective advantage of 1%. The average rate of favorable gene substitution is then $10^{-6}N$.

It would, therefore, take a population of more than 10^6 in order for the rate to exceed one gene substitution per generation.

Amino acid substitutions.   Since some nucleotide substitutions result in amino acid replacements in the protein coded for by a gene, a comparison of amino acid sequences in homologous proteins of different species can provide estimates concerning the rate of gene substitution. Such studies can also reveal ancestral relationships of present-day species. A comparative sequence analysis of the hemoglobin proteins illustrates these applications. Vertebrate hemoglobin is a tetramer composed of two α and two β (or two δ or two γ) polypeptide chains, each type coded for by a different gene. The α and β chains differ considerably in amino acid sequence. For example, human α and β chains have 65 sites with the same amino acid residues and 76 sites which are different. Among the human beta-like chains, each having 146 residue sites, β and γ have 37 sites with different amino acids while β and δ show only 10 differences. Furthermore, in a simultaneous comparison of the four polypeptide types, 26 residue sites have the same amino acids in all known hemoglobin peptides. Eleven of these, in turn, are the same as in another oxygen-carrying protein, myoglobin (Zuckerkandl, 1965).

To account for these obvious similarities, molecular evolutionists propose that globin genes are derived from a common ancestral gene following a series of gene duplications. Figure 3.13 is a phylogenetic scheme for the evolution of globin genes in man. Triangles indicate the points of gene duplication; the series of branches indicate the relative order in which the globin peptides became

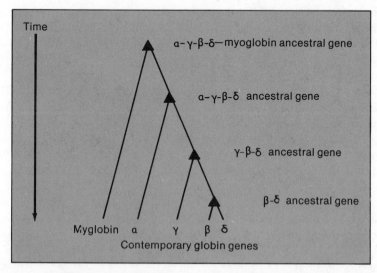

Figure 3.13. Phylogenetic scheme for the evolution of human globin genes. Triangles indicate the points of gene duplication.

distinct from each other. After an initial separation from myoglobin, a second duplication, followed by a translocation, separated the α and β-like genes. Subsequent duplications and divergence gave rise to the closely linked β, γ, and δ genes. The various hemoglobin peptide chains are produced by so-called homologous genes. Homologous genes are derived from a common ancestral gene through divergent evolution following either gene duplication (e.g., hemoglobin) or speciation (e.g., cytochrome c).

Phylogenetic or geneological trees have been constructed for many homologous proteins. Such trees can be derived showing the detailed nature of ancestral relationships of present-day species. This is accomplished solely from amino acid sequence data by depicting the minimum number of genetic events required to relate a homologous set of proteins to a single ancestral amino acid sequence (Figure 3.14). These molecular trees have the same topology (order of branches, not necessarily length or angle) as trees derived by traditional phylogenetic methods (Dickerson, 1972). Phylogeny based on molecular data thus confirms and extends the evolutionary record based on taxonomic and fossil studies. In addition, comparisons of primitive ancestral sequences inferred from phylogenetic trees for seemingly quite different protein families often provide evidence of a common, more primitive ancestor for these families, extending our knowledge of relatedness among proteins.

Finally, these studies show that different protein families evolve at their own characteristic rates. Their rate of evolutionary change is calculated by assuming that amino acid substitution proceeds as a Poisson process. Thus, if k_s is the rate of substitution per amino acid site per year, the probability that amino acid substitution does not occur at a given residue site during a period of t years is $e^{-k_s t}$. Moreover, since species behave as independent evolutionary units, the probability that substitution will not take place during this time at the same site in the proteins of two different species must be $(e^{-k_s t})^2 = e^{-2k_s t}$. Letting n be the total number of amino acid residue sites which can be compared in the two species and n_d represent the number of residue sites which differ in amino acids, we can then write

$$n_d/n = 1 - e^{-2k_s t} \quad \text{or} \quad k_s = -(1/2t)\ln(1 - n_d/n)$$

Thus, if n and n_d are measured for homologous proteins in two different species and their time of evolutionary divergence, t, is estimated from the fossil record, k_s can be evaluated directly. For example, the α hemoglobin chain in man differs from homologous chains in a number of other mammalian species at from 12% to 14% of its amino acids. Since mammals probably diverged from a common ancestor some 80 million years ago, we get approximately

$$k_s = -(1/160 \times 10^6)\ln(1 - 0.13) = 8.7 \times 10^{-10} \text{ per year}$$

Although k_s is a simple and rather useful parameter, it is customary to express the degree of evolutionary change in terms of a measure known as a unit evolutionary period (UEP). The UEP is the time required for two

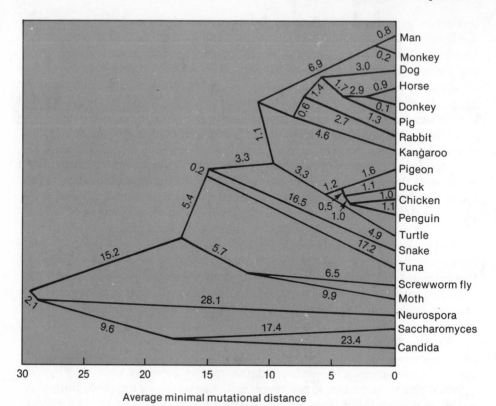

Figure 3.14. Phylogeny of 20 organisms based on the minimum mutational differences in the genes coding for cytochrome *c*. The numbers on the branches are the estimated number of nucleotide substitutions that have taken place, as inferred from the amino acid sequences of this molecule. (After W. F. Fitch and E. Margoliash. *Science* 155: 279, 20 January 1967. Copyright 1967 by the American Association for the Advancement of Science.)

proteins to diverge by 1% of their amino acid sequence. It is calculated as UEP = $0.01/2k_s$. Of those protein families which have been studied in this manner, the fibrinopeptides evolve most rapidly (UEP = 1.1×10^6 yrs), whereas histone IV evolves very slowly (UEP = 600×10^6 yrs). The UEPs for hemoglobin and cytochrome *c* are 5.8×10^6 and 20×10^6 yrs, respectively. Different evolutionary rates for different families suggests that the primary structure of some proteins (e.g., fibrinopeptides) is much more flexible in meeting functional requirements than that of other proteins (e.g., histones).

The UEP for a particular protein can be used to estimate the divergence time for that protein from a related one. Divergence times based on molecular data, however, do not always agree with those based on morphological data, since the former method assumes a similar, constant rate of evolution in the two related proteins. Such an assumption would strictly be valid only if the proteins compared had (nearly) identical functions (e.g., the cytochrome c family whose function has changed hardly at all in diverse evolutionary lines). Therefore, divergence times based on molecular data should be considered as approximations of the true divergence times.

Although selection may determine which and how many amino acid positions can be changed, it need not necessarily limit the kinds of amino acids that can be substituted at permissible positions. Such substitutions may even be selectively neutral in their effects. According to the neutral theory of molecular evolution, changes in macromolecules are the result of fixation, by random drift, of selectively neutral mutations, and diversity in evolutionary rates of different protein families is simply due to a diversity in the number of neutral sites. Because the rate of neutral gene substitution is dependent only on mutation rates (3.21), this theory predicts that the rate of amino acid substitution should be roughly constant when measured over evolutionary time. In contrast, natural selection as the agent of molecular evolution predicts that the rate of evolutionary change is dependent on the population size and degree of selective advantage, in addition to the mutation rate (3.24). When viewed over the entire evolutionary period of the protein involved, the average rate of substitution has been found to be constant per year per site, as long as the function of the molecule remains the same (Dickerson, 1971). This constancy on a chronological time basis is much more easily explained by a neutral, rather than selection, mechanism. Although the controversy between followers of the neutral and selection theories is still far from resolved, it has been most profitable in that it has stimulated a great deal of research on the mechanisms of evolution. This subject is discussed further in Chapter 14.

Evolution of genome size.   In addition to gene substitution, evolution has also involved major additions and deletions of genetic material. This is shown by the great variation in genome size in different organisms. Measurements of the DNA content in approximately 2,000 different species show that organisms can be roughly grouped into four classes, according to their amounts of DNA (Figure 3.15). The cellular DNA content among all organisms ranges from a low of less than 10^4 nucleotide pairs (some viruses) to a high of greater than 10^{12} base pairs per cell (certain primitive plants and multinucleated protozoa). Most of the diversity, however, occurs among the four classes, while organisms within each class exhibit only about a ten-fold range in DNA content.

Even though genome size does increase from viruses to prokaryotes to eukaryotes, few other evolutionary trends are obvious from the data. The amount of DNA is not necessarily correlated with organism complexity, when comparisons are made either between or within groups. For example, although fungi do indeed have a relatively low DNA content, the amoeba, *Amoeba dubias*, with 7×10^{11} nucleotide pairs, has about 100 times more DNA than man. Among the invertebrates, there is a general trend towards greater DNA contents from simple to more complex organisms. *Drosophila* is an exception,

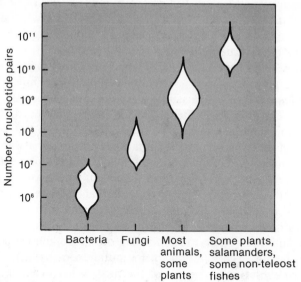

Figure 3.15. A classification scheme for organisms based on their amounts of DNA. Within each group, the majority of organisms have DNA contents within one order of magnitude. DNA amounts for all organisms vary by a factor of more than 10^5. (After R. Hinegardner. 1976. In *Molecular Evolution,* F.J. Ayala, ed. Sinauer Associates, Sunderland, Massachusetts.)

however, having one of the lowest DNA amounts among the animals (1.7 $\times$ 10^8 base pairs per haploid complement). Increases as well as decreases in genome size have occurred in the evolution of the vertebrates, so that cellular DNA content varies relatively little among reptiles, birds, and mammals (about 5 $\times$ 10^9 base pairs per haploid complement). Since a complex organism is thought to require a large number of different genes, gene diversity seems not to be strictly determined by the amount of DNA an organism possesses. Much DNA seems in fact to be genetically silent, perhaps having some yet unknown structural function.

Increases in DNA content over evolutionary time are thought to have occurred by way of duplication of genetic material. Such a process often involves small regions of chromosomes; however, entire genomes can also duplicate. Genome duplication or polyploidy has played an important role in plant evolution and will be discussed in Chapter 13.

Gene duplication, followed by the divergence in function of the duplicated segments, has already been discussed and is exemplified by the evolution of the hemoglobin genes. Other gene duplications are known to have produced multiple copies (up to several hundred per genome) of genes with identical functions. Examples of this so-called "moderately repetitive" DNA include the ribosomal RNA, transfer RNA, antibody, and histone genes. Still other duplications, resulting in the "highly repetitive" class of DNA, have occurred exclusively in eukaryotes, giving short stretches of nucleotide sequences repeated as many as a million times in the genome (Britten and Kohne, 1968). The precise function of highly repetitive DNA is unclear, although it seems a likely candidate for the regulation of gene activity. The relative proportions of single copy, moderately repetitive, and highly repetitive DNA differ widely among different organisms; no obvious correlation with evolutionary complexity has been found.

SOLVED EXAMPLE PROBLEMS

Transmission of Genes

1. Sickle-cell anemia is due to an autosomal recessive gene, Hb^S. A study of American and African adult black populations gave the following data:

	$Hb^A Hb^A$	$Hb^A Hb^S$	$Hb^S Hb^S$
American:	0.9100	0.0895	0.0005
African:	0.6000	0.3880	0.0120

    (a) Calculate the gene frequencies in each population. (b) Suggest reasons for the difference in allele frequencies between the two populations.
    solution   (a) Let p = the frequency of Hb^A and q = the frequency of Hb^S. Then in the American group, $p = 0.9100 + \frac{1}{2}(0.0895) = 0.9548$ and $q = 0.0452$. In the African population, $p = 0.6000 + \frac{1}{2}(0.3880) = 0.7940$ and $q = 0.2060$. (b) The Hb^S allele is maintained in African populations through selection (see Chapter 12).

2. Consider a population composed of 35% BB, 50% Bb, and 15% bb genotypes among both males and females. The parental generation produces 100 progeny. What proportion of the distribution of p_1 values is expected to lie between 0.67 and 0.53?
    solution   Since the parental p value is the same in both sexes, it is simply calculated as $p = 0.35 + 0.25 = 0.60$. The desired range of p_1 values then can be expressed as 0.60 ± 0.07, giving a range of x values of 120 ± 14, where $x = 2Np$. The corresponding range of the standardized variable z is

$$z_{106} = \frac{106 - 120}{6.93} = -2.02 \quad \text{and} \quad z_{134} = \frac{134 - 120}{6.93} = +2.02$$

    or about 2 standard-deviation units above and below the mean. The probability that the value of x falls within 2 standard-deviation units of the mean is 95.4% for a normal variable.

3. For the data in problem 2, compute the variance of the p_1 distribution if the ratio of males to females in the parental population is 1 to 3.
    solution   Given that $N_m/N_f = \frac{1}{3}$ and $N = 100$, we have $3N_m + N_m =$

100, or $N_m = 25$. Hence, $N_f = 75$. Using equation (3.5), the value of V_p is $V_p = (0.6)(0.4)(\frac{1}{200} + \frac{1}{600}) = \frac{4}{2500} = 0.0016$.

Gene Frequency Changes

4. Suppose that a population of 50 progeny is formed from a parental population in which $p = q = \frac{1}{2}$. What is the probability of a random change in gene frequency of absolute value greater than 0.05?

   solution $\sqrt{V_{\delta p}} = \sqrt{(0.5)(0.5)/100} = 0.05$. Since $\overline{\delta p} = 0$, a change in p of ± 0.05 corresponds to ± 1 standard-deviation units from the mean. Therefore, assuming an approximately normal variable, the probability of a δp value ≤ -0.05 or $\geq +0.05$ is $1 - 0.683 = 0.317$.

5. Determine the chance that a gene is lost due to drift in just one generation from a founding population of size (a) 10 and (b) 50, if the population gene frequency is 0.05. Repeat the calculations for a population p value of 0.15.

   solution (a) If $p = 0.05$, $p(x = 0) = (0.95)^{20} = 0.3585$. If $p = 0.15$, $p(x = 0) = (0.85)^{20} = 0.0388$. (b) If $p = 0.05$, $p(x = 0) = (0.95)^{100} = 0.0059$. If $p = 0.15$, $p(x = 0) = (0.85)^{100} = 0.0000$.

6. Study the behavior of the relationship given by equation (3.6) by calculating the $V_{p,t}/pq$ values in a population maintained at a size of 50 for 10, 100, 200, 300, 400, 500, 750, and 1,000 generations.

   solution

t	10	100	200	300	400	500	750	1,000
$1 - e^{-t/2N}$	0.0951	0.6321	0.8647	0.9502	0.9817	0.9933	0.9994	1.0000

7. Show that when s is small and $p_1/q_1 = (1 + s)p/q$, the ratio q/p can be expressed approximately as $q_1/p_1 = (1 - s)q/p$.

   solution All that needs to be shown is that $1/(1 + s)$ is approximately equal to $1 - s$ when s is small. Since $1/(1 + s) = 1 - s + s^2 - s^3 + \ldots$, and s^2 and higher-power terms will be negligible in value for small s, we have the desired result.

Origin of Variation

8. In an electrophoretic study of the amount of genic variation in humans, Harris and Hopkinson (1972) found that out of 71 loci examined in an English population, 28% were polymorphic (at least two protein forms; frequency of the most common form ≤ 0.99). Analogous studies with *Drosophila* and other organisms give similar results. Comment on the magnitude of mutational variability that appears to exist in natural populations.

   solution Since only about one-fourth to one-third of all protein variability can be detected by electrophoresis, we would estimate that essentially all of the loci are polymorphic. Hence, these studies suggest that essentially every gene locus in a population exhibits mutational differences.

9. A certain species of dipteran is differentiated into five races on the basis of overall chromosome morphology and banding patterns of individual chromosomes. The five karyotypes are given below:

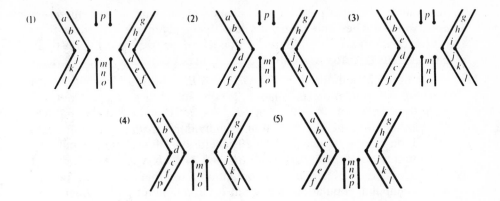

Using the letters to designate gene arrangements, postulate a scheme to account for the evolutionary relationships among these races.

solution   One possible explanation can be given as follows:

$$1 \searrow$$
$$\quad\quad 2 \longrightarrow 3 \longrightarrow 4$$
$$5 \nearrow$$

10. Suppose that 100 replica cultures of *Drosophila*, consisting of 1,000 individuals each, are examined for mutation to a new dominant allele at a particular locus. After one generation, only three cultures are found to contain the mutant gene. Estimate the mutation rate for this locus.
    solution   Using the $p(0)$ term of equation (3.8), we get $0.97 = e^{-2,000u}$. Taking the logarithm of both sides and solving, we obtain $u = 0.03046/2,000 = 1.52 \times 10^{-5}$.

11. How long will it take for gene frequencies to reach 90% of their equilibrium values in a population where $p_o = 0.10$, $u = 10^{-5}$, and $v = 5 \times 10^{-6}$?
    solution   Equation (3.11) is solved for t, where $\hat{p} = u/(u + v) = 0.67$.
    Thus, $t = \dfrac{-1}{u + v} \ln \dfrac{p_t - \hat{p}}{p_o - \hat{p}} = \dfrac{-10^5}{1.5} \ln \dfrac{(0.10)(0.67)}{(0.57)} = 1 \times 10^4$ generations.

12. For a single mutant gene that confers a 1% reproductive advantage to its bearer, calculate its ultimate chances of survival in (a) an infinitely large population, and (b) a finite population of size 40. (c) Repeat parts (a) and (b) for a selectively neutral gene. Comment.
    solution   (a) Using equation (3.14), $y = 0.020$. (b) Using equation (3.17), $y = 0.02/(1 - e^{-1.6}) = 0.025$. (c) In a large population, $y = 0$. In a population of size 40, $y = \frac{1}{80} = 0.0125$, using equation (3.15).
    We see that for a selective value of 1%, which probably is fairly typical of many loci undergoing selection, the limiting chance of survival does not depend much on population size, as long as the population is not

very small. We also note that the chance of ultimate fixation increases only two-fold when comparing this selectively advantageous gene with its neutral counterpart. This difference would be even less for smaller N (e.g., 0.061 versus 0.05 for $N = 10$).

13. Population 1 is composed of 49% BB, 42% Bb, and 9% bb genotypes. A neighboring population (population 2) consists of these three genotypes at the frequencies of 10%, 40%, and 50%, respectively. Due to a breakdown of isolating mechanisms, migration of individuals from population 2 into population 1 begins to occur. After 10 generations of migration, population 1 is found to contain 25% BB, 50% Bb, and 25% bb types. Assuming that population 2 is much larger than population 1 and that a constant fraction of the recipient population is migrant each generation, what fraction of the genes in population 1 is derived from population 2 each generation?
    solution   The assumptions mean that we can treat the donor population as essentially constant in genotype frequencies each generation, that the gene frequencies among the migrants are those of population 2 (neglect sampling error), and that M is constant. To answer the question we, therefore, solve equation (3.19) for M, where $p_m = 0.30$, $p_o = 0.70$, and $p_t = 0.50$. Hence, $(\frac{1}{10})$ log $(0.2/0.4)$ = log $(1 - M)$ = -0.0301 and $M = 0.067$. Thus, 6.7% of the genes in population 1 are derived from population 2 each generation.

14. Compute the ratio of the average time required for neutral gene fixation to that required for extinction with a population size of (a) 200 and (b) 20,000.
    solution   (a) From equations (3.22), $2N/\ln (2N)$ = $200/\ln (200)$ = 37.7 generations. (b) The same procedure yields $20,000/\ln (20,000) \simeq 2,000$. Again we see that extinction is much more likely to occur than fixation when the size of the population is large. Note that the average times for fixation and extinction are independent of mutation rates. They are consequently the same for all gene loci in a given population.

15. Comparison of the hemoglobin α polypeptides of man versus carp shows that the two have 51.4% of their amino acids in common. The divergence of the two species is thought to have occurred 375 million years ago. Estimate the average time between successive amino acid substitutions assuming that amino acid substitution proceeds as a Poisson process.
    solution   Noting   that $e^{-2k_s t} = 0.514$, $k_s = 0.667/2(375 \times 10^6) = 9 \times 10^{-10}$. Therefore, the average time between successive substitutions is

$$\bar{t} = 1/(9 \times 10^{-10}) = 1.1 \times 10^9 \text{ years}$$

16. Show that the approach taken in the derivation of equation (3.13) is equivalent to assuming that progeny number per individual mating is distributed according to a Poisson distribution.
    solution   Consider the progeny of the mating $Bb \times BB$ where b is the

single mutant gene. The probability that b is lost (i.e., all BB offspring are formed) is $(\frac{1}{2})^x$, where x is the number of offspring produced. Since population size is assumed to remain constant, let family size follow a Poisson distribution with a mean of 2. Then, $p(x) = e^{-2}2^x/x!$, and the probability of loss of b during the first generation is the summation of $p(x)(\frac{1}{2})^x$ over all x values. We get $\sum \dfrac{e^{-2}2^x(\frac{1}{2})^x}{x!} = e^{-2} \sum 1/x! = e^{-2}(e) = e^{-1}$.

PROBLEM EXERCISES

1. Calculate the gene frequencies in the following populations: (BB, Bb, bb) = (0.10, 0.25, 0.65); (0.40, 0, 0.60); (0.30, 0.60, 0.10).

2. What range of gene frequency values is expected to include 95% of the offspring, (a) in a population of 50 females and 10 males with $p_m = 0.5$ and $p_f = 0.8$? (b) In a population of 30 females and 30 males with the same gene frequencies as (a)? (c) If 1,000 populations like that in (b) are initiated, how many are expected to undergo fixation of one or the other allele after one generation? After an infinite number of generations?

3. Consider a gene locus which mutates at a rate of 10^{-5} per gamete per generation in a population of 5×10^4 individuals. What is the chance that exactly one newly arising mutant gene will be passed on to the progeny generation?

4. If a gene mutates at a rate of 10^{-6} per generation in a diploid population that remains constant in size at 10 million individuals, (a) how many mutant genes will most likely be passed on to the next generation? (b) What will be the average range (in ± 1 standard-deviation unit about the mean) of the number of mutant genes passed on?

5. Tay-Sachs disease is a degenerative brain disorder that results in death by the age of five years. The cause is a recessive lethal gene which occurs at a comparatively high frequency among Ashkenazi Jews. Assume that the forward and back mutation rates for this gene are 10^{-5} and 10^{-6}, respectively. (a) What would be the gene frequencies in the population of Ashkenazi Jews at equilibrium due solely to mutation pressure? (b) Is it realistic to expect these allele frequencies to be determined solely by mutation? Explain.

6. A particular gene locus has a foreward mutation rate of 10^{-5} per generation, negligible reverse mutation, and 90% nonmutant genes in the starting population. (a) What will be the frequency of mutant genes at this locus after 10, 1000, and 10,000 generations of continued mutation? (b) Calculate the number of generations needed for the mutant allele to increase in frequency from 0.1 to 0.5.

7. Assume a reversible mutation process with $u = v = 10^{-6}$ per generation. (a) What are the equilibrium allele frequencies due to mutation? (b) How many generations would be required to go half way to equilibrium, if the starting population consists only of nonmutant genes?

8. Viewing gene mutation at the level of the codon and using 500 codons as an average gene length, would you expect that back mutation and, therefore, mutational equilibrium, would in reality ever be a significant factor in the determination of gene frequencies? Explain.

9. Assume that two generations ago, a certain population of Indians had only blood type O (genotype ii) of the ABO blood group system. A recent study revealed that this population now contains approximately 3% I^A genes, where I^A is a dominant allele of i. A neighboring population, much larger than the one mentioned above, has maintained constant allele frequencies of 90% i and 10% I^A. Assume that all change is due solely to migration and that there is a constant migration rate per generation. (a) What proportion of genes are introduced into the Indian population through migration each generation? (b) What will be the gene frequencies in the Indian population after five more generations of migration?

10. The data below give the mean number of amino acids among the 141 in the hemoglobin α peptide that are different in humans as compared to horse, rabbit, mouse, and fish (carp). For each of the four comparisons, calculate the yearly rate of evolutionary change.

	Man	Horse	Rabbit	Mouse	Carp
Man	—	18	25	17	58

Assume that the divergence time of mammals from a common ancestor is approximately 80×10^6 years and that the divergence time of human from carp is about 375×10^6 years.

4

Random Mating and Genetic Equilibrium

Mere knowledge of gene frequencies is not sufficient to predict the way in which genes are distributed among the progeny. Before such predictions can be made, additional information is required about the mating system in the parental generation. Some of the kinds of mating patterns that can occur in biparental populations are listed in the following outline:

A. *Random mating*
B. *Nonrandom mating*
    1. *Assortative mating*—mated pairs are more similar in phenotype or in genotype (systematic inbreeding) than if chosen at random.
    2. *Disassortative mating*—mated pairs are less similar in phenotype or in genotype than if chosen at random.

These patterns vary considerably from one trait to another within the same local group. For example, human populations tend to mate at random for various blood types and a host of other traits that do not play a role in mating procedures. These same populations, however, generally mate in an assortative fashion for height, intelligence, and many traits associated with race.

RANDOM MATING FREQUENCIES

Of the patterns listed in the previous outline, random mating is the simplest to describe and serves as the primary basis for comparison. Random mating occurs when all individuals in a population have an equal chance of mating with any other individual of the opposite sex, regardless of genotype. In other words, random mating takes place when mates are selected without regard to genotype. Since mates are selected in an independent manner, the frequency of each kind of mating can be expressed as the product of the frequencies of participating genotypes. For example, a population consisting of three genotypes BB, Bb, and bb occurring at frequencies P, H, and Q among both sexes will have 3^2 or 9 possible kinds of matings when the sex of each parent is specified. These mating types and their frequencies are shown in Table 4.1.

If the sex of each parent is ignored, reciprocal crosses are equivalent and can be combined. The different kinds of matings then reduce to six: $BB \times BB$, $BB \times Bb$, $BB \times bb$, $Bb \times Bb$, $Bb \times bb$, and $bb \times bb$. In this general case, mating frequencies can be expressed by the terms of the trinomial expansion $(P + H + Q)^2 = 1$.

THE APPROACH TO GENETIC EQUILIBRIUM

In order to describe the effect of random mating on genotype frequencies, consider the case of a large population in which adults mate only once and die before the next breeding season in which their offspring reproduce. Although not essential to the argument, the assumption of nonoverlapping generations permits one to disregard the complexities of age distribution and enables one to express time conveniently in units of generations. In addition, ignore any changes that might occur as a result of mutation and migration and assume that all matings occur randomly with respect to mating partner and produce, on the average, the same number of offspring. Since matings are equally fertile, then the proportion of all progeny produced by each kind of mating should equal the frequency of that mating event. For example, of the total matings, a proportion H^2 is of type $Bb \times Bb$. Therefore, in the absence of selection, these matings will contribute a corresponding proportion of all offspring to the next generation. Of the progeny produced, however, $\frac{1}{4}$ is of genotype BB, $\frac{1}{2}$ is Bb, and $\frac{1}{4}$ bb. Hence, the total contribution of such matings to each of the three genotypes will be $\frac{1}{4}H^2$, $\frac{1}{2}H^2$, and $\frac{1}{4}H^2$, respectively. By following this procedure, the contributions of all other mating types can be determined. They are summarized in Table 4.2.

The genotype frequencies among the offspring in generation 1 can now be determined by simply taking the sum of each column in Table 4.2. The genotype frequencies become

$$P_1 = P^2 + PH + \frac{1}{4}H^2 = \left(P + \frac{1}{2}H \right)^2 = p^2$$

$$H_1 = 2PQ + PH + HQ + \frac{1}{2}H^2 = 2\left(P + \frac{1}{2}H \right)\left(Q + \frac{1}{2}H \right) = 2pq$$

$$Q_1 = Q^2 + HQ + \frac{1}{4}H^2 = \left(Q + \frac{1}{2}H \right)^2 = q^2$$

TABLE 4.1.   Random mating frequencies.

Females	Males		
	BB P	Bb H	bb Q
BB P	$BB \times BB$ P^2	$BB \times Bb$ PH	$BB \times bb$ PQ
Bb H	$Bb \times BB$ HP	$Bb \times Bb$ H^2	$Bb \times bb$ HQ
bb Q	$bb \times BB$ QP	$bb \times Bb$ QH	$bb \times bb$ Q^2

TABLE 4.2.   Mating combinations and frequencies of offspring produced under conditions of random mating.

Mating (Generation 0)	Frequency	OFFSPRING		
		BB	Bb	bb
$BB \times BB$	P^2	P^2		
$BB \times Bb$	$2PH$	PH	PH	
$BB \times bb$	$2PQ$		$2PQ$	
$Bb \times Bb$	H^2	$\frac{1}{4}H^2$	$\frac{1}{2}H^2$	$\frac{1}{4}H^2$
$Bb \times bb$	$2HQ$		HQ	HQ
$bb \times bb$	Q^2			Q^2
Sum:*	1	P_1	H_1	Q_1

TABLE 4.3.   Mating combinations and frequencies of offspring produced once equilibrium is attained.

Mating (Generation 1)	Frequency	OFFSPRING		
		BB	Bb	bb
$BB \times BB$	p^4	p^4		
$BB \times Bb$	$4p^3q$	$2p^3q$	$2p^3q$	
$BB \times bb$	$2p^2q^2$		$2p^2q^2$	
$Bb \times Bb$	$4p^2q^2$	p^2q^2	$2p^2q^2$	p^2q^2
$Bb \times bb$	$4pq^3$		$2pq^3$	$2pq^3$
$bb \times bb$	q^4			q^4
Sum:*	1	P_2	H_2	Q_2

*Data analyzed further in the text.

Thus, the genotype frequencies among the offspring after one generation of random mating are determined solely by existing gene frequencies.

Once the preceding genotype frequencies are attained, they will stay the same as long as gene frequencies remain constant. This constancy of genotype frequencies is illustrated in Table 4.3 for a second generation of random mating. In this case, summing each column yields

$$P_2 = p^4 + 2p^3q + p^2q^2 = p^2(p^2 + 2pq + q^2) = p^2$$

$$H_2 = 2p^3q + 4p^2q^2 + 2pq^3 = 2pq(p^2 + 2pq + q^2) = 2pq$$

$$Q_2 = p^2q^2 + 2pq^3 + q^4 = q^2(p^2 + 2pq + q^2) = q^2$$

since $p^2 + 2pq + q^2 = 1$. Thus we see that after one generation of random mating, an equilibrium is established in which genotype frequencies are given by the terms of the binomial expansion $(p + q)^2 = p^2 + 2pq + q^2$. For example, if the adult frequencies of (BB, Bb, bb) are (0.10, 0.20, 0.70), their frequencies in the next and all succeeding generations will be (0.04, 0.32, 0.64) as long as gene frequencies remain constant at $p = 0.20$ and $q = 0.80$.

The relationships existing between genotype and gene frequencies at genetic equilibrium are pictured in Figure 4.1 by a plot of genotype frequency versus q. The actual relations which are plotted are $P = (1 - q)^2$, $H = 2q - 2q^2$, and $Q = q^2$. As shown in the graph, the maximum values of P, H, and Q occur when q is 0, $\frac{1}{2}$, and 1, respectively.

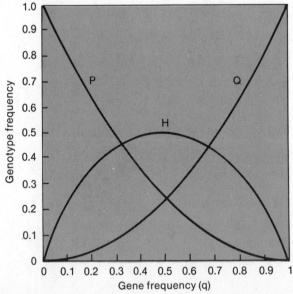

Figure 4.1. Relationship between genotype frequencies and gene frequency among the progeny of a population after one generation of random mating.

Although the preceding algebraic approach is probably the most direct way of demonstrating the attainment of genetic equilibrium, it does get to be rather long and involved. Because of this, we shall adopt two shorter methods in future discussions. One involves the development of an appropriate recurrence relation. To obtain a relationship for the present conditions, note that only two matings, $BB \times bb$ and $Bb \times Bb$, have the potential for giving rise to offspring which are different from the parents in genotype and, thus, for altering genotype frequencies in the next generation. As an example, consider the change in the frequency of heterozygotes. In this case, the value of H will increase by $2PQ$ as a result of the production of heterozygous offspring by $BB \times bb$ matings and will decrease by a factor of $\frac{1}{2}H^2$ due to the production of homozygous as well as heterozygous offspring by $Bb \times Bb$ matings. Hence, the change in the frequency of heterozygotes during the first generation of random mating can be expressed as

$$\Delta H = 2PQ - \frac{1}{2}H^2 \qquad (4.1)$$

where $\Delta H = H_1 - H$. Since $P = p - \frac{1}{2}H$ and $Q = q - \frac{1}{2}H$, then $2PQ = 2(p - \frac{1}{2}H)(q - \frac{1}{2}H) = 2pq - H + \frac{1}{2}H^2$. Substituting this expression for $2PQ$ into equation (4.1), we get

$$H_1 - H = 2pq - H \qquad \text{or} \qquad H_1 = 2pq$$

Thus, after one generation the frequency of heterozygotes is $2pq$. It is easily seen that the frequencies of homozygotes at this time are $P_1 = p - \frac{1}{2}(2pq) = p^2$ and $Q_1 = q - \frac{1}{2}(2pq) = q^2$.

A second and even shorter approach, at least for single autosomal loci, stems from a basic theorem of population genetics which states in effect that random mating is mathematically equivalent to the random union of gametes produced by randomly selected individuals in the population. The genotype frequencies of the progeny can then be calculated as the product of the gene frequencies in the gametes which combine during fertilization. Since mating proportions of the parents are $(P + H + Q)^2$, then if gametes produced by the mates combine at random, the expected genotype frequencies of the zygotes can be given as

$$[(P + \tfrac{1}{2}H) + (Q + \tfrac{1}{2}H)]^2 = (p + q)^2 = p^2 + 2pq + q^2$$

In order to picture the process more clearly, the random union of gametes is diagrammed in Figure 4.2.

The concept that a random mating population attains an equilibrium condition after one generation in which the genotype frequencies remain constant and are given by the product of their respective gene frequencies is known as the *Hardy-Weinberg law* in honor of the men who originally formulated the idea in 1908. This principle greatly simplifies the calculations of gene frequencies as well as genotype frequencies since only the frequency of one homozygote

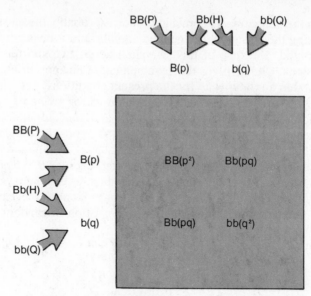

Figure 4.2.   The random union of gametes.

is needed to predict all other proportions. For example, if the frequency of *bb* homozygotes in an equilibrium population is $q^2 = 0.36$, the frequency of the *b* allele must then be the square-root of 0.36 or $q = 0.6$. Since $p = 1 - q$, the frequency of the *B* allele is simply $p = 0.4$. Thus, the frequency of homozygous dominant members of the population must be $p^2 = 0.16$ and that of heterozygotes is $2pq = 0.48$.

Multiple alleles.   The Hardy-Weinberg law can readily be extended to include the case of more than two alleles at a gene locus. To give a general example, suppose that a single locus has k alleles B_1, B_2, B_3, . . . , B_k occurring in a random mating population with frequencies $p_1, p_2, p_3, . . . , p_k$, respectively. Since random mating is equivalent to the random union of gametes produced by this population, an equilibrium will be established as in the case of two alleles after one generation. In this case, however, the equilibrium genotype frequencies will be given by the terms of the k-nomial expansion $(p_1 + p_2 + p_3 + . . . + p_k)^2$.

The presence of a multiple allelic series can lead to a tremendous variety of genotypes. For instance, with k alleles, there are k types of homozygotes and $k!/2!(k - 2)! = k(k - 1)/2$ types of heterozygotes. Therefore, the total number of genotypes produced by random mating will be $k + k(k - 1)/2 = k(k + 1)/2$. Thus, if $k = 10$, there would be 10 homozygous types and 45 kinds of heterozygotes, giving rise to a total of 55 genotypes. A partial list of the different genotypes produced from k alleles and their equilibrium frequencies is represented as follows:

Genotypes: B_1B_1 B_1B_2 B_1B_3 ·· B_1B_k · B_2B_2 B_2B_3 ·· B_kB_k
Frequencies: p_1^2 $2p_1p_2$ $2p_1p_3$ $2p_1p_k$ p_2^2 $2p_2p_3$ p_k^2

As in the problem of two alleles, the equilibrium established through random mating greatly simplifies the calculation of gene and genotype frequencies. For instance, with k alleles, it is theoretically possible to evaluate allelic proportions from knowledge of the frequencies of only $k - 1$ homozygotes. To illustrate, say that the frequencies of all homozygotes are known with the exception of B_kB_k. Then p_1 can be estimated from the square-root of the frequency of B_1B_1, p_2 from the square-root of the frequency of B_2B_2, and so on. Since the frequencies of all alleles must add to one, the frequency of the remaining allele, p_k, can finally be estimated by subtracting the sum of the frequencies of all other alleles from one. More complex situations will be illustrated later in this chapter.

DIFFERENT SEXES AND EQUILIBRIUM

In the preceding model, it was assumed that gene frequencies were the same for both sexes. If they are not the same, equilibrium genotype frequencies will not be attained among the progeny until after the second generation of random mating. To illustrate this exception to the Hardy-Weinberg law, consider a population in which gene frequencies are p_m and q_m among the gametes of the males and p_f and q_f among the female gametes. Upon random fertilization, the genotype frequencies of the progeny of generation 1 become

$$(p_m + q_m)(p_f + q_f) = p_mp_f(BB) + (p_mq_f + p_fq_m)(Bb) + q_mq_f(bb)$$

Since each kind of mating should give rise to equal numbers of males and females, on the average, the genotype frequencies will be the same for both sexes. Hence, the gene frequencies in generation 1 will then be

$$p_{m_1} = p_{f_1} = p_mp_f + \frac{1}{2}(p_mq_f + p_fq_m) = \frac{1}{2}(p_m + p_f) = p$$

$$q_{m_1} = q_{f_1} = q_mq_f + \frac{1}{2}(p_mq_f + p_fq_m) = \frac{1}{2}(q_m + q_f) = q$$

Therefore, it takes one generation just to achieve equality of gene frequencies among the sexes. Once this has been achieved, the genotype frequencies among the progeny of all the following generations will be $(p + q)^2 = p^2 + 2pq + q^2$.

A well-known example in genetics is the parental cross which is conducted between homozygous males and females of complementary genotype. Suppose that this cross involves BB males and bb females. Their offspring (the F_1) will consist of Bb heterozygotes of both sexes. It is, therefore, apparent that gene frequencies are the same for both sexes after one generation. Matings between the F_1 sibs will then produce an F_2 in which members of both sexes conform to the equilibrium frequencies: $\frac{1}{4}BB$, $\frac{1}{2}Bb$, and $\frac{1}{4}bb$. As illustrated in the above example, the net effect of different initial gene frequencies among the sexes is simply to delay the time at which equilibrium is established by one generation.

Sex-linked genes.　　　Thus far, we have dealt exclusively with the transmission of autosomal genes. An equilibrium will also be established with alleles carried on the sex chromosomes. In this case, the approach to equilibrium is complicated in some respects due to the presence of only one sex chromosome in the heterogametic sex. For the purpose of illustration, let X denote the sex chromosome and assume that females are the homogametic sex (XX) and males the heterogametic sex (XY or XO). Two-thirds of all sex-linked genes will then be present in females and the remaining one-third in males. Now consider a sex-linked locus with two alleles B and b which are distributed in a population as follows:

	Females			Males	
Genotypes:	BB	Bb	bb	B	b
Frequencies:	P	H	Q	p_m	q_m

Gene frequencies among the females are $p_f = P + \frac{1}{2}H$ and $q_f = Q + \frac{1}{2}H$, whereas in males gene frequencies are identical with genotype frequencies. Since two-thirds of sex-linked genes are carried by females, the frequencies of the two alleles among the gametes which form the next generation will be

$$p = (2/3)p_f + (1/3)p_m$$
$$q = (2/3)q_f + (1/3)q_m \qquad (4.2)$$

As in the case of an autosomal locus, when $p_m = p_f = p$, equilibrium genotype frequencies are established among the progeny within a single generation. Their values are $p(B)$ and $q(b)$ among the males and $p^2(BB)$, $2pq(Bb)$, and $q^2(bb)$ among the females. The two cases differ, however, when p_m and p_f are unequal. In the case of a sex-linked locus, an equality of gene frequencies among the sexes is approached gradually and in an oscillatory manner. During the approach to equilibrium, p and q remain the same in a large population. What does change is the distribution of the two alleles between the sexes. This is a result of the fact that a male must receive all sex-linked genes from his maternal parent while a female, on the other hand, gets genes equally from both of her parents. When written in symbolic form, these preliminary observations become

$$p_{m,t} = p_{f,t-1}$$
$$p_{f,t} = \frac{1}{2}(p_{m,t-1} + p_{f,t-1})$$

where t and $t - 1$ are successive generations. A recurrence relation can now be derived for p_m. In doing so, first observe that $p = (2/3)p_{f,t-1} + (1/3)p_{m,t-1}$ since p is the same regardless of generation. Solving for $p_{f,t-1}$, the present frequency of gene B among males can then be written as $p_{m,t} = p_{f,t-1} = (3/2)p - (1/2)p_{m,t-1}$. Upon rearrangement, we get

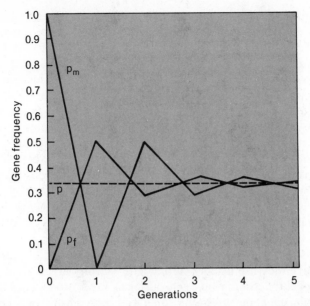

Figure 4.3.   Frequency of a sex-linked gene in both sexes during the approach to an equilibrium condition. The initial population is assumed to consist of *B* males and *bb* females.

$$p_{m,t} - p = -\frac{1}{2}(p_{m,t-1} - p) = \left(-\frac{1}{2}\right)^t (p_{m,0} - p) \qquad (4.3)$$

where $p_{m,0}$ is the frequency at $t = 0$. Observe that the difference between p_m and its equilibrial value is reduced by one-half in each generation. This is shown by a plot of gene frequency versus generation number in Figure 4.3. Starting with a population consisting of *bb* females and *B* males, an equilibrium condition is gradually approached with p_f and p_m oscillating about their equilibrium value $p = 1/3$. Since $p_{m,t} = p_{f,t-1}$, the value of p_m will always lag behind the corresponding value of p_f by one generation.

POLYPLOIDY AND EQUILIBRIUM

The attainment of random-mating equilibrium is further complicated when a population is polyploid; that is, when the population is derived from a line that has experienced an increase in number of complete sets of chromosomes. Although of little evolutionary importance among animals, polyploidy has been extremely important in the evolutionary development of plants. In fact, more than one-third of all flowering plants are believed to be polyploid. At least part of their relative success can be attributed to the tendency of polyploids to be larger in size and more vigorous in their growth than their diploid counterparts.

Polyploids are usually classified as to the origin of their multiple chromosome sets. When these sets originate from members of the same species (i.e., homologous sets), the individual that receives them is referred to as an *autopolyploid*. Thus, in more specific terms, an individual with three homologous sets of chromosomes ($3n$) would be regarded as an autotriploid, an individual with four homologous sets ($4n$) would be an autotetraploid, and so on. These chromosome changes are generally produced by the doubling of chromosome numbers in somatic cells of a sex organ (somatic doubling) or through irregularities in meiosis which lead to the production of unreduced diploid gametes. Suppose, for example, that in a mating between diploid parents ($2n \times 2n$), one parent produces a diploid ($2n$) gamete while the other contributes one which has the normal haploid (n) complement of chromosomes. In this case, the result is a triploid offspring. On the other hand, meiotic irregularities occurring in both parents could lead to offspring of tetraploid or even higher ploidy.

Triploids and other odd n plants ($5n$, $7n$, etc.) are quite rare in natural situations since they are usually sterile. This sterility arises from the unequal distribution of extra chromosome sets during meiosis, producing gametes which largely contain unbalanced chromosome numbers. Even when trivalents are produced in a triploid so that chromosomes are distributed at random in a 2:1 segregation pattern, the chance that a balanced haploid or diploid gamete is formed is usually slim, being $2(\frac{1}{2})^n$ for n number of trivalents. Since most of the gametes are genetically unbalanced in the sense that they contain unequal numbers of different genes, zygote development is impaired in the vast majority of cases. In contrast, plants with even-numbered chromosome sets have a much better chance of being fertile. For example, in tetraploids, meiotic pairing usually gives rise to quadrivalents which can produce balanced diploid gametes through a 2:2 segregation pattern. These tetraploids would be interfertile but reproductively isolated from diploids since mating between them would result in the formation of sterile triploid offspring. An autotetraploid produced in nature could then reproduce vegetatively or by self-fertilization and eventually give rise to a new species, providing that it competes successfully with its diploid counterpart.

A second major type of numerical increase in chromosomes can occur through the formation of *allopolyploids*. These are polyploids in which the multiple chromosome sets are initially derived from different species. Their origin is similar in many respects to that of autopolyploids. For example, when two species which are capable of hybridization mate, their hybrid offspring are frequently sterile. In this case, sterility is due to an insufficient genetic homology to effect pairing and provide an equal distribution of these chromosomes to gametes. However, should the hybrids undergo somatic doubling, each chromosome would have a normal pairing partner and meiosis could proceed on a regular basis. Self-fertilization would then produce an allotetraploid, commonly termed an *amphidiploid*, possessing a diploid number of chromosomes from each of the original parent species. The amphidiploid would now constitute a new species since it is interfertile and reproductively isolated from both of the species that gave rise to it. It would also behave genetically like a normal diploid and would be subject to the rules outlined in the previous sections. The sequence of events which might give rise to an amphidiploid is shown in Figure 4.4.

Random chromosome segregation.   Since amphidiploids are fundamentally diploid in their genetic characteristics, we shall restrict further discussion to autopolyploids in general, and to autotetraploids in particular. We shall also restrict our attention to a single gene locus with two alleles, B and b, and assume that the locus is completely linked to its centromere. The transmission of alleles in this case will depend only on the disjunction of chromosomes and will show a 2:2 segregation pattern generally referred to as random chromosome segregation. This segregation pattern is illustrated by the production of diploid gametes in a heterozygous autotetraploid, $BBbb$, in Figure 4.5.

In order to predict the gametic ratios of other genotypes, let k represent the number of B genes present in an autotetraploid. The genotype of an individual can then be written in general as $B_k b_{4-k}$. Now suppose that this individual produces a large number of gametes. Since sampling is without replacement during gamete formation, the probability that a diploid gamete of this individual contains exactly x B genes can be expressed as

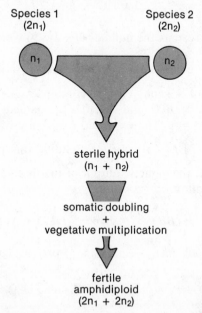

Species 1
(2n₁)

Species 2
(2n₂)

n₁

n₂

sterile hybrid
(n₁ + n₂)

somatic doubling
+
vegetative multiplication

fertile
amphidiploid
(2n₁ + 2n₂)

Figure 4.4.   Possible steps involved in the formation of a Amphidiploid.

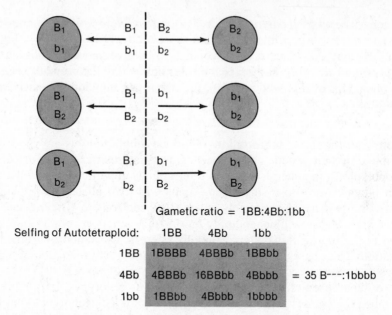

Gametic ratio = 1BB:4Bb:1bb

Selfing of Autotetraploid:	1BB	4Bb	1bb
1BB	1BBBB	4BBBb	1BBbb
4Bb	4BBBb	16BBbb	4Bbbb
1bb	1BBbb	4Bbbb	1bbbb

= 35 B---:1bbbb

Figure 4.5. Production of gametes in a heterozygous autotetraploid, *BBbb*, and consequent production of 35*B---*:1*bbbb* phenotypes upon selfing.

$$p(x) = \binom{k}{x}\binom{4-k}{2-x}\bigg/\binom{4}{2} \tag{4.4}$$

where $\binom{k}{x}\binom{4-k}{2-x}$ represents the number of ways in which x out of k B genes and $2-x$ out of $4-k$ b genes can be selected and $\binom{4}{2}$ is the total number of ways in which 2 out of 4 genes can be combined. As an example, let the genotype of the parent be B_2b_2 and say that the gamete of interest is Bb. In this case, $k = 2$ and $x = 1$. The expected frequency of this gamete type is, therefore, $p(1) = \binom{2}{1}\binom{2}{1}\bigg/\binom{4}{2} = 4/6$. Extending this procedure to all possible values of k and x, the gametic output of the five possible genotypes can then be computed as follows:

$$B_4 = \text{all } (BB) \qquad B_3b = \frac{1}{2}(BB) + \frac{1}{2}(Bb)$$

$$b_4 = \text{all } (bb) \qquad Bb_3 = \frac{1}{2}(Bb) + \frac{1}{2}(bb)$$

$$B_2b_2 = \frac{1}{6}(BB) + \frac{4}{6}(Bb) + \frac{1}{6}(bb)$$

Given these gametic ratios, the results of crossing any two particular genotypes can be readily determined by combining the appropriate gamete types at random.

Having considered the gametic output of individual genotypes, we are now in a position to describe the equilibrium characteristics of an entire population of autotetraploids. To do so, we shall assume a random mating population which at generation zero has the following gene and gamete frequencies:

	Genes			Gametes		
	B	b		BB	Bb	bb
Frequencies:	p	q		x	y	z

In this case, gene and gamete frequencies are related as $p = x + \frac{1}{2}y$ and $q = z + \frac{1}{2}y$. Since random mating is equivalent to the random union of gametes, the genotype frequencies in the next generation (generation 1) will be

Genotypes

	B_4	B_3b	B_2b_2	Bb_3	b_4
Frequencies (Generation 1):	x^2	$2xy$	$y^2 + 2xz$	$2yz$	z^2

The approach to the equilibrium condition can now be illustrated in terms of the change in the frequency of heterozygous (Bb) gametes. Letting y_1 be the frequency of Bb gametes in generation 1, we see that

$$y_1 = (1/2)(2xy) + (2/3)(y^2 + 2xz) + (1/2)(2yz)$$

$$= (1/3)(3xy + 2y^2 + 4xz + 3yz) = (1/3)(4xz + 3y - y^2)$$

From the relationship between gene and gamete frequencies, we know that $x = p - \frac{1}{2}y$ and $z = q - \frac{1}{2}y$. Therefore, $4xz = 4(p - \frac{1}{2}y)(q - \frac{1}{2}y) = 4pq - 2y + y^2$. Substituting this value into the preceding expression yields

$$y_1 = (1/3)(4pq + y) \tag{4.5}$$

Now, replacing y_1 and y in equation (4.7) with their equilibrial value, $\hat{y}$, and rearranging, we find that equilibrium is established when $\hat{y} = 2pq$. This fact enables us to obtain a simple solution for (4.5). To do so, subtract $2pq$ from both sides. We get

$$y_1 - 2pq = (1/3)(4pq + y) - 2pq$$

$$= (1/3)(y - 2pq)$$

Note that the difference between y and its equilibrium value is reduced by a factor of 1/3 in each generation. Hence, the difference existing after t generations will be

$$y_t - 2pq = (1/3)^t(y_o - 2pq) \tag{4.6}$$

where y_o is the value of y when $t = 0$. Thus we see that an equilibrium among autotetraploids is reached gradually rather than suddenly as in the case of a diploid population. Once equilibrium is reached, the frequency of BB gametes will be $x = p - \frac{1}{2}(2pq) = p^2$ and the frequency of bb gametes becomes $z = q - \frac{1}{2}(2pq) = q^2$. Therefore, the equilibrium frequencies of the diploid gametes are given by the terms of the binomial expansion $(p + q)^2 = p^2(BB) + 2pq(Bb) + q^2(bb)$.

The equilibrium proportions of the tetraploid genotypes will then be distributed as $(p + q)^4$:

Genotypes:	B_4	B_3b	B_2b_2	Bb_3	b_4
Equilibrium Frequencies:	p^4	$4p^3q$	$6p^2q^2$	$4pq^3$	q^4

MULTIPLE LOCI AND EQUILIBRIUM

So far, we have dealt only with the transmission pattern expected for alleles at a single locus. When two or more loci are considered, the results are complicated by recombination probabilities and, hence, by the distance between linked genes. To illustrate, consider a single mating between homozygous dominant and recessive parents, $AB/AB \times ab/ab$, which differ in their alleles at two linked loci. These parents can only produce nonrecombinant or parental-type gametes (AB and ab) and can thus give rise to only AB/ab offspring. These heterozygous progeny, in turn, can produce recombinant gametes (Ab and aB) as well as parental types as a consequence of crossing over during first meiotic prophase. This is pictured in Figure 4.6 as an exchange of parts between a pair of homologous chromosomes. Although merely a single exchange is shown, any chromatid with an odd number (1, 3, 5, etc.) of such exchanges between the genes in question will be recombinant. On the other hand, chromatids with an even number of crossovers and those with no crossovers will appear as parental types. Similar statements can be made concerning an $Ab/Ab \times aB/aB$ cross and their Ab/aB offspring, except that in this case, Ab and aB gametes are parental types while AB and ab are considered recombinant.

The simplest model which can be used to describe the results of genetic recombination is one in which crossovers are assumed to occur at random in any interval along the length of each chromosome pair. Thus if the probability that an exchange occurs in any particular interval is small while the number of such intervals is large, the probability that a recombinant gamete is formed (i.e., the chance of an odd number of crossovers between the genes in question) can be expressed as the sum of the odd terms of the Poisson distribution (Haldane, 1919). Hence,

$$R = e^{-d}\left(d + \frac{d^3}{3!} + \frac{d^5}{5!} + \ldots\right) = \frac{1}{2}(1 - e^{-2d}) \qquad (4.7)$$

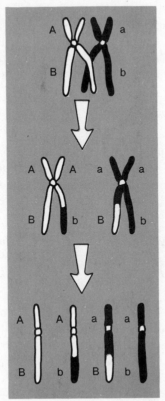

Figure 4.6.   Crossing over as the interchange of corresponding segments between chromatids of homologous chromosomes.

where R is the probability of recombination and d is the average number of crossovers occurring between the two gene loci. The value of R can be estimated directly as the proportion of recombinant types produced by a cross between a double heterozygote and a homozygous recessive (two-factor test cross). The value of d, in turn, must vary directly with distance. Thus, if genes are closely linked, d is small and e^{-2d} becomes approximately equal to $1 - 2d$; hence, R will be essentially equal to d. When the distance is large, however, e^{-2d} approaches zero and R will approach its limiting value of $\frac{1}{2}$. Since the proportion of recombinant types must also be $\frac{1}{2}$ for unlinked genes as a result of independent assortment, this means that distantly separated genes will behave as though they are unlinked. Although equation (4.7) is useful for describing the more general consequences of genetic recombination, it should be made clear that, because of the failure of adjacent crossovers to behave as independent events, recombinant frequencies frequently depart significantly from predictions based on the assumption of a Poisson distribution.

Establishment of equilibrium. Now consider these same genes within a randomly mating population in which their frequencies are $p_1(A)$, $q_1(a)$, $p_2(B.)$, and $q_2(b)$. Since A,a and B,b are allelic pairs at separate loci, it follows that $p_1 + q_1 = p_2 + q_2 = 1$. The gametes produced by this population at some arbitrary starting time (generation 0) can then be represented as

Gamete type:	AB	Ab	aB	ab
Frequency:	h	i	j	k

where $p_1 = h + i$, $q_1 = j + k$, $p_2 = h + j$, and $q_2 = i + k$. Since mating is random, these gametes will combine at random during each generation giving rise to progeny genotypes. Hence, the frequencies of the various genotypes in the next generation (generation 1) will be given by the terms of the tetranomial expansion $(h + i + j + k)^2$. For convenience, these frequencies are illustrated in terms of the following notation:

$$\begin{Bmatrix} AABB & AABb & AAbb \\ AaBB & AaBb & Aabb \\ aaBB & aaBb & aabb \end{Bmatrix} = \begin{Bmatrix} h^2 & 2hi & i^2 \\ 2hj & 2hk + 2ij & 2ik \\ j^2 & 2jk & k^2 \end{Bmatrix}$$

where $2hk$ is the frequency of the heterozygote, AB/ab, in which genes are linked in the cis arrangement, and $2ij$ is the frequency of the trans-arrangement heterozygote, Ab/aB. When using this notation, the frequencies of AA, Aa, and aa can be obtained directly from the sums of the rows which are $(h + i)^2$, $2(h + i)(j + k)$, and $(j + k)^2$. The sums of the columns, $(h + j)^2$, $2(h + j)(i + k)$, and $(i + k)^2$, give the proportions of BB, Bb, and bb. Note from the relationships existing between gene and gamete frequencies that equilibrium is established at both loci in just one generation when considered independently of each other.

Except for the double heterozygotes, the gamete types produced by different genotypes will be unaffected by crossing over. In the case of the cis-arrangement heterozygote, AB/ab, the gametes AB and ab are produced at a frequency of $1 - R$, while the gametes Ab and aB appear at a frequency R. The reverse is true of the trans-arrangement heterozygote, Ab/aB. Therefore, the gamete frequencies in generation 1 can be computed from genotype frequencies as

$$h_1 = h^2 + hj + hi + (1-R)hk + Rij = h - RD$$

$$i_1 = i^2 + ik + hi + (1-R)ij + Rhk = i + RD$$

$$j_1 = j^2 + jk + hj + (1-R)ij + Rhk = j + RD$$

$$k_1 = k^2 + ik + jk + (1-R)hk + Rij = k - RD$$

where D is the difference $hk - ij$, commonly referred to as the *coefficient of linkage disequilibrium*. Observe that an equilibrium will be established when $D = 0$ or, in other words, when the frequencies of the cis-arrangement and trans-arrangement heterozygotes are equal.

The equilibrial values of $h, i, j,$ and k can now be determined by expressing the frequencies of the gamete types in terms of gene frequencies and the linkage disequilibrium (D). For illustrative purposes, consider only one gamete type, say AB. In this case, the gamete frequency at any generation can be given as $h = D + p_1p_2$. Proof of this expression is obtained by merely substituting terms and working through the relationship as follows: $D + p_1p_2 = hk - ij + (h+i)$ $(h+j) = hk - ij + h^2 + hi + hj + ij = h$. As might be expected, similar relations can be derived for the other gamete types as well so that, in general, we can write

$$h = p_1p_2 + D$$

$$i = p_1q_2 - D$$

$$j = q_1p_2 - D$$

$$k = q_1q_2 + D$$

Thus, we see that, at equilibrium when $D = 0$, the frequencies of the gamete types are given by the products of the frequencies of their respective genes. We can, therefore, express the frequencies of the various gametes at equilibrium in the following manner:

Gamete type:	AB	Ab	aB	ab
Frequency:	p_1p_2	p_1q_2	q_1p_2	q_1q_2

These equilibrium frequencies represent the terms of the product $(p_1 + q_1)$ $(p_2 + q_2)$. Since gamete types combine at random, genotype frequencies at equilibrium can then be given by the terms of $(p_1 + q_1)^2(p_2 + q_2)^2$ as follows:

$$\begin{Bmatrix} AABB & AABb & AAbb \\ AaBB & AaBb & Aabb \\ aaBB & aaBb & aabb \end{Bmatrix} = \begin{Bmatrix} p_1^2p_2^2 & 2p_1^2p_2q_2 & p_1^2q_2^2 \\ 2p_1q_1p_2^2 & 4p_1q_1p_2q_2 & 2p_1q_1q_2^2 \\ q_1^2p_2^2 & 2q_1^2p_2q_2 & q_1^2q_2^2 \end{Bmatrix}$$

Once these frequencies are reached, different loci behave independently and the frequency of each gamete, and thus of each genotype, remains constant as long as gene frequencies stay the same.

Unlike the case when autosomal loci are considered separately, the equilibrium condition for two or more loci when considered together is not established in one generation of random mating, but gradually over many generations. To show this, consider a single gamete type, say AB, once again. We see from the equation for h, that this chromosome type will increase in frequency during each generation as a result of recombination occurring in individuals of genotype Ab/aB. Conversely, it will decrease in frequency if recombination should occur in AB/ab individuals. Therefore, the frequency of the AB gamete at generation t can be written in general as $h_t = h_{t-1} - RD_{t-1}$. Since $h_t = p_1p_2 + D_t$ and $h_{t-1} = p_1p_2 + D_{t-1}$, substitution yields

$$D_t = (1-R)D_{t-1} = (1-R)^t D_o$$

or   (4.8)

$$h_t - p_1 p_2 = (1-R)^t (h_o - p_1 p_2)$$

where $D_o = h_o - p_1 p_2$ at time-zero. Thus, when t gets large, h_t will increase monotonically to its equilibrium value. Similar equations can be derived for the other gamete types as well.

As shown by the expressions in (4.8), recombinant probabilities only affect the time required to eventually reach an equilibrium condition. For example, when genes are on separate chromosomes, $(1-R) = \frac{1}{2}$. In this case, the difference between the existing frequency of a given gamete type and its equilibrium value is halved in each generation. In contrast, much slower rates are expected for closely linked genes. This can be shown by solving for the time required to reduce D to 1% of its initial value. We get

$$t_{.01} = \log(0.01)/\log(1-R)$$

Thus when $R = \frac{1}{2}$, $t_{.01} = 6.67$, or roughly 7 generations. On the other hand, for closely linked markers separated by a map distance of, say, $100R = 1$ map unit, $t_{.01}$ is approximately 455 generations.

Immediate attainment of equilibrium.   When separate loci are considered together, equilibrium can be established in a single generation only when $D_o = hk - ij = 0$. There are several situations that satisfy this relationship. The two following cases serve as examples:

(1) Let the initial population consist of only $AaBb$ heterozygotes in which the A and B loci are unlinked. This would conform to the dihybrid cross of Mendelian genetics. In this case, each gamete type occurs at a frequency of $\frac{1}{4}$ so that $hk = ij$. The genotype frequencies will then take on the equilibrium ratio of 1:2:1:2:4:2:1:2:1 in the next generation.

(2) Suppose that two populations, both in equilibrium for two loci A and B, are mixed in proportions of M to $1-M$. If gene frequencies at one of the two loci are the same so that the populations differ at only one gene pair, equilibrium is established in the mixed population in a single generation. To show that $D_o = 0$ in this case, let p_1 and p_2 be the frequencies of genes A and B in the first population and P_1 and P_2 be their frequencies in the second. Gamete frequencies are now the average values for the two populations (i.e., $h = Mp_1 p_2 + (1-M)P_1 P_2$, etc.). Therefore, substituting these values into $hk - ij$ and taking the appropriate algebraic steps yields $D_o = M(1-M)(p_1 - P_1)(p_2 - P_2)$. Hence, D_o is zero if either $p_1 = P_1$ or $p_2 = P_2$ and equilibrium is established in the next generation.

THE ESTIMATION OF EQUILIBRIUM FREQUENCIES

Having described the theoretical consequences of random mating, we are now in a position to consider some of the more practical problems which arise when a population is sampled and tested for genetic equilibrium. The following serve to introduce a few techniques and statistical procedures which are commonly used in population genetics and to illustrate the additional complications which are encountered when genes show complete dominance.

Single locus; two alleles.   By far the simplest system to analyze is a trait determined by a single pair of codominant or incompletely dominant alleles. One example that has been studied quite extensively in the past is the MN blood group system in human populations. These particular blood types are determined by two alleles, I^M and I^N, which show codominance. One such study of the MN blood groups among Navaho Indians (Boyd, 1950) yielded the following results:

Blood type:	M	MN	N	Total
Genotype:	$I^M I^M$	$I^M I^N$	$I^N I^N$	
Observed number:	$N_1 = 305$	$N_2 = 52$	$N_3 = 4$	$N = 361$

The gene frequencies in this population can be estimated as

$$p = \frac{2N_1 + N_2}{2N} = \frac{662}{722} = 0.917 \quad \text{and}$$

$$q = \frac{2N_3 + N_2}{2N} = \frac{60}{722} = 0.083$$

with a sampling variance of $V(p) = pq/2N = (0.917)(0.083)/722 = 1.05 \times 10^{-4}$.

To determine whether these results are consistent with random-mating equilibrium, we compute the number expected of each genotype as $N'_1 = N(p^2) = 303$, $N'_2 = N(2pq) = 55$, and $N'_3 = N(q^2) = 3$ and then apply the chi-square test in which

$$\chi^2 = \frac{(N_1 - N'_1)^2}{N'_1} + \frac{(N_2 - N'_2)^2}{N'_2} + \frac{(N_3 - N'_3)^2}{N'_3}$$

$$= \frac{(305 - 303)^2}{303} + \frac{(52 - 55)^2}{55} + \frac{(4 - 3)^2}{3}$$

$$= 0.510$$

In this case, χ^2 has but one degree of freedom rather than two (i.e., two less than the number of classes) due to the fact the values of p and q which were used to predict the expected number of each genotype were also estimated from our sample data. Hence, the probability of observing deviations as large or greater than these due to chance alone can be obtained from an appropriate chi-square table as 0.45. These results are obviously consistent with the hypothesis of random mating.

In contrast to the above situation, many traits show significant differences from the results expected for genetic equilibrium. One such case is sickle cell anemia. This is a severe hemolytic anemia resulting from the homozygous expression of a codominant gene Hb^S. In this example, heterozygotes can be distinguished from homozygous unaffected types by biochemical analysis. The following table gives data from studies of this trait in a large sample from the American Negro population:

Genotype:	Hb^AHb^A	Hb^AHb^S	Hb^SHb^S	Total
Number:	2501	213	14	2728

Since codominance permits each genotype to be distinguished, gene frequencies can immediately be calculated as

$$q = f(Hb^S) = \frac{14}{2728} + \frac{\frac{1}{2}(213)}{2728} = 0.0442$$

$$\text{and} \quad p = 1 - q = 0.9558$$

At equilibrium, the expected genotype values are, therefore, $Np^2(Hb^AHb^A) = 2492.2$, $2Npq(Hb^AHb^S) = 230.5$, and $Nq^2(Hb^SHb^S) = 5.3$ ($\chi^2 = 14.8$, 1 d.f., $P < 5\%$). The expected values differ significantly from those observed, meaning that the population in question is not in random-mating equilibrium for this trait.

If heterozygotes cannot be distinguished from homozygous dominant types, as a result of complete dominance, gene frequencies are customarily estimated from sample data with an assumption of random mating. For example, suppose a population is measured for ability to taste the compound phenylthiocarbamide, PTC, where the taster character is dominant to nontaster:

Phenotype:	PTC taster	PTC nontaster	Total
Genotype:	*TT* or *Tt*	*tt*	
Observed number:	70	30	100

To calculate q, we assume genetic equilibrium in which case $f(tt) = q^2 = 0.30$ q, $= \sqrt{0.30} = 0.55$, and $p = 1 - q = 0.45$. In this example, the sampling variance of q^2 is the binomial variance $V(q^2) = q^2(1 - q^2)/N = (0.3)(0.7)/100 = 2.1 \times 10^{-3}$ while the sampling variance of q can be determined from $V(q^2)$ as $V(q) = (dq/dq^2)^2V(q^2) = (1/2q)^2V(q^2) = (1-q^2)/4N = 0.7/400 = 1.75 \times 10^{-3}$. Estimated genotype frequencies are then $p^2(TT) = 0.20$, $2pq(Tt) = 0.50$, and $q^2(tt) = 0.30$. We cannot compare these results with the observed values in a test for equilibrium, however, since an equilibrium has already been assumed in the initial calculations.

Obviously, an alternative method must be used in order to test for equilibrium when a trait shows complete dominance. One such procedure is ac-

TABLE 4.4.   Frequencies of offspring produced by random mating under conditions of complete dominance.

Mating	Frequency	Offspring	
Dominant × Dominant		Dominant	Recessive
BB × BB	p^4	p^4	
BB × Bb	$4p^3q$	$4p^3q$	
Bb × Bb	$4p^2q^2$	$3p^2q^2$	p^2q^2
Dominant × Recessive			
BB × bb	$2p^2q^2$	$2p^2q^2$	
Bb × bb	$4pq^3$	$2pq^3$	$2pq^3$
Recessive × Recessive			
bb × bb	q^4		q^4

complished by the calculation of the fraction of recessive offspring from dominant x recessive matings, S_1, and the fraction of recessive offspring from dominant x dominant matings, S_2. The fractions S_1 and S_2 are estimated from family data and are termed *Snyder's ratios*. The value expected for S_1 in an equilibrium population can be readily obtained from the following outline in Table 4.4. By summing the appropriate columns, the fraction of recessive offspring from dominant x recessive matings becomes

$$S_1 = 2pq^3/(2p^2q^2 + 4pq^3) = q/(1 + q) \tag{4.9}$$

Similarly, the fraction of recessive offspring from dominant x dominant matings is calculated as

$$S_2 = p^2q^2/(p^4 + 4p^3q + 4p^2q^2) = [q/(1+q)]^2 \tag{4.10}$$

The use of Snyder's ratios in testing for equilibrium is illustrated by an analysis of data from Weiner for inheritance of the Rh blood groups (see Table 4.5).

Although the progeny are not entirely independent of each other or of their parents, we can, for present purposes, approximate the value of q^2 by first summing over all recessives in our sample. Thus, with a total of 34 Rh^- parents and 73 Rh^- offspring, our estimate of the frequency of recessives can be calculated as $q^2 = 107/575 = 0.186$. Hence $q = 0.431$ and S_1 and S_2 become

TABLE 4.5.   Inheritance of Rh blood groups (Weiner, 1943).

Mating	Number of Families	OFFSPRING		Observed Frequency of Recessive Offspring
		Rh^+	Rh^-	
$Rh^+ \times Rh^+$	73	248	16	0.061
$Rh^+ \times Rh^-$	20	54	23	0.299
$Rh^- \times Rh^-$	7	—	34	1.000
Total	100	302	73	

$$S_1 = 0.431/1.431 = 0.302 \quad \text{and} \quad S_2 = (0.302)^2 = 0.091$$

These ratios expected at equilibrium are then compared to those observed, 0.299 and 0.061; the agreement is satisfactory, considering the approximate method used for estimating q, and we conclude that this population is in random-mating equilibrium for the Rh trait.

Single locus; multiple alleles.   If dominance is incomplete among all alleles in a multiple allelic series, all genotypes can be distinguished on the basis of phenotype alone and gene frequencies can be calculated directly from the observed genotype frequencies. It then becomes a simple matter to test the significance of the differences between the observed frequencies and those expected at equilibrium by applying a chi-square test. A more typical situation, however, is that dominance is complete among some or all alleles in the series. A numerical example involves the ABO blood system in humans. This system is determined by three alleles for which both codominance and complete dominance relationships exist. If we let p, q, and r be the frequencies of these three alleles, the blood types in this system and their frequencies expected for random mating can be given as follows:

Phenotype:	Type A	Type B	Type AB	Type O
Genotype:	$I^A I^A$ or $I^A i$	$I^B I^B$ or $I^B i$	$I^A I^B$	ii
Frequencies:	$p^2 + 2pr$	$q^2 + 2qr$	$2pq$	r^2

In a large sample of smallpox victims from a rural population of West Bengal and Bihar, India, Vogel and Chakravartti (1966) found 370 type A, 326 type B, 202 type O, and 88 type AB.

By assuming genetic equilibrium, gene frequencies can then be calculated as follows:

$$f(O) = r^2 = \frac{202}{986} = 0.205 \quad \text{and} \quad r = \sqrt{0.205} = 0.453$$

To solve for p, note that $f(A) + f(O) = f(I^A I^A) + f(I^A i) + f(ii) = p^2 + 2pq + r^2 = (p + r)^2$. Therefore,

$$(p + r)^2 = 0.580 \quad \text{and} \quad p = \sqrt{0.580} - 0.453 = 0.309$$

Similarly,

$$(q + r)^2 = 0.535 \quad \text{and} \quad q = \sqrt{0.535} - 0.453 = 0.279$$

It is apparent that the gene frequency estimates do not add to one. To eliminate this difference, Bernstein (1930) has proposed using the following adjusted estimates:

$$p^* = p\left(1 + \frac{1}{2}d\right) ; q^* = q\left(1 + \frac{1}{2}d\right) ; r^* = \left(r + \frac{1}{2}d\right)\left(1 + \frac{1}{2}d\right)$$

where p, q and r are the preliminary estimates and $d = 1 - p - q - r$. Thus, the adjusted estimates for the preceding example are

$$p^* = 0.303; \qquad q^* = 0.273; \qquad r^* = 0.424$$

which now sum to unity.

For a statistical test, we can now compute the expected numbers of individuals of the various blood types using the corrected values of p, q, and r. These are listed in Table 4.6 along with the value of chi-square. Random-mating equilibrium frequencies do not appear to exist in this population because of the poor agreement between observed and expected values.

Sex-linked loci. For a sex-linked trait, estimates of equilibrium frequencies are more readily made since the frequencies of X-linked genes in the hetero-gametic sex are immediately known regardless of the dominance relationship. For example, in a study of Norway schoolchildren, Waaler (1927) found the following data on red-green color-blindness:

Sex	Number color blind	Number normal
male	725	8324
female	40	9032

Assuming that color-blindness is due to a single sex-linked recessive gene, rg, the frequency of this gene in males is then $q_m = 725/9049 = 0.080$ and $p_m = 1 - q_m = 0.920$. These p and q values can then be used to test the female population for equilibrium. This is done by first calculating the expected number of color blind and normal females in this sample assuming random mating. If we suppose that gene frequencies are the same among males and females in this population, the expected numbers of color blind and normal females are then $q^2(9072) = 58.1$ and $(p^2 + 2pq)(9072) = 9013.9$, respectively, yielding a chi-square value of 5.675 with 1 degree of freedom. Since the probability of observing deviations as great or larger than these solely due to chance is less than 5%, we conclude that the population is most probably not in equilibrium either because mating is not at random or because gene frequency values are not equal in the sexes (or possibly both).

TABLE 4.6. Observed and expected genotype frequencies for an ABO sample of 986 individuals.

	A	B	AB	O	Total
Observed number:	370	326	88	202	986
Expected number:	343.87	301.75	163.12	177.26	986
	$\chi^2 = 41.9$ with 2 d.f., $P < 5\%$				

If a sex-linked trait shows incomplete dominance, the overall gene frequencies can be determined and used to estimate equilibrium genotype proportions. To give an example, coat color in cats is due to a sex-linked locus, where bb (or b) = black, BB (or B) = yellow, and heterozygous females (Bb) are tortoise shell. Searle found the following color frequencies in a cat population in Singapore:

Sex	Black	Tortoise shell	Yellow	Total
male	74	–	38	112
female	63	55	12	130

Thus,

$$p_f = (12 + 27.5)/130 = 0.30385; \quad q_f = 0.69615$$

$$p_m = 38/112 = 0.33929; \quad q_m = 0.66071$$

There appears to be some discrepancy in gene frequency values in the sexes. Consequently, average values of p and q must be computed. These can be determined by noting that in the entire population

$$p = \frac{2p_f N_f + p_m N_m}{2N_f + N_m}$$

since N_f does not equal N_m. Upon substituting the appropriate numerical values, we get $p = 0.314$ and $q = 1 - p = 0.686$. Using these numbers for p and q, the expected number of each genotype is then $N(BB) = p^2 N_f = 12.8$, $N(Bb) = 2pq N_f = 56.0$, $N(bb) = q^2 N_f = 61.2$, $N(B) = p N_m = 35.2$, and $N(b) = q N_m = 76.8$. These values are given in Table 4.7 for purposes of a chi-square test. Note that the probability of observing such deviations is quite large. Therefore, we conclude that the cat population is in equilibrium with respect to coat color.

Multiple loci.   Consider two loci each with two alleles, A, a and B, b, with frequencies p_1, q_1 and p_2, q_2, respectively. If both allelic pairs exhibit incomplete dominance, each of the nine possible genotypes is distinguishable phenotypi-

TABLE 4.7.   Observed and expected genotype frequencies for a sex-linked trait in cats.

	FEMALES			MALES	
	BB	Bb	bb	B	b
Observed number:	12	55	63	38	74
Expected number:	12.8	56.0	61.2	35.2	76.8

$$\chi^2 = 0.4 \text{ with 3 d.f., } P = 0.95$$

cally, allowing gene frequencies and equilibrium proportions to be determined directly. It is then a relatively simple matter to check for equilibrium by applying a chi-square test. If dominance is complete, a different procedure is required. To illustrate, consider the inheritance of wing color and body color in the beetle *Dermestes vulpinus*. In this organism, dark wing $(A-)$ is dominant to light wing (aa) and black body $(B-)$ is dominant to brown body (bb). In a sample of 152, Philip reported the following numbers (and frequencies) of the various phenotypes: $N(A-B-) = 35$, (23.03%); $N(A-bb) = 24$, (15.79%); $N(aaB-) = 61$, (40.13%); and $N(aabb) = 32$, (21.05%). Is the population in genetic equilibrium? To answer this question, at least in a statistical sense, we note that at equilibrium $f(aaB-) + f(aabb) = q_1^2(1-q_2^2) + q_1^2q_2^2 = q_1^2$. Therefore,

$$q_1 = \sqrt{0.4013 + 0.2105} = 0.7822 \qquad \text{and} \qquad p_1 = 0.2178$$

Similarly,

$$q_2 = \sqrt{f(A-bb) + f(aabb)} = \sqrt{0.3684} = 0.6070 \qquad \text{and} \qquad p_2 = 0.3930$$

The expected number of $A-B-$, $A-bb$, $aaB-$, and $aabb$ individuals within a sample of this size can then be calculated as $(1 - q_1^2)(1 - q_2^2)N = 37.3$, $(1 - q_1^2)q_2^2N = 21.7$, $q_1^2(1 - q_2^2)N = 58.7$, and $q_1^2q_2^2N = 34.3$, respectively. Comparing the observed numbers with those expected through random mating yields a chi-square value of 0.6 with 1 d.f. Since the probability of observing deviations as large or greater due only to chance is between 0.3 and 0.5, we conclude that the results are consistent with a random-mating equilibrium.

SOLVED EXAMPLE PROBLEMS

Random Mating Frequencies
1. Calculate the frequencies of the various matings in a randomly mating population with $P = 0.1$, $H = 0.2$, and $Q = 0.7$.
   solution   Expansion of the trinomial $(0.1 + 0.2 + 0.7)^2$ gives $P^2 = 0.01$, $H^2 = 0.04$, $Q^2 = 0.49$, $2PH = 0.04$, $2PQ = 0.14$, and $2HQ = 0.28$.

Approach to Equilibrium
2. A population contains adult individuals having gene frequencies of $p = 0.3$ and $q = 0.7$. What will be the genotypic proportions after one generation of random mating?
   solution   Genotype frequencies will be given by $(BB, Bb, bb) = (0.3 + 0.7)^2 = (0.09, 0.42, 0.49)$.

3. Show that genotype frequencies in randomly mating populations lie on the parabola $H^2 = 4PQ$ at equilibrium.
   solution   From equation (4.1). $\Delta H = 2PQ - \frac{1}{4}H^2 = 0$ at equilibrium. Therefore, $H^2 = 4PQ$. This can be easily verified by substituting $H = 2pq$, $P = p^2$, and $Q = q^2$.

4. In an equilibrium population in which 36% of individuals show the dominant phenotype, what fraction of the individuals is heterozygous?
    solution   Since the population is at equilibrium, $q^2 = 1 - 0.36 = 0.64$. Hence, $q = 0.8$ and the frequency of heterozygotes is then $2pq = 0.32$.

5. For a gene locus with 14 alleles, calculate the maximum (no dominance) and minimum (complete dominance) number of phenotypes possible in a population.
    solution   With no dominance, each genotype expresses a unique phenotype so that the number of phenotypes produced by random mating will equal $14(14 + 1)/2 = 105$. With complete dominance, the number of phenotypes equals the number of alleles, so that the minimum number of phenotypes is 14.

6. In rabbits, coat color pattern is determined by four alleles at a gene locus; c^+ (full color), c^{ch} (chinchilla), c^h (himalayan), and c (albino). If a population is initiated with $\frac{1}{2}c^+c^+$, $\frac{1}{4}c^{ch}c^{ch}$, $\frac{1}{8}c^hc^h$, and $\frac{1}{8}cc$ genotypes, what will be the gene and genotype frequencies expected at equilibrium?
    solution   The equilibrium gene frequencies will be the same as those in the initial population, namely $p_1 = \frac{1}{2}$, $p_2 = \frac{1}{4}$, $p_3 = p_4 = \frac{1}{8}$. The genotype frequencies will be

Genotypes:	c^+c^+	c^+c^{ch}	c^+c^h	c^+c	$c^{ch}c^{ch}$	$c^{ch}c$	c^hc^h
Frequencies:	16/64	16/64	8/64	8/64	4/64	4/64	1/64

c^hc	cc
2/64	1/64

Sexes and Equilibrium

7. Show that initial genotype frequencies of (0.1, 0.2, 0.7) in females and (0.7, 0.2, 0.1) in males yields the genotypic array (0.25, 0.50, 0.25) in the population after two generations of random mating.
    solution   After one generation, $p_{m_1} = p_{f_1} = p = \frac{1}{2}(p_m + p_f) = \frac{1}{2}(0.8 + 0.2) = 0.5$ and $q_{m_1} = q_{f_1} = q = 1 - p = 0.5$. Thus, one more generation of random mating gives the array $(p^2, 2pq, q^2) = (0.25, 0.50, 0.25)$.

8. A *Drosophila* population is started with white-eyed males and red-eyed females, where a sex-linked pair of alleles determines eye color. What are the gene frequencies in the population as a whole?
    solution   Let p = the frequency of the gene responsible for red eyes and q = the frequency of the gene responsible for white eyes. Then, $p = (\frac{2}{3})(1) + (\frac{1}{3})(0) = \frac{2}{3}$ and $q = (\frac{2}{3})(0) + (\frac{1}{3})(1) = \frac{1}{3}$.

Polyploidy and Equilibrium

9. In *Datura*, a single gene locus controls flower color, with P (*purple*) completely dominant over p (white). Autotetraploids of *Datura* are highly fertile. From a cross between $PPpp$ and $Pppp$ types, determine the expected genotypic and phenotypic ratios among the offspring.

solution $PPpp$ genotypes yield gametes: $(\frac{1}{6})(PP) + (\frac{4}{6})(Pp) + (\frac{1}{6})(pp)$. $Pppp$ genotypes yield gametes: $(\frac{1}{2})(Pp) + (\frac{1}{2})(pp)$. Therefore, the offspring genotypic ratio becomes $[(\frac{1}{6})(PP) + (\frac{4}{6})(Pp) + (\frac{1}{6})(pp)][(\frac{1}{2})(Pp) + (\frac{1}{2})(pp)] = (\frac{1}{12})(PPPp) + (\frac{5}{12})(PPpp) + (\frac{5}{12})(Pppp) + (\frac{1}{12})(pppp)$. The offspring phenotypic ratio then becomes $(\frac{11}{12})(\text{purple}) + (\frac{1}{12})(\text{white})$.

10. Calculate the genotype frequencies characterizing the approach to equilibrium by a tetraploid population initiated with equal frequencies of B_4 and B_2b_2 types.

    solution   Express the approach to equilibrium in terms of the three gamete frequencies, where in $t = 0$, $(x, y, z) = (\frac{7}{12}\ \frac{4}{12}\ \frac{1}{12})$. Assuming random chromosome segregation and utilizing equation (4.6), where $2pq = 2(\frac{3}{4})(\frac{1}{4}) = 0.375$, and the relationships $x = p - \frac{1}{2}y$ and $z = q - \frac{1}{2}y$, we get for $t = 1$: $y_1 = (\frac{1}{3})(0.3333 - 0.3750) + 0.3750 = 0.3612$; $x_1 = 0.75 - 0.1806 = 0.5694$; $z_1 = 0.25 - 0.1806 = 0.0694$. Similar calculations for the next several generations give results shown in the following table:

	Gamete Frequencies		
Generation	BB	Bb	bb
0	0.5833	0.3333	0.0833
1	0.5694	0.3612	0.0694
2	0.5648	0.3704	0.0648
3	0.5633	0.3734	0.0633
4	0.5628	0.3745	0.0628
5	0.5626	0.3748	0.0626
.			
.			
Limit	0.5625	0.3750	0.0625

At equilibrium, the genotype frequencies will be $(B_4, B_3b, B_2b_2, Bb_3, b_4) = (p + q)^4 = (0.3164, 0.4219, 0.2109, 0.0469, 0.0039)$.

Multiple Loci and Equilibrium

11. A cross $Ab/aB \times ab/ab$ yields four classes of offspring at the frequencies 37% Ab/ab, 35% aB/ab, 13% AB/ab, and 15% ab/ab. Employing the Haldane relationship, estimate the average number of crossovers occurring between the two gene loci.

    solution   There are a total of $13 + 15 = 28\%$ recombinant type offspring originating from 28% recombinant type gametes from the Ab/aB parent. From equation (4.7), $0.28 = \frac{1}{2}(1 - e^{-2d})$, giving $d = 0.45$.

12. Consider two unlinked loci in a population composed of equal frequencies of homozygous dominant, heterozygous, and homozygous recessive individuals. Calculate the genotype frequencies expected after one generation of random mating.

    solution $\frac{1}{3}$ AB/AB individuals yield $\frac{1}{3}$ AB gametes; $\frac{1}{3}$ ab/ab individuals yield $\frac{1}{3}$ ab gametes; and $\frac{1}{3}$ heterozygous individuals (AB/ab or Ab/aB) yield

$(\frac{1}{3})(\frac{1}{4}) = \frac{1}{12}$ frequency of each of the gametes AB, Ab, aB, ab. Thus, $h = \frac{1}{3} + \frac{1}{12} = \frac{5}{12}$, $i = \frac{1}{12}$, $j = \frac{1}{12}$, $k = \frac{5}{12}$, and the frequency of genotypes in the next generation is given by the expansion of $(\frac{5}{12} + \frac{1}{12} + \frac{1}{12} + \frac{5}{12})^2$, which yields

$$
\left\{
\begin{array}{ccc}
\dfrac{25}{144} & \dfrac{10}{144} & \dfrac{1}{144} \\[2ex]
\dfrac{10}{144} & \dfrac{52}{144} & \dfrac{10}{144} \\[2ex]
\dfrac{1}{144} & \dfrac{10}{144} & \dfrac{25}{144}
\end{array}
\right\}
$$

13. For the population in problem 12, compute the gene and genotype frequencies, and the values of D, during the approach to equilibrium under random mating.

    solution   Gene frequencies remain constant at $p = q = \frac{1}{3} + \frac{1}{6} = \frac{1}{2}$. Applying equation (4.8), we use the following relationships: $D_t = (\frac{1}{2})^t D_o$; $h_t = (\frac{1}{2})^t (\frac{5}{12} - \frac{1}{4}) + \frac{1}{4}$; $i_t = (\frac{1}{2})^t (\frac{1}{12} - \frac{1}{4}) + \frac{1}{4}$; $j_t = (\frac{1}{2})^t (\frac{1}{12} - \frac{1}{4}) + \frac{1}{4}$; and $k_t = (\frac{1}{2})^t (\frac{5}{12} - \frac{1}{4}) + \frac{1}{4}$. The result is the data shown below:

Gamete Frequency

Generation	AB	Ab	aB	ab	D
0	0.4167	0.0833	0.0833	0.4167	0.1667
1	0.3333	0.1666	0.1666	0.3333	0.0834
2	0.2917	0.2083	0.2083	0.2917	0.0417
3	0.2708	0.2292	0.2292	0.2708	0.0208
4	0.2604	0.2396	0.2396	0.2604	0.0104
5	0.2552	0.2448	0.2448	0.2552	0.0052
.					
.					
.					
Limit	0.2500	0.2500	0.2500	0.2500	0.0000

The equilibrium genotype frequencies among the adults will be

$$
\left\{
\begin{array}{ccc}
0.0625 & 0.1350 & 0.0625 \\
0.1350 & 0.2700 & 0.1350 \\
0.0625 & 0.1350 & 0.0625
\end{array}
\right\}
$$

14. Two populations, each in equilibrium for unlinked loci A and B, are mixed in the ratio of 1:2. In population 1, the gene frequencies are $p_1 = 0.3$ and $p_2 = 0.4$, whereas in population 2, the corresponding values are $P_1 = 0.5$ and $P_2 = 0.4$. Compute the genotype frequencies after a single generation of random mating in the combined population and note that these are the equilibrium values.

solution Since $p_2 = P_2$, $D = 0$, $h = Mp_1p_2 + (1-M)P_1P_2 = (\frac{1}{3})(0.12)$ + $(\frac{2}{3})(0.20) = 0.17$; $i = Mp_1q_2 + (1-M)P_1Q_2 = (\frac{1}{3})(0.18) + (\frac{2}{3})(0.30) = 0.26$; $j = Mq_1p_2 + (1-M)Q_1P_2 = (\frac{1}{3})(0.28) + (\frac{2}{3})(0.20) = 0.23$; and $k = Mq_1q_2 + (1-M)Q_1Q_2 = (\frac{1}{3})(0.42) + (\frac{2}{3})(0.30) = 0.34$. Note that the average p and q values for the combined population are $p_A = 0.433$ and $p_B = 0.40$, giving $h = p_Ap_B$, $i = p_Aq_B$, $j = q_Ap_B$, and $k = q_Aq_B$.

---

15. Thus far, we have assumed that random mating occurs in discrete non-overlapping generations. As we have seen, this situation leads to a sudden attainment of equilibrium in the next reproductive interval. Show that when generations overlap, equilibrium is not established suddenly but gradually as the proportion of the population derived from random mating increases.

    solution Consider a large population in which matings are equally fertile and occur randomly in time and randomly with respect to mating partner. Given a random distribution of birth and death events, we can assume that in a fraction of a generation dt, a proportion dt of the population will die and be replaced by the offspring of the remaining proportion $(1 - dt)$ of the population. Now consider the frequency of heterozygotes in the population at time $t + dt$. Letting H_t be the frequency of heterozygotes among the parents and $2pq$ the corresponding frequency among the offspring of random matings, the value H_{t+dt} can then be expressed as the mean

    $$H_{t+dt} = H_t (1 - dt) + 2pq(dt)$$

    Subtracting H_t from both sides of this expression and dividing by dt, we get

    $$\frac{H_{t+dt} - H_t}{dt} = dH_t/dt = 2pq - H_t$$

    which is the differential analog of equation (4.1). Integrating this equation over the limits of H_o at time zero to H_t at time t, we obtain

    $$H_t = 2pq - (2pq - H_o)e^{-t}$$

    Hence when t gets large so that e^{-t} approaches zero, H_t will approach $2pq$ monotonically as its equilibrium value. Equilibrium frequencies will, therefore, exist throughout the population when the last survivor of the parental generation has died.

PROBLEM EXERCISES

1. (a) Designate which of the following populations (P,H,Q) are not in random-mating equilibrium. (b) Calculate the expected Hardy-Weinberg

equilibrium proportions for those which are not. (c) How long will each population require to reach equilibrium?

(1) $\dfrac{1}{3}, \dfrac{1}{3}, \dfrac{1}{3}$ (3) 0, 0, 1   (5) 0, 1, 0

(2) $0, \dfrac{3}{4}, \dfrac{1}{4}$ (4) 0.01, 0.18, 0.81   (6) 0.64, 0.20, 0.16

2. A large randomly mating population of wild mice is found to contain 75% short-haired individuals. Does this imply that short hair is dominant over long? Explain.

3. In humans, a dominant gene at the Rh locus (autosomal) produces the D antigen and the Rh positive phenotype (Rh^+). Individuals homozygous for the recessive allele are termed Rh negative (Rh^-). In a certain randomly mating population, 16% are Rh^-. (a) What are the gene frequencies? (b) What proportion of the Rh^+ persons are heterozygous? (c) From matings between Rh^+ individuals, what is the expected frequency of Rh^- children?

4. Two different populations are composed of the following genotypes for a sex-linked locus:

	Males		Females		
	B	b	BB	Bb	bb
Population 1:	0.3	0.7	0.4	0.4	0.2
Population 2:	0.5	0.5	0.3	0.4	0.3

(a) What are the gene frequencies in each sex in each population? (b) Is either population in genetic equilibrium? (c) Calculate gene frequencies expected in population 1 over the next 5 generations. (d) What will be the equilibrium proportions expected in each population?

5. Consider three of the alleles determining fur color in mice, listed in order of decreasing dominance: A^+, agouti; a^+, black and tan; and a, black. (a) If a population is started with 100 individuals of each of the six possible genotypes, what will be the gene and genotype frequencies expected after one generation of random mating? (b) A randomly mating population of 1,000 mice is found to contain 250 black, 390 black and tan, and 360 agouti. What are the gene frequencies?

6. Prove that the following equalities hold with $p + q = 1$.

(a) $p + 2q = 1 + q = 2 - p$ (d) $p^2q + pq^2 = pq = q - q^2$
(b) $p^2 - q^2 = p - q$ (e) $q^3 + pq^2 = q^2 = (1 - p)^2$
(c) $p(1 + q) = 1 - q^2$ (f) $(1 - 2q)^2 = (1 - 2p)^2$

7. In a population undergoing random mating for a trait determined by a single locus with two alleles and complete dominance, the ratio of dominant to recessive phenotypes is found to be 8:1. What are the gene frequencies?

8. Demonstrate that for a two allele situation, if the frequency of one allele is very small, then the proportion of heterozygotes is equal to approximately twice the frequency of that allele.

9. Prove that in a randomly mating population with two alleles, half the heterozygotes have heterozygous mothers.

10. A population is in genetic equilibrium for a sex-linked locus, where the frequency of the recessive allele is 0.5. (a) What are the genotype frequencies expected? (b) Why are there so many more males than females that express a sex-linked recessive character? Would this be true of a sex-linked dominant trait? (Hint: Use male to female genotypic ratios.) (c) In another equilibrium population, the recessive phenotype occurs 10 times more frequently in males than in females. What are the allele frequencies?

11. Consider an autosomal locus with 3 alleles. Prove that (a) the maximum value of the proportion of heterozygous genotypes $(2pq + 2pr + 2qr)$ is $\frac{2}{3}$. (b) Show that the maximum value for the above proportion with n alleles is $(n - 1)/n$.

12. Suppose that a population of autotetraploids is initiated with all B_2b_2 individuals and allowed to mate at random. Calculate the gametic and zygotic proportions expected in the next generation and at equilibrium, assuming random chromosome segregation (complete linkage to the centromere).

13. A hypothetical randomly mating population of 1,000 organisms is composed of the following genotypic proportions, where the different allelic pairs assort independently:

0.20	AABB	0.06	AABb	0.01	AAbb
0.28	AaBB	0.12	AaBb	0.04	Aabb
0.16	aaBB	0.10	aaBb	0.03	aabb

(a) Determine the gene frequencies. (b) Is the population in genetic equilibrium for these two loci considered together? (c) Calculate the gamete frequencies expected from this population. (d) What is the value of D in the original population? (e) How many generations will be required for the population to go $\frac{9}{10}$ of the way to equilibrium, assuming the continuation of random mating?

14. A population is started with three genotypes, 20% AB/AB, 50% AB/ab, and 30% ab/ab, and allowed to mate at random. The loci are linked with a 25% chance of recombination between them. (a) What are the frequencies of the four kinds of gametes expected in the next generation? (b) What is the expected equilibrium frequency of each of the gamete types? (c) Determine the expected zygote frequencies in the next generation. (d) How many generations of random mating are required for the population to go half-way to equilibrium?

15. In a certain population in random-mating equilibrium, the frequency of the recessive trait is 1 in 50. Assume an autosomal locus with two alleles. What is the probability of a recessive offspring from (a) A mating between two normal individuals? (b) A mating involving one parent with the recessive characteristic and the other parent normal? (c) A normal man, who is known to have an affected mother, and a normal woman?

16. A random sample of 800 families was tested for the ability to taste PTC, with the results given below:

Mating	Number of families	OFFSPRING	
		tasters	nontasters
$T- \times T-$	376	949	110
$T- \times tt$	289	533	228
$tt \times tt$	135	–	218

Does the population appear to be in genetic equilibrium? Give reasons.

5

Components of Variation
and Resemblance

Variation in the form of phenotypic differences is observed for every trait that is studied, be it morphological, physiological, or behavioral. These differences vary in kind and degree and depend, at least in part, on the genotypes of the component organisms. Not all variation is directly a result of genotypic differences, however. Phenotypic modifications such as age variation, seasonal variation, and social or caste variation occur without a corresponding change in genotype. Moreover, environmental stress can modify a multitude of biochemical processes involved in development, producing changes which are seemingly unrelated to the genetic makeup of the organism. Thus although the genes provide directions for growth and differentiation, the appearance or phenotype of an individual is a product of the interaction between environment and genotype.

When only a single trait is studied, it is convenient to classify individual differences as either *discrete* or *continuous* variation. The variation pattern is referred to as discrete (or polymorphic) when individuals can be grouped into nonoverlapping phenotypic classes. A well-known example of discrete variation occurs in the ABO blood group system in humans for which individuals can be separated into well-defined classes on the basis of specific antigen-antibody reactions. Continuous variation, on the other hand, exists when a trait differs in degree along some continuous scale of measurement. Those traits which show continuous variation are termed quantitative (or metric) traits. Classic examples of quantitative characters are skin color and mature body height and weight in man. Measurements of such continuously varying traits usually approximate a normal probability curve when plotted in the form of a

141

frequency distribution. The basic difference between polymorphic and continuous variation involves the number of genes contributing to the trait in question and the degree to which their expression is modified by environmental factors. Discrete variation is generally a result of allelic differences at one or just a few gene loci while continuous variation occurs when a trait is determined by many genes which are highly susceptible to environmental influence.

SOURCES OF QUANTITATIVE VARIATION

Since the phenotype of an individual is the product of environmental as well as genetic effects, it is customary to express the measured or observed value of a quantitative character as the sum

$$P = G + (P - G) = G + E$$

where P is the phenotypic value, G is the genotypic value, and E is the environmental deviation. In this expression, the environment is described as producing departures in phenotype about G in either direction. Thus, in a large population which consists of a single genotype, environmental deviations are assumed to occur as often in one direction as the other so that the mean value of E is equal to zero. The mean phenotypic value will consequently equal the genotypic value of the genotype in question.

The relationship between the genotypic values of a large population and their environmental deviations is shown graphically in Figure 5.1 for the quantitative effects of a single locus. As environmental effects increase in variability, the existence of discrete genotypic values is eventually obscured, giving the appearance of a single unimodal and continuous distribution. The graphs imply that $\Sigma E = 0$ for all three genotypes. Consequently, the mean phenotypic value, $\overline{P}$, is the same as the mean genotypic value, $\overline{G}$, for the entire population.

Since the phenotypic expression of a polymorphic trait is determined by only a few genes and is relatively insensitive to normal environmental conditions, a precise phenotypic value can usually be associated with each genotypic class. In contrast, the underlying contributions of genes and the environment to the overall distribution of phenotypic expression for a quantitative trait cannot be enumerated so easily. In this case, the analysis necessarily becomes statistical in nature, concerning itself with the pattern of variability in the population. The technique usually employed is an analysis of variance, a procedure originally applied to genetic study in the 1920s by R.A. Fisher. In this procedure, the total variation observed for a character is partitioned into component parts; these parts are assigned to the variation in each causal element, and to the variation in each combination of causal elements.

The logic of the analysis is readily comprehensible if we use a particular

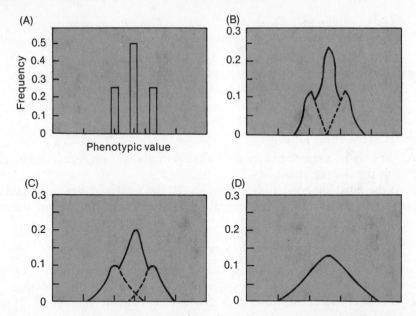

Figure 5.1   The effect of the environment on genotype expression. In the absence of environmental influence, three discrete phenotypic values are observed (A). An increasing degree of environmental effect, illustrated in (B), (C), and (D), gradually obscures the boundaries between classes, until finally enough environmental deviation occurs (D) to make the distribution continuous.

example, such as human birth weight. This is a quantitative trait, exhibiting a more or less continuous distribution of phenotypic values in any population. Considering genetic and environmental factors that could cause the weight to vary from one newborn to the next, we might include at least the following: the environment to which a mother is exposed during and prior to pregnancy; the mother's age; the number of previous children she has borne; her genotype as concerns the many, mostly undefined, gene loci that influence fetal development; and the genotype of the baby. Assuming that these factors act in an independent fashion, the total phenotypic variability observed in a population can then be expressed as the sum of the variability components due to each of the above-mentioned factors, i.e., $V_P = V_1 + V_2 + V_3 + V_4 + V_5 + V_R$, where V_P is the total phenotypic variance and V_1 through V_5 represent the variances of the five factors specifically considered as influencing birth weight. A V_R term can be included which incorporates any residual variability not attributable to defined factors. Any complex, unmeasurable effect of interaction between factors could also be included in the last term.

Human birth weight has been analyzed in such a fashion by L.S. Penrose (1954) with the following results:

Source of variance	Fraction of variance attributable to source
Maternal environment	0.24
Maternal age	0.01
Numerical position of child	0.07
Maternal genotype	0.20
Genotype of child	0.18
Residual variations	0.30

Note that, as is often the case, intangible variations contributed significantly (30%) to the overall variability.

At the most superficial level of analysis, the total variance in phenotypic values can be expressed, in general, as a linear combination of variance components

$$V_P = V_G + V_E + V_{GE}$$

in which V_P has been partitioned into a genetic variance (V_G) arising from genotypic differences within the population, an environmental variance (V_E) due to nongenetic causes, and a genotype-environment interaction variance (V_{GE}) which incorporates the lack of independence of genotype and environmental deviations. If each specific departure in environmental conditions has the same effect on all genotypes, then V_{GE} is zero and the total phenotypic variance is simply the sum $V_G + V_E$. In practice, it might also be necessary to include two additional components in the sum. One is an error variance, V_e, which incorporates the effects of random errors in measurement. A second is the genetic-environment covariance which arises when a correlation exists between genotype and environment. Such would be the case if, for example, the more desirable genotypes were consistently exposed to the more favorable environments. The covariance component can usually be eliminated with the appropriate experimental design in which genetic and environmental factors are randomized.

The environmental variance in the preceding analysis is treated as a catch-all term which includes all variation not attributable to segregating loci. Among the more common causes of nongenetic variation are nutritional and climatic factors, such as availability and quality of food for animals and suitability of light, temperature, humidity, and soil characteristics for plants. Such environmental factors continue to interact with the genotype of an organism, and they can induce variation at all stages of development. In addition to these recognizable causes of environmental variation, there are also sources of variation which differ from moment to moment within single organisms, producing differences in repeated measurements on the same individual. For this reason, it is often useful to subdivide the environmental variance into (a) a within-individual variance (special environmental variance), V_{E_s}, measuring the differences in repeated observations on the same individual, and (b) a between-individual variance (general environmental variance), V_{E_g}, measuring the non-localized variation in conditions which are common to all organisms under study. Making the above subdivision, the environmental variance can then be written as

$$V_E = V_{E_g} + V_{E_s}$$

Since the variance of the mean of n repeated measurements is $1/n$ times the variance of a single measurement, the phenotypic variance computed on the basis of n repeated measurements of each individual phenotypic value can then be expressed as

$$V_{P(n)} = V_G + V_{E_g} + (1/n)V_{E_s}$$

This reduction in the magnitude of the phenotypic variance with an increase in the number of observations points out the importance of repeated measurements in estimating the causal components of variance.

Polygenes and additive effects.   That part of the total variation that is ascribed to genetic causes is a result of a general class of genes termed polygenes (Mather, 1941). These are genes which are believed to be responsible for the expression of quantitative traits, each contributing such a small amount to the overall phenotype that their individual effects are obscured by the genotype as a whole and by the effects of the environment.

The simplest model that can be used to describe the cumulative action of polygenes in natural populations is a linear model in which some quantitative trait such as height or weight is determined by the additive contribution of polygenes at a number of loci. Assuming an additive contribution does not imply anything about the biochemical action of these genes or their chromosomal location; it only describes the statistical effects of genes on the overall phenotype. Suppose, for example, that each gene designated by a capital letter (B) contributes a units to the trait in an additive fashion while genes designated by a small letter (b) are noncontributing. Let x be the variable number of contributing genes at a locus with possible values 0, 1, and 2. If only one locus is segregating in the population, the genotypic value of an individual organism can then be expressed as a linear function of x

$$G = ax + g_0$$

where g_0 is the contribution of all nonsegregating loci which influence the trait. The model can be readily extended to n segregating loci by taking the sum. The genotypic value of an individual then becomes

$$G = \sum_{i=1}^{n} a_i x_i + g_0$$

For instance, in homozygotes of genotype $B_1B_1B_2B_2 \ldots B_nB_n$, for which the subscripts are used to designate loci that segregate in the population, the value of x will equal 2 for each locus. Therefore, the genotypic value of this homozygote will be $2n\bar{a} + g_o$ where $\bar{a}$ is the average contribution of each effective gene. In contrast, the genotypic values of the heterozygotes $B_1b_1B_2b_2 \ldots B_nb_n$ and of the homozygotes $b_1b_1b_2b_2 \ldots b_nb_n$ are $n\bar{a} + g_o$ and g_o, respectively.

The model can now be developed for an entire population by first considering the simple case of genes at a single locus. In doing so, let the frequency of the contributing allele (B) be represented by p and that of the noncontributing allele (b) by q. If we assume that the population mates at random, the possible values of x and their frequencies can be represented as follows:

Genotype	x value	Frequency
BB	2	p^2
Bb	1	$2pq$
bb	0	q^2

For this locus, the expected value and variance of x are $E(x) = (2)p^2 + (1)2pq = 2p$ and $V(x) = (2)^2p^2 + 2pq - (2p)^2 = 2pq$. The mean and variance of G will then be

$$\overline{G} = aE(x) + g_o = 2ap + g_o$$
$$V_G = a^2V(x) = 2a^2pq \tag{5.1}$$

It is apparent that the mean genotypic value, and thus the mean phenotypic value of the population, and the additive genetic variance are determined largely by two factors: the value of a and the gene frequency p. Since the value of a is fixed for any given locus, the only genetic way of changing the mean and variance is through a change in gene frequency. It should also be noted that since V_G is proportional to the product pq, its value is maximum for a given value of a when $p = q = \frac{1}{2}$. This equality holds, for example, among the progeny of a monohybrid cross.

We can now extend the model to the case of n segregating loci. The mean and variance then become

$$\overline{G} = 2\sum_{i=1}^{n} a_ip_i + g_o$$

and $\tag{5.2}$

$$V_G = 2\sum_{i=1}^{n} a_i^2p_iq_i$$

These expressions become greatly simplified when the value of a_i is the same for all loci. In this particular case, the mean and variance reduce to $\overline{G} = 2na\bar{p} + g_o$ and $V_G = 2na^2(\bar{p}\bar{q} - V_p)$, where $\bar{p}$ and $\bar{q}$ are the average allelic frequencies and V_p is the variance of gene frequencies at the loci in question.

Estimating number of loci.   The variance in (5.2) can be used in experimental situations for obtaining estimates of the number of loci contributing to a quantitative trait. Suppose, for example, that a cross is made between two inbred (and presumably homozygous) varieties of opposite phenotypic extremes. Assume also that the parental varieties differ in their genes at n independently segregating loci. Again using B and b for gene symbols, the cross can be written as

$$B_1 B_1 B_2 B_2 \ldots B_n B_n \times b_1 b_1 b_2 b_2 \ldots b_n b_n$$

Such matings will give rise to a genetically uniform F_1 of genotype $B_1 b_1 B_2 b_2 \ldots B_n b_n$ with a genotypic value intermediate between the values of the parental varieties. When F_1 hybrids are crossed, however, a variety of genotypes appear in the F_2 as a result of a reshuffling of genes during gamete formation. If the independent segregation of genes were the only cause of variation in the F_2, there would be $2n + 1$ phenotypic classes expected according to whether individuals possessed $0, 1, 2, \ldots, 2n$ contributing genes. The frequencies of these classes would correspond to the terms of the binomial expansion $(\frac{1}{2} + \frac{1}{2})^{2n}$. Thus, if n is large, the phenotype distribution in the F_2 can be approximated by a normal density function.

The genotypic mean and variance for the F_2 can be obtained from the pair of equations in (5.2) by merely substituting the value $\frac{1}{2}$ for p_i and q_i. We get

$$\overline{G} = \Sigma a_i + g_0 = n\overline{a} + g_0$$

and

$$V_G = \tfrac{1}{2} \Sigma a_i^2 = n\overline{a^2}/2$$

Since quantitative traits are also subject to variation from nongenetic causes, a more realistic picture of this series of crosses is illustrated in Figure 5.2. Observe that phenotypic variability is expected to occur in both parental varieties, even though the members of each variety are assumed to possess the same genotype. This is also true in the F_1. The F_2, on the other hand, shows variation of both genetic and environmental origin. In this case, variation due to nongenetic causes obscures all genetic discontinuities, thus converting a potentially discrete distribution into one that is continuous in nature. Since the phenotypic variance of the F_2 (V_{F_2}) measures both genetic and environmental variation while the variance of the F_1 (V_{F_1}) is a measure of environmental variation only, the genetic variance of the F_2 can be estimated as $V_G = V_{F_2} - V_{F_1} = n\overline{a^2}/2$. This assumes, of course, that environmental causes of variation remain the same from one generation to the next.

The expression for the genetic variance of the F_2 can now be used to obtain an estimate of the number of segregating loci contributing to a quantitative trait. Since the contribution of each effective gene is seldom known, the formula for number of loci is usually derived by letting $\overline{a} = R/2n$ in which R is the numerical difference between the means of the parental varieties. Assuming

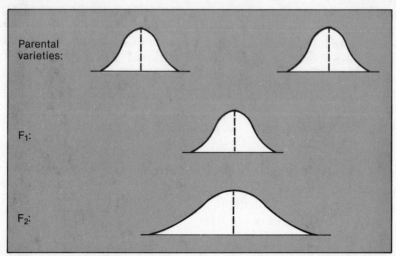

Figure 5.2. A hypothetical series of crosses involving parental varieties of opposite phenotypic extremes. The distributions represent the variability expressed in each generation, and the broken lines designate the mean phenotypic value in each case. Note that the mean phenotypic values of the F_1 and F_2 are intermediate to those of the parental varieties.

that this contribution is approximately the same at all loci such that $\overline{a^2}$ can be taken as $\overline{a}^2$, substitution into the variance formula yields

$$n = R^2/8(V_{F_2} - V_{F_1}) \qquad (5.3)$$

A number of estimates of gene loci have been published in which the preceding formula was used. For example, Falconer (1955) estimated the number of loci affecting the 6-week weight in mice as 35. Unfortunately, however, the wide variety of simplifying assumptions which have entered into the derivation of this formula means that its numerical predictions are, at best, crude approximations.

GENE INTERACTIONS

In the model outlined in the previous sections, polygenes were envisioned to act independently of each other, contributing small amounts to the phenotype in an additive fashion. Not all genes produce additive effects, however, nor are all gene actions independent of the presence of other genes. Genes may, and often do, interact with each other resulting in deviations from additivity. Such gene interactions are of two types: *dominance interactions* and *epistatic interactions*. Both dominance and epistatic interactions can be expressed as components of the genotypic value of an individual by writing

$$G = A + D + I$$

where A is the additive value of a genotype, D is the deviation from additivity due to dominance (dominance deviation), and I is the interaction deviation between two or more loci. In this expression D and I are both deviations from a straight-line relationship between G and the number of contributing genes and are defined such that their sums or mean values are equal to zero.

Having subdivided the genotypic value into an additive term and into two departures from linearity, we can now partition the genetic variance as

$$V_G = V_A + V_D + V_I$$

where V_A, V_D, and V_I are the additive genetic variance, the dominance variance, and the epistatic (or interaction) variance, respectively. In the absence of dominance and epistatic effects, the genetic variance would be entirely additive as we had assumed earlier. Of these components, the additive variance is most important to genetic theory since, once its value is known from experiment, it can be treated in the same manner as V_G in the additive model. This means that V_A will have the same simple form that can be used to estimate number of loci. Of even greater significance, the additive variance is the main cause of resemblance between relatives and is, therefore, of major consequence in describing the genetic properties of populations and their response to selection.

Since $P = G + E$, it follows that

$$V_P = V_A + V_D + V_I + V_E + V_{GE}$$

In order to show the mathematical basis for this subdivision, we will first consider the case of a single locus with dominance.

Dominance interactions.   When only a single locus is considered, the genotypic value reduces to the sum of the additive effect and the dominance deviation (i.e., $G = A + D$). Dominance deviations can be regarded as arising from nonlinear interactions between alleles, or within-locus interactions. These interactions tend to alter the effect of gene substitution so that the presence of one contributing gene at a given locus has greater than half the effect observed when both contributing alleles are together in their homozygous state. This effect is illustrated in the following scale of genotypic values:

In this general case, the genotypic value of the heterozygote can be expressed as either $a_1 + G_{bb}$ or $\frac{1}{2}(G_{BB} + G_{bb}) + \frac{1}{2}d$, where d is twice the difference between G_{Bb} and the midpoint value and is given by $a_1 - a_2$. The terms a_1 and a_2 are the effects of gene substitution and define the order of dominance. Thus, if

$d = a_1$ so that $a_2 = 0$, complete dominance exists since $G_{BB} = G_{Bb}$. The degree of dominance calculated conveniently as d/a_1 is then equal to 1. If $a_1 = a_2$ such that $d = 0$, no dominance occurs and G_{Bb} is the midpoint value. When $G_{Bb} > G_{BB}$, the degree of dominance, d/a_1, is greater than 1 and the locus is said to show overdominance.

We can now extend our basic model to a randomly mating population. To do so, let g_o be the minimum or base value (i.e., the value of G_{bb}). The genotypes and their values can then be represented as follows:

Genotype:	BB	Bb	bb
Frequency:	p^2	$2pq$	q^2
Genotypic value:	$G_{BB} = a_1 + a_2 + g_o$	$G_{Bb} = a_1 + g_o$	$G_{bb} = g_o$
Additive value:	$A_{BB} = 2a + g$	$A_{Bb} = a + g$	$A_{bb} = g$

Note that the additive value is a linear approximation of the genotypic value obtained from the expression

$$A = ax + g$$

where x is the number of contributing genes at this locus. The theoretical value of A for each genotype is obtained by fitting this straight-line relation to the actual G values by the method of least squares. This is illustrated by a plot of G versus x in Figure 5.3. In this graph, the solid circles represent the actual G values for the individual genotypes while the open circles are their theoretical additive values. A suitable linear approximation can be made by allocating as much of the total genetic variation into the additive term as possible. The remainder is then assigned to dominance deviations in much the same way as

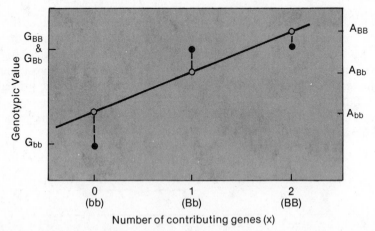

Figure 5.3. Graphical representation of genotypic values (closed circles) and fitted additive values (open circles) of the genotypes for a locus with two alleles B and b as explained in the text. Vertical departures between actual values and fitted values are treated in the same way as random errors.

error terms. Since dominance deviations will be treated as though they are random errors in a linear regression, the principle of least squares in this case is to minimize the dominance variance. For a randomly mating population, the quantity to be minimized is

$$V_D = p^2 D_{BB}^2 + 2pq D_{Bb}^2 + q^2 D_{bb}^2$$

$$= p^2 [G_{BB} - A_{BB}]^2 + 2pq[G_{Bb} - \tfrac{1}{2}(A_{BB} + A_{bb})]^2 + q^2 [G_{bb} - A_{bb}]^2$$

in which D_{BB}, D_{Bb}, and D_{bb} are the respective dominance deviations.

We can now proceed according to the standard methods by taking the derivatives $\partial V_D / \partial A_{BB}$ and $\partial V_D / \partial A_{bb}$ and setting them equal to zero. Upon further simplification, this yields the following pair of equations:

$$p(G_{BB} - A_{BB}) + q(G_{Bb} - A_{Bb}) = 0$$

$$p(G_{Bb} - A_{Bb}) + q(G_{bb} - A_{bb}) = 0$$
(5.4)

Thus, we see that $D_{Bb} = G_{Bb} - A_{Bb} = -(p/q)D_{BB} = -(q/p)D_{bb}$. Recalling that $G_{Bb} = \tfrac{1}{2}(G_{BB} + G_{bb}) + \tfrac{1}{2}d$ and that $A_{Bb} = \tfrac{1}{2}(A_{BB} + A_{bb})$, we also get $G_{Bb} - A_{Bb} = D_{Bb} = \tfrac{1}{2}D_{BB} + \tfrac{1}{2}D_{bb} + \tfrac{1}{2}d$. Using these identities to solve for the individual dominance deviations, we obtain

$$D_{BB} = -q^2 d; \qquad D_{Bb} = pqd; \qquad \text{and} \qquad D_{bb} = -p^2 d \qquad (5.5)$$

The mean dominance deviation is then

$$\overline{D} = p^2(-q^2 d) + 2pq(pqd) + q^2(-p^2 d) = 0$$

Note that by attempting to allocate as much variation as possible to the additive term, dominance deviations become variables dependent not only on d but also on gene frequency. Since $A_{bb} = g_o - D_{bb}$, we now obtain a solution for the theoretical intercept in our additive value, which is

$$g = g_o + p^2 d \qquad (5.6)$$

Thus, when dominance is lacking, $g = g_o$ as before.

In order to arrive at a solution for the value of the slope, a, rewrite the pair of equations in (5.4) as

$$p(G_{BB} - 2a - g) + q(G_{Bb} - a - g) = 0$$

$$p(G_{Bb} - a - g) + q(G_{bb} - g) = 0$$

Subtracting the two equations to eliminate g and letting $G_{BB} - G_{Bb} = a_2$ and $G_{Bb} - G_{bb} = a_1$, we get

$$a = pa_2 + qa_1 \qquad (5.7)$$

Like the intercept, the slope of our linear approximation is a variable dependent on gene frequency. The values of these parameters will, therefore, depend on the population in which they are measured.

Having obtained explicit solutions for the slope and intercept and for the various dominance deviations, we can now express the genotypic mean and the two components of the genotypic variance in terms of these parameters and their solutions. First, note that since $\overline{D} = 0$, the value of $\overline{G}$ and $\overline{A}$ will be equal. Therefore, the genotypic mean has the same form as in the additive model:

$$\overline{G} = 2ap + g$$

which, after substituting (5.6) and (5.7) for a and g and making a few algebraic rearrangements, becomes

$$\overline{G} = (a_1 + a_2)p + pqd + g_0 \tag{5.8}$$

As in the previous model, this is both the mean genotypic value and mean phenotypic value with respect to this locus. As should be expected, the mean value with dominance will be greater than that of a corresponding character with pure additive effects. Due to the pqd term, this departure is greatest when $p = \frac{1}{2}$.

Since the additive value is but a linear approximation of G, the additive variance is also of the same general form as in our additive model. Hence,

$$V_A = 2a^2pq = 2(pa_2 + qa_1)^2pq \tag{5.9}$$

Observe that when $a_1 = a_2 = a$, the variance reduces to that of the additive model. On the other hand, when dominance is complete such that $a_2 = 0$, the variance becomes $2a_1^2pq^3$ and is dependent on higher powers of the gene frequency.

The dominance variance can now be expressed in terms of our parameters with the aid of the deviations given in (5.5). It becomes

$$\begin{aligned} V_D &= p^2(-q^2d)^2 + 2pq(pqd)^2 + q^2(-p^2d)^2 \\ &= p^2q^2d^2(q^2 + 2pq + p^2) = p^2q^2d^2 \end{aligned} \tag{5.10}$$

Thus, when $d = 0$, the dominance variance is also zero as expected.

Plots of (5.9), (5.10), and their sum, the genotypic variance, are shown in Figure 5.4 for various degrees of dominance. It is apparent that the genotypic variance is greatest at intermediate gene frequencies. It is also interesting to note that, except for overdominant situations, the additive effect of genes tends to contribute more to the variance than do dominance deviations at most gene frequencies.

Until now, we have regarded the additive value of a genotype as a linear function of the number of contributing genes (x) having a measurable slope and intercept. It is frequently more convenient to eliminate the intercept by expressing the additive value as a deviation from the population mean as follows:

$$A = (ax + g) - (2ap + g)$$

$$= a(x - 2p)$$

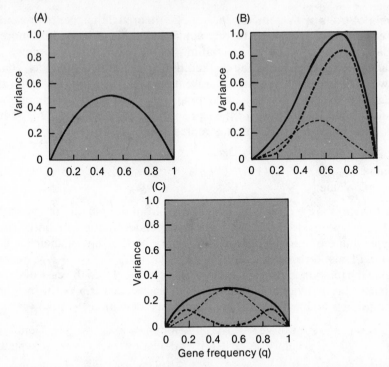

Figure 5.4. Magnitude of genetic components of variance in relation to gene frequency at a single locus. Genotypic variance—solid lines; additive variance—dotted lines; dominance variance—dashed lines. The degrees of dominance are: (A) no dominance; (B) complete dominance; (C) overdominance.

Since the x values of the genotypes BB, Bb, and bb are 2, 1, and 0, respectively, the additive values of the three genotypes would then be given as

$$A_{BB} = 2aq; \qquad A_{Bb} = a(q - p); \qquad \text{and} \qquad A_{bb} = -2ap \qquad (5.11)$$

and the mean additive value would be

$$\overline{A} = p^2(2aq) + 2pqa(q - p) + q^2(-2ap)$$
$$= 2pqa(p + q - p - q) = 0$$

When expressing additive values in this way, it is easy to show that additive effects and dominance deviations are uncorrelated. This is done by calculating the covariance of A and D as follows:

$$C(A, D) = p^2(2aq)(-q^2d) + 2pqa(q - p)(pqd) + q^2(-2ap)(-p^2d)$$
$$= -2p^2q^2ad(-q + q - p + p) = 0$$

This will be useful later when dealing with the correlation between relatives.

Analysis of traits with dominance.   The theoretical concepts presented in the preceding section can be readily applied to traits governed by more than a single locus. As a means of illustration, let us begin by considering a hypothetical character determined by the additive action of two gene loci, B and C, with two alleles at each. Assume for present purposes that environmental effects are negligible and that dominance is complete so that only four genotypes can be distinguished on the basis of their phenotypes alone. The genetic structure of this random-mating population is represented as follows:

Genotype:	$B{-}C{-}$	$B{-}cc$	$bbC{-}$	$bbcc$
Frequency:	$(1-q_B^2)(1-q_C^2)$	$(1-q_B^2)q_C^2$	$q_B^2(1-q_C^2)$	$q_B^2q_C^2$
Genotypic value:	G_{BC}	G_{Bc}	G_{bC}	G_{bc}

where G values are expressed as departures from the population mean. Since each phenotype is determined by the independent action of both loci, the genotypic value of each genotype will simply be the sum of their locus contributions. Thus, for example, $G_{BC} = G_{B-} + G_{C-}$, $G_{Bc} = G_{B-} + G_{cc}$, and so on. Applying the relationships given in (5.5), (5.7), and (5.11) to the case of complete dominance, the individual contributions of each locus can be further broken down into their additive values and dominance deviations as follows:

		Additive value		Dominance deviation		Genotypic value
G_{B-}	$=$	$2a_1q_B^2$	$+$	$-a_1q_B^2$	$=$	$a_1q_B^2$
G_{bb}	$=$	$-2a_1p_Bq_B$	$+$	$-a_1p_B^2$	$=$	$-a_1(1-q_B^2)$
G_{C-}	$=$	$2a_1'q_C^2$	$+$	$-a_1'q_C^2$	$=$	$a_1'q_C^2$
G_{cc}	$=$	$-2a_1'p_Cq_C$	$+$	$-a_1'p_C^2$	$=$	$-a_1'(1-q_C^2)$

where primes are used to indicate that genic contributions are not necessarily equal at both loci. Observe that only the additive values and dominance deviations of the homozygotes need be considered in this case since $G_{BB} = G_{Bb} = G_{B-}$ and $G_{CC} = G_{Cc} = G_{C-}$. The observed values for G resulting from the combined action of both loci are, therefore, given by the sums

$$G_{BC} = a_1q_B^2 + a_1'q_C^2; \qquad G_{Bc} = a_1q_B^2 - a_1'(1-q_C^2); \qquad G_{bC} = -a_1(1-q_B^2) + a_1'q_C^2;$$

$$\text{and} \qquad G_{bc} = -a_1(1-q_B^2) - a_1'(1-q_C^2)$$

From these relations, it is apparent that

$$G_{B-} = G_{BC}(1-q_C^2) + G_{Bc}q_C^2$$

$$G_{bb} = G_{bC}(1-q_C^2) + G_{bc}q_C^2$$

$$G_{C-} = G_{BC}(1-q_B^2) + G_{bC}q_B^2 \qquad\qquad \textbf{(5.12)}$$

$$G_{cc} = G_{Bc}(1-q_B^2) + G_{bc}q_B^2$$

Note that the single-locus values are functions of gene frequency and, therefore, depend on the population in which they are measured.

Having analyzed the above situation in symbolic form, let us now consider a specific numerical example. Suppose that we measure a random-mating population and obtain the following results:

Genotype:	$B-C-$	$B-cc$	$bbC-$	$bbcc$
Frequency:	0.63	0.21	0.12	0.04
Genotypic Value:	5	4	2	1

where the genotypic values are actual measurements in this case and not departures from the mean. The values of q_B^2 and q_C^2 are obtained directly from the data as

$$q_B^2 = 0.04 + 0.12 = 0.16$$

$$q_C^2 = 0.04 + 0.21 = 0.25$$

and the population mean is calculated to be

$$\overline{G} = (0.63)(5) + (0.21)(4) + (0.12)(2) + (0.04)(1) = 4.27$$

Subtracting the mean from each genotypic value, the values for $B-C-$, $B-cc$, $bbC-$, and $bbcc$, expressed as departures from the population average, become 0.73, -0.27, -2.27, and -3.27, respectively. We now compute the genotypic values attributable to each locus by considering the genes at each locus individually while ignoring the genes at the other. This is accomplished by substituting the appropriate values into the set of equations in (5.12). We get

$$G_{B-} = 0.48; \qquad G_{bb} = -2.52; \qquad G_{C-} = 0.25; \qquad \text{and} \qquad G_{cc} = -0.75$$

Note that by adding the proper values (i.e., $G_{B-} + G_{C-}$, $G_{B-} + G_{cc}$, etc.), we obtain the departures from the mean that were calculated for $B-C-$, $B-cc$, $bbC-$, and $bbcc$. This indicates that the two gene loci are indeed independent in their action and contribute to the trait in an additive fashion. Yet another indication of additive action is the fact that the difference in genotypic value between $B-$ and bb is the same in both $C-$ and cc genotypes. A similar pattern is observed for the difference in genotypic value between $C-$ and cc genotypes. Having calculated the genotypic values for the single-locus genotypes, we can now go back and evaluate each additive value and dominance deviation. First we compute a_1 as $G_{B-}/q_B^2 = 3$ and a_1' as $G_{C-}/q_C^2 = 1$. Note from our earlier definition of a_1 (and a_1'), that these numbers can also be obtained by subtracting the appropriate genotypic values: $G_{BC} - G_{bC}$ (or $G_{Bc} - G_{bc}$) and $G_{BC} - G_{Bc}$ (or $G_{bC} - G_{bc}$). The additive and dominance values become

Genotype:	BB	Bb	bb	CC	Cc	cc
A value:	0.96	-0.24	-1.44	0.50	0	-0.50
D value:	-0.48	0.72	-1.08	-0.25	0.25	-0.25

Finally, we can now apply equations (5.9) and (5.10) to obtain the additive and dominance variance. By adding appropriate terms, we see that

$$V_A = 2a_1^2 p_B q_B^3 + 2a_1'^2 p_C q_C^3 = 0.6912 + 0.1250 = 0.8162$$

$$V_D = a_1^2 p_B^2 q_B^2 + a_1'^2 p_C^2 q_C^2 \quad = 0.5184 + 0.0625 = 0.5809$$

To further illustrate the logic used in analyzing the variation observed for complex quantitative characters, another procedure is given at the end of this chapter which is more appropriate for the analysis of traits with varying degrees of dominance and with the added complication of environmental variation.

Epistatic interactions.   Epistatic interactions are reciprocal actions of genes at different loci that can modify the expression of one or the other or both sets of genes. One possible example would occur if the gene pair $B_1 b_1$ were to show dominance in the presence of the genotypes $B_2 B_2$ or $B_2 b_2$ at locus 2, but act additively in the presence of $b_2 b_2$. When all loci affecting a trait are considered together, many different epistatic effects are possible with loci interacting in pairs or in higher order. As a consequence of this complexity, epistatic interactions are subdivided into two-factor interactions, three-factor interactions and so forth, depending on the number of loci involved. Since three-factor and higher-order interactions are extremely difficult to measure under ordinary circumstances and are usually rather small, we shall restrict our discussion to two-factor combinations.

To illustrate the experimental analysis of epistatic interactions, consider a specific numerical example involving two interacting pairs of genes, Bb and Cc. For two interacting loci, the total genotypic value of an individual can be expressed as a departure from the population mean in the following general manner:

$$G = G_B + G_C + I_{BC}$$

where G_B is the genotypic value attributable to the B locus alone, G_C is the corresponding value of the C locus, and I_{BC} is the deviation from additivity. Thus, in the broadest sense, epistatic interactions as measured by I are absent only when the different loci contribute to a trait in an independent and additive fashion.

Now suppose that, due to complete dominance, four genotypes can be distinguished within the population with the following frequencies and genotypic values:

Genotype:	$B-C-$	$B-cc$	$bbC-$	$bbcc$
Frequency:	$(1-q_B^2)(1-q_C^2) = 0.28$	$(1-q_B^2)q_C^2 = 0.42$	$q_B^2(1-q_C^2) = 0.12$	$q_B^2 q_C^2 = 0.18$
Genotypic Value:	$G_{bc} = 4$	$G_{bc} = 3$	$G_{bc} = 1$	$G_{bc} = 1$

where the genotypic values are actual measurements, not departures from the mean, and where $q_B^2 = 0.3$ and $q_C^2 = 0.6$. In this case, the population average is $\overline{G} = 2.68$. Thus, subtracting the mean from each genotypic value, we obtain 1.32 for $B-C-$, 0.32 for $B-cc$, -1.68 for $bbC-$, and -1.68 for $bbcc$. We next compute the genotypic values attributable to each locus by applying the expressions given earlier in (5.12). They are

$$G_{B-} \ (G_B \text{ for } B-) = 0.72; \qquad G_{bb} \ (G_B \text{ for } bb) = -1.68;$$

$$G_{C-} \ (G_C \text{ for } C-) = 0.42; \qquad \text{and} \qquad G_{cc} \ (G_C \text{ for } cc) = -0.28$$

Finally, we can obtain the epistatic deviation for each genotype by the difference $I_{BC} = G - G_B - G_C$. This procedure yields

$$I_{BC} \ (\text{for } B{-}C{-}) = 1.32 - 0.72 - 0.42 \quad = 0.18$$

$$I_{BC} \ (\text{for } B{-}cc) = 0.32 - 0.72 + 0.28 \quad = -0.12$$

$$I_{BC} \ (\text{for } bbC{-}) = -1.68 + 1.68 - 0.42 = -0.42$$

$$I_{BC} \ (\text{for } bbcc) = -1.68 + 1.68 + 0.28 = 0.28$$

Note that the mean epistatic deviation is

$$\bar{I} = (0.28)(0.18) + (0.42)(-0.12) + (0.12)(-0.42) + (0.18)(0.28) = 0$$

as expected. The epistatic variance, in turn, becomes

$$V_I = (0.28) \ (0.18)^2 + (0.42) \ (-0.12)^2$$
$$+ (0.12) \ (-0.42)^2 + (0.18) \ (0.28)^2$$
$$= 0.0504$$

This value can be compared with the relative magnitudes of the additive and dominance variances for the above numerical example. Evaluating the mean value of a_1 for the B locus as $G_{B-}/q_B^2 = 2.4$ and that of a_1' for the C locus as $G_{C-}/q_C^2 = 0.7$ and applying equations (5.9) and (5.10), we get $V_A = 0.9595$ and $V_D = 0.3679$. Thus, we see that the epistatic variance constitutes a relatively minor fraction of the total variance in this case even though the original genotypic values were far from additive.

In addition to the procedures outlined in the preceding example, two-factor interactions can be analyzed further by partitioning them into the interactions between additive components, interactions between additive and dominance components, and the interactions between dominance components at the loci under consideration. We can represent these interactions by their variance components V_{AA}, V_{AD}, and V_{DD}, respectively. Thus, we can write

$$V_I = V_{AA} + V_{AD} + V_{DD}$$

Although this partitioning is purely a theoretical one, it is useful for studying the correlation between relatives as we shall see in a later section of this chapter.

CORRELATION BETWEEN RELATIVES

Due to possessing similar genotypes and to their common environment, related individuals tend to resemble each other with the degree of resemblance being directly proportional to the strength of relatedness. Determining this degree of resemblance is one of the more practical tasks confronting population geneticists since it provides an important means of measuring the additive variance. This, in turn, is crucial for estimating the heritability, a concept which is discussed in some detail later.

The degree of resemblance between relatives can be measured in a number of ways, the method used being largely one of convenience. For instance, if one works with related pairs such as parent-offspring or sib-sib pairs, it is convenient to express the degree of resemblance either in terms of the product-moment correlation coefficient

$$r_{xy} = C(x,y)/\sqrt{V(x)V(y)}$$

or by way of the regression coefficient

$$b_{y,x} = C(x,y)/V(x)$$

where $C(x,y)$ is the covariance of the phenotypic variables x and y for the related pairs, and where $V(x)$ and $V(y)$ are their respective variances. In either case, the degree of resemblance depends directly on the magnitude of the covariance of related individuals. The covariance is thus the basic unit of study. Also note that if $V(x) = V(y)$, which is true for a number of related pairs, both measures give the same results. If, on the other hand, the population is broken up into groups such as families which can consist of more than two members each, it is easier to conduct an analysis of variance and to use the information received to calculate the intraclass correlation coefficient

$$r_I = V_B/(V_B + V_W)$$

where V_B is the between-family variance, measuring the variance of family means, and V_W is the within-family variance which measures the average variance within family groups. The value of V_B can be regarded as the co-variance of family members since the greater the similarity between members of the same group, the greater the proportional difference between group means.

Parent-offspring correlation.   To illustrate how the different measures of resemblance can be computed for random-mating populations, two different kinds of relationship will be discussed: parent-offspring and full-sib correlation. Consider first the correlation between offspring and one parent. To simplify mathematical considerations, assume a single locus with completely additive gene effects (i.e., $P = A + E$). Also, assume that environmental factors do not contribute to the covariance of relatives. Both of these assumptions will be relaxed later in our discussion. Before we can compute the covariance, however, we first need to know the joint genotype distribution of offspring and a randomly chosen parent. This correlation array is shown in Table 5.1. The array of frequencies in this joint distribution was calculated directly with the aid of conditional probabilities. To give an example, suppose that the randomly chosen parent is female, written to the left in a standard cross notation, and is of

TABLE 5.1.   Joint genotype distribution of parent and offspring.

Offspring (A')	BB $(2a)$	Bb (a)	bb (0)	Total
Parent (A)				
BB ($2a$)	p^3	p^2q	–	p^2
Bb (a)	p^2q	pq	pq^2	$2pq$
bb (0)	–	pq^2	q^3	q^2

genotype BB. The probability that a BB offspring is produced given the cross $BB \times BB$ is $P(BB\backslash BB \times BB) = 1$, while the probability that a BB offspring is produced given the cross $BB \times Bb$ is $P(BB\backslash BB \times Bb) = \frac{1}{2}$. No other mating can consist of a BB female and still give rise to a BB offspring. Since the expected frequencies of these matings are $P(BB \times BB) = p^4$ and $P(BB \times Bb) = 2p^3q$, the joint occurrence of BB offspring and BB parent is

$P(BB$ offspring and BB parent)

$$= P(BB\backslash BB \times BB)P(BB \times BB) + P(BB\backslash BB \times Bb)P(BB \times Bb)$$

$$= (1)p^4 + (\tfrac{1}{2})2p^3q = p^3(p + q) = p^3$$

This numerical result is the first cell frequency in our correlation table. The frequencies of the remaining parent-offspring combinations are obtained in a similar manner. The covariance can now be calculated by taking the sum of the cross products of the additive values for the parent and offspring ($A \times A'$) times their corresponding cell frequency and subtracting the square of the mean from this sum. Since the mean phenotypes of the parent and offspring are the same ($\bar{P} = \bar{P'} = 2ap$), we get

Cov(phenotypes of parent, average offspring)

$$= C(p,o) = 4a^2p^3 + 4a^2p^2q + a^2pq - (2ap)^2$$

$$= 4a^2p^2(p + q - 1) + a^2pq = a^2pq = \tfrac{1}{2}V_A$$

It is also apparent that $V_P = V_{P'} = 2a^2pq + V_E$. Thus, the product-moment correlation coefficient and the regression coefficient become

$$r_{po} = b_{o,p} = \tfrac{1}{2}V_A/V_P$$

Full-sib correlation.   The correlation between full sibs can be calculated in much the same manner as presented above but with the aid of the frequency distribution listed in Table 5.2. In this case, the joint distribution of sib pairs was computed from the conditional probabilities of particular sib-sib combinations given different mating events. For example, the probability of the sib pair $BB-Bb$, given in order of birth, from the mating $BB \times Bb$, is $P(BB-Bb\backslash BB \times Bb) = \frac{1}{4}$. Similarly, the probability of this sib-sib combination from the mating $Bb \times Bb$ is $P(BB-Bb\backslash Bb \times Bb) = \frac{1}{8}$. Since the expected frequencies

TABLE 5.2.   Joint genotype distribution for full-sib pairs.

Sib II (A')	BB (2a)	Bb (a)	bb (0)	Total
Sib I (A)				
BB (2a)	$\frac{1}{4}p^2(1+p)^2$	$\frac{1}{2}p^2q(1+p)$	$\frac{1}{4}p^2q^2$	p^2
Bb (a)	$\frac{1}{2}p^2q(1+p)$	$pq(1+pq)$	$\frac{1}{2}pq^2(1+q)$	$2pq$
bb (0)	$\frac{1}{4}p^2q^2$	$\frac{1}{2}pq^2(1+p)$	$\frac{1}{4}q^2(1+q)^2$	q^2

of these mating events, without regard to the sex of the mating partners, are $P(BB \times Bb) = 4p^3q$ and $P(Bb \times Bb) = 4p^2q^2$, respectively, the total probability of a $BB-Bb$ sib pair will be

$P(BB-Bb$ sib pair$)$

$= P(BB-Bb\backslash BB \times Bb)P(BB \times Bb) + P(BB-Bb\backslash Bb \times Bb)P(Bb \times Bb)$

$= (1/4)4p^3q + (1/8)4p^2q^2 = \frac{1}{2}p^2q(2p + q) = \frac{1}{2}p^2q(1 + p)$

which is the first cell frequency in the second column in Table 5.2. By applying similar logic, the frequencies of the remaining sib pairs can also be obtained. The covariance for full sibs then becomes

Cov (phenotypes of sib pairs)

$= C(o,o) = a^2p^2(1+p)^2 + 2a^2p^2q(1+p) + a^2pq(1+pq) - (2ap)^2$

$= a^2p^2(2-q)(2+q) + a^2pq + a^2p^2q^2 - 4a^2p^2 = a^2pq$

$= \frac{1}{2}V_A$

Hence, as in the case of parent-offspring correlation, the correlation coefficient and the regression coefficient between full sibs will be

$$r_{oo} = b_{oo} = \frac{1}{2}V_A/V_P$$

In addition to the above method of analysis, we can also compute the intraclass correlation coefficient between full sibs by partitioning the additive variance in the manner given in Table 5.3. This table shows the expected frequencies of different families in a random-mating population along with the

TABLE 5.3.   Apportionment of additive variance among families.

Mating	Frequency	Family Pattern			Family mean	Family Variance
		BB (2a)	Bb (a)	bb (0)		
BB × BB	p^4	1	0	0	$2a$	0
BB × Bb	$4p^3q$	$\frac{1}{2}$	$\frac{1}{2}$	0	$3a/2$	$a^2/4$
BB × bb	$2p^2q^2$	0	1	0	a	0
Bb × Bb	$4p^2q^2$	$\frac{1}{4}$	$\frac{1}{2}$	$\frac{1}{4}$	a	$a^2/2$
Bb × bb	$4pq^3$	0	$\frac{1}{2}$	$\frac{1}{2}$	$a/2$	$a^2/4$
bb × bb	q^4	0	0	1	0	0

family means and family variances. Since the within-family variance, V_W, is the average variance of all family groups, this component of genetic variation becomes

$$V_W = (\tfrac{1}{4}a^2)(4p^3q) + (\tfrac{1}{2}a^2)(4p^2q^2) + (\tfrac{1}{4}a^2)(4pq^3)$$
$$= a^2pq(p^2 + 2pq + q^2) = a^2pq$$
$$= \tfrac{1}{2}V_A$$

Thus, half the total additive variance in a random-mating population is a consequence of variation among family members. The remaining half is due to differences in family means. Letting $V_P = V_B + V_W + V_E$, it follows that

$$r_I = \tfrac{1}{2}V_A/V_P$$

as in the previous cases.

The general case.   Parent-offspring and full-sib correlations can also be obtained directly for nonlinear gene effects with the aid of the joint frequency distributions given in Tables 5.1 and 5.2. Unfortunately, however, such calculations are extremely laborious and time-consuming unless simplifying assumptions are made. One useful simplification in calculating the covariance of parent and offspring is to make use of the relationship existing between the genotypic value of a parent and its average offspring value. To arrive at this relationship, consider a parent of genotype BB. It contributes only B gametes while its mate is a randomly selected individual and contributes, on the average, $p(B)$ and $q(b)$ gametes. Hence, its offspring will consist of $p(BB)$ and $q(Bb)$ genotypes with a genotypic value of $pG_{BB} + qG_{Bb} = p(2aq - q^2d) + q(aq - ap + pqd) = apq + aq^2 = aq$, which is half the additive value of the parent when expressed as a departure from the population mean. The same basic pattern emerges when parents of other genotypes are considered. Thus, if the parent in question is bb in genotype, its offspring produced from matings with randomly selected individuals will be $p(Bb)$ and $q(bb)$ with a genotypic value $pG_{Bb} + qG_{bb} = p(aq - ap + pqd) - q(2ap + p^2d) = -apq - ap^2 = -ap$. Similarly, a parent of genotype Bb will produce offspring with an average value of $\tfrac{1}{2}(pG_{BB} + qG_{Bb}) + \tfrac{1}{2}(pG_{Bb} + qG_{bb}) = \tfrac{1}{2}a(q - p)$. The preceding calculations are summarized in Table 5.4. Note that, in general, the genotypic value of an average offspring is always one-half the additive value of its parent.

Having a relationship between the parental and mean progeny values, we can now express the covariance of parent and offspring by means of the following expected value notation:

$$C(p,o) = E(A + D)(\tfrac{1}{2}A) = \tfrac{1}{2}E(A^2) + \tfrac{1}{2}E(A)(D)$$

where $A + D$ is the parental value and $\tfrac{1}{2}A$ the mean progeny value. Since additive values and dominance deviations are uncorrelated, $E(A)(D)$ must equal 0. Therefore, we get

TABLE 5.4. Genotypic values of randomly selected parent and average offspring.

Parental Genotype	Parental value	Average offspring value
BB	$G_{BB} = 2aq - q^2d$	$pG_{BB} + qG_{Bb} = aq$
Bb	$G_{Bb} = a(q - p) + pqd$	$\frac{1}{2}(pG_{BB} + qG_{Bb}) + \frac{1}{2}(pG_{Bb} + qG_{bb})$ $= \frac{1}{2}a(q - p)$
bb	$G_{bb} = -2ap - p^2d$	$pG_{Bb} + qG_{bb} = -ap$

$$C(p,o) = \tfrac{1}{2}E(A^2) = \tfrac{1}{2}V_A$$

as before. Thus, we see that dominance will not affect the covariance between parent and offspring.

When such calculations are extended over many loci to include the effects of dominance and two-factor epistatic interactions, the covariance relationships for parent and offspring and for full sibs become

$$C(p,o) = (1/2)V_A + (1/4)V_{AA}$$

$$C(o,o) = (1/2)V_A + (1/4)V_D + (1/4)V_{AA} + (1/8)V_{AD} + (1/16)V_{DD}$$

where V_{AA}, V_{AD}, and V_{DD} are the two-factor variance components. In general, if x and y are the coefficients of V_A and V_D, the covariance can be written as

$$Cov = xV_A + yV_D + x^2V_{AA} + xyV_{AD} + y^2V_{DD}$$

Note that y is zero for parent-offspring pairs, whereas it is $\frac{1}{4}$ for full sibs. This is due to the fact that one-fourth of all sib pairs are identical in genotype at each segregating locus. Thus, full sibs not only share one-half the additive effects of their genes but also one-quarter of the dominance deviations. The coefficients expected for a number of relationships in addition to parent and offspring and sibs are given in Table 5.5. Note that since x and y are always less than one, the two-factor variance components, being dependent on the

TABLE 5.5. Covariances between relatives in a random-mating population.

Relationship	Covariance coefficients of V_A	Covariance coefficients of V_D
Parent-offspring	$\frac{1}{2}$	—
Full sibs	$\frac{1}{2}$	$\frac{1}{4}$
Half sibs	$\frac{1}{4}$	—
First cousins	$\frac{1}{8}$	—

product or square of the coefficients, will tend to contribute little to the overall correlations and can usually be ignored without serious consequences. As one might imagine, higher-order epistatic interactions are even less important.

HERITABILITY

Another useful concept in population genetics is that of *heritability* (symbolized h^2). The heritability of a quantitative trait can be defined in a number of different, although related, ways. One approach is to start by defining the symbol h as the correlation coefficient between the phenotypic value (P) and the number of contributing genes (X) in the following manner:

$$h = r_{PX} = C(P,X)/\sqrt{V_P V_X}$$

This is shown more clearly by expressing the phenotypic value of an individual as $P = aX + g + \delta$ where δ is a remainder term consisting of dominance, epistatic, and environmental deviations. We know from the relationship between the correlation coefficient (h) and the theoretical slope of a linear regression of P on X, a, that $h = a\sqrt{V_X/V_P}$. We also know that $V_A = a^2 V_X$ since $A = aX + g$. Hence,

$$h^2 = a^2 V_X/V_P = V_A/V_P \qquad (5.13)$$

Thus, we see that the heritability is the proportion of the total variance that is attributable to the additive effects of genes. This is in contrast to the so-called heritability in the broad sense which is defined as V_G/V_P and gives the fraction of the total variance that is attributable to differences among genotypes.

A second and equally important approach is to define the heritability as the regression of additive value and phenotypic value:

$$A = h^2 P$$

in which A and P are expressed as deviations from the population mean. The rationale for this approach can be shown by first noting that the additive value and the dominance, epistatic, and environmental deviations are uncorrelated. Hence, the covariance between the additive and phenotypic values, $C(A,P) = E(A + D + I + E)(A)$, is simply equal to the additive variance, V_A. The regression coefficient can, therefore, be written as

$$h^2 = C(A,P)/V_P = V_A/V_P \qquad (5.14)$$

The heritability thus gives the best estimate of an individual's additive value from its phenotypic value.

Although the heritability is a useful parameter for estimating the degree to which quantitative traits are determined by additive gene effects, it should be emphasized that h^2 is a variable which not only differs from trait to trait but also varies with gene frequency and with the environment in which the population lives. This can be clarified by writing the heritability as $h^2 = V_A/(V_G + V_E)$. Since both V_A and V_G are dependent on gene frequency, h^2 will tend to be a complex function of p and q, becoming zero when all individuals are of the same genotype. The heritability is also expected to decline with an increase in environmental variation. Thus, measurements of h^2 will only apply to a particular population under a particular set of environmental conditions.

Estimating heritability.   A number of different methods have been developed for estimating values of h^2. Most of these, however, are based on some measurement of the resemblance between relatives. One such example is a regression of offspring on parent. The theoretical basis for this method was developed earlier when it was shown that the regression coefficient for the preceding analysis should be $b_{o,p} = \frac{1}{2}V_A/V_p$ and should thus equal $\frac{1}{2}h^2$. In other words, we can represent the relationship between the phenotypic value of a parent, P_p, and the mean value of its offspring, $\overline{P}_o$, as

$$\overline{P}_o = \frac{1}{2}h^2 P_p$$

where the phenotypic values are expressed as deviations from the population mean. The heritability is, therefore, a measure of the degree to which parent and offspring resemble each other.

A number of experimental difficulties are often encountered when heritabilities are estimated in the preceding manner. One is the problem of a common environment. That is to say, members of a family group are exposed to a similar environment which, in turn, contributes to family resemblance and acts to inflate the estimate h^2. This problem can be minimized by the appropriate experimental design such as randomizing environmental situations within family groups or by measuring the effect of a common environment on the covariance between parent and offspring. Yet another factor that poses some experimental difficulty is the problem of maternal effects or, in other words, the problem of a mother's nongenetic influence on progeny phenotypes. This is frequently encountered when dealing with traits which have a strong maternal influence such as birth weight in mammals. The problem of maternal effects can usually be circumvented by experimental design such as restricting the regression analysis to that of offspring on paternal parent.

Another method which has been employed quite extensively in human genetics in order to obtain estimates of the heritability in the broad sense, V_G/V_P, is that of twin studies. What is generally done is to obtain the phenotypic variance between members of monozygous (identical) twins, V_{MZ}, and compare this value with the corresponding variance between members of dizygous (fraternal) twins, V_{DZ}. It is assumed, in this case, that environmental variation is the same for both types of twins. Hence the variance for monozygous twins, being of identical genotype, will be proportional to V_E. An estimate of V_G/V_P can then be obtained from the ratio

$$H = (V_{DZ} - V_{MZ})/V_{DZ} \tag{5.15}$$

It can be shown that H tends to give an underestimate of V_G/V_p (see example exercises) and, therefore, cannot be compared directly with similar estimates obtained for other kinds of relatives.

Some heritability estimates for humans as well as for two experimental populations are listed in Table 5.6. Note that heritabilities tend to be lowest for traits which have the greatest impact on reproductive fitness such as egg production and litter size. In such cases, less adapted variants are expected to be rapidly weeded out by means of natural selection, leaving little genetic variation among the remaining members of the population. Low heritabilities are also observed for traits such as body weight in human males for which there is obviously a large environmental component.

TABLE 5.6. Some estimates of heritability.

Organism	Heritability *
Human males (Osborne and De George, 1959)	H value
Cephalic index (head width/head length)	0.9
Stature	0.8
Weight	0.05
Mice (Falconer, 1953–55)	h^2 value
Tail length (6 weeks)	0.6
Body weight (6 weeks)	0.35
Litter size	0.15
Drosophila melanogaster (Robertson, 1957)	h^2 value
Thorax length	0.4
Ovary size	0.3
Egg production	0.2

* Values are rounded to the nearest 5%.

MULTIPLICATIVE GENE EFFECTS AND THRESHOLD CHARACTERS

Many traits are known which exhibit nonadditive phenotypic patterns even though detailed analyses show them to have a polygenic basis. One common departure is one in which polygenes contribute to a trait in a multiplicative rather than additive fashion. This kind of departure is generally assumed when the phenotypic mean of an F_1 is equal to the geometric, rather than arithmetic, mean of the two parental varieties. A suitable model can be constructed by supposing that each contributing gene increases the phenotypic value by a constant multiplicative factor rather than by a constant absolute amount. For example, if a plant variety has a 10 cm height, the effect of a gene that increases height by 10% is to give an 11 cm plant; a one gene difference of 1 cm. In contrast, for a stock of 100 cm plants, this same additional gene would give a 110 cm plant; a difference of 10 cm. This geometric effect, where the increment per gene is proportional to the existing genotype, is frequently observed for traits which are the net result of the biological process of growth. Since growth is a geometric process, being the resultant so to speak of the product of a large number of random variables, the model of choice is a lognormal distribution. It is then possible to analyze multiplicative gene effects in the manner previously described by applying a logarithmic transformation of the data, thus converting a highly skewed distribution into one that is normal in character. The results of this transformation are illustrated in Figure 5.5. In this example, the original phenotypic distributions are not very noticeably skewed. Nevertheless, a strong argument can be made for the application of a lognormal distribution on the basis of the observed relationship between the phenotypic mean and standard deviation. According to statistical theory, the standard deviation of a lognormal distribution should increase directly with the mean. In other words, phenotypic distributions which lie farther up the scale of measurement will tend to show the greatest spread in measured values. This is purely a scale effect which disappears when a logarithmic transformation is made.

In a number of cases, traits that show discontinuous distribution patterns

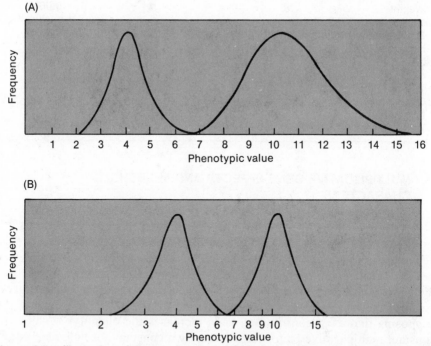

Figure 5.5. Illustration of the results of a logarithmic transformation applied to a phenotypic distribution. In (A) hypothetical data, plotted on an arithmetic scale, give skewed distributions. Plotting these data on a log scale (B) eliminates both the skewness and the scale effects observed in the variability of values.

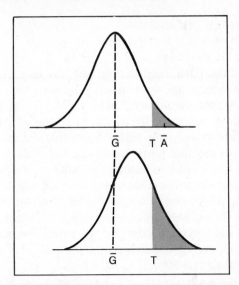

Figure 5.6. Inheritance of threshold characters. In this example, all individuals with a genotypic value above some threshold T show the trait. $\bar{G}$ is the mean value of the general population and $\bar{A}$ is the mean value of affected individuals in the general population. The lower curve shows the genotypic distribution among relatives of an affected individual.

are nevertheless thought to have a polygenic basis, the discontinuities being due to so-called *threshold effects*. The genotypic values are distributed continuously, but all values below some threshold value show the same phenotype, those above another phenotype (Figure 5.6). Thus, the phenotypic distribution does not, at first glance, indicate a polygenic character, and careful genetic analyses including cross data are necessary to detect the underlying multiple gene basis. Some disorders affecting man for which the phenotypic distributions are discontinuous but which may have a polygenic basis are listed in Table 5.7 along with their heritabilities.

TABLE 5.7. Heritabilities of some disorders of man which have a polygenic basis.

Disorder	Heritability (h^2)
Cleft lip ± cleft palate	0.76
Diabetes mellitus (early onset)	0.75
Club foot (congenital)	0.68
Hypertension	0.62
Congenital heart disease	0.35

SOLVED EXAMPLE PROBLEMS

Sources of Quantitative Variation

1. An example of the partitioning of the phenotypic variance into its component parts concerns the trait thorax length in *Drosophila*. Robertson (1957) found that the variance in length in a large, randomly mating population was 0.366, whereas the variance of the F_1 progeny of crosses between two inbred lines was 0.186. Subdivide the variance into its genotypic and environmental parts, assuming $V_{GE} = 0$.

   solution The large, random-breeding population is a heterogeneous mixture of diverse genotypes, so that its variance includes both genotypic and environmental factors and is a measure of total variability. In contrast, the offspring from a cross between homozygous parents all have the same (heterozygous) genotype, so that the F_1 variance can be used as an estimate of V_E. Hence, $V_G = 0.180$. As the proportion of the total variation, V_G is 0.492 and V_E is 0.508.

2. In a study of the components of variance of the trait bristle number on the fourth and fifth abdominal segments in *Drosophila*, Clayton, Morris, and Robertson (1957) found that the variance in their large, randomly mating base population was 10.791. The average variance specific to each individual (variance of the per individual difference between bristle numbers on the two segments) was determined to be 4.185. Previous analysis with inbred lines suggested that V_G comprised about 61% of the total variability for this trait. Comment on the relative magnitudes of the components of V_E.

   solution Taking V_{E_s} as 4.185, we have $V_{E_g} = 0.39(10.791) - 4.185 = 0.023$. Over 99% of the environmental variability is due to special effects (developmental?) on each individual; less than 1% is due to the generalized influence of environmental factors on this trait. (This disproportionate division is perhaps reflective of laboratory rearing under controlled environmental conditions.)

3. Emerson and East (1913) reported the following data on ear length in corn; the numbers within the table represent frequencies of each length.

Length of ear (cm)

	5	6	7	8	9	10	11	12	13	14	15	16	17	18	19	20	21
Parent *A*:	4	21	24	8													
Parent *B*:							3	11	12	15	26	15	10	7	2		
F_1:					1	12	12	14	17	9	4						
F_2:	1	10	19	26	47	73	68	68	39	25	15	9	1				

Calculate the number of loci determining ear length.

solution $\overline{P}_A = \Sigma\, P_{iA}\, f_{iA} = 6.63;\ \overline{P}_B = \Sigma\, P_{iB}\, f_{iB} = 16.80;\ V_{F_1} = \Sigma$

$(P_{iF_1} - \overline{P}_{F_1})^2 f_{iF_1} = 2.28$; $V_{F_2} = \Sigma (P_{iF_2} - \overline{P}_{F_2})^2 f_{iF_2} = 5.06$. Therefore,

$$n = \frac{(16.80 - 6.63)^2}{8(5.06 - 2.28)} = 5 \text{ gene loci (approximately)}.$$

4. Consider height in a certain plant to be an ideal polygenic trait determined by six independently assorting gene loci, each with two alleles. Assume that capital-letter genes contribute 2 cm each in an additive fashion, small-letter genes 0 cm each, with a residual (base) height of 3 cm. (a) From crosses among heterozygotes, what distribution of genotypic values is expected in the offspring? (b) Calculate the mean genotypic value and the genotypic variance for the offspring.

   solution (a) Represent the crosses as $B_1 b_1 B_2 b_2 \ldots B_6 b_6 \times B_1 b_1 B_2 b_2 \ldots B_6 b_6$. Letting $x =$ the number of contributing genes, $G =$ the genotypic value, and $p(x) =$ the proportion of individuals with x contributing genes, the distribution of offspring genotypes is

x:	0	1	2	3	4	5	6	7	8	9	10	11	12	
G:		3	5	7	9	11	13	15	17	19	21	23	25	27
$p(x)$:	2	3	16	54	121	193	226	193	121	54	16	3	2	($\times 10^4$)

   Frequencies are calculated using the binomial probability term

   $$p(x) = \binom{2n}{x} p^x q^{2n-x}, \text{ where } p = q = \tfrac{1}{2}.$$

   (b) Using equation (5.2), where $a = 2$ for all loci, $\overline{G} = 6(2) + 3 = 15$ cm and $V_G = 6(4)/2 = 12$ cm^2.

Gene Interactions

5. Consider a metric character determined by a single gene locus such that the genotypic values are $G_{BB} = 16$, $G_{Bb} = 12$, and $G_{bb} = 6$. Determine the effects of gene substitution, the dominance deviation, and the degree and type of dominance.

   solution Effects of gene substitution: $a_1 = G_{Bb} - G_{bb} = 6$, $a_2 = G_{BB} - G_{Bb} = 4$. Degree of dominance: $d = a_1 - a_2 = 2$, $d/a_1 = 2/6 = 1/3$. Type of dominance: incomplete $(0 < d < 1)$.

6. For the data given in Example Problem 5, determine the values of the parameters, a and g, of the additive value relationships. In addition, calculate the additive values, the mean genotypic value, and the additive, dominance, and total genotypic variances. Assume a randomly mating population composed of the genotypic array $(0.3, 0.2, 0.5)$.

   solution From equation (5.6), $g = 6 + (0.4)^2 (2) = 6.32$. Using equation (5.7), $a = (0.40)4 + (0.60)6 = 5.20$. Hence, $A_{BB} = 16.72$, $A_{Bb} = 11.52$, and $A_{bb} = 6.32$. Equation (5.8) gives $\overline{G} = 10(0.4) + 0.24(2) + 6 = 10.48$. Finally, from equations (5.9) and (5.10), $V_A = 12.98$ and $V_D = 0.230$, giving $V_G = 13.21$.

Correlation Between Relatives

7. Calculate the remaining joint frequencies of the parent-offspring combinations given in Table 5.1.

   solution $P(BB$ offspring and $\boldsymbol{Bb}$ parent$)$

   $= P(BB \backslash \boldsymbol{Bb} \times BB) \, P(\boldsymbol{Bb} \times BB) + P(BB \backslash \boldsymbol{Bb} \times Bb) P(\boldsymbol{Bb} \times Bb)$

   $= (\tfrac{1}{2})(2p^3q) + (\tfrac{1}{4})(4p^2q^2) = p^2q(p + q) = p^2q.$

   $P(Bb$ offspring and $\boldsymbol{Bb}$ parent$)$

   $= P(Bb \backslash \boldsymbol{Bb} \times BB) P(\boldsymbol{Bb} \times BB) + P(Bb \backslash \boldsymbol{Bb} \times Bb) P(\boldsymbol{Bb} \times Bb) +$
   $P(Bb \backslash \boldsymbol{Bb} \times bb) P(\boldsymbol{Bb} \times bb)$

   $= (\tfrac{1}{2})(2p^3q) + (\tfrac{1}{2})(4p^2q^2) + (\tfrac{1}{2})(2pq^3) = pq(p^2 + 2pq + q^2) = pq$

   $P(bb$ offspring and $\boldsymbol{bb}$ parent$)$

   $= P(bb \backslash \boldsymbol{bb} \times bb) P(\boldsymbol{bb} \times bb) + P(bb \backslash \boldsymbol{bb} \times Bb) P(\boldsymbol{bb} \times Bb) = (1)(q^4)$
   $+ (\tfrac{1}{2})(2pq^3)$

   $= q^3 (q + p) = q^3$

   To obtain the others, follow the same pattern as above.

Heritability

8. The data below give the mean seed size (0.01 inch) of 100 progeny reared from each of seven parental classes of sweet peas. Estimate the heritability value for this trait using a regression analysis of parent on offspring.

Parent size:	15	16	17	18	19	20	21
Mean progeny size:	15.3	16.0	15.6	16.3	16.0	17.3	17.5

   solution $b = C(P,O)/V(P) = \Sigma \, (P_i - \overline{P}) \, (O_i - \overline{O}) \, f_i / \Sigma \, (P_i - \overline{P})^2 \, f_i$

   $= [\Sigma P_i O_i - (\Sigma \, P_i)(\Sigma \, O_i)/n]/[\Sigma \, P_i^2 - (\Sigma \, P_i)^2/n]$

   $= [15(15.3) + 16(16.0) + \ldots - (126)(114)/7]/[15^2 + 16^2$
   $+ \ldots - (126)^2/7]$

   $= (2061.6 - 2052)/(2296 - 2268) = 9.6/28 = 0.343.$

   Therefore, $h^2 = 0.686.$

Multiplicative Gene Effects and Threshold Characters

9. The number of toes on the hind legs of guinea pigs is thought to be determined by a polygenic system with 4 loci and a threshold effect. An individual having 4 or less contributing genes appears phenotypically as three-toed; however, an individual possessing at least 5 effective genes exceeds the threshold and has four toes. From tetrahybrid crosses, predict the phenotypic ratio among the offspring.

   solution   The cross can be written as $B_1b_1B_2b_2B_3b_3B_4b_4 \times$ $B_1b_1B_2b_2B_3b_3B_4b_4$, so that, using the binomial expansion, the proportion of three-toed types can be calculated as $p(i \leqslant 4) = \sum\limits_{i=0}^{4} \binom{8}{1}(\tfrac{1}{2})^8$, where $i =$ the number of contributing genes. Evaluating each term and summing, we obtain $p(\text{three-toed}) = 163/256$ and $p(\text{four-toed}) = 1 - 163/256 = 93/256.$

10. Show that the statistic H is equal to $[V_A + (3/2)V_D]/[V_A + (3/2)V_D + 2V_E]$ and its value, therefore, underestimates the heritability in the broad sense, V_G/V_p.

    solution   From equation (5.15), $H = (V_{DZ} - V_{MZ})/V_{DZ}$. For any two variables x and y, recall that $V(x + y) = V(x) + V(y) - 2C(x,y,)$. Thus, regardless of the type of twins, the variance between members is $V(T_1 - T_2) = V(T_1) + V(T_2) - 2C(T_1, T_2)$, where $V(T_1) = V(T_2) = V_P = V_A + V_D + V_E$. The covariance is necessarily between the genetic effects and, since these are identical in monozygotic twins, then $C(T_1, T_2) = V_G$ due to the identity $V(x) = C(x,x)$. Thus, $V_{MZ} = 2(V_A + V_D + V_E) - 2(V_A + V_D) = 2V_E$. For dizygotic twins, $C(T_1, T_2) = \frac{1}{2}V_A + \frac{1}{4}V_D$ (see Table 5.5). Therefore, $V_{DZ} = 2(V_A + V_D + V_E) - 2(\frac{1}{2}V_A + \frac{1}{4}V_D) = V_A + (3/2)V_D + 2V_E$ and we have the desired result for H.

11. The following data are taken from Smith (1937) on corolla shape in *Nicotiana* (tobacco). In this study, comparison of the F_1 mean with that of the parental varieties, *N. sanderal* (P_1) and *N. langsdorfii* (P_2), indicated a multiplicative polygene effect, so that the data were transformed using a logarithmic scale. The variances of the parents, F_1 and F_2, were as follows: $V_{P_1} = 48$, $V_{P_2} = 32$, $V_{F_1} = 46$, and $V_{F_2} = 130.5$. In addition, backcrosses were also made involving $F_1 \times P_1$ (B_1) and $F_1 \times P_2$ (B_2). The variances of the progeny were $V_{B_1} = 85.5$ and $V_{B_2} = 98.5$. Assuming no epistatic interactions, compute the additive variance (V_A), the dominance variance (V_D), and the environmental variance (V_E) from the data given.

    solution   To analyze the data, we choose a different approach from that presented in the text, but one developed in detail by Mather and Jinks (1971). First of all, observe from equations (5.9) and (5.10) that, with $p = q = \frac{1}{2}$, the F_2 variance can be expressed as $V_{F_2} = V_A + V_D + V_E = \Sigma(1/8)(a_1 + a_2)^2 + \Sigma(1/16)d^2 + V_E$. Similar expressions can be derived for the backcross progeny. This is illustrated as follows for a single gene locus:

Backcross 1 (B_1): $Bb \times BB$

Progeny	Frequency	Value
BB	1/2	$a_1 + a_2 + g_o$
Bb	1/2	$\frac{1}{2}(a_1 + a_2 + d) + g_o$

[Mean value $= (3/4)(a_1 + a_2) + (1/4)d + g_o$]

Backcross 2 (B_2): $Bb \times bb$

Progeny	Frequency	Value
Bb	1/2	$\frac{1}{2}(a_1 + a_2 + d) + g_o$
bb	1/2	g_o

[Mean value $= (1/4)(a_1 + a_2) + (1/4)d + g_o$]

If we combine the data, the total variance becomes

$$V_{B_1} + V_{B_2} = \tfrac{1}{2}(a_1 + a_2)^2 + \tfrac{1}{4}(a_1 + a_2 + d)^2 - [\tfrac{1}{4}(3)(a_1 + a_2) + \tfrac{1}{4}d]^2$$
$$- [\tfrac{1}{4}(a_1 + a_2) + \tfrac{1}{8}d]^2$$
$$= (1/8)(a_1 + a_2)^2 + (1/8)d^2$$

By summing over all loci and including the environmental variance for each of the two above cases, we get

$$V_{B_1} + V_{B_2} = \Sigma\,(1/8)(a_1 + a_2)^2 + \Sigma\,(1/8)d^2 + 2V_E = V_A + 2V_D + 2V_E$$

Since $V_{F_2} = V_A + V_D + V_E$, the two equations can now be solved simultaneously to yield

$$V_A = 2V_{F_2} - V_{B_1} - V_{B_2} \quad \text{and} \quad V_D = V_{B_1} + V_{B_2} - V_{F_2} - V_E$$

where V_E is estimated by V_{F_1}. Thus, for the data given on corolla shape, $V_A = 2(130.5) - 85.5 - 98.5 = 77$ and $V_D = 85.5 + 98.5 - 130.5 - 46 = 7.5$.

PROBLEM EXERCISES

1. The length of the basal leaves of golden rod was measured by Charles and Goodwin in a series of controlled crosses. Representative data are given below:

    Solidaga rugosa ($\overline{P} = 5.5$) × *S. sempervirens* ($\overline{P} = 17.8$)

    F_1: $\overline{P} = 10.1$; $V_{F_1} = 4.08$

    F_2: $\overline{P} = 8.2$; $V_{F_2} = 6.66$

    Estimate the number of genes determining this trait and the average contribution per effective gene assuming additive gene effects.

2. The genetic basis of fruit weight in the tomato has been studied by Powers (1951). Data from a series of controlled crosses are reproduced below for which a logarithmic transformation has been employed:

    Danmark ($\overline{P} = 1.671515$) × red current ($\overline{P} = 0.053440$)

    F_1: $\overline{P} = 0.707441$; $V_{F_1} = 0.017856$

    F_2: $\overline{P} = 0.672012$; $V_{F_2} = 0.048285$

    B_1: $\overline{P} = 0.286961$; $V_{B_1} = 0.028038$

    B_2: $\overline{P} = 1.161870$; $V_{B_2} = 0.037797$

    Determine the number of genes controlling fruit weight and the additive and dominance variance. (See Example Problem 11.)

3. Express the additive values of the genotypes given in Example Problem 6 as deviations from the population mean.

4. Compute the remaining joint frequencies for the full-sib pairs given in Table 5.2.

5. In a population having a phenotypic mean of 55 units, a total genetic variance for the trait of 35 units^2 and an environmental variance of 14 units^2, between what two phenotypic values will approximately two-thirds of the population be found?

6. Referring to the data on *Nicotiana* given in Example Problem 11, (a) what is the heritability of the corolla shape trait? (b) What is the value of the heritability in the broad sense (V_G/V_P)?

7. Russell (1949) reported the following data on the mean size (microns diameter) of pigment granules in mice, where two gene loci, each showing complete dominance, control the expression of the trait:

Genotype:	$B-C-$	$B-cc$	$bbC-$	$bbcc$
Frequency:	0.48	0.12	0.32	0.08
Genotypic value:	1.44	0.94	0.77	0.77

Determine the additive value (A) and the dominance (D) and epistatic (I) deviations for each genotype. Determine the values for each of the components of the genetic variance.

8. The phenotypic distribution of a certain character was determined for each of two groups:

Group 1 (cm)	Group 2 (cm)
3.1	7.6
2.9	6.4
3.3	7.5
3.6	6.9
3.5	6.3

Compare the means and standard deviations of the two groups before and after a logarithmic transformation is made. Do the genes act in an additive or multiplicative fashion?

6

Inbreeding and Assortative Mating

As in the case of random mating, genotype frequencies can also be predicted in populations with a regular system of nonrandom mating. However, such predictions require information on the kind of mating system and on the degree to which it differs from randomness. Two common departures from random mating are phenotypic assortative mating and inbreeding (genotypic assortative mating). When compared with effects of random mating, both of these non-random mating patterns tend to increase the frequency of homozygotes and reduce that of heterozygotes. They differ in at least one important respect. Since inbreeding involves matings between relatives, mates possess genotypic similarities which extend over all gene pairs. Consequently, inbreeding affects all segregating loci. In contrast, phenotypic assortative mating only affects those genes which are responsible for the trait involved so long as matings are restricted to unrelated individuals.

SELFING

To illustrate the effects of an extreme but simple form of genotypic assortative mating, consider a population with nonoverlapping generations in which matings are restricted to identical genotypes as follows: $BB \times BB$, $Bb \times Bb$, and $bb \times bb$. This situation would correspond to a population of annual plants under strict self-fertilization. Since each individual will only mate with itself, the proportions of all matings will equal the frequencies at which the genotypes appear in the population. The contributions of all mating types to the next generation are summarized in Table 6.1. Note that selfing of homozygotes

174

TABLE 6.1.   Matings and frequencies of offspring produced under conditions of self-fertilization.

Mating (Generation 0)	Frequency	OFFSPRING (GENERATION 1)		
		BB	Bb	bb
BB × BB	P	P	0	0
Bb × Bb	H	$\frac{1}{4}H$	$\frac{1}{2}H$	$\frac{1}{4}H$
bb × bb	Q	0	0	Q
	$(P + H + Q)$	$P + \frac{1}{4}H$	$\frac{1}{2}H$	$Q + \frac{1}{4}H$
Sum:	$= 1$	$= P_1$	$= H_1$	$= Q_1$

results in the production of only homozygous offspring of the parental type. When heterozygotes are selfed, one-half the progeny are heterozygous and one-half are distributed equally between the homozygous classes. As a consequence of this pattern, the genotypic proportions among the offspring in the next generation will be

$$P_1 = P + \tfrac{1}{4}H$$

$$H_1 = \tfrac{1}{2}H$$

$$Q_1 = Q + \tfrac{1}{4}H$$

As shown by the above expressions, homozygous classes increase symmetrically among the offspring while the proportion of heterozygotes is reduced to one-half the parental value. If selfing were to continue, H will be reduced by one-half in each generation. Therefore, if we let H_o represent the proportion of heterozygotes in the starting population, the value of H after t generations of selfing will be

$$H_t = \tfrac{1}{2}H_{t-1} = (\tfrac{1}{2})^t H_o \tag{6.1}$$

As this expression indicates, the ultimate outcome of continued self-fertilization is the complete elimination of heterozygotes from the population. When this occurs, the frequencies of the remaining homozygotes are $P = p$ and $Q = q$. Note that inbreeding by itself does not alter gene frequencies, only genotype frequencies are changed.

Multiple loci.   The effects of selfing can be extended to include many pairs of genes. Suppose, for example, that there are k pairs of genes, all segregating independently of each other. If we start with only genotypes that are heterozygous at all k loci, the probability that any one particular locus is still heterozygous after t generations of selfing is $(\tfrac{1}{2})^t$. Hence, the probability that exactly x of these k loci remain heterozygous after t generations is

$$p(x) = \binom{k}{x} (1/2^t)^k (1 - 1/2^t)^{k-x} \tag{6.2}$$

This means that the fraction of individuals with all k heterozygous loci is reduced in each generation by

$$p(k)_t = (\tfrac{1}{2})^k \, p(k)_{t-1}$$

and that the fraction with at least one heterozygous locus will decrease with time as

$$p(x \geq 1)_t = 1 - (1 - 1/2^t)^k \tag{6.3}$$

As the latter formula helps to point out, the approach to complete homozygosity is quite rapid. For instance, with k equal to ten, the fraction with at least one heterozygous locus after ten generations of selfing is approximately equal to 0.01.

A similar analysis can be made for the case when genes are linked. Suffice it to say that linkage merely acts to reduce the rate of approach to homozygosity; the end result is unchanged.

MEASURES OF INBREEDING AND KINSHIP OF INDIVIDUALS

Coefficient of Inbreeding.   Inbreeding also produces homozygosity in bi-parental populations. In this case, however, the rate at which complete homozygosity is attained varies with the genetic correlation of mates. Therefore, in order to describe the specific consequences of inbreeding, we need a general measure of the degree to which inbreeding occurs. One such measure is the *inbreeding coefficient* (F), first proposed by Sewall Wright (1922). When applied to pedigreed populations, this parameter can be defined as the probability that two alleles in an individual are identical by descent (Malecot, 1948). Stated in an alternative way, it is the probability that two alleles arose in the past from the same gene in a common ancestor. As our definition suggests, we can subdivide members of a population into two general types: *autozygotes*—individuals in which alleles are identical by descent, and *allozygotes*—those with alleles that are independent in origin. Although autozygotes must, by definition, be homozygous, allozygous individuals may be either homozygous or heterozygous. If homozygous, allozygotes would possess alleles which are identical in state (presumably) but not identical by descent. It is, therefore, apparent that the inbreeding coefficient is merely the probability that an individual is autozygous. As such, the value of F will depend on the degree to which the parents of an individual are inbred. This can be illustrated with the aid of the single-generation pedigree given in Figure 6.1 for self-fertilization. In this example, a and b are used to designate the gametes produced by the parent, A, while gene subscripts are used only to differentiate alleles, not to imply identity or lack of it. There are three possible genotypes which individual I can have and be autozygous: $B_1 B_1$, $B_2 B_2$, and $B_1 B_2$–given that B_1 and B_2 are identical

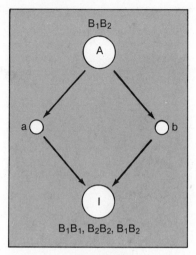

Figure 6.1.   A simple pedigree for self-fertilization. *A* and *I* denote the parent and off-spring, *a* and *b* are gametes. The genotypes possible for the offspring are listed below.

by descent from a previous generation. Using the equal sign to designate identity by descent, the inbreeding coefficient of individual I can then be expressed as the probability that $a = b$, $P(a=b)$. Applying the basic rules of probability, this becomes

$$F_I = P(a=b) = P(a=b=B_1) + P(a=b=B_2) + Pr(a=B_1, b=B_2 \backslash B_1=B_2)Pr(B_1=B_2)$$
$$+ Pr(a=B_2, b=B_1 \backslash B_1=B_2)Pr(B_1=B_2)$$

where the last two terms in the sum are the conditional probabilities given that B_1 and B_2 are identical by descent multiplied by the probability that they are, in fact, identical. Since $P(B_1=B_2)$ is, by definition, equal to the inbreeding coefficient of the parent (F_A) and all other probabilities are equal to $\frac{1}{4}$, F_I becomes

$$F_I = \tfrac{1}{4} + \tfrac{1}{4} + \tfrac{1}{4}F_A + \tfrac{1}{4}F_A = \tfrac{1}{2}(1 + F_A) \tag{6.4}$$

Thus, if A were not inbred, as might be the case if this were the first generation of selfing, F_A would be zero and the inbreeding coefficient of individual I reduces to $\frac{1}{2}$.

These calculations can be extended to analyzing more complicated pedigrees. Consider first the pedigree for half-sib mating illustrated in Figure 6.2. The diagram in part (a) represents the traditional pedigree notation in which a square is a male and a circle a female, while part (b) represents a short-hand version of the same pedigree showing only the paths taken by genes from the common ancestor to individual I. Applying the product rule for independent events, the inbreeding coefficient of individual I can then be computed as

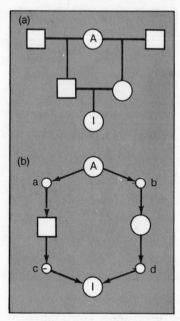

Figure 6.2. (a) Traditional pedigree notation for a half-sib mating. (b) A short-hand version of the same pedigree showing the paths taken by genes from the common ancestor A. The symbols a, b, c, and d are gametes.

$$F_I = P(c{=}d) = P(a{=}b) \cdot P(c{=}a) \cdot P(d{=}b)$$

Applying the same logic that went into the development of equation (6.4), we see that $P(a{=}b) = \frac{1}{2}(1 + F_A)$ where F_A is the inbreeding coefficient of the common ancestor. It should also be apparent that $P(c{=}a){=}P(d{=}b){=}\frac{1}{2}$. Therefore,

$$F_I = (\tfrac{1}{2})^3 (1 + F_A)$$

Thus, if individual A were not inbred, the inbreeding coefficient for half-sibs would be $(\frac{1}{2})^3 = 1/8$.

In general, we can state that if the parents of an individual have only one ancestor in common, the inbreeding coefficient of the individual can be expressed as

$$F_I = (\tfrac{1}{2})^n (1 + F_A) \tag{6.5}$$

where F_A is the inbreeding coefficient of the common ancestor and n is the number of ancestors on the path from the individual through one of his parents and back through the other. For example, in the pedigree illustrated in Figure 6.3, the total number of ancestors including the parents of the individual is 5. Hence, the inbreeding coefficient in this case is $(\frac{1}{2})^5(1 + F_A) = (1 + F_A)/32$.

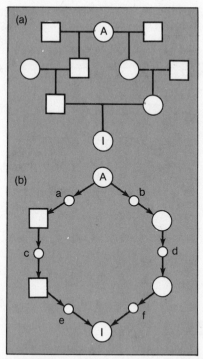

Figure 6.3.   (a) Traditional pedigree notation. (b) The same pedigree showing only the paths taken by genes from the common ancestor A. The symbols a, b, c, d, e, and f are gametes.

We can extend this procedure to include pedigrees in which the parents of an individual have more than one ancestor in common. When this is the case, the total inbreeding coefficient is the sum of the F values derived from each of the common (but unrelated) ancestors individually. In symbolic form,

$$F_I = \Sigma \left(\tfrac{1}{2}\right)^n (1 + F_A) \tag{6.6}$$

To illustrate how this expression was developed, consider the pedigree for full-sibs given in Figure 6.4. Part (a) once again shows the traditional manner of writing the pedigree, while part (b) pictures the two mutually exclusive paths taken by genes derived from each of the grandparents of the individual. Note that a pedigree can be broken up into as many circular paths as there are ancestors in common. Thus, if we use A and B to designate the grandparents of the individual, the total inbreeding coefficient can be calculated as the sum

$$F_I = \left(\tfrac{1}{2}\right)^3 (1 + F_A) + \left(\tfrac{1}{2}\right)^3 (1 + F_B)$$

where the first term is computed from the circular path involving A and the second is obtained for the path with B. Observe that if A and B are not inbred,

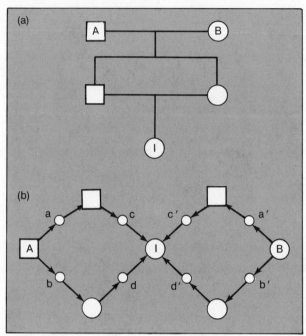

Figure 6.4. (a) Traditional pedigree notation. (b) The same pedigree showing the two mutually exclusive paths taken by genes from the common ancestors *A* and *B*.

the inbreeding coefficient for full sibs works out to be $2(\frac{1}{2})^3 = \frac{1}{4}$. It is important to note that both (6.5) and (6.6) are only applicable to those cases in which all common ancestors mate unrelated individuals.

Table 6.2 shows the inbreeding coefficients for a variety of consanguineous (i.e., inbred) matings. It is assumed in all cases that the common ancestors are not inbred.

Coefficient of kinship.   Another useful measure of inbreeding is the *coefficient of kinship* (f), introduced by Malecot (1948). This coefficient can be defined as the probability that two genes selected at random from equivalent

TABLE 6.2   Inbreeding coefficients of some consanguineous matings.

Relationship of Parents	Inbreeding Coefficient of Offspring
Unrelated individuals	$F = 0$
Full-sibs and Parent-offspring	$F = 1/4$
Half-sibs and Uncle-niece (aunt-nephew)	$F = 1/8$
First cousins	$F = 1/16$
Second cousins	$F = 1/64$

loci in separate individuals are identical by descent. For example, suppose that individual I has two parents, A and B. Let a be the gamete produced by A and b represent the gamete produced by B. The coefficient of kinship of A and B, f_{AB}, can then be expressed as $f_{AB} = P(a=b)$. Since individual I is the product of the gametes a and b, it follows that f_{AB} is the same as F_I. Thus, we see that the inbreeding coefficient of an offspring is the same as the coefficient of kinship of its parents.

The basic rules involved in calculating coefficients of kinship from pedigrees are basically similar to that of inbreeding coefficients and can be developed with the aid of the illustrations given in Figure 6.5. This example portrays the partitioning of a family pedigree into the four possible modes of inheritance of genes which are selected at random from each of the sibs C and D. In the first two patterns, the randomly selected genes come from the same parent. Thus, by applying the same rules used in calculating inbreeding coefficients, the probability that these randomly selected genes are identical by descent is equal to $\frac{1}{2}(1 + F_A)$ or to $\frac{1}{2}(1 + F_B)$ depending on the parent involved. In contrast, the

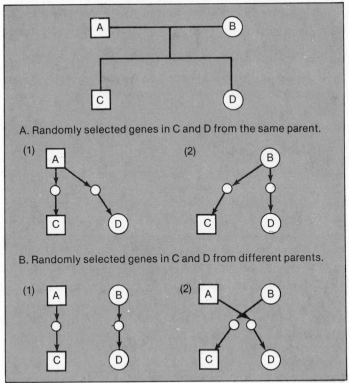

A. Randomly selected genes in C and D from the same parent.

(1)   (2)

B. Randomly selected genes in C and D from different parents.

(1)   (2)

Figure 6.5.   Four possible paths by which randomly selected genes in C and D are identical by descent. If the genes arise from different parents, identity by descent must originate in a preceding generation.

next two illustrations show genes which come from different parents. To be identical by descent, these genes would have to arise from the same gene in a previous generation. Hence, the probability of their identity must equal the coefficient of kinship of the parents, f_{AB}. Since all four inheritance patterns can occur with equal likelihood, the total probability of allelic identity in individuals C and D (i.e., the coefficient of kinship, f_{CD}) will then be

$$f_{CD} = \tfrac{1}{4}[\tfrac{1}{2}(1 + F_A)] + \tfrac{1}{4}[\tfrac{1}{2}(1 + F_B)] + \tfrac{1}{4}f_{AB} + \tfrac{1}{4}f_{AB}$$
$$= \tfrac{1}{4}[\tfrac{1}{2}(1 + F_A) + \tfrac{1}{2}(1 + F_B) + 2f_{AB}] \tag{6.7}$$

Note that if A and B are not related but are inbred, $f_{AB} = 0$ and (6.7) becomes

$$f_{CD} = (\tfrac{1}{2})^3(1 + F_A) + (\tfrac{1}{2})^3(1 + F_B)$$

which is the same as the inbreeding coefficient for full-sib matings. Thus, we see that (6.7) is a general formula which takes both the degree of inbreeding and the relatedness of mates into account.

The coefficient of kinship is known by a number of different names including the one which we are using. Two additional names which you should be familiar with are the coefficient of parentage and the coefficient of consanguinity.

BIPARENTAL POPULATIONS WITH INBREEDING

Measures of inbreeding and kinship of populations.   The coefficients of inbreeding and kinship can be used to measure the extent to which inbreeding occurs in whole populations. When applied in this manner, neither coefficient is the same for all individuals except in populations that are practicing some regular system of inbreeding such as parent-offspring or full-sib mating. If individuals vary with regard to their degree of inbreeding, the inbreeding coefficient for the population as a whole is the average value expressed as

$$F = \Sigma F_i c_i$$

where c_i is the proportion practicing a form of inbreeding with an inbreeding coefficient equal to F_i. Thus, if a population of 1,000 contained 889 individuals of random parentage, 1 individual from an uncle-niece mating, 40 individuals from first-cousin matings, and 70 individuals from second-cousin matings, the inbreeding coefficient for the entire population would be

$$F = (0.889)(0) + (0.001)(1/8) + (0.040)(1/16) + (0.070)(1/64) = 0.00372$$

Thus, as long as the proportions arising from these consanguineous matings remain constant, the value of F will stay the same from one generation to the next.

We can similarly define a coefficient of kinship for the population. It is the probability that two homologous genes selected at random from any mated pair are identical by descent. Since mates tend to vary in regard to their degree of relationship, the coefficient of kinship is defined in such a way that its value equals the average inbreeding coefficient of the following generation. In symbolic form

$$F_t = f_{t-1}$$

Genotype frequencies with inbreeding. Populations that are subject to inbreeding can be regarded as a mixture of autozygous and allozygous individuals in which the proportion of autozygotes is F and of allozygotes is $1 - F$. In other words, if we select an individual from the population at random, the probability that the individual's alleles at a particular locus are identical by descent is F. Since the probability that a given gene, say B, is present at this locus is equal to its frequency p, the chance that the individual is a BB autozygote must then be Fp. Similarly, the probability that the individual is a bb autozygote is Fq. Allozygotes, in turn, will occur with a probability equal to $1 - F$ and, since their alleles are independent in origin, the frequencies of BB, Bb, and bb allozygotes should correspond to those expected for a random-mating population. Putting these formulations together, we can represent the genetic structure of a population with inbreeding in the following manner:

Frequencies

Genotypes	Allozygotes		Autozygotes
BB	$P = p^2(1 - F)$	$+$	pF
Bb	$H = 2pq\,(1 - F)$		
bb	$Q = q^2(1 - F)$	$+$	qF

If we let $H_o = 2pq$, we see that $1 - F = H/H_o$. The coefficient $1 - F$ is often termed the *panmictic index* and measures the frequency of heterozygotes in an inbred population relative to that expected for random mating. Also, if we multiply through and rewrite the genotype frequencies as $P = p^2 + Fpq$, $H = 2pq - 2Fpq$, and $Q = q^2 + Fpq$, it becomes apparent that homozygotes increase in frequency in inbred populations at the expense of heterozygotes with the increase being greatest at intermediate gene frequencies.

Correlation between uniting gametes. By classifying inbreeding as genotypic assortative mating, we imply that a correlation exists between the genotypic values of mating individuals. This correlation between mates is responsible, in turn, for a correlation between uniting gametes. To arrive at the correlation coefficient, consider a quantitative trait with additive gene effects. Assume the genotypic values of BB, Bb, and bb to be $2a, a$, and 0, respectively. Since effects are additive, the genic values of B and b will then be a and 0. Representing the genic values of male and female gametes as g and g', their mean values can then be expressed as

$$\bar{g} = \bar{g}' = (a)p + (0)q = ap$$

while their variances become

$$V_g = V_{g'} = a^2p - (ap)^2 = a^2pq$$

The covariance of g and g' can now be obtained using the joint frequencies of uniting gametes listed in Figure 6.6. We get

$$C(g,g') = a^2(p^2 + Fpq) - (ap)^2 = a^2Fpq$$

Hence, the correlation coefficient between g and g' is

$$r_{g,g'} = C(g,g')/\sqrt{V_g V_{g'}} = F \qquad (6.8)$$

Thus, in addition to measuring the panmictic index (i.e., $1 - F = H/H_o$), the inbreeding coefficient, when applied at the level of populations, is the correlation coefficient between uniting gametes.

Since the effects of alleles are assumed to be additive, it can also be shown that the correlation coefficient for any two noninbred individuals, I and J, is twice their coefficient of kinship. Hence,

$$r_{IJ} = 2f_{IJ} \qquad (6.9)$$

For example, the coefficient of kinship for full sibs with noninbred parents is $\frac{1}{4}$. Therefore, the correlation between full sibs is $2(\frac{1}{4}) = \frac{1}{2}$, as was shown in the previous chapter for no environmental effects.

Inbreeding and rare recessive traits.   Many deleterious traits within populations are recessive and will tend to increase in frequency under conditions of inbreeding. To illustrate the extent to which inbreeding will alter the proportion of recessives, let $Q_F = q^2 + Fpq$ and $Q_o = q^2$. Dividing the first quantity by the second, we get

$$Q_F/Q_o = 1 + F(p/q)$$

This formula represents the ratio by which inbreeding increases the proportion of recessives above that expected for random mating. An analysis of this expres-

Male \ Female g \ g'	B (a)	b (0)	Total
B (a)	$p^2 + Fpq$	$(1-F)pq$	p
b (0)	$(1-F)pq$	$q^2 + Fpq$	q
Total	p	q	1

Figure 6.6.   Joint frequencies of uniting gametes. Both genic values, g and g', are assumed to be a and 0 for B and b, respectively.

sion clearly shows that if the trait in question is rare such that p is much greater than q, even a small degree of inbreeding can have a marked effect on the ratio, Q_F/Q_0. For example, with a p/q ratio of 100, an increase in F from 0 to only $1/16$ (the value expected for first-cousin matings) results in an increase in Q_F/Q_0 by over seven-fold.

Since recessives can have either random or related parentage, it is instructive and, at times, practical to partition Q_F into the various contributions made by random and consanguineous matings. Of particular interest is expressing Q_F in terms of the fraction of recessives produced by various close consanguineous matings such as full-sib or first-cousin matings. Suitable expressions can be derived if we picture a large population with inbreeding as being subdivided into a number of subpopulations each with its own characteristic inbreeding coefficient. Letting c_i and F_i be the frequency and inbreeding coefficient of subgroup i, the frequency of recessives produced in the subdivided population can then be written as

$$Q_F = (1 - F)q^2 + Fq$$
$$= \Sigma[(1 - F_i)q^2 + F_iq]c_i$$

where F is again the mean inbreeding coefficient for the entire population. If we now let k_i be the fraction of all recessives produced by mating type (or subgroup) i, we have

$$k_i = c_i[(1 - F_i)q^2 + F_iq]/[(1 - F)q^2 + Fq] \qquad \textbf{(6.10)}$$

Equation (6.10) has been useful for estimating gene frequencies of rare recessive traits in human populations. When working with human communities, it is often convenient to ignore the relatively small contributions made by consanguineous matings other than first-cousin marriages. We then express the fraction of first-cousin matings as c and of random matings as $1 - c$. The total frequency of recessives arising from both of these kinds of matings will now be $Q_F = (1 - c)q^2 + c(15q^2 + q)/16 = (16q^2 + cpq)/16$ since the inbreeding coefficient for first-cousin matings is $1/16$. Hence, the fraction of recessives from first-cousin marriages becomes

$$k = c(15q + 1)/(16q + cp) \qquad \textbf{(6.11)}$$

Plots of k versus q for different values of c are shown in Figure 6.7. Note that if the frequency of first-cousin marriages, c, and the frequency of affected children from these marriages, k, are known, the gene frequency can be estimated from (6.11) as

$$q = c(1 - k)/(16k - 15c - ck) \qquad \textbf{(6.12)}$$

without having to determine the frequency of affected children for the entire population.

Some observed values of k are shown in Table 6.3. Note that most values are within the range of 20–50% in Caucasians and are significantly higher among

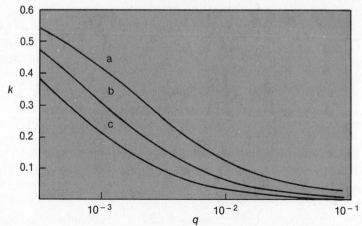

Figure 6.7.   Plots of equation (6.11) for c values of (a) 0.02; (b) 0.01; and (c) 0.005.

TABLE 6.3.   Fraction, k, of affected children from cousin marriages.

Recessive disorder	Caucasians	Japanese
Albinism	0.18–0.24	0.37–0.59
Ichthyosis congenita	0.30–0.40	0.67–0.93
Tay-Sachs disease	0.27–0.53	0.55–0.85
Xeroderma pigmentosum	0.20–0.26	0.37–0.43

Source: Neel *et al*., 1949, Amer. J. Hum. Genet., 1:156-178.

Japanese, thus indicating that a rather large proportion of these recessive disorders is among the offspring of consanguineous matings. The higher value of k in Japanese populations is due to the higher incidence of cousin marriages in Japan.

The observed values of k can be compared with theoretical expectations. Take albinism as an example. It has been estimated that in various European countries about 1 in 20,000 individuals is an albino. If this figure holds for the Caucasians for which the data in Table 6.3 apply, then the frequency of the gene for albinism can be estimated as $q = 1/141$. Taking 0.01–0.02 as a reasonable range for the proportion of cousin marriages, c, substitution into equation (6.11) yields a value for k of 0.0895 using the lower limit for c, and 0.166 using the upper limit. This discrepancy between observed and expected values is not surprising considering the fact that two different recessive genes have been shown to be capable of producing this disorder. For instance, if both recessive genotypes occurred with equal frequencies (i.e., each at 1/40,000), q would then be 1/200 rather than 1/141, yielding values for k that are more in agreement with observed results.

Inbreeding depression.   Due to the rise in the frequency of recessives, inbreeding can result in a reduction in the mean value of a quantitative trait in which dominant loci are involved. Such a reduction in the average phenotype is commonly referred to as *inbreeding depression* and can be related mathematically to F by expressing the mean genotypic value, $\overline{G}_F$, as

$$\overline{G}_F = (1 - F)\overline{G}_o + F\overline{G}_I$$
$$= \overline{G}_o - F(\overline{G}_o - \overline{G}_I)$$

In this expression $\overline{G}_o$ is the mean genotypic value among allozygotes and $\overline{G}_I$ is the mean value in the inbred or autozygous component of the population. Since $\overline{G}_F = \overline{G}_o$ for random mating, the difference $\overline{G}_F - \overline{G}_o$ can then be taken as a quantitative measure of the degree of inbreeding depression. A simple one-locus model can be derived by letting the genotypic value of BB autozygotes be given as $a_1 + a_2 + g_o$, and that of bb autozygotes be g_o (the base value). The mean of both autozygous classes will then be $\overline{G}_I = (a_1 + a_2)p + g_o$. On the other hand, the mean value of the allozygous or random-mating component is given by equation (5.8) as $\overline{G}_o = (a_1 + a_2)p + pqd + g_o$, where d is the difference $a_1 - a_2$. Making these substitutions, the change in the population mean due to inbreeding becomes

$$\overline{G}_F - \overline{G}_o = - F(\overline{G}_o - \overline{G}_I) = - Fdpq \qquad \textbf{(6.13)}$$

As this expression serves to point out, a locus can contribute to inbreeding depression only if d is not equal to zero. This would be true of any degree of dominance, including overdominance. Therefore, the physiological basis of inbreeding depression cannot be deduced simply on the nature of our equation alone.

   Equation (6.13) can be readily extended to include all loci which affect the trait in question. As long as epistatic interactions are negligible, this extension is made by merely expressing the reduction in the population mean as the sum over all contributing loci. We get

$$\overline{G}_F - \overline{G}_o = - F \sum dpq \qquad \textbf{(6.14)}$$

Thus, we see that in the absence of epistasis, inbreeding depression should vary linearly with the inbreeding coefficient; this is a relationship that has been observed experimentally in a number of cases.

Genotypic variance and inbreeding.   Picture once again a large population with inbreeding as being subdivided into a number of subpopulations, each with its own characteristic inbreeding coefficient. As inbreeding progresses, variation within subgroups will tend to diminish as a consequence of the general trend toward homozygosity. On the other hand, different subpopulations will tend to diverge in character as they undergo fixation of different alleles at a number of loci. Since the increase in between-group variation tends to exceed the reduction in genetic variation within the various subpopulations, we arrive at the paradoxical conclusion that an increase in homozygosity due to inbreeding will lead to an overall increase in genetic variability. This outcome can be expressed more precisely in mathematical terms. To do so, we shall consider a quantitative trait with additive gene effects for which the genotypic values of BB, Bb, and bb individuals are $2a$, a, and 0, respectively. If we let V_F be the genotypic variance of the entire subdivided population, it can be expressed as a linear combination of terms

$$V_F = (1 - F)V_o + FV_I \qquad (6.15)$$

where V_o is the genotypic variance among allozygotes and V_I is the corresponding variance among autozygotes. In this expression, $(1 - F)V_o$ is clearly the within-group component of variance, since only those subgroups which contain allozygotes can show individual variability. On the other hand, FV_I is the between-group component of variance, measuring the differences between groups as a consequence of fixation of different alleles. Since the mean value of a trait with additive gene effects is $\overline{G} = 2aP$ (assuming the base value to be 0) and is the same for both allozygotes and autozygotes, the values of V_o and V_I are then

$$V_o = (2a)^2 p^2 + (a)^2 2pq - (2ap)^2 = 2a^2 pq$$

and $\qquad V_I = (2a)^2 p - (2ap)^2 = 4a^2 pq$

We can now compute V_F as

$$V_F = (1 - F)(2a^2 pq) + F(4a^2 pq)$$
$$= 2a^2 pq(1 + F) = V_o(1 + F) \qquad (6.16)$$

This partitioning of variance is summarized in Table 6.4. Note that the within-group component of genetic variance declines by a factor of $(1 - F)$ below that expected for a corresponding population with random mating. The between-group component increases by $2F$, resulting in a net increase by a factor of $(1 + F)$ above that expected for a random-mating population. In a completely inbred population (i.e., $F = 1$), all individuals within each mating group will be homozygous and identical in genotype and, hence, the only source of variation is, in this case, between subgroups.

TABLE 6.4.   Partitioning of variance for populations with inbreeding.

Source of variation	Genotypic variance
Within subgroups	$(1 - F)V_o$
Between subgroups	$2FV_o$
Sum: Total population	$(1 + F)V_o$

REGULAR SYSTEMS OF INBREEDING

At the beginning of this chapter, we dealt with a regular breeding system known as self-fertilization. It should be apparent that if generations do not overlap, strict selfing will produce a population in which all members have the same probability of gene identity. Moreover, the inbreeding coefficient of each generation will be related by way of equation (6.4) to the value of F in the previous generation, yielding the recurrence relation

$$F_t = \tfrac{1}{2}(1 + F_{t-1}) \tag{6.17}$$

A solution to this expression can be obtained by writing it as follows:

$$1 - F_t = 1 - \tfrac{1}{2}(1 + F_{t-1}) = \tfrac{1}{2}(1 - F_{t-1})$$

$$= (\tfrac{1}{2})^t(1 - F_o)$$

where F_o is the inbreeding coefficient in some starting population (i.e., when $t = 0$). If we take the population back to a point in time when it is legitimate to assume that $F_o = 0$, we see that the inbreeding coefficient will increase as

$$F_t = 1 - (\tfrac{1}{2})^t \tag{6.18}$$

Note by comparison to (6.1), the panmictic index is $1 - F_t = H_t/H_o$.

In addition to selfing which can only occur among monoecious individuals, there are also a number of close inbreeding systems in biparental populations for which simple recurrence relations can be derived. We shall consider two: sib mating and parent-offspring mating. Both of these systems have practical significance in applied and experimental genetics for the development of inbred lines.

Brother-sister mating.   A population in which matings are restricted to full sibs can be thought of as being subdivided into random mating groups of two individuals each, assuming of course that the size of the population does not change from one generation to the next. A pedigree for this situation is illustrated in Figure 6.8, in which it is assumed that there are always two sibs of opposite sex that survive to mate in each successive generation. Since inbreeding is restricted to full sibs, all members of the same generation will have the same inbreeding coefficient. Similarly, the coefficients of kinship of this and every other mated pair must also be identical.

We begin our analysis of this breeding system by arriving at an expression for the coefficient of kinship for the parents in generation $t-1$ (f_{t-1}). First, observe in the pedigree that there are two possible ways in which randomly selected homologous genes can be identical by descent in the mates of generation $t-1$: (1) they are identical genes from the same parent, and (2) they are from different parents but are identical from a previous generation. Using the same logic that went into the development of equation (6.7), the probability of identity

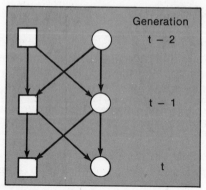

Figure 6.8. Pedigree notation for continued sib mating. Arrows show the paths taken by the genes from one generation to the next.

in case (1) is $\frac{1}{2}(1 + F_{t-2})$ where F_{t-2} is the inbreeding coefficient of the parents. On the other hand, the probability of identity in case (2) is, by definition, equal to the coefficient of kinship of the parents, f_{t-2}. Since all cases are equally likely, the coefficient of kinship of parents in generation $t-1$ is then

$$f_{t-1} = \tfrac{1}{4}(1 + F_{t-2} + 2f_{t-2})$$

Letting $F_t = f_{t-1}$ and $F_{t-1} = f_{t-2}$, we get the general recurrence relation

$$F_t = \tfrac{1}{4}(1 + F_{t-2} + 2F_{t-1}) \qquad (6.19)$$

This expression can be used directly to compute the inbreeding coefficients for a limited number of generations of brother-sister matings. For example, suppose that we start with a random-mating population which suddenly shifts to a strict regimen of full-sib matings at generation 1. We know from prior pedigree analysis that for the first two generations, $F_1 = 0$ and $F_2 = \tfrac{1}{4}$. Applying equation (6.19), we can now calculate $F_3, F_4, \ldots$ as

$$F_3 = \tfrac{1}{4}(1 + 0 + 2 \cdot 1/4) = 3/8;$$

$$F_4 = \tfrac{1}{4}(1 + 1/4 + 2 \cdot 3/8) = 1/2; \text{ etc.}$$

We can also use equation (6.19) to obtain a general solution relating F to the number of generations of inbreeding. This can be accomplished by first writing (6.19) as follows:

$$1 - F_t = \tfrac{1}{4}(4 - 1 - F_{t-2} - 2F_{t-1}) = \tfrac{1}{4}[2(1 - F_{t-1}) + (1 - F_{t-2})]$$

Substituting the appropriate value of H_{t-x}/H_o for each panmictic index $1 - F_{t-x}$ ($x = 1, 2, 3$, etc.), we get

$$H_t - \tfrac{1}{2}H_{t-1} - \tfrac{1}{4}H_{t-2} = 0 \qquad (6.20)$$

This is a second order linear difference equation for which the general solution can be written as

$$H_t = k_1\lambda_1^t + k_2\lambda_2^t \tag{6.21}$$

Here, k_1 and k_2 are arbitrary constants depending on initial conditions, and λ_1 and λ_2 are the roots of the quadratic equation $\lambda^2 - \frac{1}{2}\lambda - \frac{1}{4} = 0$. By using the methods outlined in Chapter 1, we solve and find that

$$\lambda_1 = \tfrac{1}{4} + \tfrac{1}{4}\sqrt{5} \quad \text{and} \quad \lambda_2 = \tfrac{1}{4} - \tfrac{1}{4}\sqrt{5}$$

The constants k_1 and k_2 can also be evaluated given a specified set of initial conditions. For example, suppose that the initial population consisted of only heterozygotes, Bb. In this particular case, H_o is equal to one and H_1 is one-half on the average. Substituting these values into (6.21) for times $t = 0$ and $t = 1$, along with our values of λ_1 and λ_2, we obtain the pair of equations

$$1 = k_1 + k_2$$
$$\tfrac{1}{2} = k_1(\tfrac{1}{4} + \tfrac{1}{4}\sqrt{5}) + k_2(\tfrac{1}{4} - \tfrac{1}{4}\sqrt{5})$$

Solving for k_1 and k_2, we get

$$k_1 = (1 + \sqrt{5})/2\sqrt{5} \quad \text{and} \quad k_2 = -(1 - \sqrt{5})/2\sqrt{5}$$

Thus, when all the necessary calculations and substitutions are made, our solution, exemplified in general notation by (6.21), becomes

$$H_t = (2/\sqrt{5})\,[(\tfrac{1}{4} + \tfrac{1}{4}\sqrt{5})^{t+1} - (\tfrac{1}{4} - \tfrac{1}{4}\sqrt{5})^{t+1}] \tag{6.22}$$

Since both λ_1 and λ_2 are less than 1, H_t in this expression must eventually decrease to zero. Furthermore, since λ_2 is less than zero, oscillations are expected. They are damped, however, and their amplitudes rapidly diminish as the second term in (6.22) decreases in relative importance. Ultimately, the decrease in H_t is essentially exponential and can be approximated as $H_t = k_1\lambda_1^t$. The above patterns are illustrated by plots of H_t versus t and of $\ln H_t$ versus t in Figure 6.9.

Parent-offspring mating.   Two general types of parent-offspring mating have been used in inbreeding programs. One involves the mating of the offspring of each cross to their younger parent. It can be shown that this particular series of matings gives rise to the same recurrence relation obtained for matings between sibs (6.19). A second important type of parent-offspring mating in-volves performing repeated backcrosses between an individual (usually a male) and its offspring from successive generations. This second pattern is illustrated by means of a pedigree in Figure 6.10 in which a male, designated as A, is mated successively to his daughter, then to his granddaughter, and so on. To obtain a recurrence relation for this second pattern of parent-offspring mating, we start by writing an expression for the coefficient of kinship in generation $t - 1$. First of all, note that if the gene selected from the female happens to be the one received from her father, the probability that it is identical to the gene selected again from her father in generation $t - 1$ is $\frac{1}{2}(1 + F_A)$, F_A being

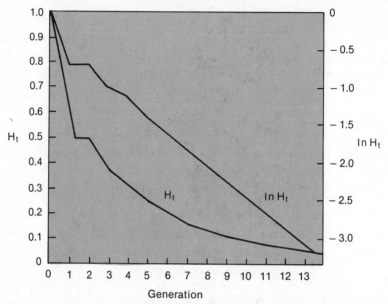

Figure 6.9. Change in heterozygosity with full-sib mating, for a population initiated with all heterozygous genotypes. The linear decrease in ln H_t after the first few generations illustrates the exponential nature of the relationship when t is at all large.

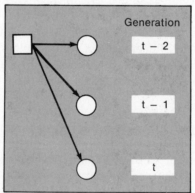

Figure 6.10. The mating between a fixed sire and his daughter, granddaughter, great-granddaughter, etc.

the inbreeding coefficient of the male parent. This can be obtained by applying logic similar to that which went into the development of (6.7). On the other hand, if the gene selected from the female happens to be the one received from her mother, it can only be identical to that selected again from her father if they were identical by descent from a previous generation. In this case, then, the probability of identity is the coefficient of kinship of the female's parents,

f_{t-2}. Since the possibilities outlined above can occur with equal likelihood, the total probability that two randomly selected genes are identical in generation $t - 1$ is

$$f_{t-1} = \tfrac{1}{4}(1 + F_A) + \tfrac{1}{2}f_{t-2}$$

Replacing the coefficients of kinship with the inbreeding coefficients of the succeeding generation, we get

$$F_t = \tfrac{1}{4}(1 + F_A + 2F_{t-1}) \tag{6.23}$$

Note that if the male is completely inbred (i.e., $F_A = 1$), the expression becomes $F_t = \tfrac{1}{2}(1 + F_{t-1})$ and is the same as the expression encountered for self-fertilization. On the other hand, if F_A is less than one, an equilibrium is established when $F_t = F_{t-1} = F$. By substitution we find that the equilibrium value is $F = \tfrac{1}{2}(1 + F_A)$. Thus, if the male were selected from a random-mating population, $F_A = 0$ and the equilibrium value becomes $F = \tfrac{1}{2}$. Since the value of F_A is not affected by the inbreeding program, we can also write for (6.23) $F_{t-1} = \tfrac{1}{4}(1 + F_A + 2F_{t-2})$. Thus, we can eliminate the common factor $\tfrac{1}{4}(1 + F_A)$ and express (6.23) as

$$F_t = \tfrac{1}{2}(3F_{t-1} - F_{t-2}) \tag{6.24}$$

This equation permits one to calculate the mean inbreeding coefficient for each generation irrespective of F_A.

INBREEDING IN FINITE POPULATIONS

Thus far, we have assumed that inbreeding occurs in very large populations such that sampling variation can be ignored. When this assumption is no longer valid, as would be the case in small populations, the average inbreeding coefficient (F) will tend to be larger in value than that expected on the basis of consanguineous matings alone. This rise in the magnitude of F in small populations is due solely to the increase in frequency of autozygotes produced as a consequence of genetic drift. Being a direct result of random fluctuations in gene frequency, this inbreeding effect is expected to occur in all finite populations, including those in which individuals mate strictly at random. This latter point can be illustrated by considering the gene pool of a random-mating population consisting of N individuals which are capable of self-fertilization. It might be helpful at this time to picture the population as one consisting of some hermaphroditic marine invertebrates, in which gametes are released into the water at one time and then unite at random. The gene or gamete pool of this population at some generation, say t, will then consist of $2N$ kinds of alleles as follows:

$$B_1, B_2, B_3, \ldots, B_i, \ldots, B_{2N}$$

where subscripts are used only to distinguish alleles, not to imply identity by descent or lack of it. There are two ways by which a zygote can receive genes which are identical by descent: (1) the random combination of two replicas of the same kind of allele such as B_1B_1, B_2B_2, etc., and (2) the random combination of two alleles which are not derived through replication in this gene pool but are identical by descent from a previous generation. Since each kind of allele makes up a fraction of $1/2N$ genes at this locus, the probability that replicas of the same kind, say B_i, combine at random is $P(B_iB_i) = (1/2N)^2$. The probability that a zygote receives replicas of the same kind without regard to subscript is then $2N(1/2N)^2 = 1/2N$. There is thus a $1 - 1/2N$ chance that they are not replicas, and a $(1 - 1/2N)F_{t-1}$ chance that they are not derived through replication in this gene pool but are identical by descent from a previous generation. Hence, the inbreeding coefficient in the next generation (generation t) can be written as

$$F_t = 1/2N + (1 - 1/2N)F_{t-1} \qquad (6.25)$$

Subtracting both sides of this equation from 1, we get

$$1 - F_t = (1 - 1/2N)(1 - F_{t-1}) = (1 - 1/2N)^t \qquad (6.26)$$

where the value of F when $t = 0$ is taken as zero. Thus, when N is fairly large in value, $(1 - 1/2N)^t \simeq e^{-t/2N}$ and F will continue to increase as

$$F_t = 1 - e^{-t/2N} \qquad (6.27)$$

Thus, we see that the ultimate outcome of this inbreeding effect is complete homozygosity, even though matings are random with regard to genotype. Also note by comparison with equation (3.6) in Chapter 3 that the inbreeding coefficient in this case can be related to the variance in gene frequency as $F_t = V_{p,t}/pq$. In other words, these are merely two different ways of describing the same process.

Biparental populations.   A similar approach can be used to describe the effects of genetic drift on the frequency of autozygotes in biparental populations. In this case, however, two uniting gametes cannot come from the same parent but may contain replicas of the same gene from a previous generation. To evaluate the effect on the inbreeding coefficient, we first compute the coefficient of kinship in generation $t - 1$ (f_{t-1}). We begin by asking the probability that two randomly selected genes (in different individuals) have come from the same parent and are replicas of the same allele. As long as mating is random and sexes are equally frequent, all individuals in generation $t - 2$ would have had an equal chance of being the parents of two randomly chosen members of the progeny generation. Hence, the probability that the two selected genes have come from the same parent is $1/N$, N being the population size. Given that the genes have come from the same individual, their probability of identity is then $\frac{1}{2}(1 + F_{t-2})$. Thus, the total probability of allelic identity is the product $\frac{1}{2}(1 + F_{t-2})(1/N) = (1 + F_{t-2})/2N$.

In addition to the preceding route, genes can also come from separate parents and still be identical by descent. In this case, the probability that they are from different individuals in generation $t - 2$ is $1 - 1/N$ and the conditional probability that they are identical, given separate parents, is the coefficient of kinship f_{t-2}. Therefore, their total probability of identity through this mode of descent is $(1 - 1/N)f_{t-2}$.

We can now combine these alternative possibilities and compute the coefficient of kinship in generation $t - 1$ as

$$f_{t-1} = (1 + F_{t-2})/2N + (1 - 1/N)f_{t-2} \qquad (6.28)$$

which, upon replacing f values with their corresponding inbreeding coefficients, yields

$$F_t = (1 + F_{t-2})/2N + (1 - 1/N)F_{t-1} \qquad (6.29)$$

A solution to this equation can be obtained by expressing each value of F in terms of its corresponding value of $1 - H/H_o$. We get

$$H_t = (1 - 1/N)H_{t-1} + (1/2N)H_{t-2} \qquad (6.30)$$

where the symbol H represents the frequency of heterozygotes. This is a linear difference equation having a solution

$$H_t = k_1\lambda_1^t + k_2\lambda_2^t$$

where

$$\lambda_1 = (N - 1 + \sqrt{N^2 + 1})/2N \qquad \text{and} \qquad \lambda_2 = (N - 1 - \sqrt{N^2 + 1})/2N$$

Note that for moderately large populations, $\lambda_1 \simeq 1 - 1/2N$ and $\lambda_2 \simeq 0$. This leads to one very important theorem of population genetics, which states that in finite populations, heterozygotes must decrease in relative frequency at a rate equal to $1/2N$ per generation. When expressed in calculus terms, this becomes

$$d(\ln H_t)/dt = -1/2N \qquad \text{or} \qquad H_t = H_o e^{-t/2N} \qquad (6.31)$$

Thus, as long as N is sufficiently small, one cannot reasonably assume a genetic equilibrium through random mating, even for relatively short periods of time.

Random and nonrandom components of F.   As we have pointed out, the increase in the frequency of autozygotes in finite populations can occur as a consequence of two different mechanisms. One involves inbreeding of varying degrees through some pattern of consanguineous mating, while the second occurs through the action of genetic drift even when mates are selected at random. Although the end result is much the same, it is often possible to distinguish between these different modes of homozygosity. To arrive at a useful relationship for F, let F_r be the random component of F defined as the probability of gene identity from random drift, and F_n be the nonrandom component, measuring the effects of nonrandom (consanguineous) matings. Since autozygosity can result from either drift or local inbreeding or both, we derive the relationship from the total probability that two alleles at a given locus are not identical by descent. This gives

$$1 - F = (1 - F_r)(1 - F_n)$$

Hence,

$$F = F_r + F_n(1 - F_r) \tag{6.32}$$

For a numerical example, calculate the inbreeding coefficient for the offspring of a full-sib mating in a population maintained with 10 males and 10 females for a period of 5 generations. In this case, we can let $F_n = 0.25$, whereas F_r can be calculated from $F_r = 1 - e^{-5/40} = 0.118$. Therefore, $F = 0.118 + 0.25(0.882) = 0.338$.

One interesting application of this formula to human populations was developed by Crow and Mange (1965). They recognized that the surname is transmitted in various groups in a regular pattern so that the total inbreeding coefficient can be estimated as $F = \frac{1}{4}I$ where I is the fraction of marriages between individuals of the same surname (isonymous marriages). For example, among first-cousin marriages $I = \frac{1}{4}$ since the relationship must extend through the male parents for the marriage to be isonymous. Thus, as expected from previous theory, $F = 1/16$. In order to calculate the inbreeding coefficient from random mating, these investigators let $F_r = \frac{1}{4} \sum a_i b_i$ in which a_i and b_i are the proportions of males and females, respectively, with a given surname. This left F_n, which could then be computed with the aid of equation (6.32). When this method was applied to the Hutterites, a religious isolate in North America, Crow and Mange obtained values of $F = 0.0495$, $F_r = 0.0445$, and $F_n = 0.0052$. Hence, the inbreeding effect in this population is largely due to random drift.

PHENOTYPIC ASSORTATIVE MATING

In addition to inbreeding (genotypic assortative mating), there are also forms of nonrandom mating which are based on phenotypic similarities between mates. For the most part, these forms of assortative mating have similar effects to those of inbreeding, producing an overall increase in homozygosity. Nevertheless, there are important quantitative differences. Some of these differences are examined in the following sections.

Complete assortative mating.   To illustrate the effects of phenotypic assortative mating, first consider a population in which dominance is complete and all matings are between individuals of the same phenotype. All mating combinations can then be classified as either dominant × dominant or recessive × recessive. Assume that the first class would comprise a fraction of $1 - Q$

of all matings and the second would occur with a frequency Q in the total population. The contributions of these matings to the next generation are given in Table 6.5. Using this table as a guide, the genotype frequencies among the offspring can now be determined by taking the sum of each column. They are

$$P_1 = (P + \tfrac{1}{2}H)^2/(1 - Q) = (P + \tfrac{1}{2}H)^2/(P + \tfrac{1}{2}H + \tfrac{1}{2}H) = 2p^2/(2p + H)$$

$$H_1 = H(P + \tfrac{1}{2}H)/(1 - Q) = H(P + \tfrac{1}{2}H)/(P + \tfrac{1}{2}H + \tfrac{1}{2}H) = 2pH/(2p + H)$$

$$Q_1 = Q + \tfrac{1}{4}H^2/(1 - Q)$$

The consequences of such a mating system can be seen more clearly by writing a recurrence relation for the proportion of heterozygotes. By changing the subscripts in the preceding expressions, it can be seen that in general

$$H_t = 2pH_{t-1}/(2p + H_{t-1})$$

We know from Chapter 1 that by repeated substitution into this recursive series, the general expression for H_t after t generations of continued assortative mating is

$$H_t = 2pH_0/(2p + tH_0) \qquad (6.33)$$

where H_o is the frequency of heterozygotes in the initial population. Note that when $t \to \infty$, $H_t \to 0$. Therefore, as in the case of inbreeding, the ultimate outcome is the complete elimination of heterozygotes from the population. Once $H_t = 0$, then $P_t = p$ and $Q_t = q$ as expected.

   If equation (6.33) is compared with equation (6.1), which describes complete genotypic assortative mating, it can be seen that assortative mating based on phenotypic similarity will result in a much slower reduction in heterozygotes than does close inbreeding. For example, if the starting population consists of $\tfrac{1}{4}BB$, $\tfrac{1}{2}Bb$, and $\tfrac{1}{4}bb$, the frequency of heterozygotes after 10 generations of self-fertilization is $(\tfrac{1}{2})^{11} = 1/2048$, while the proportion of heterozygotes is reduced to only 1/12 after the same duration of complete phenotypic assortative mating.

TABLE 6.5.   Matings and frequencies of offspring produced under conditions of complete assortative mating. It is assumed that gene *B* is completely dominant over *b*.

Mating (Generation 0)	Frequency	OFFSPRING (GENERATION 1)		
		BB	Bb	bb
BB × BB	$P^2/(1-Q)$	$P^2/(1-Q)$	—	—
BB × Bb	$2PH/(1-Q)$	$PH/(1-Q)$	$PH/(1-Q)$	—
Bb × Bb	$H^2/(1-Q)$	$\tfrac{1}{4}H^2/(1-Q)$	$\tfrac{1}{2}H^2/(1-Q)$	$\tfrac{1}{4}H^2/(1-Q)$
bb × bb	Q			Q
Sum:	1	$(P+\tfrac{1}{2}H)^2/(1-Q)$	$H(P+\tfrac{1}{2}H)/(1-Q)$	$Q+\tfrac{1}{4}H^2/(1-Q)$

Genotypic variance and assortative mating.   Many of the traits which are plainly involved in assortative mating such as height and I.Q. in human populations are polygenic characters to which the single gene models do not apply. The results of continued assortative mating on such polygenic systems were first examined by Fisher (1918) and later by Wright (1921b). They demonstrated that one major effect of assortative mating is to increase the additive genotypic variance. This effect can be illustrated if we consider a simple additive model in the absence of environmental variation. To begin with, assume a single pair of alleles (B,b) at frequencies (p,q). This is shown in Table 6.6 for the equilibrium conditions expected for random mating, and for complete genotypic and phenotypic assortative mating. It is evident that the mean phenotypic value is the same for all mating systems in this table, being equal to $\overline{G} = 2p$. In contrast, the variances differ as follows:

Random mating: $V_G = 4p^2 + 2pq - (2p)^2 = 2pq$
Inbreeding and
Assortative mating: $V_G = 4p - (2p)^2 = 4pq$ **(6.34)**

Thus, we see that at equilibrium, V_G for conditions of inbreeding and complete assortative mating is twice the value expected for random mating.

Now, suppose we extend the model to include two gene pairs (B_1, b_1) and (B_2, b_2), both occurring at frequencies (p, q). This is summarized in Table 6.7. Note that with complete phenotypic assortative mating, only the extreme homozygous types will remain at equilibrium, since they are only capable of producing offspring like themselves. This is in contrast to inbreeding which results in the fixation of all homozygous types.

Calculations of the mean and variance show that the mean is again the same in all of the above cases, being equal to $\overline{G} = 4p$. The variances differ as follows:

Random mating: $V_G = 16p^4 + 36p^3q + 24p^2q^2 + 4pq^3 - (4p)^2 = 4pq$
Inbreeding: $V_G = 16p^2 + 8pq - (4p)^2 = 8pq$
Assortative mating: $V_G = 16p - (4p)^2 = 16pq$

TABLE .6.6   The equilibrium conditions expected for a single locus under random mating, inbreeding, and complete phenotypic assortative mating.

		EQUILIBRIUM FREQUENCY		
Genotype	*Genotypic value*	*Random mating*	*Inbreeding*	*Assortative mating*
BB	2	p^2	p	p
Bb	1	$2pq$	0	0
bb	0	q^2	q	q

TABLE 6.7.   The equilibrium conditions expected for two independent loci under random mating, inbreeding, and complete phenotypic assortative mating.

Genotype	Genotypic value	EQUILIBRIUM FREQUENCY		
		Random mating	Inbreeding	Assortative mating
$B_1B_1B_2B_2$	4	p^4	p^2	p
$B_1B_1B_2b_2$, $B_1b_1B_2B_2$	3	$4p^3q$	0	0
$B_1B_1b_2b_2$, $B_1b_1B_2b_2$, $b_1b_1B_2B_2$	2	$6p^2q^2$	$2pq$	0
$B_1b_1b_2b_2$, b_1b_1, B_2b_2	1	$4pq^3$	0	0
$b_1b_1b_2b_2$	0	q^4	q^2	q

Once again, the variance for inbreeding is twice that expected for random mating; which is in agreement with theoretical expectations for any number of loci. On the other hand, the variance for complete phenotypic assortative mating is four times greater. Thus, a pattern emerges, which when extended to n gene pairs yields

$$V_G = 2nV_{G_o}$$

where V_G is the equilibrium variance for complete assortative mating and V_{G_o} is that expected for random mating. Hence, for 1 gene pair, $V_G = 2V_{G_o}$; for two gene pairs, $V_G = 4V_{G_o}$; and so on. In other words, V_G is expected to rise linearly with n.

It can be shown that if assortative mating is not complete, the expression for V_G becomes

$$V_G = 2nV_{G_o}/[2n - r(2n-1)] \qquad (6.35)$$

in which r is the phenotypic correlation between mates. Note that when assortative mating is incomplete ($r < 1$), a limit is reached where further increases in n have no effect on V_G. Once this limit is reached, V_G can be expressed approximately as

$$V_G = V_{G_o}/(1 - r) \qquad (6.36)$$

Thus, when n is large and r is small, V_G will be essentially equal to V_{G_o}.

The preceding expressions apply as long as dominance and epistasis are not contributing to phenotypic variation. Fisher demonstrated that when this is not the case, assortative mating will affect only the additive variance when n is large. The value of V_G can then be given approximately as

$$V_G = 2n\,V_{A_o}/[2n - A\,(2n-1)] + V_D + V_I \qquad (6.37)$$

where $A = rh^2$, h^2 being the heritability of the trait. Therefore, the effect of assortative mating on quantitative variation is to increase the additive variance (V_A) by a factor of $1/(1 - A)$ for large values of n.

DISASSORTATIVE MATING

As mentioned earlier, disassortative mating is said to occur when matings between dissimilar genotypes or phenotypes occur more frequently than expected for randomness. Like random mating, disassortative mating tends to maintain heterozygosity in populations. This is shown by the following special case of disassortative mating based on phenotype.

Complete disassortative mating.   Consider the case of complete phenotypic disassortative mating where matings are restricted to dominants with homozygous recessives. Only two kinds of matings are possible: $BB \times bb$ and $Bb \times bb$ which occur at frequencies of $P/(P + H)$ and $H/(P + H)$, respectively. The first kind of mating can produce only Bb offspring, while the second will produce both Bb and bb offspring in equal proportions. Therefore, only heterozygotes and homozygous recessives are present among the progeny. In all subsequent generations, matings are restricted to $Bb \times bb$, producing an equilibrium condition of $\frac{1}{2}Bb : \frac{1}{2}bb$. This is shown in symbolic form in the following recurrence relations:

Generation 1: $P_1 = 0$; $H_1 = (P + \frac{1}{2}H)/(P + H)$; $Q_1 = \frac{1}{2}H/(P + H)$

Generation 2: $P_2 = 0$; $H_2 = (P_1 + \frac{1}{2}H_1)/(P_1 + H_1) = \frac{1}{2}$; $Q_2 = \frac{1}{2}H_1/(P_1 + H_1) = \frac{1}{2}$

Note that unless $P + H = Q$ to begin with, selection will occur against one or more genotypes in the first generation, since it is not possible for all the individuals of the genotypes in excess to participate in matings. Gene frequencies are, therefore, expected to change, becoming $p = 1/4$ and $q = 3/4$ at equilibrium.

One example in which disassortative mating is complete is the maintenance of style dimorphism in many flowering plants. In this case, long style and short style phenotypes appear to be the expressions of the genotypes bb and Bb, respectively, with the BB genotype being nonviable. For the most part, pollination in this system is restricted to crosses between long-styled and short-styled flowers. Consequently, the two types of flowers are maintained at equal frequencies in natural populations.

Another mechanism that has evolved among higher plants to enforce disassortative mating is that of genetic incompatability. In a number of plant species that have evolved this mechanism, there are self-sterility alleles designated S_1, S_2, S_3, etc. These alleles inhibit growth of pollen tubes in styles with an allele in common. Thus, for example, pollen containing the S_1 allele cannot fertilize plants with genotypes S_1S_1, S_1S_2, S_1S_3, and so on, but can fertilize plants without S_1 (e.g., S_2S_2, S_2S_3, etc.). In this way out-crossing is enforced and matings between closely related individuals are prevented.

SOLVED EXAMPLE PROBLEMS

Selfing

1. Calculate the time required to reduce the level of heterozygosity by 95% in a completely self-fertilizing annual population.

   solution   Solving $H_t/H_o = 0.05 = (\frac{1}{2})^t$ for t, we obtain $t = \log(0.05)/\log(0.5) = 4.3$ generations.

2. Demonstrate that the relationship $H_{t+1} = \frac{1}{2} H_t$ for selfing can be interpreted in three ways: (1) as a description of the proportion of individuals in the population heterozygous for a single locus, (2) as a measure of the proportion of heterozygous gene pairs among k loci in a multiple locus model, and (3) as the average proportion of heterozygous gene pairs per individual.

   solution   Let $B_i b_i$ represent one of the k gene pairs at time t. At time $t + 1$, the offspring receive $\frac{1}{2}B_i b_i + \frac{1}{4}B_i B_i + \frac{1}{4}b_i b_i$ as a result of the segregation of alleles. Hence, at each locus the proportion of individuals heterozygous for a gene pair is reduced by one-half during each generation.

   To extend this analysis to more than a single locus, consider the case of $k = 3$ with $H_o = 1$. At time $t = 1$, 1/8 of all individuals will be homozyous at all loci, 3/8 will have one heterozygous locus out of three, 3/8 will have two heterozygous loci, and 1/8 will be heterozygous at all three, giving 12 total heterozygous pairs out of 24 total loci. After two generations, the corresponding proportions heterozygous for 0, 1, 2, and 3 loci will be 27/64, 27/64, 9/64, 1/64, respectively, giving 48 heterozygous pairs out of 192 total loci. Continuing this process, we see that the proportion of heterozygous gene pairs among all individuals in the population declines by one-half in each generation.

   The proportion of all loci in the population that are heterozygous is the same as the expected (average) proportion of heterozygosity per individual in the population. This is seen in terms of the expected value of the binomial formula given by equation (6.2). We have $E(x) = \frac{1}{2}k$ when $t = 1$. Thus, if an initial individual is heterozygous for k loci, the average individual in the next generation will have $\frac{1}{2}k$ heterozygous loci.

Inbreeding and Kinship of Individuals

3. Verify that the inbreeding coefficient of the offspring of first-cousin matings is 1/16, assuming that the common ancestors are not inbred.

   solution   Diagrammatically, the pedigree can be represented as either

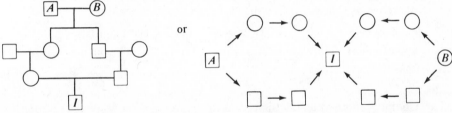

There are 5 ancestors on each of two paths, giving $F = 2(\frac{1}{2})^5 = 1/16$.

4. Demonstrate that the coefficient of kinship for first cousins can have three possible values, depending on the degree of inbreeding and relatedness of the common grandparents.

    solution   If the common ancestors are neither inbred nor related, then the coefficient of kinship of first-cousins, being the same as the inbreeding coefficient of their offspring, is 1/16. If the grandparents are themselves inbred, but are not related, then the kinship coefficient of first cousins is greater than 1/16, being $f = (1/32)(1 + F_A) + (1/32)(1 + F_B)$. Finally, if the grandparents, besides being inbred, are also related, then f is larger still, being $f = (1/32)(1 + F_A) + (1/32)(1 + F_B) + (1/8) f_{AB}$ where f_{AB} measures the degree of relatedness of the grandparents. Hence, in its most general form, f takes into account both inbreeding and relatedness.

Populations with Inbreeding

5. A population subjected to inbreeding is composed of 30% *BB*, 20% *Bb*, and 50% *bb* genotypes. Assuming that no force other than inbreeding is acting to change genotype frequencies, determine the value of F for this population.

    solution   Any of the three genotypes can be used to solve for F; however, it is simplest to use the relationship for heterozygotes, $H = 2pq(1 - F)$. Substituting $H = 0.20$, $p = 0.30 + \frac{1}{2}(0.20) = 0.4$ and $q = 0.6$, we obtain $F = 0.58$.

6. In a certain population, 40% of the children born with Tay-Sachs disease are from first-cousin matings. The frequency of first-cousin marriages is 0.01. Estimate the frequency of the recessive gene causing this disease.

    solution   Applying equation (6.12), the result is $q = (0.01)(0.60)/(6.4 - 0.15 - 0.004) = 0.001$.

7. In certain social strata in Japan, first-cousin marriages occur with as high a frequency as 9%. Consider, again, the trait albinism; assume it to be a result of a recessive condition at either of two gene loci, each occurring at a frequency of 1/40,000 in the population. Estimate the value of k for such a population using $c = 0.09$.

    solution   Assuming random mating among normally pigmented persons, $q = \sqrt{1/40{,}000} = 1/200$ for each locus. Using equation (6.11), we obtain $k = 0.57$, meaning that 57% of albinos are from cousin marriages.

8. Mettler, Moyer, and Kojima (1966) found the proportion of eggs giving rise to eclosed adults for cage populations of *Drosophila arizonensis* to decrease as follows at five different levels of inbreeding:

Genetic relationship:	Unrelated	Half-first cousins	Single-first cousins	Double-first cousins	Full-sibs
Eclosion percent:	77.0	75.1	73.3	69.1	66.2

Compute inbreeding coefficients and graph eclosion percent as a function of F, noting the form of the mathematical relationship.

solution   The inbreeding coefficients are $F = 0$, 1/32, 1/16, 1/8, and 1/4 for unrelated individuals, half-first cousins, single-first cousins, double-first cousins, and full-sibs, respectively. A graph of the data yields an approximate linear decrease in eclosion percent with F, in agreement with the theory on inbreeding depression.

Regular Systems of Inbreeding

9.   Consider equation (6.21) for which $\lambda_1, \lambda_2 = \frac{1}{4} \pm \frac{1}{4}\sqrt{5}$, and where the initial conditions include an unrelated, randomly mating population at generation zero and a population comprised of their offspring at generation one. Evaluate the roots k_1 and k_2 and determine the values of $(1 - F_t)$ over several generations if, starting at generation one, strict full-sib mating is practiced.

solution   Since generations zero and one are not inbred, we use $(1 - F_t)$ rather than H_t/H_o to represent, in general, the panmictic index. In this particular case, $F_o = F_1 = 0$, so that the pair of equations

$$1 = k_1 + k_2 \quad \text{and} \quad 1 = k_1(\tfrac{1}{4} + \tfrac{1}{4}\sqrt{5}) + k_2(\tfrac{1}{4} - \tfrac{1}{4}\sqrt{5})$$

are obtained. Solving for k_1 and k_2, we get

$$k_1 = (3 + \sqrt{5})/2\sqrt{5} \quad \text{and} \quad k_2 = -(3 - \sqrt{5})/2\sqrt{5}$$

The specific solution to equation (6.21) then becomes

$$(1 - F_t) = (1/2\sqrt{5})\,[(3 + \sqrt{5})(\tfrac{1}{4} + \tfrac{1}{4}\sqrt{5})^t - (3 - \sqrt{5})(\tfrac{1}{4} - \tfrac{1}{4}\sqrt{5})^t]$$

Substituting for $t = 2, 3, 4, \ldots$, the result is $(1 - F_t) = 3/4, 5/8, 1/2, \ldots$

10.   Starting with a randomly mating population which suddenly shifts to strict parent-offspring matings (repeated backcrosses) at generation one, calculate the values of the mean inbreeding coefficient for generations 3, 4, 5, ...

solution   From pedigree analysis, $F_1 = 0$ and $F_2 = \frac{1}{4}$. Using equation (6.24), $F_3, F_4, F_5, \ldots$ can be calculated as $F_3 = \frac{1}{2}(3/4 - 0) = 3/8$; $F_4 = \frac{1}{2}(9/8 - 1/4) = 7/16$; $F_5 = \frac{1}{2}(21/16 - 3/8) = 15/32$; etc.

Inbreeding in Finite Populations

11.   Consider a finite population in which matings are random with respect to partner and include self-fertilization. Determine the number of generations required to attain an inbreeding coefficient of 0.25 if all individuals are unrelated initially, and assuming the size of the population remains at $N = 50$.

solution   Solving equation (6.27) for t, where $F_t = 0.25$ and $2N = 100$, we obtain $t = -(2N)\ln(1 - F_t) = -(100)\ln(0.75) = 28.8$, or about 29 generations would be required.

12.   Verify that only 10 generations of mating would be required to reduce the heterozygosity by 10% within the population in Problem 11.

solution   According to equation (6.31), $0.90 = e^{-t/100}$, giving $t = 10.5$ generations.

Phenotypic Assortative Mating

13. A population that previously underwent random mating suddenly switches
     to complete phenotypic assortative mating. Calculate the fractional re-
     duction in heterozygotes after two generations, if $p = q = 0.5$.
     solution $H_o = 2pq = 0.5$. Therefore, by equation (6.33), $H_2 = 2(\frac{1}{2})(0.5)/$
     $(2 \cdot \frac{1}{2} + 2 \cdot \frac{1}{2}) = 0.25$; a reduction in the frequency of heterozygotes by one-
     half.

14. Burt and Howard (1956), in an analysis of variation in IQ among humans,
     found that the correlation coefficient between mates was 0.3875. Calculate
     the V_G/V_{G_o} ratio if the number of gene pairs responsible for this trait is
     $n = 10$, $n = 20$, . . ., ∞.
     solution   Using equation (6.35), where $r = 0.3875$, we obtain $V_G/V_{G_o} =$
     1.58 for $n = 10$; 1.61 for $n = 20$; and, using equation (6.36), 1.63 when
     n is very large. Note that little change occurs in the ratio when n is larger
     than 20.

---

15. Show that, for an equilibrium population, $F = r/(2 - r)$ where r is the
     correlation coefficient between mates.
     solution   Let the genotypic values of BB, Bb, and bb individuals be 2,
     1, and 0, respectively. The genotypic variance, from equation (6.16), is
     then $V_F = 2pq(1 + F)$. Since the variance is the same for both mating
     partners, the correlation coefficient between mates can then be expressed
     as r = covariance/variance. Using mating frequencies from Table 4.1, the
     covariance becomes $C_F = (2 \times 2)P^2 + (2 \times 1)2PH + (1 \times 1)H^2 - (2p)^2$ in
     which $2p$ is the mean genotypic value. Recalling that $H^2 = 4PQ$ for
     an equilibrium population, the covariance can then be written as $C_F =$
     $4P^2 + 4PQ + 4PH - 4p^2 = 4(p^2 + Fpq) - 4p^2 = 4Fpq$. Thus, $r =$
     $4Fpq/2pq(1 + F) = 2F/(1 + F)$. Solving for F, we get $F = r/(2 - r)$.

PROBLEM EXERCISES

1. An annual, strictly self-fertilizing population consists of equal frequencies
    of the three genotypes at a single locus. (a) What will be the genotype
    frequencies expected in the population after four generations of continued
    selfing? (b) How long (in generations) will be required to achieve approx-
    imately 99% homozygotes?

2. Consider a population heterozygous for three independently assorting gene
    loci, Aa, Bb, Cc, which practices self-fertilization. (a) What is the prob-
    ability that locus Bb is heterozygous after four generations of selfing? (b)
    What is the chance that one of the three loci is heterozygous after four
    generations? (c) What fraction of the population is expected to have no
    heterozygous loci after four generations?

3. A sample is selected at random from a population and consists of 82 *BB*, 44 *Bb*, and 34 *bb* types. Estimate the value of *F* for the population.

4. One percent of the marriages in a certain population are between cousins. If the population has a frequency of 1 in 3,600 recessive phenotypes, estimate the expected proportion of cousin marriages among the parents of such recessives.

5. In a large randomly mating population, the frequencies of the members of a pair of alleles controlling a quantitative trait are $p = 0.8$, $q = 0.2$. Assume that *B* is completely dominant over *b* and that the genotype values are $BB = Bb = 1$ and $bb = 0$. (a) What is the average value for this trait? (b) What would be the average genotypic value if the population were the result of one generation of 50% full-sib matings? (c) What would be the average genotypic value if the population were the result of first-cousin matings? (d) What is the predicted population variance if 50% full-sib matings occur?

6. In a population undergoing continued sib-mating, show that the heterozygosity is given by $H_t = H_{t-1} - (1/8)H_{t-3}$.

7. A self-fertilizing population is initiated with a single heterozygous type. (a) How many generations will be required to reduce the heterozygote frequency below 1%? (b) What will be the gene frequency values at this time, assuming no forces act to change genotype frequencies other than inbreeding?

8. Calculate the inbreeding coefficients for each of the following pedigrees, assuming that the original parents in each case are unrelated.

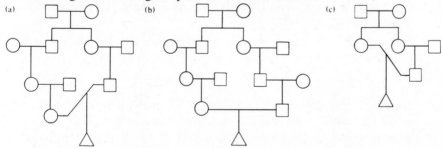

9. A population contains a constant proportion of 5% individuals from first-cousin matings, 14% individuals from second-cousin matings, and 81% individuals of random parentage. If the gene frequency values are $p = q = 0.5$, determine the genotype frequencies in the population.

10. The gene frequency values in a population practicing inbreeding are $p = 0.6$, $q = 0.4$. (a) What will be the genotype frequencies when the total inbreeding coefficient attained is 0.3? (b) What will be the inbreeding coefficient when the genotype frequencies after inbreeding are (0.456, 0.288, 0.256)?

11. A population composed of 1% homozygous recessives, that has been randomly mating in the past, undergoes 25% second-cousin matings in one generation. What is the expected percent increase in the frequency of recessives, Q?

12. One-third of the members of a particular plant population practice selfing; the rest undergo random cross-fertilization. If the present frequency of homozygotes is $P = 0.4$, $Q = 0.1$, (a) what will be the frequency of homozygous types after three generations of continued breeding under the mixed mating system? (b) What will be the expected frequency of heterozygotes and the value of F at equilibrium?

13. Consider a small population of 50 hermaphroditic marine invertebrates, all diploid and unrelated to each other. (a) What would be the inbreeding coefficient of the next generation if gametes, released into the water at the same time, underwent random fertilization? (b) If the population size remained constant and there were no outside forces acting to change the frequencies of genes or genotypes, what would be the inbreeding coefficient after ten generations? (c) If self-fertilization were impossible in this group, what would be the inbreeding coefficient after one generation? After ten generations?

14. In a large, randomly mating population, 4 out of every 10,000 individuals are affected with cystic fibrosis (recessive disorder). However, a certain smaller population has an increased incidence of the disease, 0.25%. Assuming that the gene frequency is the same in both populations, what value of F would characterize the inbred population?

15. For a population of 20 individuals (sex ratio = 1), plot H_t/H_o as a function of time (see equation 6.31).

16. Show that one locus undergoing complete phenotypic assortative mating changes heterozygote frequency per generation as

$$\Delta H_t = -H_t^2/(2p + H_t)$$

17. An annual population practices complete phenotypic assortative mating. (a) If the initial population consists of equal frequencies of the three genotypes at a single locus, what will be the genotype frequencies after four generations of continued assortative mating? (b) How many generations will be required to reduce the frequency of heterozygotes by a factor of three?

18. Consider a hypothetical trait having a correlation coefficient between mates of 0.1. Calculate the proportionate increase in the genotypic variance for $n = 10$, $n = 20$, $n = \infty$ genes specifying the trait.

Part Three

Ecology of Populations

7

Ecology of Populations: Spatial Distribution

Unlike population genetics, which has in the past been more concerned with the relative frequencies of genes and genotypes than with total numbers, the study of population ecology has centered on the variables that influence the distribution and abundance of organisms. Among these variables are the factors responsible for the broad geographic limits of a population such as predation, competition, disease, the dispersal ability and behavioral characteristics of the species, and the physical and chemical features of the environment. In many instances, these factors play a dual role by limiting not only the size of the geographic range but also the density of the population within this area of distribution. Thus, the principle factors governing distribution and abundance may be one and the same (Andrewartha and Birch, 1954).

In this chapter, we begin the discussion of population ecology with a consideration of the variables affecting the spatial patterns of single-species populations and some of the methods used in the analysis of these patterns. Since the concepts apply to a broad range of biological phenomena, the discussion will start with a theoretical treatment of the general nature and mode of action of limiting factors. Later sections will then deal, more specifically, with the limits to the distribution and spacing of organisms, placing special emphasis on the physical factors related to climate.

LIMITING FACTORS: THEORETICAL CONSIDERATIONS

The principle of limiting factors.   The limiting effect of environmental factors on various biological processes was first generalized in the "law of the minimum'' by von Liebig (1840) and later, in more explicit terms, with the ''law of limiting factors'' by F. F. Blackman (1905). Freely translated, these principles state that the rate of a biological process will be limited by the requisite in least supply. Taken literally, this implies that if x is the concentration or intensity of a factor which is limiting some process under study, then the rate of the process should increase with x up to a point where yet another factor becomes limiting. A modern interpretation of the principle of limiting factors is shown graphically by a series of plots in Figure 7.1. These curves illustrate the effect of a continuous increase in the intensity or concentration of one limiting factor for each stepwise change in another. All additional controlling elements, except for the two which are shown in each case, are assumed to be present in constant excess. Observe that the biological response depends largely on just one factor level only at the extremes of each curve. If we take plot A as an example, we observe that at a high light intensity, there appears to be a direct relation between the rate of photosynthesis and the carbon source for a fairly broad range of CO_2 concentrations. The relationship is not linear, however, as the observed increases in rate diminish progressively, ultimately becoming zero once the plateau level is reached. This feature has been aptly described as the ''law of diminishing returns.'' Note also that the stepwise change in light intensity alters the shape of the curve by raising the asymptote when increased

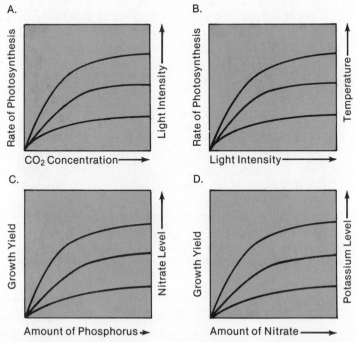

Figure 7.1. Principle of limiting factors illustrated in terms of various saturation curves. Principle discussed in text.

to higher levels. The plateau cannot be raised indefinitely, however, since the rate will eventually be limited by another factor such as temperature (see plot B). Therefore, at saturating CO_2 concentrations, light intensity serves as the principle limiting factor; whereas, carbon dioxide is, for all practical purposes, limiting the rate of photosynthesis when present at low concentrations. Since the principles apply equally well to the other plots illustrated in Figure 7.1, similar statements can be made regarding their overall characteristics.

   One of the first, and probably the most influential, attempts to quantify the principle of limiting factors was the model proposed by Mitscherlich in 1909. He proposed that an observed increase in yield (dy) is directly proportional to an increase in the lowest factor level (dx) and to the amount by which the yield falls below some maximum set by the amount of the factor at the next higher level. Stated symbolically.

$$dy = u(Y - y)dx$$

where Y is the maximum yield and u is a constant. When integrated over the limits from 0 to y and from 0 to x, the expression becomes

$$y = Y(1 - e^{-ux}) \tag{7.1}$$

Thus, when the quantity of the limiting reactant (x) is small, the yield can be expressed approximately by the linear relationship $y = Y(ux)$. On the other hand, when x is large, y approaches its upper limiting value, Y. The overall features of the curve described by this relation are shown in Figure 7.2, where the values of the parameters were chosen to arrive at a fit to experimental data.

   Although the Mitscherlich equation has been found to fit some yield data very well, there is now extensive experimental evidence which indicates that many factor effects, such as that of nutrient supply on the growth of bacteria

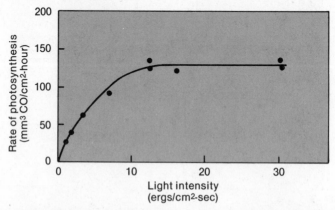

Figure 7.2.   Rate and efficiency of photosynthesis in a sugarbeet leaf at varying incident light intensities. The data are fitted to the equation $y = Y(1-e^{-ux})$ by choosing appropriate values for the parameters Y and u. (Data from P. Gaastra. 1958. Medeleel. Landbouwhogeschool Wageningin 58(4): 1.)

and plants, and that of prey density on the feeding response of predators, can be described more precisely by an expression similar in form to the Michaelis-Menten equation of enzyme chemistry (Monod, 1942; Ikusima, 1962; Holling, 1959b). In this case, the yield can be expressed as

$$y = Y\frac{ux}{1 + ux} \tag{7.2}$$

where x is again a factor level and u is a constant. This is an equation for a rectangular hyperbola shown graphically in Figure 7.3 in which the equation is fitted to experimental data. Note when ux is small in comparison to 1, the equation reduces to a linear form $y = Y(ux)$. Conversely, when ux is much greater than 1, y approaches its limiting value, Y. In regard to these limiting properties, both yield equations (7.1) and (7.2) are mathematically similar. They can be differentiated, however, by a suitable linear transformation. For instance, the Mitscherlich equation can be written in a linear form as $\ln[Y/(Y-y)] = ux$. Thus, if data were to follow this expression, a plot of $\ln[Y/(Y-y)]$ versus x should yield a straight line with a slope equal to u. The rectangular hyperbola, on the other hand, is usually transformed into a linear relation by expressing it in terms of its reciprocal: $1/y = (1/uY)(1/x) + 1/Y$. In this case, a plot of $1/y$ versus $1/x$ yields a straight line with a slope equal to $1/uY$ and an intercept of $1/Y$.

In addition to the curvilinear responses that we have just considered, many dose-response curves tend to show a sigmoidal or S-shaped appearance. This type of response can be generated, in theory, when u is no longer constant but

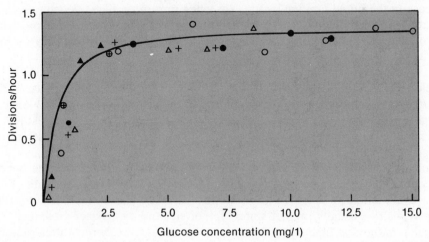

Figure 7.3.   Hyperbolic relationship between the multiplication rate of bacteria and the concentration of food. Values for the parameters Y and u were chosen to fit the data. The different symbols represent different experiments. (Data from J. Monod, 1942. Reproduced, with permission, from the Annual Review of Microbiology, Volume 3. Copyright 1948 by Annual Reviews Inc.)

is a function of x. Suppose, for example, that $u = u_o x$ in equation (7.2). The yield equation would then be converted to:

$$y = Y\frac{u_o x^2}{1 + u_o x^2} \tag{7.3}$$

This expression will give rise to an S-shaped curve when y is plotted against x. Numerous other relations can produce similar plots including the cumulative normal, gamma, and logistic distribution functions. If the distribution is normal, or nearly so, the sigmoid curve can be converted into a straight line when the proportions, $F(x)$, are transformed into probits (Finney, 1947).

It should be pointed out that, at present, a complete understanding of the co-action of all environmental factors is impossible, especially with regard to the influence exerted on processes as complex as growth. One must, therefore, proceed with caution when choosing a mathematical model for purposes of analysis and prediction. Making such a choice can be quite frustrating, however, in view of the fact that a number of relationships give rise to saturation curves which are similar in appearance. Nevertheless, using only one or just a few models to the exclusion of others should be avoided in the absence of adequate data.

Tolerance limits.   There is one important aspect of limiting factors which is not included in the previous models and which restricts their usefulness in practice. The models in their present form predict that the rate of a biological process will approach a maximum value asymptotically with a continued increase in the initial limiting factor. Yet when present in high enough intensity or concentration, most factors influencing biological activities exert a depressing or inhibitory effect. In other words, processes may be limited not only by too little of a factor but also by too much.

Many attempts have been made to quantify this secondary reduction in yield at high factor levels, but few have met with any success in giving reasonable fit to experimental data or in providing additional insight into the problem. A large percentage of the theoretical attempts have followed the "weakest link" interpretation of biological phenomena. Since most biological activities are dependent on a complex series of many reactions, if any one reaction is adversely affected by an excess of some environmental factor, so is the entire process. Thus, the rate of a complex process is limited through the rate of its slowest reaction (or weakest link). Models based on these theoretical considerations alone usually predict some type of sigmoid or inverted S-shaped reduction in yield at high factor levels. For instance, Mitscherlich attempted to account for the harmful effects by postulating that the secondary reduction in yield could be described by the quantity e^{-kx^2} where k is a constant. By introducing this quantity into, say, equation (7.1), a plot can be produced in which there is a unique optimum level determined by a balance between the beneficial and harmful effects of the limiting factor. In more recent years, one procedure which has been used with some limited success in providing a reasonable fit to experimental data is to express the secondary reduction in yield by means of the logistic model given by equation (2.27). Although this model does provide a satisfactory fit to some experimental data, it does not have a sound physiochemical basis and must be regarded as strictly empirical.

CLIMATIC FACTORS

The components of weather are among the most important variables affecting terrestrial populations. They include such factors as temperature, humidity, wind velocity, and light intensity, all of which can be readily measured and quantified. Of these, temperature and moisture appear to have the greatest impact on the distribution of plant and animal types. This is seen in Figure 7.4 by the close correlation that exists between the different vegetation types and these two climatic factors. Note that most biomes can be ordered neatly on a two-dimensional scale of moisture and temperature. Thus, a reasonably accurate picture of the broad-scale distribution of plant and animal types can be obtained simply from knowledge of temperature and moisture patterns. Numerous other factors are undoubtedly involved, as in any relationship as complex as this. For example, soil conditions have often been cited as a major contributing factor, as a result of the fact that a very similar correlation can be drawn between soil type and vegetation differences. In this case, however, it is difficult to separate cause from effect since the major types of soil are themselves determined to a large degree by the action of plants and climate.

Temperature as a limiting factor.   Of the climatic factors that have an important influence on biological activities, temperature is probably the most

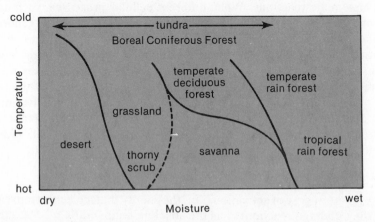

Figure 7.4. Distribution of vegetation type with respect to moisture and temperature. (Adapted from J.L. Richardson, 1977. *Dimensions of Ecology.* Williams and Wilkins, Baltimore.)

extensively studied. This is due, in part, to its ease of measurement. The best known instances where temperature acts to limit species distribution involve plants and those animals that cannot regulate their own body temperature (poikilotherms). The distribution of the mosquito *Aedes aegypti* provides one such example. This mosquito is found only between the latitudes of 45° north and south of the equator, but its range extends world-wide over all land surface within this belt. These northern and southern boundaries of the species range coincide with winter isotherms of 10°C. Temperatures below this level are lethal to the larvae and adults. In this case, it is fairly obvious that the factor limiting distribution is the lower lethal temperature. Other situations may not yield such clear-cut results. Since organisms respond differently to environmental variables at different stages of their life cycles, one problem which can lead to ambiguity is a failure to identify the stage with the greatest temperature sensitivity. Without this information, no apparent correlation with the extent of distribution may exist. Another source of potential difficulty is a failure to measure all temperatures of ecological importance (e.g., minimum, mean, and maximum temperatures). In many cases the ecologically relevant variable is the daily or seasonal, rather than the average, fluctuation in temperature. Furthermore, it is often difficult to separate the effects of temperature from those of moisture. Thus, although it might seem obvious that temperature is a major limiting factor on a global level, its precise relation to the extent of distribution of individual species is much more obscure.

The temperature tolerance range of living organisms tends to be considerably less than the 150°C, or so, range of environmental temperatures on earth. Although some bacteria and algae can remain active at temperatures as low as 0°C and, in hot springs, at levels as high as 85°C, most organisms are restricted to a range from about 0° to 40°C or less. For single-celled organisms, the temperature effects between these extremes are similar to those observed for simple enzymatic reactions. When different cellular processes, such as respiration and growth, are studied as functions of temperature, one generally receives a unimodal curve like that shown in Figure 7.5. In this case, the temperature response is depicted as the resultant of two temperature-dependent relationships: one representing a promotive process that increases with temperature in a manner expected for a catalyzed reaction (possibly the reaction at the rate-limiting step) and a second describing thermal inactivation (e.g., protein denaturation). The increase in rate (v) to the left of the optimum quite often follows that predicted by the Arrhenius equation for single enzymatic reactions. This expression is written as follows:

$$v = Ae^{-E_a/RT}$$

where E_a is the energy of activation (i.e., the energy that molecules must acquire before they undergo reaction), T is the absolute temperature, and A and R are constants, R being the gas constant (1.98 calories/mole-degree). Values of E_a have been measured for a large number of enzymes and, on the whole, tend to fall within the range of 1,000 to 25,000 calories/mole.

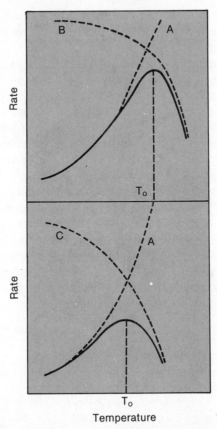

Figure 7.5.   Interpretation of temperature-limited response typical of a number of physiological processes. Curve A in both plots represents the increase in the rate of the limiting reaction as predicted by the Arrhenius equation, while curve B (short-time exposure) and curve C (long-time exposure) depict the reduction in rate due to thermal inactivation of enzymes. The observed rate is the resultant of the two opposing effects.

Since the continued existence of life depends ultimately on enzymatic reactions, the above considerations can be regarded as the crux of temperature relations in all organisms. At low temperatures, approaching the freezing point of water, most enzymatic reactions are very sluggish and the various physiological activities of an organism are correspondingly reduced. At the other extreme, enzymes denature and become inoperative as catalysts. This is, then, the upper thermal limit for sustaining life for any prolonged period of time. Most organisms, however, are capable of maintaining some degree of independence of the limitations imposed by this thermal strait jacket. For example, birds and mammals (i.e., homeotherms) are capable of maintaining their body temperatures higher than that of their surroundings by the energy released during metabolic activities. All other organisms conform to the environment with respect to body temperature. Although most organisms are conformers in this regard, many are able to compensate for temperature extremes. Some of the survival strategies used by various organisms include: (1) physiological adaptations such as shivering and evaporative cooling (sweating, panting, etc.), (2) acclimation through physiological changes in temperature tolerance when subjected to prolonged thermal stress, and (3) behavioral adaptations which move an organism towards its optimum temperature (seeking sun or shade, burrowing, etc.). In addition, many homeotherms compensate for cold by reducing conductive heat loss through the increase in subcutaneous fat or by producing thick layers of fur or feathers. Also, extremes in temperature may simply be avoided through migration or by hibernation.

In a general sense, all of the aforementioned strategies can be regarded as homeostatic mechanisms which help the organism balance its heat budget. In other words, they help in balancing the rate at which energy is gained and lost, and thereby help to maintain a suitable internal temperature for enzymatic reactions. Generally, organisms gain energy through metabolism and by the absorption of solar energy and infrared thermal radiation. On the other hand, energy is lost by convection, evaporation, and the emission of infrared radiation from the organism. Once the budget is balanced, the energy gained equals the energy lost. This can be summarized as follows:

$$E_M + E_S + E_{IR} = E_C + E_E + E_{IR'}$$

where
E_M = metabolic energy
E_S = energy absorbed from sunlight (solar energy)
E_{IR} = energy received from infrared radiation
E_C = energy lost by convection
E_E = energy lost by evaporation
$E_{IR'}$ = energy lost by infrared radiation

On the input side of this equation, E_M can be adjusted by homeotherms through appropriate changes in metabolic rate; whereas, E_S can be altered by poikilothermic animals as well as homeotherms by means of heat-seeking or avoiding behavior. On the output side, both convective and radiative energy exchange depend to a large extent on the surface temperature of the organism since E_C is proportional to the difference between the surrounding temperature and the temperature of the organism's surface, while $E_{IR'}$ is dependent on the fourth power of the surface temperature. Therefore, any adaptation which would diminish heat transfer from the body core to its surface, such as increased insulation, would tend to reduce energy losses by these mechanisms. Another adaptive strategy which achieves basically the same end is a reduction in the surface area to volume ratio through an overall increase in body size, thereby minimizing heat loss to the environment. This is a common adaptation and serves as the basis of Bergmann's ecogeographic rule which states that for homeotherms, body size tends to increase along a gradient from warm to cold temperatures.

Moisture as a limiting factor.   Moisture, in the form of water vapor, drinking water, or soil water, can be an important limiting factor for terrestrial organisms. This is reflected in the observed correlation between mean annual rainfall and major vegetation types. In the case of plants, distribution can often be limited by lack of sufficient soil moisture for seed germination or the establishment of seedlings. For example, studies indicate that the tolerance of seedlings to drought is a critical factor in setting lower limits to the distribution of trees in mountainous areas (Daubenmire, 1943). Soil moisture is also important in limiting the metabolic activity of established plants. Although water is required directly for photosynthesis, the indirect effects of water shortage are generally more important. This is seen by the fact that 97% or more of the water absorbed by a plant is lost through transpiration. Thus, if water is not supplied at a rate sufficient to offset this evaporative loss, the ensuing gradual dehydration of the tissues will eventually result in permanent injury and finally death. Even under less restrictive conditions, prolonged periods of water stress can significantly reduce photosynthetic rates through the activation of stomatal closure.

Nowhere are the effects of water shortage more acute than in desert environments. Yet, few deserts are truely barren of life; in fact, some are quite diverse despite the temperature extremes and low annual rainfall. To survive in such hostile conditions, desert plants have evolved numerous adaptations to avoid the more severe effects of water stress. They include: (1) germination and growth only during "rainy seasons" (desert annuals), (2) accumulation and storage of water in certain tissues (succulents such as the cactus), (3) morphological adaptations such as small leaves which reduce the transpiration to absorption ratio (xerophytes such as the creosote bush), and (4) reduction of water loss by shedding leaves during dry periods. In addition, stomatal closure under conditions of water deficit and the development of a thick cutin layer serve to retard water loss by stomatal and cuticular transpiration.

Moisture availability is one of many environmental factors that influence the shape of plants and their parts. Orians and Solbrig (1977) have studied the adaptations of desert leafs to moisture availability and have proposed a model to account for the high proportion of desert plants with deciduous, mesophytic leaves. They analyze the limiting effects of water in terms of the tight association that exists between the rate of transpiration and the rate of carbon uptake through stomata, assuming that the primary goal of natural selection is to maximize the rate of photosynthesis of a plant within the constraints of its available resources. Considerations of leaf morphology and physiology lead one to suspect that the maximum rate of photosynthesis is inversely related to the ability to photosynthesize under conditions of low water availability (Figure 7.6). They postulate that all plants perform better when moisture is available, but that plants with xerophytic leaves are able to photosynthesize at greater water stresses than plants with mesophytic leaves. According to their model, this means that the maximum photosynthetic rate of xerophytic leaves is lower than that of mesophytic leaves under conditions of high moisture availability.

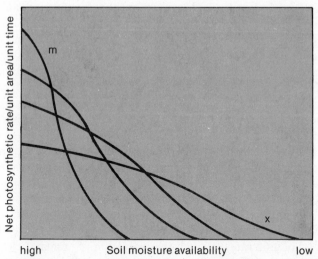

Figure 7.6. Predicted relationship between photosynthetic rate and soil water availability for leaves variably adapted to extract water from the soil. (m) mesophytic leaves, (x) xerophytic leaves. (From G.H. Orians and O.T. Solbrig. 1977. Am. Nat. 111: 677. Copyright 1977 by The University of Chicago Press. All rights reserved.)

For example, leaf shapes conducive to photosynthesis under a moist regime, such as large surface area and high leaf conductivity, necessarily enhance transpiration, so that such a plant could not be flexible enough to adjust to dry conditions. Conversely, plants able to withstand low moisture levels are characterized by small cells and thick cell walls, which would prevent a high photosynthetic rate even during periods of water availability. The coupling of photosynthesis and transpiration thus means that plants will be narrowly adapted to particular moisture conditions.

The model used by Orians and Solbrig is applied to plant distributions based on comparisons of the cost of constructing mesophytic and xerophytic leaves and the incomes accrued by each. Figure 7.7A shows the cost-income curves for both types of leaf. The cost of construction per unit surface area of a mesophytic leaf is assumed to be less than that of a xerophytic leaf, since the former is simpler in morphology. Costs are high during leaf construction but become constant per unit time once the leaf has matured (maintenance cost). Assuming that income can be measured as calories gained from photosynthesis, it will accumulate linearly, with the precise slope depending on water availability. For both leaves, profits begin to accumulate once income exceeds costs (points a and b on graphs). Figure 7.7B shows the profit curves expected from the relationships in part A. Note that the less costly mesophytic leaves yield profit sooner in the year than the more expensive xerophytic leaves, and that, given constant moisture, the superiority of mesophytic leaves increases with time. The total amount of yearly profit should depend on the total length of

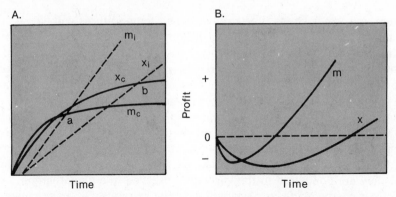

Figure 7.7. (A) Cost-income curves for mesophytic and xerophytic leaves. Costs are shown as solid lines, incomes as dashed lines. Break-even points are designated *a* and *b*. (B) Profit curves based on the cost-income relationships shown in (A). (From G.H. Orians and O.T. Solbrig. 1977. Am. Nat. 111: 677. Copyright 1977 by The University of Chicago. All rights reserved.)

moisture availability (total time in which profits accumulate), and also on the frequency and regularity of dry periods, since income is depressed in these stages. Hence, even though mesophytic leaves yield profits early, xerophytic leaves can be expected to yield profits long after mesophytic types cease accruing benefits, if the yearly period consists of any prolonged or erratic dry periods. The model thus predicts that mesophytic leaves will be found in deserts with regular rainy periods because they provide higher profits, but that in areas with low or unpredictable rainy periods, xerophytic leaves will be favored.

Adaptations to conditions of water shortage are not restricted to plants but occur in many animals as well. They include estivation and diapause during the driest periods and behavioral mechanisms such as burrowing to reduce water loss. In addition, desert animals such as kangaroo rats, *Dipodomys*, are able to survive without drinking water by efficient use of metabolic water and moisture present in food stuffs. They are able to balance their water budget by minimizing water loss through such mechanisms as a nocturnal habit, lack of sweat glands, and excretion of a very concentrated urine and nearly dry feces. Although most desert animals are characterized by having highly impermeable body coverings, a few have permeable integuments to facilitate water uptake. For example, the cockroach *Arenivaga* can absorb moisture from the air beneath the desert surface when the relative humidity is 82% or higher. Similarly, desert toads can absorb moisture by capillarity while sitting on a wet surface.

Combined effects.   So far, we have considered a few of the limiting effects exerted by climatic factors and some of the strategies organisms have evolved to cope with them. Limiting factors do not always act alone, however. They sometimes even interact in a synergistic manner. Such is the case with temperature and water stress. For example, high temperatures can aggravate the detrimental effects of water shortage through increased evaporative loss. In fact, many of the effects of temperature in limiting species distributions may operate through the water balance of an organism. These interactive effects serve as the basis for the use of climatographs to assess the habitat suitability of an organism from knowledge of its tolerance levels to the combined effects of temperature and moisture. A climatograph is usually just a plot of the mean monthly temperature within a given region as a function of the mean monthly rainfall. Therefore, if the tolerance limits for the combined effects of temperature and moisture are known for the critical parts of the life cycle of an organism, and if they are compared to the variation observed in a climatograph, certain predictions can be made concerning the habitat suitability of the organism with regard to these parameters. This is shown in Figure 7.8 by means of climato-graphs for two ecogeographic regions. Included in the diagram is a plot of the reproductive tolerance shown by a hypothetical population to the combined effects of temperature and moisture. In this example, it is apparent that con-tinued existence in a desert habitat is not possible due to the inability of the organism to withstand the dry, hot summers. It is also possible to use clima-tographs to obtain information about the temperature and moisture tolerances of a species. One approach is a transplant experiment, illustrated in terms of a particular example in Figure 7.9. This represents a climatograph for the

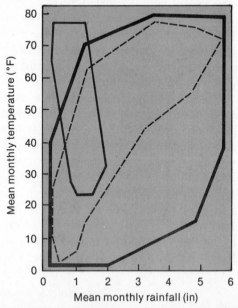

Figure 7.8. Climatographs for sagebrush desert (solid line) and tall grass prairie (dashed line) ecogeographic regions. The heavy line gives the reproductive tolerance of a hy-pothetical population to the combined effects of temperature and moisture.

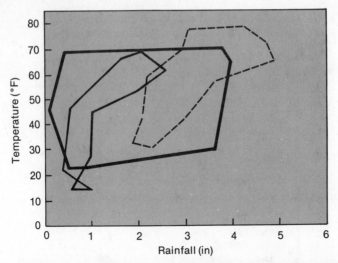

Figure 7.9. Climatograph for Havre, Montana (solid line) where the Hungarian partridge (*Perdix perdix*) has been successfully introduced and Columbia, Missouri (dashed line), where it has failed, compared with average conditions in its European breeding range (heavy line). (After A.C. Twomey. 1936. Ecology 17: 122.)

Hungarian partridge, *Perdix perdix*, in its native European habitat. Superimposed are climatographs of two areas, one in Missouri and the other in Montana, where the species was introduced. Although neither climatograph is completely within that of the native habitat, the fact that the introduction failed in Missouri but not in Montana would make one suspect that the hotter and wetter summers of Missouri may have served as a limiting factor for one or more of those critical activities such as nesting, incubation, and chick survival.

The interaction of temperature and moisture has been used by Thornthwaite (1948) to devise a quantitative system for classifying climates. The classification scheme involves the concept of potential evapotranspiration, which is the amount of water that would be evaporated from the soil and transpired from vegetation if it were available. The potential evapotranspiration is calculated as an empirical function of temperature and daylight hours, since areas with high temperatures and long photoperiods are subjected to greater evaporative water losses than cooler, shorter daylength regions. The relationship between potential evapotranspiration and actual evaporation and transpiration then determines seasonal surpluses or deficiencies of water and, in effect, whether a climate is truly wet or dry. Although actual measurements of potential evapotranspiration are not extensive enough for a world-wide classification of climates, Thornthwaite's method (Figure 7.10) has been used to determine the climatic conditions for a wide variety of regions. It is generally found that major vegetation types such as grasslands, temperate deciduous forests, and deserts tend to correlate well with this classification scheme.

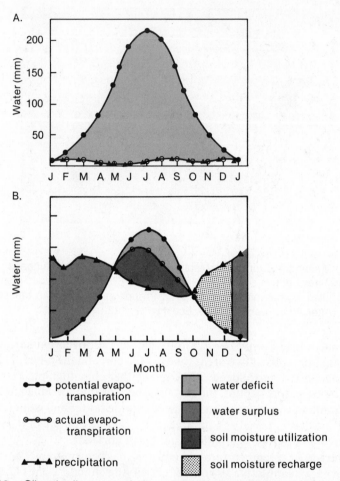

Figure 7.10. Climatic diagrams of (A) a desert regime (Blythe, California) and (B) a temperate, deciduous forest (Memphis, Tennessee). (A—Adapted from J. Major. 1963. Ecology 44: 485; B—Adapted from H.J. Critchfield. 1974, and used with permission of C. W. Thornthwaite Associates.)

PHENOTYPE AND ENVIRONMENTAL STRESS

As the preceding discussions on temperature and moisture tolerance are meant to convey, the key to the persistence of any population is its ability to withstand the existing range of conditions and to cope with environmental change. This ability depends, in turn, on the morphological, physiological, and behavioral characteristics of its members and on the plasticity of these characteristics. Since animals are free to move about and because their morphological flexibility is not usually great, short-term responses of animals to environmental change are mainly behavioral and physiological. Plants, on the other hand, are usually fixed to their immediate environment and must, therefore, possess enough developmental flexibility to respond by morphological as well as physiological means. This is illustrated in Figure 7.11 by the changes in morphology of the arrowleaf *Sagittaria sagittifolia* when growth occurs under different environmental conditions. This plant is capable of producing aquatic as well as terrestrial leaves depending on whether it is submerged or growing on dry land. When submerged, thin aquatic leaves develop which lack a cuticle. These are able to absorb nutrients directly from the water but have little structural strength and must be supported by the water to remain erect. In contrast, the terrestrial leaves which develop on land do have the normal structural strength attributed to plants, but they are ill adapted to a submerged existence since they tend to break off in water currents. Thus, phenotypic plasticity permits individuals to respond to changes which are very short in duration, as compared to evolutionary time, without the need for genotypic change.

Ultimately, the limits of tolerance of the individual organism are determined by its genotype, and because of genetic differences, individuals of each kind tend to vary in their ability to respond to environmental stress. This is evident

Figure 7.11.   Adaptive responses in the arrowleaf. The drawings illustrate the variation in the morphology of the arrowleaf, *Sagittaria sagittifolia,* that is exhibited when it grows on land, when it is partially submerged, and when it is completely submerged. This variation is not hereditary but stems from the interaction of the genotype of the plant and its environment. From B. Wallace and A.M. Srb, *"Adaptation,"* 2nd ed. Reprinted by permission of Prentice-Hall, Inc., Englewood Cliffs, New Jersey.)

in species that are spread over a broad range of conditions. Such species often include locally adapted populations in different portions of their geographic range which show measureable differences in their average limits to stress. Variation also exists within each local population although these differences are usually less pronounced.

Species also tend to vary in their tolerance ranges to different environmental factors. In other words, an organism may have a broad range of tolerance for one condition and a narrow range for another. These differences have led to the development of a variety of descriptive terms. For instance, a species that has a wide range of tolerance to one or more factors is said to be euryoecious, while a species with narrow tolerance limits is stenoecious. The prefixes eury- and steno- may also be applied to a specific type of tolerance. Thus, for example, a species showing a broad tolerance range to temperature would be eurythermal, whereas one with, say, a narrow tolerance to salt water is stenohaline.

THE ECOLOGICAL NICHE

Many of the topics that we have discussed thus far relate to the concept of the ecological niche. The term niche was introduced by Grinnell in 1917 while attempting to explain the distribution of the California Thrasher, *Toxostoma redivivum*. He later defined it in 1928 as "the ultimate distributional unit, within which each species is held by its structural and functional limitations." When defined in this way, the concept of a niche is basically the same in meaning as the word "habitat." At about the same time, Elton (1927) developed what is now known as the functional concept of the niche in which "the niche of an animal means its place in the biotic environment, its relations to food and enemies." Thus, Elton emphasized what an animal is doing (i.e., its "occupation" in a biotic community), not just the place where it lives or what it looks like.

In 1958, Hutchinson attempted to clarify these rather vague concepts by redefining the niche as an n-dimensional hypervolume which we call the *fundamental niche*. To illustrate the construction of the fundamental niche, suppose we measure the tolerance limits of some terrestrial plant to, say, temperature and moisture, and plot these in the form of a climatograph. This is illustrated in Figure 7.12A. Now assume that we measure its tolerance limits to some other environmental variable such as the amount of some specific soil nutrient and include this as a third dimension. We then get a three-dimensional plot which might look like that in Figure 7.12B. If we were to continue to measure the limits to all environmental variables which affect the species and include them as niche parameters, we would eventually obtain the fundamental niche of the species in the form of a multidimensional plot that describes the total range over which the species can function.

The fundamental niche can be regarded as the pre-interactive or potential

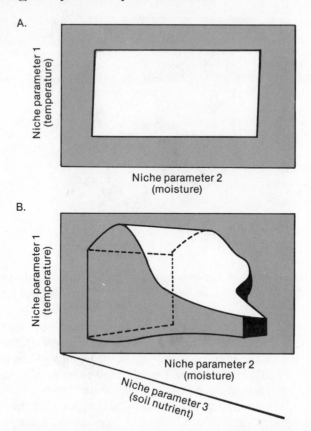

Figure 7.12.   Multidimensional niche concept. (A) A two-dimensional niche established by minimal and maximal values for each of two environmental variables. (B) A three-dimensional niche established by including the minimal and maximal values for a third environmental variable.

niche since it fails to take into account the effects of interactions with other species. Species, of course, do not live alone but interact in ways that can be either beneficial or detrimental to their fertility and survival. One form of interaction which alters the extent to which a species fills its fundamental niche is competition. If two species compete for some environmental resource, their fundamental niches must overlap. To minimize the detrimental effects of this competitive interaction, natural selection tends to act in a way so as to reduce the extent to which each niche is actually filled (Figure 7.13). This reduced niche space which is actually occupied by the species and which describes the species in its biotic community is then the post-interactive or *realized niche*.

Though elegant in approach and intellectually satisfying, the niche concept of Hutchinson does have its drawbacks. First of all, it assumes that all niche variables can be ordered along linear coordinates. This is suitable for many

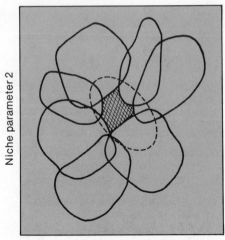

Niche parameter 1

Figure 7.13. Overlapping of two-dimensional niches. The broken curve indicates the fundamental niche of a species, while the cross-hatched interior is the realized niche.

physical parameters such as temperature and moisture, but can be difficult in the case of some biological variables. Secondly, it suggests that there is an equal probability of the species persisting in all regions of the niche. This is obviously not the case since survival would tend to be maximum towards the center and significantly reduced towards the outer limits of tolerance. This problem can be lessened to some extent by adding another dimension which measures the relative success of the species in its environment which we call fitness. Thus, if we were to plot fitness against temperature first and then add, say, moisture as another coordinate, we get the plots shown in Figure 7.14 in

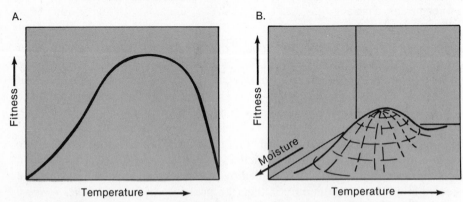

Figure 7.14. Species niche. Graph *A* illustrates a one-dimensional temperature tolerance niche. Graph *B* pictures a possible two-dimensional niche with a peak of maximum fitness.

which the height of the plots is a measure of the probability of success in terms of survival, fertility, etc. Since a number of niche parameters will be uncorrelated, an n-dimensional plot (or hypervolume) will have coordinates radiating in all directions, giving rise to a structure which can be likened to a sphere. This actually constitutes a probability cloud in which the greatest density of points (i.e., the highest probability of success) will be towards the center. This optimal niche region has been referred to as the *preferred niche* of the species and would constitute the range of environmental conditions in which the species, when given the opportunity, would most likely be found in the absence of competition.

A third problem with the multidimensional niche concept, as presented thus far, is its failure to account for genetic variation in tolerance which exists within each and every species. Different models have been suggested to account for the effects of genetic variation on niche space (e.g., Emlen, 1973), but rather than making an attempt to reproduce these, we shall simply modify our present model to illustrate where genetic variation comes into play. If we assume that it is possible to determine the tolerance curves and resource spectra for all phenotypes existing within a species population at any moment in time, we might arrive at a series of distributions like those illustrated along the one-dimensional niche in Figure 7.15. Furthermore, if we assume that selection intensity increases with distance above or below some optimum level, those phenotypes with tolerance levels closest to the optimum should occur in the greatest frequency, whereas they should decline in frequency toward the extremes. The final fitness curve is then the resultant of the various distributions of included phenotypes. Note also that the total variance (σ^2) for the distribution will be given by the sum of the within-phenotype component of variance, which measures the average variance in the phenotype curves, and the between-phenotype component of variance, measuring the variability in the niche lo-

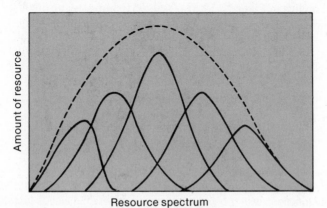

Resource spectrum

Figure 7.15.   Genotypic variation in niche characteristics along a single dimension. The resultant for the population is shown by the broken curve.

cations of different phenotypes. This view helps to illustrate the transient nature of a species niche. As conditions change, genotype frequencies and, hence, phenotype frequencies are expected to change as well, resulting in an alteration of niche dimensions. It is, therefore, apparent that a multidimensional niche can only apply to a species at one particular time.

Due to the potentially infinite number of niche parameters that must be measured in order to completely describe a species, the concept, as presented above, would appear to have little practical value. In some cases, however, it is possible to restrict attention to one or just a few niche parameters (MacArthur, 1968). For example, in the case of a food-limited predator, the relevant niche parameter might be the size of available food items. The niche relationship could then be represented in terms of a one-dimensional resource utilization curve in which the amount of prey eaten is plotted against prey size. This simplification is helpful when describing certain niche characteristics such as *niche breadth* and *niche overlap*. Niche breadth, or niche width as it is often called in the one-dimensional case, refers to the extent that the realized niche spreads across a set of niche dimensions. If the tolerance curve or resource utilization spectrum is normally distributed, or approximately so, the niche breadth of a one-dimensional niche can be expressed in terms of some simple measure of variability or uncertainty such as the standard deviation (σ). In this case, a generalist, having a broad range of tolerance to the principle limiting factor, would be characterized by a large value of σ. Conversely, a specialist, with narrow tolerance, would be typified by a comparatively small niche width. Since σ^2 depends on both the within-phenotype and between-phenotype components of variation, it can be seen that a generalized or broad-niched species might actually evolve through the acquisition of many highly specialized variants rather than through the development of a single flexible phenotype.

Niche overlap, on the other hand, refers to the extent to which two species share a common niche. This is pictured in terms of the overlapping one-dimensional niches in Figure 7.16. If d is used to indicate the distance separating niches from peak to peak, the extent of overlap can then be related to the ratio

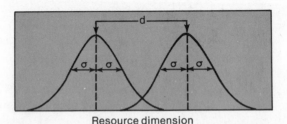

Resource dimension

Figure 7.16. Quantification of niche overlap. The niche curves are assumed to be normal density functions with d being the distance separating niches from peak to peak and σ is the standard deviation. The degree of overlap can then be expressed by the ratio d/σ.

d/σ (May and MacArthur, 1972). In this case, small values of d/σ imply substantial overlap, while for large values, the reverse is true. The ecological and evolutionary implications of niche overlap will be considered later in Chapter 11.

SPATIAL ATTRIBUTES OF POPULATION STRUCTURE

The term *population structure* is used to denote those features of populations that affect the pattern of mate selection, and thereby govern the way in which gametes unite during fertilization. Such features include age and sex distribution and the spacing of the individual members of a population. These structural attributes are influenced, in turn, by a host of other factors such as spatial and temporal variation in environmental conditions, courtship and mating behavior, and dispersal ability and, as we shall see in later chapters, play a major role in the growth and regulation of populations.

Patterns of dispersion.   One of the more important aspects of population structure is the dispersion pattern of its members. At any instant in time, dispersion can be viewed in terms of a hierarchy of levels, ranging from relative variations in density throughout an area of distribution down to the spacing of individuals of a local group. This is illustrated by the hierarchy of aggregates shown in Figure 7.17. When considered on a sufficiently broad scale, it is often convenient to ignore individual spacing and to simply represent a dispersion pattern by way of a map which is stippled or shaded to differing degrees in order to illustrate relative variations in population density. Such widespread and general patterns are determined, in part, by spatial variation in the physical and biotic factors which make up the environment. Where the environment is extremely heterogeneous, conditions can differ from place to place to levels beyond the limits tolerated by the species. Such variation in habitat conditions serves to produce discontinuities and irregularities in population density. As one passes from this extreme to one of greater uniformity, the density pattern, as pictured in terms of the shading on our map, may change from a collection of isolated patches to a continuum with scattered regions of high density. These spatial patterns will also vary in time. As conditions change, and they always do, certain patches become vacant as local groups go extinct. Some of these are later reestablished through colonization by migrants from surrounding areas. Others may, by chance, remain unoccupied. The net effect is a complex series of spatial and temporal changes in dispersion pattern which are partly due to variations in habitat conditions and are partly a result of historical accident.

  Since no species of organism is uniformly distributed over a large geographical area, the more resolution required of a dispersion analysis, the more difficult the task. The ultimate level of resolution is to describe the dispersion pattern of a population in terms of the spacing of individuals relative to one

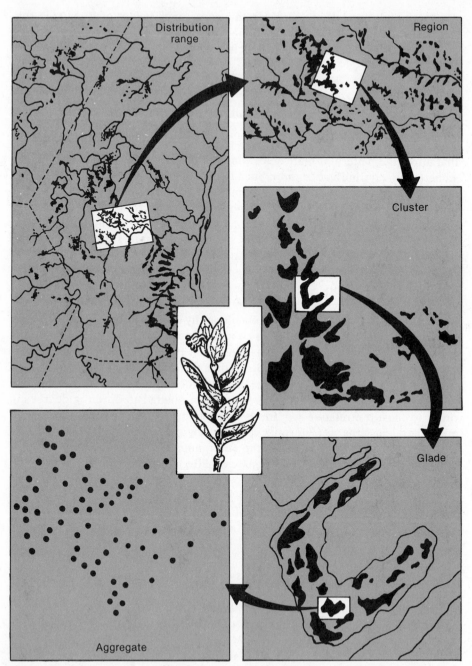

Figure 7.17.   Hierarchy of aggregates of *Clematis fremontii* var. *riehlii*. (From Erickson, 1945. Ann. Missouri Bot. Gar. 32.)

another. Such spatial patterns can be conveniently divided into different categories which are illustrated in a simplified manner in Figure 7.18 and listed in the following outline:

A.   *Random dispersion*
B.   *Nonrandom dispersion*
  1.   Regular (or infradispersed)—spacing is more uniform than expected for randomness.
  2.   Clumped (or contagious)—spacing is less uniform than expected for randomness (i.e., aggregation of individuals).

In the case of clumped spacing, the aggregates may also be distributed randomly, uniformly, or in clumps. Since motile organisms are free to move about, their positions will constantly change. When applied to such organisms, the spatial patterns illustrated in Figure 7.18 merely represent the spatial arrangements

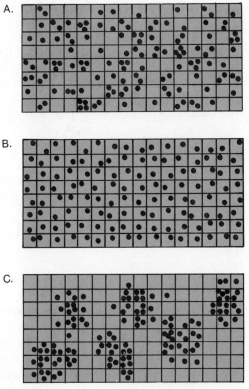

Figure 7.18.   Three spatial patterns of individual organisms (represented as points) on a grid of unit squares. *A.*—random spacing, *B.*—regular spacing, *C.*—clumped spacing. In each diagram, the average number of individuals per square is one.

that might be observed at one moment in time, such as seen with the aid of aerial photos. Analysis of the spatial patterns of aerial and aquatic species requires the use of three dimensions and will not be considered here.

Mathematics of random spacing.　　If spacing is truly random, the number of individuals per sampling unit should be distributed according to a Poisson distribution. To show this, consider a local population consisting of N individuals scattered at random throughout a favorable area. Now, suppose that we subdivide the space into a large number of squares or quadrats of equal size as illustrated in Figure 7.18A. Assume that the squares are sufficiently large so that every square contains a large number of locations, each having an equal chance of being occupied by a single individual. If the number of locations per square is n and the probability of each location being occupied is p, the probability that exactly x locations are occupied will then be

$$p(x) = \frac{n!}{x!(n-x)!} p^x (1-p)^{n-x}$$

where $n!/x!(n-x)!$ represents the number of different ways in which x locations can be filled. Implicit in the assumption of randomness is that the occupation of one site has no effect on the chance that an individual is present in a neighboring location. In other words, these are independent events.

When n is large and p is very small, which is generally the case, the expected proportion of squares with exactly x individuals becomes

$$p(x) \simeq \frac{(np)^x}{x!} (1-p)^n \rightarrow \frac{(np)^x}{x!} e^{-np}$$

Letting $m = np$ represent the average number of individuals per sampling unit, $p(x)$ can be expressed as the Poisson probability

$$p(x) = \frac{m^x}{x!} e^{-m} \tag{7.4}$$

for which the variance is also equal to m.

One important feature of random spacing is the lack of dependence of the sampling distribution on quadrat size. This lack of dependence on sampling area stems from the requirement that all locations must have an equal likelihood of being occupied for dispersion to be random. Thus, if we were to choose two quadrats, one being twice as large as the other, the distribution should still be Poisson in both. In this case, doubling the quadrat size merely doubles the average number of individuals per sampling unit. This relationship between the mean and the area which is sampled can be taken into account by writing the mean as $m = aN$ where a is the area of the sampling unit and N is the population density.

Spacing in patchy environments.   In contrast to the pattern expected for randomness most spatial patterns observed in nature do depend to some extent upon the area of observation or quadrat size. On a sufficiently large scale, all species tend to exhibit some degree of clumping due to the variable or discontinuous nature of suitable habitats within any large geographical area. As a consequence of the patchy environment, each species which can exist only in certain ecological conditions will tend to vary in average density from one location to another or may be subdivided into a series of discontinuous local populations when conditions are sufficiently diverse. As the scale of observation is reduced so as to include only a small part of a favorable area, spacing may then approach either a random or infradispersed pattern.

The effect of a patchy environment on the overall pattern of dispersion can be illustrated in terms of a commonly used model in population biology known as the island model. This model describes one extreme case of environmental patchiness in which a given segment of a species range is pictured as being subdivided into "habitat islands" or favorable regions surrounded by different habitats which are not occupied normally by the species except for occasional migrants. This model is pictured in terms of a mosaic in Figure 7.19 in which cross-hatched areas represent habitable regions within the field of observation.

Now, suppose that we subdivide this space into a checkerboard of squares.

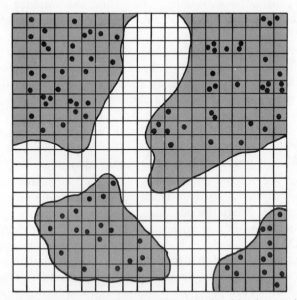

Figure 7.19. An infradispersed spatial pattern obtained by increasing the scale of observation to include uninhabitable squares. The points are assumed to be distributed at random throughout cross-hatched "habitat islands."

By doing so, we would likely observe a highly clumped spatial pattern with individuals present only in squares which overlap suitable habitats. Although the total scale of observation has been increased, the size of each square is assumed to be the same as in Figure 7.18. Now assume as before that individuals are spaced at random throughout the habitable squares with a mean and variance equal to m. If the proportion of habitable squares is q and of uninhabitable squares is $1-q$, then the proportion of all squares with exactly x individuals will now be

$$p(x) = (q)\frac{m^x}{x!} e^{-m} \tag{7.5}$$

Empty squares must include all uninhabitable squares as well as those habitable squares that are, by chance, unoccupied. Therefore, the proportion of empty quadrats will be $p(0) = (1-q) + qe^{-m}$.

If we consider the entire grid without regard to habitat, as would be the case if we failed to recognize unsuitable habitats, the mean number of individuals per sampling unit would now be $m_t = qm$. The total variance can be determined by noting that the average variance within the two distinctive regions (V_w) is $qm + (1-q)0 = qm$; whereas the variance of group means (V_B) is $q(m-qm)^2 + (1-q)(0-qm)^2 = q(1-q)m^2$. Since the total variance is simply the sum of the within-group and between-group measures of variation, then $V_t = qm + q(1-q)m^2 = m_t + mm_t - m_t^2$. Thus, the variance in this case is greater than what is expected for complete randomness by an additional factor of $q(1-q)m^2$.

As illustrated in the previous model, a distinguishing feature of a clumped spatial pattern is that the variance of the distribution exceeds the mean. This property has been used by population biologists to measure the degree of clumping or aggregation in terms of the variance/mean ratio. A purely random pattern will yield a variance/mean ratio which is not significantly different from unity. Clumped patterns, on the other hand, yield ratios which tend to be significantly greater than one.

Lloyd (1967) has proposed another measure of aggregation which he calls *mean crowding* symbolized by $\overset{*}{m}$. This parameter measures, in effect, the average number of individuals with which each member of a population shares its square or quadrat. When the positions of the individuals are random within clumps, the mean crowding is analogous to the mean number per habitable square (m) in the island model. This correspondence stems from the fact that if the total mean remained unchanged, aggregated individuals must share their quadrat with an average of m/m_t times as many other members of the population as they would if the distribution were entirely random throughout the area of observation. Thus, if we replace m with the symbol $\overset{*}{m}$, the total variance can be expressed as $V_t = m_t + \overset{*}{m}m_t - m_t^2$. Solving for $\overset{*}{m}$, we get

$$\overset{*}{m} = m_t + (V_t/m_t - 1) \tag{7.6}$$

For example, if $m_t = 1$ and $V_t = 10$, then $\overset{*}{m} = 1 + (10 - 1) = 10$. In this case, a mobile animal organism would encounter 10 times as many individuals, on the average, as it would for completely random spacing.

One probability distribution which frequently seems to fit populations in which members are grouped into clumps is the negative binomial. As pointed out in Chapter 2, this is a discrete distribution which can be derived from the Poisson by assuming that the mean is itself a random variable. Suppose, for example, that a population is potentially capable of random dispersion given uniform environmental conditions. If conditions were uniform, its pattern per unit sampling area would then be described by the Poisson formula

$$p(x) = \frac{N^x}{x!} e^{-N}$$

Now assume that, due to environmental heterogeneity, the mean or average density of the population varies in a random fashion throughout the entire habitat area. Thus, N can be treated as a random variable with its own probability distribution. Whatever the actual distribution of N, it is likely that a gamma distribution could serve as a reasonable approximation because of its ability to generate such a variety of shapes and patterns. The assumed density function can then be written as

$$f(N) = \frac{v^k}{\Gamma(k)} N^{k-1} e^{-vN}$$

with parameter v and having a mean and variance of k/v and k/v^2, respectively. Since N is a variable, the probability of x individuals per unit sampling area will then be the sum of all Poisson distributions with specific values of N times their expected frequency $f(N)$. When expressed in calculus notation, this becomes

$$p(x) = \frac{1}{x!} \int_0^\infty N^x e^{-N} f(N) dN = \frac{v^k}{x!\,\Gamma(k)} \int_0^\infty N^{k+x-1} e^{-N(1+v)} dN$$

Recall that the gamma function can be expressed as

$$\Gamma(n) = a^n \int_0^\infty N^{n-1} e^{-aN} dN$$

Letting $n = k + x$ and $a = 1+v$, we see that the terms within the integral are simply $\Gamma(k+x)/(1+v)^{k+x}$. By making this substitution, we get

$$p(x) = \frac{\Gamma(k+x)}{x!\,\Gamma(k)} \left[\frac{v}{1+v}\right]^k \left[\frac{1}{1+v}\right]^x$$

This is the probability mass function of the negative binomial distribution for which the mean and variance are

$$m = k/v \quad \text{and} \quad V = k/v + k/v^2 = m + m^2/k$$

Thus, we see that the variance exceeds the mean by an additional factor of m^2/k.

We can now express this distribution in terms of its mean as

$$p(x) = \frac{\Gamma(k+x)}{x!\,\Gamma(k)} \left[\frac{k}{k+m}\right]^k \left[\frac{m}{k+m}\right]^x \qquad (7.7)$$

Consequently, to specify such a distribution requires two parameters, the mean m and a constant k which measures the variability in population density. The value of k determines the degree of aggregation. When k approaches infinity (usually a value greater than eight is sufficient), the negative binomial distribution approaches the Poisson and spacing is essentially random. As the value of k decreases (usually within the range of 1 and 8), spacing becomes progressively more clumped in pattern. Thus, low values of k are associated with a high degree of aggregation in populations which conform to this distribution. The goodness-of-fit of the negative binomial distribution to the spacing of an actual population is pictured graphically in Figure 7.20. Observed frequencies are also compared with those expected from the Poisson distribution derived for the island model (7.5). In this case, the best fit is obtained with the negative binomial.

When the negative binomial distribution is applied to field data, the value of k is frequently estimated by way of the sample mean ($\bar{x}$) and the sample variance (s^2). This is accomplished by replacing the mean and variance in the relation $V = m + m^2/k$ with their sample estimates. The estimate of k is then

$$k = \bar{x}^2/(s^2 - \bar{x})$$

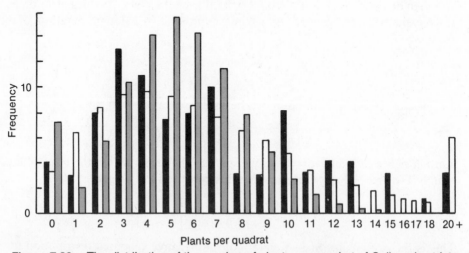

Figure 7.20. The distribution of the number of plants per quadrat of *Salicornia stricta*. Solid bars: observed. Open bars: fitted negative binomial distribution. Hatched bars: fitted Poisson distribution with added zeros. (Data from C.I. Bliss and R.A. Fisher. 1953. Biometrics 9: 176. With permission of the Biometric Society.)

Usually, this method of estimating k is only reliable for low density populations where $\bar{x}$ is small and $k/\bar{x}$ is greater than 6. For high density populations, k should be obtained by iterative solution from the distribution formula.

So far, our discussion has dealt primarily with clumped patterns arising from environmental patchiness. It should be emphasized, however, that clumped spatial patterns are not restricted to heterogeneous environments. Even within a uniformly favorable area, aggregation might occur as a result of the social nature of animal organisms. Clumping may also arise as a result of vegetative reproduction or from limited dispersal of seeds, spores, or larval forms of sedentary organisms. The dispersal of heavy wind-borne seeds, for example, tends to produce clusters or groves in the vicinity of the parental plant. Generally, these spatial patterns can also be approximated by means of the negative binomial distribution. In fact, several models leading to the negative binomial have been developed which start out with the assumption that organisms are naturally grouped into clusters within a uniformly favorable space. This illustrates, of course, that a good fit to experimental data does not necessarily verify the assumptions in a specific model, since a variety of models can be developed which predict basically the same distribution.

SPACING SYSTEMS IN ANIMALS

The preceding discussion has treated the units of dispersion as fixed points. This is an obvious oversimplification, but one which permits the use of conventional statistical analyses. With mobile animals, a more accurate and complete picture of spacing can be gained by sampling individual (or group) locations at different times. These estimates are usually provided by visual and radio-tracking methods and by repeated trapping. The collection and analysis of such data can yield useful information about the spatial behavior of individuals (and groups) with respect to food and shelter and how they relate to others of the same species.

Home range.   Individual animals often restrict their wanderings to a limited space with familiar surroundings. This area to which an animal normally confines its movements in search of food and mates and for caring of young is referred to as its *home range*. Not all parts of the home range get equal use. The region of greatest activity is usually toward the center and is appropriately termed the core area. This typically includes the nest or den or some preferred resting site. Surrounding the core is the foraging area in which resource acquisition takes place. Since the general trend in movements tends to proceed radially to and from the core, the probability of finding the animal will generally be greatest towards the center of its home range and will tend to decline with distance to the outer limit. For this reason, the computation of home range size should be based on a fairly large number of sightings or recaptures in order to obtain a reasonable estimate of range boundaries.

The home range is not a hard and fast geographical area but has been shown to vary with the season, the breeding cycle, and the sex of the individual. It also varies considerably from one species to another. For example, Hamilton (1937) found the home range of the meadow vole *Microtus pennsylvanicus* to be only 0.7 acre. On the other hand, estimates of the home range of, say, the whitetail deer are as large as 160 acres (Jewell, 1966). Much of this variation in home range can be attributed to differences in body size and mobility. A large body size means greater metabolic demands and, thus, a large foraging area is needed to fill them. One would, therefore, expect that home range size, A, should vary with body weight, W, in much the same manner as metabolic rate. Studies have shown that this is indeed the case, yielding the general power relationship $A = kW^b$ (Schoener, 1968). It is generally observed, however, that b tends to be greater in magnitude in this relationship than in the corresponding metabolic rate equation. This probably reflects the greater energy costs involved in the search for required resources in larger areas. Consideration of such energy costs can also explain the observation that b is greater for predators, with their more sparsely distributed food supply, than for herbivores.

Several other factors are known which can influence the distance which an organism will travel in search of food and mates. Two of the most obvious are the availability of resources and the risk of predation. Recently, Covich (1976) has proposed a model to account for their effects. The model is shown graphically in Figure 7.21. In this illustration, the curve designated Y describes the changes in resource yield (i.e., the amount of resources available to a

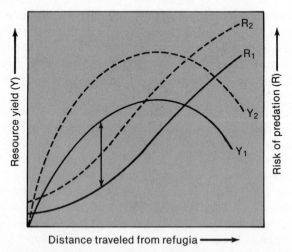

Figure 7.21.   A graphical model illustrating the effects of increased resource yields (Y_1, Y_2) and/or increased risks of predation (R_1, R_2) on the optimal distance traveled within a foraging area. One optimal distance is indicated by the vertical line. (From A.P. Covich. 1976. Ann. Rev. Ecol. System. 7: 235. Reproduced, with permission, from the Annual Review of Ecology and Systematics, Volume 7. Copyright 1976 by Annual Reviews Inc.)

consumer in a fixed period of time) as a function of the distance from the core or place of refuge. Since resources tend to be rapidly depleted in and around the place of refuge, the resource curve is expected to increase with distance up to a maximum and then decline due to increased competition with other individuals in overlapping foraging areas. In contrast, the risk curve, designated as R, is a cost function, measured in terms of the reduction in feeding rates at a given level of predation. It, in turn, will most probably increase with distance into less familiar areas. The optimal distance which the organism is expected to travel will then correspond to the maximum difference between these two curves. Note that an increase in resource yield will tend to shift the optimal distance farther away from the central area, while increases in the levels of competition and predation decrease the distance, moving it closer to the place of refuge.

Territoriality.   A regular spatial pattern can arise among animals through a form of social behavior known as *territoriality*. This is a space-oriented form of behavior in which an animal actively defends a particular area known as its territory from intruders of the same species and, in some cases, closely related species. In most instances, actual fighting is minimized through the use of accoustical and visual displays in order to advertise territorial boundaries or by marking territories with special scents, as is typical of many mammalian species with their well-developed sense of smell.

Territorial behavior is a common pattern among reptiles, birds, and mammals, and occurs occasionally in some lower vertebrates and invertebrates as well. It has been studied most extensively among birds, where it takes on a variety of forms. Some species are territorial only at the time of mating, while others defend a territory throughout the year. Species also vary with respect to the size of their territories. In colonial sea birds, for example, small nesting territories are the rule where territorial space is restricted to just an area in the immediate vicinity of the nest. Small territories are also characteristic of lek systems, like that of the prairie chicken *Tympanuchus cupido*, in which males gather in territorially subdivided communal mating areas, or leks, and try to attract females by their elaborate displays. Other birds, such as the European robin *Erithacus rubecula*, have all-purpose territories and defend an area large enough to sustain mating, feeding, and breeding activities. Except in the case of an all-purpose territory, which is identical in extent with home range, the area defended is usually less than the entire foraging area.

Apart from its significance in the regulation of population size, which is considered in a later chapter, territoriality appears to serve three main functions: protection of the nest or den, improvement of mating success, and insurance of an adequate food supply. In support of the latter function, Schoener (1968) found that territory size for a variety of birds increased with body weight as $A = kW^b$ for which the value of b was equal to 1.09, thus indicating that birds with greater metabolic needs require larger territories in order to sustain their food requirements.

Organization into groups.   Animals frequently exhibit behavior patterns which lead to the formation of groups. These include family groupings; mating groups, exemplified by harems and leks; and various social aggregations such as colonies, herds, flocks, schools, and packs. Numerous advantages accrue to individuals by joining with others to form such groups. Among the more obvious factors favoring group-forming behavior are hunting and mating success and protection against predators. For example, wolves in packs benefit from teamwork by running down and killing much larger animals than a single individual can safely handle. Schooling in fish can facilitate escape from predation by serving to lower the frequency of contacts between the prey and their predators. Escape from predation is also a factor with large herbivores such as musk oxen, *Ovibos muschatus*, which can successfully protect themselves and their young against predators when present in herds by using shoulder-to-shoulder defense tactics. Protection against the cold is yet another benefit accrued from group formation which seems to account for the aggregation tendency of many snakes during winter dormancy.

One factor that is currently regarded as of prime importance in the evolutionary development of groups is the distribution of food resources. A major stimulus in this regard has been the work of Horn (1968) which suggests that flocking in birds is favored in habitats where resources are clumped and unpredictable. An idealized model which Horn proposed to compare the energetics of foraging trips for territorial and colonial nesting is represented schematically in Figure 7.22. To illustrate the logic behind the model, consider two types of resource distribution: (1) uniform in space and predictable in time, and (2) clumped in space and unpredictable in time. Compute the cost of foraging trips as the minimum average distance that a nesting pair must travel to resource sites. Thus, if we designate the location of the nest as (x_o, y_o) and that of a particular resource site as (x_i, y_j), the cost will then be

$$\sum_i \sum_j \sqrt{(x_i - x_o)^2 + (y_j - y_o)^2}\, p(x_i) p(y_j)$$

where the sum is taken over all sites at which a nesting pair can feed.

(1) First, consider a uniform and predictable distribution of food resources. In the case of territorial spacing, only the four resource locations which surround the nest site need to be visited in order to provide an adequate supply of food. Thus, if we let $2d$ be the minimum distance between resource sites, the average foraging distance for territorial spacing is

$$\sqrt{d^2 + d^2} = 1.41d$$

This is in contrast with colonial spacing, in which an average pair must now visit all sixteen sites. The average distance traveled from the central nesting location is then

$$\tfrac{1}{4}\sqrt{d^2 + d^2} + \tfrac{1}{2}\sqrt{d^2 + (3d)^2} + \tfrac{1}{4}\sqrt{(3d)^2 + (3d)^2} = 3.00d$$

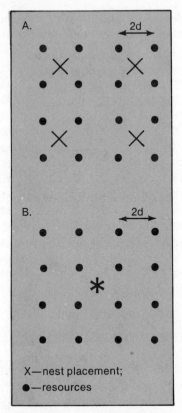

Figure 7.22. Diagrammatic representation of nest placement with respect to resources for territorial (A) and colonial (B) nesting.

(2) Now, assume that resources are clumped and unpredictable as to where they may appear. This means that an average pair must visit all sixteen feeding sites, regardless of nest location, to be certain of finding a sufficient food supply. The average foraging distance for territorial spacing is then

$$\tfrac{1}{4}\left[\sqrt{d^2 + d^2} + \sqrt{d^2 + (3d)^2} + \sqrt{d^2 + (5d)^2}\right] + \tfrac{1}{16}\left[\sqrt{(3d)^2 + (3d)^2}\right.$$
$$\left. + 2\sqrt{(3d)^2 + (5d)^2} + \sqrt{(5d)^2 + (5d)^2}\right] = 3.86d$$

Colonial spacing, on the other hand, yields an average distance of 3.00d, as before.

If we now assume that, with other things being equal, selection should act to minimize the expenditure of energy in foraging, it becomes apparent that territorial spacing of nests is favored with an even dispersion of food resources, while colonial nesting is favored when food is clumped. It is, therefore, possible that groups develop in response to spatial and temporal clumping of resources. In less patchy conditions, regular spacing is optimal and territorial defense is worth the effort. As patchiness increases, an increasingly larger area is needed to sustain each individual and the maintenance of territories becomes overly expensive. A more aggregated grouping of organisms would then be optimal for foraging success.

While territoriality provides a mechanism by which solitary individuals or mated pairs partition a limited resource supply, the development of *dominance hierarchies* permits a sharing of resources by members of social groups. A dominance hierarchy is a form of social differentiation in which individuals are ordered in rank, with those of higher rank intimidating those below them on the dominance scale. This type of organization has been intensively studied in domestic chickens where it is referred to as the peck order. In such hierarchies, subordinates typically avoid dominants or show some form of submissive behavior if in danger of being attacked. This reduces actual fighting as well as other forms of internal disruption. For this social system to work, each member of the group must recognize others and respond to them as individuals. Consequently, large groups, which continually change in composition, do not establish stable dominance hierarchies. In such cases, aggressive encounters take the form of threat displays or attacks.

PATTERNS RESULTING FROM DISPERSAL

In addition to environmental patchiness and the behavioral characteristics of the species, the distribution of a population in time and space is also influenced by dispersal. Dispersal is the mechanism by which a population spreads into surrounding areas, either by the active movements of its members or through the dissemination of propagules such as seeds or spores. It is, therefore, the mechanism for gene exchange between local breeding groups and the method by which new areas are colonized. When viewed in terms of a single plant or animal population, dispersal is often directly related to growth rate since an efficient dispersal mechanism would provide for the rapid occupation and utilization of all available living space. It is also intimately related to continued adaptation and reproductive success since it serves as the mixing process by which genetically dissimilar mates are encountered or brought into close proximity, thus providing for the establishment of new and possibly more adaptive gene combinations among the offspring.

In their simplest form, dispersal patterns are usually described in terms of the way in which the fraction of individuals (or their propagules) drops off with distance from the source of dispersal. Although numerous regression models have been applied to the analysis of dispersal data, many dispersal patterns can be distinguished on the basis of the following form of distribution function:

$$\log G(x,t) = -\,[(x - v)/a]^b \tag{7.8}$$

where $G(x,t)$ is the fraction having traveled at least a distance x from the source in time t. In this expression, a and v are often time-dependent parameters, v being a measure of the tendency to move in a specific direction, termed drift. The simplest dispersal patterns are those which occur in the absence of drift ($v = 0$) and for which b is an integer. Two such patterns that have been intensively studied are (1) the *exponentially-distributed* pattern in which the logarithm of the fraction of disseminating organisms or propagules falls off linearly with distance ($b = 1$), and (2) the *normally-distributed* pattern in which the logarithm of this fraction decreases with distance-squared ($b = 2$).

The exponential pattern quite often characterizes passive dispersal in plants and insects in which seeds, spores, or adult forms are carried by wind and water currents. A suitable working model is also simple to formulate mathematically. Suppose, for example, that dispersal is accomplished by propagules which move in a given direction and have a fixed probability per unit distance that they will cease moving (e.g., fall from the air). The resultant distribution will then be exponential and, when measured in the direction of movement, the fraction of propagules which travel at least a distance x from the source in time t can be expressed as

$$G(x,t) = 1 - (1/a) \int_0^x e^{-x/a} \, dx = e^{-x/a}$$

where a is now the average distance traveled by the propagules. Thus, if we plot $\ln G(x,t)$ versus x, the equation predicts a linear decrease with distance.

A normally-distributed pattern, on the other hand, would develop from seemingly random movements of animals over extended periods of time. A useful model in this regard can be developed if we assume that dispersal is accomplished by active movements in a randomly changing course. The net effect is like that expected for the diffusion of inanimate objects, giving rise to a distribution about the center of dispersal like shots around a bullseye. Since dispersal occurs by a long succession of random movements, we would expect by way of the central limit theorem that, regardless of the distribution of the individual movements, the resultant distribution should be that of a normal random variate. Thus, in two-dimensional space, the density function can be expressed as

$$f(x) = (1/2\pi\sigma^2) \, e^{-x^2/2\sigma^2}$$

The fraction of the population lying outside a circle of circumference $2\pi x$ centered on the source of dispersal at time t is then

$$G(x,t) = 1 - (1/\sigma^2) \int_0^x x e^{-x^2/2\sigma^2} \, dx = e^{-x^2/2\sigma^2}$$

where $2\sigma^2$ is equivalent to a^2 in equation (7.8). It can be shown that the variance in this model increases in direct proportion to time. Thus, we can write $\sigma^2 = 2Dt$ where D is a measure of dispersal rate. Observe that the logarithm of the proportion of dispersing individuals is expected to fall off with distance-squared. One obvious objection to the use of this model in describing the dispersal of higher animal forms is the assumption of complete statistical randomness. As any biologist is quick to point out, successive directional movements in animals are not independent as visualized in the model but are generally correlated. Moreover, dispersal does not take place in a uniform space, but must occur in a changing environment. Despite the obvious simplifications, the model has been useful in describing the spread of some populations into unoccupied areas when dispersal was measured over extended time intervals. To exemplify its application in this regard, consider a boundary circle about the center of dispersal which includes all but one member of the dispersing population at time t. If N_t is the number of individuals in the population, the proportion expected to be farther than x from the center of dispersal will now be

$$1/N_t = e^{-x^2/4Dt}$$

Letting $A = \pi x^2$ represent the area of the boundary circle, this equation reduces to

$$A = 4\pi Dt (\ln N_t) \tag{7.9}$$

When N_t is large, the boundary circle can be thought of as a contour showing the relative extent of a spreading population after a given time of dispersal. An important point to note in this model is that the area of the boundary circle is proportional to the size of the spreading population. Therefore, larger populations will tend to expand into uninhabited areas more rapidly than smaller ones. Dispersal will thus be related to growth rate. As an example, suppose that a population increases as $N_t = N_o e^{rt}$, or $\ln N_t - \ln N_o = rt$, where r is a measure of growth related to the doubling time of the population as $r = (\ln 2)/T_d$ (see Chapter 8). When N_o is small in comparison to the present size of the population, $\ln N_o$ can be ignored and equation (7.9) can be given approximately as $A = 4\pi Drt^2$. Hence, A will depend directly on growth rate as given in terms of $1/T_d$. Also note that under these conditions, the square-root of the area including the population, and thus the radius of the boundary circle, will increase linearly with time. Such a pattern has been described by Skellam (1951) for the expansion of the muskrat after its escape from captivity in Central Europe (Figure 7.23). In this case, the spread of the population was quite uniform with time despite irregularities in the terrain.

Although the model derived for a normally-distributed pattern has been extensively applied to the spread of natural populations, values of b in equation (7.8) are more generally found to be less than 2. This gives rise to a leptokurtic, or peaked, distribution as compared to the normal, and suggests a definite tendency of organisms to remain close to the center of dispersal. This is exemplified by the results of a classic experiment conducted by Dobzhansky and

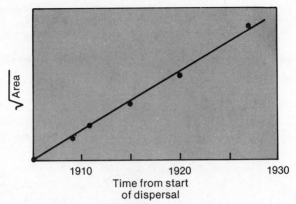

Figure 7.23. Geographic expansion of the muskrat after its escape from captivity in Europe. (From J.G. Skellam. 1951. Biometrika 38: 196.)

Wright (1943) on the dispersal of the fruit fly, *Drosophila pseudoobscura*. In this experiment, large numbers of flies were released at a given point on one day. Recaptures were then made on following days in traps which were spaced 20 meters apart in a cross-shaped pattern centered on the point of release. To avoid confusion from the capture of native, wild-type flies, only flies of the eye-color mutant orange were released. Although the recapture data were initially described in terms of a leptokurtic distribution, more recently Wallace (1966) has subjected the results to regression analysis using a model analogous to equation (7.8). He found that the results form a straight line when plotted as log number of flies per trap versus the square-root of distance, suggesting a value of $b = \frac{1}{2}$. Other dispersal data have also been analyzed which tend to suggest similar results. A particularly interesting example is that of matrimonial migration in man which is illustrated graphically in Figure 7.24. In this case, the dispersal pattern is expressed as the probability of marriage as a function of the distance between the birth-places of marriage partners. The data give a remarkably good fit to a square-root relationship and indicate that the persons in this sample, like *Drosophila* in the preceding study, tend to remain close to the center of dispersal and mate with individuals of their proximate group.

As with the growth equations that were considered earlier, the parameters in any simple dispersal model are expected to vary with environmental conditions. For instance, the activities of many plants and animals are correlated with daily and seasonal changes in temperature, light intensity, and a host of other variables. In such instances, dispersal is often confined to only a fraction of the entire seasonal cycle. Moreover, dispersal can be induced in animals by biotic factors such as overpopulation and food shortages, resulting in a complex relationship between dispersal facility and population size. Spatial variation in the biotic and physical environment can also act as barriers and thus limit the distance which an organism can safely travel and still survive and reproduce. For example, Janzen (1970) suggests that the dispersion of rain-forest trees in

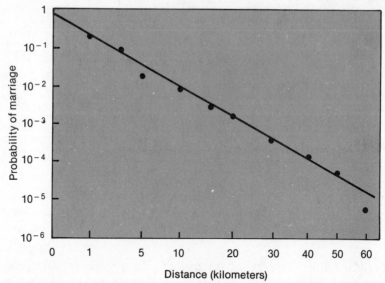

Figure 7.24. The probability of marriage in man as a function of the square root of the distance between the birthplaces of the marriage partners. (After L.L. Cavalli-Sforza. 1959. Proc. 10th Intern. Congr. Genet. 1: 389.)

the tropics is limited by seed predation by various insects, mammals, and birds. Since seed predation tends to be concentrated in the vicinity of the parent plant where seeds and fruits are most likely to fall, seed survivorship increases with distance from the source of dispersal (Figure 7.25). When considered together

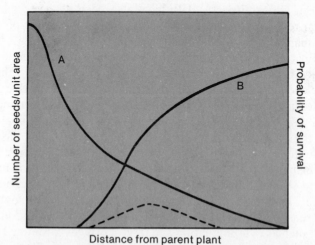

Figure 7.25. Hypothetical model to account for the high diversity of tropical rain-forest trees. Curve *A* represents dispersal of seeds from the parent plant, and *B* shows the probability of seed survival. Their product (dashed curve) gives the resultant survivorship as a function of the distance from the parent plant where a new tree can grow.

with the dispersal relationship, this yields a peak region of highest realized probability of seed survival near the point of intersection of the two curves.

SOLVED EXAMPLE PROBLEMS

Limiting Factors

1. Suppose that the growth (y) of a particular plant variety varies with the amount of a limiting nutrient (x) in the manner described by equation (7.2). Show that u can be evaluated from the reciprocal of x when y is equal to one-half its maximum value.

   solution   Let $y = \frac{1}{2}Y$. We have $\frac{1}{2} = ux/(1 + ux)$. Solving for u, we get $u = 1/x$.

2. A number of different mathematical models have been proposed to give empirical fit to the photosynthesis-light relationship observed during saturation. For instance, Smith has shown that some data concerning the rate of photosynthesis (y) as a function of the incident light intensity (I) fit the equation $y = Y(aI)/\sqrt{1 + (aI)^2}$, where a and Y are constants. (a) Show that at low values of aI, y increases linearly with I and that at high intensities, y approaches Y. (b) Compare the curve predicted by the above function with that of the Mitscherlich equation (7.1). (c) Show that if data should follow the preceding relation, a plot of $y/\sqrt{Y^2 - y^2}$ versus I will yield a straight line having a slope equal to a.

   solution   (a) When $(aI^2) << 1$, $y \approx Y(aI)$. When $(aI)^2 >> 1$, $y \approx Y$. (b) The curves are similar in appearance except the above function remains approximately linear over a greater range of I values and breaks more sharply in its approach to the upper asymptote. (c) First square the function. We get $y^2 = Y^2(aI)^2/[1 + (aI)^2]$. Solving for $(aI)^2$, we obtain $y^2/(Y^2 - y^2) = (aI)^2$. Taking the square-root then yields the desired linear relationship.

Climatic Factors

3. Suppose that the growth rate of a microbial population doubled with an increase in temperature from $27°–37°C$. Employing the Arrhenius equation, determine the temperature coefficient (E_a) for the growth process.

   solution   First, let $v_1 = Ae^{-E_a/RT_1}$ and $v_2 = Ae^{-E_a/RT_2}$ where $T_2 > T_1$. The fractional increase in rate can then be expressed in terms of its logarithm as $\ln(v_2/v_1) = -(E_a/R)(1/T_1 - 1/T_2)$. Solving for E_a, we get $E_a = RT_1 T_2 \ln(v_2/v_1)/(T_2 - T_1)$ which, for $v_2/v_1 = 2$, $T_1 = 300°K$, and $T_2 = 310°K$, becomes $(1.98)(300)(310)(0.639)/10 = 12,760$ calories.

Population Structure

4. An investigator is interested in the distribution of a particular species of snail in a large tidal pool. The snails burrow into the mud as the tide goes out. The number of snails per quadrat was then determined for each of 418 quadrats:

$$x: \quad 0 \quad 1 \quad 2 \quad 3 \quad 4 \quad 5 \quad 6$$
$$\text{Quadrats:} \quad 305 \quad 75 \quad 22 \quad 12 \quad 3 \quad 1 \quad 0$$

Is there significant departure from a random spacing pattern?

solution   If the snails are randomly dispersed, the number per quadrat will follow a Poisson distribution with m estimated as $172/418 = 0.41$. We can then calculate the expected values of $p(x)$ on the basis of the Poisson formula and use a chi-square test to determine the significance of the differences between observed and expected values.

$$x:\quad 0\quad\ 1\quad\ 2\quad 3\quad 4\quad 5\quad 6$$
$$(418)p(x):\quad 277.0\ \ 114.0\ \underbrace{23.5\ \ 3.2\ \ 0.3\ \ 0.0\ \ 0.0}_{27.0}$$

$$\overline{\chi^2} = (277 - 305)^2/277 + (114 - 74)^2/114 + (27 - 38)^2/27 = 21.35.$$

$P < 0.01$ so reject the hypothesis of a random spacing pattern.

5. When spacing corresponds to a negative binomial distribution, show that the parameter k can be expressed in terms of the mean crowding as

$$k = m/(\overset{*}{m} - m)$$

solution   The variance of the negative binomial distribution is $V = m + m^2/k$. But, from the definition of mean crowding, the total variance can be expressed as $V = m + \overset{*}{m}m - m^2$. Thus, $m^2/k = \overset{*}{m}m - m^2$ and rearrangement of terms gives the desired result.

Patterns Resulting from Dispersal

6. Suppose that an experiment, similar to that of Dobzhanṣky and Wright, is performed in which several thousand flies (marked with an eye-color mutant) are released at a given point on one day, followed by the subsequent daily recapture and release of these flies at regularly spaced traps. Assume that by the first day following release, 63% of the recaptured flies are trapped within a circle of area 1 m² centered on the point of release. If dispersal follows a normally distributed pattern, (a) what is the dispersal coefficient (D) in m²/day? (b) What proportion of the recaptured flies will be expected to be trapped within the dsignated circle by the second day following release? By the third day?

solution   (a) Assuming a normally distributed pattern of dispersal, $2D = \sigma^2$ at day 1. The fraction of the population lying outside a circle of circumference $2\pi x$ is $G(x,1) = 0.37$ for $x^2 = 1/\pi$. Hence, $0.37 = e^{-1/2\pi\sigma^2}$ and $\sigma^2 = 0.16$. Thus, $D = 0.08$ m²/day. (b) On the second day, σ^2 will equal 0.32 and the fraction of recaptured flies trapped within the designated circle is expected to be $1 - G(x,2) = 0.39$. Similarly, at 3 days, $\sigma^2 = 0.48$ and $1 - G(x,3) = 0.28$.

7. Assume that the directional dispersal pattern of a particular insect species is exponential when carried long distances by wind. If half of the dispersing insects travel a distance of at least 2 miles from the source in 1 day, what is the average distance traveled by the insects per day?

solution Let x be the distance traveled. Then $\frac{1}{2} = e^{-x/\bar{x}}$. Setting x equal to 2 and solving for $\bar{x}$, we get $\bar{x} = 2/\ln 2 = 2.89$ miles.

8. Show that, in the case of random dispersion, the square of the distance between nearest neighbors is an exponential random variable.

   solution Consider an individual chosen at random and a circular sampling unit of area a centered about this individual. First determine the probability that, by increasing the area to $a + da$, the position of another individual is included within the circle. Since spacing is random, the probability that area a is empty is e^{-aN}, whereas the probability that area da contains one individual is Nda. Hence, the total probability is $Ne^{-aN}da$. The density function of the variable a is thus exponential, given as $f(a) = Ne^{-aN}$. Since $a = \pi z^2$, where z is the radius of the circle, we have the desired result. The probability density function of z can also be obtained, using $da = 2\pi z\,dz$, giving $f(z) = 2\pi Nze^{-\pi Nz^2}$.

PROBLEM EXERCISES

1. Many bacteria can grow on a simple, defined medium consisting of certain inorganic salts, plus a carbon and energy source such as glucose. If the inorganic constituents are supplied in excess, then the carbon source can become the factor limiting the growth of the population. In a study of the effect of glucose concentration on the growth rate of a bacterial population growing in such a medium, the following data were obtained:

Glucose: (mg/1)	1	3	5	7	9	11	13	15	17	19	21	25
Growth rate: (divisions/min)	0.22	0.49	0.65	0.76	0.84	0.89	0.94	0.98	1.00	1.03	1.05	1.08

   (a) Plot the data as growth rate versus glucose concentration. (b) By use of a suitable linear transformation, determine whether the Mitscherlich equation (7.1) or a rectangular hyperbola (7.2) best fits the data. (c) From the graphs constructed in part (b), estimate the values of the parameters Y and u. (Use only the function that best fits the data.) (d) Can you suggest some possible limiting factors at high-glucose concentrations?

2. To account for the harmful effects of high-factor levels, Mitscherlich postulated the following relationship between yield (y) and the amount of limiting factor (x):

$$y = Y(1 - e^{-ux})e^{-kx^2}$$

   Show that y is maximum for intermediate values of x, becoming zero when x is zero and when x is very large.

3. Mitscherlich also proposed that if two independent limiting factors, x_1 and x_2, are varied simultaneously, their combined effect on yield would follow the expression

$$y = Y(1 - e^{-u_1 x_1})(1 - e^{-u_2 x_2})$$

(a) Show that when both factors are increased proportionally, the response curve will tend to have a sigmoid appearance. (b) Suggest an experiment to test if the factors influence yield independently as implied in the model.

4. The effect of temperature on the rate of bacterial growth was measured. Growth rates were determined for seven bacterial populations, each growing maximally at a different temperature. The data are given below:

Culture:	1	2	3	4	5	6	7
Temperature (°C):	16	21	25	30	35	40	45
Growth rate: (divisions/hr)	0.19	0.31	0.53	0.84	1.20	1.33	1.05

(a) Illustrate the effects of temperature by a plot of $\ln v$ versus $1/T$. (b) Determine the value of E_a from the plot for temperatures below 40°C.

5. It has been suggested that, for widely distributed species, temperature tends to act as the primary limiting factor towards the poles, while water balance does so towards the tropics. How might this be the case? Explain.

6. An ecologist subdivided a meadow into a checkerboard of squares, each of unit area, and proceeded to count the number of squares which contained at least one individual of a certain plant species. She observed that 18% of the quadrats contained this plant. Assuming that members of this plant population are distributed at random over their range, (a) what is the average number of plants per square? (b) What is the variance of the plant distribution?

7. Suppose that, upon closer examination, the ecologist in Problem 6 observed that one-half of the quadrats were uninhabitable by this species due to adverse soil conditions. If individuals are distributed at random throughout habitable squares, (a) what is the average number of plants per habitable square? (b) What is the total variance for the distribution of plants throughout the meadow? (c) What fraction of the habitable squares are empty? (d) What fraction of the empty squares are habitable? (e) Calculate the value of the mean crowding index, $\overset{*}{m}$.

8. Bliss and Fisher (1953) determined the number of adult red mites on each of 150 apple leaves. The results are given below:

Mites per leaf:	0	1	2	3	4	5	6	7	≥8
Number of leaves:	70	38	17	10	9	3	2	1	0

(a) Compute the sample mean and sample variance and use them to estimate the value of k, assuming mites are distributed according to a negative binomial probability function. (b) Determine the freqencies expected for a negative binomial distribution with $k = 1$.

9. A few individuals of an animal species were released into a previously uninhabited region. The population size and area of distribution were then examined on two occasions, once at 20 years and again at 40 years following release. By 20 years after release, the population had grown to a size of 750 individuals, having a mean density of 2 per square-kilometer. During the time that elapsed between the 20 and 40 year observations, the area occupied by the population increased by a factor of 2.8. (a) Assuming that dispersal approximates a normally distributed pattern, what is the dispersal coefficient (D) in units of kilometer-squared per year? (b) Assuming that the population continues to grow with a constant doubling time, what is the population size expected 40 years after release?

10. Describe the important factors which can influence spacing of individuals within a species range. List the factors that affect the dispersal pattern of a population.

8

Population Growth

Due to the reproductive ability and finite lifespan of individual organisms, populations tend to show temporal as well as spatial variation in density. Interest, therefore, lies not only in the number of individuals in a particular space at a particular moment but also in how this number changes in time. Of special concern to ecologists is the development of a quantitative theory which adequately describes the affects of age and sex composition and the different components of the physical and biotic environment on population growth. The usefulness of such a theory in providing accurate predictions concerning future population trends is readily apparent. Although the development of a single, widely applicable growth model has yet to be realized, many of the basic theoretical concepts pertaining to population growth processes have already been quantified, yielding useful, albeit crude models of population increase. These concepts serve as the subject material for the present chapter.

PARAMETERS OF NUMERICAL CHANGE

When considered over time, the size of a population will depend on the numbers gained through birth (natality) and immigration, and on the numbers lost through death and emigration. Stated symbolically, the growth rate of a population can be expressed as

$$\triangle N_t = N_{t+1} - N_t = B - D + I - E$$

where $\triangle N_t$ designates the net change in population size per unit time interval (expressed in any convenient unit of time such as days, months, years, etc.) and where B, D, I, and E are the birth rate, death rate, immigration rate, and emigration rate, respectively. At times it is more convenient to express the growth of populations in terms of relative rates of change. This is accomplished by dividing through by N_t as follows:

$$\Delta N_t / N_t = \beta - \delta + \iota - \epsilon$$

where β, δ, ι, and ϵ are the finite rates of birth, death, immigration, and emigration, respectively, expressed on a per individual basis.

When ι and ϵ are negligible in comparison to the other parameters, or when ι is approximately equal to ϵ, population growth is essentially a result of a simple birth and death process. Under these conditions, the growth equations can be written as

$$N_{t+1} = N_t + (\beta - \delta)N_t$$

$$= (1 + \beta - \delta)N_t \qquad \textbf{(8.1)}$$

$$= \lambda N_t$$

where λ is termed the *finite rate of increase*, the factor by which a population increases during a single unit interval. The growth rate now becomes

$$\Delta N_t = (\beta - \delta)N_t = (\lambda - 1)N_t \qquad \textbf{(8.2)}$$

Thus, when $\lambda = 2$, the population would double in size during the specified time interval. The relative growth rate, on the other hand, would equal one. Note that when $\beta = \delta$, $\lambda = 1$. When this happens, $\Delta N_t = 0$ and the size of the population is the same at times t and $t+1$.

Equations (8.1) and (8.2) are suitable when population growth occurs in discrete time intervals as in seasonal breeders. As long as time intervals are kept short so as to include only a single breeding season, β and δ can then have a simple meaning as the average birth and death rates per individual. On the other hand, when generations overlap and births and deaths occur at any time (i.e., continuous growth), members of different generations may reproduce and/ or die during the same time interval. In this case, the meanings of β and δ become somewhat nebulous. One way to circumvent this problem is to express the growth parameters as instantaneous rates of change. This is accomplished by merely writing the growth rate, ΔN_t, in terms of the derivative, dN_t/dt. For a simple birth and death process, we get

$$dN_t/dt = (b - d)N_t = rN_t \qquad \textbf{(8.3)}$$

where b and d are now the instantaneous birth and death rates per individual and r is a commonly used measure of population growth generally referred to as the *intrinsic rate of increase* (also known as the Malthusian parameter). Note that since $\lambda - 1 = \beta - \delta$ and $r = b - d$, the finite and instantaneous birth and death rates can be related by means of the expressions

$$b = r\beta/(\lambda - 1) \qquad \text{and} \qquad d = r\delta/(\lambda - 1) \qquad \textbf{(8.4)}$$

Thus, if β and δ are known for a continuous breeder, b and d can be calculated by means of these relationships when given values for r and λ.

It should be pointed out that the two methods of expressing growth of populations are not mutually exclusive. In fact, the finite and intrinsic rates of increase are readily interchangeable on most occasions. This is shown by integrating equation (8.3) over the time interval from t to $t+1$. We then obtain

$$N_{t+1} = e^r N_t \qquad \text{or} \qquad r = \triangle (\ln N_t) \tag{8.5}$$

where $\triangle (\ln N_t) = \ln N_{t+1} - \ln N_t = \ln N_{t+1}/N_t$. By comparison with equation (8.1), we see that if $\lambda = e^r$, the formulae are equivalent. Thus, if a unit time interval were chosen so that $r = \ln \lambda$, a seasonally breeding population would then increase as though growth occurred continuously during this period. Because of the logarithmic relationship existing between r and N, the intrinsic rate of increase (or $\ln \lambda$) is often termed the logarithmic growth rate. It should also be noted that when r is very small (i.e., when $b - d$ is close to zero), e^r can be expressed approximately as $1 - r$. Under these conditions, $r = \lambda - 1$ and equations (8.2) and (8.3) are equivalent. Some examples of finite and intrinsic rates of increase are shown in Table 8.1 along with the mean duration of a generation, commonly known as the *generation time* and symbolized by T_c. Except for man, all growth parameters which are given were measured under controlled laboratory conditions.

TABLE 8.1.   Comparison of fundamental growth parameters for a few animal species.

Organism	r Intrinsic rate (per week)	λ Finite rate (per week)	T_c Generation time (weeks)
Tribolium castaneum* (flour beetle)	0.71	2.03	7.9
Rattus norvegicus** (brown rat)	0.104	1.11	31.1
Man*** (world, 1975)	0.019 (per year)	1.02 (per year)	—

*—From Leslie and Park (1949); **—From Leslie (1945); ***—From Boughey (1975)

Although the parameters given in these fundamental growth equations are very useful in describing population change, it should be stressed that they are rarely constant for any extended period of time since they depend upon the physical, chemical, and biotic factors which make up the environment. This is illustrated in Figures 8.1 and 8.2 by the effects of temperature and moisture on the intrinsic rate of increase of the grain beetle *Calandra oryzae*. Note that in the latter graph, the approximate contour plotted for $r = 0$ designates the effective tolerance limits of this species.

Because of the importance of environmental changes on population growth, many of the growth models presented in this and later chapters will be derived

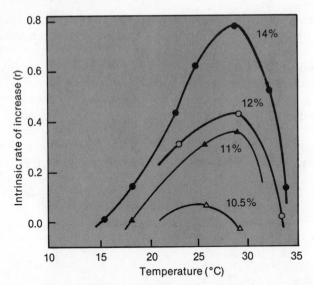

Figure 8.1. Effect of temperature and moisture on the intrinsic rate of increase of *Calandra orvae.* (Data from L.C. Birch. 1953. Ecology 34: 698.)

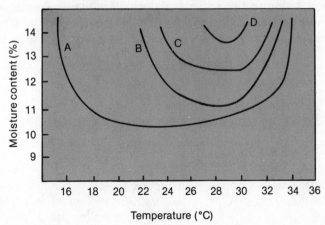

Figure 8.2. Approximate contours plotted for four different values of *r* for *C. oryzae* living at different moisture and temperature conditions. (A) *r* = 0; (B) *r* = 0.34; (C) *r* = 0.47; (D) *r* = 0.69. (From L.C. Birch. 1953. Ecology 34: 698.)

for species in which breeding occurs seasonally, rather than throughout the year. Therefore, several of the models will take the form of recurrence relations that can be solved algebraically or by graphical methods. For the most part, these growth equations are derived for closed populations so that population changes can be accounted for on the basis of survival and fertility.

Variable reproductive rates.   In the preceding section, the parameters of population growth were presented as though all individuals in a population have the same probability of producing offspring or of dying within a reproductive interval. This is seldom the case since most populations are composed of several kinds of individuals (different ages and different genotypes) that vary in survival and fertility. In addition, populations are rarely homogeneous in reproductive potential throughout their area of distribution. Physical as well as biotic components of the environment can vary significantly within the spatial boundaries of a population, thus producing differences in reproductive rates. When such differences are taken into account, the appropriate measure of growth is the arithmetic mean of all finite rates of increase. Thus, if there are n different kinds of individuals (or groups of individuals in distinct environmental settings) in the population at time t with densities $N_1, N_2, \ldots, N_n$ and reproductive rates $\lambda_1, \lambda_2, \ldots, \lambda_n$, the size of the population at time $t+1$ can then be given as

$$N_{t+1} = \lambda_1 N_1 + \lambda_2 N_2 + \ldots + \lambda_n N_n = \sum_{i=1}^{n} \lambda_i N_i = \bar{\lambda} N_t$$

where $N_1 + N_2 + \ldots + N_n = N_t$ and $\bar{\lambda}$ is the average rate defined as $\bar{\lambda} = \Sigma \lambda_i N_i / N_t$. Therefore, with contemporary differences in survival and fertility, the entire population will increase as though all individuals possessed the average finite rate of increase. It is important to note that if type-specific reproductive rates are inherited, individuals with the largest values of λ_i will increase in frequency in the next generation and the reproductive rate of the population as a whole will change even when growth conditions remain constant.

METHODS OF ESTIMATING POPULATION PARAMETERS

A number of methods have been devised to estimate population densities. Most of them involve sampling only a small part of a population rather than attempting to make a total count. One such procedure, which is suitable for plants and certain immobile animal species, is the *quadrat sampling method*. This involves subdividing a habitat into a large number of sampling areas (or quadrats) of equal size and shape and counting the number of individuals in randomly selected quadrats. If individuals are dispersed randomly in space (i.e., follow a Poisson distribution pattern), the total population size can then be determined by simply multiplying the average number per sampling area by the total area occupied by the population. Since most populations tend to show nonrandom dispersion patterns, this procedure can give rise to unreliable estimates of total size unless sampling is done over a sufficiently large area.

Another sampling technique frequently used in the study of mobile animal species is the *mark-recapture method*. Probably the simplest of these procedures is one which yields a population estimate known as the Lincoln (or Petersen) Index. This technique involves a preliminary trapping period in which animals are marked (dye patches, banding, ear notching, toe clipping, etc.) and then released into their natural environment. This is followed by a final trapping period (census period) in which the number of marked and unmarked animals are recorded. An estimate of the population size can then be made by using the ratio of marked to unmarked animals in each sample. If the number of recaptures is relatively large, this ratio can be given as

$$N/M = n/m \qquad \text{or} \qquad N = Mn/m$$

where N = the estimate of the total number of animals in the population, n = the number of animals trapped in the census period, M = the total number of marked animals, and m = the number of marked animals trapped during the census period. To illustrate numerically, suppose that 42 adults of the deer mouse, *Peromyscus maniculatus*, were captured during one night in traps dispersed over a habitat area of 10^4 square-meters. They were marked by toe-clipping and then released. During the next night, 39 adults were captured in the same traps of which 22 were marked. Upon substituting these values into the general formula, the population estimate from the Lincoln Index would then be $(42)(39)/22 = 74$ adults per 10^4 square-meters.

Implicit in the Lincoln Index is the assumption that marked animals do not show a tendency to avoid or seek out traps during the census period. It is also assumed that when animals are captured and marked, their release will result in a random mixing among the population as a whole. Neither assumption is always correct. One principle violation is that individuals of a population tend to behave quite differently toward a capturing device. For instance, some are trap-shy and are extremely difficult to capture; whereas others are trap-happy and behave as though they regard the trap as a good source of food and/ or a suitable form of shelter. In addition to these, other complications can arise if the population is rapidly changing in composition through births, deaths, or as a result of migration. As might be expected, however, more complex approaches have been developed to avoid or measure these effects. To illustrate how the mark-recapture technique can be used to estimate changes due to loss (deaths and emigration) and to dilution (births and immigration), we shall consider a stochastic *multiple-recapture method* devised by Jolly (1965). Suppose that animals are captured at several consecutive time periods, (e.g., on successive weeks, months, years, etc.). At the first trapping period, the number is recorded and the animals marked and released. At the second trapping period (first census period), the numbers of marked and unmarked animals are recorded and again marked and released. This procedure is repeated during the third trapping period (second census period), and so on, up to a final trapping period L. The data, including the time when each captured animal was last caught for analysis, can be tabulated as follows:

Trapping period (i)	Total captured (n_i)	Total released (s_i)	Time last captured (j)			
			1	2	3 .... $L-1$	
1	n_1	s_1				
2	n_2	s_2	m_{21}			
3	n_3	s_3	m_{31}	m_{32}		
4	n_4	s_4	m_{41}	m_{42}	m_{43}	
⋮	⋮	⋮	⋮	⋮	⋮	
L	n_L	s_L	$m_{L,1}$	$m_{L,2}$	$m_{L,3}$ .... $m_{L,L-1}$	

where, in general, m_{ij} is the number of animals captured in trapping period i which were last caught in trapping period j. The population density at period i can then be estimated as

$$N_i = M_i n_i / m_i$$

which is the simple Lincoln Index with m_i = the total number of marked animals recaptured at period i (i.e., $m_i = \sum_{j=1}^{i-1} m_{ij}$) and M_i = the estimate of the total number of marked animals in the population at period i. To compute M_i, one first has to determine the number of marked animals in the population which were not captured at period i. This number can be estimated by noting that its value is related to the numbers marked before time i, which are not captured during trapping period i but are caught subsequently (Z_i), as s_i is to the number of animals released from the ith sample which are subsequently recaptured (R_i). Hence, the number of marked animals not recaptured at period i is simply $s_i Z_i / R_i$. The estimate of the total number of marked animals can then be made:

$$M_i = s_i Z_i / R_i + m_i$$

The loss rate $(1 - \phi_i)$ due to deaths and emigration and the dilution rate (B_i) due to births and immigration can now be computed from consecutive estimates of N and M. To do so, first note that since the number of marked animals in the population can only decrease between successive trapping periods through mortality and emigration, the fraction surviving from time i to time $i+1$ can be calculated from the ratio of marked animals at these time periods:

$$\phi_i = M_{i+1}/(M_i - m_i + s_i)$$

where $M_i - m_i + s_i$ represents the total number of marked animals at time i after s_i are marked and released. The dilution rate during this same time interval can be estimated by subtracting the population size expected at time $i+1$, assuming no births and immigration, from the population size which is actually measured. We get

$$B_i = N_{i+1} - \phi_i (N_i - n_i + s_i)$$

Observe that reliable estimates can be made by this procedure even when the number released during a trapping period does not equal the number captured.

For a numerical example, suppose that an animal population is sampled and marked according to the above procedure, yielding the following results:

Trapping period	Total captured	Total released	Time last captured						
			1	2	3	4	5	6	7
1	73	73							
2	97	96	9						
3	101	90	3	14		Z_4			
4	99	95	4	7	10 /	R_4			
5	110	110	1	5	6	19			
6	111	110	0	3	2	10	20		
7	122	120	0	0	1	4	13	25	
8	136	135	1	0	0	3	7	16	23

The calculation of ϕ_4 and B_4 will serve to illustrate the desired data analysis. From the table, we get:

$$m_4 = 4 + 7 + 10 = 21; \quad m_5 = 1 + 5 + 6 + 19 = 31;$$

$$R_4 = 19 + 10 + 4 + 3 = 36; \quad R_5 = 20 + 13 + 7 = 40;$$

$$Z_4 = 1 + 5 + 6 + 3 + 2 + 1 + 1 = 19;$$

$$Z_5 = 3 + 2 + 10 + 4 + 3 + 1 + 1 = 24$$

Given that $s_4 = 95$ and $s_5 = 110$, the estimates of M_4 and M_5 can then be calculated as

$$M_4 = (95)(19)/36 + 21 = 71.1; \quad M_5 = (110)(24)/40 + 31 = 97.0$$

Hence,

$$N_4 = (71.1)(99)/21 = 335.2; \quad N_5 = (97)(110)/31 = 344.2$$

Employing the above values, we then compute

$$\phi_4 = 97/(71.1 - 21 + 95) = 0.668$$

$$B_4 = 344.2 - (0.668)(335.2 - 99 + 95) = 123.0$$

The variances of these estimates can be computed using the relationships developed by Jolly (1965). Jolly has shown that the variances are due both to stochastic fluctuations in population numbers and to errors of parameter estimation. As expected, errors in estimation tend to be minimal when the number of recaptures is large.

EXPONENTIAL GROWTH MODELS

Semelparity.   When the density of a population is small in comparison to the limit set by environmental conditions, growth tends to proceed exponentially with time. To illustrate this fundamental pattern of growth, first consider a population in which parents reproduce only once in their lifetime and are no longer present at the completion of the next reproductive cycle (semelparous reproduction). Such is the case in annual plants and many kinds of insects as well as for microorganisms where reproduction occurs by fission. Since the extent of a reproductive interval varies considerably for different species (from as small as 20 minutes for bacteria to as large as 17 years for cicadas), assume only for the purpose of deriving a model that reproduction occurs annually during discrete breeding seasons. In order to formulate this process mathematically, let $N_0, N_1, \ldots, N_{t-1}, N_t$ be the number after $0, 1, \ldots, t-1, t$ years of growth. Now, as long as conditions remain favorable, average yearly birth and death rates will remain the same so that the population increases each year by a constant multiple of the number present at the end of each reproductive period. Thus, after one year of growth, the size of the population will be $N_1 = \lambda N_0$, and after two years of growth, $N_2 = \lambda N_1 = \lambda^2 N_0$, and so on. Continuing this process over t years yields the general growth formula:

$$N_t = N_0 \lambda^t = N_0 e^{rt} \tag{8.6}$$

where λ now takes on the additional meaning of the factor by which a population increases from one generation to the next (one year in the above case). Thus, for example, if $\lambda = 10$, $N_0 = 10$, and $t = 5$ generations, the size of the resulting population would be $N_5 = (10)(10)^5 = 10^6$, illustrating the tremendous potential of such a species for numerical increase.

     Equation (8.6) provides a method to evaluate λ (or r) from experimental data. This is shown by rewriting the equation in logarithmic form as $\ln N_t = rt + \ln N_0$ for which a plot of $\ln N_t$ versus t will be a straight line with a slope equal to r. This graphical analysis has found practical use in microbiology for evaluating the growth rates of microorganisms and is illustrated by the plots in Figure 8.3. In the case of bacteria, exponential growth is extremely rapid and is essentially continuous throughout a reproductive cycle. Therefore, density measurements can be taken at rather short and somewhat arbitrary time intervals. Since $\lambda = 2$ for binary fission, an analysis of growth can then be made on the basis of the growth relation $N_t = N_0 2^{t/T_d} = N_0 e^{(\ln 2)t/T_d}$ where t is now a continuous variable and T_d, the doubling time. By comparision with equation (8.6), it can be seen that an evaluation of r will yield the doubling time by way of the relation $r = (\ln 2)/T_d$. This procedure is not as useful in the case of annual plants and animals, however. Not only is the method time consuming, it also requires that density measurements be made at identical or very similar stages of the life cycle. If not measured in this way, density changes which occur through mortality between successive breeding intervals could

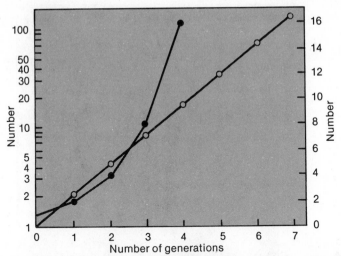

Figure 8.3. Exponential growth of bacterial populations, plotted on arithmetic (closed circles) and logarithmic (open circles) coordinates.

produce a highly irregular or saw-toothed growth curve that would be difficult to analyze. A more useful procedure is that of estimating λ from the fertility rate (m), or litter size, defined as the average number of female offspring produced per female at the reproductive age. Suppose that in a population with a 1:1 sex ratio, a constant fraction p of progeny survive to the reproductive age and then produce an average of m offspring per individual during each breeding season. By generation t, pN_t offspring will survive to sexual maturity. The number of births accrued during generation t (the finite birth rate) is then $B = mpN_t$; and since generations do not overlap, all members of this generation will die before their progeny reproduce. Hence, the total number of deaths during the generation interval (the finite death rate) must be $D = N_t$. Recalling now that, for a simple birth and death process, the growth rate is the difference between birth and death rates, ΔN_t must then be equal to $mpN_t - N_t = (mp - 1)N_t = (\lambda - 1)N_t$. Thus, we see that $\lambda = mp$, in this case, and can be measured directly from experimentally determined values of m and p. For example, suppose that the average litter size of an annual population is 20. If only 0.1 of the progeny survive to reach the reproductive age, this population will then increase by a factor of $\lambda = (20)(0.1) = 2$ in each yearly generation, assuming, of course, that conditions remain unchanged.

Iteroparity.   Exponential growth is also a potential characteristic of populations with overlapping generations where reproduction occurs several times in a lifetime (iteroparous reproduction). This is illustrated in Figure 8.4 by the increase in number of ring-necked pheasants (*Phasianus colchicus*) following their introduction on Protection Island, Washington. In this instance, however,

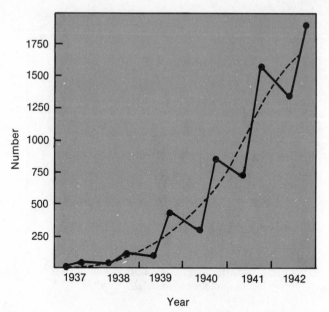

Figure 8.4.   Increase in the number of pheasant (*Phasianus colchicus*) on Protection Island, Washington, from 1937 to 1942. (Data from A.S. Einarsen. 1945. Murrelet 26:39.)

the data show a definite departure from pure geometric increase at high densities. Presumably, the population was approaching its environmental limit prior to the last recorded census. In such populations, a complete analysis of exponential growth is complicated because reproduction occurs in different age groups with different survivorship and fertility values. To illustrate, say that all members of a population have the potential to survive to a maximum attainable age of n years and produce offspring in discrete annual intervals starting at their minimum reproductive age. Designate the number of individuals born x years back at the start of breeding season t as $N_{x,t}$ and let their fertility rate and the fraction of this age group that survives during the year be m_x and p_x, respectively. If we now let p be the fraction of newborn that survive during their first year, the contribution of age x to the size of the population at the start of breeding season $t+1$ will then be $pm_xN_{x,t} + p_xN_{x,t} = (pm_x + p_x)N_{x,t}$. Hence, the total population at the start of $t+1$ will be the sum of $(pm_x + p_x)N_{x,t}$ over all age groups. Letting c_x represent the fraction of individuals of age x (i.e., $c_x = N_{x,t}/N_t$), the summation becomes

$$N_{t+1} = \sum_{x=1}^{n} (pm_x + p_x)N_{x,t} = \left[\sum_{x=1}^{n} (pm_x + p_x)c_x \right] N_t \qquad (8.7)$$

where values of m_x can be taken as zero for individuals in their prereproductive and postreproductive ages. Comparing this equation with (8.1), we see that the finite rate of increase of a seasonal-breeding population with overlapping generations can be given as

$$\lambda = \sum_{x=1}^{n} (pm_x + p_x)c_x \qquad (8.8)$$

Recalling that λ must be constant for a pure geometric increase in population size, it should be apparent that not only must pm_x and p_x remain constant for exponential growth, implying constant growth conditions, but c_x must stay the same as well. The problem of a constant age distribution will be considered in detail in a later section.

The value of iteroparity.   Lamont Cole (1954b) pointed out the fact that, despite the seeming advantage of repeated reproduction, little difference actually exists in reproductive potential between iteroparity and semelparity when growth proceeds under optimal conditions. This is shown by the following procedure. Assume that, in a perennial population, fertility and survivorship values are constant and independent of age and represent them as m and p, respectively. The maximum finite rate of increase for this perennial population is then $\lambda = (m + 1)p \sum_{x=1}^{n} c_x = (m + 1)p$. Comparing this relation with $\lambda = mp$ for an annual yields the rather surprising result that, whatever inherent advantage repeated reproduction might confer on a perennial population, the same growth potential could be achieved by an annual population with identical values of m and p by the addition of at most one offspring to the average litter size. Also note that, by letting λ_p represent the finite rate of increase of a perennial population and λ_a for an identical population but with an annual reproductive habit, the maximum fractional gain from repeated reproduction is then simply

$$(\lambda_p - \lambda_a)/\lambda_a = (m + 1)/m - 1 = 1/m$$

Thus, if $m = 2$, an annual could achieve a 50% gain in reproductive potential if its members had the chance of continued survival and reproduction. On the other hand, if $m = 20$, only a 5% gain could be achieved. It would appear from this analysis that an evolutionary switch, if physiologically possible, from an annual to a perennial mode of reproduction is of little adaptive significance when fertility rates are high as they often are in natural populations. If so little is gained by repeated reproduction, then why are perennial species so common? Several models have been proposed in recent years which directly bear on this question. It was first pointed out by Charnov and Schaffer (1973) that the assumption of equal adult and juvenile mortality rates (or no mortality for either, as in the case of Cole's original derivation) is unrealistic. Instead, survival probabilities among juveniles in natural populations tend to be lower than those of mature individuals. If we let p' represent a constant survival probability at maturity, the finite rate of increase for the perennial population can then be expressed as $\lambda_p = mp + p' = (m + p'/p)p$. The fractional gain from repeated reproduction is then

$$(\lambda_p - \lambda_a)/\lambda_a = (m + p'/p)/m - 1 = p'/mp$$

For example, the perennial buttercup *Ranunculus bulbosus*, for which $p = 0.05$, $m = 30$, and $p' = 0.8$, adds, in theory, $(0.8)/(30)(0.05)$, or about 53%, to its total reproductive output by reproducing over several seasons.

The relative adaptive value of iteroparity can also be viewed from the standpoint of environmental uncertainty and its effect on age-specific mortality rates (Schaffer and Gadgil, 1975). Suppose, to begin with, that only adult survivorship probabilities vary, equaling $p'(1 + s)$ in good years and $p'(1 - s)$ in bad. Because of the geometric nature of population increase, the finite rate of growth for the perennial population, when averaged over both good and bad years, will be given as the geometric mean

$$\lambda_p = [(mp + p' + sp')(mp + p' - sp')]^{1/2}$$
$$= [(mp+p')^2 - (sp')^2]^{1/2}$$

assuming, of course, that good and bad years contribute equally to the overall rate. The fractional gain from repeated reproduction will then be

$$(\lambda_p - \lambda_a)/\lambda_a = [(1 + p'/mp)^2 - (sp'/mp)^2]^{1/2} - 1$$

Clearly, increases in year-to-year variation, as measured by s, produce a reduction in the reproductive advantage of iteroparity even without a change in the average value of p'. Temporal variation in adult survivorship can, therefore, shift the balance in favor of the annual reproductive habit. Schaffer and Gadgil point out that this situation has probably been important in the evolutionary development of annual plants in desert environments. In this case, annuals are favored since seeds are better able to cope with the extreme aridity and unpredictable nature of this environment than mature plants.

Now suppose that only juvenile survivorship varies, having the same general pattern of $p(1 + s)$ in good years and $p(1 - s)$ in bad. In this case,

$$\lambda_a = [(mp)^2 (1 + s)(1 - s)]^{1/2} = [(mp)^2(1 - s^2)]^{1/2}$$

and

$$\lambda_p = [(mp + p')^2 - (mp)^2(s^2)]^{1/2}$$

The fractional gain now becomes

$$(\lambda_p - \lambda_a)/\lambda_a = [(1 + p'/mp)^2 - s^2]^{1/2}/[(1 - s^2)]^{1/2} - 1$$

Since $1/(1 - s^2)$ will increase without limit as s approaches unity, it is apparent that any increase in temporal variation in juvenile mortality will tend to favor a perennial mode of reproduction.

To summarize the preceding analyses: it is predicted that iteroparity will be favored when juvenile mortality is large in comparison to that of adults. Moreover, the reproductive advantage associated with repeated reproduction can be further enhanced by temporal variation in juvenile survivorship values. Thus, only by spreading reproduction out over several years, the population reduces the risk of total reproductive failure in any given year.

LIMITS TO POPULATION GROWTH

The growth equations developed in the previous sections describe the numerical consequences of reproduction under conditions suitable for exponential growth. It should be obvious, however, that no population can continue to increase in an exponential fashion for very long. Ultimately, population size will be limited by the supply of food or space if for no other reason.

Several approaches have been taken to model the effects of resource limitation on population growth. One of the first attempts was that of Lotka (1925) who expressed the growth rate of a single species population as a function of the entire set of limiting factors affecting numerical change. Thus, the growth rate of species i, for example, could be written as

$$\Delta N_i = F_i (N_1, N_2, N_3, \ldots; C_1, C_2, C_3, \ldots) \qquad (8.9)$$

where the Ns are variables such as species abundances, nutrient levels, concentrations of toxic by-products, etc. and the Cs compose a series of parameters such as growth rate constants, feeding efficiencies, and so forth, which would incorporate the effects of such factors as temperature and moisture on growth. Though the preceding expression serves as a helpful shorthand way of identifying the various factors which influence growth, it is completely impractical to measure all the different variables that would normally be included in this function. A far simpler and more useful starting point is to assume that all factors are constant except those which are altered in the intensity of their effects with a change in population density (the so-called responsive factors of Nicholson, 1954). This is a valid assumption to make when studying population growth under controlled laboratory conditions and serves as a useful first approximation for growth events in the field. Since the niche parameters which are now being considered are all functions of the size of the population in question, the growth relation then simplifies to $\Delta N = F(N)$. Such functions can usually be approximated by expressing them as infinite series. Thus, expanding $F(N)$ as a series of increasing powers of N, and writing ΔN as the derivative dN/dt, in the continuous case,

$$dN/dt = aN + bN^2 + cN^3 + \ldots \qquad (8.10)$$

where $a, b, c, \ldots$ are constants which can take on positive or negative values. These expressions can produce curves which mimic the growth of populations to any desired degree of accuracy by including a sufficient number of terms. The first two terms in the expansion have biological meaning. For instance, if only the first term is included in our growth formula, we have an expression which describes exponential growth. If we were to include the second, N-squared term, the equation would then additionally describe some form of interaction between organisms, being beneficial to growth if b is positive or detrimental when b is negative. The biological meaning of the higher terms is obscure. To provide further insight into the factors which affect population growth, what follows is a discussion of some specific models which describe the process reasonably well in a number of populations.

Sigmoid growth: the logistic model.   Many populations, when introduced into a limited environment, show a sigmoid pattern of growth that is typified by an S-shaped curve when population density is plotted arithmetically against time. Such a curve is illustrated in Figure 8.5 along with some frequently occurring modifications of this classic growth pattern. One may think of sigmoid

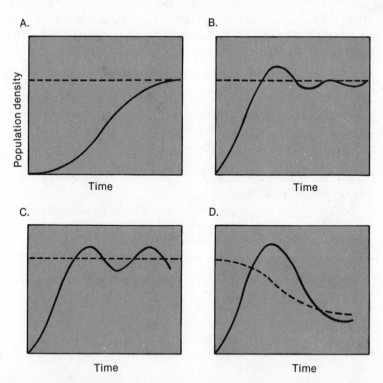

Figure 8.5.   Sigmoid growth (graph A) and several modifications (graphs B, C, and D). In each case the dashed line represents the upper limit to population density (carrying capacity). Graph D illustrates an overshoot-crash pattern which occurs when herbivores overgraze their range.

growth as the result of two opposing "forces": (1) the biotic potential, or in other words, the tendency of populations to grow exponentially at their maximum rate when conditions permit, and (2) the resistance imposed by environmental factors to unlimited growth, thus resulting in a gradual leveling off of population densities to an upper limit at which the growth rate is equal to zero. This upper limit to population density has been aptly called the *carrying capacity*, designated by the letter K.

In order to describe some of the conditions which are responsible for this sigmoid pattern of growth, consider a population which is limited by habitat space. Such a population might include a plant species that is limited by the number of safe microsites provided for its seeds on the soil surface, or by the supply of some nutrient such as phosphorus. It could also represent a group of herbivores limited by the availability of a certain type of vegetation or some species of microorganism that is limited by the accumulation of toxic products in its growth medium. In such cases, competition will take the form of crowding. For instance, a plant might crowd out the root systems of its competitors or deny sunlight to competitors by the shade it casts. Animals, on the other hand, may crowd out competitors by merely being more efficient in locating, acquiring, and metabolizing foodstuffs which are in limited supply.

One of the first attempts at describing the effects of crowding on growth rate was by way of the logistic equation mentioned in Chapter 1. This growth model is frequently derived for continuous breeders by assuming that the relative rate of growth, expressed by the derivative dN/Ndt, is directly proportional to the amount of some critical resource which is still available for use by the growing population. Suppose that a population of size N_o is introduced into a habitat area which is capable of supporting K individuals over an extended period of time. When the population reaches a size equal to N, the fraction of the available living space being used at that moment can be expressed as N/K. The fraction not in use, or in other words, the fractional amount that is capable of supporting additional members in the population, is then $1 - N/K = (K - N)/K$. Hence, we can write

$$dN/Ndt = d(\ln N)/dt = r(K - N)/K \tag{8.11}$$

where r is the intrinsic rate of increase under conditions of exponential growth (i.e., when N is small in comparison to K). Note that, if we let $r = a$ and $- r/K = b$, the expression can be written as $dN/dt = aN + bN^2$. The logistic equation is, therefore, an abbreviated version of (8.10) in which the series has been terminated after the N^2-term. An explicit solution to the logistic equation can be obtained by integrating over the limits of N_o at time 0 to N_t at time t. We get

$$N_t = N_o\, e^{rt}/[1 + (e^{rt} - 1)N_o/K] \tag{8.12}$$

When plotted as N_t versus t, this equation yields the smoothed version of the sigmoid growth curve. Note that, when t is close to zero and N_o is small in comparison to K, the population density is expected to rise exponentially according to the expression $N_t = N_o e^{rt}$. On the other hand, when t is large, N_t gradually approaches K, the upper asymptote. Equation (8.12) can also be written in linear form as

$$\ln[(K - N_t)/N_t] = \ln[(K - N_o)/N_o] - rt \tag{8.13}$$

Thus, if growth should follow the logistic pattern, a plot of $\ln[(K - N_t)/N_t]$ versus t will yield a straight line with a slope equal to r and an intercept of $\ln[(K - N_o)/N_o]$. When this procedure is used, K must first be estimated by eye from data points which appear to have reached the plateau level.

    The growth patterns of numerous populations have been studied in the laboratory where conditions can be monitored and kept reasonably constant. Many of these laboratory populations appear to follow the logistic pattern of growth quite well. The goodness-of-fit is illustrated in Figure 8.6 by the population growth curves of two diverse organisms of differing complexity.

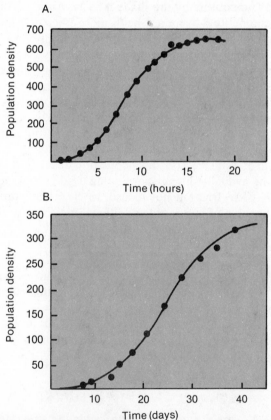

Figure 8.6. Sigmoid growth curves for (A) yeast cells, and (B) fruit flies (*Drosophila*). (Data from R. Pearl, 1927. Quart. Rev. Biol. 2: 532.)

The logistic model is derived in the form of a differential equation and is, therefore, limited in the strictest sense to populations which show continuous growth. When growth is seasonal, population changes can best be described by means of finite difference equations that attempt to relate the population size at one year (or generation) to that of the next. One approach is to employ the discrete analog of the logistic equation expressed in terms of the following difference equation

$$\Delta N_t = (\lambda - 1) N_t (1 - N_{t+1}/K) \tag{8.14}$$

or by way of the recurrence relation

$$N_{t+1} = \lambda N_t / [1 + (\lambda - 1) N_t/K] \tag{8.15}$$

In both expressions, N_{t+1}/N_t is the finite rate of increase which is realized under limited conditions and λ (or e^r) is the finite rate of increase under conditions of exponential growth. A general solution can be obtained by expressing (8.15) in terms of N_t and N_{t-1} and rewriting it as follows:

$$N_t/(K - N_t) = \lambda N_{t-1}/(K - N_{t-1}) = \lambda^t N_o/(K - N_o)$$

When solved for N_t, this solution is equivalent to equation (8.12).

The logistic equation and its discrete analog contain several simplifying assumptions which seriously limit their usefulness. For this reason, their broad application as growth models has been severely criticized in the past. Three of the more questionable assumptions are: (1) the environment is constant except for crowding effects: (2) the detrimental effects of crowding do not alter the age distribution of a population; and (3) the response to changes in population density is instantaneous (i.e., there are no time lags).

Asymmetrical growth curves.   The logistic growth equation predicts that the relative growth rate, dN/Ndt, decreases as growth proceeds as a linear function of N. This results in an S-shaped growth curve which is asymptotic at its ends to $N = 0$ and $N = K$ and having its point of inflection at $N = K/2$. When considered in its entirety, the logistic growth curve is symmetrical since rotation about the inflection point through 180° leaves the curve unchanged. Not all population growth fits this pattern. In a number of cases, inflection points have values that are less than $K/2$, giving rise to curves that are asymmetrical in appearance. In addition, measurements of dN/Ndt in such cases tend to decrease in a curvilinear manner with N. One example is shown in Figure 8.7. A growth model that has been used with some success in the past to model such situations is that of Gompertz (1825). This expression is derived by assuming that the relative rate of growth is proportional to the difference $\ln K - \ln N$ rather than $K - N$ as in the logistic model. This leads to the following equation:

$$dN/Ndt = d (\ln N)/dt = -b (\ln N/K) \tag{8.16}$$

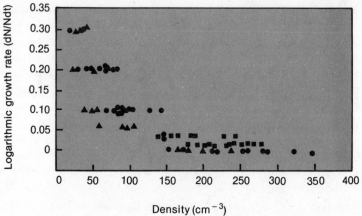

Figure 8.7. Logarithmic growth rate of *Daphnia magna* as a function of population density, illustrating a curvilinear function of density. Data from F.E. Smith. 1963. Ecology 44: 651.)

where b is a constant equal to $r/\ln K$. When integrated over the limits of N_o at time 0 to N_t at time t, this yields

$$N_t = Ke^{Ce^{-bt}} \tag{8.17}$$

in which $C = \ln(N_o/K)$. When plotted as N_t versus t, this expression produces an asymmetrical growth curve in which N_t is equal to N_o when $t = 0$ and approaches its upper asymptote, K, when t gets large. The inflection point of this curve is at K/e.

As in the case of the logistic model, the Gompertz growth function can also be expressed in terms of a finite difference equation. This can be written in either one of the following forms:

$$N_{t+1} = N_t\,(K/N_t)^b \quad \text{or} \quad \Delta\,(\ln N_t) = -b\,(\ln N_t/K) \tag{8.18}$$

A general solution is obtained by expressing the model in terms of N_t and N_{t-1} and rewriting it as follows:

$$\ln(N_t/K) = (1 - b)\ln(N_{t-1}/K) = (1 - b)^t \ln(N_o/K)$$

Thus, if b is small in value such that $(1 - b)^t$ can be taken essentially as e^{-bt}, the solution is the same as (8.17) which was obtained for a continuous model.

Other models have also been derived for populations showing asymmetric growth patterns (e.g., Smith, 1963). Most are three-parameter equations, however, requiring knowledge of a constant in addition to r and K. Although a few of these will be presented later in the text, none have received the widespread use of the simpler Gompertz function.

AGE STRUCTURE

In most populations with overlapping generations, reproductive rates tend to vary with the age of the individual. In human populations, for example, birth rates are highest in the early and mid-twenties, dropping to zero in the prereproductive and postreproductive ages. Death rates, on the other hand, are greatest during the first year and at old age. Thus, unless a constant fraction of the population is present in each age class, the growth rate will vary even when conditions remain the same. In order to gain a precise estimate of growth, we must then need to know the pertinent life history features affecting reproductive potential. These are usually summarized by way of life and fertility tables.

For the sake of clarity, assume that a population consists of $n+1$ age classes, each of unit interval, and possesses a fixed schedule of age-specific fertility and survival values. The survival and fertility schedule of this population can then be described in terms of a *cohort* (a group of individuals born at the same time) which is followed to the maximum attainable age (n). In order to construct an actual life table of this cohort, survivorship values must first be measured and tabulated. For convenience, we define the survivorship value of a cohort as

l_x = the proportion of an original cohort surviving from birth to age x

where the proportion surviving at birth (l_o) is unity. Once the survivorship values are known, they are often plotted against age to yield what is known as a *survivorship curve*. Three simple types of survivorship curves are shown by the semilogarithmic plots in Figure 8.8. Since different species vary considerably in their maximum attainable age, the graph is plotted as log l_x versus the fraction of the total life span to avoid confusion. The curve designated as type I illustrates survivorship data in which mortality is greatest during infancy

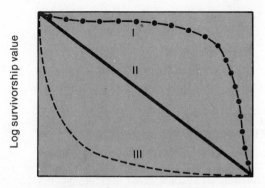

Fraction of total lifespan

Figure 8.8.   Three general types of survivorship curves. Curves are explained in text.

and at old age. This survivorship curve is typical of modern man. The type II curve, on the other hand, is typical of microbial populations and a number of birds. In this instance, l_x decreases as an exponential function of age. The final extreme is shown by the type III curve. In this case, mortality is greatest in the youngest age categories. The type III curve exemplifies the general survivorship pattern of many species of plants, invertebrates, and fishes. It should be pointed out that the survivorship curves of actual populations tend to vary in shape for different growth conditions. Thus, a survivorship curve should not be regarded as a fixed characteristic of a species, but rather as a temporary pattern which can be altered by environmental change. This dynamic view of a survivorship schedule is illustrated graphically in Figure 8.9 by the effects of increasing density on age-specific mortality in the water flea *Daphnia pulex*. As shown by this series of curves, there is at first a general increase in survivorship values with increasing density. This is eventually followed by an overall decrease in survival with the greatest mortality change occurring in the younger age groups.

In addition to l_x statistics, four other quantities are also used in life tables that can be calculated directly from survivorship data. They are defined as follows:

$d_x = l_x - l_{x+1}$ = the proportion of the total population dying in the age interval x to $x+1$.

$q_x = d_x/l_x$ = the proportion of survivors at age x dying in the age interval x to $x+1$.

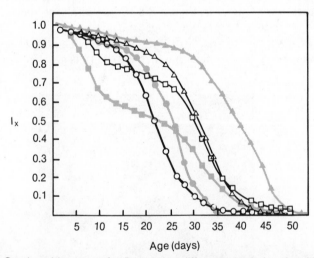

Figure 8.9. Survivorship curves for *D. pulex* at different population densities. Densities are (○) 1, (●) 2, (△) 4, (▲) 8, (□) 16, (■) 32 per ml. (Data from P.W. Frank, C.D. Boll, and R.W. Kelly. 1957. Physiol. Zool. 20: 287. Copyright 1957 by The University of Chicago. All rights reserved.)

$p_x = 1 - q_x$ = the proportion of survivors at age x surviving to reach age $x+1$.

e_x = the mean expectation of life for survivors at age x.

Of these derived statistics, e_x is by far the most difficult to compute and to conceptualize. As long as age intervals are sufficiently short, however, e_x can be calculated by first taking the sum of the mean number of survivors during an age interval, $\frac{1}{2}(l_x + l_{x+1})$, from x to the maximum attainable age, n. This yields the total lifetime remaining to the survivors at age x in units of individuals multiplied by time. To obtain the average lifetime remaining to each individual, we then simply divide by the number surviving at age x, l_x. This procedure yields

$$e_x = \frac{1}{l_x} \sum_{y=x}^{n} (l_y + l_{y+1})/2 \tag{8.19}$$

Thus, for example, if $l_{n-1} = 0.12$ and $l_n = 0.04$, an individual of age $n-1$ would have a mean expectation of life equal to $e_x = [\frac{1}{2}(0.12 + 0.04) + \frac{1}{2}(0.04 + 0)]/0.12 = 0.83$ age interval.

The preceding concepts apply directly to the construction of a survivorship schedule known as a *cohort life table* (also termed a horizontal life table). The data for a life table of this sort are compiled by recording the number of survivors in a cohort, followed until all of its members are dead. In practice, the development of cohort life tables is restricted to species with short lifespans. On the other hand, survivorship data for long-lived species, such as man, are compiled in the form of a *current life table* (or vertical life table). This is a life schedule which is based on a cross section of the population at one particular point in time. In this case, the l_x values are computed indirectly from age-specific death rates. As we shall see in the next section, the two types of life table only approach identity in populations which develop a stable age distribution under constant growth conditions; usually they are different.

Like the life table, a fertility table can be constructed from a single vital statistic. In this case, the statistic is the fertility rate defined as

m_x = the mean number of daughters born per unit time to each female at age x.

Two types of fertility schedules are shown in graphical form in Figure 8.10 Curve I in this plot is typical of organisms that reach sexual maturity at a definite age and continue to produce offspring throughout their remaining lifespan. Curve II, on the other hand, is typical of most higher organisms, including modern man. Here, birth rates are greatest shortly after the attainment of sexual maturity, decreasing to zero at old age. It should be emphasized that, like survivorship schedules, these curves merely represent two general patterns that might be expected to change when growth conditions vary. This is shown in Figure 8.11 by a plot of the measured m_x values for *Daphnia pulex* at different

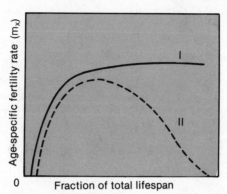

0   Fraction of total lifespan

Figure 8.10.   Two general types of fertility curves. Curves are explained in text.

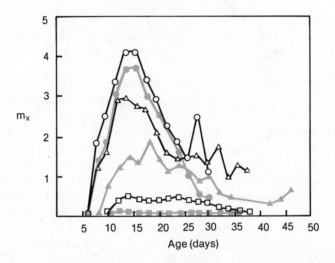

Figure 8.11.   Fertility schedule for *D. pulex* females at different population densities. Densities are (o) 1, (●) 2, (△) 4, (▲) 8, (□) 16, (■) 32 per ml. (Data from P.W. Frank, C.D. Boll, and R.W. Kelly. 1957. Physiol. Zool. 20: 287. Copyright 1957 by The University of Chicago. All rights reserved.)

population densities. It is apparent in this case that an increase in density results in a marked reduction in fertility of most ages as well as an increase in the age of first reproduction.

Once survivorship and fertility values are known for all age groups, they can then be incorporated into one compound $l_x m_x$ distribution, the construction of which is illustrated theoretically in Figure 8.12 and for an actual population in Figure 8.13. In the case of seasonal breeders (or any population which is arbitrarily grouped into age intervals of unit length), the distribution function is defined by the sum of all $l_x m_x$ products as

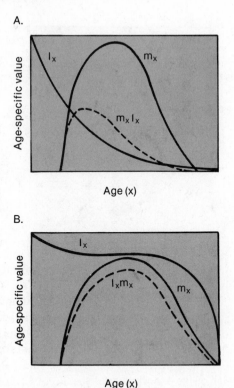

Figure 8.12. Two different types of $l_x m_x$ distributions. Graph A illustrates a case in which the shape of the distribution is strongly influenced by the sharp reduction in survival. Graph B shows a case in which the shape of the distribution is determined largely by changes in fertility.

$$R_o = \sum_{x=0}^{n} m_x l_x \qquad (8.20)$$

where R_o is termed the *net reproductive rate*. This is yet another growth parameter which measures the average number of daughters born to each female during her entire lifetime. To see how summing all $l_x m_x$ products will provide such information, suppose we start with a group of females born at time t and follow this cohort through several age intervals. Designate the number born at time t as $N_{0,t}$ and assume that they reproduce at regular yearly intervals. The number surviving at age 1 will be $l_1 N_{0,t}$; and if each surviving female produces an average of m_1 female offspring, the number of daughters produced by this cohort at age 1 is $m_1 l_1 N_{0,t}$. Similarly, the number of daughters produced by this cohort at age 2 is expected to be $m_2 l_2 N_{0,t}$; and at age 3, $m_3 l_3 N_{0,t}$; and so on. If we continue to follow this cohort, the total number of daughters that it will produce during its existence is then simply the sum of all possible $l_x m_x N_{0,t}$

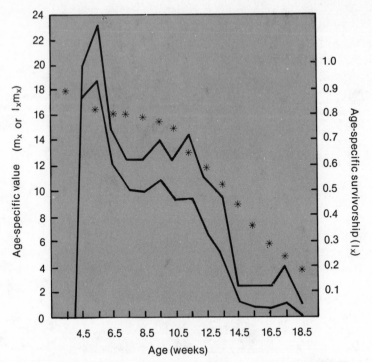

Figure 8.13. Distribution of age-specific survivorship (l_x, crosses) and fertility (m_x, upper curve), and their product, $l_x m_x$ (lower curve), for the rice weevil *Calandra oryzae*. (Data from L.C. Birch. 1948. J. Anim. Ecol. 17: 15.)

values. Thus, dividing this sum by $N_{0,t}$ gives the average number of daughters born to each member of the cohort during its lifetime, which is the same as equation (8.20). It should be apparent that, in the case of seasonal breeders with nonoverlapping generations, R_o is the same as the finite rate of increase when expressed in terms of a generation interval.

The mean of the $l_x m_x / R_o$ distribution, in which the sum of all values must equal one, is frequently taken as a measure of the generation time, T_c, of a population. Thus

$$T_c = \frac{1}{R_o} \sum_{x=0}^{n} x m_x l_x \qquad (8.21)$$

When defined in this way, the generation time represents the average reproductive age of females.

Stable age distribution.   The effects of age variation on population growth can be visualized most clearly for birth-pulse populations in which reproduction is highly seasonal and occurs during a short period each year. For the purpose of illustration, consider some hypothetical animal population with specific breeding seasons. Assume for convenience that individuals are counted shortly after the time of reproduction, where the offspring at time t, $N_{0,t}$, can be expressed as either young born alive, eggs laid, or young hatching, depending on the species studied. The population at time t can then be represented by the following table:

Age (x):	0	1	2	$\cdots$	n
Number ($N_{x,t}$):	$N_{0,t}$	$N_{1,t}$	$N_{2,t}$	$\cdots$	$N_{n,t}$
Survivorship value (l_x):	1	l_1	l_2	$\cdots$	l_n
Fertility rate (m_x):	0	m_1	m_2	$\cdots$	m_n

where $N_{0,t} + N_{1,t} + N_{2,t} + \ldots + N_{n,t} = N_t$, and where n is the maximum attainable age.

Now, assume that a number of individuals of a single reproductive age are introduced into a new and favorable environment. How will the presence of only a single reproductive age affect population growth? Considered over time, reproduction occurring in the represented age class will only contribute to newborn individuals of age 0; whereas, ages 1, 2, 3, etc. will begin to increase in size as a result of aging of individuals in younger age categories. Eventually, the rate of increase in the number born during each reproductive period will equal the rates of increase in other age classes as a result of aging and the proportion in each age category will remain constant. When this occurs, the population is said to have a *stable age distribution* and will increase under conditions of exponential growth according to the expression $N_t = N_o \lambda^t = N_o e^{rt}$.

The approach to a stable age distribution is illustrated in Table 8.2. This table gives the data on a hypothetical population with three age classes of one

TABLE 8.2.   The age distribution of a hypothetical population starting with 200 at age 1 and their 400 offspring at age 0. The population is enumerated after each breeding season. Survival values are assumed to be $p_0 = 0.5$, $p_1 = 0.5$, and $p_2 = 0$. Age-specific birth rates are $m_0 = 0$, $m_1 = 2$, and $m_2 = 2$.

Time (years) t	Age (years) 0	1	2	3	N_t	N_t/N_{t-1}
0	400	200	0	0	600	—
1	600	200	100	0	900	1.500
2	800	300	100	0	1200	1.333
3	1100	400	150	0	1650	1.375
4	1500	550	200	0	2250	1.364
5	2050	750	275	0	3075	1.367
6	2800	1025	375	0	4200	1.366
7	3825	1400	512	0	5737	1.366

year each. The population is assumed to have a single breeding season concentrated at the end of each year so that time intervals have the same duration as age intervals. The proportion surviving each year in the age intervals
0–1, 1–2, 2–3 years are $p_0 = 0.5$, $p_1 = 0.5$, and $p_2 = 0$; while the proportion
surviving from birth at 0, 1, and 2 years of age are $l_0 = 1$, $l_1 = 0.5$, and $l_2 = 0.25$.
Moreover, the age-specific birth rates are assumed to be $m_0 = 0$, $m_1 = 2$, and
$m_2 = 2$. From these values, the net reproductive rate can be calculated using
equation (8.20) as $R_o = (0.50)(2) + (0.25)(2) = 1.50$ and the generation time
can be obtained by equation (8.21) as $T_c = [(1)(0.50)(2) + (2)(0.25)(2)]/1.5$
$= 1.33$ years.

Starting with 600 individuals (200 one-year-olds and their offspring born
just prior to time zero), the population increased to 5,737 individuals over a
period of 7 years. During this period of growth, the finite rate of increase
(N_t/N_{t-1}) varied in an oscillatory manner gradually attaining a value of 1.366.
This is pictured graphically in Figure 8.14 in which the increase in total population size is plotted as $\ln N_t$ versus t. Note that, at first, there are oscillations
in population size. The oscillations are damped, however, and the data gradually
approach a straight-line relationship with a limiting slope of $r = 0.312$ per year.

The data in Table 8.2 are also shown in Figure 8.15, where the proportion
in each age category after 0, 3, and 6 years of growth is plotted in the form of
a histogram. As shown in this plot, little change occurs after 3 years of growth,
and by 6 years, the population age distribution has essentially reached a constant
proportion for each age.

The changes occurring in each age category during the approach to the

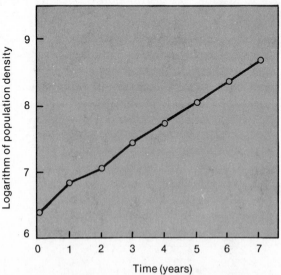

Figure 8.14.   A plot of the population given in Table 8.1 during seven years of growth.

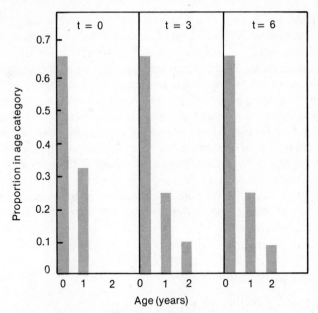

Figure 8.15. A plot of the age distribution given in Table 8.1 after 0, 3, and 6 years of growth.

stable age distribution can be predicted by first noting that, for three age classes, the number of offspring present at time t ($N_{0,t}$) can be expressed as

$$N_{0,t} = m_1 p_0 N_{0,t-1} + m_2 p_1 N_{1,t-1}$$

But $N_{1,t-1} = p_0 N_{0,t-2}$. Therefore, we can write

$$N_{0,t} = m_1 p_0 N_{0,t-1} + m_2 p_1 p_0 N_{0,t-2}$$

$$= m_1 l_1 N_{0,t-1} + m_2 l_2 N_{0,t-2}$$

(8.22)

or, generalizing for any number of ages,

$$N_{0,t} = \sum_{x=0}^{n} m_x l_x N_{0,t-x}$$

(8.23)

Note that equation (8.22) is a second-order difference equation of the form $x_{t+2} + bx_{t+1} + cx_t = 0$. Hence, its general solution is $N_{0,t} = k_1 \lambda_1^t + k_2 \lambda_2^t$ where

$$\lambda_1 = \tfrac{1}{2}m_1 l_1 + \tfrac{1}{2}\sqrt{(m_1 l_1)^2 + 4 m_2 l_2} \quad \text{and} \quad \lambda_2 = \tfrac{1}{2}m_1 l_1 - \tfrac{1}{2}\sqrt{(m_1 l_1)^2 + 4 m_2 l_2}$$

Solving for k_1 and k_2 from the initial conditions given in Table 8.2 and substituting the appropriate numbers in for m_x and l_x values, the specific solution for $N_{0,t}$ becomes

$$N_{0,t} = (430.9)(1.366)^t - (30.9)(-0.366)^t$$

where $\lambda_1 = 1.366$ and $\lambda_2 = -0.366$. Since λ_2 has a negative value, the system is expected to oscillate. But, since the absolute value of λ_2 is less than 1, the amplitude of these oscillations will diminish with time. Eventually, the effect of the second term in our solution will become negligible in comparison to the first, and the number born during each time interval will be expected to increase exponentially with an apparent finite rate of increase of $\lambda_1 = 1.366$. This is basically a mathematical verification of the pattern observed in Figure 8.14.

Once a stable age distribution is established, the number in each age category will increase under conditions of exponential growth according to the expression $N_t = N_o e^{rt}$. Therefore, the number born at time t can be expressed in terms of the number born at time $t-x$ by $N_{0,t} = e^{rx} N_{0,t-x}$ or, upon rearrangement, $N_{0,t-x} = N_{0,t} e^{-rx}$. Also note that during the intervening x time units, individuals born at time $t-x$ will age to form the survivors of age x at time t $(N_{x,t})$. Hence, we can write

$$N_{x,t} = l_x N_{0,t-x} = l_x N_{0,t} e^{-rx}$$

or, when divided by $N_t = \Sigma N_{x,t}$,

$$c_x = c_o l_x e^{-rx} = l_x e^{-rx} / \sum_{x=0}^{n} l_x e^{-rx} \qquad (8.24)$$

where $c_x = N_{x,t}/N_t$ and $c_o = N_{0,t}/N_t$. Since c_x is now the proportion of the total population at age x, the relationship described by equation (8.24) defines the stable age distribution. Note that when r is a large positive value, which is true for rapidly growing populations, the distribution will be skewed toward younger age categories. Also, observe that when $r = 0$, $c_x = c_o l_x$ and the stable age distribution will be basically similar to the survivorship curve for the population at that time. Some of the various kinds of stable age distributions which are predicted by equation (8.24) are illustrated graphically in Figure 8.16.

As the numerical example in Table 8.2 clearly demonstrates, the finite and intrinsic rates of increase are not only functions of physical conditions through survivorship and fertility values, but also depend on the initial age distribution even when conditions are basically uniform. Thus, fertility, survivorship, and age distributions must all be stationary if these growth parameters are to remain the same during successive breeding seasons. Once these conditions apply, the age distribution calculated from a cross-section of the population at one specific time will be the same as that computed from a cohort when followed throughout life. The finite and intrinsic rates of increase can then be estimated directly from experimentally determined values of l_x and m_x at one point in time without having to measure changes occurring over several reproductive intervals. The desired relationship can be obtained by letting $N_{0,t-x} = N_{0,t} e^{-rx}$ and substituting this expression into equation (8.23). The number of offspring at time t can then be written as

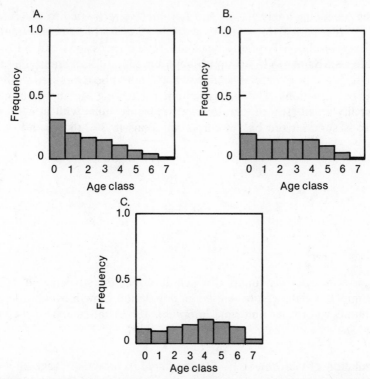

Figure 8.16. Three types of stationary age distributions represented in terms of seven age classes. Graph A illustrates the type of age distribution characteristic of an exponentially growing population ($r = 0.2$) having a high proportion in the younger age categories. Graph B represents a population that remains constant in size ($r = 0$). Graph C shows a declining population ($r = -0.2$) having a high proportion in the older age categories. All graphs were constructed using equation (8.24) and assuming the same l_x distribution.

$$N_{0,t} = \sum_{x=0}^{n} m_x l_x N_{0,t} e^{-rx}$$

Now dividing by $N_{0,t}$, we get

$$\sum_{x=0}^{n} m_x l_x e^{-rx} = 1 \qquad (8.25)$$

Given fertility and survivorship data, r can be calculated from this equation by a trial and error process (iterative solution). For example, using the l_x and m_x data given for the simple example in Table 8.2, we get $(0.50)(2)e^{-r} + (0.25)(2)e^{-2r} = 1$. The value of r that will satisfy the equality is 0.312, in agreement with the value obtained from the plot in Figure 8.14.

In the preceding analysis, m_x and l_x values were treated as discrete variables. The mathematical formulations are thus suited for birth-pulse populations in which reproduction is highly seasonal. The expressions can be used as reasonable approximations for continuous breeders if sufficient ages are included; but, for a more precise analysis, they should be expressed in the form of differential equations. This is easily done by making age and time intervals infinitesimally small (say of size dx) and replacing sums with integrals. This procedure is summarized by rewriting equations (8.20), (8.24) and (8.25) as follows:

$$\int_0^n m_x l_x \, dx = R_o$$

$$b l_x e^{-rx} = c_x$$

$$\int_0^n m_x l_x e^{-rx} dx = 1$$

where c_x is now a density function which describes the stable age distribution of a continuous breeder. Note that when population growth is continuous, the relative number born per unit time interval is the instantaneous birth rate per individual, b.

The calculation of vital rates.   One example of how the foregoing analysis is applied to real populations is represented in the work of Birch (1948) on the rice weevil *Calandra oryzae*. Table 8.3 shows m_x and l_x data obtained when *C. oryzae* is reared under conditions of exponential growth in wheat of 14% moisture content and at 29°C. Note that by summing the $l_x m_x$ products, the net reproductive rate is calculated as $R_o = 113.56$. Thus *C. oryzae* will multiply 113.56 times in each generation under these conditions. The value of r was then estimated by iteration using equation (8.25). It was found that r lies between 0.76 and 0.77 but so much closer to the former than the latter that 0.76 can be taken as a suitable approximation. Hence, $\lambda = e^r = 2.14$. It was also found from the various $m_x l_x e^{-rx}$ values that this value of r is determined to a large extent by the rate of oviposition in the first couple of weeks of adult life, being 56% accounted for by the first week of adulthood. The instantaneous birth and death rates were then obtained from the age distribution data given in the same table. As before, l_x values were taken at the mid-points of each age. It should be noted in this example, age is given from the time the egg is laid; and since eggs were not laid at regularly spaced times, population size will gradually increase during each week by a factor of e^r. The finite birth rate per individual (i.e., the number of eggs laid during an interval divided by the population size at the start of that interval) could then be expressed as $\beta = c_o e^r$. This results in the age distribution function

TABLE 8.3.   The life table and age distribution of *Calandra oryzae* at 29°C. The value of *r* is taken as 0.76.

Age (weeks)	l_x	m_x	$l_x m_x$	$l_x e^{-r(x+1)}$	Age Distribution
0.5	0.95	—	—	0.4443150	0.54740
1.5	0.90	—	—	0.1968300	0.24249
2.5	0.90	—	—	0.0920520	0.11341
3.5	0.90	—	—	0.0430470	0.05304
4.5	0.87	20.0	17.400	0.0194619	0.02398
5.5	0.83	23.0	19.090	0.0086818	0.01070
6.5	0.81	15.0	12.150	0.0039609	0.00488
7.5	0.80	12.5	10.000	0.0017944	0.00221
8.5	0.79	12.5	9.875	0.0008453	0.00104
9.5	0.77	14.0	10.780	0.0003850	0.00047
10.5	0.74	12.5	9.250	0.0001769	0.00022
11.5	0.66	14.5	9.570	0.0000726	0.00009
12.5	0.59	11.0	6.490	0.0000301	0.00004
13.5	0.52	9.5	4.940	0.0000125	0.00002
14.5	0.45	2.5	1.125	0.0000050	0.00001
15.5	0.36	2.5	0.900	—	—
16.5	0.29	2.5	0.800	—	—
17.5	0.25	4.0	1.000	—	—
18.5	0.19	1.0	0.190	—	—

$$R_o = 113.560 \quad 1/\beta = 0.8116704$$

Source: From L. C. Birch. The Intrinsic Rate of Natural Increase of an Insect Population. J. Anim. Ecol. 17: 15–26. 1948.

$$c_x = \beta l_x e^{-r(x+1)}$$

which was used in making these calculations. Since $\Sigma c_x = 1$, $1/\beta$ was calculated from the expression

$$1/\beta = \sum_{x=0}^{n} l_x e^{-r(x+1)}$$

as 0.81167. Therefore, $\beta = 1.23067$. The instantaneous birth rate can then be computed from $b = r\beta/(\lambda - 1)$ as 0.82. Finally, the instantaneous death rate is estimated from the difference $d = b - r$ as 0.06.

Reproductive value.   The relative success of a population in becoming established in a complex and changing environment often depends on its ability to reproduce and fill its ecological space as rapidly as possible. If such is the case, the relative "worth" of an individual would then depend on the number of offspring that it is capable of producing. Since age-specific survivorship values and fertility rates tend to vary, the relative contribution of an individual to the future success of the population will depend upon its age. This idea has been incorporated into a quantity referred to as the *reproductive value*, symbolized by v_x/v_o. One can define the reproductive value as the number of offspring that an individual of age x is expected to produce during the remainder of its lifespan, relative to an individual at age 0. In other words, if we removed an individual of a given age from a population, what effect would it have on the future growth of the population? The concept of reproductive value can be formulated mathematically by first obtaining an expression for the present number of offspring produced by individuals of age x and older, and then dividing this expression by the present number of individuals of age x. First of all, the number of offspring produced by individuals of age x and older at time t can be obtained by rewriting equation (8.23) as

$$N_{0,t} = \sum_{y=x}^{n} m_y l_y N_{0,t-y} = \sum_{y=x}^{n} m_y l_y N_{0,t} e^{-ry}$$

An appropriate expression for the present number of individuals of age x can be acquired by noting that the individuals of age x which are alive at time t are the survivors of the progeny born at time $t-x$. Hence, we can write

$$N_{x,t} = l_x N_{0,t-x} = l_x N_{0,t} e^{-rx}$$

Dividing the first equation by the second and then rearranging terms, we get our definition of the reproductive value as

$$v_x/v_o = \frac{e^{rx}}{l_x} \sum_{y=x}^{n} m_y l_y e^{-ry} \tag{8.26}$$

A plot of this equation is shown in Figure 8.17 for *Calandra oryzae* when grown at 29°C (Birch, 1948). The graph is subdivided into prereproductive and reproductive age categories for easier interpretation. First note that within the prereproductive age category, m_x values must be zero. Consequently, the summation term in equation (8.26) remains constant in this region of the graph. The initial rise in reproductive values is thus a consequence of the e^{rx}/l_x term. Since l_x values are approximately constant for the prereproductive ages (see Table 8.3), v_x/v_o tends to rise exponentially with age. Once the reproductive age category is reached, m_x values are greater than zero and reproductive values will decline due to the effect of the summation term, eventually reaching zero for postreproductive ages. As a result of the combined effects of age-specific survival and fertility, the removal of a female from such a population would thus have its greatest effect shortly after she has attained a reproductive age.

The concept of reproductive value has a number of important implications in population biology. Take predation as an example. From the standpoint of efficiency, a truly skillful predator would be one which could maximize its rate of exploitation without seriously reducing the productivity of its prey. This feat

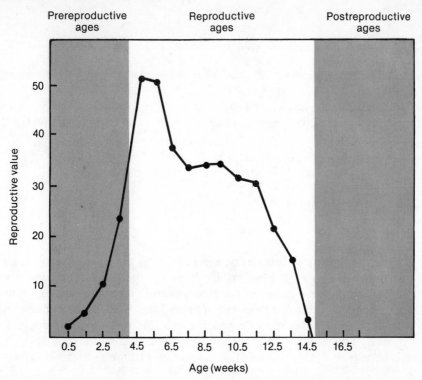

Figure 8.17. Plot of reproductive values for *Calandra oryzae*, based on data given in Table 8.3 and equation (8.26).

could be accomplished in theory if the predator were to select those individuals for consumption with the lowest reproductive values. This is what one generally observes since predators normally feed on the old, sick, and very young. Whether this is merely a coincidence or of basic importance to the evolution of predator-prey systems is still open to conjecture.

Leslie's model.   When more than three age groups are involved, the use of matrices greatly facilitates analyses of temporal changes in population size and structure. Such procedures were originally developed by Leslie (1945). For the readers who are not familiar with matrix algebra, we suggest that you first study the material in Appendix IV before proceeding, or simply skip to the next section.

     To illustrate the use of the Leslie matrix in population biology, we begin by analyzing the development of a stable age distribution in a population which is growing exponentially. The procedure is basically similar to that taken in the analysis of Table 8.2. Let the number of individuals of all ages in the population at time *t* be represented by the column matrix

$$\vec{N}_t = \begin{bmatrix} N_{0,t} \\ N_{1,t} \\ \vdots \\ N_{n,t} \end{bmatrix}$$

where, as before, $N_{x,t}$ designates the number of individuals of age x at time t and no individual can live longer than age n. Now, define the projection (Leslie) matrix, L, as

$$L = \begin{bmatrix} F_0 & F_1 & F_2 & \dots & F_{n-1} \\ p_0 & 0 & 0 & \dots & 0 \\ 0 & p_1 & 0 & \dots & 0 \\ \multicolumn{5}{c}{\dots\dots\dots\dots\dots\dots} \\ 0 & 0 & 0 & \dots & p_{n-1} \end{bmatrix}$$

where F_x is the fertility of females of age x and p_x is the fraction surviving the unit time interval x to $x+1$. The fertility F_x is not the same as m_x which was used earlier, but is the number of daughters born in one time unit to a female of age x that survives into the next unit of time. Thus, if births are concentrated into a short season at the end of each time unit, then F_x can be expressed as $F_x = p_x m_{x+1}$. The number of young born at time $t+1$ from females of age x at time t is then $p_x m_{x+1} N_{x,t}$. Hence, the population at time $t+x$ can be given as

$$\vec{N}_{t+1} = L\vec{N}_t = \begin{bmatrix} p_0 m_1 & p_1 m_2 & p_2 m_3 & \dots p_{n-1} m_n \\ p_0 & 0 & 0 & \dots 0 \\ 0 & p_1 & 0 & \dots 0 \\ \multicolumn{4}{c}{\dots\dots\dots\dots\dots\dots} \\ 0 & 0 & 0 & \dots p_{n-1} \end{bmatrix} \begin{bmatrix} N_{0,t} \\ N_{1,t} \\ N_{2,t} \\ \vdots \\ N_{n,t} \end{bmatrix}$$

Following the rules of matrix multiplication,

$$\vec{N}_{t+1} = \begin{bmatrix} p_0 m_1 N_{0,t} + p_1 m_2 N_{1,t} + \dots + p_{n-1} m_n N_{n}+_{,t} \\ p_0 N_{0,t} \\ p_1 N_{1,t} \\ \vdots \\ p_{n-1} N_{n-1,t} \end{bmatrix} = \begin{bmatrix} N_{0,t+1} \\ N_{1,t+1} \\ N_{2,t+1} \\ \vdots \\ N_{n,t+1} \end{bmatrix}$$

From this relationship, the population size and the proportion in each age group can be calculated at any time, regardless of whether a stable age distribution has been attained. Consider a hypothetical example of a population starting with 100 individuals of age 0 and 50 individuals of age 1 and with 5 possible age groups for which $p_0 = 0.75$, $p_1 = 0.5$, $p_2 = 0.25$, $p_3 = 0.1$ and $m_0 = 0$, $m_1 = 2$, $m_2 = 2$, $m_3 = 2$:

$$L = \begin{bmatrix} 1.5 & 1.0 & 0.5 & 0 \\ 0.75 & 0 & 0 & 0 \\ 0 & 0.5 & 0 & 0 \\ 0 & 0 & 0.25 & 0 \\ 0 & 0 & 0 & 0.1 \end{bmatrix} \text{ and } \overrightarrow{N_0} = \begin{bmatrix} 100 \\ 50 \\ 0 \\ 0 \\ 0 \end{bmatrix}$$

Then

$$\overrightarrow{N_1} = L\overrightarrow{N_0} = \begin{bmatrix} 1.5(100) + 1(50) + 0 + 0 + 0 \\ 0.75(100) \\ 0.5(50) \\ 0 \\ 0 \end{bmatrix} = \begin{bmatrix} 200 \\ 75 \\ 25 \\ 0 \\ 0 \end{bmatrix} ; N_1 = 300$$

Similarly,

$$\overrightarrow{N_2} = L\overrightarrow{N_1} = \begin{bmatrix} 1.5(200) + 1(75) + 0.5(25) + 0 + 0 \\ 0.75(200) \\ 0.5(75) \\ 0.25(25) \\ 0 \end{bmatrix} = \begin{bmatrix} 387.5 \\ 150 \\ 37.5 \\ 6.2 \\ 0 \end{bmatrix} ; N_2 = 581.2$$

Continuing this process, we get the data plotted in Figure 8.18. In this particular example, a stable age distribution is attained essentially by the seventh

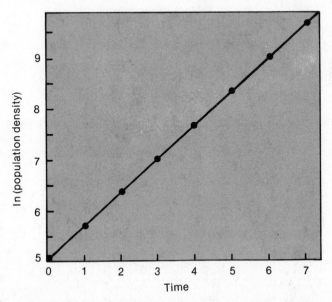

Figure 8.18.   Growth curve of a population starting with 100 individuals of age 0 and 50 of age 1, with 5 possible age groups, where p_x and m_x values are given in text.

unit interval. The population then increases exponentially with a finite rate $\lambda = 1.9371$ per unit interval.

This procedure is not restricted to an analysis of exponentially growing populations but can also be applied to populations which are growing in a limited environment. For example, suppose that age-specific survival is affected by an increase in population size in a manner expected in the logistic model. Furthermore, assume that density has the same effect on all age groups such that all age-specific survivorship values can be divided by the term $q_t = 1 + aN_t$. Population growth can then be described as $N_{t+1} = LQ_t^{-1} N_t$ where Q_t is the diagonal matrix

$$Q_t = \begin{bmatrix} q_t & 0 & 0 & \ldots & 0 \\ 0 & q_t & 0 & \ldots & 0 \\ 0 & 0 & q_t & \ldots & 0 \\ \hdotsfor{5} \\ 0 & 0 & 0 & \ldots & q_t \end{bmatrix}$$

As an example, let $a = 0.0002$. Then $q_0 = 1 + 0.0002(150) = 1.03$ and

$$Q_0^{-1} = \begin{bmatrix} 0.971 & 0 & 0 & \ldots & 0 \\ 0 & 0.971 & 0 & \ldots & 0 \\ 0 & 0 & 0.971 & \ldots & 0 \\ \hdotsfor{5} \\ 0 & 0 & 0 & \ldots & 0.971 \end{bmatrix}$$

Thus

$$\overrightarrow{N_1} = LQ_0^{-1}\overrightarrow{N_0} =$$

$$\begin{bmatrix} 1.5 & 1.0 & .50 & 0 \\ .75 & 0 & 0 & 0 \\ 0 & .50 & 0 & 0 \\ 0 & 0 & .25 & 0 \\ 0 & 0 & 0 & .10 \end{bmatrix} \begin{bmatrix} .971 & 0 & 0 & 0 & 0 \\ 0 & .971 & 0 & 0 & 0 \\ 0 & 0 & .971 & 0 & 0 \\ 0 & 0 & 0 & .971 & 0 \\ 0 & 0 & 0 & 0 & .971 \end{bmatrix} \begin{bmatrix} 100 \\ 50 \\ 0 \\ 0 \\ 0 \end{bmatrix}$$

$$= \begin{bmatrix} 194.2 \\ 72.8 \\ 24.3 \\ 0 \\ 0 \end{bmatrix} \text{; and } N_1 = 291.3$$

We also have $q_1 = 1 + 0.0002(291.3) = 1.058$. Thus,

$$\overrightarrow{N_2} = LQ_1^{-1}\overrightarrow{N_1} = L \begin{bmatrix} .945 & 0 & 0 & 0 & 0 \\ 0 & .945 & 0 & 0 & 0 \\ 0 & 0 & .945 & 0 & 0 \\ 0 & 0 & 0 & .945 & 0 \\ 0 & 0 & 0 & 0 & .945 \end{bmatrix} \begin{bmatrix} 194.2 \\ 72.8 \\ 24.3 \\ 0 \\ 0 \end{bmatrix} = \begin{bmatrix} 356.5 \\ 137.6 \\ 34.4 \\ 5.8 \\ 0 \end{bmatrix} \text{;}$$

and $N_2 = 534.3$.

The results of 14 such calculations are shown in Figure 8.19 by a plot of N_t versus time, and by a plot of the age distributions at times 0, 7, and 14 in Figure 8.20. Note that the results yield a sigmoid growth curve much like that predicted by the logistic model. Also note that as the population approaches its upper asymptote, its age distribution includes a greater proportion of older ages.

EVOLUTION OF DEMOGRAPHIC TRAITS

In population genetics theory, r (or R_0) is usually treated as a phenotypic parameter that will vary with the genetic makeup of the population. This means that populations of different genotypes or of different species will vary with respect to their intrinsic rates of increase even when grown under the same conditions. Since selection involves differential reproduction, those populations with the greatest r value will have the selective advantage and will form a greater proportion of the total in each generation of exponential growth. This is easily shown by considering two species populations with densities N_1 and N_2 and reproductive rates r_1 and r_2. Letting p_t be the proportion of species 1 at time t and p_0, the frequency at time zero, it can be seen that

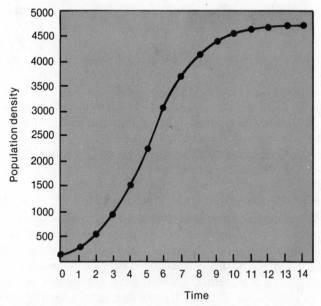

Figure 8.19.   Growth curve of a population starting with 100 individuals of age 0 and 50 of age 1, with 5 possible age groups, where p_x and m_x values are given in text. Growth is assumed to be limited by population density according to the expression $q_t = 1 + aN_t$ for all age groups, $a = 0.0002$.

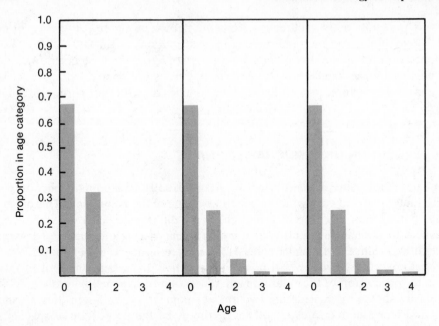

Figure 8.20.   Plot of the age distributions at times 0, 7, and 14, for the data shown in Figure 8.12.

$$p_t = N_{1,t}/(N_{1,t} + N_{2,t})$$

$$= N_{1,0}e^{r_1t}/(N_{1,0}e^{r_1t} + N_{2,0}e^{r_2t})$$

$$= p_o/[p_o + (1-p_o)e^{-(r_1-r_2)t}]$$

Thus, if $r_1 > r_2$, the proportion of species 1 will approach unity as its limiting asymptote. The reverse is true when $r_2 > r_1$. In either case, however, the mean for the combined population, which is $\bar{r} = r_1p + r_2(1-p)$, must increase in value. Hence, when growth proceeds exponentially, selection will tend to act so as to maximize the average intrinsic rate of growth.

r as a function of life history traits.   The adaptive changes which occur in r are achieved through a variety of different mechanisms. Many of these can be demonstrated by relating the intrinsic rate of increase to parameters describing the l_xm_x distribution. By far the simplest relationship is that between r, R_o, and T_c. To arrive at this expression, assume a population of continuous breeders undergoing exponential growth. Since conditions are constant, this population must increase R_o times its existing size in each generation. Thus, after t/T generations, the population size will be

$$N_t = N_oR_o^{t/T} = N_oe^{(\ln R_o)t/T} \tag{8.27}$$

where N_o is the density at $t/T = 0$ and T is a growth parameter roughly equal to the generation time (T_c) as defined by equation (8.21). By comparing this expression with previous equations for exponential growth and replacing T with T_c, it can then be seen that, to a reasonable approximation,

$$r = (\ln R_o)/T_c \tag{8.28}$$

This suggests two different, though not mutually exclusive, ways of increasing r: (1) by increasing the number of offspring per parent and (2) by reducing the average reproductive age of females. A more detailed analysis is made possible by relating R_o and T_c, in turn, to basic demographic characteristics. To help reduce mathematical complexity, assume m_x and l_x to be

$$m_x = m_A \quad \text{and} \quad l_x = l_o e^{-kx} = l_A e^{-ky}$$

where k is a constant and $y = x - A$, A being the age of first reproduction. These expressions are plotted in Figure 8.21 along with the resulting $m_x l_x$ distribution. Using these expressions to evaluate R_o, we get

$$R_o = m_A \int_A^W l_x dx$$

$$= m_A l_A \int_0^L e^{-ky} dy \tag{8.29}$$

$$= R_A(1 - e^{-kL})$$

where $R_A = m_A l_A / k$ and L is the length of reproductive life, that is, $L = W - A$, W being the age of last reproduction. Similarly, T in equation (8.27) can be approximated as

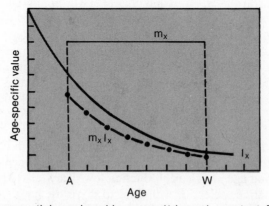

Figure 8.21. Exponential survivorship curve (l_x), and constant fertility (m_x), with the resulting $m_x l_x$ distribution. A and W are the ages of first and last reproduction, respectively.

$$T_c = (1/R_o) \int_A^W x l_x m_x dx$$

$$= (R_A/R_o) \left[\int_0^L yke^{-ky}dy + A \int_0^L ke^{-ky}dy \right] \tag{8.30}$$

$$= A + 1/k + L(1 - R_A/R_o)$$

It is apparent from the first expression that selection can act to increase R_o by an enlargement of litter size (increase m_A), through a reduction of prereproductive mortality (increase l_A), or by prolonging the length of reproductive life (lengthen L). Of course, any combination of these is also possible. The second solution indicates that selection can lower T_c by a reduction in development time (decrease A) and/or through a reduction in the total number of reproductive ages (decrease L). Note that, in either case, changing the length of reproductive life tends to have opposing effects on r. Hence, the ultimate strategy will depend to a large degree on initial conditions. For example, consider two hypothetical populations for which kL is small enough so that $R_o \simeq m_A l_A L$ and $T_c \simeq W$. In one population, let $R_o = 1.5$, $A = 1$, and $W = 2$ so that $r = \ln(1.5)/2 = 0.202$. In the second, assume that $R_o = 15$, $A = 1$, $W = 2$, and $r = \ln(15)/2 = 1.35$. Now suppose that a lengthening of reproductive lives doubles the age of last reproduction in both populations. This will triple the value of R_o and double T_c. Thus, its overall effect is to increase r in the first population, since after the change, $r = \ln(4.5)/4 = 0.375$, and decrease r in the second population, since its value is now $\ln(45)/4 = 0.950$. Obviously, a more effective approach to increasing r in the second population is through an increase in litter size or a reduction in the age of first reproduction (or both) if physiologically possible.

The relationship between r and T_c (or more precisely, T) for different values of R_o is shown in Figure 8.22. It can be seen that when R_o is large, changes in T_c have a profound effect on r; whereas, changes in T_c have little influence on the value of r when R_o is close to one. This suggests that organisms with large litters have more to gain by increasing r through a reduction in T_c, possibly by decreasing the prereproductive period. In contrast, slow maturing organisms with small litters are influenced little by changes in an already large value of T_c, and would benefit more from an increase in R_o by prolonging the length of reproductive life. Similar conclusions were drawn by Cole (1954b) and Lewontin (1965). Both found that r is quite sensitive to changes in the length of the prereproductive interval, with the greatest impact occurring when fertility is high and age at first reproduction low. They also pointed out that in a growing population, selection will tend to drive the length of the prereproductive period (i.e., development time) to its physiological minimum. This appears to be the case for many small organisms living in fluctuating environments. Many seasonal insects, for example, reproduce early in life, laying large

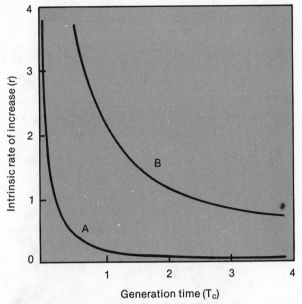

Figure 8.22.   Graph of the relationship $r = (\ln R_o)/T_c$ for different values of R_o. Graph A, $R_o = 1.2$, graph B, $R_o = 10$.

numbers of eggs after comparatively short development times. The effect of organism size on reproductive rate is shown in a general way by the log-log plot of r versus T_c in Figure 8.23. This has been investigated more fully by Fenchel (1974) who found r to be inversely proportional to body weight and directly proportional to metabolic rate per unit weight. The relationship between r and body weight (W, in grams) can be expressed as

$$r = kW^b$$

where b is about -0.275. Moreover, Fenchel found that k takes on three different values characteristic for unicellular organisms, poikilotherms, and homeotherms. The direct proportionality between r and metabolic rate per unit weight probably stems from the inverse relationship between metabolic activity and development time as measured by T_c.

Timing the amount of reproductive effort.   Selective increases in r cannot continue indefinitely. Eventually, an organism will be limited by the amount of energy that it can devote to reproductive effort. This is seen more clearly by assuming that an organism receives a maximum total amount of energy (E_t) of which E_r is devoted to reproduction, E_g to growth, and E_m to maintenance such that $E_t = E_r + E_g + E_m$. Since E_t is fixed, shunting more of the available energy to reproductive purposes can only reduce the amount that can be ex-

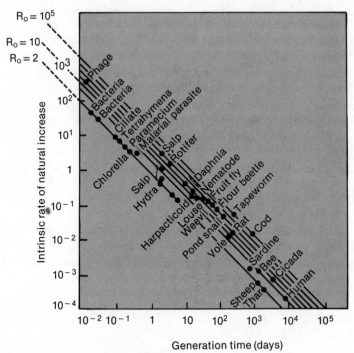

Figure 8.23.   Log-log plot of the intrinsic rate of natural increase (r) versus generation time (T_c) for a wide variety of organisms. The slopes represent different values of R_o. (From A.C. Heron. 1972. Oecologia 10: 294.)

pended on growth and maintenance and, hence, decrease the chances of survival. Data on some insects, for example, show an inverse relation between total fecundity and subsequent life span (Loschiaro, 1968), indicating that intensive reproduction can have a detrimental effect on future growth. Thus, each type of organism is faced with a trade-off between a large reproductive effort at an early age—which would maximize r—and less emphasis on reproduction. The question then arises as to how might the organism apportion this energy so as to optimize its return in the form of offspring. One approach which can be taken in an attempt to answer the question is the cost-benefit analysis of Schaffer (1974). This is based on the result of Fisher (1930) that r is maximized when the expression

$$m_x + p_x V_{x+1}$$

is maximal at every age. Here, $p_x = l_{x+1}/l_x$ while the value $V_{x+1} = v_{x+1}/v_o$ and is the reproductive value at age $x+1$. In this sum, m_x will tend to rise monotonically in value with an increase in the amount of reproductive effort. We can, therefore, regard m_x as the profit or benefit accrued to the population in increased current fecundity as a result of x-year-olds diverting a greater fraction of total energy to reproduction. On the other hand, $p_x V_{x+1}$ will decline with increasing effort and can be treated as the cost to the population in subsequent fertility and mortality losses. The sum of the two terms is simply the net gain to the population. This is shown by the plots in Figure 8.24. In graph A, both m_x and $p_x V_{x+1}$ curves are concave. Here, optimal reproductive effort is either 0 or 1 (i.e., all or none). The population could then benefit most, in theory, by either diverting all its resources into reproduction during the current season or skipping a year. In this case, single stage or semelparous reproduction would be selected for with maximum effort occurring at an early age, assuming r is to be maximized. In graph B, both m_x and $p_x V_{x+1}$ are convex. Optimal

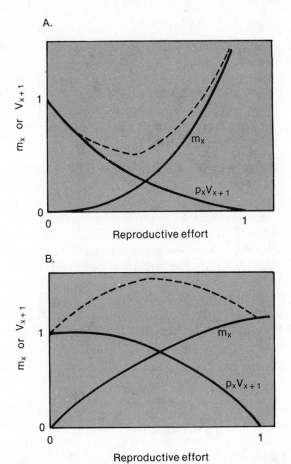

Figure 8.24.   Benefit (m_x) and cost $(p_x V_{x+1})$ as a function of reproductive effort. The resultant is shown by the dashed line and represents the net gain to the population.

effort is now intermediate. Thus, an iteroparous form of reproduction would be selected in which the amount of resources diverted to reproductive purposes is spread out over more than a single season. Since the cost function, $p_x V_{x+1}$, decreases with age, reproductive effort should increase with age in an iteroparous species. It is important to note that it may be possible to have two optima occurring, one intermediate and the other all-or-none, depending on the shapes of the cost and profit curves. Which strategy evolves in this situation depends on initial conditions, or, in other words, on the reproductive strategy of the ancestral population.

SEX DISTRIBUTION AND DEMOGRAPHY

In addition to age structure, sex distribution can also have a significant impact on population growth. For instance, if males outnumber females among adults, the growth rate will tend to decline below that predicted on the basis of total density, without regard to sex ratio. Excess males, under these conditions, would merely compete for essential resources without contributing directly to reproduction. On the other hand, an adult male-to-female ratio of less than one might actually enhance population growth in some ungulates, for example, where the normal breeding structure involves one reproducing male with a harem of females.

Like birth and death rates, sex ratio tends to vary with age. This is particularly well-documented in mammals where the sex ratio in older cohorts tends to be imbalanced in favor of females. In elk, for example, the prenatal ratio of males to females is 53:47, whereas the adult ratio is 23:77 (Cowan, 1950). Similar, though much less spectacular, changes occur in humans. Because of age-specific differences, the sex ratio is usually considered at up to four separate stages of the life cycle. The primary sex ratio is the ratio at conception. Variations in this ratio can either occur through the differential rate of production of X and Y sperm (meiotic drive) or as a result of their differential ability to achieve fertilization (gametic selection). Both are known to be under genetic control (i.e., Sandler and Novitsky, 1957). The secondary sex ratio, in turn, is the ratio at birth and is the one most often quoted for man. The secondary ratio may differ from that at fertilization as a consequence of differential viability during fetal development. Factors such as X-linked recessive, lethal mutations could be instrumental here since they do not affect the viability of heterozygous females. In addition to the preceding changes, decreases in the secondary sex ratio are known to occur with increasing parental age and with birth order. Finally, the tertiary and quaternary ratios are those measured at the respective stages of juveniles and adults. Again, the changes which occur are a result of differential mortality and are reflected in the differences existing in the male and female survivorship curves shown in Figure 8.25.

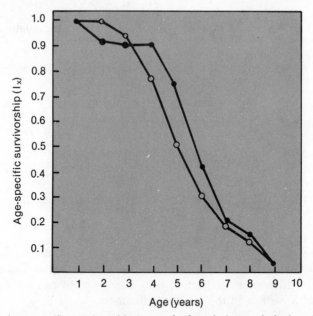

Figure 8.25. Age-specific survivorship curves for female (open circles) and male (closed circles) Red Dear (*Cervus elaphus*) on the Isle of Rhum, Scotland. The values of l_x are based on a cohort of 1,000 individuals of age 1 in 1957. The sex ratio is 1 at age 1, increases to 1.48 at age 5, and then decreases to slightly less than 1 at age 9. (Data from V.P.W. Lowe. 1969. J. Anim. Ecol. 38: 425.)

The evolution of sex ratio.   Despite the age-specific differences which exist in sex ratio, the average ratio tends to conform to the theoretical value of 1:1 expected on the basis of random chromosome segregation and equal viability of all sex genotypes. Since group variation in sex ratio is presumably under genetic control, it is reasonable to question the adaptive significance of maintaining a ratio which is typically near 1:1. A solution to this question was first proposed by Fisher in 1930 and the problem has since been studied by numerous other investigators with a variety of theoretical approaches (Shaw and Mohler, 1953; Bodmer and Edwards, 1960). The approach that we shall take is patterned after that of Crow and Kimura (1970).

Consider an annual population consisting of N individuals in which a proportion P are males and $Q = 1 - P$ are females at the time of conception. Now, suppose that within this population there exists a group of n individuals (group i) with a primary sex ratio that differs from the total, consisting of p males and $q = 1 - p$ females. Letting l_m and l_f be the survivorship fractions for males and females and m_m and m_f represent their respective fertilities, the life history of the group and that of the total population can be represented as follows:

	Group i		Total Population	
Generation t:	Males	Females	Males	Females
Number of				
Zygotes:	np	nq	NP	NQ
Adults:	npl_m	nql_f	NPl_m	NQl_f
Generation $t + 1$:				
Total Zygotes:	$n(pl_m m_m + ql_f m_f)$		$N(Pl_m m_m + Ql_f m_f)$	

From this, the finite rates of increase of the group (λ_i) and the total population (λ) become

$$\lambda_i = n(pl_m m_m + ql_f m_f)/n(p + q) = pl_m m_m + ql_f m_f$$

$$\lambda = N(Pl_m m_m + Ql_f m_f)/N(P + Q) = Pl_m m_m + Ql_f m_f$$

Assuming that type-specific differences in sex ratio are inherited, then, what will eventually happen to the primary ratios in the group and the total population? Due to differences in growth rate, the problem can be readily solved by comparing λ_i with λ in the following manner:

$$(\lambda_i - \lambda)/\lambda = (n_{t+1}/n_t - N_{t+1}/N_t)/(N_{t+1}/N_t)$$

$$= (n_{t+1}/N_{t+1} - n_t/N_t)/(n_t/N_t)$$

$$= \Delta f_i/f_i$$

where f_i is the existing frequency of group i. Now, recalling that the total contribution of males in the population must equal that of females, we see that $Pl_m m_m = Ql_f m_f$. Hence,

$$\Delta f_i/f_i = [(pl_m m_m + ql_f m_f) - (Pl_m m_m + Ql_f m_f)]/(Pl_m m_m + Ql_f m_f)$$

$$= p/2P + q/2Q - 1 \qquad\qquad (8.31)$$

$$= (p - P)(Q - P)/2PQ$$

Note that $\Delta f_i/f_i = 0$ when $p = P$ and when $P = Q = \frac{1}{2}$. This means that an equilibrium can only be established when the primary sex ratio in the group is the same as the total population, at which time, the primary sex ratio in the total population is 1:1. According to this model, differences existing in secondary, teritary, and quaternary ratios are merely a result of differential survival of males and females. Should the population compensate for losses occurring predominantly in one sex, however, by producing more offspring than normal, it is possible to shift the expected 1:1 ratio to a later age. In this case, the sex ratio would be equal at some age prior to the age when compensation is no longer possible (Crow and Kimura, 1970).

SOLVED EXAMPLE PROBLEMS

Parameters of Numerical Change

1. A certain continuously breeding rat population increases in size by a factor of 1.50 per month. The average relative monthly death rate is 0.50. Estimate the values of b and d for this population.

   solution   Since $\lambda = 1.50$ and $\delta = 0.50$, $\beta = \lambda - 1 + \delta = 1.00$. Similarly, $r = \ln \lambda = 0.40$. Thus, the instantaneous birth and death rates per individual can be calculated as $b = 0.4(1)/0.5 = 0.8$ and $d = 0.4(0.5)/0.5 = 0.4$.

2. Census taken on two different seasonally breeding populations on each of two consecutive years show the following:

	N_1	N_2
Pop. *A*	5,000	5,400
Pop. *B*	80	180

   Determine the value of r for each population and compare these values with the values of $\lambda - 1$.

   solution   In the more slowly growing population A, $\lambda = 5{,}400/5{,}000 = 1.08$ per year, so that $r = \ln \lambda = 0.0768$, which approximates the value of $\lambda - 1$. In contrast, the more rapidly growing population B gives $\lambda = 2.25$ and $r = \ln \lambda = 0.8101$, so that $\lambda - 1$ is not a good approximation of r.

3. Show that contemporary differences in survival and fertility in a continuously growing population also imply that the population will increase as though it possesses the average reproductive rate, $\bar{r}$.

   solution   If the densities of the n different kinds of individuals in the population at time t are $N_1, N_2, N_3, \ldots, N_n$, and their reproductive rates are $r_1, r_2, r_3, \ldots, r_n$, then

   $$dN_t/dt = r_1 N_1 + r_2 N_2 + r_3 N_3 + \ldots + r_n N_n$$

   $$= \sum_{i=1}^{n} r_i N_i = \bar{r} N_t, \quad \text{where} \quad \bar{r} = \sum_{i=1}^{n} r_i N_i / N_t$$

Estimating Population Parameters

4. The Lincoln-Peterson index is a biased estimate of population size. Unless all three parameters M, n, and m (particularly m) are large relative to the population density, the estimate of N made by the index may not be a good one. To help overcome this bias, Bailey (1951) has proposed a modified estimate given as $N' = M(n + 1)/(m + 1)$. Suppose that 20 organisms are trapped, marked, and released. A subsequent trapping yields 18 individuals, of which 5 are marked. Estimate the population size using both forms of the Lincoln-Peterson index.

solution   Applying the relationship $N = Mn/m$, the result is $N = (20)(18)/5 = 72$. Using Bailey's formula, we obtain $N' = (20)(19)/6 = 63$.

5. The marking-recapture method of estimating population size depends on the assumption that all captured individuals represent a random sample of the population. If this condition holds, the probability that a marked individual is recaptured x times during a series of successive trials will equal the Poisson term $p(x) = m^x e^{-m}/x!$, where m is the average number of times an individual is recaptured. Suppose that 500 marked individuals of a species of small mammals were released, and the number of times that each was recaptured was recorded:

Number of times recaptured:	0	1	2	3	4	5
Number of individuals:	434	39	14	9	3	1

(a) Is there a significant departure from randomness in the sampling procedure? (b) What explanations can be given for observed departures from randomness?
solution   (a) $m = [39 + 2(14) + 3(9) + 4(3) + 5]/500 = 0.22$. Working out the Poisson terms gives expected values (based on randomness) of 400.35, 88.08, 9.69, 0.71, 0.04, and 0.002. Comparison with observed numbers indicates a considerable departure from randomness ($\chi^2 > 200$). (b) The most marked departures are for the $x = 1$ (too low) and $x \geq 2$ (too high) classes, suggesting that perhaps some animals are trap-happy.

Exponential Growth Models
6. Consider a population of four seasonally breeding insects that invades a favorable ecological area and increases by a factor of five each generation. Calculate the number of individuals expected over each of the first several generations.
solution   Applying equation (8.6) with $N_o = 4$ and $\lambda = 5$, we obtain $N_1 = 20$, $N_2 = 100$, $N_3 = 500$, $N_4 = 2,500$, $N_5 = 12,500$, ..., $N_{10} = 9.8 \times 10^6$.

7. A particular population of iteroparous individuals, having constant fertility and survivorship values, reproduces at the rate of 10 offspring per female per year. Assume that young attain reproductive age in one year. Calculate the value of the finite rate of increase for this population and compare the growth potential of this population with that of a semelparous counterpart if (a) juvenile and adult survivorship per year are both 0.30, and if (b) juveniles have one-tenth the chance of survival as adults.
solution   Using the relationship $\lambda_p = mp + p'$, we obtain $\lambda_p = 0.30(11) = 3.30$ per year. The semelparous population would have $\lambda_a = mp = 3.0$, only 10% less than the iteroparous group. For the semelparous population to attain the reproductive potential of the iteroparous group, its value of m would have to be increased by p'/p per litter, which, if $p' = p$, means adding just one offspring per litter, so that $m = 11$ rather than 10. If $p' = 0.30$

and $p = 0.03$, then $\lambda_p = 0.60$ and $\lambda_a = 0.30$. Since $p'/p = 10$, 10 offspring would have to be added per litter for the semelparous population to have the reproductive potential of the iteroparous population. The semelparous population would be expected to double its reproductive value if it switched to reproducing over several seasons before death of adults.

Limits to Population Growth

8. Suppose that a population of 100 individuals is introduced into a habitat capable of supporting 5,000 individuals over a long period of time. The intrinsic exponential growth rate is $r = 0.50$ per unit time interval for this population. Using equation (8.12), calculate the population size expected over the first several time intervals and compare these values with those expected if growth is unlimited.

   solution   Calculating the number expected for unlimited growth, $N_o e^{rt}$, and the number expected for logistic growth, when $r = 0.50$ and $K = 5000$, we get:

t	$N_o e^{rt}$	$N_o e^{rt}/[1 + (e^{rt} - 1)N_o/K]$
1	164.9	162.8
2	271.8	262.8
3	448.2	419.0
4	738.9	655.2
5	1218.2	995.6
6	2008.6	1453.7
7	3311.5	2016.4
8	5459.8	2635.1
9	9001.7	3237.6
10	14841	3758.9
15	180800	4868.1
20	2202600	4988.9

   We see that over the first two or three time periods, growth is not much affected by resource utilization. Differences between unlimited and limited growth then become obvious. By time 8, the unlimited growth curve has passed 5,000 individuals but the logistic curve is only about halfway there. The rate of change in population size per unit time begins to decrease by this time, so that only after approximately 20 time intervals is the carrying capacity reached.

9. A hypothetical population of invertebrates, reared in the laboratory, gives the following population densities as a function of time:

t(days):	10	15	20	25	30	35
N_t:	30	80	140	180	200	200

   Is the population following a logistic growth pattern?

solution The carrying capacity, K, can be estimated as 200. Using the appropriate logarithmic transformation, points for a plot of $\ln[(K - N_t)/N_t]$ versus time are obtained:

t:	10	15	20	25	30	35
$\ln[(K - N_t)/N_t]$:	1.735	0.405	−0.848	−2.200	−	−

The plot is obviously linear, meaning that the logistic model fits the data. From the slope, $r = 0.262$. Extrapolation and evaluation of the intercept gives N_o of approximately 2 or 3 starting individuals.

10. Given a sigmoid growth curve, how could you determine whether a Gompertz model would be appropriate to describe the data?

solution Equation (8.17) can be transformed into a linear form by taking successive logarithms, giving $\ln(\ln N_t/K) = \ln C - bt$. Therefore, a plot of $\ln(\ln N_t/K)$ versus time yields a straight line with a slope equal to b. If the data exhibit a good fit to a linear relationship when plotted on these coordinates, then the Gompertz function can be used and r can be estimated as $b(\ln K)$.

Age Structure

11. Current life tables are constructed from age-specific death rates, M_x, defined as the number of deaths occurring during a unit time interval to individuals of age x, divided by the number of individuals alive in the age class at the mid-point of the time interval. Show that, if population size remains constant, l_x can be calculated from M_x by means of the recurrence relationship:

$$l_{x+1} = [(1 - \tfrac{1}{2}M_x)/(1 + \tfrac{1}{2}M_x)]\,l_x$$

solution By the above definition, M_x can be written as $d_x/\tfrac{1}{2}(l_x + l_{x+1})$. Since $d_x = l_x - l_{x+1}$, then $M_x = 2(l_x - l_{x+1})/(l_x + 1_{x+1})$ and solving for l_{x+1} gives the desired result.

12. Based on the curves in Figure 8.10, suggest simple mathematical models to describe the two fertility patterns.

solution We can express m_x as a simple function of L, the length of reproductive life, by the proportionalities:

case I: $m_x \propto 1 - e^{-kL}$ and   case II : $m_x \propto Le^{-kL}$

where $L = x - A$, A being the age of first reproduction, and k is a constant.

13. Lowe (1969) obtained the following life history data on a cohort of Red Deer aged one year in 1957:

age (yrs):	3	4	5	6	7	8	9
m_x:	0.311	0.278	0.302	0.400	0.476	0.358	0.447
l_x:	0.939	0.752	0.507	0.305	0.187	0.131	0.025

Determine the values of R_o and T_c for this population.

solution Applying equation (8.20), $R_o = \sum\limits_{x=0}^{n} l_x m_x = (0.311)(0.939) +$
$(0.278)(0.752) + \ldots + (0.477)(0.025) = 0.923$.

Using equation (8.21), T_c is calculated by first computing $\sum\limits_{x=0}^{n} x m_x l_x$
$= 3(0.939)(0.311) + 4(0.278)(0.752) + \ldots + 9(0.447)(0.025) = 4.307$,
so that $T_c = 4.307/0.923 = 4.67$ years.

14. From the life history data given in Table 8.2, calculate the stable age distribution expected for this population.
    solution The plot shown by Figure 8.14 gives the value of 0.312 for r so that $e^{-r} = 0.732$. Substituting this into equation (8.25), we obtain
    $$\sum_{x=0}^{n} l_x e^{-rx} = (1)(0.732)^0 + (0.5)(0.732)^1 + (0.25)(0.732)^2 = 1.50.$$ The
    proportions in the various age categories are then easily calculated as

    $c_o = 1/1.5 = 0.67;$ $\quad c_1 = 0.366/1.5 = 0.24;$ $\quad c_2 = 0.134/1.5 = 0.09$

    Comparison of these expected proportions with the numbers in each age group at year 7 in Table 8.2 verifies that, by this time, the population has essentially attained a stable age distribution.

15. A hypothetical population is composed of three age classes, the proportion surviving each of the first 2 years being 0.5. Age-specific birth rates are $m_o = 0$, $m_1 = 2$, and $m_2 = 1$. Estimate the value of r for this population.
    solution Applying equation (8.25), we obtain $(0.50)(2)e^{-r} + (0.25)(1)e^{-2r} = 1$, or $0.25e^{-2r} + e^{-r} - 1 = 0$. Writing e^{-r} as z, this is equivalent to the quadratic equation $0.25z^2 + z - 1 = 0$, which upon solving for z, gives $z = e^{-r} = 0.828$. Thus, $r = 0.189$.

16. A population starts with 200 individuals of age 0, 100 individuals of age 1, and 5 possible age groups, where $p_0 = 1$, $p_1 = 0.5$, $p_2 = 0.25$, $p_3 = 0.1$ and $m_0 = 0$, $m_1 = 2$, $m_2 = 3$, $m_3 = 2$. (a) Give the Leslie projection matrix for this population. (b) Calculate the age distribution and population size over the first 5 generations. Check whether a stable age distribution has been attained. (c) Estimate the value of r for the stable age distribution.

    solution (a)
    $$L = \begin{bmatrix} 2 & 1.5 & 0.5 & 0 \\ 1 & 0 & 0 & 0 \\ 0 & 0.5 & 0 & 0 \\ 0 & 0 & 0.25 & 0 \\ 0 & 0 & 0 & 0.1 \end{bmatrix}$$

(b)   Age

time	0	1	2	3	4	N_t	N_t/N_{t-1}
0	200	100	0	0	0	300	2.666
1	550	200	50	0	0	800	2.609
2	1425	550	100	12	0	2087	2.609
3	3725	1425	275	25	1	5451	2.612
4	9725	3725	712	69	2	14233	2.611
5	25394	9725	1862	178	7	37166	2.611

(c) $r = \ln(N_t/N_{t-1}) = \ln(2.611) = 0.959$.

17.   Comment on the significance of the reproductive value to natural selection.
      solution   Since v_x/v_o is a measure of the relative contribution of individ-
      uals to the next generation, selection will have its greatest impact on the
      genetic characteristics of a population when acting on ages with the largest
      reproductive value. Thus, for example, genes which cause the death of
      individuals with the largest v_x/v_o will be removed from the population
      faster than if mortality occurred at another age.

18.   Show that r can be written as $r = (1/A)\ln(l_A v_A/v_o)$, where A is the age
      of first reproduction, and l_A and v_A/v_o are the survivorship and reproductive
      values at that age.
      solution   Applying equation (8.26), the reproductive value at the age of
      first reproduction can be written as

      $$v_A/v_o = \frac{e^{rA}}{l_A} \sum_{y=0}^{L} m_y l_y e^{-ry}$$

      But $\sum\limits_{y=0}^{L} m_y l_y e^{-ry} = 1$, so that $l_A v_A/v_o = e^{rA}$, and rearranging after taking
      the ln gives the desired expression for r.

19.   Demonstrate that T_c and T [in equation (8.27)] are the same in value when
      r is small.
      solution   There are several approaches that can be taken, a simple one
      being to start with the relationship $\Sigma e^{-rx} l_x m_x = 1$. If r is small, $e^{-rx} \simeq$
      $1 - rx$ and we can write that $\Sigma (1 - rx) l_x m_x = 1$. Multiplying, we obtain
      $\Sigma l_x m_x - r \Sigma x l_x m_x = 1$. From equations (8.20) and (8.21), we then have
      $R_o - r R_o T_c = 1$. But, when r is quite small, $R_o - r R_o T_c \simeq R_o/(1 + r T_c)$
      so that $1 + r T_c = R_o$ and $T_c = (R_o - 1)/r$. Also, when r is small, the
      relationship between R_o and T becomes $R_o = e^{rT} \simeq 1 + rT$. Thus, $T = (R_o - 1)/r = T_c$.

PROBLEM EXERCISES

1.   The adults of a certain species of insect lay their eggs in the autumn and
     die before the eggs hatch during the following spring. A certain population

of 1,000 individuals was observed to increase to 1,400 during a period of one year. Predict the population size after (a) one more year; (b) five more years.

2. For a population of human lice undergoing exponential growth, the intrinsic rate of increase is 0.122 per day under optimal conditions. The generation time of a human louse is 31 days. Starting with 10 lice at time zero, how many would be present at the end of six generations of exponential growth?

3. Suppose that 100 pond snails, *Physa gyrina*, are introduced into a large area. If growth could continue at a constant relative rate for 10 weeks, we would expect to find a population size of up to 2.17×10^8 individuals. (a) What is the factor of increase in population size per day? (b) How many days are required for each doubling of population size?

4. Reconsider the population in Example Problem 7 where $m = 10$, $p' = 0.30$, and $p = 0.03$. If there is a 50% variation from year to year in juvenile survivorship, determine the reproductive advantage of iteroparity over semelparity.

5. The capture-per-unit-effort technique that can be used to estimate population size is based on counting the number of unmarked individuals in successive random samplings of the population. Captures are made at regular intervals over a period of time; the number of previously unmarked individuals is recorded for each sample and these individuals are then marked and the entire capture is returned to the population. The number of new (unmarked) organisms should decrease with each successive capture, following a linear relationship $y_t = - ax_t + b$, where y_t is the number of unmarked individuals in a sample taken at time t, and x_t is the cumulative catch through time t. Extrapolation to $y_t = 0$ gives an estimate of the population size. Suppose a hypothetical situation in which 100 individuals of a certain insect population were trapped daily, those previously unmarked were tallied and marked, and the catch then released into the general population, resulting in the following data:

t	number marked	number unmarked	cumulative catch
1	0	100	100
2	12	88	200
3	24	76	300
4	36	64	400
5	48	52	500

Construct a graph of data, with number unmarked plotted against cumulative catch, and estimate the total population size from the extrapolated x_t intercept.

6. Assume that 10 individuals of a uniform species population are introduced into an environment having a carrying capacity of 10^4. During the first 10

years of growth, the population increases by a factor of 100. If the population grows in accordance with the logistic equation, (a) at what time (in years) will dN/dt be maximum? (b) What will be the population size after 20 years of growth?

7. Twenty individuals of a particular species were introduced into a space-limited environment. During its initial (approximate) exponential growth phase, the population doubled in size every 23 years. By the time the population reached a size of 1,000 individuals, however, it took 30 years to double in size. If we assume that growth proceeds in a manner described by the logistic equation, (a) what is the carrying capacity of this environment? (b) What is the maximum growth rate (dN/dt) of this population in its limited environment? (c) At what time (in years) will the growth rate be maximum? (d) How long would it take an initial population of size 20 to reach the same growth rate as in (b) if growth were to continue at an exponential rate?

8. A commonly used technique for fitting the logistic equation to data collected on slowly growing populations is to approximate $d(\ln N_t)/dt$ by $\Delta(\ln N_t)/\Delta t$ and plot calculated values of $\Delta(\ln N_t)/\Delta t$ versus $\overline{N_G}$, where $\overline{N_G}$ is the geometric mean of population size during the specified time interval. Since, according to theory, $d(\ln N_t)/dt = r - rN_t/K$, this plotting procedure will yield estimates of r and K by determining the slope (r/K) and the intercept (r) of the line. For a numerical example, the population size of the United States from 1790 to 1950 is given below in column 2 at each of 20-year intervals (taken from U.S. census data). Determine the best fitting logistic curve for the data. (Note: Obviously the U.S. population now exceeds the carrying capacity value predicted by these data. The good fit of the population to a logistic growth curve prior to 1950 is not matched today.)

year	N_t	$(1/20)(\ln N_{t+20} - \ln N_t)$	$\overline{N_G}$
1790	3930000	0.0305	5334000
1810	7240000	0.0288	9654000
1830	12870000	0.0294	17280000
1850	23190000	0.0270	30390000
1870	39820000	0.0229	50060000
1890	62950000	0.0190	76090000
1910	91970000	0.0144	106630000
1930	122775000	0.0103	136000000
1950	150700000		

9. For a population composed of 100 individuals with $r = 0.5$ per unit time interval and $K = 5,000$, calculate the population sizes expected as the population approaches its limiting value if growth proceeds according to

the Gompertz function. Compare with the population in Example Problem 8.

10. Prove that the inflection point of the Gompertz growth function occurs at $N = K/e$.

11. The table below gives the probability of death at different ages in the U.S. population from 1959 to 1961:

Age (x)	Chance of death (d_x)
0 – 10	0.0323
10 – 20	0.0065
20 – 30	0.0121
30 – 40	0.0184
40 – 50	0.0431
50 – 60	0.0969
60 – 70	0.1821
70 – 80	0.2728
80 –	0.3358

(a) What is the probability that a person of age 40 will survive to reach age 50? (b) What is the mean expectation of life for individuals of age 20? Of age 40? Of age 60?

12. Consider the following data for a hypothetical seasonally breeding population:

Age (yrs)	l_x	m_x	Initial Size (at reproduction)
0	1.0	0	800
1	0.6	2	200
2	0.3	1	200
3	0.0	0	0

(a) What is the net reproductive rate of this population? (b) What is the generation time of this population? (c) Work out the age distribution over time, until the population approximates a stable age distribution (as in Table 8.2). (d) What is the intrinsic rate of increase expected under conditions of a stable age distribution? (e) How many years (approximately) will be required for the population to reach a stable age distribution?

13. Consider the definition of reproductive value as expressed by equation (8.26). (a) Show that the reproductive value of a cohort at birth is equal to one when the age distribution is stable. (b) Calculate the reproductive values of the various age classes in Problem 12. (c) It has been pointed out that the age of maximum reproductive value is also the age of greatest sensitivity to natural selection. Give an explanation for this correlation.

14. Krebs (1978) cites the following data from Connell (1970) on the barnacle *Balanus glandula*:

Age (yrs)	l_x	m_x	Age (yrs)	l_x	m_x
0	1.0	0	5	0.0000110	12700
1	0.0000620	4600	6	0.0000065	12700
2	0.0000340	8700	7	0.0000020	12700
3	0.0000200	11600	8	0.0000020	12700
4	0.0000155	12700			

Calculate the values of the net reproductive rate, the intrinsic rate of increase, the finite rate of increase, and the instantaneous birth and death rates of this population. Also determine the proportion expected in each age group for a stable age distribution.

15. Consider again the starting population of Example Problem 16. Assume that a density-related factor limits growth by affecting survival in a linear fashion, such that all survivorship values are divided by the term $1 + aN_t$ in which $a = 0.0002$. Determine the age distribution and population size over the first 9 generations. Plot N_t versus time.

16. The following is a representation of the female age distribution of the human population in the United States in 1970:

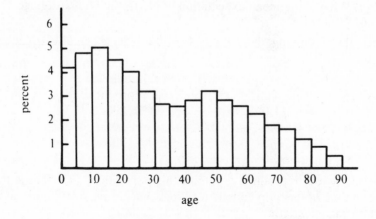

(a) Has the population attained a stable age distribution? (b) From your knowledge of past demographic trends, what specific factors have contributed to the "unevenness" of the age distribution? (c) Demographic projections indicate that if females start to bear children at replacement level ($R_o = 1$) now, the U.S. population would not stop growing for another 70 years or so, assuming no migration. What explanations can be given for this time delay in attaining zero population growth? (d) Demographers often express birth rates in terms of total fertility rates, defined as the projected average number of infants born to each female during her lifetime. At replacement level, the total fertility rate would be approximately equal to 2.1 for the U.S. population. Why is the index greater than 2 at replacement level?

9

Population Fluctuations
and Regulatory Mechanisms

The logistic pattern of growth described in an earlier chapter is closely approximated by many populations while under controlled laboratory conditions. It may also be approached by some populations in the field that are invading new habitats. Most populations in nature, however, are not in the process of filling unoccupied habitats but are already established residents of biotic communities. In such cases, population size is usually observed to fluctuate about some average value; this value, in turn, showing little tendency for any long-term growth or decline. Those observations quite obviously lead to questions about the nature of the factors responsible for density variation and for maintaining a relatively constant average size. In an attempt to answer these questions, we begin our discussion with an analysis of population fluctuations. This is then followed by a consideration of the nature of density regulation, including some of the hypotheses that have been proposed to account for it.

DENSITY FLUCTUATIONS AND THEIR ANALYSIS

Ecological studies have confirmed that most natural populations tend to fluctuate in size. But as Lack (1954) points out, the magnitude of growth and decline tends to be far less than might be expected on the basis of reproductive potential alone. For example, insect populations are known that can fluctuate in density by as much as 1,000-fold or more over several seasons (Varley, 1949). Yet, this is small when compared to their innate capacity for numerical change. In contrast, other organisms, such as large mammals, show much smaller variation in numbers, rarely differing by more than a magnitude over several years.

The fact that populations fluctuate in size tends to complicate the analysis of census data. Williamson (1972) has emphasized the advantages of subjecting all census data to logarithmic transformation. Other than the tendency of populations to increase exponentially when conditions permit, there are three main reasons for the conversion to logarithms. First of all, logarithmic transformations represent a convenient way of organizing highly variable data in compact form. This is particularly useful when populations vary by several orders of magnitude during the census period. Secondly, if two populations are compared which fluctuate in size by the same relative magnitude, changes in the logarithms of their densities ($\Delta \ln N_t$) will be the same, while the corresponding arithmetic changes (ΔN_t) will tend to differ, depending on the existing sizes of the populations being considered. For a numerical example, say that one population increases by a factor of ten from 100 to 1,000 while another increases by the same factor but from 10 to 100. Obviously $\Delta \ln N_t$ is the same for both populations, being equal to $\ln(10)$. In contrast, ΔN_t is equal to 900 for the first population and 90 for the second. This basic principle is also shown by the population fluctuations graphed in Figure 9.1. Note that plotting census data on arithmetic coordinates will tend to give the impression that the most abundant population is also the most variable. The third reason for a logarithmic transformation is the fact that population changes tend to be more symmetrically distributed when plotted on a logarithmic scale. This is frequently observed when several estimates of population size are made at different times and then plotted in the form of a frequency distribution, such as number of observations as a function of measured density. The resulting graph is often highly skewed, having the general appearance of a lognormal function. Converting the density estimates to logarithmic values transforms the plot into one that is more normally distributed in appearance.

Several statistical measures of density variation (or stability) have been proposed. Possibly the most frequently used is the coefficient of variation defined as $CV = \sqrt{V(N)}/\overline{N}$, where $\overline{N}$ and $V(N)$ are the mean and variance of N. This yields the relative variation of N about the mean. When a logarithmic transformation is used, a more suitable measure of variation is the coefficient of fluctuation, CF. This measure is computed from the standard deviation of the logarithm of population density, termed the logarithmic deviation, D_l. Letting $N_1, N_2, N_3, \ldots, N_t$ be the measurements of population density at t different times, the logarithmic deviation can be calculated from sample data as

$$D_l = \sqrt{\sum_{i=1}^{t} (\log N_i - \log \overline{N}_G)^2/(t-1)}$$

where $\overline{N}_G$ is the geometric mean density. From this we get the coefficient of fluctuation by taking the antilogarithm:

$$CF = \text{antilog } D_l$$

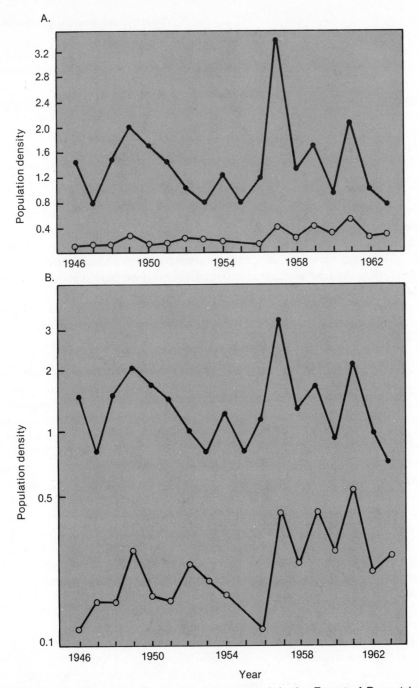

Figure 9.1. Density of breeding pairs of the great tit in the Forest of Dean (closed circles), England, and de Hoge Veluwe (open circles), Netherlands, plotted on arithmetic (A) and logarithmic (B) coordinates. (Data from D. Lack. 1966. *Population Studies of Birds*.)

Unlike the coefficient of variation which is used to indicate variation in plus and minus values above and below the mean, the coefficient of fluctuation gives the multiplicative factor by which the density is expected to vary from some minimum to maximum value. Thus, if we assume that log-density variation conforms to a normal distribution, we would expect to observe, about 95% of the time, a maximum change in log N of 4 times the logarithmic deviation (2 standard deviation units above and below the mean, log $\overline{N}_G$). This corresponds to a total change in N by a factor of $(CF)^4 =$ antilog $4D_l$. When annual observations are made, this relative change would represent the factor by which the population might vary from its minimum to maximum value over a twenty-year period, since only a fraction of 0.05 or 1 out of every 20 observations is expected to fall outside this range. In the case of the fluctuations in Figure 9.1, both populations are about equal in variability, having CF values of approximately 1.5. This would indicate that maximum density changes about the mean of $N/(1.5)^2$ to $N(1.5)^2$ are expected over a twenty-year period at both locations. Other CF values that have been calculated from data on natural populations range from almost 1 in very stable populations (e.g., the oyster catcher, *Haematopus ostralegus*, $CF = 1.15$), to values greater than 10 in some highly variable insect populations.

Seasonal fluctuations.   Seasonal variation in environmental conditions is among the major causes of population change. It is, therefore, convenient at the outset to separate such density changes from those which are unrelated to any seasonal cycle. In temperate regions, seasonal changes in population density are usually correlated with the cyclic variation in temperature, while in the tropics, seasonal fluctuations generally occur in response to an alteration of wet and dry periods. Regardless of the geographic locality, however, populations tend to respond to seasonal changes in resource quality and abundance by decreasing when these resources are scarce or present in an unsuitable form, and by increasing during favorable periods when required resources are in excess.

Various types of seasonal fluctuations are shown graphically in Figure 9.2. Graph (A) represents a population with discrete nonoverlapping generations in synchrony with the environmental cycle. This pattern is common among insects and herbaceous plants which are at the mercy of their physical environments. The life cycles of such organisms are correlated with climatic changes with mature forms participating in reproduction during favorable seasons and escaping the harsh environmental conditions at other times by remaining in a temporary state of dormancy (eggs, seeds, pupae, etc.). Graph (B), on the other hand, illustrates the case of many seasonal breeding animal populations with overlapping generations, as well as some perennial plants. In this case, critical stages in the development of the young generally coincide with the season which is most favorable in terms of food and climate. Finally, graphs (C) and (D) picture two possible responses of a continuously breeding population under conditions of seasonality. If the natural response time, T_R, of the population

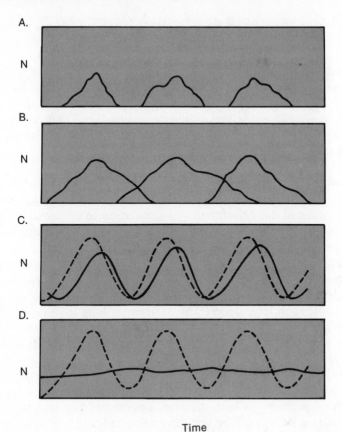

Time

Figure 9.2. Responses of populations to seasonal fluctuations. The number of adults in each population is plotted as a function of yearly seasonal cycles. Dashed lines in (C) and (D) represent the environmental cycle.

is short in comparison to the environmental cycle (i.e., a comparatively short generation time), the population tends to "track" the environmental variations (graph (C)). For example, suppose that the environmental cycle follows a sine curve. The carrying capacity of the population could then be modeled as

$$K = K_o + K_1 \cos(2\pi\, t/\tau)$$

where τ is the period of the environmental oscillations. Conversely, if T_R is long in comparison to the seasonal cycle, then the carrying capacity becomes approximately (May, 1976)

$$K = \sqrt{K_o^2 - K_1^2}$$

Thus, when environmental fluctuations are short in comparison to the generation time, the population will maintain itself at a level less than the average, K_o, expected in the preceding case.

TIME LAGS, UNSTABLE AGE DISTRIBUTIONS, AND CHANCE

Population fluctuations can occur in theory even in the absence of environmental change. They include random or stochastic fluctuations and density oscillations resulting from time delays in the response of organisms to the detrimental effects of crowding. Since these density changes can only be predicted on theoretical grounds, what follows is a description of some of the models that have been used to account for them.

Time-lag models of population change.   Since biological systems rarely, if ever, respond instantaneously to change, it is reasonable to expect that time delays will occur in the adjustment of a population to its resource supply. For instance, maturation delays might develop, depending on the time required for newborn offspring to increase in size and in feeding capacity and attain the same space requirements of breeding adults. This would serve to postpone the full impact of crowding on birth and death rates. Time lags could also result from delays in the adjustment of age structure to departures from a stable age distribution. If such time delays are sufficiently long in duration, one might expect the population to "overshoot" its equilibrium level and recover in an oscillatory pattern. An analysis of the behavior of a population about the carrying capacity level could then provide valuable information on how rapidly it responds to density checks with appropriate changes in survival and fertility.

Probably the simplest approach to take is to analyze time-lag effects on the growth of populations with discrete, nonoverlapping generations. In this case, maturation delays will be one generation in length. This is illustrated by expressing the growth equation in either one of the following general forms:

$$N_{t+1} = N_t f(N_t) \qquad \text{or} \qquad \Delta(\ln N_t) = \ln f(N_t)$$

where $f(N_t)$ is some decreasing nonlinear function of density. These equations predict that reproductive success will be inversely related to the density at the start of the reproductive cycle. Hence, N_{t+1}/N_t and $\Delta(\ln N_t)$ will decrease as growth proceeds and competition for living space becomes more intense.

Some possible effects of a one-generation time delay on population growth are shown in Figure 9.3 by way of plots of a growth relation that has been frequently used in population biology to describe birth-pulse populations. The model is commonly expressed in either one of the following equations:

$$N_{t+1} = N_t e^{r(1 - N_t/K)} \qquad \text{or} \qquad \Delta(\ln N_t) = r(1 - N_t/K) \qquad \textbf{(9.1)}$$

with a characteristic return time of $T_R = 1/r$. Each curve in Figure 9.3 represents a plot of the population densities in two consecutive generations, N_{t+1} and N_t. This is a plotting procedure used extensively by Ricker (1954) to form what is known as a *reproductive curve*. Such curves are drawn in reference to a diagonal 45° line ($N_{t+1} = N_t$) which corresponds to the replacement level of the popu-

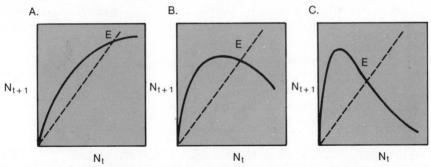

Figure 9.3.   Graphical analysis of density-dependent regulation. The graphs represent a series of reproductive curves illustrating the effects of crowding on consecutive generations. An equilibrium is established where each curve intersects the 45° diagonal.

lation. When the reproductive curve lies above the replacement line, the population is increasing in size, since N_{t+1} is then greater than N_t. Conversely, the population undergoes a reduction in size when the curve lies below the line. Consequently, point K on the graph represents an attracting equilibrium point in that, if the system is disturbed in any way, the population density will eventually return to this equilibrium value. At this point, both N_{t+1} and N_t will equal the carrying capacity level. Observe that when r is large (i.e., T_R is small), the curve has a critical point, $dN_{t+1}/dN_t = 0$, to the left of the replacement line. As was pointed out in Chapter 1, this is a characteristic feature of many finite difference models in which the effect of the time delay is sufficiently great to produce an overshoot of the equilibrium. The overshoot will then lead to oscillations about K. Such density changes are shown in Figure 9.4 in terms of a plot of the time course of a population as predicted from a trace of its reproductive curve.

The influence of r on the tendency of a population to oscillate can be shown more directly by expressing equation (9.1) in terms of its derivative. We get

$$dN_{t+1}/dN_t = (1 - rN_t/K) \exp r(1 - N_t/K)$$

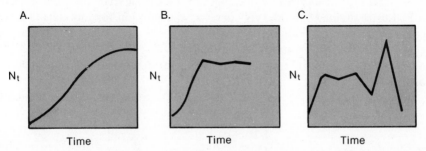

Figure 9.4.   Graphical analysis of density-dependent regulation. The graphs illustrate how the populations shown in Figure 9.3 will approach their equilibrium level with time.

Extrema can now be evaluated by setting the derivative equal to zero. When this is done, we find that each reproductive curve described by this model has a maximum at $N_t = K/r$ with a value $N_{t+1} (max.) = (K/r) e^{r-1}$. Thus, an increase in r would cause a shift in maximum reproductive potential toward lower parental densities. This suggests that when r is greater than one, a selective reduction in the size of the parental stock below its equilibrium level could actually enhance the recruitment of new reproductive members to the population as a consequence of a reduction in density-related mortality. This result has important implications in the exploitation of populations by man and other predators and is considered in detail in a later chapter.

Oscillatory tendencies can now be tested by evaluating the slope when N_t is equal to K (see Chapter 1). We find that at the equilibrium point, $dN_{t+1}/dN_t = 1 - r$. This implies that density oscillations will occur when r is greater than one. Oscillations do occur when r is between 1 and 2; however, they are damped. Note when r is very small, $\Delta(\ln N_t)$ can be approximated by the derivative $d(\ln N_t)/dt$. When this occurs, equation (9.1) is the same as the logistic model.

May (1975b) has also analyzed the global stability of equation (9.1) for the conditions $N_{t+2} = N_t = N_{t-2}$, $N_{t+4} = N_t = N_{t-4}$, etc. and has found that by increasing the value of r between 2 and 2.692, stable limit cycles are produced which proceed from stable cyclic oscillations between two population points, to cycles with four points, then eight points, and so on. On the other hand, values of r greater than 2.692 lead to a chaotic regime with cycles of arbitrary period, or aperiodic behavior, depending on initial conditions. As May points out, "even if the natural world was 100% predictable, the dynamics of populations with density-dependent regulation could nonetheless in some circumstances be indistinguishable from chaos, if the intrinsic growth rate r is large enough."

Models like equation (9.1) can be extended to populations with overlapping generations. However, in this case, different ages are likely to experience different density effects and a full generation time lag is probably much too long. Leslie (1959) took a less approximate approach, though one that is more complex, by modifying his age group model to include a time lag with regard to age-specific density effects. Using the model described earlier in Chapter 8, Leslie divided the interval survivorship fraction for individuals of each age, say age x, by $q_{x,t} = 1 + aN_{t-x-1} + bN_t$ where a and b are constants. Thus, he assumed that the quantity q is dependent not only on the density of the population at the present moment but also on its size when each age group was born.

As explained in Chapter 8, the q values form a diagonal matrix such that

$$Q_t = \begin{bmatrix} q_{0,t} & 0 & 0 & \cdots & 0 \\ 0 & q_{1,t} & 0 & \cdots & 0 \\ 0 & 0 & q_{2,t} & \cdots & 0 \\ \cdots\cdots\cdots\cdots\cdots\cdots \\ 0 & 0 & 0 & \cdots & q_{n,t} \end{bmatrix}$$

where, again, $\vec{N}_{t+1} = LQ_t^{-1}\vec{N}_t$.

Figure 9.5 gives a numerical example in which specific values of a and b are used. Note that oscillations occur as a consequence of the delayed density effects on age distribution. Their amplitudes decline, however, as the population approaches a stable age structure characteristic of its carrying capacity level. Once the age distribution is stable, $N_{t-x-1} = N_t = K$ and it can be shown that the population density will be given as $K = (\lambda - 1)/(a + b)$.

Another approach to modeling the population growth of organisms with complex life histories has been to employ a logistic equation in which different time lags have been incorporated. This type of model serves as a useful approximation when generations overlap and when growth is essentially continuous. One such growth model can be expressed as follows:

$$dN_t/dt = rN_t(1 - N_{t-T}/K) \tag{9.2}$$

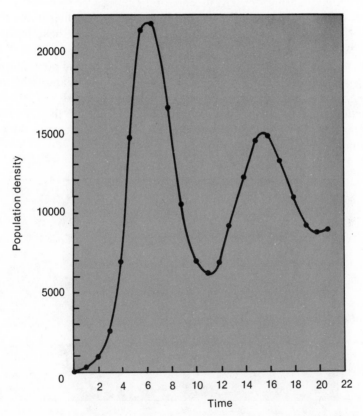

Figure 9.5.   Growth curve of a population starting with 81 individuals of age 0, 21 of age 1, 5 of age 2, and 1 of age 3. In the Leslie projection matrix, $F_0 = 0$, $F_1 = 45/7$, $F_2 = 18$, $F_3 = 18$, $p_0 = 7/9$, $p_1 = 5/7$, and $p_2 = 3/5$. Growth is assumed to be limited by population density according to the expression $q_{x,t} = 1 + aN_{t-x-1} + bN_t$, where $a = 0.000148148$ and $b = 0.000037037$. (From P.H. Leslie. 1959. Physiol. Zool. 32: 151. Copyright 1959 by The University of Chicago. All rights reserved.)

where T is the reaction time lag which measures the time delay in the response of a population to the effects of crowding. For example, N might represent the density of a herbivore population that is limited by vegetation which takes time T to recover from being grazed. Hutchinson (1948) has shown that the equilibrium K, in this case, is stable as long as rT (or T/T_R) is less than $\frac{1}{2}\pi$. More specifically, monotonic damping occurs when $0 < rT < e^{-1}$ while oscillatory damping is the case when $e^{-1} < rT < \frac{1}{2}\pi$. When rT is greater than $\frac{1}{2}\pi$, stable limit cycles develop with periods of roughly $4T$ (May, 1976).

The time lag in equation (9.2) is assumed to be exactly T in length. Hence, the extent of resource limitation is dependent on the population at some particular instant in past time. It is more realistic, however, to think of T as some average value since the population is likely to be affected by resource use in the past in a continuous manner. An improvement of basic theory might then be made by expressing N_{t-T}/K in equation (9.2) as $\int N_{t'} \, f(t-t')dt'$ where $f(t-t')$ is a density function (or weighting factor) which distributes the effect of resource utilization at past times. For a more detailed description of this approach see May (1973).

A good example of how time lags can alter the pattern of population growth is shown in Figure 9.6 by the growth of laboratory populations of the water flea *Daphnia magna*. In this example, oscillations occur due to the presence of a reaction time lag, which is illustrated in the graph by the lags present in the time it takes the populations to compensate for increases in birth rate by corresponding increases in death rate.

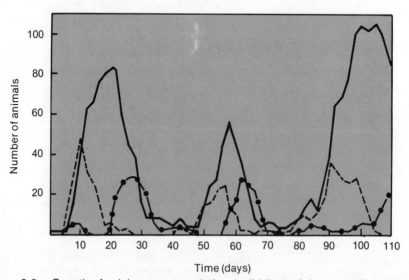

Figure 9.6. Growth of a laboratory population (solid line) of the water flea (*Daphnia magna*) at 25°C. The numbers of births (dashed line) and deaths (dashed-dotted line) have been doubled to make them visible on the graph. (Data from D.M. Pratt. 1943. Biol. Bull. 85: 116.)

Stochastic models I: demographic stochasticity.   In addition to time-lag-induced oscillations, it is also possible in theory for populations to exhibit random fluctuations due to the stochastic nature of population change. This stems from the fact that births and deaths are not events which happen in time with absolute certainty but can only be predicted with a certain level of probability. To illustrate the nature of chance effects on population growth, consider, first, the relatively simple case of continuous growth resulting from a pure birth process. This might be exemplified by cell divisions occurring in a population of microorganisms while under optimal conditions. Assume N_o individuals to start with and let k represent the number of births (or cell divisions) ocurring during t time units of growth. These k births will then be distributed among N_o clones at time t. Since deaths are assumed not to occur during this time, the probability that N individuals exist at time t can be expressed as $P_N(t) = P_{k+N_o}(t)$ where $k = N - N_o$. In order to obtain the exact distribution of births at time t, we first take note of the fact that the number of ways in which k births can be ordered in N_o clones (i.e., the number of ways of dividing k events or things into N_o subsets, some of which may be empty), is given by the combination term $\binom{k + N_o - 1}{N_o - 1} = \binom{N - 1}{N_o - 1}$. The probability of any one such arrangement can then be given as the probability that k individuals in this arrangement were born during time interval t and N_o were not. Thus, if we let p_t represent the probability that a randomly selected individual was born in this time interval, the probability of any one specific arrangement then becomes $p_t^k (1 - p_t)^{N_o} = p_t^{N-N_o}(1 - p_t)^{N_o}$. When all possible arrangements are taken into account, this yields

$$P_N(t) = \binom{N - 1}{N_o - 1} p_t^{N-N_o}(1 - p_t)^{N_o}$$

This expression is simply a negative binomial distribution in which the expected value of N at time t is $E(N\backslash t) = N_o/(1 - p_t)$. We also know from deterministic theory that the expected value of N in the present situation should be $E(N\backslash t) = N_o e^{bt}$, where b is the birth rate per individual. Combining these expressions and eliminating $E(N\backslash t)$, we see that $p_t = 1 - e^{-bt}$. The distribution now becomes

$$P_N(t) = \binom{N - 1}{N_o - 1} e^{-bN_o t}(1 - e^{-bt})^{N-N_o} \tag{9.3}$$

The mean and variance of this distribution are

$$E(N\backslash t) = N_o e^{bt} \quad \text{and} \quad V(N\backslash t) = N_o e^{bt}(e^{bt} - 1) \tag{9.4}$$

Hence, the relative variation about the mean will be

$$\sqrt{V(N\backslash t)} / E(N\backslash t) = [(1 - e^{-bt})/N_o]^{\frac{1}{2}}$$

which approaches $N_o^{-\frac{1}{2}}$ as $t\to\infty$. Thus, for large populations, the relative variation is negligible and the deterministic approach should suffice.

The relationship between the deterministic prediction of population growth in this example and the probability distribution of the corresponding stochastic model are shown in Figure 9.7. Observe that the actual path taken by the population is governed strictly by the probabilities of succeeding events and can thus give rise to random fluctuations in population size.

The preceding model can be extended to include both births and deaths. Pielou (1977) has shown that this situation leads to a distribution similar to that of a pure birth process in which the mean and variance are

$$E(N\backslash t) = N_o e^{rt} \quad \text{and} \quad V(N\backslash t) = \frac{(b+d)}{(b-d)} N_o e^{rt}(e^{rt} - 1) \qquad (9.5)$$

where d is the death rate per individual and $r = b - d$. Again we see that the

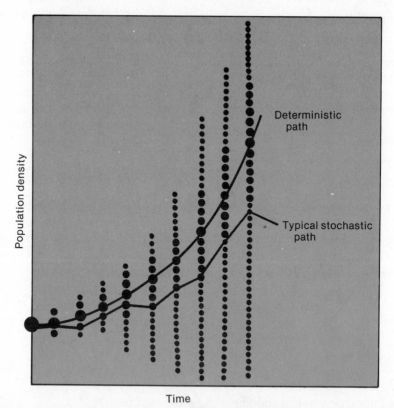

Figure 9.7.   Comparison of deterministic and stochastic population growth. The circles extending vertically from points on the deterministic curve represent the probability distribution of population size at that time.

relative variation for this stochastic approach becomes proportional to $N_o^{-\frac{1}{2}}$ when t gets large.

So far, we have only considered models which apply to populations undergoing exponential growth. A stochastic approach can also be applied to logistic growth. One such model was developed by Bartlett (1960) for which the probabilities of birth and death are computed separately for each random event. The derivation of this model is made easier if we first make note of the fact that the logistic equation incorporates the assumption that birth and death rates are linear functions of population density. This is shown by expressing b and d as follows:

$$b = b_o - a_b N \qquad \text{and} \qquad d = d_o + a_d N \qquad \text{(9.6)}$$

in which b_o, d_o, a_b, and a_d are constants. Thus, birth rates are expected to decline in a linear fashion as growth proceeds. The reverse is true of the death rate. Since $dN/Ndt = b - d$, the logistic equation can then be written as

$$dN/Ndt = (b_o - a_b N) - (d_o + a_d N)$$
$$= (b_o - d_o) \quad - (a_b + a_d)N \qquad \text{(9.7)}$$

Now, consider a single birth or death event, disregarding for the moment the time taken for this event. Since birth and death rates are linear functions of density, we can assume that the probability of this event being a birth and resulting in an increase in density of, say, N to $N+1$, $P(N \rightarrow N+1)$, is proportional to $b_o - a_b N$. Similarly, we can assume that the probability of a death, $P(N \rightarrow N-1)$, is proportional to $d_o + a_d N$. Since these events are mutually exclusive and are the only outcomes which are assumed possible, the sum of their probabilities must add to one. This is achieved by dividing through by the sum of the birth and death rates. The probabilities then become

$$P(N \rightarrow N+1) = \frac{b_o - a_b N}{(b_o + d_o) - (a_b - a_d)N}$$
$$P(N \rightarrow N-1) = \frac{d_o + a_d N}{(b_o + d_o) - (a_b - a_d)N} \qquad \text{(9.8)}$$

Thus, we see that the probability of birth will decrease and the probability of death will increase as the population expands in numbers.

Now consider the time required for each event. Since growth is continuous, each event should be of random duration. This is equivalent to treating births and deaths as random variables which are exponential functions of time. We can, therefore, write

$$F(t) = 1 - e^{-p_N t} \qquad \text{or} \qquad t = (1/p_N)\ln[1 - F(t)] \qquad \text{(9.9)}$$

where $F(t)$ is the cumulative distribution function and p_N is the rate at which events occur once the population has reached size N. The value of p_N can be computed by first expressing the probability of either a birth or death in a time interval dt. This will be $p_N dt = (b) N dt + (d) N dt = [(b_o + d_o) - (a_b - a_d) N] N dt$. It then follows that

$$p_N = (b_o + d_o) N - (a_b - a_d) N^2 \qquad (9.10)$$

In order to simulate the growth of a population with the aid of this model, the following procedure is generally taken:

(1) Calculate $P(N \rightarrow N+1)$.
(2) Select a number in the range (0,1) from a table of random numbers.
(3) If the number is greater than $P(N \rightarrow N+1)$, the next event is a death and the population decreases by one; if it is smaller, the next event is a birth and the population increases by one.
(4) Calculate p_N using equation (9.10).
(5) Pick a number for $F(t)$ in the range (0,1) from a table of random numbers and calculate the expected time for the event.
(6) Continue the above procedure for the next event.

For a numerical example of this procedure, let $N_o = 10$, $b_o = 0.7$, $d_o = 0.4$, $a_b = 0.002$, and $a_d = 0.001$. For this case,

$$P(N \rightarrow N+1) = \frac{0.7 - (0.002)(10)}{1.1 - (0.001)(10)} = 0.6126$$

Now suppose our random number is less than 0.6126. The next event is then a birth and the population advances to $N_1 = 11$. The value of p_N can now be calculated as

$$p_N = (1.1)(10) - (0.001)(10)^2 = 11.1$$

and, if we select a number for $F(t)$ equal to, say, 0.667, the expected time for this event is then

$$t = (1/11.1)\ln(1 - 0.667) = 0.1 \text{ time unit}$$

When this procedure is again applied to this example and repeated to include several birth and death events, we ultimately get a stochastic version of a sigmoid curve in which the randomly selected data points are scattered about the deterministic prediction. If the above procedure were continued for a sufficient period of accumulated time, the density of the population in our example would eventually reach the carrying capacity and continue to fluctuate about this level as a result of chance events. Bartlett (1960) has evaluated the probability distribution for a population which undergoes logistic growth once the carrying capacity has been reached. One specific example of this distribution is shown graphically in Figure 9.8. Although discrete and not entirely symmetrical, the distribution does resemble a normal curve in overall appearance.

Since density fluctuations described by this distribution are assumed to be random, a population at its carrying capacity level has a chance of ultimately

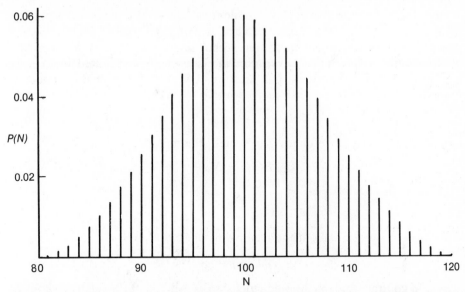

Figure 9.8.   Distribution of probabilities of a population containing N individuals once a stochastic equilibrium has been reached. The mean and variance of the distribution are $E(N) = 99.5$ and $V(N) = 50$. (From E. Pielou. *Mathematical Ecology*. Copyright © 1977 by Wiley-Interscience. Reprinted by permission of John Wiley & Sons, Inc., New York.)

dropping to zero density and undergoing extinction. In fact, it can be shown that the approximate chance of eventual extinction, given $b \geqslant d$, is $(d/b)^{N_0}$. Thus, for example, if a population were undergoing exponential growth with $b = 0.8$, $d = 0.4$, and $N_0 = 10$, the chance of eventual extinction is $(\frac{1}{2})^{10} = 1/1024$. On the other hand, when $b = d$, as would occur at the carrying capacity level, the chance of ultimate extinction equals one, regardless of the initial size of the population. In other words, extinction is an ultimate certainty for any population that is held in check by environmental limits for any extended period of time.

Stochastic models II: environmental stochasticity.   Stochastic density changes can also arise in populations that are exposed to randomly fluctuating environments. The stochastic nature of the process is readily seen by treating one or more of the growth parameters as random variables. To illustrate, consider a population within a randomly changing environment in which the fluctuations can be treated as "white noise"; that is, an environment in which there is no correlation between fluctuations at successive instants. The effects of such environmental changes on population growth can be taken into account by expressing the intrinsic rate of increase as a time-dependent variable by way of the equation $r = \bar{r} + \gamma(t)$, where $\bar{r}$ is the rate of increase averaged over some specified period and $\gamma(t)$ is a random variable with a mean value of zero. In this case, r might be assumed to vary as a consequence of short-term perturbations in local weather conditions. Since $\ln N_t = \ln N_o + rt$ when growth is exponential, then as long as variation in r is normally distributed about $\bar{r}$, the variation in N will be lognormal. Letting $f(N,t)$ be the probability density function of N at time t, it can be shown that

$$f(N,t) = (2\pi\sigma^2 t)^{-\frac{1}{2}} N^{-1} \exp\{-[\ln(N/N_o) + \tfrac{1}{2}\sigma^2 t - \bar{r}t]^2 / 2\sigma^2 t\} \qquad (9.11)$$

where σ^2 is the variance of r. As expected, the mean value of N is

$$E(N) = N_o e^{\bar{r}t}$$

while the variance of N is

$$V(N) = N_o^2 e^{2\bar{r}t}(e^{\sigma^2 t} - 1)$$

The relative variation about the mean will, therefore, be

$$\sqrt{V(N)}/E(N) = (e^{\sigma^2 t} - 1)^{\frac{1}{2}}$$

Thus, in contrast to demographic stochasticity for which the relative variation approaches $N_o^{-\frac{1}{2}}$, fluctuations arising from environmental stochasticity are independent of population size. Observe as well, that unless $\bar{r} = 0$, growth (or decline) will continue to occur independent of the size of the population. Thus, changes in weather might increase or decrease growth rate about some average value but can never produce a balanced condition in which $dN/Ndt = 0$ for any extended period of time.

Probability models have also been derived for populations which are limited by factors such as food or space, when r or K or both parameters undergo random variation. Although weather is not directly responsible for density limitation, variation in the carrying capacity level due to environmental changes leads to a reduction in maximum average density, below that expected on the basis of the arithmetic mean of K. For example, logistic growth with a randomly varying value of K does not lead to a mean population of $\bar{K}$ but rather to $\bar{K} - \tfrac{1}{2}\sigma_K^2$ where σ_K^2 is the variance of K (May, 1974).

POPULATION CYCLES

Of the density fluctuations that have been studied and recorded, the most striking are those in which the fluctuating populations reach peak densities at fairly regular intervals. Two of the most common patterns encountered among populations are the three- to four-year cycles reported to occur among lemmings, mice (e.g., *Microtus agrestis*), and other small rodents; and the nine- to ten-year cycles reportedly common among a variety of fur-bearing mammals in the northern forest regions of Canada. Much of the evidence for the longer cycles has been based on the analyses of fur returns or hunting-kill statistics.

For example, the nine- to ten-year cycles illustrated for the six mammals in Figure 9.9 are based on fur returns from all Canadian provinces.

The appearance of cycles of similar average length among the growth patterns of different species has stimulated considerable research in this area and its share of polemics. At first, the causes of cycles were attributed to climatic changes and to meteorological phenomena such as sunspot cycles (Elton, 1924). Since known climatic and meteorological changes have not been satisfactorily correlated with the periodicity exhibited by most long-term cycles, ecologists have generally looked toward other explanations. These alternative hypotheses can be outlined as follows: (1) random-fluctuations hypotheses, (2) time-lag hypotheses, and (3) predation hypotheses. Probably the greatest proponent for random fluctuations as an explanation has been Cole (1951, 1954a). In 1951, Cole published a paper which jolted ecologists by demonstrating that random changes in population size could produce so-called cycles which are very similar to a number of published results. The logic is as follows: Suppose that random fluctuations give rise to yearly numbers which are random and independent such that the size in one year has no influence on the size in the following year. A peak will occur whenever a number is larger than both the preceding and following numbers. A cycle is then simply the distance between consecutive peaks. Now, consider three random numbers labeled a, b, and c which are assumed to be different, with a being the largest. There are $3! = 6$ possible arrangements or ways in which the numbers can appear (abc, acb, bac, bca, cab, and cba) but only two (bac and cab) produce a peak. Hence,

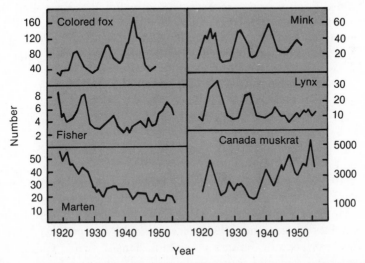

Figure 9.9. Nine- to ten-year cycles in populations of arctic and boreal North American animals. Population densities were measured as the number of pelts received by the Hudson Bay Company. (From L.B. Keith. 1963. *Wildlife's Ten-year Cycle.* University of Wisconsin Press, Madison.)

the probability of getting a peak with three consecutive, random numbers is $2/6 = 1/3$. Now, assume that n estimates of population size are made during consecutive years. With n total numbers, there are $n - 2$ groups of three consecutive numbers of which $(n - 2)/3$ constitute peaks. The number of cycles being one less than the number of peaks is then $(n - 2)/3 - 1 = (n - 5)/3$. Since the mean cycle length $(\overline{L})$ is simply n divided by the number of cycles, we can now express this as

$$\overline{L} = \frac{n}{(n - 5)/3} = 3n/(n - 5)$$

In addition to these fundamental cycles, there are also cycles of so-called dominant peaks, defined whenever one fundamental peak is greater than both preceding and following peaks. The above theory for analyzing fundamental peaks also applies here in that the probability of a dominant peak, given a group of three fundamental peaks, is $1/3$. In this case, however, the number of groups of three fundamental peaks is two less than the total number of peaks, or $(n - 2)/3 - 2 = (n - 8)/3$. The expected number of dominant peaks can then be written as $(1/3)(n - 8)/3 = (n - 8)/9$, and the number of cycles is $(n - 8)/9 - 1 = (n - 17)/9$. Hence, the mean cycle length for dominant peaks becomes

$$\overline{L} = \frac{n}{(n - 17)/9} = 9n/(n - 17)$$

Note when n is large, the mean cycle lengths for fundamental and dominant peaks become 3 and 9 years, respectively, in good agreement with the cycle lengths most frequently recorded.

In contrast to the random-fluctuations hypotheses, all other major explanations generally assume some underlying biological cause of cycles and tend to picture the "statistical cycles" of Cole as merely bumps in the numbers, which make the underlying pattern appear less regular. For instance, time-lag hypotheses suggest that cycles are created when populations overshoot some threshold level, thus triggering overpopulation phenomena such as disease, starvation, and/or social strife. Due to inherent time delays, the populations then recover in an oscillatory pattern, producing a more-or-less regular sequence of overpopulation periods, each followed by a population crash. As indicated in Figure 9.10, even simple time-lag models such as equation (9.2) fit population cycles surprisingly well, thus lending support to this hypothesis. For the most part, time-lag explanations differ in regard to the factors which are assumed to limit population size. Lack (1954), for example, has proposed that food is of primary importance in limiting population density, while Christian (1950), on the other hand, believes that populations, particularly rodent populations, are limited by a combination of behavioral and physiological changes brought on by social stress. As with most of the hypotheses in this area, experimental evidence can be cited both for and against these ideas. For example, studies

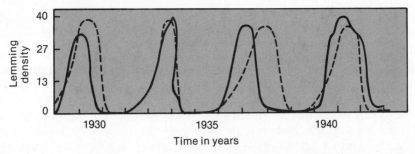

Figure 9.10. A comparison of Shelford's (1943) data on lemming cycles in Canada (solid line) with cycles predicted by the simple time-lag equation (9.2) (broken line). The time delay, *T*, is taken as 0.72 year. (From R.M. May. 1976. *Theoretical Ecology: Principles and Applications*. Saunders, Philadelphia.)

on Alaskan lemmings (Pitelka, 1964) have shown that food is severely depleted when lemmings reach their peak numbers and suggest that the supply of food may be a major cause of their decline. During peak periods, many important chemicals are tied up in living organisms and their waste products and are recycled only after a certain lag time has elapsed (Schultz, 1969). In contrast, work conducted on other rodents, in particular that of Chitty (1960), has tended to show that populations have an ample supply of food even at their peaks of abundance. Contradictory evidence has also been supplied in the case of Christian's social stress hypothesis. Detailed laboratory studies on rodents by Christian and others have shown a rise in aggressive phenomena, such as fighting and other forms of social strife, with an increase in population density. This eventually leads to physiological stress due to stimulation of pituitary-adrenocortical activity, followed by a reduction in survival and fertility. Experiments on mice, for example, indicate a delay in spermatogenesis, delayed sexual activity, diminished ovulation and implantation, and increased intrauterine mortality under crowded conditions (see Christian and Davis, 1964). These effects of endocrine strain appear to have prolonged consequences which extend even into periods of low density, thus providing a lag which is necessary for cycling. Much of the criticism that has been directed against Christian's social stress hypothesis centers around the findings that field data fail to show similar changes with increases in density (Clough, 1965), suggesting that these effects are artifacts of unrealistically high densities.

Predation hypotheses, on the other hand, propose that cycles are produced as a consequence of the oscillatory nature of predator-prey interactions. These ideas are based, for the most part, on predator-prey models that predict oscillations in both predator and prey densities even in the absence of time lags and on laboratory results from simple predator-prey systems which tend to support these predictions (see Chapter 10). Some field studies have also implicated predation in the maintenance of population cycles. For example, Pearson (1966), in studies of the California vole (*Microtus californicus*) and its predators (feral cats, raccoons, gray foxes, and skunks), found a very close correlation between the number of *Microtus* present and the number eaten, both apparently cycling with the same frequency, but with the latter lagging behind the former. According to Pearson, predators influence the cycle length of their prey by reducing the rate at which the prey recovers from the low point of each cycle. A similar oscillatory pattern is observed in the density cycles of the lynx and its principal prey, the snowshoe hare, in which the cycle lengths average 9.7 and 9.6 years for the lynx and hare, respectively (Fig. 9.11). However, in this case, the predator cannot be responsible for the cycles, since snowshoe hares show similar density changes in areas where no lynx are found.

At present, there does not appear to be a completely satisfactory explanation for the origin and maintenance of population cycles. In fact, none of the hypotheses that have been mentioned so far have been consistently documented in the field. In recent years, other explanations have been given in which the genetic structure of the population is assumed to be important in both limiting population size and promoting oscillations. These are discussed in some detail later in connection with population regulation.

POPULATION REGULATION

Probably no concept in population ecology has generated more controversy than has the regulation of population size. Since the mechanisms that are involved in controlling plant and animal numbers are not completely understood, the controversy in the past has centered around two opposing viewpoints. According to one view, populations are limited by factors which make up the physical environment and, therefore, act in a manner which is *density-inde-*

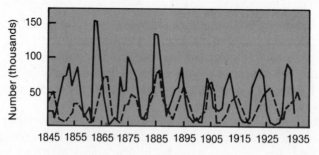

Figure 9.11. Population cycles in the lynx (dashed line) and its principal prey, the snowshoe hare (solid line). Population densities were measured as the number of pelts received by the Hudson Bay Company. (From E.P. Odum. 1971. *Fundamentals of Ecology.* Saunders, Philadelphia.)

pendent. For example, variations in climatic conditions such as sudden storms or sudden drops in temperature can alter birth and death rates in a manner not directly related to the existing size of the population. Such fluctuations, as is commonly believed, will produce a more or less random scatter of measured densities.

A logical alternative is that of *density-dependent* regulation. This view holds that population densities are subject to the law of diminishing returns, so that the average growth rate per individual will decrease as growth proceeds and as competition for some resource in limited supply becomes more intense. This permits a form of regulation through a rise in the death rate or by a decline in birth rate (or both) as the density of the population increases. This concept is illustrated by graphical means in Figure 9.12. Here, it is assumed that individual birth and death rates are linear functions of population density as in the logistic model. Note that an equilibrium level is attained at the point of intersection of the two lines (i.e., where the birth rate equals the death rate). Thus, if we let $b = b_o - a_bN$ and $d = d_o + a_dN$ in which all but b, d, and N are constants, the equilibrium level, K, then becomes

$$b_o - a_b K = d_o + a_d K \qquad \text{or} \qquad K = (b_o - d_o)/(a_b + a_d)$$

Generally speaking, the main proponents of density-independent regulation have been concerned with the ecology of small animals, especially insects, which are influenced to a greater degree by the vagaries of the weather. Their arguments are largely based on the close association between variations in population densities and changes in climate. For example, studies conducted by Andrewartha (1944) on the Australian grasshopper, *Austroicetes cruciata*, indicated that the distribution of this insect is determined by the length and favorableness of the season. At its northern boundary, conditions were too dry and the grasshoppers died due to lack of food; while at its southern extreme, the insects failed to survive due to excessive moisture. Abundance was also observed to vary in response to weather, with large numbers persisting only

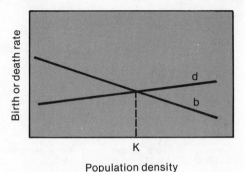

Figure 9.12.   One simple relationship between birth and death rates and population density.

in the central parts of the range where variations in climatic conditions were less extreme. This led Andrewartha and Birch (1954) to conclude that the same components of climate which determine the distribution of this insect are also responsible for limiting its abundance. A similar correlation can be observed in the seasonal variation of a species of thrips, *Thrips imaginis*, which feeds on pollen and the soft tissue of flowers in southern Australia (Fig. 9.13). Populations of this insect increase essentially unchecked during the spring when flowers are abundant. This is followed by a sharp decline after the onset of the summer drought when plants in bloom are relatively scarce. During this decline, large numbers of the insect die while searching in vain for new flowers. The insect populations are then kept at fairly low levels throughout the dry summer and cool winter, until the following spring. Hence, the pattern of periodic outbreaks in population size is set by seasonal changes in weather, whereas peak numbers are determined largely by the intrinsic rate of natural increase of this species, and by the density of survivors at the start of the spring season.

Many of the original arguments against weather as a controlling factor were presented by A. J. Nicholson in a paper published in 1933. In this publication,

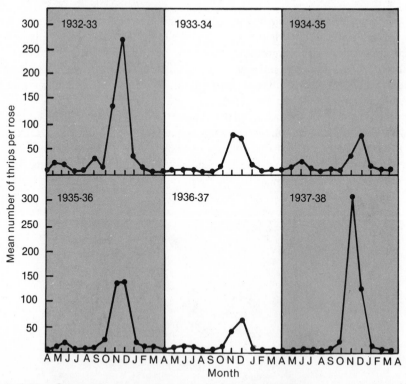

Figure 9.13. Seasonal variation in a population of adult thrips on roses. (Data from J. Davidson and H.G. Andrewartha. 1948. J. Anim. Ecol. 17: 193)

Nicholson likened the size of a population to the depth of the ocean and density fluctuations resulting from changes in weather to the waves on the ocean surface. As he so aptly pointed out, the surface of the ocean is constantly in motion, rising and falling with the position of the moon. Nevertheless, one would not conclude from this that the position of the moon determines the depth of the ocean. Neither should one conclude that population size is determined by climate, but merely the change in size. He went on to clarify the distinction between destruction and control by using an example of a hypothetical population which is capable of increasing by 100-fold in each generation if left unchecked. Assuming that weather destroys 98% of this population in a manner unrelated to density, the population would still be capable of doubling in each generation. Now, if some other factor, such as a predator, were to act in a density-dependent fashion, its kill would increase as growth proceeds and would soon reach the 1% level necessary to achieve a balance. Thus, although weather is the most important factor in terms of total destruction, only the destruction caused by the predator population actually serves to control the size of its prey.

In more recent years, ecologists have attempted a synthesis of the important ideas from both sides of the controversy. The one that follows is patterned after Horn (1968). Suppose that a population increases on the average according to a modified form of the logistic equation as

$$dN/dt = rN(1 - N/K) - d_iN$$

where d_i is the death rate resulting from the density-independent effects of weather. Note that an equilibrium is expected when $rN(1 - N/K) = d_iN$. The equilibrium density will then be $N_e = K(r - d_i)/r$. These equilibrium conditions are shown in Figure 9.14 by dN/dt versus N plots of the parabola $dN/dt = rN(1 - N/K)$ and of the straight-line relationship $-dN/dt = d_iN$. The equilibrium density occurs at the point at which the plots intersect.

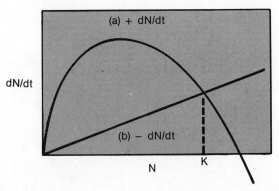

Figure 9.14. Rate of population change as a function of population size. (a) Only density-dependent factors are operating; (b) Only density-independent factors are operating. An equilibrium is established at the point of intersection.

Now, suppose that we follow the population over several generations. Since environmental conditions will most probably change, we can expect to observe temporal changes in the values of both d_i and K. Such variations are illustrated by the plots in Figure 9.15 in terms of the average and the maximum and minimum values observed during this period of time. These are given for both high (graph A) and for low (graph B) effects of density-independent factors. In both graphs, the differences $a - b$ and $c - d$ represent the maximum ranges of variation in N_e due to changes in density-dependent factors while $a - c$ and $b - d$ are the corresponding ranges as a result of changes in density-independent effects. Note that $a - c$ and $b - d$ tend to be considerably greater than $a - b$ and $c - d$ when the effects of density-independent factors are high. The reverse is true when their effects are low. Thus, in the former case, variation in N_e will tend to be closely correlated with changes in the weather, giving the impression that climate is solely responsible for limiting population growth. In the latter case, variation in N_e will tend to follow changes in density-dependent factors such as food, predators, and the like.

So far, we have treated weather as strictly a density-independent factor.

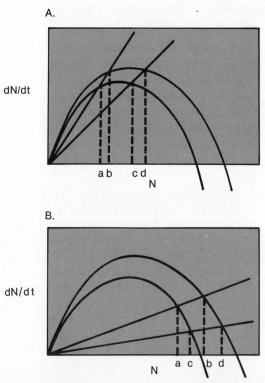

Figure 9.15.   High (A) and low (B) effects of density-independent factors on population regulation. See text for explanation.

However, it has been shown by Smith (1961) and others that weather does not have to act entirely in a density-independent manner. For instance, if shelter areas are limited in number or are difficult to find in a hurry, the percentage of the population destroyed by weather would not be constant, but would tend to increase with density. Under these conditions, mortality due to inclement weather would be density-dependent and could, in theory, produce a stable equilibrium level.

REGULATION THROUGH INTRASPECIFIC COMPETITION

During the long debate over the nature of population regulation, several ecologists stressed the importance of intraspecific competition in the limitation of population growth. As was pointed out repeatedly during this period, competition serves as the one mechanism by which increases in population density lower the chance of survival of an average individual. This prompted a number of investigators to examine the effects of crowding on the survival and fertility of different species when maintained under controlled laboratory conditions. In order to illustrate some of their findings, what follows are a few selected examples. The results of these studies not only demonstrate the effects of specific types of competitive interaction, but have also served in the past as laboratory tests of density dependence.

Scramble competition.   Ecologists have recognized different types of competition operating in animal populations. Probably the simplest is a form known as *scramble competition*. In this case, all members of a population have general access to essential resources. Therefore, any increase in density will intensify competition through a reduction in the average amount of resources available to each individual. Such might be the case when food is scarce and limiting to growth. Gross crowding would then reduce nutrition to a level bordering on starvation. In such instances, high density effects are felt throughout the group, and only a fraction of existing members can obtain enough food to survive and take part in sustaining the population.

One example of how scramble competition can affect population growth is illustrated by Nicholson's experiments on the Australian sheep-blowfly, *Lucilia cuprina* (1948). Figure 9.16 shows the survivorship pattern observed when different numbers of blowfly larvae are introduced into glass tubes containing a fixed amount of food. Note that the number of emerging adults actually declines with increases in the number of larvae at high larval densities. This results from an insufficient amount of food for all the larvae to reach a size needed for pupation. Observe also, that if each emerging adult can produce a large and fixed number of eggs which hatch into larvae, this survivorship pattern will generate a reproductive curve which is typical of populations that show violent fluctuations in density. To test the possibility of density oscillations,

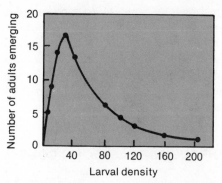

Figure 9.16. The relationship between larval density and adult emergence with regard to mortality in *Lucilia cuprina* (Blowfly). (From A.J. Nicholson, 1948. Proc. 8th Intern. Congr. Entom., 277.)

Nicholson placed small numbers of *L. cuprina* into population cages and supplied them with 50 grams of liver per day for the larvae, and water and dry sugar for the adults as well. A careful day-to-day record of the numbers of individuals was then made. The results are shown graphically in Figure 9.17. In this case, density oscillations were observed and could be accounted for by the intense competition between larvae for food. This is shown by the fact that a doubling of the food supply to the larvae approximately doubled the average

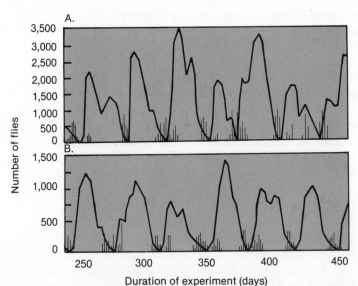

Figure 9.17. Density oscillations of Blowfly adults as a result of competition for food between larvae. Curves represent the number of adults and vertical lines the number of adults eventually emerging from eggs laid on that day. The amount of food available to larvae in *A* is twice the amount in *B*. (From A.J. Nicholson, 1957, Cold Spring Harbor Symp. Quant. Zool., 22, 153.)

number of surviving adults. Since adults had an adequate supply of food, oscillations apparently developed because too many eggs were laid for the food source when numbers of adults were high, causing larvae to starve before pupation. Thus, if egg production were reduced, fewer competing larvae could give rise to a greater number of surviving adults. This was later shown to be the case. Nicholson found that if 50% of the adults are destroyed on every second day, the reduction in eggs, and thus in larval competition, produced a compensatory increase in all of the later stages of development.

Nicholson also tested the effect of competition on total egg production. Cultures were set up in which the adults were excluded from the larval food and given a restricted and constant supply; whereas the larvae were supplied with an excess. Since each adult fly requires a certain amount of protein food before it can produce eggs, the result was again oscillations, but in this case it was due to competition between adults. When adult densities were high, fewer eggs were produced per individual, on an average, resulting in a reduction in the number of larvae emerging. This served to lower the number of adults in the next generation and helped to restore egg production back to its upper level. Because few of the larvae survived to reach pupation in cultures governed by larval competition, Nicholson reasoned that the oscillatory effects of competition on the fecundity of the adults should be opposed by competition among the larvae. He found that, by restricting the food supply to the larvae and decreasing the food ration to the adults to 1 gram liver per day, he could indeed effect a reduction in the extent of oscillations and obtain a growth pattern in which there are comparatively small fluctuations about an equilibrium level (Fig. 9.18).

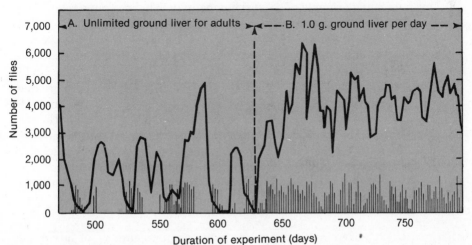

Figure 9.18.   Effect on a Blowfly culture of restricting adult food supply. Curves and vertical lines are as indicated in the legend for Figure 9.17. (From A.J. Nicholson, 1957, Cold Spring Harbor Symp. Quant. Zool., 22, 153.)

Several attempts have been made to model the experimental results of Nicholson on the sheep blowfly. The most successful are those which have used differential growth equations that include a time delay for maturation (developmental lag) and incorporate the threshold effect of some minimum quantity of protein needed for egg production. An example is the model developed by Oster, Auslander, and Allen (1976) which was derived specifically for the blowfly system. The model was found to display limit cycles which reproduced much of the fine structure observed in experimental results, thus indicating that a large part of the variation that has traditionally been attributed to environmental noise or experimental error can be simulated by a deterministic approach.

Contest competition.   In contrast to the density oscillations observed when individuals scramble for food, a more stable pattern of growth results from a type of competitive interaction known as *contest competition*. Contest competition occurs when each successful competitor claims sufficient resources for self-maintenance and reproduction. The surplus individuals without territorial claims migrate to other areas or are forced to occupy less suitable sites in which the chance of success is much reduced. The deleterious effects of crowding are then confined to that fraction of the population which has failed to procure suitable living space and defend it against encroachment. Similar effects can occur with the establishment of dominance hierarchies. Under crowded conditions, subordinates may be forced to leave the group, only to enter less familiar surroundings in which they are more susceptible to predation. It is easy to see how such behavior could keep a population from over-exploiting its food supply and also provide a selective mechanism to insure that only the strong contribute offspring to the next generation.

One interesting example of contest competition in which contests are often lethal, is illustrated by the experiments of Crombie (1944) on the beetle, *Rhizopertha dominica*, and the moth, *Sitotroga cerealella*. In both of these species, females oviposit on cereal grains. The developing larvae then bore their way in to feed and complete their larval and pupal stages within a single grain. Under crowded conditions, individual seeds can, by chance, be infested by more than a single larva. Nevertheless, Crombie found that in most instances of multiple infestation only one insect completed its development within the seed. The rest were generally forced to migrate or died of wounds received from attacks by other larvae of the same species. These contests thus give rise to a density-dependent form of regulation in which the probability of survival per infested grain varies inversely with the initial density of larvae (Fig. 9.19). This survivorship pattern can be expressed as

$$S_L = c/N_L$$

where S_L is the surviving fraction, N_L is the average number of larvae per infested grain, and c is a constant. Under conditions of strict contest competition in which only one individual will survive per sampling unit, the constant c

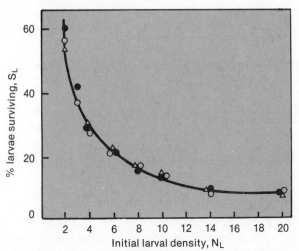

Figure 9.19.   Relationship between initial density and survival of *Sitotroga* (open circles) and *Rhizopertha* (closed circles) larvae alone, and mixed together (triangles). (From A.C. Crombie, 1944, J. Exp. Biol. 20: 135.)

should equal 1. Crombie found that the experimental values of c agreed very closely with this theoretical expectation, being 1.16 for *Rhizopertha* and 1.1 for *Sitatroga*.

Although many ecologists believe that social factors such as territoriality can regulate animal numbers, controversy still remains over the importance of their role in nature. Part of the problem lies in the variation of territorial effects with population density (Brown, 1969). When densities are low so that all members of the population are able to claim desirable sites, territoriality may actually promote population growth by improving the dispersion pattern of individuals relative to their food supply. At intermediate densities, all individuals might still obtain territories but some may be excluded from preferred sites and forced to breed in less favorable areas. This could create a buffer effect which would help to limit growth if the death rate from other sources is large enough. Only when the density is sufficiently high so as to create a nonbreeding surplus will competition for territorial space exert its full impact as a limiting factor. Several attempts have been made to demonstrate the presence of a nonbreeding surplus, but for one reason or another, such as failure to show a surplus of females, interpretations of most results are open to debate.

Interference.   In addition to a mutual exploitation of resources, intraspecific competition can also involve some form of direct interference, often arising as a by-product of social behavior. For instance, subordinates in a dominance hierarchy may have so little time for foraging that they lose weight and eventually starve to death. Interference can also affect survival and fertility in more

solitary species. For example, a searching predator may react to chance encounters with others of its own species by temporarily ceasing to search or by
dispersal from the area, thus reducing its chance of capturing prey. Since such
interactions will reduce the chance of successful reproduction, the relative
growth rate of a population is expected to decrease in proportion to the rate
of such encounters and, hence, to population density.

Although there is little direct experimental evidence to support the role of
interference as a density-regulating factor, one situation where it is thought to
be important is in limiting the fecundity or egg production of many kinds of
insects. In this case, frequent encounters at high population densities can lead
to the general disturbance of females and may cause them to squander a greater
proportion of their energy on movement as opposed to reproduction. The results
of one such study, conducted by Boyce (1946) on the fecundity of the flour
beetle, *Tribolium confusum*, are shown in Figure 9.20. In this experiment, adult
beetles were kept on a flour medium to maintain an environment as uniform
as possible and to permit a simple determination of daily egg production. Each
sample differed only in the number of pairs of males and females, ranging from
1 to 128. Furthermore, to reduce the detrimental effects of flour contamination
and the problem of adults eating their own eggs, the medium was frequently
changed and the eggs were counted at daily intervals. These precautions served
to reduce the number of variables acting concurrently on the growth of egg
production in this species.

As expected for density-dependent regulation, egg production per adult
per day decreases with increasing density, but not in the linear manner predicted

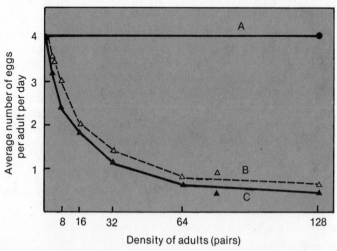

Figure 9.20.   Daily egg production of *Tribolium confusum*. *A*—fecundity if there were
no cannibalism and no density effects. *B*—average real fecundity including cannibalism.
C—average apparent fecundity without the effects of cannibalism. (After J.B. Boyce.
1946. Ecology 27: 290.)

by the logistic model. Egg cannibalism does have an effect; however, it is slight when compared to the general influence of crowding. Also note in Figure 9.21 that the data tend to fit a straight line when the ordinate value is expressed as its reciprocal. These results can be readily explained on the basis of interference with egg production if we assume that egg-laying activities are depressed in direct proportion to random encounters between adults. A suitable model can be derived if we first define an intrinsic rate of oviposition, u, in terms of the expression

$$u = dE/Ndt$$

in which E is the number of eggs, N is the number of adults, and t is time. Now, suppose that after each encounter there is a time during which the activity effectively ceases and the individual is not available for further interference. If we assume the relationship between "wasted" time and rate of encounters to be approximately linear, the average time required to perform the given activity can then be expressed as

$$T_a = T_o + b(N - 1)$$

where T_o is the average time required for the same activity in the absence of interference and b is a constant, $b(N-1)$ being proportional to the rate of encounters with $N - 1$ others in the population. If we assume further that egg-laying occurs randomly in time, $1/u$ can then be taken as the average time for oviposition. Thus, replacing T_a with $1/u$ and T_o with $1/u_o$, we can write $1/u = 1/u_o + b(N-1)$ in which u_o is a constant. Solving for u, we get the alternative form of this equation

$$u = \frac{dE}{Ndt} = \frac{u_o}{1 + u_o\, b(N-1)} \tag{9.12}$$

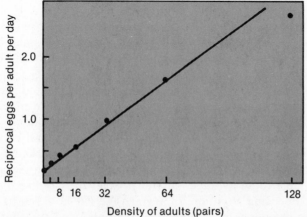

Figure 9.21.   A reciprocal plot of the data in Figure 9.20 (C).

Note that, in agreement with the data, a plot of the reciprocal egg production per individual per day versus the existing size of the population will yield a straight line. Other data tend to support these results (Sokal, 1967).

Numerous studies have also demonstrated the importance of general interference on survival and fertility among mammals. For example, studies by Christian (1950) and others on rats have shown that frequent encounters can lead to increased aggression and fighting among males. There was also a reduction in breeding effort under crowded conditions. In this case, animals were frightened too often or engaged too much in social activity, ultimately leading to a change in hormone balance (the general adaptation syndrome).

Competition in plants   Although much of the theory concerning the role of intraspecific competition in the regulation of population size has originated from studies on animal populations, considerable evidence has also accumulated for the importance of competition in higher plants. Of particular importance in this regard are the studies of Kira, Shinozaki, and others of this Japanese school on the influence of density on plant production. These studies have shown that the total yield of many terrestrial plants tends to follow a logistic pattern during the growing season. For example, Shinozaki and Kira (1956) found that the reciprocal of the average individual weight w in even-aged plants increased linearly with density, N. This implies that the total population yield, y, where $y = wN$, is related to N in the form of a rectangular hyperbola (i.e., $y = AN/(1+BN)$). When total yield was measured at different days after sowing, they obtained the peculiar time trends illustrated in the y versus N plots in Figure 9.22. These data concerning the density and time relationships for plant growth strongly suggest that total yield can be expressed by way of the following equation:

$$y = e^{kt}y_o/[1 + (e^{kt} - 1)y_o/y_m]$$
$$= e^{kt}w_o N/[1 + (e^{kt} - 1)w_o N/y_m]$$

(9.13)

where y_m is the maximum yield obtainable under a specific set of initial growth conditions and k is a constant. Note when N and t are small in value, y is directly proportional to N as shown in Figure 9.22. When N and/or t are large, y becomes independent of N. Thus, by letting $y_o = w_o N$, where w_o is the average individual weight of seeds or seedlings initially planted, we get a logistic expression which relates biomass to initial density and to time, in the same manner as that proposed for the density of many animal populations.

Unlike animals in which growth of individuals is comparatively fixed, plants tend to exhibit developmental plasticity and can vary markedly in per capita yield. This permits survival even under conditions where the amount of resources available to an average individual is severely reduced as a result of competition. Focusing attention on average individual yields fails to account for the plastic development of individuals and obscures the effects of compe-

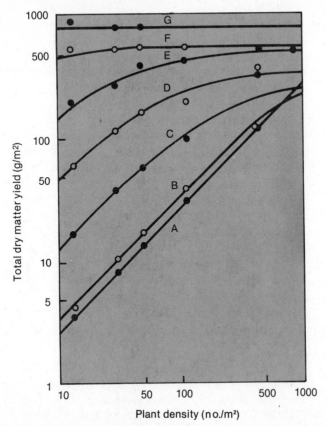

Figure 9.22. The density effect on the yield of dry matter in a spacing experiment with soybeans, plotted on log-log scale. (A) 0; (B) 12; (C) 21; (D) 31; (E) 45; (F) 84; and (G) 119 days. (From K. Shinozaki and T. Kira. 1961. J. Biol, Osaka City University. 12:69.)

tition on plant-to-plant variation. Such effects are illustrated in Figure 9.23 by the influence of population density on individual yield in the flax *Linum usitatissimum.* Observe that conditions of density stress produce a hierarchy consisting of a few large individuals and many more smaller ones. Thus, as population densities increase, there is a progressive shift from an almost normal to a highly skewed or lognormal distribution of individual plant dry weight. Although terrestrial plants are known to show considerable plasticity in both vegetative growth and seed number, variation in seed size is often quite small. Since there exists an optimal size for effective seed germination, these results suggest that a successful adaptive strategy in plants is one in which reproductive and vegetative yields can be sacrificed under conditions of stress in order to produce seeds with maximum survival probabilities.

In addition to density-related changes in individual yields, intraspecific competition in terrestrial plants may also be detected by changes in plant-to-

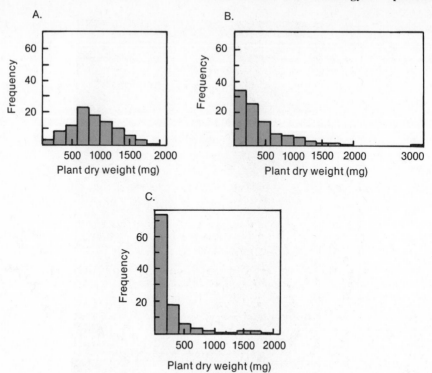

Figure 9.23. The influence of density on the frequency distribution of individual plant dry weight in *Linum usitatissimum*. The seeds were sown at densities of (A) 60/m², (B) 1440/m², and (C) 3600/m², and harvested at seed maturity. (From Obeid, 1965.)

plant distances. Since plants require some minimum quantity of space for growth and survival, there will tend to be some lower limit on nearest-neighbor distances, within which the presence of one individual will inhibit the establishment of another. Thus, crowding will tend to produce a uniform distribution pattern with plant-to-plant distances being more regular than expected on the basis of randomness. This tendency towards regular spacing in dense populations can be expressed in terms of a ratio, R, of the average measured distance between nearest neighbors, $\bar{r}_A$, to the expected distance, $\bar{r}_E$, if all plants are dispersed at random. Since, for random spacing, the square of the distance between a randomly chosen individual and its nearest neighbor is an exponential random variable (see Chapter 7), it can be shown that the expected nearest-neighbor distance is simply $\bar{r}_E = 1/2\sqrt{N}$. Thus, for a population of density N, we have

$$R = \bar{r}_A/\bar{r}_E = 2\bar{r}_A\sqrt{N} \qquad (9.14)$$

Note that the value of R will equal 1 when spacing is random. It will be greater than 1 when spacing is more uniform, with a maximum occurring at 2.149. The maximum occurs with uniform, hexagonal spacing when $\bar{r}_A = 1:0745/\sqrt{N}$. This is a closest-packing arrangement in which all nearest-neighbor distances are the same, and each plant is at the center of a regular hexagon.

LOW DENSITY EFFECTS

Growth models describing density-dependent regulation are usually developed with the idea that survival and fertility are inverse functions of density. Such models must always predict that the relative growth rate of a population will be maximum when N approaches zero. Among many sexually reproducing populations, however, reproductive rates tend to be maximum at intermediate values of N, decreasing at both high and low densities. One example is shown in Figure 9.24 for the effect of adult density on the fecundity rate in the moth *Anagasta kuhniella*. Factors such as competition probably account for the observed reduction in reproductive potential at high densities. Various other limiting factors have been proposed which may act at low population levels. For instance, small populations may result in reduced protection from predators which greater numbers afford, while in other cases reduced densities may mean a greater exposure to inclement weather (a factor important to many animals which huddle together for warmth). The effect that will concern us here is the reduction in mating success. For example, if an individual searches randomly for mates, it follows that the probability of finding one must decline with decreasing densities. Hence, mate procurement could serve as an important factor limiting the rate of reproduction.

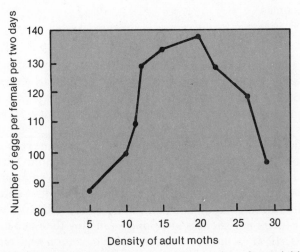

Figure 9.24. The effect of adult moth density on the number of eggs laid in a population of *A. kuhniells*. (From Ullyett, 1945.)

A simple model describing the drop in mating success at low population densities can be derived by expressing the instantaneous birth and death rates of a population as

$$d(\ln N)/dt = b_o p - d_o$$

where p is the fraction of females (or female gametes) impregnated at time t. To arrive at a value for p, consider the effect of increasing density by an increment ∂N. If matings are random with respect to time and to mating partner, any corresponding change in p will be proportional to the number of contacts with potential mates, which increase directly with ∂N, and to the fraction of unfertilized females, which limit the number of contacts that are successful in mate procurement. Hence, we can write

$$\partial p = c(1 - p)\partial N$$

in which c is a constant. This integrates to

$$p = 1 - e^{-cN}$$

Making this substitution, we get

$$d(\ln N)/dt = b_o(1 - e^{-cN}) - d_o$$
$$= r - b_o e^{-cN} \qquad \textbf{(9.15)}$$

Thus when N is small, approaching zero, the logarithmic growth rate approaches $-d_o$; whereas when N is large, $d(\ln N)/dt$ becomes equal to r. This growth expression can be further modified by letting $N = M$ when $d(\ln N)/dt = 0$. By making these substitutions, we see that $c = \ln(b_o/r)/M$. Equation (9.15) then becomes

$$d(\ln N)/dt = r[1 - (r/b_o)^{(N - M)/M}] \qquad \textbf{(9.16)}$$

Since r is less than b_o, this latter equation indicates that $d(\ln N)/dt$ is positive when N is greater than M. Thus, growth will proceed to its environmental limit. On the other hand, when N is less than M, $d(\ln N)/dt$ is negative and the population must continue to undergo a decline in density. Hence, the value $N = M$ represents a point of unstable equilibrium since, when the density is above this value, the population will increase, but if for some reason the density should fall below M, the population is doomed to extinction. This could serve as an important limiting factor under conditions of extreme environmental stress or during colonization. For example, when a population first enters a suitable habitat, its initial density is quite often low. The reproductive success of its members and hence their success at colonization may then depend entirely on the value of M. If M is large, a successful colonization will require a fairly large starting population. Conversely, when M is small, only a few migrants may be sufficient to establish the population.

Combined effects   Both high and low density effects can be incorporated into a single model by assuming that the logarithmic growth rate is also some decreasing function of N. For example, if the population is limited at high densities as a consequence of competition, the logarithmic growth rate might be approximated as

$$d(\ln N)/dt = r - b_o e^{-cN} - aN \qquad (9.17)$$

or in terms of $\Delta(\ln N_t)$ for seasonal breeders. A plot of this expression is shown in Figure 9.25. Observe that as N rises, $d(\ln N)/dt$ increases initially due to an increase in the probability of finding mates. As N continues to rise, $d(\ln N)/dt$ attains a maximum value and then declines to zero as the detrimental effects of crowding become more intense. There are, therefore, two points at which the reproductive curve intersects the replacement line: point E', an unstable equilibrium point, and point E, a stable one.

THE ANALYSIS OF DENSITY LIMITATION IN NATURAL POPULATIONS

Unlike the laboratory populations that were considered earlier in which the causes of mortality and losses in fertility can be at least partially controlled, many factors can and often do act concurrently on natural populations. To complicate matters further, these factors tend to vary with the season and with the age of the individual. Thus, when considered in its entirety, the pattern of regulation in natural populations becomes a complex system with many inter-acting components. An attempt to illustrate the many factors affecting popu-

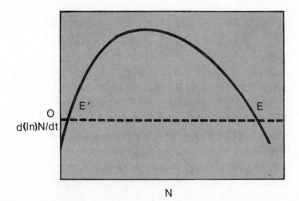

N

Figure 9.25.   Representative plot of equation (9.17) showing both high and low density effects on population growth. Point E represents a stable equilibrium point since populations slightly greater than E tend to drop toward this level, while those slightly less than E tend to rise to meet it. Point E' is an unstable equilibrium point since populations slightly greater than E' tend to increase while those slightly less tend to decrease.

lation growth is shown in Figure 9.26 for an insect species with nonoverlapping generations. In the first part (a), we see some of the major factors influencing fecundity and egg survival. This is followed in part (b) by a representation of the variables affecting mortality during any one stage of growth. Observe that, in order to relate the size of the population in one generation (N_{t+1}) to that of the preceding generation (N_t), one needs to know all the pertinent life-history data for the generation interval. Therefore, any description of density regulation in natural populations must include an analysis of the action of all the major factors which contribute to fecundity losses and to mortality at all stages of growth. In attempting such a study, it is often convenient to employ a method developed by Varley and Gradwell (1960) known as *k-factor analysis*. This procedure has become popular for the study of insect populations with annual generations where seasonal changes are not a problem. It consists of an analysis of the causes of age-specific mortalities and of fecundity losses, and involves estimating the numbers at the start of each specific stage of the life cycle and then calculating the successive losses as

$$k_i = \log(N_i) - \log(N_{i+1}) = -\Delta(\log N_i)$$

where N_i and N_{i+1} are the numbers at the start of age intervals i and $i + 1$ and k_i is the logarithmic measure of mortality at the ith stage. When this notation is used, k_0, though not a true mortality, is the measured reduction from the maximum possible fecundity, k_1 is the estimated egg mortality, k_2, the early larval mortality, and so on. The total generation mortality is then calculated as

$$K = \sum_{i=0}^{n} k_i$$

In addition to analyzing the causes of age-specific mortality, this technique provides a means of predicting future trends in populations. This is illustrated by the mortality data in Figure 9.27 on the cinnabar moth, *Tyria jacobaeae*. By such a plot, it is easy to see which stages are the most variable and which contribute most to overall mortality. The major causes of such mortality on the larval stages are shown in Figure 9.28. It is readily apparent in this case that the key factor in determining trends in population size has been larval loss due to starvation, particularly on the fourth- and fifth-instar larvae. It must be stressed, however, that the key factor that accounts for the major fluctuations in population size is not necessarily the principal factor regulating growth. Quite often, the key factor and the so-called regulatory factor are not the same.

The method of *k*-factor analysis has several useful applications. One is in the area of pest control. By recognizing the key factors controlling variability in an insect pest, for example, it may be possible to predict the occurrence of sudden outbreaks of the organism and, thereby, reduce economic losses. Similarly, from knowledge of the age-specific mortality data that are provided by a *k*-factor analysis, one is better able to judge what stages in the life history of the pest are most susceptible to control.

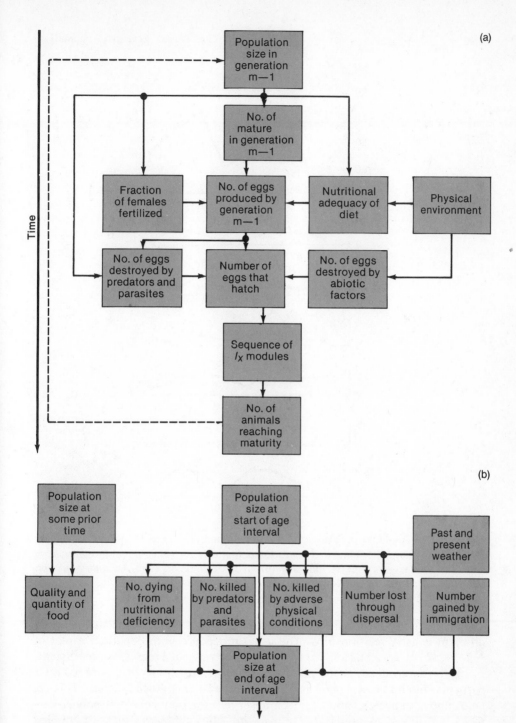

Figure 9.26. Block diagrams showing the major factors determining (a) how many offspring are produced in each generation, and (b) how many offspring survive each generation. (From B.D. Collier et al., *Dynamic Ecology.* Prentice-Hall Inc. Reprinted by permission of Prentice-Hall Inc., Englewood Cliffs, New Jersey.)

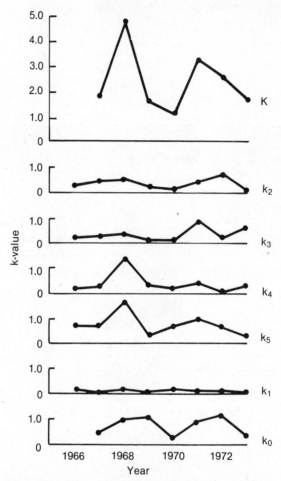

Figure 9.27. A k-factor analysis of the cinnabar moth. k_o = failure to reach maximum fecundity; k_1 = egg mortality; k_2 = early larval mortality; k_3 = mid-larval mortality; k_4 = late larval mortality; k_5 = pupal mortality. (From J.P. Dempster. 1975. *Animal Population Ecology.* Academic Press, New York.)

Another useful feature of this model is that it enables one to recognize different density relationships. The usual procedure is to construct a plot of $-\Delta(\log N_i)$ or k_i versus $\log(N_i)$ from which the value of a regression coefficient, b, can be determined. Some possible variations are shown in Figure 9.29. Of particular interest is the pattern labeled delayed-density dependence. This relationship is expected (and has been observed) for prey (or host) populations which are linked to predators (or parasites) through some form of coupled oscillation. In this case, the magnitude of the delay will depend upon the extent of the lag between changes in prey density and corresponding changes in the density of predators.

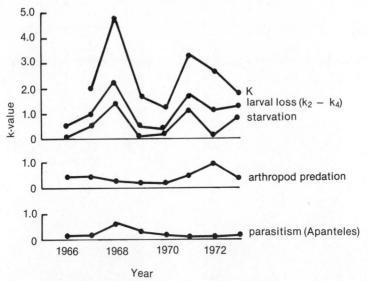

Figure 9.28.   The impact of *k*-factors for starvation, predation, and parasitism on total larval mortality in the cinnabar moth. (From J.P. Dempster. 1975. *Animal Population Ecology*. Academic Press, New York.)

As long as generations do not overlap, many of the patterns observed for direct-density dependence can be modeled by the following three-parameter equation:

$$N_{t+1} = \lambda N_t(1 + aN_t/b)^{-b} \tag{9.18}$$

where λ is the finite rate of increase and a and b are constants. This equation can be derived from the logistic model of population growth (see example problem 9) for which the parameter b is used to measure the relative exent of a time delay in the system. By letting $N_t = N_{t+1} = K$ in the model, it can be seen that an equilibrium condition develops when the population density reaches the value $K = b(\lambda^{1/b} - 1)/a$.

The value of b in the growth model can be estimated from the limiting slope of a $-\Delta(\log N_t)$ versus $\log(N_t)$ plot and describes competition for resources where "pure" scramble and "pure" contest competition simply become two extreme types of interactions within a continuum of theoretical possibilities. If competition is of the scramble type, much of the resource supply is wasted during early stages of development in maintaining individuals that ultimately fail to gain enough resources to reproduce. Hence, time-lag effects in such systems will tend to be quite large. The growth equation describing pure scramble competition can then be obtained from (9.18) by letting b approach infinity. We get

$$N_{t+1} = \lambda N_t e^{-aN_t} = N_t e^{r-aN_t}$$

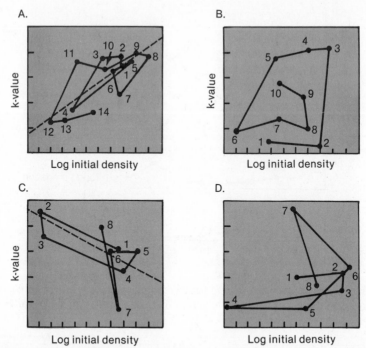

Figure 9.29.   Time sequence plots showing the relation of *k*-factors to population density with different density relationships. (A) Density-dependent predation (winter moth pupae), (B) Delayed density-dependent predation (rock ptarmigan eggs), (C) Inverse density-dependent parasitism (gypsy moth eggs), and (D) Density-independent predation (cinnabar moth larvae). (From J.P. Dempster. 1975. *Animal Population Ecology*. Academic Press, New York.)

Observe that if $a = r/K$, this expression is identical to equation (9.1) which, as we have shown earlier, gives rise to an oscillatory pattern of growth when r is large. Conversely, when competition is of the contest type, little is wasted on nonproductive members of the population and time-lag effects will tend to be small. This can be modeled by letting $b = 1$ in (9.18). Thus, for pure contest competition,

$$N_{t+1} = \frac{\lambda N_t}{1 + aN_t}$$

Setting $a = (\lambda - 1)/K$, we now have the discrete form of the logistic equation. This always gives rise to a stable pattern of growth, characterized by monotonic damping.

The general growth model expressed by equation (9.18) has been studied extensively by Hassell (1975) and others and has been shown to give rise successively to oscillatory damping, then to stable limit cycles, and finally to chaotic fluctuations as λ and b increase in value. This is shown by a plot of b versus λ in Figure 9.30. The model has also been applied to several insect

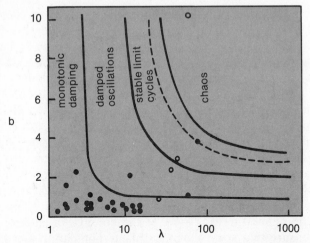

Figure 9.30. Dynamical behavior of equation 9.18 in terms of a plot of b versus λ. The solid circles come from the analysis of life table data on field populations and the open circles from laboratory populations. (From M.P. Hassell et al., 1975. J. Anim. Ecol. 45: 471.)

populations with discrete generations. For the most part, those populations that have been examined in light of this model tend to show rather stable growth patterns, having relatively low values of b (Hassell, Lawton, and May, 1976). Obvious exceptions include laboratory populations, such as the blowfly *L. cuprina*, which tend to scramble for food in close confinement and lack the large density-independent mortalities characteristic of natural populations.

ON THE THEORY OF SELF-REGULATION

Thus far, we have assumed that whatever the mechanism of regulation, extrinsic environmental factors such as food levels, predation, and climate are the primary means of control. It is variability in these environmental factors that results in changes in population size over time. Nevertheless, it might also be possible that populations are regulated through intrinsic conditions. The genetic, behavioral, and physiological properties of the population constitute a part of its environment and these internal environmental factors could act to control population size. It would then be variability among the members of the population in these intrinsic properties that results in changes in birth and death rates over time, and this could conceivably occur even in a perfectly constant external environment. This is the concept embodied by the term *self-regulation*.

Several different authors have invoked self-regulation in their attempts to explain observed instances of population control which are apparently not based on predators, harsh climatic conditions, or overexploitation of environmental resources. According to one such idea advanced by Wynne-Edwards (1962), a population is able to limit its own numbers below the carrying capacity level of its habitat, despite potentially large numbers in the population, by some form of social behavior (e.g., territoriality or dominance hierarchy), the evolution of which avoids direct intraspecific competition for food and the threat of starvation in the future. If all individuals were to compete directly (scramble) for the food supply in a given area, the result, if food were the only limiting factor, would be regulation at the starvation level due to exhaustion of the resource supply. A behavioral pattern such as territoriality, however, eliminates overexploitation of food so that the supply is not exhausted and starvation levels are not attained. Other forms of social organization also allow only a limited quota of individuals to share a limiting resource, thereby preventing the possible depletion of future levels. For example, the colonial nature of nesting in many oceanic birds prevents surplus individuals from breeding, by excluding them from the defined nesting sites of the colony. In addition, dominance hierarchies ensure that some members of the population are well-fed when there is not enough food for all. Theoretically, any species with some form of dispersal mechanism is capable of self-regulation.

There are well-documented examples of density-dependent qualitative changes in populations that are linked with dispersal; for example, "phase" changes in locusts (Uvarov, 1966). Individuals living in low-density populations exhibit solitary behavior, whereas at high densities locusts are quite gregarious. The solitary and gregarious phases differ in behavioral, physiological, and morphological characteristics as well as coloration. A sequential alteration of these apparently accompanies the shift in phase from solitary to gregarious, behavioral changes being followed by physiological changes, followed, in turn, by changes in color and, finally, in morphology. Alterations in wing length and size give increased mobility and are accompanied by lowered fecundity and shortened developmental time. The gregarious phase thereby becomes fitted for a migratory existence, allowing successful emigration from a crowded population.

Although it is not clear how locusts undergo phase transformation, there appear to be several factors involved. These include an increase in population size as a result of successful reproduction, an increase in density, aggregation, and mutual habituation (addiction to living together). The result is swarm formation and enhanced development of the gregarious phase. Weather factors— particularly moisture levels—rather than predators, parasites, or disease, seem to be the major ecological components involved in phase transformation (Dempster, 1963).

Chitty (1960) has proposed that all species are capable of self-regulation of their population densities, even though in certain (e.g., marginal) habitats, other mechanisms of regulation may be more important. According to Chitty, any increase in population size that results in proportionally more of the weaker genotypes and, therefore, in a deterioration in the quality of the population, will be countered by an increased sensitivity to normal mortality factors in the environment. Chitty's behavioral-genetic poymorphism hypothesis proposes that as the size of the population increases, so does mutual interference among its members. Selection for the ability to withstand crowding is necessarily accompanied by a deterioration of the overall adaptiveness of the organisms to their environment and, consequently, in lowered viability (e.g., lowered resistance to climatic stress). Further enhancement of mutual interference propagates the deterioration of the overall quality of the population and reproductive rates decline. Eventually, the population stops growing and may actually decrease in density to low levels where there are few interferential effects. Then, an increase in numbers can occur and the cycle can repeat itself. A modified version of Chitty's hypothesis, incorporating the effects of dispersal, has been proposed by Krebs and Myers (1974) and is diagrammed in Figure 9.31.

Support for a genetic basis to population regulation comes from biochemical studies which use electrophoretically-detectable protein variants to determine changes in allele frequencies at a gene locus. For example, Gaines and Krebs (1971) have found alterations in protein composition associated with density changes in cycling vole populations. As will be pointed out in Chapter 14, the levels of genetic variation present in natural populations are certainly high enough to serve as a basis for large-scale selective changes over relatively short

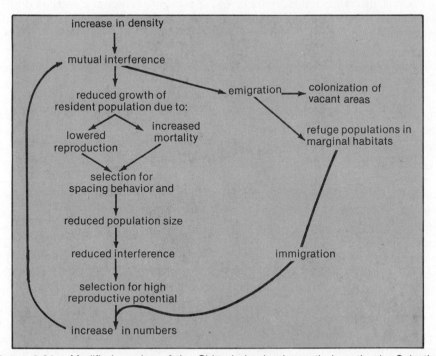

Figure 9.31. Modified version of the Chitty behavioral-genetic hypothesis. Selection acts through behavioral interactions to change the genetic composition of the population as the density fluctuates. (From C.J. Krebs and J.H. Myers. 1974. Population cycles in small mammals. In Advances in Ecological Research 8:268.)

time periods. Whether or not such genetic changes are the cause of demographic changes in populations is, however, not known at the present time.

The idea that self-regulation occurs through the effects of crowding on the endocrine system has been advanced by Christian, based on studies of microtene populations. Basically, this hypothesis states that mutual interference takes the form of stress which directly results in a reduction in population growth by causing rapid and reversible changes in adrenal functions. (Resorption of embryos in the uterus as a result of stress as occurs in rabbits and deer could be a part of this kind of self-regulatory mechanism.) The validity of the stress hypothesis still remains unproven, however, since experimental studies have so far failed to show a necessary correlation between physiological changes of adrenal functions and reproduction, mortality, dispersal, or growth characteristics in natural populations (Krebs and Myers, 1974; Krebs et al., 1977).

Self-regulation might also be possible through interspecific interactions such as herbivore-plant, predator-prey, and parasite-host systems. Pimental (1968) has proposed that a genetic feedback mechanism operates in such cases to influence population size. Suppose, for example, that a new species of parasite is introduced into an area containing a suitable host to which infection by the parasite is ultimately lethal. Initially, parasite numbers increase and competition within the population intensifies. Hosts become increasingly scarce, which makes their location by parasites more difficult. If competition within the parasite population for the relatively scarce hosts can limit its numbers before the host population is destroyed, then evolutionary changes can occur. Strong selective pressures created on the host can result in the evolution of types more resistant to the parasites. If the latter can respond genetically by alterations in survival and reproductive rates so as to improve its chances of infection, then the parasite density can become stably adjusted to the change in the genetic constitution of the hosts.

The well-documented case of interaction between European rabbits and the myxomatosis virus in Australia provides an example of such genetic feedback. To control high rabbit populations, the virus, in its original virulent form, was introduced into existing populations of the host. At first, the virus was very effective, proving fatal to some 98% of the rabbits. Due to selection for individuals more resistant to viral infection, however, rabbit mortality has gradually decreased to about 25%. This reduction in mortality has been accompanied by genetic change and consequent altering of density within the viral population. In the latter case, attenuated forms have been selected for, increasing the average life span of the host and thereby improving the chance of viral transfer.

In closing, it should be pointed out that most published ideas regarding self-regulation are still highly speculative. The hypothesis developed by Wynne-Edwards in which territoriality and many other forms of social behavior have supposedly evolved for the purpose of regulating population size is presently discounted, since it postulated the need for some form of group selection to override selection acting on the individual. Until much more field data are available on a broad scale of organisms, the possible role, if any, of self-regulation in the biology of populations will remain obscure.

SOLVED EXAMPLE PROBLEMS

Density Fluctuations and Their Analysis

1. Compare the density fluctuations in the following two hypothetical populations by computing the coefficients of variation (CV) and fluctuation (CF) for both sets of data.

	t_1	t_2	t_3	t_4	t_5
Population A:	10	30	10	20	10
Population B:	1	5	2	5	2

solution The arithmetic means and variances are $\overline{N}_A = 16.0$, $V(N_A) = 80.0$, and $\overline{N}_B = 3.0$, $V(N_B) = 2.8$. Thus $CV_A = 0.56$ and $CV_B = 0.62$. Moreover, since $\log(\overline{N}_{G,A}) = 1.1556$ and $\log(\overline{N}_{G,B}) = 0.4000$, we have $D_{l,A} = 0.222$ and $D_{l,B} = 0.299$. This gives $CF_A = 1.67$ and $CF_B = 1.99$. Thus, population B fluctuates by a greater average factor than population A does. Note that a simple comparison of variances would suggest that population A is more variable than B. However, elimination of the effect of population size shows that this is not the case.

2. A model that has been used to illustrate seasonal variation of population growth is $dN/dt = Nr_o\cos(t)$, where t is measured in radians. Using this model, describe the characteristics of population growth.

   solution According to this model, N_t/N_o varies as $e^{r_o\sin(t)}$. Thus, N_t fluctuates in a regular fashion between maxima of $t = \pi/2, 5\pi/2, 9\pi/2, \ldots$ ($\sin(t) = +1$) and minima of $t = 3\pi/2, 7\pi/2, 11\pi/2, \ldots$ ($\sin(t) = -1$). The model describes the delayed effect of resource availability on population size when $t = 0, 2\pi, 4\pi, \ldots$ are taken as times of greatest food availability and $t = \pi, 3\pi, 5\pi, \ldots$ as times of greatest food shortage.

Time Lags, Unstable Age Distributions, and Chance

3. Suppose that the reproductive potential of a herbivore population in the present generation depends upon the amount of vegetation consumed by the population in the preceding generation. One way to model this time-delayed density effect is to express growth as $\Delta \ln N_t = r(1 - N_{t-1}/K)$. Conduct a local stability analysis on this relationship, determining the value of r which leads to divergent oscillations. Compare your results with those obtained for equation (9.1).

   solution First rewrite the expression as $N_{t+2} = N_{t+1}e^{r(1 - N_t/K)}$. Now define x_{t+2}, x_{t+1}, and x_t as departures from the equilibrium density K (see Chapter 1 for details). The expression can then be written as

$$x_{t+2} + K = (x_{t+1} + K)\, e^{r(1 - x_t/K - K/K)} = (x_{t+1} + K)\, e^{-rx_t/K}$$

Since only small departures are considered in a local stability analysis, products of x values can be ignored and $e^{-rx_t/K} \simeq 1 - rx_t/K$. Thus.

$$x_{t+2} + K = (x_{t+1} + K)(1 - rx_t/K) \simeq x_{t+1} + K - rx_t$$

Rewriting:

$$x_{t+2} - x_{t+1} + rx_t = 0$$

The solutions are: $\lambda_1, \lambda_2 = \frac{1}{2} \pm \frac{1}{2}\sqrt{1 - 4r}$. Thus, if $r < \frac{1}{4}$, the system is stable and nonoscillatory. The system oscillates when $r > \frac{1}{4}$, the oscillations becoming divergent when $r > 1$. It should be noted that the incorporation of a reaction time lag causes the system to show a greater tendency to oscillate than does the relationship shown in equation (9.1).

4. According to equation (9.4), the variance of the $P_N(t)$ distribution increases with time, so that the farther into the future that population size is predicted, the less precise will be the numerical estimate. Demonstrate that this is true by calculating the probability of there being 10 cells after 30 minutes and 20 cells after 60 minutes in a bacterial population for which $N_o = 5$ and $b = 0.023$ per minute.

   solution Using equation (9.3), at time 30 min, the probability of 10 individuals is $P_{10}(30) = \dfrac{9!}{4!5!}(e^{-3.45})(1 - e^{-0.64})^5 = 0.123$. The probability that there will be 20 individuals at time 60 min is $P_{20}(60) = \dfrac{19!}{4!15!}(e^{-6.9})(1 - e^{-1.38})^{15} = 0.051$. Therefore, we see that, if there is a stochastic element in reproduction, prediction of population sizes at future times is not very precise, especially when long time periods are involved. The smaller the initial population size, the greater the relative variation about the mean, and the less adequate is a deterministic approach.

Regulation through Intraspecific Competition

5. Assume that the eggs of a particular annual insect species are distributed randomly throughout habitat units (e.g., seeds, leaves, or stems of a plant). If the food available in each habitat unit is only sufficient to support one developing insect to the reproductive age, survivors will be limited to those habitat units that are infested by a single individual. Show that the growth of this insect population can be modeled by means of equation (9.1).

   solution Let N_t be the average number of eggs per habitat unit at generation t. Since insect dispersion is random, the number of individuals per habitat unit is Poisson distributed. Thus, if there are n habitat units in the total field of observation, the number of survivors will be $(n)(N_t e^{-N_t})$. The fraction that survive is then $(n)(N_t e^{-N_t})/nN_t = e^{-N_t}$. If each survivor produces λ progeny, the density of eggs at generation $t+1$ will be $N_{t+1} = \lambda N_t e^{-N_t} = N_t e^{r(1 - N_t/K)}$.

6. Anderson (1965) has suggested that in the presence of interference, the
    time required to accomplish a biological process, T_a, can be expressed as
    $T_a = T_0 e^{(b/T_0)(N - N_0)}$, where N_0 is the lowest population density having an
    interference effect. Show that the model presented in the text is simply one
    special case of Anderson's expression.

    solution   The model presented in the text assumes that there is no lower
    population size limit to interference, i.e., that $N - N_0 = N - 1$. If we then
    consider the case where b/T_0 is small, then Anderson's model becomes T_a
    $= T_0[1 + (b/T_0)(N - 1)]$. Solving for T_a gives $T_a = T_0 + b(N - 1)$. This
    represents the situation when the ratio of the time delay per individual
    encounter to the minimum time required to perform the activity is small.

7. Show that for uniform, hexagonal spacing, illustrated below, $\bar{r}_A = 1.0745/$
    $\sqrt{N}$.

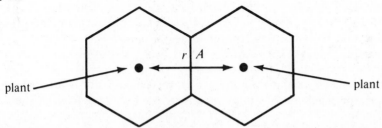

    solution   Uniform hexagonal spacing means that we can treat each indi-
    vidual as being centered in a hexagonal area. Such an arrangement allows
    the closest packing of uniformly-spaced individuals. To find the area con-
    taining each individual, recall from geometry that the area of a hexagon
    equals $\frac{1}{2}rp$, where p is the perimeter and r is the distance from the center
    to a side. Since $p = 6s$, s being the length of a side, the area then can be
    given as $3rs$. Consider each of the six equilateral triangles in a hexagon:

    By the Pythagorean theorem, $s^2 = r^2 + (\frac{1}{2}s)^2$, so that $s = 2r/\sqrt{3}$ and the
    area of the hexagon becomes $6r^2/\sqrt{3}$. Since the area occupied by each
    individual is $1/N$, we have that $1/N = 6r^2/\sqrt{3}$ and $r_A = 2r = 1.0745/$
    $\sqrt{N}$.

8. Southwood (1966) cites data of Varley and Gradwell on the survival of a
    moth over different stages of a single generation:

Stage	Number/$10m^2$
reproducing adults*	30
eggs laid	1,260
eggs hatching	850
larvae	170
pupae	90
adults emerging	45
adults reproducing	20

*Assume maximum fecundity per female is 100 eggs.

Calculate the specific k values and the total generation mortality, K.

solution   To calculate k_o, first determine the maximum potential fecundity which is $\frac{1}{2}(30)(100)$ = 1,500 eggs. Thus, k_o = log(1,500/1,260) = 0.076. Similarly, k_1 (egg loss) = log(1,260/850) = 0.171; k_2 (early larval mortality) = log(850/170) = 0.699; k_3 (larval losses due to parasitism and predation) = log(170/90) = 0.276; k_4 (pupal losses) = log(90/45) = 0.301; k_5 (mainly dispersal) = log(45/20) = 0.352; and $K = \Sigma k_i$ = 1.875.

---

9. One approach to modeling the growth of a population with discrete non-overlapping generations is by means of the following form of the logistic equation:

$$\Delta (\ln N_t) = \ln \lambda - a \int_0^1 N_{t+t'} \, dt'$$

in which the last term is proportional to the average number of competitive encounters per individual during generation t and measures the effects of competition for a limited resource supply on survival and on the ability to reproduce at the end of the generation interval. The symbol $N_{t+t'}$ is used to designate the number of survivors at some time t' after the start of generation t. Show that equation (9.18) is a solution to this relationship when resources are assumed to be wasted on nonproductive members of a population.

solution   Assume that the rate of reduction in the number of survivors is directly proportional to the number of competitive encounters between them. This yields the expression $dN/dt = -kN^2$. Integrating over the limits of t and $t+t'$, we get $N_{t+t'} = N_t/(1 + kN_t t')$. Making the substitution for $N_{t+t'}$ and integrating, the expression for $\Delta (\ln N_t)$ becomes

$$\Delta (\ln N_t) = \ln \lambda - (a/k)\ln(1 + kN_t)$$

Letting $a/k = b$ and rearranging, the expression can be written as $N_{t+1} = \lambda N_t(1 + aN_t/b)^{-b}$. Note that $a/k > 1$ when resources are wasted in maintaining individuals that survive but fail to gain enough of the resource supply to reproduce at an optimal level. This would be characteristic of scramble competition where all members of the population have general access to resources. In pure contest competition, on the other hand, many may die, but those that survive have sufficient resources to reproduce fully. In this latter case, $a/k = 1$.

PROBLEM EXERCISES

1. Plot N_t versus t over several cycles using equation (9.1) with $r = 2$ and $K = 100$. Do the same with $r = 2$ and $K = 1,000$. Compare the cycles in these plots with those obtained when the same data are graphed as $\ln N_t$ versus t. (Note that by making a logarithmic transformation, the cycles are less skewed and retain about the same amplitude regardless of the value of K.)

2. Show that when all values of N_i are the same, the coefficient of variation equals zero, while the coefficient of fluctuation equals unity.

3. Show that equation (9.1) becomes approximately the same as the logistic equation when r is very small in value.

4. Demonstrate mathematically that if growth proceeds according to equation (9.1), oscillations in the variable $X_t = N_t/K$ will be bounded above by $X_{max} = (1/r)\exp(r - 1)$ and bounded below by $X_{min} = (1/r)\exp(2r - 1 - e^{r-1})$.

5. Consider a population of microorganisms undergoing exponential growth. Using equation (9.3), compute the probability that the population remains constant in size over 6 intervals of time knowing $b = 0.05$ and $N_o = 10$.

6. Derive a modified version of the logistic growth equation by assuming that the instantaneous birth rate of a population decreases through interference effects in a manner similar to that described by equation (9.12).

7. Show that when individuals search at random for food (or some other requisite), each traversing an area a, the area of successful search, i.e., the area covered which is not already searched by competitors, is $(1 - e^{-aN})/N$.

8. Evaluate the expected population size and variance using equation (9.5) for $t = 6$, $b = 0.7$, and $d = 0.05$, starting with an initial population of $N_o = 100$ individuals.

9. Applying Bartlett's stochastic model for logistic growth, simulate population growth over four successive birth and/or death events, computing the time required for each event. Use $N_o = 11$, $b_o = 0.7$, $d_o = 0.4$, $a_b = 0.002$, and $a_d = 0.001$.

10. It is possible to develop a discrete analogue of equation (9.17) by writing the expression as $\Delta \ln N_t = r - b_o e^{-cN_t} - aN_t$. Construct plots of N_{t+1} versus N_t and ΔN_t versus N_t for $a = 0.02$, $b_o = 2.4$, $c = 0.02$, and $r = 2.0$. Determine the points of density equilibrium for the population. Which equilibrium points are stable and which are unstable?

11. Richards and Waloff (1961) collected the following data on the broom
     beetle (*Phytodecta olivacea*):

Year:	1954	1955	1956	1957	1958
Number of adults:*	11,820	16,184	17,027	6,343	6,759
(sex ratio)	(0.474)	(0.565)	(0.500)	(0.583)	(0.565)
Number of eggs and larvae:	460,169	659,554	701,563	201,760	125,039
Number of pupae:	63,939	137,610	7,140	44,826	10,454
Number of adults (pre-winter):	34,055	37,844	5,297	7,344	5,356
Number of adults (post-winter):	13,516	12,047	2,839	4,875	2,742

*Assume 250 eggs per female as maximum fecundity.

Perform a k-factor analysis and determine, by inspection of the graph, the
stage contributing most to total mortality.

10

Interspecies Relationships: Interactions Between Trophic Levels

In addition to the self-imposed limiting effects of crowding, there are also a variety of interactions with other species that influence the size of populations. These interactions can be beneficial or detrimental, one-way or reciprocal, and may involve species at the same as well as different feeding levels.

If two interacting species populations, designated as 1 and 2, are introduced into the same environmental space, the growth rate of each population will be modified to an extent depending on the density of the other. This can be represented symbolically by the following set of growth equations:

$$dN_{1,2}/dt = dN_1/dt \pm a_{1,2}N_1N_2$$

$$dN_{2,1}/dt = dN_2/dt \pm a_{2,1}N_1N_2$$

where $dN_{1,2}/dt$ is the growth rate of species 1 in the presence of 2, $dN_{2,1}/dt$ is the growth rate of species 2 in the presence of 1, dN_1/dt and dN_2/dt are the growth rates of species 1 and 2 in the absence of any interacting species, and $a_{1,2}$ and $a_{2,1}$ are the respective interaction coefficients. If growth is discrete, the derivative, dN/Ndt, in each case, can be replaced by the difference expression $\Delta(\ln N)$. Also note that these equations are general and do not imply which particular growth model would be appropriate for each species when growing alone.

Five different kinds of interspecific interactions can be recognized on the basis of whether the interaction coefficients are positive, negative, or zero. These five kinds of interactions correspond to the six different combinations of $+$, $-$, and 0, less (0,0), and are listed in the following outline:

Interaction	Species 1	Species 2
1. Mutualism	+	+
2. Commensalism	+	0
3. Amensalism	0	−
4. Predation (and Parasitism)	+	−
5. Competition	−	−

The first two forms of interactions are frequently grouped under a more inclusive title—*symbiosis*—since they usually involve a close association between two species. Mutualism occurs when the growth and survival of both species are benefited by the interaction. For example, the relationship between the fungal and algal components of a lichen and the relationship between a legume and the nitrogen-fixing bacteria in its root nodules are mutualistic. Commensalism, on the other hand, is said to occur when the growth and survival of only one of the participants is benefited while neither is harmed. Examples of commensal species include a variety of epiphytes, such as bromeliads, which use trees as a point of attachment. The epiphytes do not harm the trees in any way and benefit from their support.

Amensalism, predation, and parasitism are interactions in which one of the species is affected in a negative way. Amensalism quite often involves some form of antibiosis in which a population produces a chemical which adversely affects the growth and survival of other species, whereas predation and parasitism are forms of exploitation in which one species derives nourishment from the tissues of another. Predation and parasitism are usually distinguished by the fact that a typical predator captures, kills, and eats individuals of another species, while a typical parasite resides on or in the body of its host without necessarily killing it.

Of the various forms of species interactions, two have been studied extensively by population ecologists. These are the "vertical" or feeding relationships between species and the "horizontal" interactions exemplified by interspecific competition. Since competition is considered in some detail in the next chapter, we shall restrict our discussion in this section to feeding interactions.

TROPHIC RELATIONSHIPS

All populations within ecosystems participate in food chains or nutritional series in which consumers at one level (predators and parasites) feed on producers or other consumers at a different level (prey and hosts). Food chains are, in turn, linked together to form an interlocking network known as a food web. Each step in the food chain (or food web) constitutes a trophic level. For example, green plants or producers which perform the necessary process of photosynthesis must occupy the first trophic level, herbivores or plant eaters the second, primary carnivores which eat herbivores the third, and so on. Although it is often convenient to think of a species as occupying a single trophic level, one should keep in mind that many animals have highly varied diets and cannot be neatly categorized in this way.

As a result of the feeding interactions between trophic levels, part of the energy originally stored in plant tissues is transferred to herbivores, then to primary carnivores, and so on. This is shown diagramatically in Figure 10.1. Observe that at each step of a food chain only a fraction of the total energy made available to the organisms is actually stored in the form of food material. A large part of this energy intake is used simply for respiratory purposes and is lost as heat. Part is also lost through export of dead organic matter by wind

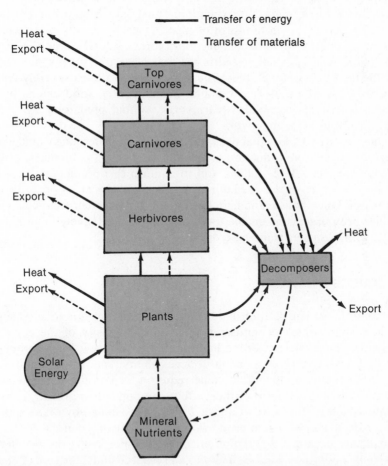

Figure 10.1.   Transfer of energy and materials through an ecosystem. Energy is gradually lost as heat. Materials are lost through export by wind and water. Observe that mineral nuturients are recycled while energy transfer is a one-way process.

and water and is, therefore, no longer available to the community. That fraction of the total energy used by one step in the food chain in unit time which is made available to the next higher step is termed the *ecological efficiency*. Thus, for example, when reference is being made to predators and their prey, the ecological efficiency is defined by the ratio

$$\frac{\text{Calories of prey consumed by predators per unit time}}{\text{Calories of food consumed by prey per unit time}}$$

Estimates of ecological efficiencies vary considerably, ranging up to 20%. For plants, measurements of the energy available in plant growth divided by the energy present in incident light usually lie in the neighborhood of 1%. In contrast, ecological efficiencies of the higher trophic levels average around 10%, which can be used as a rough approximation. Thus, only about 0.1 of the energy consumed by herbivores in the form of plant tissue is actually transferred to primary carnivores, 0.01 to secondary carnivores, etc. Since only a limited amount of solar energy is converted in the first place to a form which can be used by the next trophic level, these successive energy drains severely restrict the number of steps in any food chain. Consequently, food chains linking herbivores to terminal carnivores (carnivores without predators) are usually not more than four steps in length.

Because of the 90% loss that occurs with energy transfer, one would expect to observe a successive reduction in the standing crop (or biomass) at each higher trophic level. Field studies tend to confirm this prediction, except in cases where the size of the predator is much greater than its prey. In such cases, the rapid metabolism and high reproductive rates often characteristic of the smaller prey organisms enable them to support a relatively large mass of predators with a smaller standing crop.

RESOURCE DYNAMICS

General theory.   The relationship between a population and its food supply is a dynamic one which depends not only on the density of the consumer population but on properties of the limiting nutrient as well. These properties include such characteristics as quality, accessibility, rate of generation, and density relative to some threshold value required for consumer maintenance. For a quantitative description of their effects on population growth, consider a requisite which is generated at a rate F, being consumed by organisms and leaving (or decaying) at a rate proportional to its existing density R. If each member of the consumer population encounters and exploits the resource at random, thus having equal accessibility to all resource units, the rate of change in R can be expressed as (individual terms referring to rates):

$$dR/dt = \text{input} - \text{output} - \text{consumption}$$

$$= F \quad\quad - vR \quad\quad - aRN$$

(10.1)

where a and v are constants. The factor a in the last term is a measure of procurement rate. For example, if N is the density of some predator species, the value of a would then represent the average area effectively searched for prey by each predator per unit time. Observe that in the absence of consumers, $dR/dt = F - vR$. Thus if F is constant, R would approach its equilibrial value F/v monotonically, according to the expression $R = (F/v)(1 - e^{-vt})$. Alternatively, when consumers are present and $dR/dt = 0$, R attains the value $\hat{R} = F/(v + aN)$. Note when aN is small in comparison to v, $\hat{R}$ is then independent of population density and approaches the value F/v expected in the absence of competition. In this event, the absolute quantity of requisite is unaffected by the numbers "searching" for it and the apparent shortage of the resource limiting growth is merely a reflection of the low procurement field of individuals (i.e., low value of a) relative to the distribution and dynamics of R. Observations such as these have led workers to distinguish between an "absolute" shortage that would occur under conditions of intense competition, and a "relative" shortage that can occur at low population densities and depends solely on the procurement field of each individual and on the resource supply that it encounters.

Now consider the growth of consumers. Since the population is supposed to be limited by resource R, the population growth rate should vary directly with the amount consumed. Thus, assuming that some threshold quantity q is required per consumer for maintenance, the rate of growth becomes

$$dN/dt = uRN - qN \tag{10.2}$$

in which u is a constant. The population will, therefore, decrease at a rate equal to $-qN$ when in the absence of its resource supply. Note also that by making the growth rate directly proportional to the rate of consumption, we are assuming a constant "conversion efficiency" in turning resource into offspring. This efficiency is measured in terms of the ratio u/a.

There is one extension of this model that is of special interest since it yields the logistic equation for population growth. This is obtained by setting $F = vR$ and $q = 0$; a condition that might be approximated in certain microbial populations. Equations (10.1) and (10.2) then simplify to $dR/dt = -aRN$ and $dN/dt = uRN$. Hence, $dR/dt = -(a/u)dN/dt$ or, upon integration, $R = C - (a/u)N$ where C is an integration constant. Substituting this latter expression into the equation for dN/dt, we obtain

$$dN/dt = uN(C - aN/u)$$
$$= uCN(1 - aN/uC)$$

Thus, by letting $uC = r$ and $uC/a = K$, we obtain the basic equation for logistic growth.

It is possible to distinguish between two basic types of relationship existing between a population and its resource supply. They are *noninteractive* and *interactive* systems. A noninteractive system is one in which the exploiting population has no direct effect on the rate at which the resource is produced.

It is typical of plants and their limiting resources, and of herbivores that feed on the fallen leaves or seeds of plant populations that have reached their carrying capacity levels. This exploitation system tends to give the exploiting population a quasi-logistic pattern of growth (see example problem 10).

In contrast to the above situation, interactive systems are those in which the consuming population influences the rate of resource production. Hence, the components of the system interact. This is typical of most predator-prey (including herbivore-plant) systems where the growth rate of the prey population is influenced by predator density and vice versa. Such interacting systems quite often produce a system of coupled oscillations due to the linkage between the two changing populations.

It is possible to subdivide interactive systems further into *laissez-faire* and *interferential* systems. A laissez-faire system is where resources are independently procured by consumers. This is the pattern of resource consumption assumed in the development of the preceding models. In contrast, interferential systems occur when consumers interfere with each others' search for food. One approach that can be taken, so as to incorporate the effects of interference into the model, is to assume that the parameters u and a vary with N in a manner described by equation (9.12). Thus, in the case of the consumer population, we can write

$$dN/dt = uRN/(1 + cN) - qN \qquad (10.3)$$

Similar changes can be made in the equation for dR/dt. Regardless of the model, however, the rate of increase for the consumer population must always be less with interference than without.

Continuous culture of microorganisms: an application and test of theory. The continuous culture of microorganisms is a method that has become extremely important in research and for producing microbes and microbial products in industry. This technique usually entails growing bacterial populations in sterile liquid medium under equilibrium (i.e., steady-state) conditions. To accomplish this, various devices have been designed to provide bacteria with a medium that is constant (or nearly so) in aeration, temperature, pH, and nutrient composition. One such apparatus is shown schematically in Figure 10.2. In this device, sterile medium contained in a reservoir is pumped into the growth chamber at a constant rate and agitated to permit adequate mixing. Excess medium (containing bacteria) is then released into a receiving vessel by way of an overflow device. Since inflow equals outflow, a constant culture volume is, therefore, maintained.

Two methods have been commonly employed to control the equilibrium state. One is to adjust the flow rate so that the number of bacteria washed out in the effluent per unit time equals the rate of growth. This serves as the basis for the continuous culture device known as a turbidostat. In this case, a photocell is used to detect deviations in the turbidity of the culture and pass a signal to

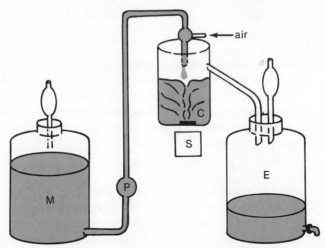

Figure 10.2.   An apparatus for continuous culture. Sterile medium (M), contained in a reservoir, is added to the culture (C) at a predetermined rate by means of a metering pump (P). The culture is agitated with a magnetically coupled stirrer (S) and aerated. The culture volume is maintained constant by a constant level overflow device and effluent culture (E) is collected in a receiver bottle.

a pump or valve calling for compensatory increases or decreases in flow rate. Another means of control is by maintaining the concentration of some nutrient at a level low enough to limit growth so that the growth rate adjusts itself to the flow rate. This second type of apparatus is known as a chemostat and is the device to which the following discussion applies.

The theory of a chemostat is basically similar to that presented in the preceding section. Monod (1942) first showed that, in batch culture, the growth rate of bacteria is related to the density of the limiting requisite according to the equation

$$dN/dt = uRN/(K_s + R)$$

where K_s is the saturation constant numerically equal to R when $dN/Ndt = \frac{1}{2}u$. Note that growth rate is not a linear function of R as predicted in the earlier model but varies instead as a rectangular hyperbola. Thus, growth rate becomes limited by yet another factor at high values of R. Also in batch culture, the requisite is consumed at a rate

$$dR/dt = -aRN/(K_s + R)$$

Additional factors have to be considered when growth occurs in a device designed for continuous culture. In this case, bacteria increase in density through growth and decrease as a consequence of dilution. The resource, in turn, is gained through incoming culture medium, and is lost by way of growth and in the effluent. This leads to the following equations:

$$dN/dt = uRN/(K_s + R) - DN$$
$$dR/dt = D(S - R) - aRN/(K_s + R)$$

(10.4)

where D is the dilution rate defined as $D = f/V$ in which f is the flow rate and V, the culture volume. In (10.4), S is the maximum resource concentration. Hence, $DS - DR$ is the difference between the rates at which the resource within the growth chamber is gained through inflow and lost by outflow. Once the equilibrium condition is reached, the relative growth rate of the population is balanced by the dilution rate. This gives

$$\hat{R} = DK_s/(u - D) \qquad \text{and} \qquad \hat{N} = Y(S - \hat{R}) = Y[S - DK_s/(u - D)] \quad (10.5)$$

where $Y = u/a$ and is commonly referred to as the yield constant.

When viewed in terms of total production, the performance of a continuous culture system is judged by two criteria. One is the *output rate*, defined as the total quantity of bacteria produced per unit time, and a second is the *effective yield*, measured in terms of the quantity of cells produced per unit of resource added to the growth chamber. In terms of the parameters already defined, these criteria are

$$\text{Output rate} = D\hat{N} = DY[S - DK_s/(u - D)]$$
$$\text{Effective yield} = Y_c \quad = \hat{N}/S$$

(10.6)

Their values are plotted as a function of D in Figure 10.3 along with the steady-state values of R and N. Note that the output rate increases linearly with dilution rate up to a maximum value, and then drops rapidly to zero. The value of D when the output rate is zero is termed the critical value (D_c) and corresponds to

$$D_c = uS/(K_s + S)$$

The effective yield, on the other hand, varies little until D becomes large. Thus, maximum production efficiency with high output and maximum effective use of the limiting resource occurs at a dilution rate only slightly below that giving the maximum output rate.

Several studies have been performed in order to test the validity of these equations. One by Herbert *et al.* (1956), using the bacterium *Aerobacter cloacae* and glycerol as the growth-limiting requisite, demonstrated little departure from theoretical expectations except at high dilution rates. These deviations from theory appeared to be the fault of the apparatus, such as imperfect mixing, and not the mathematical model.

PREDATION

Allocation of energy.   In the broadest sense, all animal populations, or consumers, can be regarded as predators since they must feed on other living

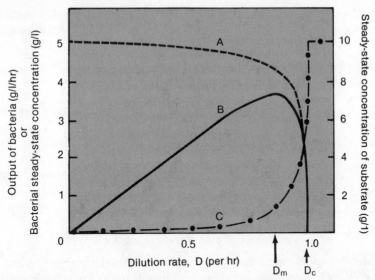

Figure 10.3.   Steady-state relationships in a continuous culture. Curve *A* is the concentration of bacteria (N), curve *B* is the output rate (DN), and curve *C* is the substrate concentration (R). The curves are drawn for an organism with $u = 1.0/\text{hr}$, $Y = 0.5$, $K_s = 0.2$ g/l, and $S = 10$ g/l. The effective yield (Y_c) would simply be $1/10$ that of N. D_m marks the maximum output of bacteria.

organisms or their remains in order to survive. However, most biologists restrict the use of this term to heterotrophs that search for live food and then kill and eat the individuals which they attack. In this regard, predation can be viewed in two different ways: one as a feeding response on the part of the predator, and a second as a source of mortality for the prey. From the standpoint of the predator, the capture and consumption of prey is merely a means to offset the energy costs of body maintenance and growth. This is shown more directly in terms of the energy budget of an individual animal. To begin with, most predatory animals do not eat all of the prey which they kill; some parts of a prey organism are inedible while others are simply left once the predator has reached satiation. Of that actually eaten, some is eventually lost through the inevitable production of wastes. Consequently, the energy budget of a predator must be written in terms of the food that is actually ingested less the amount lost in the form of waste products. A suitable expression in this regard is given as follows:

$$E_c - E_w = E_g + E_r$$

where E_c = energy value of prey consumed
E_w = energy value of waste products (feces, urine, etc.)
E_g = energy value of stored food (stored fat) and materials used in the elaboration of new tissues (proteins, etc.)
E_r = energy value of food metabolically degraded (energy for work)

The total energy expenditure of a single individual in excess of wastes is thus the sum of the energy required for growth and respiration. Additional insight into the fate of energy expended in the course of metabolism can be gained by writing

$$E_r = E_s + E_d + E_a$$

where E_s = energy expended in an unfed and resting animal (standard metabolism)

E_d = energy expended in the digestion, assimilation, and storage of food materials

E_a = energy expended in muscular activity above the resting level

Thus we have

$$E_c - E_w = E_g + E_s + E_d + E_a$$

This final expression can be taken to represent the total energy gains and losses encountered by a predator over some convenient time of measurement. Of the variety of energy requirements included in this equation, E_s can be regarded as a measure of the energy needed for body maintenance. Its value has been shown to be dependent on a number of factors, such as temperature and oxygen supply, as well as on the body size of the organism. As with other energy relations, the dependence on body size is generally expressed by means of a power function $E_s = kW^b$, where the value of b varies around 0.75 for animals with a wide range of body weights.

A diagram depicting the relation between energy intake and expenditure is shown in Figure 10.4. Observe that when an animal is receiving less than its

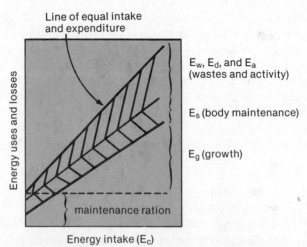

Figure 10.4. A model depicting the relative uses and losses of energy as a function of energy intake.

maintenance ration, it incurs an energy deficit since energy use exceeds that taken in. This will place a drain on tissue stores and the organism will lose body mass. If this deprivation continues, it must obviously lead to death as a result of starvation. Also, note that materials excreted as wastes and the energy expended in other miscellaneous activities tend to increase with food consumption. Consequently, a simple one-to-one relationship between growth (or reproductive output) and energy intake need not be observed. Nevertheless, it is often possible to assume a constant conversion efficiency and express the reproductive output as a linear function of E_c, such as,

$$\text{Reproductive output} = i(E_c - M)$$

where M is the maintenance ration in energy units and i is a constant. One example of this relationship is plotted in Figure 10.5.

Of the variety of energy expenditures of a predator, E_a is probably the most complex and difficult to measure in its entirety, since it includes any muscular activity over and above that of a resting animal. Although activity may be directed in many ways, those which have the greatest effect on the well-being of the predator and on the persistence of its more inclusive population are food gathering and the functions associated with reproductive success. Such activity can be taken into account by expressing E_a as follows:

$$E_a = E_{sp} + E_{re} + E_{a'}$$

where E_{sp} = energy expended in hunting (search for and pursuit of prey)
E_{re} = energy expended in reproductive functions (search for mates, courtship, care and training of young, etc.)
$E_{a'}$ = energy expended in all additional activity

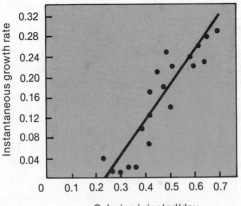

Calories injested/day

Figure 10.5.   Instantaneous growth rate of a population of *Hydra pseudoligactis* Hyman as a function of the rate of food injestion. (Data from L. Schroeder, 1969. Ecology 50: 81. Copyright 1969 by the Ecological Society of America.)

It should be apparent that the relative magnitude of each of these components depends on the availability of prey. When prey is abundant, less energy is needed for the capture of food and a correspondingly greater amount can be expended on reproductive activity. On the other hand, when suitable prey is rare, considerable energy must be spent on search and pursuit, and little can then be devoted to assuring reproductive success. These difficulties have been reduced in part by feeding strategies which tend to lower the energy costs of search and pursuit. For example, when a certain kind of prey is common, predators may develop a search image and restrict their feeding activities to that species. Likewise, most predators feed largely on the young, old, and sick for which the costs of pursuit are minimal.

Functional and numerical components of predation.   A variety of environmental factors are known which can influence the rate at which predators feed on a particular species of prey. They include the food preferences of the predator, the palatability of the prey, and the density and quality of alternative foods. Possibly the simplest variable which can be measured under experimental conditions is the quantity of prey. Solomon (1949) recognized two responses of predators to increasing prey density. They are (1) a *functional response*, by which the amount of prey consumed by each individual predator is altered, and (2) a *numerical response*, which results in a change in the density of predators within a given feeding area. Three common functional responses are pictured graphically in Figure 10.6 by plots of the number of prey killed per predator per unit time versus prey density. The first (curve A) is a linear response in which the amount of prey killed increases in direct proportion to the density present up to some saturation level. This is often designated as a type 1 response and is typical of filter-feeding animals, such as brine shrimp which filter out a constant fraction of their prey up to the limit of their filtering capacity. Curve B, on the other hand, represents a type 2 (or hyperbolic) response in which observed increases in the rate of attack diminish progressively. This is a common response among insect predators (Fig. 10.7). Finally, curve C shows a type 3 (or sigmoid) response. In this case, the predator responds only slightly to changes in the abundance of prey at low-prey densities. This is then followed by a rise in the relative rate of attack such that the fraction of prey killed per predator per unit time increases to a maximum at intermediate numbers of prey. The sigmoid response is typical of predators which eat several kinds of food and exhibit a switching response; that is, the tendency to hunt the more abundant prey in preference to the less abundant one. For instance, many vertebrate predators lack specialization and learn from frequent contact to hunt the prey in greatest abundance. Such predators are expected to exhibit a rapidly increasing kill rate as the prey in question becomes the most readily obtainable food source. The specific nature of this increase will tend to vary from one species of predator to another, however, since animals learn to discriminate between foods not only by ease of hunting but also by palatability of prey (Fig. 10.8).

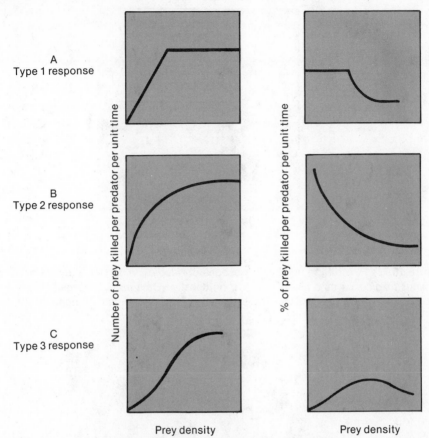

Figure 10.6.   Three common functional responses of predatory animals. Each response is shown by a pair of graphs, one (left) representing the rate of change in prey number killed, the other (right) the rate of change in the percent of prey killed, per predator per unit time.

The various factors contributing to the overall shape of a functional response curve can be formulated in terms of a mathematical model. Perhaps the most useful in this regard is the model proposed by C. S. Holling (1965). Holling has proposed that the major factor limiting the attack rate of predators is the time a predator spends handling each prey (i.e., time spent in pursuit of prey, time spent eating, and digestive pause during which the predator is not hungry enough to attack). If we represent this time as t_h, we can then represent the fraction of the total time which an individual predator spends searching as $1 - t_h n_a$ where n_a is the number of prey attacked per predator per unit time. The value of n_a should increase directly with the total density of prey and with the fraction of time available for search. Hence,

$$n_a = aN(1 - t_h n_a)$$

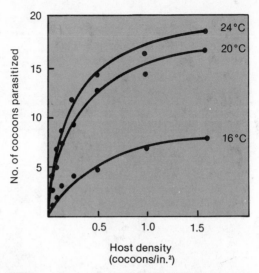

Figure 10.7. Plots of the number of cocoons of *Neodiprion sertifer* attacked by *Dahlbominus fuliginosus* as a function of cocoon density. (Data from T. Burnett, 1951. Am. Nat. 85: 337. Copyright 1951 by The University of Chicago Press. All rights reserved.)

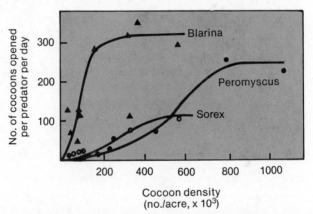

Figure 10.8. Plots of the rate of attack on *N. sertifer* cocoons by various small mammals as a function of cocoon density. (Data from C.S. Holling. 1959. Can. Entomol. 91: 293.)

in which a is the instantaneous rate of attack given as $a = kp$ where k is the rate of encounters and p is the probability of attack once an encounter takes place. Solving for n_a, we get

$$n_a = \frac{aN}{1 + at_h N} \tag{10.7}$$

Note, in this case, we get a hyperbolic response in which the number of prey (n_a) attacked per unit predator per unit of time increases with prey density (N)

up to a limiting asymptote equal to $1/t_h$. Observe also that the fraction of prey attacked per unit time, n_a/N, is a function of prey density, decreasing as $1/t_h N$ when the density of prey is high. This reduces the efficiency with which a predator population can limit the density of its prey.

Holling's model can be modified in various ways in order to describe a sigmoid functional response. For example, if the predator shows a tendency to hunt the more abundant prey, then the probability with which it attacks a particular prey organism at each encounter should increase with a rise in the density of that prey. This density dependence can be taken into account by expressing the rate of attack in our model as some increasing function of N. The simplest assumption to make is to let $a = a'N$. The number of prey attacked per predator per unit time can then be expressed as

$$n_a = \frac{a' N^2}{1 + a' t_h N^2} \tag{10.8}$$

We now have an equation describing a sigmoid response in which the limiting asymptote is again $1/t_h$. The value of n_a/N now varies in a complex pattern as $a'N/(1 + a' t_h N^2)$. In this case, the fraction of prey attacked per unit time is maximum at intermediate values of N, decreasing at both high and low densities. This reduction at low prey densities is of obvious advantage to the prey in that it permits them to recoup their losses, should they be reduced to low levels by the predator population, and, thus, protects them from annihilation.

In addition to changes in the individual rate of attack, predators can also respond to increases in prey density through changes in their own abundance. This so-called numerical response can come about by two possible mechanisms. The first is by way of migration to or from surrounding areas. This is often an immediate behavioral response in which the predators aggregate in regions of high prey density. Such behavior is common among some insectivorous birds, for example, which flock onto locust swarms. A second mechanism available for numerical change is through an alteration in the reproductive activity of the predators already in the area. This is an intergeneration response and, since the generation time of the predators is usually greater than that of their prey, it tends to give rise to a delayed density-dependent change in predator numbers due to the time lag existing between the two populations.

Three basic kinds of numerical response can be recognized. They are as follows: (1) a direct response, (2) no response, and (3) an inverse response. In the latter case, a reduction in numbers could result from an increase in competition with other predatory animals. The three different forms of numerical response are plotted as predator density versus prey density in Figure 10.9 next to each of the three functional responses. By plotting each functional response as the fraction of prey killed per predator, a total response can be calculated directly by multiplying the corresponding numerical values for the numerical and functional responses. This yields the fraction of prey killed at each prey density, referred to as percent predation. Observe that with an inverse response,

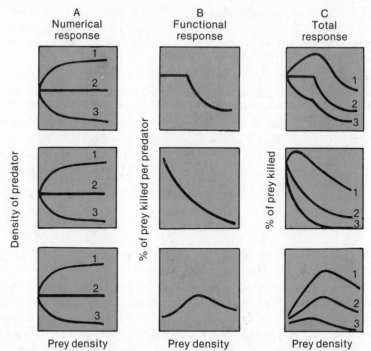

Figure 10.9. (A) Three kinds of numerical response: (1) direct response, (2) no response, and (3) inverse response. (B) Functional responses plotted as % prey killed per predator. (C) Total response, obtained by taking the product of the numerical and functional responses.

and in the absence of any change in predator density, only a sigmoid functional response can act in a density-dependent way as a curb on the prey population. Therefore, vertebrate predators can exert control through both their functional and numerical responses, whereas insect predators with a hyperbolic functional response can only control their prey through changes in numbers.

Exploitation and optimum yield.   From the standpoint of the prey, predation can be regarded as either an additional or substitutional source of mortality. If substitutional—that is, if predation merely substitutes one source of mortality for another—the predator will have little effect on the size of its food supply. In this case, the predator would merely be eating prey which are already destined to die from other causes. On the other hand, when predation acts as an additional source of mortality, it will lead to a reduction in numbers of prey and must then be accompanied by some compensatory change in survivorship or fertility (or both) if the prey is to persist. Some compensatory changes are possible when prey populations are limited by density-dependent factors such as food or space. Exploitation under these conditions would mean that fewer individuals will be present to compete for essential resources, thus insuring greater reproductive success for the remaining members of the prey population. This compensatory increase in reproductive potential will then serve to restore a new equilibrium level at a somewhat lower density.

The above mechanism is shown by way of a reproductive curve in Figure 10.10. It is assumed, in this case, that a constant fraction of each generation is lost to man or other predators as implied by the lowered reproductive curve under exploitation. The results are shown in terms of three consecutive harvests designated C_1, C_2, and C_3 and, by following the arrows along the spiral, the

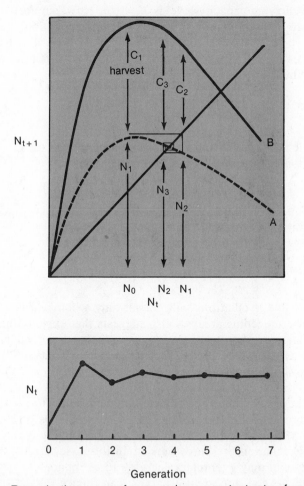

Figure 10.10.   Reproductive curve of prey under a constant rate of predation (A) including the number harvested (B). The bottom graph demonstrates that the new equilibrium level of prey is approached with damped oscillations. It is constructed by following the spiral lines shown in the upper graph.

sequences of harvests can be read directly off the graph. These changes are then plotted directly on the lower graph as a time series to show an oscillatory approach to a new equilibrium level.

The actual time path taken by the prey population will, of course, depend on the slope of the new reproductive curve at its point of intersection with the 45° diagonal. This can be shown by employing a specific growth model. Assume, for example, that in the absence of predators, the growth of the prey population can be expressed as

$$N_{t+1}/N_t = \exp(r - aN_t)$$

in which the carrying capacity level is $K = r/a$. Now, suppose that a constant fraction of prey is removed by predators in each generation. Let this fraction be $1 - e^{-d}$ where d is some constant greater than zero. The fraction of prey which survives predation will then be e^{-d}. We can now incorporate this source of mortality into our equation by writing

$$N_{t+1}/N_t = (e^{-d})(e^{r-aN_t})$$

$$= \exp(r - d - aN_t)$$

and, since the new equilibrium level can now be written as $K_d = (r-d)/a$, our growth relation becomes

$$N_{t+1}/N_t = \exp[(r-d)(K_d - N_t)/K_d] \qquad \textbf{(10.9)}$$

This represents the equation for the new reproductive curve under the present form of exploitation. The slope of the curve at its point of intersection with the replacement line can then be evaluated by solving the derivative, dN_{t+1}/dN_t, for $N_t = K_d$. This procedure yields

$$dN_{t+1}/dN_t = 1 - (r-d)$$

Thus, we see that oscillations will persist only when $r-d$ is greater than or equal to 2. The preceding analysis also suggests that exploitation may actually enhance the stability of prey populations by reducing their tendency to oscillate. For instance, if r is greater than 2 in the absence of predators, the population is expected to show permanent oscillations, as in equation (9.1). But, if predation is sufficiently intense so as to reduce the apparent rate, $r-d$, to a value less than 2, oscillations may then be damped or nonexistent. The rate of exploitation cannot be increased indefinitely, however, since when d is greater than r, N_{t+1}/N_t is less than 1 and the prey population will continue to decrease in size as long as such predation pressures persist. In this case, the prey population is overexploited and may eventually decrease to extinction.

As we have seen, too great a harvest can reduce the density of the prey below its replacement level and may eventually decimate the population, while a much smaller rate of predation generally results in wastage of prey through other sources of mortality. The optimal strategy for any predator, including man, is then to maximize its harvest (or yield) of prey without impairing the ability of the prey population to replace itself. This optimal level of exploitation is referred to as the *maximum sustainable yield* (or optimum yield), and is commonly used in reference to man who has the capacity to willfully choose and control his method of harvest. The concept is illustrated graphically in Figure 10.11. Observe that at each prey density, there exists an exploitable surplus of prey equal to ΔN_t. Since this is in excess of the level of prey required for maintenance, a prudent predator could continue to harvest this amount in each generation without producing a directional change in the density of the prey population. The optimum yield is then the maximum value of ΔN_t and represents the maximum amount of prey which can be harvested when the rate of exploitation and the growth rate of the prey are balanced (e.g., when $d = r - aN_t$ in the previous model).

The preceding analysis of optimum yield is adequate for prey populations with nonoverlapping generations. But, when applied to populations with complex life histories, age-specific birth and death rates must also be considered since predation will alter the age structure of the prey. More than one optimal strategy is then possible depending on the m_x and l_x distributions and on the form of density regulation normally operating in the prey population. To illustrate this point, two alternatives are shown by means of fertility and survivorship curves in Figure 10.12. The first plot (curve A) illustrates survivorship data in which mortality is normally greatest among the postreproductive ages with the lowest reproductive values. In this case, the optimum strategy for a predator would be to concentrate its efforts on older members of the prey population and thus maximize productivity. Conversely, when mortality is normally great-

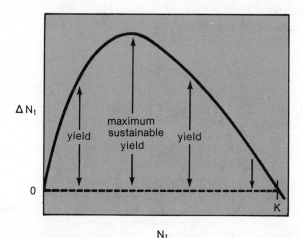

Figure 10.11. A sustainable yield curve. This shows the exploitable surplus of prey which can be harvested without producing a directional change in population density. The maximum value of ΔN_t corresponds to the maximum sustainable yield.

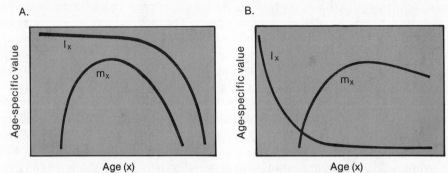

Figure 10.12. Fertility and survivorship curves of prey illustrating optimum harvesting strategy of predators. Graph *A* represents a case where the predator might maximize productivity by restricting the harvest to postreproductive ages. Graph *B* represents a situation where wastage could be minimized by harvesting prereproductive ages.

est in the youngest age categories as pictured in curve B, the optimal goal would be to remove as large a yield as possible from the younger ages so as to minimize wastage. The predator would then compete with other sources of mortality for its harvest without endangering the reproductive potential of its prey.

Lotka-Volterra equations. So far, we have considered how a constant rate of predation will influence the density of prey. Needless to say, if the predator population is food-limited, the prey population will also influence the density of its predators. Numerous models have been proposed in the past in order to describe this interdependency of a population and its multiplying food supply. One of the earliest models proposed, and also one of the most influential, was a set of equations derived independently by Lotka (1925) and Volterra (1926). Both considered the simple case of a food-limited predator population (N_1) which searches randomly for prey, and a predator-limited prey population (N_2). The derivation of the model is, therefore, the same as for equations (10.1) and (10.2) except, in this case, the limiting resource is a reproductive requisite which is assumed to multiply at its maximum relative rate in the absence of consumers. Hence, the predator and prey growth equations for this interactive system can be written as

$$(\text{predator}) \quad dN_1/dt = uN_1N_2 - qN_1$$
$$(\text{prey}) \quad\quad dN_2/dt = rN_2 - aN_1N_2$$

(10.10)

where r is the intrinsic rate of increase of the prey in the absence of predation. Observe that an equilibrium is established when $dN_1/dt = dN_2/dt = 0$. The equilibrium densities of predator and prey are then $\hat{N}_1 = r/a$ and $\hat{N}_2 = q/u$.

A solution can be obtained by dividing the first equation by the second. We get

$$(r - aN_1)d(\ln N_1) + (q - uN_2)d(\ln N_2) = 0$$

which, upon integration, yields

$$a(\hat{N}_1 \ln N_1 - N_1) + u(\hat{N}_2 \ln N_2 - N_2) = \text{const.}$$

By plotting the integrated expression as N_1 versus N_2, we obtain a family of closed curves in Figure 10.13. The intersecting lines in this graph are the equilibrium solutions (zero-growth lines or isoclines) $N_1 = r/a$ and $N_2 = q/u$. Since we obtain a closed curve as a solution, any pair of values (N_1, N_2) is restricted to one of the family of curves. Moreover, since each population must decrease above (or to the left of) its zero growth line and increase below (or to the right of) its isocline, the pair of values will continue to follow the cyclical path in an anticlockwise direction indefinitely. This, of course, leads to continued oscillations in predator and prey densities of constant amplitude. To show this more precisely, rewrite the pair of equations in (10.10) in terms of small departures from their equilibrium levels. By letting $x = N_1 - \hat{N}_1$ and $y = N_2 - \hat{N}_2$, the equations then become

$$dx/dt = [uy + u(q/u) - q](x + r/a) \simeq (ur/a)y$$

$$dy/dt = [r - ax - a(r/a)](y + q/u) \simeq -(qa/u)x$$

Differentiating with respect to t, we get

$$d^2x/dt^2 = (ur/a)dy/dt \quad = -qrx$$

$$d^2y/dt^2 = -(aq/u)dx/dt = -qry$$

These equations describe simple harmonic motion. Thus, if we let $x = 0$ when $t = 0$, their solutions are (Chapter 1):

$$N_1 = \hat{N}_1 + A_1\sin(\sqrt{qr}\, t)$$
$$N_2 = \hat{N}_2 + A_2\cos(\sqrt{qr}\, t)$$

(10.11)

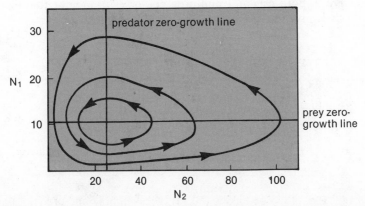

Figure 10.13. Three of the family of curves following equations (10.10), where $u = 0.02$, $q = 0.50$, $r = 1.00$, and $a = 0.10$. The equilibrium point is $N_1 = 10$, $N_2 = 25$.

In this case, predator and prey densities continue to vary sinusoidally with a period of $2\pi/\sqrt{qr}$. A plot of these equations is given in Figure 10.14. Note that the predator population lags behind its prey by $\frac{1}{4}$ cycle. Consequently, the predator population is increasing most rapidly when the prey population has attained its maximum size.

Volterra's principle.   There are several interesting aspects of predator-prey interactions that can be demonstrated by means of the Lotka-Volterra equations. One that concerns us here is a generalization, first given by Volterra, which states that any factor which increases the individual death rates of both predator and prey populations in an indiscriminate fashion will eventually result in an increase in the prey population and a corresponding decrease in its predator population. In order to show this, suppose that both predator and prey populations experience an additional source of mortality, such as hunting or the use of pesticides by man. The logarithmic growth rates of the predator and prey populations can then be written as

$$d(\ln N_1)/dt = uN_2 - q - d_1$$
$$d(\ln N_2)/dt = r - aN_1 - d_2$$

where N_1 and N_2 are the densities of the predator and prey populations, and d_1 and d_2 are the corresponding reductions in logarithmic growth rates caused by the outside agency. Once equilibrium is achieved, the predator density will be $\hat{N}_1 = (r - d_2)/a$, whereas the prey density is $\hat{N}_2 = (q + d_1)/u$. When compared to the equilibrium values in the absence of the additional source of mortality, it becomes apparent that the predator density has decreased by d_2/a and the prey density has increased by d_1/u. This, of course, has important consequences in man's tinkering with the normal regulatory mechanisms found in nature. For example, many destructive insect pests are normally subject to regulation by insect predators. Indiscriminate application of insecticides which are destructive to both predator and prey could result in an actual increase in the level of the prey, thus defeating one's initial purpose.

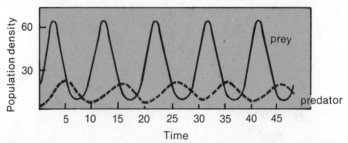

Figure 10.14.   Plot of the equations (10.11), showing prey and predator population densities over time. The population is that shown as the middle curve in Figure (10.13).

Experimental studies on predation.   One of the earliest experimental tests of the Lotka-Volterra model was conducted by Gause (1934), using the protozoans *Didinium nasutum* (the predator) and *Paramecium caudatum* (the prey). The results of these experiments are summarized in graphical form in Figure 10.15. Note that when the two species were cultured in an infusion of oats (plot A), *Didinium* quickly eliminated its prey from the medium and then died of starvation. This result would correspond in mathematical terms to a case of divergent oscillations followed by extinction. Similarly, when Gause provided a sediment in the culture medium as a place in which the prey could

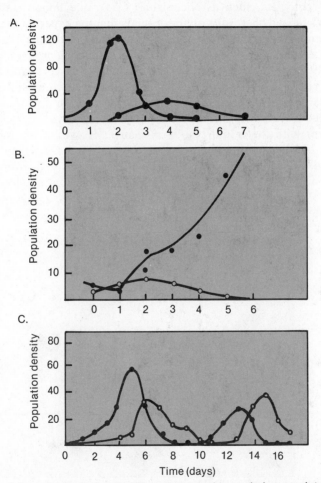

Figure 10.15.   Interaction between *Didinium nasutum* (open circles, predator) and *Paramecium caudatum* (closed circles, prey). (A) Oat medium; (B) oat medium with sediment; (C) with immigration, where (1 *Didinium* + 1 *Paramecium*) were added on days 0, 3, 6, 9, 12, and 15. (From G.F. Gause, 1934. *The Struggle for Existence*. Williams and Wilkins, Baltimore.)

hide (plot B), *Didinium* again eliminated its prey from the clear portion of the medium and then starved to death. However, in this latter case, the surviving *Paramecium* in the sediment later repopulated the culture. The only way Gause found that density oscillations could be maintained in this experimental setup was by introducing one *Didinium* and one *Paramecium* as immigrants every third day (plot C). From these results, Gause concluded that oscillations in the numbers of predators and their prey are not an inherent property of the predator-prey interaction itself as implied by the Lotka-Volterra equations, but occur as a result of interference from without.

Other ecologists, such as Nicholson (1954), questioned Gause's experiments and criticized his results on the grounds that the experimental microcosm which he employed was far too simple to conform to theory. To see if environmental complexity was indeed important in stabilizing predator-prey cycles, Huffaker (1958) performed a series of experiments using a predator-prey system in which predatory mites (*Typhlodromus occidentalis*) were used which fed on herbivorous mites (*Eotetranychus sexmaculatus*) which, in turn, fed on oranges. At first, Huffaker found that the predator always eliminated its prey, in agreement with the initial results of Gause. However, by increasing the complexity of his experimental universe, he and his co-workers were finally able to devise a configuration of oranges interspersed with rubber balls and with artificial barriers of vaseline which gave rise to continued oscillations in the numbers of predator and prey (Fig. 10.16) without doing anything more than replace old oranges with fresh ones.

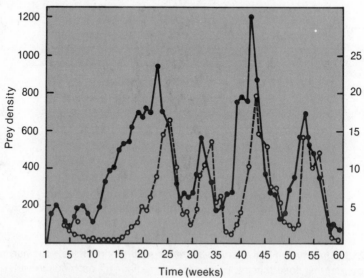

Figure 10.16.   Interaction between predator and prey mite populations, *T. occidentalis* (open circles, predator) and *E. sexmaculatus* (closed circles, prey), in a highly complex laboratory environment (see text for details). (From C.B. Huffaker, K.P. Shea, and S.G. Herman. 1963. Hilgardia 34: 305.)

As the results of Huffaker and others (e.g., Utida, 1957) indicate, predators can indeed regulate the density of their prey and will do so in an oscillatory pattern, given a sufficiently complex spatial environment. Just how important such interactions are in nature is difficult to assess, however, and is still a matter of controversy. For example, after spending years studying the muskrat, *Ondatra zibethicus*, Errington (1963) concluded that predators, notably minks *Lutreola vison*, have little effect on muskrat densities. Although predators may take large numbers as prey, most muskrats that are killed by predators are those which are forced out of suitable habitat as a consequence of territorial hostility and stood little chance of finding a secure place to live. It might be argued, in this case, that the predators are acting as scavengers and are feeding on individuals that are already doomed to die. Similar conclusions have been drawn with respect to predation on African game herds (Talbot and Talbot, 1963). Thus, in some instances at least, predators simply act as a substitutional source of mortality and may actually serve to dampen any oscillatory tendencies on the part of their prey.

Improvements on basic theory.   Although it has been tempting to use the Lotka-Volterra equations in order to account for various natural cycles as exemplified by the snowshoe hare and the lynx (Fig. 9.11), there are problems in doing so. First of all, most large mammalian predators have significantly lower growth rates than their prey. It is, therefore, doubtful that a population of large, slow-growing predators such as the lynx could ever reproduce rapidly enough to overtake and control its faster-growing prey population without some additional environmental limit serving as a brake to prey reproduction. Secondly, the cycles predicted by the model are unrealistic for any natural population, since they are conservative (or neutral) oscillations. As pointed out in Chapter 1, the amplitudes of such oscillations are dependent on initial conditions and will only stay the same as long as conditions do not change. If the environment is perturbed in any way, the amplitude of the cycles will most likely increase, eventually leading to the extinction of the predator and prey. This is in contrast to stable limit cycles which are independent of initial conditions and show a tendency to return to the same basic pattern, with the same average value, after an environmental disturbance.

A number of improvements can be made on the Lotka-Volterra equations. The following outline lists a few possibilities.

1.   Carrying capacity. The applicability of predator-prey models can be generally improved by including a carrying capacity level for the prey population. One approach is to apply the logistic growth function as follows:

$$\text{(predator)}\quad dN_1/dt = uN_1N_2 - qN_1$$
$$\text{(prey)}\quad dN_2/dt = rN_2(1 - N_2/K) - aN_1N_2$$

$$(10.12)$$

These equations predict a stable equilibrium level with both N_1 and N_2 exhibiting damped oscillations with time. As Caughley (1976) has pointed out, the inclusion of the logistic term into the prey growth equation is most appropriate for herbivore-plant systems and is only a rough approximation, at best, for higher trophic levels.

2.   Time lags. Most predator and prey populations are expected to exhibit time lags in the way they respond to changes in their resource supply. Such time delays can be included into a predator-prey model as follows:

$$\text{(predator)} \quad dN_{1,t}/dt = uN_{1,t-T}N_{2,t-T} - qN_{1,t}$$

$$\text{(prey)} \quad dN_{2,t}/dt = rN_{2,t}\,(1 - N_{2,t-T'}/K) - aN_{1,t}N_{2,t}$$

$$(10.13)$$

where T is the developmental time lag of the predator population and T' is the reaction time lag of the prey. When time delays are sufficiently long, these equations predict a growth pattern characterized by stable limit cycles.

3.   Functional response. A greater degree of flexibility and realism can be incorporated into a predator-prey model by including a term which sets a limit on the number of prey that a predator will attack. The predation rate will then depend on the functional as well as the numerical response of the predator. For example, if the predator shows a type 2 response, the appropriate model might be

$$\text{(predator)} \quad dN_1/dt = uSN_1N_2 - qN_1$$

$$\text{(prey)} \quad dN_2/dt = rN_2(1 - N_2/K) - aSN_1N_2$$

$$(10.14)$$

where S is a saturation factor which can have forms such as $(1 - e^{-bN_2})/bN_2$ (Ivlev, 1961) or $1/(1 + bN_2)$ of Holling. In general, models such as the one above which include a term for the functional response of the predator and a carrying capacity level for the prey describe a form of interaction with either a stable equilibrium point or stable limit cycles, depending on the values of the different parameters.

4.   Prey refuge. Yet another situation that may be encountered in predator-prey interactions is where some of the prey have suitable places to hide from their predators while others do not. In this case, predators might depend on the density of prey above a certain number that finds suitable cover. The effect of a refuge can be taken into account by letting M be the density of prey which is protected from predation. A suitable model might then be expressed as

$$\text{(predator)} \quad dN_1/dt = uN_1(N_2 - M) - qN_1$$

$$\text{(prey)} \quad dN_2/dt = rN_2(1 - N_2/K) - aN_1(N_2 - M)$$

$$(10.15)$$

These equations describe a stable equilibrium situation.

5.   Alternative food. An improvement of the basic theory can be made by assuming that the predator population has an additional source of food capable of supporting the predator in the absence of the prey in question. If the predator searches indiscriminately for prey, the prey population under consideration should contribute to the growth of the predator in an additive

fashion. By incorporating the effects of additional prey into a single intrinsic rate of increase r_1, we can write

$$\text{(predator)} \quad dN_1/dt = r_1N_1 + uN_1N_2 - qN_1$$
$$\text{(prey)} \qquad dN_2/dt = r_2N_2(1 - N_2/K) - aN_1N_2$$

$$(10.16)$$

This model describes a stable equilibrium point when $q > r_1$. Predation results in the elimination of the prey when $q \leq r_1$.

In addition to the modified versions of the Lotka-Volterra equations that have just been considered, another model that has received even more attention in recent years is one proposed by Leslie (1948). Leslie used a simple modification of the logistic equation by expressing the growth rate of the predator population in terms of a prey-dependent carrying capacity level. His equations are

$$\text{(predator)} \quad dN_1/dt = r_1N_1(1 - N_1/cN_2)$$
$$\text{(prey)} \qquad dN_2/dt = r_2N_2(1 - N_2/K) - aN_1N_2$$

$$(10.17)$$

This is basically an interferential model which best applies to situations where predators interfere with each other's search for food. Note when dN_1/dt and dN_2/dt are both equal to zero, the predator and prey densities are $N_1 = cN_2$ and $N_2 = K(1 - aN_1/r_2)$, respectively. These zero-growth lines (isoclines) are plotted in Figure 10.17. Observe that an equilibrium situation develops at the point of intersection of these lines. Bearing in mind that each population must decrease above its isocline and increase below it (note the arrow showing the direction of change of predator and prey), a (N_1, N_2) combination given by the point on the graph should then roughly follow the path that is marked by the

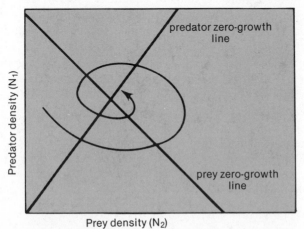

Figure 10.17.   Plot of equations (10.17) showing predator and prey isoclines, and the convergence of the system on the equilibrium point.

open curve. Since the trajectory of this path forms a closing spiral that converges on the equilibrium point, both N_1 and N_2 will tend to exhibit damped oscillations with time. Hence, unlike the Lotka-Volterra case (Fig. 10.13) which leads to constant metastable cycles, the equilibrium condition in this case is stable in that, if the system is disturbed in any way, predator and prey densities eventually come back to the same equilibrium values. If such disturbances arise from a time lag between the change in one population and the response in the other, oscillations in both predator and prey densities can occur. In such instances, predation can be regarded as being responsible for the density fluctuations since in its absence these coupled-lag oscillations would cease. Density fluctuations can also arise when only the prey species show time lags in the adjustment of birth and death rates to environmental change. In this case, the predator population will oscillate because the prey are oscillating, but it is not the cause of the density fluctuations.

It should be stressed that all the models presented above are based on the assumption of random search on the part of the predator. When prey are clumped and the predator distribution is also nonrandom and numerically correlated with that of their prey, the stability of predator-prey interactions tends to increase (Murdie and Hassell, 1973). These equations are also deterministic models and, as a consequence, do not take random density fluctuations into account. This latter point could be quite important when attempting to simulate actual data. For example, the failure of the Lotka-Volterra equations to mimic the results of Gause's experiments could be due to the chance extinction of the prey population. Stochastic simulation of the Lotka-Volterra model tends to bear this out, since the chance of extinction is very great, especially when a population is at the low point of its cycle. Leslie and Gower (1960) have also investigated several hypothetical predator-prey interactions by employing stochastic and discrete-time versions of equations (10.17). They found that the chance of a small population surviving when being preyed upon in a highly restricted space and uniform environment is indeed small, in agreement with the results of Gause.

Many of the modifications that have been presented thus far by means of separate sets of equations can be summarized in terms of a single model. One such approach is illustrated by the plots in Figure 10.18. What is shown is a graphical method patterned after that developed by Rosenzweig and MacArthur (1963) for analyzing the results of different predator-prey interactions from the nature of the predator and prey isoclines. The curves which are shown are roughly similar to those constructed by Rosenzweig (1969) and Maly (1969) from actual experimental data and are based to a large degree on the following set of growth equations:

(predator) $dN_1/dt = uN_1N_2/(1 + bN_2 + cN_1) - qN_1$

(prey) $dN_2/dt = rN_2(1 - N_2/K) - aN_1N_2/(1 + bN_2 + cN_1)$

$$(10.18)$$

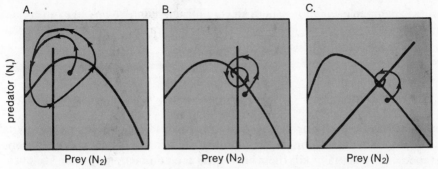

Figure 10.18.   Plots of predator and prey isoclines for equations (10.18). Graphs A and B represent laissez-faire systems ($c = 0$), whereas graph C illustrates the effects of predator interference.

where the constant c measures the effects of interference. The predator and prey isoclines for this system are, respectively,

$$N_1 = (1/c)(u/q - b)[N_2 - 1/(u/q - b)]$$ **(10.19)**

$$N_2 = r(1 + bN_2)(1 - N_2/K)/[a - cr(1 - N_2/K)]$$

Note that in the case of a laissez-faire system ($c = 0$), the predator isocline is a vertical line, like that predicted by the Lotka-Volterra equations. In contrast, the prey isocline has a hump, increasing at low prey densities, passing through a maximum, and then decreasing to zero when the density of prey is high. The initial rise in the value of N_1 required for prey maintenance is due to the reduction in predation efficiency with increasing prey densities. This is a characteristic pattern for predators which exhibit a hyperbolic functional response. The subsequent fall at high levels of prey can simply be ascribed to the results of competition between members of the prey population. A somewhat different pattern emerges in the case of an interferential system ($c > 0$). In this case, we see a linear rightward tilting of the zero-growth line of the predator population. There is also a change in the shape of the prey isocline, resulting from an increase in height and a leftward shift of the peak value.

The outcome of predation can now be predicted by determining the path taken by the two populations in the region of the intersection point of the predator and prey isoclines. If the intersection point is to the left of the peak for a laissez-faire system, the populations take an outwardly spiraling path (graph A). In this case, the predators are so efficient that the system destabilizes. Although such intersection points will produce stable limit cycles, progressive departures to the left of the peak quickly lead to a situation where the lower bound of the limit cycle is so close to zero that extinction of one or both of the populations is virtually certain. When the point of intersection is to the right of the peak, the path taken by the populations spirals inward (graph B). This results in damped oscillations about an equilibrium point. Note that even greater stability develops with an interferential system (graph C). In this case, oscillations are quickly damped.

PARASITISM

Host-parasite interactions.   Although parasites can only persist on living organisms, they are often responsible for the death of their hosts. In some instances, they actually kill their host upon the completion of their life cycle, as in many insect parasites (or parasitoids) which lay their eggs in their host's pupae or larvae. While in others, they weaken their host to such an extent that death becomes inevitable from other sources. In either case, the end result of parasitism is basically similar to predation and may be described by analogous sets of equations.

Several mathematical models have been derived specifically for host-parasite relationships. However, the type of interaction which lends itself best to mathematical treatment is the relationship between a parasitoid and its host. Unlike the situation usually encountered with most predator-prey systems, the generation times of the host and parasitoid are often the same. Hence, the interaction can be effectively described by means of a discrete-time model. A classical example of such a model is one derived by Nicholson and Bailey (1935). They proposed a random-search model, in which it was assumed that when a parasitoid encountered a suitable host only a single egg was laid, or if more than one egg is laid, only one survives. Since search is assumed to be random, the area effectively covered by each parasitoid (a_c) in search of hosts can then be related to the total area it traverses (a) by way of the differential equation

$$da_c = (1 - a_c P_t)da$$

in which P_t is the density of parasites at the start of generation t and $1 - a_c P_t$ is the fraction of the total area which is still available for effective search. Hence, the fraction of the total area covered by the parasite population is obtained by integration as follows:

$$a_c P_t = 1 - e^{-aP_t}$$

Now, if eggs are laid in all hosts in this area, the fraction of hosts that escape infection and survive to reproduce is simply $1 - a_c P_t = e^{-aP_t}$. Thus, letting R_o be the net reproductive rate of the host population in the absence of parasites, the density of hosts in the presence of parasites at generation $t+1$ (H_{t+1}) can be related to the density at generation t (H_t) by way of the expression

$$H_{t+1} = R_o H_t e^{-aP_t} \tag{10.20}$$

and, since each infected host gives rise to one adult parasite, the density of parasitoids in generation $t+1$ will be

$$P_{t+1} = R_o H_t - H_{t+1} \tag{10.21}$$

$$= R_o H_t(1 - e^{-aP_t})$$

The results of one experimental test of this model, using the housefly *Musca domestica* and its pupal parasite, the wasp *Mormoniella vitripennis*, are shown in Figure 10.19. Although the fit is reasonably good over a period of seven generations, the model fails to account for apparently stable host-parasitoid interactions in nature since it predicts a series of oscillations of ever-increasing amplitude (see Example Problem 9). This difficulty can be alleviated to some extent by employing models which place a limit on the number of hosts and, consequently, on the number of parasites. For example, one possible alternative to the Nicholson-Bailey model is the set of equations studied by Beddington *et al.* (1976). Their model takes the form

$$H_{t+1} = H_t \exp[r(1 - H_t/K) - aP_t]$$
$$P_{t+1} = R_o H_t[1 - \exp(-aP_t)] \tag{10.22}$$

in which $R_o = e^r$ and K is the carrying capacity level for the host population in the absence of parasites. Despite the upper limit on host density, the interaction is still highly unstable at large values of r. A less realistic, though highly stable, alternative is provided by the discrete-time versions of the Leslie equations in (10.17), derived by Leslie and Gower (1960). They are

$$H_{t+1} = R_h H_t/(1 + a_h H_t + a'_p P_t)$$
$$P_{t+1} = R_p P_t/(1 + a_p P_t/H_t) \tag{10.23}$$

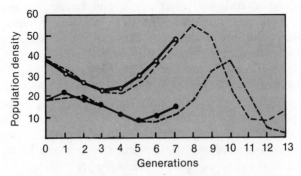

Figure 10.19. Interaction between *M. domestica* (host, open circles) and *M. vitripennis* (parasite, closed circles). The solid lines represent experimental data; the dashed lines are estimates using the Nicholson-Bailey model (equation (10.21)). (From P. DeBach and H.S. Smith. 1941. Ecology 22: 363.)

These equations predict a stable equilibrium point preceded by oscillations of decreasing amplitude. It should be noticed that both of the preceding models are discrete-time versions of predator-prey equations. They can, therefore, be applied to predator and prey populations with overlapping generations by replacing net reproductive rates with the appropriate finite rates of increase.

Epidemics and infectious disease.   In addition to the host-parasite interactions that have been discussed thus far, in which it was assumed that the host is infected by way of the free-living adult stage of a parasitoid, numerous parasitic infections of viral, bacterial, and fungal etiology can also be transmitted directly by contact between members of the host population. When a disease-producing microorganism is introduced initially into a population, essentially all potential hosts are susceptible to the disorder. Consequently, such an introduction is often followed by an epidemic wave in which new cases rise to a peak and then decrease in frequency as the number of susceptibles within the population declines. The rate at which susceptibles contract a disease can be quite spectacular. A good example is the spread of a viral disease termed myxomatosis among rabbits in Australia after its introduction in 1950. In just one locality where 100 infected rabbits were released, the rabbit population dropped from 5,000 to 50 within six weeks after the appearance of the first new case.

Many factors are known which influence the rate at which individuals contact a disease. They include factors which limit the rate of encounters, such as spatial distribution and the extent of crowding, as well as factors which influence the probability of transmission once a contact is made. The latter group would include active individual immunity. If a sufficient portion of a population is immune to a disease as a result of the buildup of antibodies from a prior infection, the resistance of the entire group would be of a high order. Other factors could act to lower resistance of individuals. For example, when large groups are undernourished and exposed to inclement weather, the disease can spread quite rapidly once sufficient contacts are made. Age distribution can also be a factor in limiting the severity of epidemics due to age-specific differences in susceptibility to disease.

Various attempts have been made to describe the development of an epidemic wave through the use of mathematical models. Due to the complexity of these models, however, the discussion which follows is limited to highly simplified deterministic approaches which describe the probability of contracting a disease independent of any variation in the virulence of the parasite or in the resistance of the host population. Possibly the simplest model that can be used to describe the nature of an epidemic wave is one which is based on a population in which individuals are infectious as soon as they contract the disease (i.e., no latent period), and remain as infectives throughout the course of the epidemic. This situation might correspond to epidemics of mild though highly infectious diseases that occur within small groups of very mobile individuals.

Suppose that an epidemic starts with one infectious individual within a population of size N. Let X be the number of susceptibles and $Y = N - X$ be the number of infectives at some time t. The rate of change in the number of susceptibles can then be expressed as

$$-dX/dt = kXY = kX(N - X)$$

Integrating over the limits from $N - 1$ at time zero to X at time t, we then get

$$X = N(N-1)/(N+ e^{Nkt} - 1) \qquad (10.24)$$

which describes a sigmoid reduction in susceptibles with time (Fig. 10.20). Since the rate of increase in the number of new cases, dY/dt, must equal the rate of reduction in the number of susceptibles, the equation for the epidemic wave can then be expressed by differentiating (10.24) as

$$dY/dt = -dX/dt = k(N-1)N^2 e^{Nkt}/(N + e^{Nkt} - 1)^2 \qquad (10.25)$$

This equation describes the curve in Figure 10.20, which shows a peak in the development of new cases when $X = \frac{1}{2}N$. The values of dY/dt and t which correspond to the maximum are $\frac{1}{4}kN^2$ and $\ln(N-1)/kN$, respectively.

An even more realistic model can be developed if we assume that infectives are removed during an epidemic as a consequence of death, isolation, or through recovery and subsequent development of active immunity. Suppose, for example, that in a population of N individuals at time t there are X susceptibles,

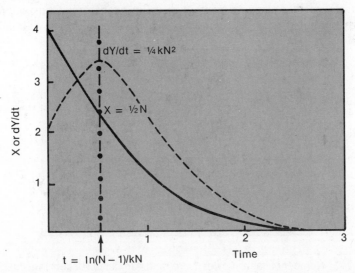

Figure 10.20. Plots of equations (10.24, solid line) and (10.25, dashed line).

Y infectives, and Z who are isolated, dead, or recovered and immune so that $X + Y + Z = N$. Expressing the number of infectives in time dt as k_1XYdt and the number of removals as k_2Ydt, the course of the epidemic can be described by the differential equations

$$dX/dt = -k_1XY$$

$$dY/dt = k_1XY - k_2Y \tag{10.26}$$

$$dZ/dt = k_2Y$$

An approximate solution for the epidemic curve in this model has been given by Kermack and McKendrick (1939) and is shown by the bell-shaped curve in Figure 10.21. They have also shown that no epidemic can start in this system unless the number of susceptibles is greater than k_2/k_1. When X is greater than this threshold density, e.g., $X = k_2/k_1 + C$, the total size of the epidemic (i.e., the total number of individuals removed by the time the epidemic has run its course) will be $2C$. The epidemic will thus reduce the number of susceptibles to a value as far below the threshold density as it was above it initially.

EVOLUTION OF FEEDING SYSTEMS

In a system in which one species feeds on another, the interacting populations will become jointly adapted to each other. Any modification in the characteristics of one will tend to be followed by a compensatory change in the other. For example, in prey populations, a selective premium is placed on traits which provide a means of escape or protection from predators. Consequently, the prey will become better at not being eaten. However, those individuals in the

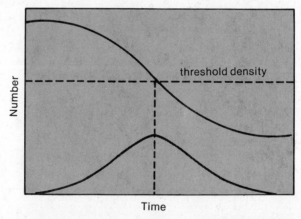

Figure 10.21. Number of cases (lower curve) and number of susceptibles (upper curve) during the time course of an epidemic. Note that the peak of the epidemic wave occurs at the time of the threshold density of susceptibles.

predator population that can cope effectively with such evolutionary advances in their prey will then have the adaptive advantage and will increase in relative abundance. Thus, an evolutionary race occurs with the prey becoming more efficient at avoiding predators and the predators, correspondingly, more efficient at capturing prey. This process of evolutionary change that occurs jointly in two or more interacting populations is termed *coevolution* and is the subject of present concern.

What follows are four topics dealing with different evolutionary aspects of predator-prey systems. The first two are largely descriptive and are concerned primarily with various mechanisms that have evolved for defense against predation. The last two are highly theoretical, introducing models that are used to relate the theory of feeding dynamics to the concept of predator evolution.

Defense mechanisms in plants.   Immobile plants would seem to be easy targets for mobile herbivores. Yet, most plants have developed some form of defense against predation. These defense mechanisms include protective anatomical features, such as thorns or a tough, leathery surface, and the production of secondary metabolites which are either toxic to potential herbivores or otherwise affect the palatability of plant parts. The secondary metabolic products which are used in defense by plants are diverse, ranging through the alkaloids, phenolics, terpenes, steroids, and a variety of glycosides. Their relation to primary metabolism is diagrammed in Figure 10.22.

The alkaloids are a heterogeneous collection of nitrogenous compounds which constitute some of the better-known feeding deterrents. They include nicotine, colchicine, and strychnine, which are known for their toxicity, as well as opium and peyote, which are famous for their hallucinogenic properties

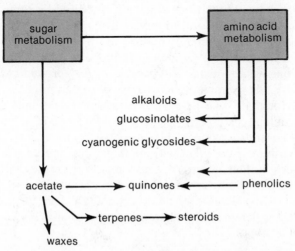

Figure 10.22.   Relationship of secondary plant metabolites to primary metabolism.

in man. This group is relatively common with up to 40% of the flora, in some places, containing alkaloid-bearing plants (Levin, 1976).

Even more widespread are the phenolics, varying in relative complexity from the vesicants present on the leaves of poison ivy to polymeric phenolic constituents such as tannins. The importance of tannins as a deterrent to feeding is shown by the negative correlation between the degree of insect infestation and the tannin content in the leaves of the oak, *Quercus robur*. It has been found, for example, that the period of highest infestation occurs in the spring when leaves are relatively free of tannins (Feeny, 1970). The level then drops during the summer as the tannin content increases. The fact that tannins form heterogeneous complexes with proteins, including digestive enzymes, probably accounts for their ability to provide a defense against herbivore attack.

The volatile terpenes often serve as odorants and are largely responsible for the feeding deterrence of resin vapors emanating from the leaves of some plant species. Plant terpenoid substances are also known which have molting hormone activity in insects. These substances, named phytoecdysones, can alter metamorphosis in insects when present in sufficient quantity.

The storage of glycosides is also an effective defense mechanism against herbivores. One group, the steroid cardiac glycosides, are powerful heart toxins in vertebrates, causing convulsive heart attacks when consumed in sufficient dose. These are produced by a variety of plants including the foxglove, *Digitalis purpurea*. Cyanogenic glycosides, such as amygdalin, are also stored for the plant's defense. Their toxicity is a result of the release of HCN upon digestive hydrolysis. Like the better-known alkaloids, glycosides tend to have a bitter taste. This serves as a cue for conditioning herbivores.

Despite a broad potential range for toxicity, considerable variation exists in the effectiveness of many secondary plant products as feeding deterrents. Part of this variation results from the ability acquired by some herbivores, or their gastrointestinal microflora, to metabolize or detoxify plant poisons. This is generally accomplished either by hydrolysis, in the case of amides and esters, or through a combination of oxidation-reduction and conjugation reactions.

In situations where a plant produces secondary products with a restricted range of toxicity, the plant metabolites may be used by animals, which can feed on the plant, for their own defense. For example, the milkweed *Asclepias curassavica* contains cardiac glycosides which are toxic to vertebrates. Yet, the larvae of an entire group of insects, the *Danainae*, which includes the monarch butterfly, eat the plant with no apparent adverse effects. By storing these glycosides in their tissues, the insects acquire protection from potential predators. Birds which attempt to feed on the insects find them distasteful and learn to avoid eating them after one or two unpleasant encounters. Thus, a chemical used for defense in plants can also be used for a similar purpose at a higher trophic level.

Cryptic, warning, and mimetic patterns.   One of the better-known ways in which animals avoid predation is by means of camouflage. This can involve a structural resemblance to another organism (or part of an organism) or to an inanimate object. In insects, for example, general resemblance to parts of trees or other plants is quite common. Thus, species such as the orthopterous insect *Phyllium siccifolium*, as well as lepidopterans (e.g., Kallima), look remarkably like leaves. Others are known which resemble flowers, bark, twigs, and even lichen. Camouflage can also occur through cryptic (or protective) coloration. Many animals have colors and body markings which blend with the landscape. In some birds and mammals, these colors vary to fit the season, while in certain kinds of fishes, amphibians, lizards, and invertebrates, chromatophore responses can produce rapid changes in coloration to blend with the immediate background. Counter-shading is another important component of camouflage which, in vertebrates, typically involves combining a darkly colored back or top with a lighter ventral surface. This helps to avoid shadow effects since, when illuminated from the top, a counter-shaded animal tends to appear more uniformly colored than one with little color contrast to begin with.

Whereas some species escape from predators by blending with their environment, others gain a similar advantage by advertising their presence with bright, contrasting colors. Such warning coloration is common among bad-tasting and poisonous animals and serves as a signal to remind potential predators of earlier bad experiences. For example, in the case of distasteful species, inexperienced vertebrate predators quickly learn after one or two trials to avoid all food items which look like the noxious prey. Thus, by reducing the number of attacks on prey and by decreasing the amount of time wasted by the predators in pursuit of an unpalatable food item, warning coloration is of benefit to both interacting populations.

When several distasteful prey species live in the same general area, they frequently participate in a warning system known as *Mullerian mimicry*. This is a system in which two or more species with unpleasant attributes share a common warning pattern. It is quite common in tropical insects, especially butterflies, where unpalatable species from several different genera can show similar morphology and behavior. Mullerian mimicry is clearly of benefit to the prey since, by having only one warning pattern to remember, predators will make fewer mistaken attacks. Additionally, less frequent encounters on a per species basis will occur with inexperienced predators. Hence, fewer deaths will transpire in each of the participating groups as a consequence of predator-related incidents.

Species with unpleasant attributes may also be involved in another mimetic system known as *Batesian mimicry*. In this case the unpleasant or distasteful species serves as a model for one or more palatable species, the mimics. By resembling an unpleasant species, the mimics gain protection from predation' since a predator will tend to confuse them with the model and, therefore, avoid them. A well-known example of a Batesian system in North America is that of the monarch butterfly, *Danaus plexippus*, (the model) and the viceroy butterfly, *Limenitus archippus*, (the mimic). The monarch butterfly can retain the cardiac glycosides which it receives from milkweeds and is, therefore, unpalatable to birds. Since the monarch and its mimic, the viceroy, are very similar in appearance, birds do not distinguish between them and, after feeding on a monarch, subsequently reject both the model and the mimic on later encounters (Brower, 1958).

So far, we have emphasized the role of camouflage and mimicry as protective devices for prey. It should be noted that these mechanisms also evolve to the benefit of the predator. Even top predators, such as tigers, gain from a camouflaged appearance, since this helps to provide the concealment necessary for an undetected approach to prey. Similarly, predators which look and act like harmless organisms or objects will gain a selective advantage by deceiving their prey. This latter example serves as the basis for another mimetic pattern known as *aggressive mimicry*. This is a form of mimicry in which a predator tricks its prey by having the appearance of a nonpredator. For instance, the Malaysian mantid, *Hymenopus coronatus*, mimics a flower, and thus traps and eats insects which alight on its petal-like legs. Another intriguing example, where the prey is the model and the predator the mimic, is the case of the predaceous fireflies of the genus *Protinus* in which females mimic the flash pattern of females in the related genus *Photurus*. By responding to the flash of the male *Photurus*, it is permitted to land close enough to its unsuspecting prey to launch a successful attack.

Evolution of predator isoclines.   Natural selection tends to favor highly efficient predators that can be supported by low levels of prey. In terms of the jargon used in the earlier-mentioned models, this means that predator populations (or predator genotypes) with the lowest isoclines will be adaptively superior. This is readily seen by way of a simple predator growth relationship. Suppose that two predator populations (or genotypes within the same population) feed on a single species of prey and grow according to the following set of equations:

$$d(\ln N_1)/dt = u_1 R - q_1 = u_1(R - Q_1)$$
$$d(\ln N_2)/dt = u_2 R - q_2 = u_2(R - Q_2)$$

$$(10.27)$$

in which R is the density of prey and $Q_1 = q_1/u_1$ and $Q_2 = q_2/u_2$ are the prey densities required for the maintenance of predators 1 and 2, respectively (i.e., the zero-growth lines or isoclines of the two competing predator types). Which population has the selective advantage? An answer can be obtained by first setting $u_1 = ku_2$ and then solving the equations simultaneously. This gives rise to

$$d(\ln N_1)/dt - kd(\ln N_2)/dt = d(\ln N_1/N_2^k)/dt = u_1(Q_2 - Q_1)$$

Letting $X = N_1/N_2^k$, we get

$$d(\ln X)/dt = u_1(Q_2 - Q_1)$$

which, upon integration, yields

$$X_t = X_o \exp [u_1(Q_2 - Q_1)t]$$

Thus, if the predator isocline of population 1 (Q_1) is less than that of population 2 (Q_2), the ratio of N_1 to N_2^k, and hence the ratio of N_1 to N_2, will increase without limit with population 1 being the sole survivor. The opposite will happen if $Q_2 < Q_1$, implying that the most successful type is the one which can maintain an equilibrium on the least amount of prey. Similar arguments can be made for populations which exhibit a type 2 functional response; except, in this case, increases in exploitation efficiency can lead to instability. If the prey isocline has a hump and the predator isocline is vertical, as expected for laissez-faire systems, a lowering of the predator isocline to the left of the prey maximum results in rapid destabilization with extinction being a very likely possibility. Then how have the relatively stable systems in the real world evolved? Gilpin (1975) has provided one explanation in which he proposes that the stability of real predator-prey systems evolves through the development of self-stabilizing interferential mechanisms, such as fighting or social dominance, by way of group selection. This is illustrated by the series of graphs in Figure 10.23. It is assumed that the primitive predator isocline is vertical and intersects at the peak of the prey isocline. Selective increases in exploitation efficiency then cause a leftward drift of the predator isocline and, as long as coevolution in the prey population can not keep pace, many local predator populations become extinct. Selection will then favor the more stable groups in which the development of aggression between individual predators has created interference competition. This causes a clockwise rotation of the predator isocline about its intersection with the prey axis and has an overall stabilizing effect. Additional increases in exploitation efficiency are now possible, making the predator isocline shift farther leftward. The net effect is a rightward tilting zero isocline that intersects the prey axis near the origin.

Two other factors should be mentioned that affect the stability of predator-

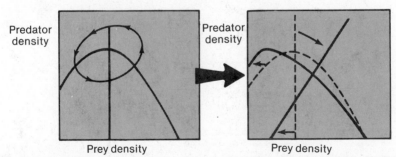

Figure 10.23. Possible changes in predator and prey isoclines during the evolution of an interferential predator-prey system from a less efficient and less stable laissez-faire system.

prey systems. One is territoriality on the part of the predators. This mechanism reduces the chance of oscillations by placing a ceiling on the predator population. The dampening effect that such a ceiling provides is illustrated in Figure 10.24. Another factor that can influence stability is the type of functional response shown by the predators. Although changes in the functional response do not necessarily alter the shape of the predator isocline, they will change the isocline of the prey, with the type 3, or sigmoid, response contributing most to stability.

Specialization of predators.   When, might we ask, is it profitable for a predator to specialize and narrow its range of acceptable prey? Conversely, under what conditions is it more rewarding for a predator to be a generalist, with a broad range of items in the diet? These questions were first formally addressed by MacArthur and Wilson (1967). Their conclusions can be expressed explicitly in terms of a model patterned after that of J. Maynard Smith (1974). Suppose that a predator population of density N feeds on a variety of food resources with densities R_1, R_2, R_3, . . . Let the number of prey killed per predator per unit time of type i be

$$n_i = kp_iR_i(1 - \Sigma t_{h,i}n_i)$$

or, upon manipulation,

$$n_i = kp_iR_i/(1 + k \Sigma p_iR_it_{h,i}) \tag{10.28}$$

where k is the encounter rate, p_i is the probability that the predator attacks type i prey once an encounter is made, and the $t_{h,i}$'s are the respective handling times. Assuming, as before, that reproductive output is a linear function of energy intake, we can also write

$$d(\ln N)/dt = \Sigma w_in_i - q \tag{10.29}$$

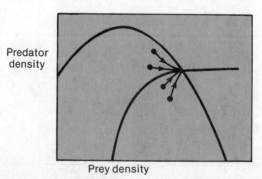

Figure 10.24.   Effect of territorial behavior on the predator isocline. This places a ceiling on the predator population and prevents oscillations altogether.

in which w_i is the contribution of prey i to predator production. Using (10.28) to eliminate n_i in equation (10.29), we then get

$$d(\ln N)/dt = k \Sigma w_i p_i R_i/(1 + k \Sigma p_i R_i t_{h,i}) - q \qquad (10.30)$$

Consider two extreme situations. First assume that $R_i t_{h,i}$'s are small so that $k \Sigma p_i R_i t_{h,i} \ll 1$. Then,

$$d(\ln N)/dt \simeq k \Sigma w_i p_i R_i - q$$

In this case, little time is spent in handling food items, such as in pursuit, eating, etc., and most of the predator's time will be devoted to search. Since the intrinsic rate of increase of the predator population is proportional to the factor $k \Sigma w_i p_i R_i$, selection will act to maximize predator growth by increasing the probability of attack to $p_i = 1$ for all food items. Hence, when resources are difficult to find but relatively easy to catch and consume, the optimal strategy will be that of a generalist, having a broad range of acceptable prey.

Now suppose that $R_i t_{h,i}$'s are large such that $k \Sigma p_i R_i t_{h,i} \gg 1$ and

$$d(\ln N)/dt \simeq \Sigma w_i p_i R_i/\Sigma p_i R_i t_{h,i} - q$$

Here, little time is available for search. Selection will then act to maximize $\Sigma w_i p_i R_i/\Sigma p_i R_i t_{h,i}$. This is accomplished by increasing the probability of attack to $p_i = 1$ for those food items which yield the largest ratio of w_i to $t_{h,i}$ and reducing the probability to $p_i = 0$ for all others. Thus, when the time available for search is low, while a great deal of energy is spent on pursuit, selection will act to produce specialists.

SOLVED EXAMPLE PROBLEMS

Trophic Relationships

1. Suppose that a predator population requires a diet of 10,000 kilocalories of prey per day. Each prey organism weighs an average of 50 grams and each gram yields 5 kilocalories. If the average lifespan of the prey before being consumed by predators is 100 days, what is the standing crop in number of prey required for predator maintenance?

   solution   The number of calories available per prey organism is $(50)(5) = 250$ kilocalories. The predator population, therefore, requires $10,000/250 = 40$ prey per day. This is the turnover rate of the prey population; it is the amount of prey biomass that must be replaced daily. Since predators consume $1/100$ of the prey population per day, we have that $(0.01)(\text{standing crop}) = 40$. Thus, the prey population size required to support the predators is 4,000 individuals.

Resource Dynamics

2. Show how limitation by a transient resource such as light is basically the same as limitation by habitat space and, therefore, gives rise to a logistic type of relationship.

   solution   Let I be the light intensity impinging on plants, expressed in terms of energy transmitted per unit area per unit time, and i represent the intensity used for maintenance by a single plant. The proportion used for maintenance by a population of size N is then iN/I, leaving $1 - iN/I$ available for growth. Hence, the growth of the plant population will be

$$d(\ln N)/dt = r(1 - iN/I) = r(1 - N/K)$$

   where $K = I/i$.

3. Consider a population of bacteria growing in continuous culture with $u = 1.0$ per hr, $Y = 0.5$, and $K_s = 0.1$ g/l. If the dilution rate is 0.5 per hr and the substrate concentration flowing into the culture is 6 g/l, determine the equilibrium values of the substrate concentration ($\hat{R}$) and the bacterial concentration ($\hat{N}$). Also, calculate the values of the output rate, the effective yield, and the critical value of D.

   solution   Using equations (10.5), with $D = 0.5$ and $S = 6$, we obtain $\hat{R} = 0.05/0.5 = 0.1$ g/l and $\hat{N} = (0.5)(5.9) = 2.95$ g/l. Therefore, the output rate is $(0.5)(2.95) = 1.475$ g/l per hour and the effective yield is $Y_c = 0.49$. The output rate would be zero at a dilution rate of $D_c = 6/6.1 = 0.98$ per hr.

Predation

4. Demonstrate that when the functional response is hyperbolic and exploitation is included, the number of prey successfully attacked in time t, N_a, can be given as

$$N_a = N\{1 - \exp[-a(Pt - t_h N_a)]\}$$

   where N is the total density of prey and P is the predator density.

   solution   When exploitation is included in the model, unconsumed prey will decrease with time. Thus, when N_a prey have been consumed, the number of prey attacked per predator per unit time becomes

$$n_a = dN_a/Pdt = a(N - N_a)/[1 + at_h(N - N_a)]$$

   This yields

$$\int \frac{dN_a}{N - N_a} + at_h \int dN_a = aP \int dt$$

   Upon integration and rearrangement, we get the desired result.

5. Show that an introduction of a time lag (however slight) into the Lotka-Volterra equations leads to instability.

solution   First express the Lotka-Volterra equations as

$$\Delta\ln N_{1,t} = uN_{2,t} - q$$

$$\Delta\ln N_{2,t} = r - aN_{1,t}$$

Now, let $N_1 = x + Q_1$ and $N_2 = y + Q_2$, where x and y are departures from the equilibrium values Q_1 and Q_2, respectively. Since x and y are assumed to be small, so that each $\Delta\ln N$ is approximately $\Delta N/N$, and because $Q_1 = r/a$ and $Q_2 = q/u$, the equations become

$$x_{t+1} + Q_1 = (x_t + Q_1)(1 + uy_t) \simeq x_t + Q_1 + (ru/a)y_t$$

$$y_{t+1} + Q_2 = (y_t + Q_2)(1 - ax_t) \simeq y_t + Q_2 - (aq/u)x_t$$

Hence, we can write $\Delta^2 x_t = (ru/a)\,\Delta y_t = -\,rqx_t$. This yields

$$x_{t+2} - 2x_{t+1} + (1 + rq)\,x_t = 0$$

for which the solutions are $\lambda_1, \lambda_2 = 1 \pm \sqrt{-rq}$. Since $-rq < 0$ and $1 + rq > 1$, the ultimate outcome will be oscillations which increase initially in amplitude.

6. Demonstrate that if reproductive output is a linear function of energy intake, the rate of increase in a predator population (N_1), with a type 2 functional response, can be given as

$$d(\ln N_1)/dt = awN_2/(1 + at_h N_2) - q$$

where N_2 is the prey density and w is the efficiency with which prey is converted into predator offspring.
solution   Let $d(\ln N_1)/dt = wn_a - q$ where n_a is the number of prey attacked per predator per unit time. Since $n_a = aN_2/(1 + at_h N_2)$, substitution yields the desired expression.

7. Show that when the Leslie model is applied to Volterra's principle, prey are not necessarily expected to increase above their original level following an additional source of indiscriminate mortality.
solution   Equations (10.17) can be modified to include an additional source of mortality by writing them as

$$d(\ln N_1)/dt = r_1(1 - N_1/cN_2) - d_1$$

$$d(\ln N_2)/dt = r_2(1 - N_2/K) - aN_1 - d_2$$

where d_1 and d_2 are, as before, the reductions in logarithmic growth rate caused by the additional mortality. When $d(\ln N_1)/dt = d(\ln N_2)/dt = 0$, we have

$$\hat{N}_1 = Kc(r_1 - d_1)(1 - d_2)/[r_1 r_2 + aKc(r_1 - d_1)] \qquad \text{and}$$

$$\hat{N}_2 = r_1(1 - d_2)/[r_1 r_2 + aKc(r_1 - d_1)]$$

Since the predator population is reduced by both d_1 and d_2, it must decrease in abundance. However, the equilibrium value of N_2 is reduced by d_2 in the numerator and increased by d_1 in the denominator. The ultimate outcome will depend on the relative magnitudes of these effects.

8. Derive equation (10.18) for the predator population by assuming that the fraction of the total time available for search declines with the number of attacks on prey and encounters with other predators.

    solution   Let n_p = the rate of encounters each predator makes on the average with other predators. If encounters are entirely random, $n_p/n_a \simeq N_1/N_2$ where n_a is, again, the rate of attack per unit predator and N_1 and N_2 are the densities of the predator and prey, respectively. We can then write

$$n_a = aN_2(1 - t_N n_p - t_h n_a)$$
$$= aN_2[1 - t_N(N_1/N_2) n_a - t_h n_a]$$

in which t_N = the time lost from search following an encounter with another predator. Solving for n_a and expressing $at_h = b$ and $at_N = c$, we get $n_a = aN_2/(1 + bN_2 + cN_1)$. Substituting into the expression $d(\ln N_1)/dt = wn_a - q$ and letting $u = aw$, we then get the desired equation.

Parasitism

9. Considering small displacements from the equilibrium state, show that the host-parasite model of Nicholson and Bailey is unstable and oscillatory.

    solution   Let y and x represent departures from the equilibrium values $P_e = (1/a)\ln R_o$ and $H_e = (1/a)(\ln R_o)/(R_o - 1)$, respectively. For small displacements, we can then write $x_{t+1} + H_e = (x_t + H_e)e^{-ay_t} \simeq x_t + H_e - aH_e y_t$. Thus,

$$x_{t+1} = x_t - \left(\frac{\ln R_o}{R_o - 1}\right) y_t$$

Similarly, $y_{t+1} + P_e = R_o(x_t + H_e) - (x_{t+1} + H_e)$, or, since $P_e = (R_o - 1)H_e$.

$$y_{t+1} = R_o x_t - x_{t+1}$$

Replacing y_{t+1} with $[(R_o-1)/\ln R_o](x_{t+1} - x_{t+2})$ from the first solution, we get

$$x_{t+2} - \left(\frac{\ln R_o}{R_o - 1} + 1\right) x_{t+1} + R_o\left(\frac{\ln R_o}{R_o - 1}\right) x_t = 0$$

Since $4R_o(\ln R_o)/(R_o - 1)$ must be greater than $[(\ln R_o)/(R_o - 1) + 1]^2$ as long as R_o is greater than 1, the interaction must inevitably lead to oscillations. Moreover, since $c = R_o(\ln R_o)/(R_o - 1)$ is greater than 1, the oscillations will increase in amplitude.

10. The growth pattern expected for a noninteractive exploitation system can be illustrated by that predicted for a population of algae which is limited

by a micronutrient such as phosphorus. Assume a closed system such as a lake and that the total phosphorus tied up in living matter is rapidly returned back into the system upon the death of algal cells. Let S be the constant total concentration of resource. The concentration in current use is then $S - R$. Thus if we let q be the individual death rate of the algal population, the rate at which phosphorus is returned to the system becomes $q(S - R)$. Hence, the approximate rates of change in resource and population densities can then be written as

$$dR/dt = q(S - R) - aRN$$

$$dN/dt = uRN - qN$$

for which the equilibrium solutions are

$$\hat{R} = q/u \quad \text{and} \quad \hat{N} = q(S - R)/aR = (uS - q)/a$$

Demonstrate that this model must predict a growth curve, similar to that of the logistic equation, in which the approach to equilibrium is without oscillations.

solution   To predict the behavior of the model in the vicinity of the equilibrium state, let $x = R - \hat{R}$ and $y = N - \hat{N}$ be departures from equilibrium and assume that x and y are small so that terms in x^2, xy, and y^2 can be ignored. Since $dx/dt = dR/dt$ and $dy/dt = dN/dt$, we can write

$$dy/dt = [(u)(q/u) + ux - q](uS - q)/a$$

$$= ux(uS - q)/a$$

By a similar procedure,

$$dx/dt = -uSx - qay/u$$

If we differentiate the latter equation with respect to t and substitute the preceding expression for dy/dt, we get

$$d^2x/dt^2 + uS(dx/dt) + q(uS - q)x = 0$$

This is a second order differential equation which has the solution

$$x_t = k_1 e^{\lambda_1 t} + k_2 e^{\lambda_2 t}$$

Since the roots λ_1 and λ_2 are real and negative, the model must predict a nonoscillatory approach to equilibrium.

PROBLEM EXERCISES

1. Reconsider Example Problem 1. What effect would doubling the average lifespan of prey have on the number of prey required for predator maintenance?

2. Under what conditions could it be possible for the standing crop of prey to be less (in terms of total biomass) than that of the predator population? Analyze in terms of the Lotka-Volterra equations.

3. Using the appropriate expression in (10.6), determine the value of D which will yield a maximum output rate of bacteria.

4. The efficiency of utilization of a resource supplied in the inflowing growth medium can be defined as Y_c/Y. Relate the efficiency to D and S and show that the maximum utilization of a resource occurs at low values of D and at high S.

5. In the derivation of equation (10.8), it was probably unreasonable to assume that the rate of attack will continue to increase linearly with prey density. Show that a sigmoid functional response will also develop when the rate of attack is a hyperbolic function of the number of prey (e.g., $a = a'N/(1+a'bN)$).

6. Demonstrate why the metabolic rate of an organism should be proportional to the two-thirds power of its body weight under ideal conditions.

7. Draw the sustainable yield curve for a prey population which grows in a logistic manner and compute the density of prey which corresponds to the maximum sustainable yield.

8. From studies on the functional and numerical responses of small mammal predators to the density of prey (sawfly cocoons), Holling (1959a) found that the proportion of prey destroyed (expressed as percent predation) varied with prey density in a curvilinear manner similar to the curve presented below:

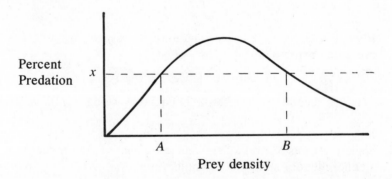

Assuming that the value x represents the intensity of predation required to keep the prey population constant in size, then there are two possible equilibrium levels of prey, designated A and B in the graph. (a) Which is a stable equilibrium point and which is not? Explain. (b) Is it possible in this case for the prey to escape control by predators? If so, how might this occur?

9. Show how equation (10.7) can be transformed into a straight-line rela-
    tionship so that both the rate of attack, a, and the handling time, t_h, can
    be determined by a simple plotting procedure. Do the same for equation
    (10.8).

10. Suppose that the densities of a predator population and its prey oscillate
    in a manner described by the Lotka-Volterra equations with a period of
    ten years. Given that the logarithmic growth rate of the prey population
    in the absence of predators is 1.8 per year, at what relative rate will the
    predator population decline in the absence of its prey?

11. Develop a simple model in which the predators are assumed to act strictly
    as a substitutional source of mortality on their prey.

12. Suppose that prey are subject to low-density effects so that the growth
    rate of their population in the absence of predators is given by equation
    (9.17). Predict the consequences of different levels of predation on such
    a population from the points of intersection of the predator and prey
    isoclines. Assume a *laissez-faire* system.

13. Show that the maximum sustainable yield for a population which obeys
    the Gompertz growth equation occurs when the density is K/e.

14. Differentiate between predation as it occurs between herbivores and
    plants, and between carnivores or carnivores and herbivores. Make a list
    of differences and similarities.

15. Suppose that 36 pupae of the housefly, *Musca domestica*, are distributed
    within an appropriate experimental setting and 18 pupal parasites (*Nasonia
    vitripennis*) are added. After 24 hours (1 generation), only 16 unparasitized
    pupae are found. Ignoring any effects of interference, what is the area of
    search of the parasite?

11

Interspecies Relationships: Organization into Communities

Populations occur together in mixtures of differing species composition, size, and complexity which are termed communities. Like the populations which compose them, communities have structure, perceived in both time and space. Its spatial components of structure are the vertical and horizontal distributions of species. Due to the presence of growth forms which vary in height, such as trees, shrubs, and grasses, plant communities tend to be stratified into vertical layers with animal populations concentrating their activities at different depths. In a forest community, for example, some species are ground feeders and concentrate their activities on the forest floor, while others feed in the forest canopy. In addition to vertical structure, each layer of the community is further differentiated by the dispersion of its members in horizontal space. Some pairs of species show distributions which are seemingly unrelated, while others, such as parasites and their hosts, tend to be closely correlated in spatial distribution. The degree of association between two species (i.e., the degree to which species are present together in the same sampling unit) can be measured with the use of a 2×2 contingency table. Letting $n = a + b + c + d$ represent the total number of quadrats examined, the contingency table can be represented as follows:

		Species B		
		Present	Absent	Total
Species A	Present	a	b	$a+b = h$
	Absent	c	d	$c+d = i$
	Total	$a+c = j$	$b+d = k$	n

for which the chi-square statistic is

$$\chi^2 = \frac{(ad - bc)^2 n}{(h)(i)(j)(k)}$$

For a numerical example, suppose that 20 quadrats contain both species, 60 contain species A but not species B, and so on; giving rise to the following table:

| | | Species B | | |
		Present	Absent	Total
	Present	20	60	80
Species A				
	Absent	80	40	120
	Total	100	100	200

Given independence, it is apparent, in this case, that we should expect cell frequencies of $a = b = 40$ and $c = d = 60$. Applying the chi-square test, we obtain

$$\chi^2 = \frac{[(20)(40) - (60)(80)]^2(200)}{(80)(120)(100)(100)} = 33.3$$

When compared with a chi-square table with one degree of freedom, it is apparent that there is a strong negative correlation between the two species. This could be due to differences in environmental tolerance or to negative interactions such as interspecies competition.

In addition to vertical and horizontal differentiation, community structure also exhibits a temporal component in terms of daily and seasonal cycles. For example, some species are active in daytime, other forms at night, and still others during the twilight hours. Different seasonal rhythms for the flowering and fruiting of plants and for mating of animals occur as well. As the seasons progress, different flowers come in bloom and these, in turn, are visited by different groups of pollinating insects. A community is, therefore, a dynamic entity, changing in response to the physical environment.

INTERSPECIFIC COMPETITION

Competitive exclusion principle.   Community structure is influenced by species interactions, since the presence of one species may very well depend on the presence or absence of another. One of the most important in this regard is interspecific competition. It is said to occur when two species living in the same region (sympatric species) seek a common limiting resource, such as food or space. As with intraspecific competition, competition between species can take the form of either exploitation or interference. In the former category, species affect each other's growth rate indirectly by merely using a common limiting factor, while in the latter, they produce direct detrimental effects as would be the case when one predator drives off a competing species from its feeding territory. Regardless of the precise nature of the interaction, the eventual outcome is the same and can be phrased in a basic theorem of biology known as the *competitive exclusion principle* (or Gause's principle). It states that two sympatric species cannot continue to utilize a limited resource in the same way in that the competitive superiority of one must eventually lead to the extinction of the other. In other words, no two species can continue to occupy the same ecological niche. To give a hypothetical example, consider two plant species with very similar requirements for some limited resource such as light or soil moisture which is present in fixed amounts. In this case, the populations will compete for suitable growing space and the result of this competitive interaction will depend on the tolerances of the two species to the detrimental effects of crowding. Now, let K_1 and K_2 represent the carrying capacity levels of species 1 and 2, respectively. Once the species have reached densities of N_1 and N_2, the total space momentarily in use can be expressed as being proportional to $N_1 + bN_2$, where the factor b is used to allow for differences in the efficiency with which the species use their limited resources. In this example, each individual of species 2 would require b times the amount of growing space as an individual of species 1. Hence, the fraction of the total habitable space still available for the growth of species 1 will be $[K_1 - (N_1 + bN_2)]/K_1$, while that for species 2 is $[bK_2 - (N_1 + bN_2)]/bK_2 = [K_2 - (N_2 + b^{-1}N_1)]/K_2$. Assuming that the growth of both species can be approximated by way of the logistic model, the logarithmic growth rates of the two populations can then be written as

$$d(\ln N_1)/dt = r_1(K_1 - N_1 - bN_2)/K_1 \tag{11.1}$$
$$d(\ln N_2)/dt = r_2(K_2 - N_2 - b^{-1}N_1)/K_2$$

To predict the outcome of this competitive interaction, let $r_1/K_1 = k(r_2/bK_2)$. Multiplying the second equation by k and subtracting it from the first, we get

$$d(\ln N_1/N_2^k)/dt = (r_1/K_1)(K_1 - bK_2)$$

which integrates to

$$N_1/N_2^k = Ce^{(r_1/K_1)(K_1 - bK_2)t}$$

where C is a constant. Note that the result of competition in this case depends only on the carrying capacity levels of the interacting species and the value of b. If $K_1 > bK_2$, N_1/N_2^k, and hence the ratio of N_1 to N_2, will increase without limit with species 1 being the sole survivor. Conversely, species 2 will ultimately replace species 1 if $bK_2 > K_1$.

Numerous experiments have been performed that lend support to the exclusion principle. One of the first investigations of this type was that of Gause (1934) using mixed-species populations of various yeasts and protozoans. Probably his best-known study was with the closely related ciliate protozoans *Paramecium aurelia* and *P. caudatum*. Gause found that both species could grow well separately at 26°C on a balanced physiological salt solution, buffered at a pH = 8.0, in which bacteria were added daily as a food source. By starting each culture with 2 cells per 0.5 ml and taking daily counts beginning after day 1, Gause was able to measure a carrying capacity level and intrinsic rate of increase of $K_1 = 105$ and $r_1 = 1.1244$ for *P. aurelia* and of $K_2 = 64$ and $r_2 = 0.7944$ for *P. caudatum* when each was grown alone. Since *P. aurelia* was smaller in size and in individual food requirements, K values and population densities were calculated in terms of total "volume" expressed relative to a volume of 1 for a *P. caudatum* cell. Two factors were apparently limiting growth in this system. One was competition for food, and the second was an accumulation of waste products which was more detrimental to *P. caudatum* than to *P. aurelia*. Having measured the growth characteristics of each separate population, Gause then focused his attention on the growth of mixtures of the two species. To permit the exclusion of one species by another, a constant relative death rate was simulated by removing one-tenth of the population mixture each day. This yielded the results illustrated by the example in Figure 11.1. As the data indicate, *P. aurelia* was found to be competitively superior since *P. caudatum* was consistently eliminated from mixed cultures. Moreover, these results could be simulated using simple logistic theory. Although the competitive effects of each species on the other were found to vary during the course of each experiment, competition in this case is reasonably described by equation (11.1) in which b is taken as approximately 1.64. The species, therefore, appear to be sharing a niche in which the inhibitory effects of crowding on the growth rate of both species are measured by *P. aurelia*'s density plus 1.64 times *P. caudatum*'s density. Thus, not only do these results support the validity of competitive exclusion, they also indicate that the conclusions derived from the logistic model are in agreement with actual experimental data.

In addition to the experiments of Gause on various microorganisms, an immense amount of work has been done on competition occurring between species of the flour beetle (*Tribolium*). Of particular importance have been the studies by Park on the species *T. confusum* and *T. castaneum*. Park found that one or the other species always eliminated its competitor when allowed to reproduce in the same flour medium. This is expected from the exclusion principle. However, the actual winner in each case varied depending on the climate and on the particular genetic strains used. For example, when he exposed the beetles to a range of climatic conditions using different combinations of temperature and relative humidity, he found that both species could grow separately in all experimental climates, although the maximum densities for *T. confusum* and *T. castaneum* were obtained at 34°C and 70% humidity and 29°C

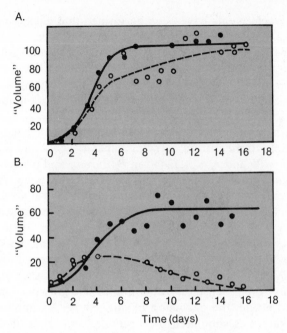

Figure 11.1. Growth of *P. aurelia* and *P. caudatum* in separate and mixed cultures. (A) *P. aurelia,* alone (solid circles) and in a mixed population (open circles); (B) *P. caudatum,* alone (solid circles) and in a mixed population (open circles). (From G. F. Gause. 1934. *The Struggle for Existence.* Williams and Wilkins, Baltimore.)

and 70% humidity, respectively. When the species were grown together, however, they produced the results shown in Table 11.1. As the data indicate, one species or the other is always a winner, but the percentage of wins varies for both species from 100% at one climatic extreme to 0% at the other. Thus, at intermediate climatic regimes, the outcome of competition in this system is indeterminate and can only be predicted on the basis of chance. Probabilistic outcomes such as these can best be analyzed by way of stochastic models which provide a means of predicting the chance of extinction for each species under different sets of conditions. A number of stochastic models have been used to analyze Park's data. One, proposed by Leslie, Park, and Mertz (1968), provides a good approximation to the observed results. This model is based on logistic equations presented in the next section and assumes a condition of unstable equilibrium in which the eventual outcome is affected by the initial densities of the two species.

Park has also investigated the mechanisms involved in competitive exclusion. He found that the probability of elimination in this system is determined largely by the resultant of two opposing rates. One is the intrinsic rate of increase under the conditions employed, and the other is the rate of egg and pupal cannibalism by larvae and adults. Park studied several different genetic

TABLE 11.1   The outcomes of competition between species of *Tribolium* in six different climates.*

Temperature (°C)	Humidity (%)	Climate	% Wins	
			T. confusum	T. castaneum
34	70	Hot-moist	0	100
34	30	Hot-arid	90	10
29	70	Temperate-moist	14	86
29	30	Temperate-arid	87	13
24	70	Cold-moist	71	29
24	30	Cold-arid	100	0

*Adapted from Park, 1962.

strains of both species and found that in most cases the strains that consistently won in competition experiments were those with the highest value of r and the highest relative cannibalistic tendency. It thus appears that the primary mechanism for exclusion in this case is one of interference, in the form of mutual predation, rather than one of exploitation.

Other forms of interference competition have been observed in the field. One example concerns the direct exclusion of the barnacle, *Chthamalus stellatus,* by another barnacle, *Balanus balanoides* (Connell, 1961). In Scotland, adult *Chthamalus* occur in the intertidal zone between the levels of mean high water of neap and spring tides. This is above the zone occupied by *Balanus*. Although young *Chthamalus* can settle and attach to rocks in the lower *Balanus* zone, they seldom survive to adulthood. Direct observations by Connell have shown that *Balanus* settled in greater densities in the lower zone and, as a consequence of faster growth, smothered, undercut, and crushed the *Chthamalus*.

Interference competition is also known to occur in plants where it takes the form of poisoning or *allelopathy*. Plants frequently produce poisons (or allelopathic agents) which interfere with the growth of other species. A classic example is the black walnut, *Juglans nigra*, which can inhibit the growth of other plants, including some grasses, alfalfa, and certain other trees, as far as 80 feet away. The allelopathic agent, in this case, is a compound known as juglone (5-hydroxy-α-napthaquinone) which is secreted by the roots of the tree. The action of the chemical is highly selective with some species, e.g., Kentucky blue grass, experiencing no ill effects.

The problem of coexistence.   In nature, species having similar resource requirements frequently occupy different geographic regions (allopatric species) or tend to occupy different habitats when in the same region. Competition is also avoided by temporal differences in feeding activities. For example, the staggering of life cycles in some closely related species enables them to concentrate their activities at different seasons. Nevertheless, actually or potentially competing species are often observed occupying the same habitat at the same time in apparent contradiction to the exclusion principle. It is, therefore, of interest to consider what conditions permit the coexistence of competing species.

Studies conducted on natural populations have shown that competing species can coexist if there is enough variation in habitat conditions to allow specialization on the part of each competitor. For example, consider two plant species in direct competition for growing space. Assume that the competitors differ sufficiently in their tolerance levels to soil moisture so that they prefer somewhat different growing conditions, with species 1 favoring the wet lowlands and species 2 the drier portions of their range. The proposed variation in tolerance limits is pictured graphically in Figure 11.2. It is assumed that the entire range of tolerance exhibited by both species approximates the variation in growing conditions within their habitat. Since tolerance variations do overlap, the species are obviously competitors. However, only those individuals of both species growing under conditions corresponding to the region of overlap are actually in direct competition. If the region of overlap is not too large, the overall effects of intraspecific competition will be more detrimental than the effects of interspecific competition on both populations. As a result, the two competing species can coexist indefinitely.

The preceding example can be phrased more precisely in the form of a mathematical argument. In doing so, let K_1 and K_2 again represent the carrying capacity levels of the two species when growing alone. When present together, their growth equations may then be expressed as

$$d(\ln N_1)/dt = r_1(K_1 - N_1 - \alpha N_2)/K_1$$
$$d(\ln N_2)/dt = r_2(K_2 - N_2 - \beta N_1)/K_2$$

(11.2)

In this set of equations, α and β are *competition coefficients*, measuring the degree to which the presence of each competitor inhibits the reproductive rate of the other. If competition is strictly exploitative in nature, their numerical

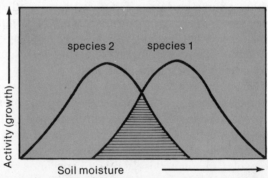

Figure 11.2. Comparison of the relative tolerance limits of two hypothetical plant species. The hatched area represents the region of overlap in growth preferences.

values depend on the amount of overlap in the growing preferences of the two species; the greater the overlap, the larger their numerical values. For example, if no overlap exists so that growing preferences are entirely different, both α and β are zero and no competition occurs. If the species have identical preferences, competition coefficients are reciprocals of each other (i.e., $\alpha\beta = 1$) and will equal unity when resource requirements are quantitatively the same. For these conditions, the logistic model requires but a single parameter, in addition to the different values of r and K, such as b in equation (11.1). In certain situations, both coefficients can attain values such that $\alpha\beta > 1$. Suppose, for example, that the plant species give off allelopathic agents that are toxic to their competitors but have little effect on the metabolism of the producing species. Each poison would tend to enhance the detrimental effects of inter-specific competition and the population which can produce it could reduce the reproductive rate of the competing species to a greater extent than it would its own.

The conditions required for coexistence can be determined by setting $d(\ln N_1)/dt = d(\ln N_2)/dt = 0$. This would correspond to a situation in which

$$(\text{Isocline of species 1}) \qquad N_1 = K_1 - \alpha N_2$$

$$(\text{Isocline of species 2}) \qquad N_2 = K_2 - \beta N_1$$

These zero-growth equations are pictured graphically by N_1 versus N_2 plots in Figure 11.3. In every case, each species will decrease above its zero-growth line and increase below it. Consequently, any starting combination of the two species corresponding to a point (N_1, N_2) which is above the line $d(\ln N_2)/dt = 0$ will move up and to the left. The change in composition is just the opposite for the reverse situation. The graphs in Figure 11.3 picture four possible results of competition summarized as follows:

(1) Either species wins in competition, depending on initial conditions, when

$$\alpha > K_1/K_2 \qquad \text{and} \qquad \beta > K_2/K_1$$

(2) Species 1 always wins in competition when

$$\alpha < K_1/K_2 \qquad \text{and} \qquad \beta > K_2/K_1$$

(3) Species 2 always wins in competition when

$$\alpha > K_1/K_2 \qquad \text{and} \qquad \beta < K_2/K_1$$

(4) The two species coexist when

$$\alpha < K_1/K_2 \qquad \text{and} \qquad \beta < K_2/K_1$$

Note that equilibrium situations are possible for both cases (1) and (4) at the point of intersection of the zero-growth lines. The equilibrium is unstable in case (1), however, since any disturbance in the numbers of the two competitors

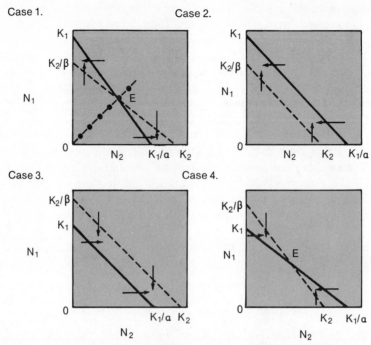

Figure 11.3. Competition between two species. The solid line in each case represents a plot of the zero-growth line of species 1 ($N_1 = K_1 - \alpha N_2$) and the broken line represents a plot of the zero-growth line of species 2 ($N_1 = K_2/\beta - N_1/\beta$). K_1 and K_2/β are the N_1 intercepts of the two equations, and K_1/α and K_2 are the N_2 intercepts, respectively. Since each species must decrease above its zero-growth line and increase below it, the densities of the competing species will move in the directions indicated by the arrows.

will eventually result in the elimination of species 2 if their densities should move to the left of the line OE and in the extinction of species 1 to the right of this line. Consequently, cases (1), (2), and (3) all conform to the principle of competitive exclusion. A situation of interest develops in case (4) where the equilibrium state is stable. Here, any starting combination of the two species will converge on the point of intersection of the isoclines. The zero-growth equations can now be used to solve for the equilibrium densities of both species. These densities become $\hat{N}_1 = (K_1 - \alpha K_2)/(1 - \alpha\beta)$ and $\hat{N}_2 = (K_2 - \beta K_1)/(1 - \alpha\beta)$. These equations allow us to make the same predictions that were alluded to earlier, namely that the smaller the values of α and β and thus, the greater the degree of specialization on the part of each competitor, the larger the equilibrium densities of both species. This is particularly important if growing conditions should vary, since α and β must be small enough to insure that one species is not eliminated while the other has a temporary competitive advantage.

Resource partitioning and feeding strategies.   Several studies have shown that similar species can coexist if they can differentiate in various ways so as to reduce the detrimental effects of competition. One of the earliest was that of Gause (1935) who demonstrated that a mixed-species population of *P. caudatum* and *P. busaria* could coexist while feeding on yeast as their only food source. In this case, coexistence was made possible by the different feeding habits of the two protozoa: *P. caudatum* feeding in the liquid medium and *P. busaria* in the bottom layers.

Observations in the field have also given support to this idea. One classic study was that of MacArthur (1958) on five species of the wood warbler (*Dendroica*); the Cape May warbler, *D. tigrina*; the myrtle warbler, *D. coronata*; the black-throated green warbler, *D. virens*; the blackburnian warbler, *D. fusca*; and the bay-breasted warbler, *D. castanea*, which can be present together in spruce forests of eastern United States. These species are very similar in size and shape and are mainly insectivorous. Although feeding habits do overlap, each species tends to feed in a different zone of the tree. Thus MacArthur found that he could subdivide average-sized trees into six vertical zones, each of ten-foot regions; and branches into three zones, one of bare or lichen-covered base, a middle zone of old needles, and a zone of new needles or buds (Figure 11.4). He also found that within vegetative zones, overlapping species use different feeding movements: a radial movement along branches, a tangential or circumferential movement around outer branches, and a vertical movement between branches at different heights. For example, the Cape-May spends its time foraging primarily in the outer zone of the top 40% of each tree, and moves vertically obtaining mainly those insects exposed on the tops and undersides of limbs, while the black-throated green warbler forages in the mid 20% of trees and moves tangentially, probably getting most of its insect-food along the sides of branches. Thus, by spatially and behaviorally dividing their environment, wood warblers are able to coexist by avoiding (or at least minimizing) the effects of competition through specialization.

Several studies indicate that niche diversification can proceed along more than one dimension. For example, Cody (1968), in his study of grassland bird communities, found three primary modes of specialization: (1) food-type separation through morphological and behavioral specialization for the types of foods eaten, (2) vertical habitat separation through occupation of different vertical vegetative zones, and (3) horizontal habitat separation by occupation of different habitat patches. The average niche separation along these three dimensions in ten grassland bird communities is shown graphically in Figure 11.5. Although the relative degree of separation along each dimension varies from one community to the next, food-type separation appears to be the most common mechanism, in this case, for resource partitioning. Schoener (1974) has conducted an extensive review of the relative importance of different resource dimensions in the separation of species. His considerations include food-type dimensions (separation by food taxon, size, texture, etc.), habitat dimen-

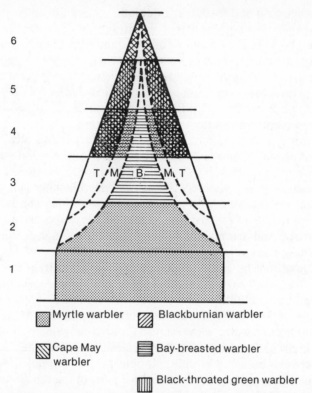

6
5
4
3   T /M B M\ T
2
1

▦ Myrtle warbler   ▨ Blackburnian warbler

◺ Cape May   ▤ Bay-breasted warbler
  warbler

                        ▥ Black-throated green warbler

Figure 11.4. Feeding positions of five species of warblers in spruce forests of the eastern United States. The tree is divided into six vertical zones and the branches into three zones, (B) base, (M) middle, and (T) terminal. The zones in which each species spends the majority of its foraging time are shaded. (After R.H. MacArthur. 1958. Ecology 39: 599. Copyright 1958 by the Ecological Society of America.)

sions (separation by horizontal habitat, vertical strata, etc.), and temporal dimensions (daily and seasonal separation). From this study, five major patterns emerged. They are: (1) "habitat dimensions are important more often than food-type dimensions, which are important more often than temporal dimensions," (2) "predators separate more often by being active at different times of the day than do other groups," (3) "terrestrial poikilotherms relatively often partition food by being active at different times of the day," (4) "vertebrates segregate less by seasonal activity than do lower animals," and (5) "segregation by food type is more important for animals feeding on food that is large in relation to their own size than it is for animals feeding on relatively small food items." Patterns in addition to these were observed but were not statistically significant. One which may be real is the observation that habitat dimensions appeared to be less important for aquatic animals than for terrestrial animals. This may simply reflect the lack of habitat heterogeneity in aquatic systems.

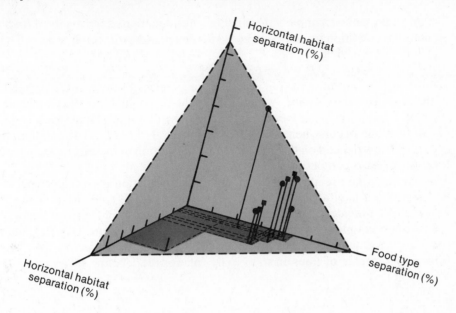

Figure 11.5. Average niche separation along three dimensions in ten grassland bird communities. (After M. Cody. 1968. Am. Nat. 102: 107. Copyright 1968 by The University of Chicago Press. All rights reserved.)

Competition and predation.   Another mechanism which enables competing species to coexist is through predation. Imagine, if you will, two competing species with similar resource requirements, both serving as food for a generalized predator. As the losing competitor becomes scarce, the predator will feed more heavily on the more abundant species. This, in turn, will serve to reduce the density of the species with the competitive advantage and gives the less abundant species a chance to multiply. Consequently, neither species will be eliminated.

The above example can be translated into mathematical terms for a more precise analysis. In doing so, we shall again designate the competitors as species 1 and species 2. Since both serve as a food source for a predator population their growth rates can be given as

$$d(\ln N_1)/dt = r_1(K_1 - N_1 - \alpha N_2)/K_1 - a_1 P$$
$$d(\ln N_2)/dt = r_2(K_2 - N_2 - \beta N_1)/K_2 - a_2 P$$

$$(11.3)$$

In the above equations, α and β are competition coefficients, P is the abundance of the predator, and a_1 and a_2 are presumed constants depending on the rate at which the predator feeds on the respective prey species. If the predator is food-limited, its density will also be governed by the abundance of prey, but this need not concern us here.

As in previous examples, the simultaneous equations can be solved for an equilibrium condition by setting $d(\ln N_1)/dt$ and $d(\ln N_2)/dt$ equal to zero. This yields the zero-growth planes $K_1 - N_1 - \alpha N_2 - (a_1 K_1/r_1)P = 0$ and $K_2 - N_2 - \beta N_1 - (a_2 K_2/r_2)P = 0$. Letting $K_1(1 - a_1 P/r_1) = K_1'$ and $K_2(1 - a_2 P/r_2) = K_2'$ (these are now the apparent carrying capacity levels in the presence of the predator), the equilibrium densities of the two competitors now become: $\hat{N}_1 = (K_1' - \alpha K_2')/(1 - \alpha\beta)$ and $\hat{N}_2 = (K_2' - \beta K_1')/(1 - \alpha\beta)$. Note that a stable equilibrium can occur when $\alpha < K_1'/K_2'$ and when $\beta < K_2'/K_1'$. The equilibrium conditions now depend on the predation rate in addition to the carrying capacity levels of the two competitors.

One important feature of this model is that predation may enable species to coexist in a habitat in which only one would be the sole survivor in the absence of a predator. An example of this is pictured graphically by a plot of the zero-growth planes of the two competing species in Figure 11.6. To better visualize the graph, equations are given for a number of projection lines. As shown by the pair of lines in the N_1ON_2 plane, the isocline of species 1 is

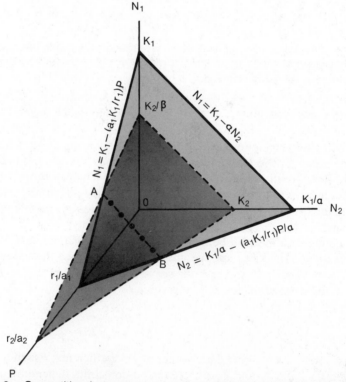

Figure 11.6.   Competition between two species subject to predation. The P axis represents the density of the predator. Since r_2/a_2 is greater than r_1/a_1, an equilibrium will be established at some point on the line AB.

greater than that of species 2 in the absence of predators ($P = 0$). Thus, without predation, species 1 would continue to increase to its carrying capacity level with the concurrent elimination of species 2. Note that the zero-growth planes pass through the P axis at r_1/a_1 and at r_2/a_2. Therefore, if the zero-growth planes are to intersect in this example, r_2/a_2 must be greater than r_1/a_1. This could happen if species 2 has the larger intrinsic rate of increase or if species 1 is preyed upon more heavily than species 2. The line AB in the plot represents the intersection of the two planes. There will be some point or set of values (N_1, N_2, P) that will satisfy the condition $d(\ln N_1)/dt = d(\ln N_2)/dt = 0$. This will represent a stable equilibrium condition, thus permitting coexistence of the two competitors.

The idea that competing species can coexist when exposed to an additional source of mortality such as predation has been verified by the studies of Utida (1953) on competition between two species of the bean weevil, *Callosobruchus chinensis* and *C. quadrimaculatus*. When mixed populations were fed on the azuki bean, *C. chinensis* was excluded by the fifth generation. In contrast, when a pteromalid wasp, *Neocataolaccus namezophagus*, was used to parasitize the larvae of both populations, both species of weavils existed together and were held at relatively low levels of density. This result occurs regardless of the initial densities of the host species relative to each other.

Character displacement and ecological release.   When two closely related species have partially overlapping geographic ranges, they are often very similar in zones of allopatry; whereas in regions where they occur together, they typically diverge in one or more characteristics so as to promote a greater separation of resource requirements. This intensification of species differences in regions of sympatry is referred to as *character displacement*. Any one of a large number of character differences can be involved since the mechanisms for achieving resource separation can be quite varied. An outstanding illustration of morphological discontinuities is provided by the different species of Darwin's finches on the Galapagos Islands. The largest islands are 80 miles long, and the maximum altitude is 4,000 feet. Vegetation changes from semi-arid thorn shrub at the lower elevations to humid forest at the higher levels. The larger islands possess from 7 to 11 species each, exemplifying well-defined systems of resource separation. While a few species appear to be separated by spatial (altitudinal) or behavioral factors, the most prominent mechanism is morphological. Beak size and conformation are highly adapted to food type, the beaks of species on the same island showing little or no overlap (Fig. 11.7). Species of *Geospiza*, a genera that occurs at low elevations, are seed eaters and differ from one another in the proportion of the various seed types consumed. For example, *G. magnirostris* has a massive beak, eating proportionally more large thick-walled seeds than *G. fuliginosa*, whose smaller beak is adapted to smaller, thin-walled seeds. The genus *Camarhynchus* is found at higher elevations and is insectivorous; the beaks of its species are adapted to texture

Figure 11.7. The Galapagos finches. (From D.L. Lack. 1953. "Darwin's finches." Scientific American 188, No. 4: 66.)

of plant tissue and depth to which it must be excavated to obtain larvae. The warbler finch, *Certhidea olivacae*, is isolated from all other species in both feeding habit and behavior. It forages through tree and shrub foliage for small insects in the manner of a warbler, and thus is characterized by a small and slender beak. When pair-wise comparisons are made, character differences tend to be greater when the species compared are from the same island than when they are taken from different islands (Table 11.2). These morphological differences, therefore, appear to have been acquired in sympatry through the

TABLE 11.2   Bill lengths (mm) of *G. fortis* and *G. fuliginosa* in areas of sympatry and allopatry.*

Species	Indefatigable	(Island) Daphne	Crossman
G. fortis	12.0	10.5	—
G. fuliginosa	8.4	—	9.3

*Data from Lack (1947).

selective effects of interspecific competition. The results of more recent studies help to support this view (e.g., Fenchel, 1975).

While interspecific competition produces shifts in niche location through character displacement, intraspecific competition tends to promote a broadening of a species niche along a resource axis. Therefore, in an open environment, a newly colonized species may expand its niche by selecting a greater variety of food types than are utilized in the source habitat. This phenomenon has been termed *ecological release* by Wilson (1961). The distinction between the two phenomena is shown by way of a graphical model in Figure 11.8. In this model,

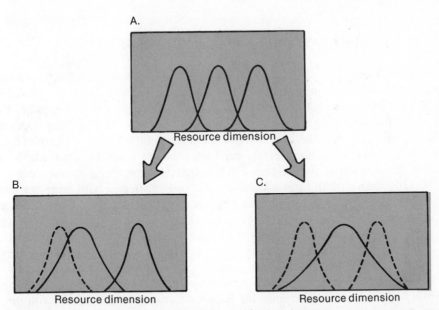

Figure 11.8. Diagrammatic representation of resource partitioning under the influence of competition. In (A), intense interspecific competition favors a narrow niche width. In (B), the absence of one species (dashed line) enhances the relative degree of intraspecific competition and the resulting increase in the amount of genetic variation broadens niche width and alters mean location. Still further reduction in the number of competitors (C) expands niche width in both directions (competitive release).

species are assumed to divide their resources along a single dimension. More-over, the width of each resource utilization curve is assumed to be an increasing function of the amount of genetic variation, which is in turn dependent on the existing balance between interspecific and intraspecific competition pressures. If extensive overlap occurs on both sides of the resource curve (graph A), intense interspecific competition will favor greater specialization through a reduction in niche width. In a more open environment, there is a relaxation of interspecific competition and a corresponding increase in the relative impor-tance of intraspecific competition. This can result in a shift in mean niche location (graph B) or an expansion in both directions (graph C) upon further reduction of species diversity. It should be kept in mind that changes in niche width and mean niche location occur through alterations in the phenotypic (and hence genotypic) variation pattern of each species population. Thus, it is pos-sible for niche expansion to proceed through either (or both) an increase in the between-phenotype component of variation, by increasing the variety of pheno-types, or an enlargement of the within-phenotype component, by widening the range of resources selected by each phenotype. It is possible for the latter alternative to occur through greater behavioral or developmental plasticity on the part of the specialized phenotypes.

LIFE HISTORY PATTERNS AND COMPETITIVE ABILITY

r and *K* selection.   Thus far, we have only considered the effects of com-petition on equilibrium species, or those species that live in an environment which is stable enough to permit them to reach and remain at their equilibrium levels. Such species are generally maintained at or near the carrying capacity of their environment. The outcome of exploitation competition will then depend on which species has the greatest carrying capacity level. In other words, in stable environments the selective advantage of competing species centers around K values, with little advantage accrued to species with large intrinsic rates of increase. Since equilibrium populations must exist on a limited energy supply, natural selection will proceed in such a way so as to maximize K and reduce r, thereby permitting the most efficient use of environmental resources without expending excess energy in converting food into offspring. This process is referred to as K *selection*. Consistent with the emphasis on efficiency, rather than productivity, K selection will tend to favor iteroparity and longer lifespan (providing a greater opportunity for learning to exploit the limited resources), delayed reproduction and small litters or clutches of offspring (reduced birth rate), and large body size, with few large young and parental care (increased survival because of fewer predators and greater buffering against environmental change). Due to high survival rates, density regulation will be largely through changes in litter or clutch size, or by altering the length of the developmental period.

In unstable environments, where conditions change in an unpredictable manner, populations generally vary in density below their carrying capacity level. In such instances, a species might specialize in exploiting new environmental situations as they appear. Such opportunistic species would multiply rapidly when required resources are in abundance and depend on their dispersal ability to invade other areas when conditions become less favorable. In such instances, a premium would be placed on a high reproductive rate and the species that can fill its environment more rapidly than others would have a selective advantage. One would imagine that here natural selection proceeds to maximize r (r selection). In this case, the traits that are favored are those which promote rapid rates of reproduction, such as early age at first reproduction, short generation time, large clutches or litters, and small body size with small, numerous offspring and no parental care, thus maximizing productivity rather than efficiency. Since r-strategists are not exposed to the pressures of crowding, there is little advantage in the evolution of mechanisms for strong competitive ability.

Pianka (1970) has stressed the point that r and K strategies are simply the end points on a continuum of possibilities. He has also suggested that whole groups of terrestrial organisms tend to fall on one side or the other of the r-K continuum. Terrestrial vertebrates and perennial plants appear to be relatively K-selected, while insects and annual plants tend to be r-selected. Additionally, Southwood *et al*. (1974) has pointed out that the spectrum of demographic strategies that characterize the r-K continuum should give rise to different forms of density regulation. These should fall between the patterns illustrated by means of reproductive curves for extreme r and K-strategists in Figure 11.9.

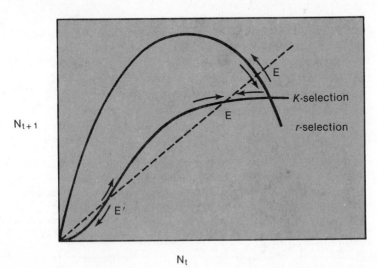

Figure 11.9. Reproductive curves for extreme r- and K-strategists, showing stable (E) and unstable (E') equilibrium points.

Since equilibrium species tend to remain at or around the carrying capacity level, quite stable regulatory mechanisms should evolve for high densities. These same populations will be relatively inefficient in their ability to reproduce at low densities, being subject to irreversible decline should their level drop below a critical point. Conversely, opportunist species should evolve efficient mechanisms for mate procurement and reproduction at low densities, but, under rare bursts of growth, they will tend to overshoot their upper equilibrium levels and subsequently crash.

Table 11.3 summarizes some of the correlates of r and K selection. Although many of the conclusions are borne out in field data on birds and wildflowers (e.g., Cody, 1971; Gadgil and Solbrig, 1972), other approaches to determining life history patterns have generated markedly different predictions. For instance, Schaffer (1974), employing the model described earlier in Chapter 8, concluded that environmentally induced fluctuations which have their impact on juvenile mortality favor iteroparity, long life, late maturity, and reduced reproductive effort. On the other hand, high or variable adult mortality favors semelparity, short life, early reproduction, and increased reproductive effort. Hence, the assumption that increased environmental uncertainty necessarily selects for increased reproductive effort does not appear to be justified.

TABLE 11.3   Some of the correlates of r- and K-selection.

	r-selection	K-selection
Climate	Variable and/or unpredictable	Constant and/or predictable
Mortality	Density-independent; uncertain adult survival	Density-dependent; uncertain juvenile survival
Survivorship	Often type III (see Fig. 8.1)	Usually types I and II (see Fig. 8.1)
Population size	Variable in time, nonequilibrium; usually below carrying capacity; frequent recolonization necessary	Constant in time, equilibrium; at or near carrying capacity; no recolonization necessary
Competition	Often lax	Usually keen
Selection favors	1. Rapid development 2. High maximum r value 3. Early reproduction 4. High resource thresholds 5. Small body size 6. Semelparity 7. Increased birth rate	1. Slow development 2. Competitive ability 3. Delayed reproduction 4. Low resource thresholds 5. Large body size 6. Iteroparity 7. Decreased death rate
Length of life	Short, usually less than one year	Long, usually greater than one year
Leads to	Productivity	Efficiency

Source: After Pianka (1970)

Evolution of competitive ability.   A number of experiments have been performed which indicate that competitive ability is itself subject to evolutionary change. One such study by Pimental *et al.* (1965) was conducted to determine whether interspecific competitors, which differ slightly in competitive ability, could undergo selective change so that both species would compete yet still coexist. It was postulated that when the losing competitor is rare, most of its competitive interactions are with members of the winning species. Thus, selection should act to improve the interspecific competitive ability of this less abundant population. By the same token, most of the competitive interactions in the dominant species are between its own members. As a result, its interspecific competitive ability will remain unaltered (or possibly decline) as it acquires an improved ability to counter intraspecific competition. As this process continues, the competitive abilities of the two species may eventually reverse, with what was once the losing population becoming a winner and vice versa. This would then give rise to a coevolving system which, after an alternating series of species dominance and changing competitive ability, ultimately develops into a stable state of equilibrium.

To test this hypothesis, Pimental and co-workers studied the effects of competition between the housefly, *Musca domestica*, and a blowfly, *Phoenicia sericata*. These species have a similar life cycle which is about 14 days in length at 80°F. When houseflies and blowflies are taken from wild populations and mixed in a small population cage, competitive exclusion invariably occurs with the housefly winning in slightly more than half the trials. It was found that the two species could be kept together for a prolonged period in a large population cage in which the ratio of housefly adults to blowfly adults averaged about 10:1. To determine whether the less abundant blowfly gained in competitive ability during its stay in the mixed population, samples of the two species were taken after a 38-week period and tested against each other and against wild populations in various combinations in small cages. The results are listed in Table 11.4.

TABLE 11.4   Results of competition tests in small cages using wild stocks and experimental flies which had been maintained for 38 weeks in a mixed species cage in which blowflies were relatively rare and houseflies common.*

| | | | Number of tests | |
| | | | Won by Housefly | Won by Blowfly |
Houseflies		*Blowflies*		
wild	x	wild	6	3
experimental	x	experimental	0	5
wild	x	experimental	0	5
experimental	x	wild	3	2

*Data from Pimental et al. (1965)

Note that, as predicted by theory, blowflies improved significantly in compet-itive ability during the 38-week period, while little change is noticed in samples taken from the more abundant housefly population. Further evidence for a coevolving competitive system was obtained from two of the reported tests which lasted for over 70 weeks before exclusion occurred. During this time, both of these test systems exhibited alternating periods of species dominance, each lasting from about 10 to 24 weeks (5 to 12 generations) in length. When samples were taken and further tested, it was found that, as expected, the blowfly possessed the greatest competitive ability at the end of periods of housefly dominance. The housefly then regained the competitive advantage during periods of blowfly dominance. As these studies show, significant changes in competitive ability are possible over periods of just a few generations.

Gill (1974) has proposed a model in which species evolve competitive ability through a process known as α *selection*. Gill suggests two basic mech-anisms by which an individual can be selected. One is an improvement of its own capabilities by way of r and/or K selection, and a second is an impairment of its competitor's capabilities through the acquisition of interference phenom-ena such as allelopathy or agonistic behavior. The latter mechanism serves as the basis for α selection, since it gives rise to an increase in the competition coefficient α (or β), the measure of interspecific competitive ability. Thus, species populations will evolve competitive ability by increasing their selection coefficients, through interferential mechanisms, to values greater than one, thereby reducing the logarithmic growth rate of the competing species.

The deterministic consequences of α selection are illustrated graphically in Figure 11.10 along with the effects of r and K selection. These plots are based on the following pair of equations:

$$d(\ln N_1)/dt = r_1(K_1 - N_1 - \alpha_{12}N_2)/K_1$$

$$d(\ln N_2)/dt = r_2(K_2 - N_2 - \alpha_{21}N_1)/K_2$$

where α_{21} measures the interferential effects of species 1 on species 2, the reverse being true for α_{12}. Observe in graph B that by increasing α_{21}, the less efficient but more productive competitor (species 1) can create a situation where it can win in competition if it gains a numerical advantage at the outset. Here, the value of r or the probability of first colonization can determine the outcome. Also note in graph C that if species 1 escapes from the interferential effects of species 2 (e.g., develops an immunity to the allelopathic substances of the competing species), K_1/α_{12} can increase to a level where a stable equilibrium is possible.

Since interferential mechanisms require an additional input of energy and often have inhibitory effects on the growth rates of populations that use them, changes in α usually affect other growth parameters. Thus, increases in α through some interferential mechanism may require changes in the energy

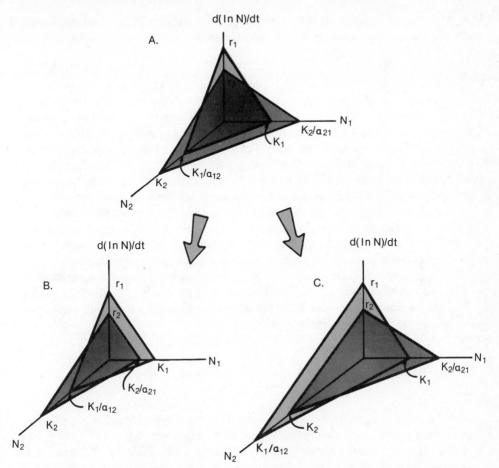

Figure 11.10. Graphical representation of α selection. The value of α_{21} increases in B and that of α_{12} decreases in C. See text for details.

budget, resulting in a reduction in the species' own values of r and K. These compensatory changes in growth parameters, along with the ability to escape from the competitor's interferential effects, provide a mechanism for a feedback process which permits coexistence under a regime of changing competitive ability.

MULTISPECIES COMMUNITIES

Competitive interactions. It is possible to extend the logistic model to competition among three or more species. However, if more than two species are competing, the possible interactions between the various species must also be considered. This leads to the appearance of a number of interaction terms, which is seen by writing the logistic equation as

$$d(\ln N_i)/dt = r_i(K_i - N_i - \Sigma\alpha_{ij}N_j - \Sigma\alpha_{ijk}N_jN_k - \ldots - \Sigma\alpha_{ijk..m}N_jN_k. .N_m)/K_i$$

in which j, k, etc. do not equal i and where greek letters denote interaction coefficients (e.g., α_{ijk} designates the joint effect of species j and k on species i). The meaning of the various interaction terms can be clarified by a simple example. Suppose that each competitor added to the system randomly overlaps one-half the niche space of species i. Thus, after the addition of one competitor, species i will have only one-half of its former niche free of competition; the other half will be involved in a two-way interaction. With the addition of a second competitor, the former niche occupied without competition will then be reduced to $(\frac{1}{2})(\frac{1}{2}) = \frac{1}{4}$. In this case, one-half of the former niche is shared with each of the added competitors, resulting in two-way interactions, and one-fourth with both, the latter giving rise to a three-way interaction. Similar computations would have to be made if another competitor were added.

Because of the number of possible interactions, the preceding equation is extremely cumbersome to use and difficult to apply in real situations. For this reason, it is generally assumed that higher-order interaction terms are negligible. This leads to the fairly simple expression:

$$d(\ln N_i)/dt = r_i(K_i - N_i - \Sigma\alpha_{ij}N_j)/K_i \tag{11.4}$$

At equilibrium, all $d(\ln N_i)/dt = 0$. This results in:

$$\hat{N}_i = K_i - \Sigma\alpha_{ij}N_j$$

which can be used to analyze the results of competition. Coexistence of all m interacting species is theoretically possible; however, Strobeck (1973) has shown that, for this to happen, $2(m - 1)$ inequalities must be satisfied. This is highly unlikely in any large community, unless interactions are ordered and nonrandom.

The study by Vandermeer (1969) provides a useful example of how the preceding model can be applied to experimental systems. Vandermeer conducted an empirical test of the importance of higher order interactions employing a four-way experiment. For experimental organisms, he used the four ciliate protozoans, *Paramecium caudatum*, *P. bursaria*, *P. aurelia*, and *Blepharisma* sp. Values of r_i and K_i were first evaluated from single-species cultures. The four were then grown in pairs for the evaluation of competition coefficients using the relationship:

$$\alpha_{ij} = (1/N_j)[K_i - (K_i/r_i)dN_i/N_idt - N_i]$$

In this case, dN_i/dt was estimated as $\frac{1}{2}(N_{t+1} - N_{t-1})$ from the appropriate plots of experimental data. The four ciliates were finally cultured together and the results compared with the theoretical curves predicted by equation (11.4). The resulting data are plotted in Figure 11.11. Although minor deviations do occur, the basic model is obviously a good predictor of the results of competition in this artifical community.

Feeding interactions.   It is also feasible to describe food chain interactions with the use of rather simple mathematical models. Consider, for example, the following primary carnivore, herbivore, plant system:

(plant) $d(\ln N_1)/dt = r(1 - N_1/K) - a_{12}N_2$

(herbivore) $d(\ln N_2)/dt = u_{21}N_1 - q_2 - a_{23}N_3$

(carnivore) $d(\ln N_3)/dt = u_{32}N_2 - q_3$

A solution can be obtained by setting all logarithmic growth rates equal to zero. This yields

$$\hat{N}_1 = K - (a_{12}K/r_1)N_2$$

$$\hat{N}_2 = q_3/u_{32}$$

$$\hat{N}_3 = (u_{21}/a_{23})N_1 - q_2/a_{23}$$

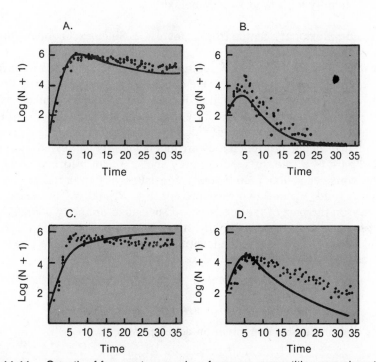

Figure 11.11.   Growth of four protozoans in a four-way competition experiment. (A) *P. aurelia;* (B) *P. bursaria;* (C) *P. caudatum;* and (D) *Blepharisma* sp. The theoretical curves predicted by equation (11.4) are shown for comparison. (From J.H. Vandermeer. 1969. Ecology 50: 362. Copyright 1969 by the Ecological Society of America.)

By solving these equations simultaneously, it is possible to obtain equilibrium values for N_1, N_2, and N_3. Due to density dependence in the plant population, the equilibrium condition is stable.

May (1971) and others have extended these Lotka-Volterra-type models to the study of stability in complex communities. Take the case of a system with n predators, with the population of the ith species being N_i, and the same number of resource species with populations R_i. The analogue of the Lotka-Volterra equations for this community is

$$d(\ln R_i)/dt = r_i - \Sigma a_{ij} N_j$$

$$d(\ln N_i)/dt = \Sigma u_{ij} R_j - q_i$$

May has shown that the behavior of this mathematical model is either one of neutral stability, as in the two species case, or the system is unstable. Thus, in general, the multispecies system is unstable rather than merely oscillatory. Similar conclusions were drawn for other predator-prey models, indicating that the more species in a trophic-level interaction, the less stability there is. This is in contradiction to the "folk wisdom" of contemporary ecology, which relates increased stability with food-web complexity.

Limits to complexity at a single trophic level.   Since exclusion occurs when there is sufficient overlap in the niche space of competing species, it is reasonable to suspect that interspecific competition will place a limit on the number of species that can stably coexist. One conclusion to this effect was drawn by Volterra (1926) who pointed out that for resource-limited populations, there can be no more species in a community than there are kinds of resources (i.e., food items, prey species, etc.) on which they depend. In this case, resources are classified as being different if they are independently harvested (e.g., leaves, nuts, and bark of a tree, or separate prey species). For a formal proof of this theorem, consider a simple community consisting of two predator species, of densities N_1 and N_2, and two resource species, R_1 and R_2, in which there is a tendency on the part of the predators to specialize on the two kinds of prey. If the resources are consumed in direct proportion to the frequency at which they occur in the community, the logarithmic growth rates of the two predator species can be approximated as

$$d(\ln N_1)/dt = u_{11}R_1 + u_{12}R_2 - q_1$$

$$d(\ln N_2)/dt = u_{21}R_1 + u_{22}R_2 - q_2$$

Observe that an equilibrium situation develops when

$$u_{11}R_1 + u_{12}R_2 = {}'q_1$$

$$u_{21}R_1 + u_{22}R_2 = q_2$$

These are the isoclines for the predators which are represented by the solid lines in Figure 11.12. Since all points on each line represent a growth rate of

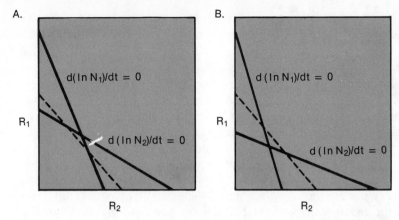

Figure 11.12. Isoclines for two predator species (N_1 and N_2) which specialize on two resource species (R_1 and R_2) are shown by the solid lines. The dashed lines represent a generalist predator isocline, which crosses the other two (A) below their point of intersection, and (B) above their point of intersection.

zero for the predators in question, each predator population must increase in size for all (R_1,R_2) combinations above its isocline and decrease below it. A predator will, therefore, eat the prey down to levels which correspond to some point on its own zero-growth line. Should the two isoclines intersect, the point of intersection will then correspond to the prey levels which maintain both predator species at equilibrium. Since there can only be one point of intersection, given two species of prey, this result, therefore, implies that two resource types cannot support more than two consumer species.

The preceding proof only applies to coexistence at fixed densities. Without this restriction, it is possible for, say, n consumer species to be supported by less than n food items. It also assumes that different resources are encountered several times by each consumer and used in proportion to their densities. It is possible to include a wider range of strategies by introducing the concept of *environmental grain*. This relates to the manner in which a species perceives and exploits its environment. According to MacArthur (1968), an environment is "fine-grained" relative to a species if its resources are encountered in the proportion in which they occur. This is the strategy assumed in the preceding model. On the other hand, the environment is "coarse-grained" if the species spends a major part of its time on just one resource. For example, food differences, as in the form of different seed sizes or of different insect species, would be fine-grained to an organism if encountered randomly and several times during its lifespan. This organism would be a generalist if it also selects and eats the different food items, such as different insect species, as they are encountered. In contrast, alternative hosts would tend to be coarse-grained for a specific parasite which might reside on one host during a major part of its life cycle. The concept of fine-grained resources does not alter the previously stated relationship between number of resources and maximum number of species. The main new feature introduced by this classification scheme is the possibility of habitat subdivision. Thus, for a coarse-grained mixture of n grain types, a single resource can potentially support n different specialists.

When resources are fine-grained, the optimal number of consumer species which can be maintained may be less than the maximum limit set by the number of resource types. Suppose, for example, that a generalist predator invades the preceding community. If the invading generalist has an isocline that crosses inside those of the previously established species (Figure 11.12A), an unstable situation develops with two points of intersection and the invader will ultimately replace at least one of the two specialists. On the other hand, the specialists will starve out the invading species if the specialist isoclines intersect inside that of the generalist (Figure 11.12B). Note, however, that if the generalist can utilize both species of prey with high degree of efficiency, it may reduce their levels to such an extent that neither of the specialists can survive in the community for very long. Hence, under certain circumstances, two prey species can support only a single species of predator.

SPECIES ABUNDANCE AND DIVERSITY

Measures of abundance.   An important part of the study of community ecology is the elucidation of the number of species within a community, and the number of individuals of each of these species. Characterization of species abundance can be done in several ways, perhaps the best of which involves fitting the data by a distribution function. If a particular frequency distribution were found to accurately describe the relative abundance of species in different communities, then these communities could be characterized by the values of the distribution parameters specific to each. This would be especially useful if the parameters have biological meaning. Unfortunately, there appears to be no one single probability function that describes a majority of species abundance relationships. We discuss here several of the distributions that have been found to apply.

Fisher, Corbet, and Williams (1943) proposed a *logarithmic series* to mathematically describe the species abundance distribution of 197 species in a sample of 6,814 moths captured within a light trap in England. The major feature of these data, and of much of the data collected on other organisms as well, is that most species are represented by just a few individuals, the frequency of species having more members becoming progressively less. The logarithmic series

$$\alpha x, \alpha x^2/2, \alpha x^3/3, \ldots, \alpha x^n/n$$

describes such a distribution having n abundance classes, where α is a measure of species diversity (number of species relative to the number of individuals), and x is a constant related to the mean number of individuals per species.

The total number of species in the sample S is, therefore, given as $\sum_{r=1}^{n}\alpha x^r/$ $r = -\ln(1 - x)$, and the total number of individuals in the sample is calculated as $N = \sum_{r=1}^{n} r\alpha x^r/r = \alpha x/(1 - x)$. Solving these two equations simultaneously gives estimates of the values of α and x. Although the value of x depends on sample size, that of α does not. It can, therefore, be used in a comparative fashion as an index of species diversity.

Another distribution frequently applied to small communities with homogeneous groups of species is the *geometric distribution* of the niche preemption model. In this case, species are ranked from most to least abundant; abundance, in theory, is based solely on success in procuring resources. Each species is envisioned to preempt for its own use a constant fraction, x, of the resources left available for use by more successful species. Thus, the relative abundance of the rth species is $N_r/N = x(1 - x)^{r-1}$, and a plot of log (N_r/N) versus species rank, r, is linear. Figure 11.13 shows the patterns of relative abundance in five different successional plant communities in Southern Illinois. The earlier stages appear to follow a niche preemption pattern.

In larger, more complex communities, relative species abundance is often found to follow a *lognormal distribution* (Fig. 11.13, 40 years). In this case, very rare and very common species are less frequent than species having intermediate levels of abundance. The number of individuals per species might be expected to be lognormally distributed if the multiplicative interaction of a large number of independent factors determined resource utilization. Species diversity can then be measured as the population variance, σ^2, calculated from sample estimates of the mean and standard deviation. One useful property of the lognormal is that it allows estimation of the total number of species (including those so rare as to not be included in the sample) in the community. If species abundance data are plotted using a logarithmic scale on the abscissa (Figure 11.14), the total number of species can be determined by extrapolating the bell-shaped distribution back to zero and finding the area under the curve. Preston (1948) has suggested scaling the abscissa in octaves representing successive population doublings, so that the distribution can be expressed as $f(R) = f(R_o)e^{-a^2 R^2}$, where R expresses abundance calculated as $\log_2(N/N_o)$, R_o being the mode octave. Since the lognormal distribution stated in this fashion is uniquely characterized by the values of $f(R_o)$ and a, it should be useful in comparing relative species abundance in different communities. However, as May (1975c) has pointed out, the values of these parameters are more a mathematical property of the lognormal distribution than a biological property of the system, making the distribution useful mainly in a descriptive sense.

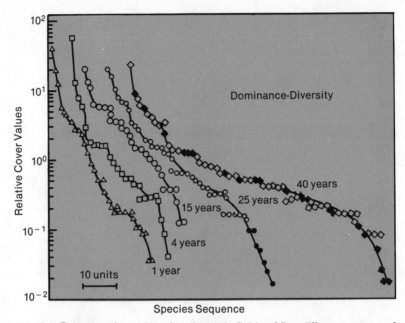

Figure 11.13. Patterns of species abundance in fields of five different stages of abandonment in southern Illinois. The percentage of the total community area contributed by a given species is plotted against that species' rank, ordered from most to least abundant. Symbols are open for herbs, half-open for shrubs, and closed for trees. (From Bazzaz, F.A. 1975. Ecology 56: 485. Copyright 1975 by the Ecological Society of America.)

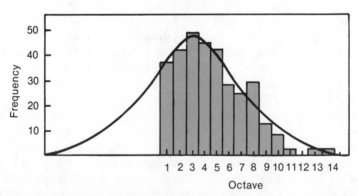

Figure 11.14. Species abundances in a sample of moths caught in a light trap. The abscissa is scaled geometrically into octaves representing successive population doublings. The data fit a lognormal distribution truncated at a species abundance of 1. If the distribution is extrapolated back to 0, rare species can be included for a better estimate of the total number of species in the community. (After F.W. Preston. 1948. Ecology 29: 254.)

Measures of diversity.   Once the distribution of species abundance is determined, it is possible to express species diversity or variability in terms of a single population parameter. As was pointed out in Chapter 2, the variance of the distribution is uniquely suited for this purpose. Because many species abundance relationships do not seem to fit any empirical or theoretical distribution, however, ecologists consider it desirable to have some distribution-free measure of the diversity of species. One such measure is *Simpson's diversity index, C.* If the proportion of individuals in a community that are of species i is p_i, then the chance that, in choosing two members of the community at random, both are of the ith species is p_i^2. The chance that both are of the same species is then $\sum_{i=1}^{S} p_i^2$. Species diversity is thus defined as $C = 1 - \Sigma p_i^2$. This measure is related to the variance of the observed species abundance distribution, giving relatively more weight to the common species, so that it is sometimes used to express the relative dominance of one or two species in the community. For general application, some workers prefer to use $1/\Sigma\, p_i^2$ as the measure of diversity, interpreting this as the number of equally likely species required to produce the same diversity value as observed in the sample being studied.

Simpson's index accomplishes one goal of a diversity index—its value depends not only on the number of different species in a community but also on the relative abundance of each. The latter is termed the evenness or equitability of the observed distribution. Its effect can be seen by comparing two communities, the first having two species with 90 members in one and 10 in the other, and the second having two species with 50 members each. In the first community, $C = 1 - (0.9^2 + 0.1^2) = 0.18$. In the second, $C = 1 - (0.5^2 + 0.5^2) = 0.5$. It is, therefore, apparent that the greater equitability or evenness of species in the second community makes it more diverse.

One common interpretation of diversity is the degree of uncertainty in predicting the species of an individual drawn at random from a community. The greater the uniformity of species abundance, the less predictable is the species identity of each individual sampled. This idea is the basis for the use of an information measure of diversity known as the *Shannon index, H'*, defined as

$$H' = -\sum_{i=1}^{S} p_i \ln p_i \qquad\qquad (11.5)$$

where p_i is, again, the proportion of the ith species. This index of diversity, like that of Simpson, depends on both the number of species and their relative abundance, the value of H' being maximum when all species are represented by the same number of individuals. While insensitive to the underlying distribution of species abundance and thus useful for comparing diversity in different communities, H' is strictly defined in information theory for large populations.

The Shannon index is particularly useful when hierarchical diversity is being measured. Suppose, for example, that both the species and the genus of the members of a community are being determined, and that the investigator desires to partition the total diversity into its genus and species components. Let p_{ij} be the proportion of individuals belonging to the jth species of the ith genus and let q_i be the proportion of the ith genus. Then, the total diversity of the sample is

$$H'(GS) = -\sum_i \sum_j q_i p_{ij} \ln (q_i p_{ij})$$

Multiplying and sorting terms, we obtain

$$H'(GS) = -\sum_i q_i \ln q_i - \sum_i \sum_j q_i p_{ij} \ln p_{ij}$$

But $-\Sigma \, q_i \ln q_i$ is simply the genus diversity, and $-\Sigma \, p_{ij} \ln p_{ij}$ is the species diversity with the ith genus. Hence

$$H'(GS) = H'(G) + H'_G(S)$$

where $H'_G(S)$ is the average species diversity over all genera.

MECHANISMS MAINTAINING DIVERSITY

The mechanisms that govern or regulate the abundance and diversity of species in a community are varied and often complex. At least six factors can be considered to influence species abundance to varying degrees, depending on the particular community. These include time, spatial heterogeneity, environmental stability, productivity, competition, and predation.

Time.   If we consider area on a global scale and long time periods, it is clear that the animal and plant kingdoms have diversified themselves, by evolution. On a shorter time scale, biotic changes caused by gradual changes in the world's climates may also influence diversity. Both paleontological data and studies on living oganisms show a latitudinal gradient in global species diversity being high in the tropics and decreasing towards the poles. This has been interpreted as evidence for evolutionary time as a regulator of diversity, diversity being proportional to both the rapidity of evolution in a location (dependent on environmental "favorability") and the length of time through which an area has been allowed to develop under stable conditions. The lack of glaciation in the tropics would then be one of the factors contributing to the continued accumulation of species.

It seems more instructive, from both experimental and theoretical standpoints, to consider the effects of time in an ecological, rather than evolutionary sense. The ecological time hypothesis of species diversity postulates that diversity is limited by the dispersal of species into new areas of suitable habitat. If dispersal is the major factor determining species diversity, then its effects should be most pronounced in geographic localities physically separated from other areas, such as islands.

If we exclude the origin of species through speciation, then the only way in which a species can enter a new habitat is by immigration, resulting from its various dispersal mechanisms. Assuming that conditions are within the tolerance range of the species, then once present in the new habitat, it must compete effectively and withstand new predation pressures if it is to survive. If it cannot, the ultimate outcome is extinction. These concepts are embodied in the *species equilibrium theory* formulated by MacArthur and Wilson (1967). This theory was first proposed to explain those factors which regulate the number of species on oceanic islands where the mainland serves as a continued source of new species. If the analogy is not carried too far, the theory is also useful in explaining the build-up of species in any semi-isolated habitat during its colonization period. This theory simply states that the number of species which are present on an island is determined by opposing immigration and extinction rates.

In order to formulate the model mathematically, let S_t represent the number of species already present on an island at time t and let P equal the total number of species present in surrounding source areas (i.e., the mainland). The rate of build-up in the number of new species can then be written as the immigration rate minus the extinction rate. Now, the extinction rate will depend on the number of species already present on the island (S_t); whereas the immigration rate will depend on the number of species located in source areas but not presently existing on the island ($P - S_t$). Hence, we get

$$\Delta S_t = m(P - S_t) - uS_t = mP - (m + u)S_t \qquad \textbf{(11.6)}$$

where $\Delta S_t = S_{t+1} - S_t$ and where m and u are the average immigration and extinction rates per species, respectively. Since immigration and extinction have opposing effects, an equilibrium will be established when $\Delta S_t = 0$. When this occurs, the equilibrium number of species will be given by

$$\hat{S} = mP/(m + u)$$

Thus, $\hat{S}$ varies hyperbolically with m, approaching a limiting value of P when the average immigration rate per species is very high. On the other hand, when average extinction rates are very high, $\hat{S}$ becomes approximately equal to mP/u.

The approach to an equilibrium situation can be seen more clearly by first writing the number of species presently existing on the island in terms of a recurrence relation. By changing subscripts, it can be seen that, in general,

$$S_t = mP + (1 - m - u)S_{t-1}$$

where t and $t-1$ represent successive time intervals (months, years, etc.). Substituting $(m + u)\hat{S}$ for mP and subtracting $\hat{S}$ from both sides, the expression can now be written in terms of the departure from equilibrium as

$$S_t - \hat{S} = (1 - m - u)(S_{t-1} - \hat{S})$$

As long as average immigration and extinction rates remain constant, this difference is further reduced by the factor $1 - m - u$ in each additional time interval. Therefore, the difference existing after t time intervals will be

$$S_t - \hat{S} = (1 - m - u)^t (S_o - \hat{S}) \tag{11.7}$$

assuming $\hat{S}$ is constant. Since $(1 - m - u)^t$ approaches zero as t gets large, the number of species on the island will approach the value of $\hat{S}$ exponentially.

As shown in the preceding equations, both the magnitude of $\hat{S}$ and the rate at which this equilibrium level is approached depend on the numerical values of m and u. The magnitude of m, in turn, is a function of the distance from the source area. Recall that for random dispersal, the number of individuals or propagules decreases with the distance away from the source of dispersal. It follows that m should also decrease with distance. This is illustrated in Figure 11.15 by a plot of total immigration rate versus S for islands of varying distances from the mainland. Note that a stable equilibrium is established where the immigration and extinction curves intersect. In this illustration the immigration rate is represented as a concave curve rather than as a straight line as assumed in equation (11.7). This is to account for the greater likelihood that more rapidly dispersing species would successfully invade an island first, thus producing an initial drop in the average immigration rate of the remaining colonists. The application of equation (11.7) is, therefore, limited to predicting values of S

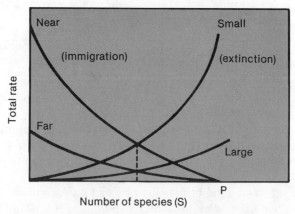

Figure 11.15. Representative immigration and extinction rates of species colonizing islands of varying distances from the mainland and of different areas. An equilibrium number of species is reached at the point of intersection of any pair of immigration and extinction curves.

near the point of equilibrium, where m and u values are not expected to change significantly.

There are only a few experimental studies of island species diversity that are applicable to testing the species equilibrium theory. One such study, by Simberloff and Wilson (1970), involved following the recolonization of six mangrove islands in the Florida Keys after they had been fumigated to remove all their fauna. On each island, the colonization curve rose rapidly with time (Fig. 11.16), approaching an equilibrium level very close to that originally on the island. The rate of approach to equilibrium is fairly smooth and both this rate and the final equilibrium value are inversely related to the distance of an island from the mainland. All of these findings are in general agreement with the species equilibrium theory.

We can also test the theory using the extinction rate. The value of u is a function of the area of the island being colonized; the smaller the area, the smaller the size of existing species populations, and, hence, the greater the chance of a species undergoing extinction. Thus, the average extinction rate per species will tend to be inversely related to an island's area. This is also illustrated in Figure 11.15. In this case, the graph predicts that the extinction rate should be a curvilinear relationship rising steeply as S approaches P. Thus at first, most invading species are successful in colonization. As habitats fill, it becomes increasingly more difficult for invading species to establish a beach-head since the invader must then compete successfully for the limited number of resources which are partitioned among the species already present on the island. These curves predict that the equilibrium number of species should increase with the area being colonized. This prediction conforms to the observed species-area relationships for oceanic islands shown in Figure 11.17. Studies

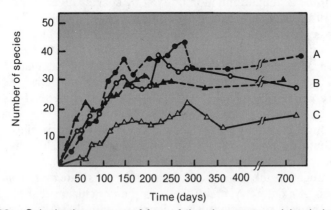

Figure 11.16. Colonization curves of four of the six mangrove islands in the Florida Keys which had previously been fumigated to remove all fauna. Island *A is nearest to the mainland, island* C farthest from the mainland, and islands *B* are at intermediate distance. (After D.S. Simberloff and E.O. Wilson. 1970. Ecology 51: 934. Copyright 1970 by the Ecological Society of America.)

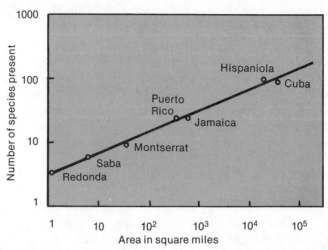

Figure 11.17. Area-species curve of reptiles and amphibians in the West Indies. The regression line corresponds to the equation log S = 0.301 log A + constant, where A is the island's area and S is the number of species. (After R.H. MacArthur and E.O. Wilson. *The Theory of Island Biogeography,* copyright © 1957 by Princeton University Press. Reprinted by permission of Princeton University Press.)

have shown that the number of species on an oceanic island is roughly proportional to the cube-root of the island's area.

Rosenzweig (1975) has discussed continental equilibrium species diversity, building on MacArthur's argument (1969) that continental species diversity will be a product of the rates of speciation and extinction. The speciation rate is postulated to be a sigmoid function of existing species diversity, dependent on the rate of formation of effective geographic barriers. The chance of occurrence of a barrier is greater the larger the species range, but the chance of complete dissection of the range depends inversely on its size. Therefore, the probability of formation of a geographic isolate should peak at intermediate range sizes. Whether or not speciation then takes place depends on barrier effectiveness and the divergence rate of the isolate. The latter might depend on the rate of occurrence of beneficial mutations in the population, which would be low when diversity is high (population sizes small). The ability of a species to recognize a barrier should increase with diversity when diversities are low, as wide niches are narrowed, and then reach some stationary value.

Putting together the chance of formation of an isolate and its effectiveness as a function of existing diversity leads to the conclusion that at low species diversities, the rate of speciation will increase with diversity. As species accumulate, however, a maximum speciation rate is reached, after which the increase in the rate of speciation slows, finally reaching a more-or-less constant value—in other words, a sigmoid relationship (Fig. 11.18). Assuming that continental extinction rates are dependent on species diversity in a manner similar

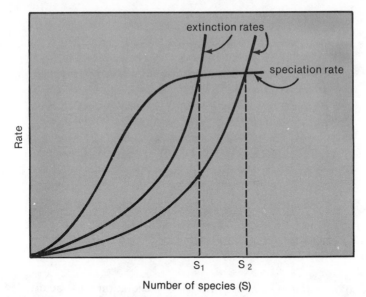

Figure 11.18.   The postulated effect of number of species on speciation rate (sigmoid curve) and extinction rates (concave curve). The equilibrium number of species occurs where the speciation curve and extinction curve intersect.

to those characterizing islands, the result is an equilibrium species diversity value where the two curves intersect.

Spatial heterogeneity.   A second mechanism by which diversity can be maintained is through spatial variation in community structure. If some limiting resource varies in such a way that a variety of microhabitats are formed, for which different species can specialize, then competition will be avoided and the species can coexist. For example, MacArthur and MacArthur (1961) found that insectivorous woodland birds partition their environment vertically into zones of foliage height. By dividing foliage height into three layers (litter and ground foliage, shrub zone, and tree zone), they were able to calculate the foliage height diversity (FHD). The bird species diversity was strongly correlated with FHD (Fig. 11.19). There was only a weak correlation between horizontal plant diversity (plant species types) and BSD. The results suggest that stratification of the environment provides the microhabitats necessary for a variety of bird species to coexist.

Similar studies of birds in other latitudinal regions have shown the same positive correlation between bird and plant height diversities, but not necessarily the same number of zones characterizing vertical stratification. Puerto Rican species were found to partition their environment into just two vertical layers, whereas Panamanian birds subdivide their foliage into four layers and are more specific in their choice of layer. Although it is not clear what meaning may be

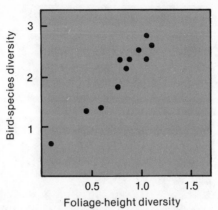

Figure 11.19. The relationship between bird-species diversity and foliage-height diversity in deciduous forests of the Eastern United States. (Data from R.H. MacArthur and J.W. MacArthur. 1961. Ecology 42: 594.)

ascribed to the number of zones into which vegetation must be divided in order to obtain a good fit to bird species diversity, these results are at least consistent with the idea that the latitudinal gradient in overall species diversity mentioned earlier can, in part, be accounted for by more habitat diversity and/or finer subdivision of habitat space by species nearer the equator.

Environmental stability.   This hypothesis simply proposes that the degree of stability of the environment (physical or biological) determines the degree of specialization of resource requirements by a species. The more restricted these requirements, the finer the subdivision of the environment, and thus the greater the species diversity. Stability in this sense refers to either yearly environmental fluctuations of small amplitude or to small variances of the period and amplitude of these fluctuations (predictability). Increased species diversity in the tropics would be explained as being the result of the relative climatic stability of this area. In contrast, zones of higher latitudes would favor broader adaptations by species so that they are flexible enough to meet seasonal climatic conditions. The stability-time hypothesis proposes that environmental stability and evolutionary time interact in determining species diversity.

Despite the apparent simplicity of this proposed mechanism, there is little, if any, unambiguous experimental evidence on the relationship between niche size and environmental stability or certainty. Thus, the importance of stable environmental conditions in promoting species diversity remains obscure.

Productivity.   It might seem reasonable to think that species diversity will be positively correlated with the productivity of the environment: the higher the rate of energy flow per area of habitat, the greater the potential for specialization in resource use. Although this idea is appealing, there is little evidence to support it and, in fact, some directly contradicts it. The role of productivity in determining species diversity may instead be coupled with that of environmental constancy. If environmental stability increases the opportunities for specialization on the part of organisms, it might do so through a stabilization of productivity. For example, if constant favorable weather conditions exist throughout the year, primary production will be high and constant. In the tropics, the resulting long growing season may promote coexistence of species by allowing them to partition the environment temporarily.

Competition.   The environmental stability hypothesis suggests that organisms are more specialized in stable, predictable climates, so that their narrower niches allow more species to coexist in the same locality. This result can also be viewed from the standpoint of competition being the primary mechanism that influences diversity. In regions where physical factors are not important in regulating populations, natural selection may operate primarily through biological mechanisms such as competition. Selection acting in this manner would lead to a redistribution of species niches along one or more resource dimensions. This is shown for a two-dimensional case in Figure 11.20. Note that pairs of

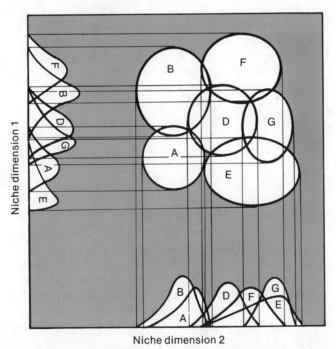

Figure 11.20.   Diagrammatic representation of resource utilization of six hypothetical species along two niche dimensions. Species which overlap extensively along one dimension can avoid competition by niche separation along the other dimension.

species with substantial niche overlap along a single resource axis can avoid competition by separation along another dimension, thus permitting greater species packing.

Predation.   The basis of the predation explanation is that predators, by lowering prey levels, reduce the intensity of competition among the prey and thereby promote the coexistence of potential competitors. The predation hypothesis thus proposes that species diversity is negatively correlated with the intensity of competition. Theoretical justification for the predation idea is derived from models, such as the one presented earlier in this chapter, which predict that moderate predation pressure can allow for coexistence of species in situations where one would otherwise be excluded. Of course, for predation to be a significant factor in this respect, it must be the primary factor limiting abundance of prey.

An interesting example of species diversity being associated with predation has been provided by Paine (1966). Among the intertidal invertebrates along the Washington coast, the food web is well-defined and constant, so that it is possible to determine the effects of alterations in particular members of the web. Paine removed the predator starfish *Pisaster* from the shore and found that the number of species in the web dropped from 15 to 8 as a result. One explanation for these findings is that in the absence of *Pisaster*, competition among its prey intensifies and many species are eliminated.

Predation might be just one of several factors that control diversity by keeping individual species population sizes below levels they would otherwise attain. For example, periodic climatic disasters could decimate populations to the extent that niche space is opened to species that otherwise would be eliminated by competition. If such an explanation is correct, we would expect climatic instabilities to increase, rather than decrease, species diversity.

It should be obvious from the preceding discussion that it is not possible to explain species diversity using any single mechanism. Many of the six factors mentioned interact, so that it is unrealistic to pick out any one as the basic determinant of diversity patterns. For example, diversity might be regulated in some cases by competition, but competition, in turn, might be a function of spatial heterogeneity and environmental stability. Spatial heterogeneity could be, in part, related to environmental stability. However, it could also be a function of the intensity of competition, competitive interactions forcing species to perceive a finer subdivision of their environment. The complexity of the situation makes it difficult to sort out its various components, although some progress has been made in relatively simple communities. As an illustration, we consider the studies by Pianka (1966, 1967) on North American desert lizards.

In North America, 12 species of flatland desert lizards are distributed over the Northern Great Basin, Mojave, and Sonoran deserts. The areas differ in lizard species diversity, ranging from just four species in Oregon, Idaho, and

Utah in the north, to ten species in Southern California and Western Arizona. Since lizards have been present in all three deserts for about the same length of time, evolutionary time is not a factor determining diversity. Ecological time is not a factor either, except in the one case of the genus *Uma*, which does appear to be limited in its distribution by dispersal. All other species have had ample time to disperse into the available habitats. Pianka thus looked for physical and biological mechanisms to explain the observed diversity pattern.

Rainfall does not seem to influence lizard diversity, either as the determinant of desert productivity or as a component of environmental stability. Since rainfall amounts are less in the Mojave than in other areas of the lizards' range, it appears that productivity does not limit diversity. Rainfall is most variable in the Mojave, where diversity is highest. Species diversity was found to be correlated with mean July temperature and length of the frost-free period, however, so that environmental stability does appear to play a role in regulating the relative abundance of these lizards. Pianka found no evidence of any difference in the degree of competition among lizards from the various deserts, and little conclusive evidence of predation. The major factor limiting diversity was spatial heterogeneity. Lizard species diversity was found to be strongly correlated with plant volume diversity, environments with high plant structural variability possessing the greatest diversity of lizard species.

SOLVED EXAMPLE PROBLEMS

1. Given a 2×2 contingency table with h of the n quadrats having species A and j of the n quadrats having species B, show that the probability of a given set of cell frequencies is

$$Pr = h!i!j!k!/a!b!c!d!n!$$

solution For a given n, h, and j, the number of ways of choosing h quadrats which contain species A is $\binom{n}{h}$, and the number of ways of choosing j quadrats which contain species B is $\binom{n}{j}$. Thus, the number of ways of obtaining both the observed totals h and j is the product of these two quantities, $\binom{n}{h}\binom{n}{j}$. Since the number of different ways of partitioning n into its four cell components is $n!/a!b!c!d!$, the probability of any particular set of cell frequencies, given n, h, and j, is

$$Pr = \frac{n!/a!b!c!d!}{\binom{n}{h}\binom{n}{j}} = \frac{h!i!j!k!}{a!b!c!d!n!}$$

Competition

2. In 1934, Gause conducted a study on competition between two species of yeast when grown together under anaerobic conditions. Let N_1 and N_2 be the amounts of the two species and let their growth equations be

$$d(\ln N_1)/dt = 0.218 - 0.0168\,N_1 - 0.0528\,N_2$$

$$d(\ln N_2)/dt = 0.0607 - 0.0105\,N_2 - 0.00459\,N_1$$

Compute the competition coefficients and predict the carrying capacity levels of the two species when grown separately.

solution   Comparison with equation (11.2) shows that for species 1, $r_1 = 0.218$. Thus, $K_1 = 13.0$ and $\alpha = 3.15$. Similarly, for species 2, $r_2 = 0.0607$. Hence, $K_2 = 5.8$ and $\beta = 0.439$.

3. Consider a simple form of competitive interaction described by the equations:

$$\Delta\ln N_{1,t} = r_1(1 - N_{1,t}/K_1 - \alpha N_{2,t}/K_1)$$

$$\Delta\ln N_{2,t} = r_2(1 - N_{2,t}/K_2 - \beta N_{1,t}/K_2)$$

Show that, in contrast with predation, competitive interactions of this sort do not produce oscillations; that is, they will not cause oscillations in populations which do not oscillate in the absence of competition.

solution   Rewrite the expressions in terms of small departures from equilibrium: $x = N_1 - \hat{N}_1$ and $y = N_2 - \hat{N}_2$. We get

$$x_{t+1} + \hat{N}_1 = (x_t + \hat{N}_1)\exp[\,r_1(1 - x_t/K_1 - \hat{N}_1/K_1 - \alpha y_t/K_1 - \alpha\hat{N}_2/K_1)\,]$$

$$y_{t+1} + \hat{N}_2 = (y_t + \hat{N}_2)\exp[\,r_2(1 - y_t/K_2 - \hat{N}_2/K_2 - \beta x_t/K_2 - \beta\hat{N}_1/K_2)\,]$$

Noting that $\exp[\,r_1(1 - \hat{N}_1/K_1 - \alpha\hat{N}_2/K_1)\,] = \exp[\,r_2(1 - \hat{N}_2/K_2 - \beta\hat{N}_1/K_2)\,] = 1$, then, for small displacements,

$$x_{t+1} = x_t - (r_1\hat{N}_1/K_1)x_t - \alpha(r_1\hat{N}_1/K_1)y_t$$

$$y_{t+1} = y_t - (r_2\hat{N}_2/K_2)y_t - \beta(r_2\hat{N}_2/K_2)x_t$$

Observe that by letting $a = r_1\hat{N}_1/K_1$ and $b = r_2\hat{N}_2/K_2$, we get a pair of relations similar to equations (1.26). Eliminating y gives

$$x_{t+2} - (2 - a - b)x_{t+1} + (1 - a - b + c)x_t = 0$$

where $c = ab(1 - \alpha\beta)$. The general solution is $x_t = k_1\lambda_1^t + k_2\lambda_2^t$ in which

$$\lambda_1, \lambda_2 = 1 - \tfrac{1}{2}(a+b) \pm \tfrac{1}{2}\sqrt{(a+b)^2 - 4c}$$

Since $(a+b)^2 - 4c$ is positive, divergent oscillations will only occur if λ_1 or λ_2 is less than -1. Such oscillations can also happen in the absence of competition when either r_1 or r_2 is greater than 2, but are not promoted by the competitive interaction.

4. Employing the linear model graphed in Figure 11.3, show that the equilibrium point E must lie above the line $N_1/K_1 + N_2/K_2 = 1$.

    solution   The above expression is the line connecting the intercepts $N_1 = K_1$ and $N_2 = K_2$. Referring to case 4 in Figure 11.3, it can be seen that such a line must always pass below the point of intersection of the two isoclines, unless $K_1 = K_2/\beta$ and $K_2 = K_1/\alpha$. Note that the reverse will be true for an unstable equilibrium represented by case 1; that is, the line will always pass above the point of intersection of the isoclines for unstable equilibria.

Multispecies Communities

5. Consider a simple food chain consisting of plants (N_1), herbivores (N_2), and carnivores (N_3). Assume that plants are limited solely by predation so that the growth equations can be expressed as

    $$d(\ln N_1)/dt = r - a_{12}N_2$$

    $$d(\ln N_2)/dt = u_{21}N_1 - q_2 - a_{23}N_3$$

    $$d(\ln N_3)/dt = u_{32}N_2 - q_3$$

    Show that such a simple feeding relationship will not continue to exist since herbivores cannot simultaneously maintain their prey and predators in equilibrium.

    solution   A solution is obtained by equating all logarithmic growth rates to zero. This yields

    $$\hat{N}_2 = r/a_{12}$$

    $$\hat{N}_2 = q_3/u_{32}$$

    $$\hat{N}_3 = (u_{21}/a_{23})N_1 - q_2/a_{23}$$

    Since $\hat{N}_2$ cannot simultaneously possess two different values, a stable equilibrium cannot exist.

Species Abundance and Diversity

6. Suppose that 4,365 individuals of a collection of 203 species of insects fit a logarithmic series distribution. Estimate the quantities x and α.

    solution   Since $S = -\alpha \ln(1 - x)$ and $N = \alpha x/(1 - x)$, then x can be estimated by an iterative procedure using the relationship $S/N = -(1 - x)\ln(1 - x)/x$ obtained from the preceding expressions. By applying this method, we get $x = 0.99$ for $S/N = 203/4,365 = 0.0465$. The value of α is then $(4,365)(0.01)/0.99 = 44.09$. Thus, $\alpha x \simeq 44$ is the expected number of species represented by a single individual; $\alpha x^2/2 \simeq 22$ is the number of species with two individuals, and so on.

7. Suppose that a large island, with 200 plant species, serves as the source of new species for a small neighboring island. If $m = u = 0.01$ per year, what is the total extinction rate on the smaller island once an equilibrium is established?

solution   The total extinction rate is the number of species lost per year and can be computed at equilibrium as $u\hat{S}$. Since $\hat{S} = mP/(m + u) = \frac{1}{2}(200) = 100$, the total extinction rate becomes $(0.01)(100) = 1$ species per year.

8.   The frequency distribution of trees that had established themselves in an abandoned quarry was observed to be as follows:

Species	Number
Shingle oak	5
Slippery elm	10
Black walnut	13
Shagbark hickory	30
White oak	42

Assuming this to be a representative sample of the surrounding community, estimate the diversity by computing H'. The observed diversity, in this case, is what fraction of the maximum diversity?
solution   Using the equation $H' = -\Sigma(N_i/N) \ln (N_i/N)$ where $N = 100$, we obtain $H' = -0.05 \ln 0.05 + 0.1 \ln 0.1 + 0.13 \ln 0.13 + 0.3 \ln 0.3 + 0.42 \ln 0.42 = 1.371$. The maximum diversity occurs when all $N_i = 20$, giving $H'_{max} = -\ln 0.2 = 1.609$. Hence, $H'/H'_{max} = 0.85$.

9.   May (1973b) has suggested the following model as a first approximation for a mutualistic form of interaction:

$$d(\ln N_1)/dt = r_1[1 - N_1/(K_1 + aN_2)]$$

$$d(\ln N_2)/dt = r_2[1 - N_2/(K_2 + bN_1)]$$

In this case, each species grows logistically and has its carrying capacity increased by the presence of the other. Show that such a simple model cannot describe a stable equilibrium unless $ab < 1$.
solution   Solve for the equilibrial values of the two species by setting both logarithmic growth rates equal to zero. This yields

$$\hat{N}_1 = (K_1 + aK_2)/(1 - ab) \quad \text{and} \quad \hat{N}_2 = (K_2 + bK_1)/(1 - ab)$$

If $ab = 1$, both populations are predicted to grow without bounds. Thus a finite equilibrium only exists for $ab < 1$.

PROBLEM EXERCISES

1.   Predict the outcome of competition for the pair of species in Example Problem 2.

2.   Predict the outcome of competition when $\alpha = \beta = 1$ and $K_1 = K_2$. What is implied when $\alpha = \beta$? When $\alpha = 1/\beta$?

3. The discrete time version of Gause's competition model (11.2) is the pair
    of difference equations

    $$N_{1,t+1} = \lambda_1 N_{1,t}/(1 + A_1 N_{1,t} + B_1 N_{2,t})$$
    $$N_{2,t+1} = \lambda_2 N_{2,t}/(1 + A_2 N_{1,t} + B_2 N_{2,t})$$

    (see Leslie, 1958). Predict the outcome of competition for $\lambda_1 = \lambda_2 = 4$,
    $A_1 = 0.03$, $B_1 = 0.02$, $A_2 = 0.06$, and $B_2 = 0.04$. Plot the results as $N_{1,t}$
    and $N_{2,t}$ versus t starting with populations of 10 each.

4. It was pointed out in Example Problem 4 that for Gause's competition
    model, a stable equilibrium point must lie above the line connecting the
    intercepts $N_1 = K_1$ and $N_2 = K_2$. An exception to this condition has been
    reported by Ayala (1969) for competition between *Drosophila pseudoob-
    scura* and *D. se rata*. Show how the existence of a stable equilibrium point
    below the line $N_1/K_1 + N_2/K_2 = 1$ can be explained by assuming that
    isoclines are curvilinear rather than linear as in the model.

5. Calculate Simpson's diversity index and the Shannon information measure
    of diversity for the following hypothetical communities:

	Species (i)											
Proportion of species in:	1	2	3	4	5	6	7	8	9	10	11	12
Community A -	0.30	0.20	0.20	0.10	0.05	0.04	0.03	0.02	0.02	0.02	0.01	0.01
Community B -	0.15	0.15	0.15	0.15	0.15	0.15	0.10					

6. One approach which can be taken to incorporate curvilinear immigration
    and extinction rates into the species equilibrium model is to assume
    that the average immigration rate per species declines with S as $m = m_o (P - S_t)$ and the average extinction rate per species increases with S
    as $u = u_o S_t$. Substitute these expressions into equation (11.6) and plot the
    relationship as S_t versus t for $P = 100$, $S_o = 0$, $m_o = 0.02$, and $u_o = 0.01$.
    How does the approach to equilibrium compare with that predicted by
    equation (11.7)?

7. On a small island containing 8 arthropod species, the total immigration rate
    equals the total extinction rate at 1 species per year. The island is close
    to a larger source island with 25 species of arthropods. If the small island
    is suddenly defaunated, how long will it take for the number of arthropod
    species to return to one-half its original value?

Part Four

Evolution of
Populations

12

Natural Selection

From a genetic point of view, evolution can be described at its most elemental level as any progressive change in gene frequency. Such changes in the genetic makeup of populations are basically a result of four evolutionary "forces": (1) mutation, (2) migration, (3) selection, and (4) genetic drift. The first three are *systematic processes*, producing changes which are predictable both in magnitude and direction. Genetic drift, on the other hand, is a *dispersive process*, predictable only in the degree to which gene frequencies are changed. Of these, mutation, migration, and drift produce changes which are largely nonadaptive in character since they do not occur as an adaptive response to environmental conditions. Consequently, selection is the only elemental process of evolution having a direct and causal relationship with adaptation.

Natural selection can be defined as the differential (nonrandom) reproduction of genotypes. In other words, selection occurs when individuals of a given genotype consistently leave a greater or lesser number of surviving offspring than others. Such variation in reproductive success, or fitness as it is generally called, is a direct consequence of differences in genotype-specific reproductive and survival values. These differences, in turn, stem from a variety of causes including differential fecundity and mating success, variability in the onset and duration of reproductive periods, and the differential effects of competition, predation, and changes in the physical environment.

MEASUREMENT OF FITNESS

Ideally, the fitness of an organism should express its adaptability to environmental change and, thus, its ability to survive over many generations. Unfortunately, no such measure has been devised that can be deduced without recourse to the known evolutionary record. For this reason, fitness is usually expressed in terms of the short-term reproductive success of a species population extending over one or just a few generations. One useful measure in this regard is the net reproductive rate (R_o). As defined in an earlier chapter, R_o gives the average contribution of each individual in terms of number of progeny to the next generation. Hence, the genotype possessing the largest value of R_o and thus, the largest fitness value, will tend to have the greatest impact on the composition of the gene pools of succeeding generations. Suppose, for example, that at generation t a population is composed of n genotypes with numbers N_1, N_2, N_3, . . ., N_n and reproductive rates $R_{0,1}$, $R_{0,2}$, $R_{0,3}$, . . ., $R_{0,n}$. The size of the population in the next generation $(t+1)$ will then be

$$N_{t+1} = \sum_{i=1}^{n} R_{o,i} N_i = \bar{R}_o N_t$$

where $\bar{R}_o$ is the reproductive rate of the entire population defined as the arithmetic mean $\bar{R}_o = \Sigma \, R_{o,i} N_i / N_t$. Thus, if $R_{o,i}$ is greater than $\bar{R}_o$, the relative contribution of the ith genotype must then be greater than the population average and its genes will increase in frequency in the next generation.

There are a number of advantages to using R_o as an indicator of fitness. One is its ability to fit well into the general theory of population genetics where time intervals are usually expressed in terms of whole generations. It also yields a common-sense estimate of reproductive rate which applies to both annual and perennial populations. On the other hand, the fact that this parameter is based on an entire generation cycle limits its usefulness when comparing the fitness of genotypes that differ in generation time. When such comparisons are to be made, it is better to express the fitness of each genotype in terms of either its finite or intrinsic rates of increase. To illustrate, consider a population with overlapping generations that undergoes continuous exponential growth. Since the population will increase R_o times its existing size in each generation, the three growth parameters can be related, approximately, as

$$R_o = \lambda^{T_c} = e^{rT_c}$$

where λ and r are the finite and intrinsic rates of increase and T_c is the generation time. These measures of fitness are, therefore, interchangeable under most conditions.

The genetic basis of fitness or reproductive success is a property of the actions and interactions of all genes which make up the genotype of an individual. Thus, ideally, fitness should be expressed in terms of whole genotypes. Although this characterizes much of the modern thinking about the selective process, it is still highly theoretical and impossible to quantify since each individual is essentially unique. Consequently, fitness is generally measured in terms of the relative contributions of individual loci or of small groups of genes to the total reproductive rate. When expressed in this way, the results of selection can be modeled by rather simple mathematical equations.

Fitness is relative in another way. In populations that are limited by food, space, or predators, the net reproductive rate of the whole population ($\bar{R}_o$) is usually close to unity; however, the genotype-specific reproductive rates may vary anywhere from zero to values greater than one. It is, therefore, convenient to express the fitness of each genotype as a ratio of R_o values relative to some standard of comparison. The standard commonly used is the genotype with the largest reproductive rate. In this way, the reproductive potential of each genotype can be measured in terms of a *relative fitness* or *adaptive value* (W) and that of the entire population by the *mean fitness* ($\bar{W}$). The calculation of adaptive values is illustrated by means of the following hypothetical population:

Genotype:	BB	Bb	bb
Frequency (f_i):	$P = \frac{1}{4}$	$H = \frac{1}{2}$	$Q = \frac{1}{4}$
Net Reproductive Rate ($R_{o,i}$):	1.25	1.00	0.75
Relative Fitness (W_i):	$\frac{1.25}{1.25} = 1.00$	$\frac{1.00}{1.25} = 0.80$	$\frac{0.75}{1.25} = 0.60$

$$R_o = \Sigma\, R_{o,i}\, f_i = (1.25)\tfrac{1}{4} + (1.00)\tfrac{1}{2} + (0.75)\tfrac{1}{4} = 1.00$$

$$\bar{W} = \Sigma\, W_i\, f_i = (1.00)\tfrac{1}{4} + (0.80)\tfrac{1}{2} + (0.60)\tfrac{1}{4} = 0.80$$

Observe that W_i and, consequently, $\bar{W}$ can range in value along a scale running from 0 to 1. Also note that by expressing fitness in a relative manner, we tend to cancel many of the mortality and fertility losses which are independent of genotype (i.e., nonselective deaths). For example, consider a population with discrete nonoverlapping generations. Let k be the fraction of each genotype surviving nonselective deaths and designate the genotype-specific fertility and survivorship values as m_i and l_i, respectively. Assuming that genotype 1 is the most fit, the mean fitness then becomes $\bar{W} = k\Sigma m_i l_i f_i / k m_1 l_1 = \Sigma m_i l_i f_i / m_1 l_1$. The value of $\bar{W}$ is, therefore, a measure of the probability of genetic survival; that is, the probability that a randomly selected individual does not experience death or any fertility loss because of the properties of its genome.

The preceding method of calculation can be extended to situations where fitness is expressed in terms of the finite (or intrinsic) rate of increase. As long as the generation time is constant, the relative fitness of the ith genotype can be expressed as

$$W_i = e^{r_i T_c}/e^{r_m T_c} = e^{(r_i - r_m)T_c}$$

where r_m is the intrinsic rate of increase of the genotype with the largest reproductive rate. Note when the difference in intrinsic rates is small, W_i becomes approximately

$$W_i = 1 + (r_i - r_m)\,T_c$$

Should genotypes differ in their generation times as well, T_c values must also be treated as genotype-specific variables.

   Although selection, as defined earlier, merely implies a difference in reproductive success, it is customary to speak of selection as though it were operating against one or more genotypes (or genes). In this regard, the degree of disadvantage can be measured by the selection coefficient, s, which is the proportional reduction in relative fitness of a genotype in question. Hence, the relative fitness of an adaptively inferior genotype can be expressed as $W = 1 - s$ where s can vary from 0 (no selection) to 1 (complete selection). When expressed in this way, s represents a measure of selection intensity.

GENERAL SELECTION MODELS: CONSTANT RELATIVE FITNESS

In the classical theory of natural selection as developed by J. B. S. Haldane, R. A. Fisher, and S. Wright, mathematical expressions are derived assuming a constant relative fitness independent of population size. This implies either that reproductive rates remain constant (a highly unlikely possibility considering the time periods involved), or that density limiting factors are independent of genotype and cancel when one reproductive rate is divided by another. These expressions are also derived in one of two forms: discrete-time models and continuous-time models. As with population growth equations, discrete-time models are appropriate for seasonal populations when generations do not overlap or, if they do, when age distribution is constant. Continuous-time models, on the other hand, describe selection as occurring in populations with continuous births and deaths. In the sections that follow, most of the models are derived for seasonal breeding populations for which age structure is assumed to be constant. Thus, time is treated as a discrete variable. As we shall see, however, the two types of models are readily interchangeable under most conditions.

Haploid populations.   The simplest form of selection occurs in haploid populations where results are not complicated by dominance interactions. This situation applies not only to bacteria and many forms of algae but also to gametes of diploid populations (gametic selection) when differences exist in their abilities to survive and undergo fertilization.

   The genetic consequences of selection in haploid organisms can be illustrated by means of a selection model. To do so, consider a population at generation $t-1$ consisting of two genotypes B, and b having frequencies and adaptive values as follows:

Genotype:	B	b
Frequency:	p_{t-1}	q_{t-1}
Relative Fitness:	$W_1 = 1$	$W_2 = 1-s$

Since adaptive values measure the relative contribution of genotypes to the gene pool of their progeny, the ratio of q to p in the next generation and, hence, the ratio of q_t to $1-q_t$ will be given as

$$\frac{q_t}{1 - q_t} = \frac{W_2 q_{t-1}}{W_1(1 - q_{t-1})} = \frac{(1 - s)q_{t-1}}{1 - q_{t-1}}$$

Thus, if s remains constant, the ratio of q to p will decrease by a factor of $1-s$ in each generation. The expression can then be solved in terms of t as

$$\frac{q_t}{1 - q_t} = (1-s)^t \frac{q_o}{1 - q_o}$$

where q_o is the frequency of gene b at generation zero. Assuming s is small, $(1-s)^t \simeq e^{-st}$ and q_t becomes

$$q_t = \frac{q_o}{q_o + (1-q_o)e^{st}} \qquad (12.1)$$

Hence, the value of q must eventually reduce to zero and will do so in a sigmoid fashion with time. Note that gene B will increase in frequency according to equation (3.7).

Diploid populations.   A general selection model can also be obtained for diploid populations but is further complicated by the system of mating in the group of organisms under study. Therefore, to avoid mathematical complexity, the following discussion will be limited to random-mating populations.

Consider a single locus with two alleles B and b which are distributed among genotypes as follows:

Genotype:	BB	Bb	bb
Frequency:	p^2	$2pq$	q^2
Relative Fitness:	W_1	W_2	W_3

Gene frequencies in the next generation will then be

$$p_1 = (W_1 p^2 + W_2 pq)/(W_1 p^2 + W_2 2pq + W_3 q^2) = p(W_1 p + W_2 q)/\bar{W}$$

$$q_1 = (W_3 q^2 + W_2 pq)/(W_1 p^2 + W_2 2pq + W_3 q^2) = q(W_3 q + W_2 p)/\bar{W}$$

where $\bar{W}$ is the mean fitness of the population given in this case as $\bar{W} = W_1 p^2 + W_2 2pq + W_3 q^2$. The ratio of q_1 to p_1 now becomes

$$\frac{q_1}{1 - q_1} = \left[\frac{W_3 q + W_2(1 - q)}{W_1 (1 - q) + W_2 q}\right] \frac{q}{1 - q} = \left[\frac{W_b}{W_B}\right] \frac{q}{1 - q}$$

where $W_B = W_1(1 - q) + W_2 q$ and $W_b = W_3 q + W_2(1 - q)$. The factors, W_B and W_b, are the adaptive values of genes B and b, or more specifically, the average fitness values of all genotypes containing each of these genes. Note that for diploid populations, W_B and W_b are themselves functions of gene frequency. Consequently, the equation as it stands cannot be solved directly except when the three relative fitness values form a geometric progression such that $W_1:W_2:W_3 = 1:(1-s):(1-s)^2$. The W_b/W_B ratio then works out to be $1-s$. When this simplification does not hold, a more useful form of this equation can be obtained by expressing it in terms of the change in gene frequency per generation (Δq). To do so, we first solve for q_1 and get

$$q_1 = \frac{W_b q}{(1-q)W_B + qW_b} = \frac{W_b q}{\bar{W}}$$

Note that the mean fitness of the population, $\bar{W}$, can also be expressed as the average fitness of both alleles (i.e., $\bar{W} = pW_B + qW_b$).

Subtracting q from both sides of the preceding expression, we now obtain $q_1 - q$ expressed as

$$\Delta q = q(W_b - \bar{W})/\bar{W} \qquad (12.2)$$

Note that this expression consists of two fundamental relationships. First of all, Δq is related linearly to q. Hence, the rate of change in the frequency of genes as a result of selection is expected to be large when these genes are common and rather small in magnitude when these genes are rare. Secondly, Δq is directly related to the fractional excess in fitness of a gene over the population average. This excess in fitness is expressed as $(W_b - \bar{W})/\bar{W}$. Thus, if a gene is selectively advantageous to its carrier, it must increase in frequency within a population. The reverse would be true of adaptively inferior genes.

It is sometimes useful to express the fractional excess in fitness of a gene in equation (12.2) in the form of a derivative. This can be done by noting that $d\bar{W}/dq = 2(W_b - W_B)$. Since $p(W_b - W_B) = (W_b - \bar{W})$, the change in q per generation becomes

$$\Delta q = (pq/2\bar{W})d\bar{W}/dq = \tfrac{1}{2}pqd(\ln \bar{W})/dq \qquad (12.3)$$

where $d\bar{W}/dq$ represents the slope at a point on a $\bar{W}$ versus q plot. Since the factor $pq/2\bar{W}$ is always positive, the direction of change will now depend on $d\bar{W}/dq$. Thus, q will increase when $d\bar{W}/dq > 0$, decrease when $d\bar{W}/dq < 0$, and remain constant when $d\bar{W}/dq = 0$.

Since selection operates on the phenotype of organisms and not directly on the naked genotype, the effectiveness of selection in diploid populations depends on the degree of dominance exhibited by a character. Varying degrees of dominance can be taken into account by assigning the following adaptive values:

Genotype:	BB	Bb	bb
Relative Fitness:	1	$1 - hs$	$1 - s$

The factor h is a measure of the degree of dominance shown by either of the two alleles. For example, when $h = 0$, gene B is dominant and gene b is recessive; when $h = 1$, gene b is dominant and gene B is recessive; and when

$h = \frac{1}{2}$, no dominance exists and the fitness of the heterozygotes is exactly intermediate between the two homozygous types. We can now express $\bar{W}$ and W_b in terms of both h and s as follows:

$$\bar{W} = p^2 + 2pq(1-hs) + q^2(1-s) = 1 - 2hsq + (2h-1)sq^2$$

$$W_b = (1-s)q + (1-hs)(1-q) \quad = 1 - hs(1-q) - sq$$

Substituting these values into equation (12.2), we get

$$\Delta q = \frac{sq(1-q)[q(2h-1) - h]}{1 - 2hsq + (2h-1)sq^2} \tag{12.4}$$

This represents a very general relationship which can be used to determine the change in gene frequency per generation of selection for various conditions of dominance. Three special cases are given in the following outline:

Case 1.   Partial selection against recessives ($h = 0$).

$$\Delta q = -\, sq^2(1-q)/(1-sq^2) \tag{12.5}$$

Case 2.   Partial selection with intermediate heterozygotes ($h = \frac{1}{2}$).

$$\Delta q = -\tfrac{1}{2}sq(1-q)/(1-sq) \tag{12.6}$$

Case 3.   Partial selection against dominants ($h = 1$).

$$\Delta q = -\, sq(1-q)^2/(1-2sq+sq^2) \tag{12.7}$$

These formulae are plotted as Δq versus q in Figure 12.1. Note that the effectiveness of selection for these different degrees of dominance varies markedly with gene frequency with cases 1, 2, and 3 showing maximum rates of change when q is approximately 2/3, 1/2, and 1/3, respectively. In all cases, Δq is zero only when $q = 0$ and $q = 1$. Consequently, when both alleles are present in a population, selection will proceed with the eventual elimination of the disadvantageous gene.

    The effectiveness of selection can also be measured in terms of the number of generations required for a specified change in gene frequency. If s is small, the denominator in each of the preceding cases will not differ significantly from 1. The numerator of each expression can then be written in the form of a differential equation by replacing Δq with dq/dt. The approximate expressions along with their integrated forms are listed as follows:

Case 1.   Partial selection against recessives ($h = 0$, $s < 1$).

$$\frac{dq}{dt} = -\, sq^2(1-q) \quad \text{and} \quad t = \frac{1}{s}\left[\frac{q_o - q_t}{q_o q_t} + \ln \frac{q_o(1-q_t)}{q_t(1-q_o)}\right]$$

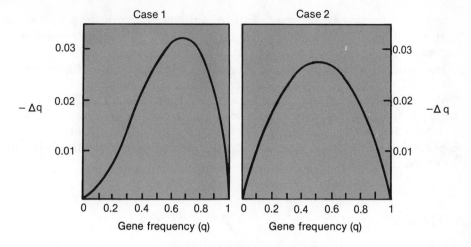

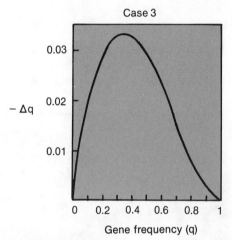

Figure 12.1. Change in gene frequency in diploid populations for different conditions of dominance. The curves are representative plots of three special cases: case 1, partial selection against recessives; case 2, partial selection with intermediate heterozygotes; case 3, partial selection against dominants.

Case 2.   Partial selection with intermediate heterozygotes ($h = \frac{1}{2}, s < 1$).

$$\frac{dq}{dt} = -\tfrac{1}{2}sq(1-q) \text{ and } t = \frac{2}{s}\left[\ln\frac{q_o(1-q_t)}{q_t(1-q_o)}\right]$$

Case 3.   Partial selection against dominants ($h = 1, s < 1$).

$$\frac{dq}{dt} = -sq(1-q)^2 \text{ and } t = \frac{1}{s}\left[\frac{q_o - q_t}{(1-q_t)(1-q_o)} + \ln\frac{q_o(1-q_t)}{q_t(1-q_o)}\right]$$

In all cases, q_t is the frequency of the disadvantageous gene at generation t and q_o represents its frequency when $t = 0$. For example, the number of generations required to reduce the frequency of a detrimental gene from $q_o = 0.7$ to $q_t = 0.1$ when $s = 0.02$, is 581 generations for case 1, 304 generations for case 2, and 263 generations for case 3. This is illustrated by the q_t versus t plots in Figure 12.2. Note that t is inversely proportional to s. Therefore, an increase in s will produce a reduction in t by the same order of magnitude.

Solutions can also be obtained for the three special cases when selection is complete ($s = 1$). These solutions are given in the form of recurrence relations as follows:

Case 1.   Complete selection against recessives ($h = 0$, $s = 1$).

$$\Delta q = -q^2/(1 + q); \; q_t = q_{t-1}/(1 + q_{t-1}) = q_o/(1 + tq_o); \; t = (q_o - q_t)/q_o q_t$$

Case 2.   Complete selection with intermediate heterozygotes ($h = \frac{1}{2}$, $s = 1$).

$$\Delta q = -\tfrac{1}{2}q; \; q_t = \tfrac{1}{2}q_{t-1} = (\tfrac{1}{2})^t q_o; \; t = \ln (q_o/q_t)/\ln 2$$

Case 3.   Complete selection against dominants ($h = 1$, $s = 1$).

$$\Delta q = - q; \; \text{(gene eliminated in a single generation)}.$$

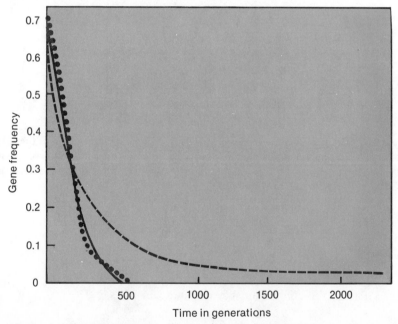

Figure 12.2.   Patterns of gene frequency changes for recessive (dashed line), semi-dominant (solid line), and dominant (dotted line) genes under selection. The initial gene frequency is 0.7 and the selection coefficient is 0.02 in all cases.

As these expressions illustrate, complete selection is most effective when acting on a gene which shows complete or partial dominance. When completely dominant, both homozygous and heterozygous carriers of the gene are lethal or effectively sterile. Consequently, the gene is lost in a single generation. When dominance is lacking or when there is complete selection against a recessive trait, the rate of reduction in gene frequency is limited by the rate at which heterozygotes are removed from the population. This is especially critical at low gene frequencies. When q is small so that $1 - q \simeq 1$ and $2pq \simeq 2q$, the proportion of bb homozygotes is negligible and essentially all of the deleterious genes are present in heterozygous combinations. The effectiveness of selection will then depend entirely on the reproductive success of heterozygotes. Thus, when $h = \frac{1}{2}$, $2q_t = H_t = (\frac{1}{2})^t H_o$ and one-half the heterozygotes are eliminated or fail to reproduce in each generation. When $h = 1$, $2q_t = H_t = H_o/(1 + tq_o)$ and the frequency of heterozygotes is reduced at a very slow rate. In the latter case, the reduction in heterozygotes is due solely to the selective elimination of bb offspring from $Bb \times Bb$ matings.

Evidence for selection.   Numerous attempts have been made to obtain support for the general theory of selection by means of laboratory experiments. Generally speaking, however, agreement between theory and observation is most satisfactory for selection against lethal genes. One such example is shown in Figure 12.3. In this case, a starting population of *D. melanogaster* was used

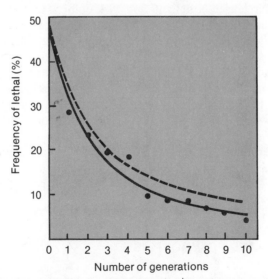

Figure 12.3.   Selection against an autosomal lethal gene in an experimental population of *D. melanogaster.* Closed circles represent observed lethal frequencies. The dashed line is the theoretical expectation for a completely recessive lethal; the solid line designates the results expected for a lethal gene that reduces heterozygote fitness by 10%. (From B. Wallace. 1963. Am. Nat. 97: 65. Copyright 1963 by The University of Chicago. All rights reserved.)

which was heterozygous for an autosomal lethal gene allelic to the recessive eye-color mutation light (lt). Since the value of the selection coefficient cannot exceed 1, the greater rate of reduction in frequency than that expected for a recessive lethal can only be explained on the basis of a slight reduction in the fitness of heterozygotes. The fact that experimental results on non-lethal genes are even less satisfactory implies that selection is generally more complex than predicted on the basis of classical theory.

Although natural selection tends to be a slow and gradual process, some rather rapid selective changes have been observed and recorded in the field. Probably the most extensively studied of these concerns the rapid increase in the melanic form of the peppered moth *Biston betularia*. This change has occurred during the past one hundred years in several urban areas of England where the surrounding terrain has been darkened with the soot of industrial pollution. During the first part of the nineteenth century, this species was typified by a light-colored form which blended quite nicely with the lichen-covered tree trunks dotting the countryside (Figure 12.4). Then, in 1848, the first melanic form was collected in Manchester. At that time, the melanic form probably comprised less than 1% of the population. Fifty years later, it had increased to a frequency of about 95%. Since the species has one generation per year, this spectacular change actually occurred in 50 generations.

Much of what we know regarding the nature of the selective agent has been gained through the extensive studies of H. B. D. Kettlewell. For example, Kettlewell (1958) released both light- and dark-colored forms into industrialized and nonindustrialized areas and then recaptured samples with the use of light traps. The results of his studies clearly demonstrate that the melanic form has the selective advantage in sooty environments. Moreover, photographs taken by Kettlewell and Tinbergen revealed that a major cause of the selective action was differential predation by birds. In these well-documented cases, the melanic form possessed the selective advantage of protective coloration on the soot-darkened trees within industrialized areas, while the opposite was true of the light-colored form.

Breeding experiments have indicated that these color differences are largely determined by a single pair of alleles with the melanic condition being the dominant trait. This accounts, in part, for the rapid rise of the dark-colored form as a result of selection.

EQUILIBRIA AND POLYMORPHISM

In addition to producing systematic changes in gene frequency which we generally associate with evolution, selection, when acting alone or in combination with other evolutionary forces, can also give rise to conditions of stable equilibria. The maintenance of equilibria is probably the most important role of selection since the majority of selective changes are directed towards the elim-

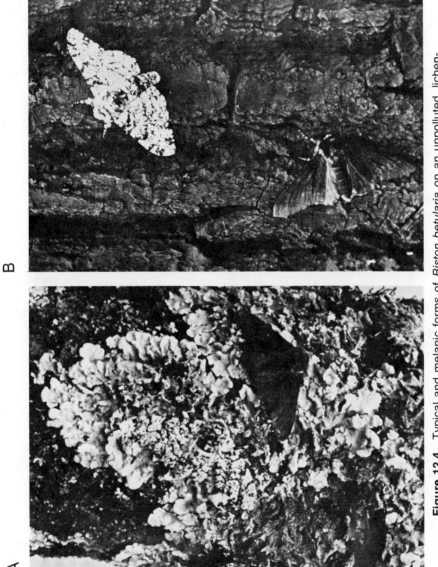

Figure 12.4 Typical and melanic forms of *Biston betularia* on an unpolluted, lichen-covered tree trunk (A) and on a soot-covered tree trunk (B). (After Kettlewell, 1958, Proc. X. Int. Cong. Ent. 2.)

465

ination of detrimental genes from populations that are already adapted to their environment. What follows are a few of the selective mechanisms which can act on a single locus and lead to equilibria in a homogeneous environment.

Balance between mutation and selection.   If the effects of mutation and selection oppose each other, an equilibrium condition is eventually established in which the number of detrimental genes arising by mutation equals the number lost through selection. For example, consider the case of selection against a recessive genotype. The reduction in gene frequency per generation due to selection is

$$\Delta q_s = -spq^2/(1 - sq^2)$$

Counteracting this reduction will be the change in gene frequency due to mutation (u and v being forward and reverse mutation rates)

$$\Delta q_m = up - vq$$

The net change in gene frequency will then be

$$\Delta q = \Delta q_m + \Delta q_s = up - vq - spq^2/(1 - sq^2)$$

Equilibrium between selection and mutation occurs when

$$up = vq + spq^2/(1 - sq^2)$$

Since mutation rates are generally much smaller in value than selection coefficients, q will tend to be small at equilibrium. Consequently, vq and sq^2 (in the denominator) can be safely ignored. Thus,

$$up = spq^2$$

which, upon simplification, becomes

$$\hat{q}^2 = u/s \quad \text{or} \quad \hat{q} = \sqrt{u/s} \tag{12.8}$$

If the recessive trait were lethal ($s = 1$), these expressions would reduce to $\hat{q}^2 = u$ and $\hat{q} = \sqrt{u}$. Thus, if $u = 10^{-6}$, $\hat{q} = 10^{-3}$ or about 1 in every 1,000 gametes carry a mutant gene of this type. In this instance, essentially all the mutant genes will be present in heterozygous combinations and, therefore, not directly exposed to the effects of selection.

A somewhat similar situation occurs when selection is against a gene with partial dominance. In this case, the change in gene frequency due to selection can be expressed by equation (12.4). When q is very small, this expression can be written approximately as

$$\Delta q = - shpq$$

Therefore, at equilibrium,

$$up = shpq$$

Simplifying, we get

$$\hat{q} = u/sh \qquad (12.9)$$

Note that as the degree of dominance increases, the equilibrium frequency of the gene is reduced proportionately. For example, when $s = 1$, $u = 10^{-6}$, and $h = \frac{1}{2}$, then $\hat{q} = 2 \times 10^{-6}$. On the other hand, when $s = 1$, $u = 10^{-6}$, and $h = 1$, then $\hat{q} = 10^{-6}$. In both cases, the equilibrium frequencies are so low that the expected number of gametes carrying mutant genes ($2N\hat{q}$) is usually less than 1 for most breeding populations.

Selection favoring heterozygotes.   In addition to the joint effects of selection and mutation, selection when acting alone can also be important in the maintenance of genetic variability. One example is where heterozygotes show superior fitness (overdominance). This occurs when h in equation (12.4) is greater than 1. We can represent an overdominant locus in terms of adaptive values as follows:

	BB	Bb	bb
Relative Fitness:	$1 - s_1$	1	$1 - s_2$

Using these fitness values, we obtain

$$\bar{W} = (1-s_1)p^2 + 2pq + (1-s_2)q^2 = 1 - s_1(1-q)^2 - s_2q^2$$

and

$$W_b = (1-s_2)q + (1 - q) = 1 - s_2q$$

Substituting these expressions into equation (12.2), we have

$$\Delta q = -(s_1+s_2)pq[q - s_1/(s_1+s_2)]/(1 - s_1p^2 - s_2q^2) \qquad (12.10)$$

Note that an equilibrium is established when

$$\hat{q} = s_1/(s_1 + s_2) \quad \text{and} \quad \hat{p} = 1-\hat{q} = s_2/(s_1 + s_2) \qquad (12.11)$$

The equilibrium condition is stable as shown by a plot of Δq versus q in Figure 12.5.

   To better visualize the process, assume random mating and think of selection as acting through the differential survival of genotypes prior to the age of reproduction. At equilibrium, the genotype frequencies among zygotes and breeding adults can then be represented as

	Frequency	
Genotype	Before Selection	After Selection
BB	p^2	$(1-s_1)p^2/\bar{W}$
Bb	$2pq$	$2pq/\bar{W}$
bb	q^2	$(1-s_2)q^2/\bar{W}$

Since adults mate at random, this see-saw process continues to occur in each succeeding generation. For example, consider the case where homozygous gene

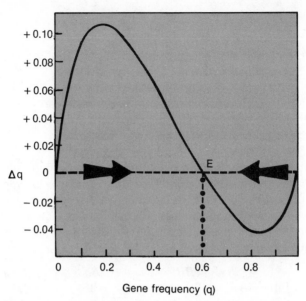

Figure 12.5. Change in gene frequency in diploid populations in which heterozygotes show superior fitness. An equilibrium is assumed to be established at a gene frequency of 0.6. Point *E* represents a stable equilibrium point since Δq is positive when *q* is less than *E*; whereas, Δq decreases when *q* is greater than *E*.

combinations are lethal ($s_1 = s_2 = 1$). Since $\hat{p} = \hat{q} = \frac{1}{2}$ in this case, the genotype frequencies before selection are $p^2 = \frac{1}{4}$, $2pq = \frac{1}{2}$, and $q^2 = \frac{1}{4}$, while only heterozygotes remain after selection. This balanced-lethal condition is maintained by the production of homozygous offspring from matings between the surviving heterozygotes.

The preceding example of heterozygote superiority represents one important mechanism for the maintenance of two or more alleles of varying fitness at relatively high frequencies. Such a situation gives rise to a stable variation pattern usually referred to as *balanced polymorphism*. An example of this phenomenon in human populations is the sickle-cell polymorphism prevalent in parts of Africa and Asia. Homozygotes ($Hb^S Hb^S$) are afflicted with a form of erythrocyte destruction known as sickle-cell anemia and tend to die in early childhood. This sickle-cell condition is due to a mutational replacement of glutamic acid with valine in the beta chain of hemoglobin which, in turn, leads to the sickling and ultimate destruction of red blood cells. Individuals which are heterozygous for the sickle-cell gene ($Hb^A Hb^S$) have a milder condition of sickling without anemia. There is now considerable evidence to indicate that sickle-cell heterozygotes are more resistant to malaria caused by the parasite *Plasmodium falciparum* than are homozygotes with normal hemoglobin ($Hb^A Hb^A$). Thus, in areas of the world where falciparum malaria is endemic, heterozygotes are at less of a disadvantage than either homozygous type, and the sickle-cell gene is maintained in native populations at relatively high frequencies.

Probably the most extensively investigated examples of balanced polymorphism are the inversions in the third chromosome of *Drosophila pseudoobscura*. Of these, the three most widely mentioned in the literature are Standard (*ST*), Arrowhead (*AR*), and Chiricahua (*CH*), all of which can be detected by examination of banding patterns in the larval salivary chromosomes. When samples are taken from the same natural population, in which any two of these arrangements are present, the chromosomes appear to be held in equilibrium as a result of their different selective values. Several experimental tests of this hypothesis were made by Dobzhansky and co-workers. The data from one population cage experiment by Dobzhansky and Pavlovsky (1953) are plotted in Figure 12.6. In this study, replicate populations, originally from Piñon Flats, California, were started initially with 20% *ST* and 80% *CH*. It was subsequently observed that the *ST* arrangement increased in frequency in all populations, gradually approaching an equilibrium value of 86%. By assuming a simple case of overdominance, fitness values for both chromosome types were then estimated by way of an iterative procedure developed earlier by Levene (Dobzhansky and Levene, 1951). In this technique, data are fitted to a linear equation of the form

$$W_3 = (x_t^2/x_{t+1}) W_1 + (x_t/x_{t+1} - x_t) \qquad (12.12)$$

where x_t and x_{t+1} are gene frequency ratios in two successive generations (i.e., $x_t = p_t/q_t$ and $x_{t+1} = p_{t+1}/q_{t+1}$). This equation can be derived directly from the p_{t+1}/q_{t+1} ratio in which $W_2 = 1$. Note that, by computing x values for two different successive sets of generations, both W_1 and W_3 can be estimated (see Example Problem 6). From their data, Dobzhansky and Pavlovsky estimated

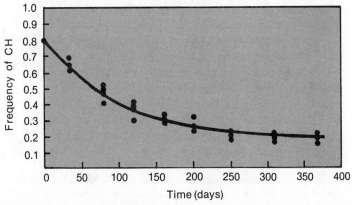

Figure 12.6. Frequency of the *CH* chromosome in replicate populations of *D. pseudoobscura* initiated with 80% *CH* and 20% *ST* arrangements. (From Th. Dobzhansky and O. Pavlovsky. 1953. Evolution 7: 198.)

W_1 and W_3 to be 0.41 and 0.90, respectively. The expected equilibrium frequency of ST is then $(1 - 0.41)/(2 - 0.41 - 0.90) = 0.86$, in excellent agreement with observation.

Selection against heterozygotes.   A particularly interesting situation develops when heterozygotes are selectively inferior to homozygous types. To illustrate, consider the simplest possible case where $W_1 = 1$, $W_2 = 1 - s$, and $W_3 = 1$, where W_1, W_2, and W_3 are, again, the fitness values of the genotypes BB, Bb, and bb, respectively. The mean fitness for the population will then be

$$\bar{W} = p^2 + (1-s)2pq + q^2 = 1 - 2spq$$

and

$$W_b = q + (1-s)p$$

By substituting these expressions into equation (12.2), we obtain

$$\Delta q = spq(q - \tfrac{1}{2})/(1 - 2spq) \tag{12.13}$$

This equation is plotted in Figure 12.7. Note that an equilibrium will develop at $\hat{q} = \tfrac{1}{2}$. The equilibrium condition is unstable, however, since Δq is negative for all values of q less than $\tfrac{1}{2}$, and it is positive when q is greater than the equilibrium value. Thus, any departure from the equilibrium point will result in the elimination of one or the other allele.

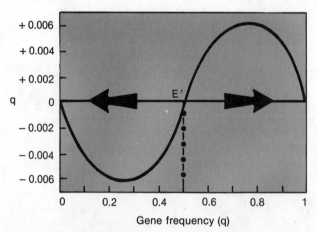

Figure 12.7.   Change in gene frequency in diploid populations when selection is against heterozygotes. An equilibrium is established at a gene frequency of 0.5. Point E' represents an unstable equilibrium since Δq is negative when q is less than E'; whereas, Δq increases when q is greater than E'.

EXTENSIONS OF BASIC THEORY

Multiple alleles.   The simple theory that has been presented so far can be extended to more complex situations. One situation that frequently arises is the case of multiple alleles. Suppose there are k alleles at a given locus with frequencies $p_1, p_2, p_3, \ldots, p_k$. Employing the same general procedures outlined for the case of two alleles, the frequency of, say, the ith allele in the next generation (generation 1) can then be given by

$$p_{i,1} = [W_{ii}p_i^2 + \sum_{i \neq j} W_{ij}p_ip_j]/\bar{W}$$

$$= p_i[\sum_j W_{ij}p_j]/\bar{W}$$

Hence, the change in p_i becomes

$$\Delta p_i = p_i \ (W_i - \bar{W})/\bar{W} \tag{12.14}$$

where $W_i = \sum_j W_{ij}p_j$ and represents the fitness of the ith allele. For a numerical example, say that there are three alleles, B_1, B_2 and B_3, occurring at frequencies 0.2, 0.3, and 0.5, respectively. Assume, further, that fitness values are as follows:

	B_1B_1	B_1B_2	B_1B_3	B_2B_2	B_2B_3	B_3B_3
Fitness:	0.8	1	1	0.7	1	0.9

What is the expected frequency of B_1 in the next generation? To obtain the answer, first compute the mean fitness as

$$\bar{W} = (0.8)(0.2)^2 + 2(0.2)(0.3) + 2(0.2)(0.5) + (0.7)(0.3)^2$$
$$+ 2(0.3)(0.5) + (0.9)(0.5)^2 = 0.94$$

Next, calculate the fitness of B_1. This yields

$$W_1 = (0.8)(0.2) + (1)(0.3) + (1)(0.5) = 0.96$$

The frequency of B_1 in generation 1 is then

$$p_{1,1} = (0.2)(0.96)/0.94 = 0.204$$

Note that only a change in gene frequency of $+ 0.004$ is expected during the course of the generation.

Wright (1942, 1945) has developed a more general expression in order to describe the effects of selection on an autosomal gene. He has shown that, when dealing with multiple alleles in a k-ploid organism, the change in the frequency of the ith allele can be expressed as

$$\Delta p_i = [p_i(1 - p_i)/k\bar{W}]\partial \bar{W}/\partial p_i \tag{12.15}$$

in which $\partial \bar{W}/\partial p_i$ stands for the partial derivative of $\bar{W}$ with respect to p_i and where $k = 1$ for haploids, $k = 2$ for diploids, $k = 4$ for autotetraploids, etc. Implicit in this equation is the assumption that selection intensity is weak enough so that genotype frequencies do not depart significantly from Hardy-Weinberg proportions.

Selection on sex-linked genes.   As long as the frequencies and fitnesses of all alleles are the same in both sexes, equation (12.15) can also be used to describe the effects of selection on sex-linked genes by letting $k = 3/2$. This is shown by writing the change in gene frequency among males (Δq_m) and among females (Δq_f) in terms of separate equations. With two alleles, the equations are

$$\Delta q_m = (p_m q_m / \bar{W}_m)\, d\bar{W}_m / dq_m \quad \text{and} \quad \Delta q_f = (p_f q_f / 2\bar{W}_f)\, d\bar{W}_f / dq_f$$

Note that, since males carry only a single dose of each sex-linked gene, they will behave collectively as a haploid population in response to selection. The total change in gene frequency is then

$$\Delta q = (2/3)\Delta q_f + (1/3)\Delta q_m$$

Thus, when $q_f = q_m = q$ and $\bar{W}_f = \bar{W}_m = \bar{W}$,

$$\Delta q = (2pq/3\bar{W})\, d\bar{W}/dq \qquad \qquad (12.16)$$

Observe that selection is more efficient when operating against a sex-linked gene than against a gene at an autosomal locus.

Effect of inbreeding.   The preceding theory can also be applied to populations in which inbreeding occurs. In this case, it is useful to view the population as consisting of an inbred (autozygous) component, which behaves as a haploid population with respect to selection, and a random mating (allozygous) component. Letting the subscript I stand for the inbred component and the subscript o for the random-mating component, then $\bar{W} = F\bar{W}_I + (1 - F)\bar{W}_o$ or $F(\bar{W}_I/\bar{W}) + (1 - F)(\bar{W}_o/\bar{W}) = 1$. Hence, for an autosomal locus with two alleles,

$$\Delta q = F(\bar{W}_I/\bar{W})\Delta q_I + (1 - F)(\bar{W}_o/\bar{W})\Delta q_o$$

where Δq is the change in gene frequency for the population as a whole. Thus, we can write

$$\Delta q = (pq/\bar{W})[Fd\bar{W}_I/dq + \tfrac{1}{2}(1 - F)d\bar{W}_o/dq]$$
$$= (pq/2\bar{W})[d\bar{W}/dq + Fd\bar{W}_I/dq] \qquad (12.17)$$

It is clear from the above expression that selection is more effective in populations with inbreeding than in those in which mating is strictly random. This is due to the rise in the frequency of homozygotes in inbred populations.

SELECTION WITH MULTIPLE LOCI

Up to this point, we have been largely concerned with the effects of selection on single gene loci. It is important to realize, however, that selection acts on individuals by virtue of their phenotype. Consequently, its effects are often influenced by the actions and interactions of genes at many loci. Several attempts have been made at quantifying the influence of linkage and nonallelic interactions on selection but, due to the mathematical complexity which arises, no one has developed a general model which provides a complete analytic solution. For this reason, only a few specific cases will be considered in the discussions that follow.

Linkage equilibrium; noninteracting loci.   By far the simplest case to describe is one in which nonalleles are functionally independent and exist in linkage equilibrium (i.e., $D = 0$). Nonallelic genes can then be treated as though they are transmitted independently. Consider, for example, two gene loci, each with two alleles. By treating each locus separately, the genotypic fitnesses and genotype frequencies before selection can be designated as follows;

	Locus 1			Locus 2		
	AA	Aa	aa	BB	Bb	bb
Frequency:	p_1^2	$2p_1q_1$	q_1^2	p_2^2	$2p_2q_2$	q_2^2
Fitness:	W_1	W_2	W_3	W_1'	W_2'	W_3'

After selection, gene frequencies in each case will then be

$$p_1(\text{after selection}) = p_1(W_1p_1 + W_2q_1)/\bar{W}_A$$
$$p_2(\text{after selection}) = p_2(W_1'p_2 + W_2'q_2)/\bar{W}_B$$

where $\bar{W}_A$ and $\bar{W}_B$ are the mean fitness values for the two respective loci.

Now consider both loci together. If the population mates at random, the genotypes, frequencies, and fitnesses of the progeny can be expressed in a 3 × 3 table (Table 12.1) in which the symbols h, i, j, and k represent the frequencies of the AB, Ab, aB, and ab gametes, respectively.

TABLE 12.1   A 3 × 3 table showing genotype frequencies after random mating and selection.

	AA	Aa	aa
BB	h^2 W_{11}	$2hj$ W_{21}	j^2 W_{31}
Bb	$2hi$ W_{12}	$2(hk + ij)$ W_{22}	$2jk$ W_{32}
bb	i^2 W_{13}	$2ik$ W_{23}	k^2 W_{33}

When loci are independent, each fitness value in Table 12.1 is just the product of fitnesses of separate genes. Thus, $W_{11} = W_1 W_1'$, $W_{21} = W_2 W_1'$, etc. Similarly, $\bar{W} = \bar{W}_A \bar{W}_B$. Moreover, once linkage equilibrium is achieved, $h = p_1 p_2$, $i = p_1 q_2$, $j = q_1 p_2$, and $k = q_1 q_2$. Recurrence relations can then be written for gamete frequencies by simply taking the products of the post-selection frequencies of the appropriate genes. For example, a recurrence relation for the frequency of AB is obtained by multiplying the post-selection values of p_1 and p_2. We get

$$h_1 = h[(W_1 p_1 + W_2 q_1)(W_1' p_2 + W_2' q_2)]/\bar{W}_A \bar{W}_B$$

$$= [W_{11} h^2 + W_{12} hi + W_{21} hj + \tfrac{1}{2} W_{22}(hk + ij)]/\bar{W}$$

Similar expressions can be obtained for the other gamete types. Since $hk - ij = D = 0$, we have

$$h_1 = h\bar{W}_{AB}/\bar{W}; \quad i_1 = i\bar{W}_{Ab}/\bar{W}; \quad j_1 = j\bar{W}_{aB}/\bar{W}; \quad \text{and} \quad k_1 = k\bar{W}_{ab}/\bar{W} \qquad \textbf{(12.18)}$$

where

$$\bar{W}_{AB} = W_{11}h + W_{12}i + W_{21}j + W_{22}k$$

$$\bar{W}_{Ab} = W_{12}h + W_{13}i + W_{22}j + W_{23}k$$

$$\bar{W}_{aB} = W_{21}h + W_{22}i + W_{31}j + W_{32}k \qquad \textbf{(12.19)}$$

$$\bar{W}_{ab} = W_{22}h + W_{23}i + W_{32}j + W_{33}k$$

and are the average fitness values attributable to the different gametes.

As long as both loci contribute to total fitness independently, a simple expression can also be written for the change in the frequency of each gene due to selection. In doing so, recall that $\bar{W} = \bar{W}_A \bar{W}_B$. Hence, $\ln \bar{W} = \ln \bar{W}_A + \ln \bar{W}_B$. The change in gene frequency at, say, locus A can then be expressed as

$$\Delta p_1 = \tfrac{1}{2} p_1 q_1 d(\ln \bar{W}_A)/dp_1 = \tfrac{1}{2} p_1 q_1 \partial(\ln \bar{W})/\partial p_1 \qquad \textbf{(12.20)}$$

Thus, the change in p depends only on the frequencies of the genes at the locus in question and the contribution of the allele to total fitness.

The above theory can be exemplified in terms of the following system:

Genotype:	$A\text{-}B\text{-}$	$A\text{-}bb$	$aaB\text{-}$	$aabb$
Frequency:	$(1-q_1^2)(1-q_2^2)$	$(1-q_1^2)q_2^2$	$q_1^2(1-q_2^2)$	$q_1^2 q_2^2$
Fitness:	1	$1-s_2$	$1-s_1$	$(1-s_1)(1-s_2)$

In this case, it is readily apparent that each locus contributes to fitness in an independent and multiplicative fashion. Hence, the change in the frequency of, say, the A gene is given by equation (12.20) in which the total mean fitness is now $\bar{W} = (1 - s_1 q_1^2)(1 - s_2 q_2^2)$. It should be noted, however, that the preceding example will conform to theory only as long as selection coefficients are sufficiently small so as not to disturb linkage equilibrium. Also observe that, when the contribution of each locus to fitness is small, independently acting loci will behave in an additive fashion. This is seen by writing, for small s,

$$(1-s_1)(1-s_2) \simeq 1 - s_1 - s_2 \quad \text{and} \quad (1-s_1q_1^2)(1-s_2q_2^2) \simeq 1 - s_1q_1^2 - s_2q_2^2$$

Thus, fitness values in the above situation will be expressed in the ratio of $1:1-s_2:1-s_1:1-s_1-s_2$. Note that the lack of interlocus interaction is now evidenced in the fact that the difference (rather than the ratio) between A- and aa is the same in both B- and bb individuals.

Linkage disequilibrium; interacting loci.   When nonallelic genes show functional interdependence, linkage equilibrium cannot always be assumed since selection will tend to enhance the association of favorably interacting genes. In the situation where $D \neq 0$, gamete frequencies can be expressed by way of genotype frequencies in Table 12.1. For example, in the case of the AB gamete,

$$h_1 = [h^2 W_{11} + hi W_{12} + hj W_{21} + (hk(1-R) + ijR) W_{22}]/\bar{W}$$

Similar expressions can be derived for the other gamete types. By letting $D = hk - ij$, the frequencies of the different gamete types become (Lewontin and Kojima, 1960)

$$h_1 = [h\bar{W}_{AB} - RW_{22}D]/\bar{W}$$
$$i_1 = [i\bar{W}_{Ab} + RW_{22}D]/\bar{W}$$
$$j_1 = [j\bar{W}_{aB} + RW_{22}D]/\bar{W} \qquad\qquad \text{(12.21)}$$
$$k_1 = [k\bar{W}_{ab} - RW_{22}D]/\bar{W}$$

Note that these relations differ from the expressions derived earlier in (12.18) by the term $RW_{22}D$. Thus, when $D = 0$, the two are the same.

The changes in gamete frequencies per generation can also be obtained as

$$\Delta h = [h(\bar{W}_{AB} - \bar{W}) - RW_{22}D]/\bar{W}$$
$$\Delta i = [i(\bar{W}_{Ab} - \bar{W}) + RW_{22}D]/\bar{W}$$
$$\Delta j = [j(\bar{W}_{aB} - \bar{W}) + RW_{22}D]/\bar{W} \qquad\qquad \text{(12.22)}$$
$$\Delta k = [k(\bar{W}_{ab} - \bar{W}) - RW_{22}D]/\bar{W}$$

Since changes in the joint frequencies of genes at interacting loci are dependent on the magnitude of D, an investigation of the factors which influence its value is now in order. This can be done in terms of an expression for ΔD. Writing $D = hk - ij$ as $(D + \Delta D) = (h + \Delta h)(k + \Delta k) - (i + \Delta i)(j + \Delta j)$ and ignoring higher order terms, we get

$$\Delta D = k\Delta h + h\Delta k - j\Delta i - i\Delta j$$

Substituting the expressions for the changes in gamete frequencies from (12.22), the equation becomes

$$\Delta D = (1/\bar{W})[hk(\bar{W}_{AB} + \bar{W}_{ab} - 2\bar{W}) - ij(\bar{W}_{Ab} + \bar{W}_{aB} - 2\bar{W}) - RW_{22}D]$$

$$= (1/\bar{W})[\tfrac{1}{2}H(\bar{W}_{AB} - \bar{W}_{Ab} - \bar{W}_{aB} + \bar{W}_{ab})$$

$$+ \tfrac{1}{2}D(\bar{W}_{AB} + \bar{W}_{Ab} + \bar{W}_{aB} + \bar{W}_{ab} - 4\bar{W}) - RW_{22}D]$$

where $H = hk + ij$ and is the total frequency of heterozygotes, $AaBb$. Note that ΔD is zero when

$$\hat{D} = -H(\bar{W}_{AB} - \bar{W}_{Ab} - \bar{W}_{aB} + \bar{W}_{ab})/(\bar{W}_{AB} + \bar{W}_{Ab} + \bar{W}_{aB} + \bar{W}_{ab} - 4\bar{W} - 2RW_{22})$$

The numerator of this expression, $\bar{W}_{AB} - \bar{W}_{Ab} - \bar{W}_{aB} + \bar{W}_{ab}$, has been shown to represent the additive x additive epistatic deviation (Kojima and Kelleher, 1961), and is zero only when the locus contributions to fitness are additive (or multiplicative, if higher order terms are included in the derivation of ΔD). For example, in a previous case that we considered, in which the fitnesses of $A\text{-}B\text{-}$, $A\text{-}bb$, $aaB\text{-}$, and $aabb$ were 1, $1-s_2$, $1-s_1$, and $1-s_1-s_2$, respectively, gamete fitnesses become $\bar{W}_{AB} = 1$, $\bar{W}_{Ab} = 1 - s_2(i + k)$, $\bar{W}_{aB} = 1 - s_1(j + k)$, and $\bar{W}_{ab} = 1 - s_1(j + k) - s_2(i + k)$. Thus, $\bar{W}_{AB} - \bar{W}_{Ab} - \bar{W}_{aB} + \bar{W}_{ab} = 0$. It is, therefore, possible to assume that, under such a regimen of selection, there will be no permanent linkage disequilibrium. This is not the situation when epistatic interactions occur. In order to illustrate this point, consider the following symmetric case of overdominance (Lewontin and Kojima, 1960):

$$\begin{Bmatrix} W_{11} & W_{21} & W_{31} \\ W_{12} & W_{22} & W_{32} \\ W_{13} & W_{23} & W_{33} \end{Bmatrix} = \begin{Bmatrix} a & c & a \\ b & 1 & b \\ a & c & a \end{Bmatrix}$$

From symmetry considerations, it should be apparent that the model must ultimately give rise to an equilibrium state at which $h = k$ and $i = j$. These equalities imply that $h + i = j + k$ and $h + j = i + k$ (of course, $h + k$ will only equal $i + j$ when the frequencies of cis and trans heterozygotes are equal). Since $p_1 = h + i$, $q_1 = j + k$, $p_2 = h + j$, and $q_2 = i + k$, it is also apparent that $p_1 = q_1 = \tfrac{1}{2}$ and $p_2 = q_2 = \tfrac{1}{2}$ at equilibrium.

To simplify calculations, let $h = k = x$ and $i = j = \tfrac{1}{2} - x$. The value of D then becomes

$$D = x^2 - (\tfrac{1}{2} - x)^2 = x - \tfrac{1}{4}$$

Similarly,

$$\bar{W} = x(\bar{W}_{AB} + \bar{W}_{ab}) + (\tfrac{1}{2} - x)(\bar{W}_{Ab} + \bar{W}_{aB})$$

$$= x[2(a - b - c + 1)x + (c + b)]$$

$$- (\tfrac{1}{2}-x)[2(a - b - c + 1)x - (a+1)] \tag{12.23}$$

$$= 4(a - b - c + 1)x^2$$

$$- 2(a - b - c + 1)x + \tfrac{1}{2}(a + 1)$$

$$= 4Ex^2 - 2Ex + \tfrac{1}{2}(a + 1)$$

where E is a measure of the epistatic deviation in this symmetric case. When $E = 0$, $(\bar{W}_{AB} - \bar{W}_{Ab} - \bar{W}_{aB} + \bar{W}_{ab})$ is also zero and no permanent linkage disequilibrium can occur. Since $\Delta x = 0 = x(\bar{W}_{AB} - \bar{W}) - RD$ at equilibrium (12.22), then $x\bar{W} = x[Ex + \frac{1}{2}(c + b)] - R(x - \frac{1}{4})$. Multiplying (12.23) by x and making the preceding substitution for $x\bar{W}$, we then obtain the cubic equation:

$$4Ex^3 - 3Ex^2 + \tfrac{1}{2}Ex + R(x - \tfrac{1}{4}) = 0 \qquad (12.24)$$

This expression has three possible solutions. One, $x = \frac{1}{4}$, is obtained by factoring (12.24) as follows:

$$(x - \tfrac{1}{4})(4Ex^2 - 2Ex + R) = 0$$

Observe in (12.24) that this solution exists regardless of the value of E. In fact, when $E = 0$, $x = \frac{1}{4}$ is the only permissible equilibrium point under these special conditions. Note also that, since $D = x - \frac{1}{4}$, there will be linkage equilibrium (i.e., $D = 0$).

Two additional solutions can be found by solving the quadratic equation $4Ex^2 - 2Ex + R = 0$. This yields

$$
\begin{aligned}
x &= [2E \pm \sqrt{4E^2 - 16RE}]/8E \\
&= \tfrac{1}{4} \pm \tfrac{1}{4}\sqrt{1 - 4R/E}
\end{aligned}
\qquad (12.25)
$$

These solutions can only exist when $4R/E$ is a positive fraction. Since $E = a - b - c + 1$, the conditions required for (12.25) are then

$$a + 1 > b + c \qquad \text{and} \qquad R < \tfrac{1}{4}E \qquad (12.26)$$

These potential equilibria are, therefore, important when genes are closely linked and show significant epistatic interactions. Observe, as well, that D will depart from zero by a factor of $\pm \frac{1}{4}\sqrt{1 - 4R/E}$. Hence, a permanent linkage disequilibrium will exist under these conditions.

The above model is summarized in Figure 12.8 by plots of the expressions

$$f(x) = 4Ex^3 - 3Ex^2 + \tfrac{1}{2}Ex$$

$$g(x) = R(x - \tfrac{1}{4})$$

for specified values of E and R. Points of intersection between the cubic equation, $f(x)$, and the linear equation, $g(x)$, then give possible equilibrium states. In both graphs, the adaptive values were taken as

$$
\left\{
\begin{array}{ccc}
0.8 & 0.5 & 0.8 \\
0.4 & 1 & 0.4 \\
0.8 & 0.5 & 0.8
\end{array}
\right\}
$$

These give an E value of $E = 0.8 - 0.4 - 0.5 + 1 = 0.9$. Hence, $f(x) = 3.6x^3 - 2.7x^2 + \frac{1}{2}x$ in both cases. Since $a + 1 > b + c$, in the example, the number of possible equilibrium points will depend on the value chosen for R relative to 0.225 (i.e., $\frac{1}{4}E$). In the first plot (graph A), R is taken as 0.05, indicating strong

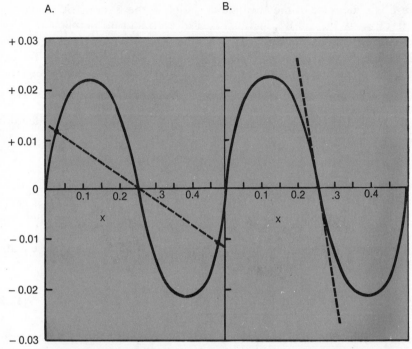

Figure 12.8. Equilibria under selection pattern for two autosomal loci. The graphs represent plots of the expressions $f(x) = 4Ex^3 = 3Ex^2 + \frac{1}{2}Ex$ (solid line) and $g(x) = R(\frac{1}{4} - x)$ (dashed lines) for $E = 0.9$. In A, $R = 0.05$, whereas in B, $R = 0.225$.

linkage. This gives three equilibrium points. However, only two stationary points, corresponding to $x = \frac{1}{4} \pm \frac{1}{4}\sqrt{1 - 4R/E}$, are stable, since any departure from $x = \frac{1}{4}$ will result in the system moving to either one of these exterior points. In graph B, on the other hand, $R = 0.225$, causing the line to rotate in a clockwise direction. There will be only one stable equilibrium point, under these conditions, at $x = \frac{1}{4}$. The value $R = 0.225$ is, therefore, a critical point separating a condition of permanent linkage disequilibrium from linkage equilibrium.

So far, we have only considered symmetrical equilibria for which $h = k$ and $i = j$. Solutions can also be found for asymmetric stationary states for which $h = k$, $i \neq j$ (or $h \neq k$, $i = j$) or, in the more general case, $h \neq k$, $i \neq j$. For example, Karlin and Feldman (1970) studied a symmetric viability model expressed in the form:

$$\begin{Bmatrix} 1 - \delta & 1 - \beta & 1 - \alpha \\ 1 - \gamma & 1 & 1 - \gamma \\ 1 - \alpha & 1 - \beta & 1 - \delta \end{Bmatrix}$$

They found that, in addition to the three symmetrical equilibria, there may also be up to four asymmetric equilibria under certain conditions. Thus, it is possible that as many as seven equilibria may exist simultaneously for a two-locus system. It must be noted, however, that at most, only two are stable.

In summary, there are two principal points brought out by the preceding two locus models. (1) First of all, some form of epistasis is required for maintaining a nonrandom association of gametic combinations, the strength of this association being directly dependent on the degree of departure from strictly additive (or multiplicative) gene effects. (2) Secondly, although the genes involved do not have to be on the same chromosome, linkage increases the chance of disequilibrium. Thus, linkage plays a supporting role in maintaining a gametic phase imbalance.

Linkage effects on neutral genes.   The fact that linked genes tend to remain together on the same chromosome provides a mechanism for selection, while acting on a closely linked marker, to increase the frequency of a neutral (or slightly detrimental) gene. As an example, consider a selectively neutral locus, A, at which all genotypes, AA, Aa, and aa, have unit fitness. Now suppose that at a closely linked locus, B, the genotypes BB, Bb, and bb have fitness values 1, 1, and $1 - s$, respectively, independent of the A locus. The rate of change in the frequency of the b allele will then be

$$\Delta q_2 = \Delta j + \Delta k = - sp_2q_2^2/(1 - sq_2^2)$$

The frequency of the A gene is also expected to vary by a rate equal to

$$\Delta p_1 = \Delta h + \Delta i = sq_2D/(1 - sq_2^2) = - (\Delta q_2/q_2p_2)D$$

Thus we find that, even though the A gene is selectively neutral, its frequency will continue to change as long as linkage disequilibrium persists. Such might be the case for a newly arising neutral mutation, say A, which is closely linked to some beneficial gene, B, in the process of replacing its selectively inferior allele. Initially, D will not equal zero. Hence, A will start to increase in frequency, hitching a ride, so to speak, by virtue of its proximity to B. Since $D = D_o(1 - R)^t$, linkage disequilibrium must eventually disappear. However, this may take a considerable period of time if the markers are closely linked. Thus, selection acting on closely linked genes may provide selectively neutral mutations with a greater survival probability than expected on the basis of strictly independent transmission.

EFFECTS OF SELECTION ON QUANTITATIVE TRAITS

Much of the experimental and theoretical work on natural selection has dealt with simple qualitative traits. These characteristics are particularly suitable for study, since it is possible through breeding tests and by various biochemical procedures to identify genotypes and, thereby, calculate the frequencies of genes and genotypes and assign genotype-specific fitnesses to individuals. Such genetic dissection is extremely difficult to perform with continuously distributed, polygenic characters where each unit on the phenotypic scale can include several genotypes. Consequently, methods used for measuring selection effects on qualitative and quantitative traits tend to differ. What follows is a brief description of some of the approaches used on polygenic systems with an attempt at relating their underlying principles to the concepts derived from single locus models.

Response to selection.   The effects of selection on polygenic variation can be illustrated by means of a simply inherited quantitative trait portrayed in terms of a continuous distribution in Figure 12.9. In this instance, genotypic differences are extremely small and are obscured by environmental effects. It is, therefore, virtually impossible to measure the fitness of individual genotypes or to measure changes in gene frequencies. For this reason, the phenotypic response to selection is expressed in terms of the change in mean phenotypic value per generation. Suppose, for example, that individuals having values which exceed the population mean are better equipped to withstand the rigors of their environment. These individuals will consistently have a greater chance of surviving to serve as parents of the next generation. If the trait is sufficiently heritable, we would then expect to observe a shift in the mean phenotypic value

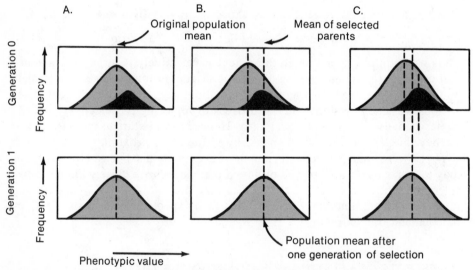

Figure 12.9.   The effect of selection on population variation. The large curve represents the entire population, the small curve (top row), the selected parents. In *A*, phenotypic variation is caused entirely by environmental variation, so that the population mean does not change after selection. In *B*, phenotypic variation is entirely genetic, so that the population mean after one generation of selection is equal to that of the selected parents. In *C*, phenotypic variation has both genetic and environmental components so that the mean after selection is between the mean of the selected parents and the original mean.

of the progeny in the direction of the mean of the selected parents. This can be shown in more explicit terms by means of an example breeding experiment. To do so, consider a trait determined entirely by additive gene effects at n independent loci. The mean phenotypic value can then be expressed as $\bar{P} = 2na\bar{p} + g_o$ (equation 5.2). Now, suppose that from a large population, individuals are selected to serve as parents of the next generation. Assume that parents have a mean of $\bar{P}_s = 2na\bar{p}_s + g_o$. The difference between the mean of the parents and the population mean, $\bar{P}_s - \bar{P}$, constitutes a measure of selection intensity known as the *selection differential*, S. It should be apparent that if gene frequencies do not change from parents to offspring, the mean of the next generation ($\bar{P}_1$) will equal that of the selected parents. Therefore, when genes exert strictly additive effects, the *selection response*, measured by the change in the mean phenotypic value, $\bar{P}_1 - \bar{P}$ (usually symbolized as R, but which we shall designate as $\Delta\bar{P}$ to avoid confusion with the frequency of recombination), will equal the selection differential. Usually $\Delta\bar{P}$ is less than S. Due to the presence of environmental effects and to dominance and epistatic interactions, the progeny generation tends to slip back (i.e., undergoes regression) towards the mean of the population from which the parents were selected. Hence, we can write as a general relationship

$$\Delta\bar{P} = (b_{o\bar{p}})S \qquad (12.27)$$

for $0 < b_{o\bar{p}} \leq 1$. In this expression, $b_{o\bar{p}}$ is the regression coefficient of offspring on the mean of the selected parents, measuring the strength of correlation between the selection differential and the selection response. Although (12.27) is useful for descriptive purposes, geneticists prefer a relationship that can be predicted on the basis of genetic principles. One such expression can be derived by relating $b_{o\bar{p}}$ to the heritability. In doing so, first recall that the covariance between the phenotypic values of a randomly selected parent and average offspring, $C(P,O)$, is $\frac{1}{2}V_A$. The covariance between the values of an average parent and average offspring must be the same, i.e., $C(\bar{P},O) = \frac{1}{2}[C(P_m,O) + C(P_f, O)] = \frac{1}{2}[\frac{1}{2}V_A + \frac{1}{2}V_A] = \frac{1}{2}V_A$, since variances are equal among the parents. The phenotypic variance of an average parent can also be derived as $V(\frac{1}{2}P_m + \frac{1}{2}P_f) = V(\frac{1}{2}P_m) + V(\frac{1}{2}P_f) = 2(\frac{1}{4})V_P = \frac{1}{2}V_P$. The regression coefficient, which is the covariance divided by the phenotypic variance, can then be expressed as

$$b_{o\bar{p}} = (\tfrac{1}{2}V_A)/(\tfrac{1}{2}V_P) = h^2 \qquad (12.28)$$

This yields, for selection response,

$$\Delta\bar{P} = h^2S \qquad (12.29)$$

The response to selection can, therefore, be predicted once the heritability of the trait is known (or, conversely, h^2 can be estimated once $\Delta\bar{P}$ and S are known).

Probably the simplest form of directed selection on a quantitative character is that of truncation selection, illustrated in Figure 12.10. This is common in plant and animal breeding experiments in which all individuals above a certain threshold, say T, are saved for breeding purposes. Let $y = (P_s - \overline{P})/\sigma_P$, where P_s is the variable phenotypic value of potential parents and σ_P, the standard deviation. If phenotypic values are normally distributed, y will have a density function

$$f(y) = (1/\sqrt{2\pi})e^{-y^2/2}$$

Assume that q is the proportion of the population selected as parents. Hence,

$$q = (1/\sqrt{2\pi}) \int_T^\infty e^{-y^2/2}dy$$

The mean of y then becomes

$$\bar{y} = (\overline{P}_s - \overline{P})/\sigma_P = S/\sigma_P$$

$$= (1/q)(1/\sqrt{2\pi}) \int_T^\infty ye^{-y^2/2}dy$$

$$= z/q$$

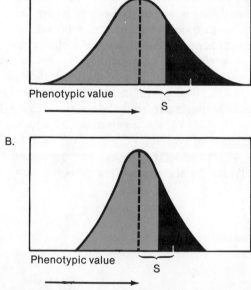

Phenotypic value

Phenotypic value

Figure 12.10. Diagrams depicting truncation selection. 20% of the population is selected in both cases; however, due to the greater variation existing in *A*, the selection differential is greater than in *B*.

where z is the ordinate at the point of truncation. Solving for S, we get

$$S = (z/q)\sigma_P \tag{12.30}$$

Thus, if q and σ_P are known, S can be evaluated using a table of ordinates of a normal curve. Note that z is fixed for a given value of q. This leaves only two approaches which can be taken by a breeder to improve selection response. One is to increase the heritability by carefully controlling environmental conditions. A second is reducing the proportion saved for breeding purposes. Although the latter method is by far the simplest and the most straightforward in approach, it also has its limits. Such limits are set by the numbers needed to avoid inbreeding and to maintain the existing size of the population.

Fundamental theorem of natural selection.   Unlike the case of artificial selection experiments, in which individuals might be saved for breeding purposes above a certain threshold, selection in nature will depend, in a statistical sense, on the relative fitness of individual members of a population. This will only rarely correspond to a situation which can be likened to that of truncation selection. Usually, fitness will tend to change in a gradual, rather than abrupt, manner. In order to show how the selection differential is related to the concept of fitness as applied to natural populations, consider the following model for noninteracting polygenic loci. First note that, since $\bar{P} = 2\Sigma a_i p_i + g_o$,

$$\Delta \bar{P} = 2\Sigma a_i \Delta p_i \quad \text{and} \quad \partial \bar{P}/\partial p_i = 2a_i$$

where the sum includes all pertinent loci. Moreover, $\Delta p_i = (p_i q_i/2\bar{W})\partial \bar{W}/\partial p_i \simeq (p_i q_i/2\bar{W})(\partial \bar{W}/\partial \bar{P})(\partial \bar{P}/\partial p_i)$. Thus, we can write

$$\Delta \bar{P} = \Sigma (2a_i)^2 (p_i q_i/2\bar{W})\partial \bar{W}/\partial \bar{P}$$

and, since $V_A = 2\Sigma a_i^2 p_i q_i$, we have

$$\Delta \bar{P} = (V_A/\bar{W})\partial \bar{W}/\partial \bar{P} = h^2 (V_P/\bar{W})\partial \bar{W}/\partial \bar{P} \tag{12.31}$$

Observe that if W is linearly related to P (i.e., $W =$ constant multiplied by P), $\partial \bar{W}/\partial \bar{P}$ would be constant and the selection differential would then be directly proportional to $V_W/\bar{W}$. Also note that in the case where $W = P$ and $h^2 = 1$, the expression becomes

$$\Delta \bar{W} = V_W/\bar{W} \tag{12.32}$$

This equation can be derived directly for simple additive traits in the absence of environmental deviations. It serves to point out the importance of genetic variation to evolutionary change and represents a version of Fisher's *fundamental theorem of natural selection* (1958). This theorem states that the rate of improvement of fitness is directly proportional to the additive variance in fitness for the population. In other words, a population will cease to respond to selection once its additive variation is depleted. Also note that, since V_W

and $\bar{W}$ must have positive values, $\Delta \bar{W}$ must always increase in magnitude. Thus, selection will tend to proceed so as to maximize $\bar{W}$.

Modes of Selection.   When acting on continuous variation, selection is often classified as either (1) directional, (2) stabilizing (or centripetal), or (3) disruptive (or centrifugal). These modes of selection are illustrated pictorially in Figure 12.11, along with their corresponding relationships between fitness and the phenotypic value.

Directional selection is the type of selection dealt with in the previous model and is of particular interest to animal and plant breeders. As the name implies, directional selection involves selection for an extreme type and results in a gradual directional change in the population mean. It is, therefore, limited by the potential genotypic variation of a population. This potential is usually much greater than that actually expressed at any one time. For example, with two alleles occurring with equal frequency at each of 20 loci, the expected proportion of the most extreme and, presumably, most favorable genotype is $(\frac{1}{2})^{40}$. It is highly unlikely that such a genotype would normally appear in a population. However, as selection proceeds in that direction, with a concomitant increase in the frequencies of the selectively superior genes, the likelihood increases and, eventually, this extreme may represent the most commonly occurring type. An example of the extent to which directional selection can proceed before a limit is reached is shown in Figure 12.12, in terms of the results from a study by Falconer (1955) on six-week body weight in mice. This is a two-way selection in which the upward data represent what happened when heavier mice were selected at six weeks of age and then interbred, while the downward data are the results of a corresponding series of selection experiments

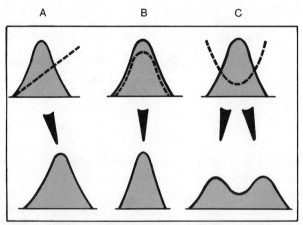

Figure 12.11.   Three modes of selection on a quantitative character and their effects. Solid lines show the frequency distributions of the quantitative character, and the dashed lines the fitness, as a function of phenotypic value.

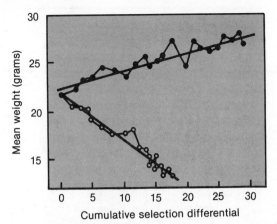

Figure 12.12. Two-way selection for body weight in mice. The upward sloping points represent selection for heavier weight, and the downward sloping points, selection for lighter weight. (Data from D.S. Falconer, 1955. Cold Spring Harbor Sympos. Quant. Biol. 20: 178.)

for lighter-weight mice. In this case, selection response continued over 20 generations resulting in about a two-fold difference in body weight between the high and low lines.

Stabilizing selection (also known as balancing selection) represents selection for intermediate types or, in other words, against extremes. It is selection for the status quo and, therefore, represents a form of selection operating on populations which are adapted to their immediate environments. A classic example of this type of selection is shown by the data from Karn and Penrose (1951) on the relationship between the birth weight distribution in humans and percent survival before the 28th day of age (Fig. 12.13). It is evident that the optimal birth weight corresponds to that with the lowest mortality.

Unlike the case of a balanced polymorphism at a single locus, selection for intermediate types in a polygenic system tends towards homozygosity rather than heterozygosity, with intermediate homozygotes being the predominant genotypes once a balance is reached. This is readily seen in terms of a simple additive system consisting of two gene pairs, A,a and B,b, with genotypes $AaBb$, $AAbb$, and $aaBB$ having the optimum phenotype. Note that, due to the production of suboptimal types, the mean fitness of a mixture of the three genotypes must be less than that of a population consisting of only $AAbb$ or $aaBB$ types (because of gene assortment, a population cannot consist of only $AaBb$ types). Thus, selection will act in such a way so as to produce a homozygous population, consisting of either all $AAbb$ or all $aaBB$. In this case, the repulsion gamete type, Ab or aB, with the highest initial frequency is the one destined to undergo fixation.

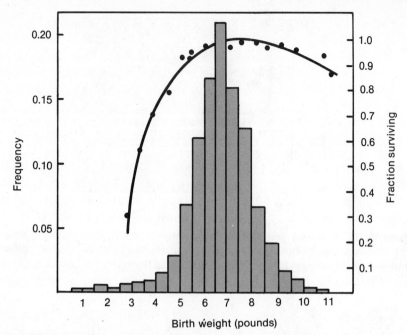

Figure 12.13. Distribution of human birth weight (bars) and percent survivorship to the 28th day of age (solid line). (Data from M.N. Karn and L.S. Penrose, 1951. Ann. Eugenics 16(1): 147–164.)

Disruptive selection can be regarded as the converse of stabilizing selection, since what is involved is the selection against intermediate types or, in other words, selection for extremes. Such selection could occur in an environment which is heterogeneous in space, with opposite extremes being selected for in different localities. Although disruptive selection can occur in random-mating populations, matings between extremes tend to erase any changes that have taken place by the production of intermediate types. Therefore, if it is to produce evolutionary divergence, it must be associated with some degree of reproductive isolation resulting from such factors as spatial isolation or assortative mating. The fact that reproductive isolation can actually develop as a consequence of disruptive selection has been demonstrated by the classic experiments of Thoday and Gibson (1962) on the numbers of sternopleural bristles in *D. melanogaster*. In these experiments, eight males and eight virgin females were selected with the highest number of bristles and then placed together for 24 hours, for mating purposes, with eight males and eight virgin females with the lowest bristle number. Males were then discarded and females were again separated on the basis of bristle number into "high" and "low" cultures. This same mating procedure was used, along with disruptive selection, during the next several generations by always selecting the eight males and eight virgin females with the highest bristle number from the "high' culture and those with the lowest bristle number from the "low" culture. Thoday and Gibson found that, by 12 generations of selection, flies diverged in bristle number into high and low lines despite the opportunity for random mating in each selection cycle. It was also shown that, in one strain, reproductive isolation occurred after 10 generations of disruptive selection, apparently through the development of assortative mating.

MATING SYSTEMS AND SEXUAL SELECTION

The behavioral mechanisms that determine the way in which males and females come together for mating purposes are collectively known as mating systems. These systems can be divided into three major types: (1) monogamy, in which mating is restricted to one member of the opposite sex, (2) polygamy, where bonds can be formed with two or more individuals of the opposite sex, and (3) promiscuity, where no pair bond is formed and copulations can occur with one to several members of the opposite sex.

Monogamy, the most restrictive pattern, is the predominant form among birds, occurring in 91% of all avian species (Lack, 1968). Two general types are recognized. Among swans, cranes, and certain other large birds, for example, mates tend to remain together throughout life, even during the non-breeding season. The above pattern has been referred to as perennial monogamy (Brown, 1975). Many small migrant birds, on the other hand, separate from their mate after each breeding season and may or may not pair with the same individual in the following year. This latter type is termed seasonal monogamy by Brown to distinguish it from the perennial pattern.

The less restrictive polygamous system can also be divided further into two different types. One is polygyny, in which one male mates with two or more females. The bonds, in this case, may be formed at the same time or in series. A second type is polyandry, which occurs when one female mates with two or more males. As might be expected from the respective reproductive roles of males and females, this second system is relatively rare.

Sexual selection.   In polygamous and, to a different degree, promiscuous systems, males are in competition for mates. When two or more females are acquired by a single male, at least one other male must fail to reproduce, assuming an even sex ratio. Consequently, those hereditary characteristics which contribute to mate procurement will be of adaptive value and, due to the greater reproductive contribution which they provide, will tend to appear in greater frequency among adults in succeeding generations. This selective process which results from competitive mating is what Darwin (1859, 1871) referred to as *sexual selection*. Sexual selection includes two recognizable forms. One is intrasexual selection which results from an active form of competition between members of the same sex for attracting and holding mates. These competitive interactions usually involve aggressive encounters between males, such as fighting and threat displays, which are especially frequent and conspicuous during the mating season. This form of selection is generally believed to be responsible for the evolutionary development of larger size and aggressiveness in the males of many species and for various structures used in combat with other males such as the antlers of deer. A second form is termed intersexual selection. This involves the selection of male characteristics which females find sexually attractive. For example, males of some species perform courtship displays in order to attract mates. In many of these cases, certain male attributes have evolved, such as colorful plumage in male birds, for example, which serve to catch the female's attention and stimulate her sexually. As Orians (1969) has pointed out, sexual selection in mammals and birds is largely a consequence of female choice. While males produce large numbers of gametes during each generation, females produce only a small number but at a considerably greater energy cost. Thus, to avoid the chance of wasting the reproductive effort of an entire season on an erroneous interspecific mating or one with a sterile male, it is to the advantage of the female to exercise much greater discrimination in mate selection than does the male.

The genetic consequences of sexual selection can be illustrated in terms of a simple model. Suppose that a fraction u of females will mate only with BB males; the remaining $1 - u$ mates at random. Letting P, H, and Q represent the genotype proportions in the population, the six possible matings will then have the following frequencies:

Mating type	Frequency
$BB \times BB$	$uP + (1 - u)P^2$
$BB \times Bb$	$uH + (1 - u)2PH$
$BB \times bb$	$uQ + (1 - u)2PQ$
$Bb \times Bb$	$(1 - u)H^2$
$Bb \times bb$	$(1 - u)2HQ$
$bb \times bb$	$(1 - u)Q^2$

The frequencies of the genotypes among the offspring can then be calculated as:

$$P_1 = u(P + \tfrac{1}{2}H) + (1 - u)(P + \tfrac{1}{2}H)^2$$

$$H_1 = u(Q + \tfrac{1}{2}H) + (1 - u)2(P + \tfrac{1}{2}H)(Q + \tfrac{1}{2}H)$$

$$Q_1 = (1 - u)(Q + \tfrac{1}{2}H)^2$$

Letting $p = P + \tfrac{1}{2}H$ and $q = Q + \tfrac{1}{2}H$, the frequency of the b allele then becomes

$$q_1 = (1 - u)q + \tfrac{1}{2}uq = (1 - \tfrac{1}{2}u)q$$

After t generations, we get

$$q_t = (1 - \tfrac{1}{2}u)^t q_o \quad \text{and} \quad p_t = 1 - (1 - \tfrac{1}{2}u)^t(1 - p_o)$$

Thus the favored allele, B, will eventually be fixed in the population.

The above model suggests that u is constant. According to Fisher (1930), however, the sexual preference will itself be subject to selection since those females which mate with the favored males will leave more genes to future generations due to the favored status their sons will possess. O'Donald (1962, 1967) has proposed a model involving two loci, one locus determining the preferred character and the other the mating preference. The model indicates that sexual selection can proceed at a very rapid rate when the two loci are closely linked and when the genes responsible are recessive rather than dominant. Furthermore, when sexual selection is opposed by "ordinary" natural selection, as might be the case when a gaudy trait is preferred but where survival is favored by concealed coloration, very high intensities of natural selection are needed to prevent fixation of a recessive gene by sexual selection.

SELECTION MODELS: VARIABLE RELATIVE FITNESS

So far, we have only considered selection models which incorporate the concept of a constant relative fitness. As mentioned earlier, this concept is equivalent to the assumption that net reproductive rates are constant or, possibly, that density-limiting factors are independent of genotype and cancel when one reproductive rate is divided by another. It should be apparent from previous discussions on population growth that the first alternative can never be true for very long and the second is rather unlikely. Hence, it can generally be asserted that fitness values are variables which depend on the myriad of factors which affect the size and spatial distribution of a population. What follows are some models that take such factors into account.

Competitive selection.   If a population is resource-limited, the members of the population must compete for those requisites that are in least supply. This means that growth is density dependent. Thus, if genotypes differ in competitive ability, selection will occur since genotypic fitnesses must then be different functions of population density.

Several models have been proposed recently for competitive selection (also termed density-dependent selection or "soft selection" by Wallace, 1968), but due to the complexity of factors involved in density regulation, all make simplifying assumptions about the growth form of the population. As long as growth is sufficiently slow so that the one-generation time lag is not a critical factor, a useful approximation is that of discrete-time logistic growth (Charlesworth, 1971; Roughgarden, 1971). Genotypic fitnesses can then be expressed as linear functions of N. Furthermore, by assuming a random-mating population in which genotypic differences are limited to fertility, zygotes will exist in Hardy-Weinberg proportions despite density-dependent growth (Smouse, 1976). To illustrate the development and analysis of such a model, consider a single locus exhibiting complete dominance. The population can then be represented as follows:

Genotype: $B-$ bb
Frequency: $1-q^2$ q^2
Density: N_1 N_2
Fitness: $W_1 = 1 + r_1(K_1 - N_1 - \alpha N_2)/K_1$ $W_2 = 1 + r_2(K_2 - N_2 - \beta N_1)/K_2$

in which W_1 and W_2 are adaptive values expressed in the form of finite rates of increase and where $N_1 + N_2 = N$. We can, therefore, write

$$\Delta N_1/N_1 = W_1 - 1 = r_1 - r_1 N_1/K_1 - \alpha r_1 N_2/K_1$$
$$= r_1 - r_1 N(1-q^2)/K_1 - \alpha r_1 N q^2/K_1$$
$$\Delta N_2/N_2 = W_2 - 1 = r_2 - r_2 N_2/K_2 - \beta r_2 N_1/K_2$$
$$= r_2 - r_2 N q^2/K_2 - \beta r_2 N(1-q^2)/K_2$$

Note that genotypic fitnesses are frequency-dependent (i.e., dependent on gene frequency) as well as density-dependent.

The rate of change in gene frequency can now be obtained. First, solve for $\bar{W}$ and W_b as follows:

$$\bar{W} = W_1(1-q^2) + W_2 q^2$$
$$W_b = W_1(1-q) + W_2 q$$

Substituting these expressions into equation (12.2), we get

$$\Delta q = pq^2(W_2 - W_1)/\bar{W}$$

If we now assume that $\bar{W}$ is close to unity, the change in q becomes, approximately,

$$\Delta q = pq^2[\Delta N_2/N_2 - \Delta N_1/N_1]$$
$$= pq^2[(r_2 - r_1) - q^2 N(r_2/K_2 - \alpha r_1/K_1) \qquad \textbf{(12.33)}$$
$$- (1-q^2)N(\beta r_2/K_2 - r_1/K_1)]$$

A stable equilibrium, in this case, is reached once N_1 and N_2 attain constant and positive values. The value of q at equilibrium can be obtained by setting $\Delta N_1/N_1 = \Delta N_2/N_2 = 0$. This results in the pair of equations

$$K_1 = N(1-q^2) + \alpha N q^2$$
$$K_2 = N q^2 + \beta N(1-q^2)$$

Solving these equations simultaneously yields

$$\hat{q} = \sqrt{(K_2 - \beta K_1)/[K_1(1-\beta) + K_2(1-\alpha)]} \qquad \textbf{(12.34)}$$

Since this model is basically the same in form as the expressions used to describe the effects of interspecific competition, it should come as no surprise that equilibrium conditions are the same in both cases. Thus, a stable equilibrium develops when

$$\alpha < K_1/K_2 \quad \text{and} \quad \beta < K_2/K_1$$

The above equilibrium would occur if genotypes differ sufficiently in their ecological requirements so that the effects of competition between individuals of the same genotype would be more detrimental to reproductive success than the effects of competition between dissimilar genotypes. As a result, each genotype gains an advantage when rare and is selected against when common. Any such minority advantage will ultimately lead to a state of balanced polymorphism.

Selective predation.   As pointed out in Chapter 10, several different kinds of adaptations have arisen as a consequence of predation. Many of these, e.g., adaptive coloration, lead to polymorphism in the prey species. Clarke (1962, 1969) has noted that learning on the part of the predator can be responsible for maintaining variation in the prey by providing a minority advantage. Through a learning process, the predator develops a search image for the most frequently encountered types of prey and searches for them preferentially. The less frequently occurring types will then have a chance to increase in density until they too become abundant enough to be favored by the predator. This results in a form of frequency-dependent selection, often referred to as *apostatic selection*, which can lead to the development of balanced polymorphism.

For a simple model of apostatic selection, consider a trait determined by a single pair of genes exhibiting incomplete dominance. If the fitness of each morph is linearly related to its frequency, the prey population can be represented as follows:

	BB	Bb	bb
Frequency:	p^2	$2pq$	q^2
Fitness:	$W_1 = 1 - sp^2$	$W_2 = 1 - 2spq$	$W_3 = 1 - sq^2$

The expressions for $\bar{W}$ and W_b become

$$\bar{W} = 1 - s(1-q)^4 - 4s(1-q)^2q^2 - sq^4$$

$$W_b = 1 - 2sq(1-q)^2 - sq^3$$

Using equation (12.2), we then get, after some algebraic manipulation,

$$\Delta q = -2spq(6q^3 - 9q^2 + 5q - 1)/(1 - sp^4 - 4sp^2q^2 - sq^4) \quad \textbf{(12.35)}$$

Note that $\Delta q = 0$ when

$$6q^3 - 9q^2 + 5q - 1 = (2q - 1)(3q^2 - 3q + 1) = 0$$

Since $q = \frac{1}{2}$ is the only real root of this cubic equation, this is the value of q at equilibrium. A plot of equation (12.35) is shown in Figure 12.14 which can

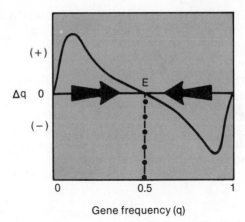

Figure 12.14. Plot of equation (12.35) illustrating the effects of frequency-dependent selection.

be compared with the results expected for heterozygote superiority in Figure 12.5. Observe that frequency-dependent selection, of the type examined here, is more efficient than simple overdominance in changing gene frequencies when q is close to zero or to one, but less efficient when q is near its equilibrium point.

Another, though more complex type of frequency-dependent selection occurs in Batsian mimicry where mimetic and nonmimetic forms are maintained in a population through selective predation (see Chapter 10). Like apostatic selection, Batsian mimicry requires prey recognition and learning on the part of the predator; however, in the latter case, mimetic forms are protected from predation by the predator developing an avoidance image, due to the distastefulness of the model, rather than a searching image. Despite the similarities in the two processes, the preceding model does not apply to both since fitness values in Batsian mimicry are not only functions of the frequencies of the mimetic forms but depend on the frequencies of the models as well.

Frequency-dependent sexual selection.   Selection not only involves differential viability and fecundity but also depends on the successful acquisition of mates. Those hereditary characteristics which contribute to this success will be of adaptive value to the individuals that possess them. Of special interest here are those mechanisms for attracting mates which provide the carriers of certain genotypes with a mating advantage when they are in the minority. Recent studies have provided evidence that pheromones may play such a role among insects. Pheromones are chemical signals (airborne "hormones") which affect the behavior of conspecific individuals. They include releaser substances (e.g., sex attractants and alarm pheromones) which cause an immediate behavioral response on a receptor organism; primer substances (e.g., queen substance of the honeybee) which can alter the physiological state of an organism so as to produce a response at a later time; and recognition substances which permit insects to discriminate between different kinds of individuals. It is this latter type of chemical signal that we are concerned with in this section. The effects of recognition substances on mate selection have been studied quite extensively in species of *Drosophila*. For example, Ehrman and her co-workers, working with *D. pseudoobscura*, have found female flies can recognize a variety of different male genotypes by way of olfactory cues. This discriminatory ability exists even in the absence of prior experience, although experience has been shown to influence female response (Pruzan and Ehrman, 1974). Moreover, the chemical signals provide a recognition system that is frequency-dependent. In a series of studies on flies carrying the *AR* and *CH* chromosome arrangements, it was found that female preference was always given to rare males, providing the males in lowest frequency with a mating advantage. This frequency-dependent mating behavior served as the mechanism for chromosomal polymorphism, since the mating advantage of the rare type decreases as minority-males become commoner, thus leading to a state of equilibrium. Some of the results obtained by Ehrman (1967) from mating tests are summarized in Figure 12.15. The data for each genotype are fitted to an adaptive function $W_i = 1 + X_i/G_i$ where W_i is the fitness of the ith genotype, G_i is the genotype frequency, and X_i is a constant (Anderson, 1969). This adaptive function is simply an approximation of a more general growth rate expression $W_i - 1 = A_i/(1 + B_iN_i) = A_i/(1 + B_iNG_i)$, where N_i is the density of the ith genotype. Thus, when the total density, N, is sufficiently large, the population will behave as though fitness values are inverse functions of genotype frequency. To illustrate the predicted outcome of such mating behavior, assume that density is suffi-

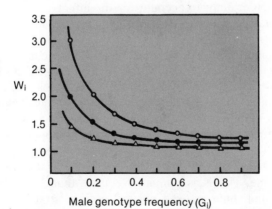

Male genotype frequency (G_i)

Figure 12.15.   Predicted male mating success as a function of male genotype frequency for 3 different values of X_i; open circles, $X_1 = 0.2$; closed circles, $X_2 = 0.1$; triangles, $X_3 = 0.05$. (From L. Ehrman. 1967. Am. Nat. 101: 415–424. Copyright 1967 by The University of Chicago. All rights reserved.)

ciently large so that the genotypes among the males will have the following fitness values:

	BB	Bb	bb
Frequency:	p^2	$2pq$	q^2
Fitness:	$W_1 = 1 + X_1/p^2$	$W_2 = 1 + X_2/2pq$	$W_3 = 1 + X_3/q^2$

The values of $\bar{W}$ and W_b in this case are

$$\bar{W} = 1 + X_1 + X_2 + X_3$$

$$W_b = 1 + \tfrac{1}{2}X_2/q + X_3/q$$

Applying equation (12.2), we then get

$$\Delta q = [X_3(1 - q) + \tfrac{1}{2}X_2(1 - 2q) - X_1q]/(1 + X_1 + X_2 + X_3) \quad \text{(12.36)}$$

An equilibrium will be established when

$$\hat{q} = (X_3 + \tfrac{1}{2}X_2)/(X_1 + X_2 + X_3)$$

Using the values of $X_1 = X_2 = 0.1$ and $X_3 = 0.3$ from Anderson's analysis, the predicted equilibrium frequencies for these experimental results are $\hat{q} = 0.7$ and $\hat{p} = 0.3$.

Selection in heterogeneous environments.   Essentially all of the selection models presented thus far have emphasized the mechanisms of genetic change and have more or less ignored the problem of environmental heterogeneity. In the real world, environments are patchy, tending to vary in both time and space. Hence, it is expected that genotypic fitnesses will change, not only from season to season but also from place to place. Several models have been proposed in recent years which attempt to account for the effects of temporal and spatial variation in habitat conditions. Much of the thinking along these lines can be summarized in terms of the concept of fitness sets, devised by Richard Levins (1968). This is a theoretical approach to the analysis of adaptive strategies which incorporates the idea that selection will act in a heterogeneous environment so as to maximize fitness. Consider, for example, the fitness distribution of some quantitative character such as body size in an invertebrate species for a uniform set of climatic conditions. If the range of measurements is sufficiently broad, we might expect to see something akin to the bell-shaped distribution shown in Figure 12.16. The optimal adaptive strategy under those conditions is rather straightforward. It would be a population consisting of the phenotype with the largest fitness value. This is assuming, of course, that the optimum phenotype can exist in a homozygous state. If not, the optimal strategy may be a state of balanced polymorphism.

Now, suppose that the population is exposed to two different environmental situations such as two different climatic conditions; one hot, the other cold. The hypothetical fitness distributions which correspond to this case are shown

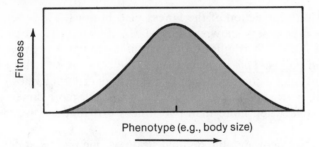

Figure 12.16.   Hypothetical fitness distribution showing plot of fitness versus body size under uniform climatic conditions.

in graphs A and B of Figure 12.17. Since large body size is adaptive in cold environments, due to the low surface area to volume ratio, and the reverse is true for warm climates, then what would be the optimal strategy for an environment which is sometimes hot and sometimes cold? Predictions concerning this and many related problems of environmental heterogeneity can often be made by constructing a fitness set. This is simply a plot of the fitness variable in one environment, W_1, along one axis against the corresponding fitness in the second environment, W_2, along the other axis. Each point (W_1, W_2) would then represent a pair of fitness values for the same phenotype but under different environmental conditions. Two general types of plots are possible, depending

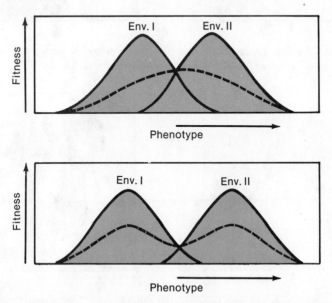

Figure 12.17.   Hypothetical fitness distributions under two climatic conditions. The dashed lines represent the mean fitness in the two environments.

on the point of intersection of the fitness distributions. These are the convex and concave fitness sets shown in Figures 12.18 and 12.19. A convex set develops when fitness distributions intersect at some value between their peaks and inflection points. This is in contrast to the concave set which is produced if the point of intersection between two fitness distributions lies outside their inflection points. It should also be noted that three or more dimensional fitness sets are possible when more than two fitness distributions are considered at one time.

Before one can predict the optimal strategy, one must first define an adaptive function which relates the mean fitness of the population within a mixture of conditions (or patches, as we shall call them) to the fitness value in each

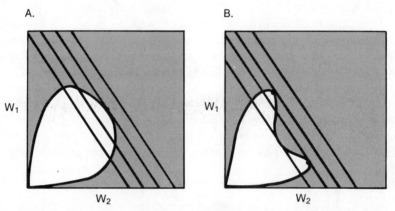

Figure 12.18. Convex (A) and concave (B) fitness sets. The straight lines represent plots of the linear adaptive function for a fine-grained environment.

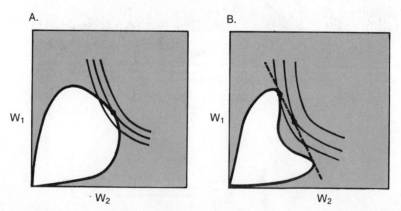

Figure 12.19. Convex (A) and concave (B) fitness sets. The curved lines represent plots of the hyperbolic adaptive function for a coarse-grained environment. The dashed line is the mean fitness of a mixture of genotypes.

environment alone. The exact nature of the adaptive function will depend on the frequency of each patch type and on the grain of the environment. Consider a fine-grained environment first. Recall that this is one in which an organism encounters the different patch types several times during its lifespan and in proportion to the frequency at which they occur. What is fine-grained will, of course, depend on the lifespan, size, and mobility of the organism. For example, seasonal fluctuations in temperature might be regarded as fine-grained to a long-lived terrestrial mammal but not to an annual plant. To arrive at the appropriate adaptive function, let c = the proportion of time spent in the first environmental situation (patch type 1). Since each patch type is encountered several times during the life cycle, the mean fitness will be $\bar{W} = cW_1 + (1 - c)W_2$. Solving for W_1, we then get the adaptive function for these conditions

$$W_1 = [\bar{W} - (1 - c)W_2]/c \tag{12.37}$$

Note that a W_1 versus W_2 graph of this function yields a family of lines for which the slope, $(1 - c)/c$, depends on the relative importance of each patch type (Figure 12.18). Assuming that selection will act to maximize $\bar{W}$, the optimal phenotype will be represented by the point of intersection between the adaptive function and the outermost point on the fitness set. Thus, in the case of fine-grained differences, the optimal strategy is a generalist, having an intermediate phenotype, in the case of a convex set; and a phenotype which is specialized for one or the other habitat conditions in the case of a concave set. For example, a single generalized phenotype in a long-lived animal species could respond behaviorally to very rapid (e.g., daily) fluctuations in temperature or physiologically and through migration to less rapid (e.g., seasonal) changes. On the other hand, if conditions are sufficiently different (i.e., a concave set), behavioral and physiological responses may no longer be adequate and a specialist might evolve that is adapted to, say, the warmer season and escape the harsher periods through a temporary state of dormancy.

At the other extreme is a coarse-grained environment in which patch size (or temporal duration) is sufficiently large so that an individual will spend an entire lifetime under one set of conditions. (Bear in mind that fine-grained and coarse-grained differences are simply two extremes in a continuum of possibilities with most situations falling somewhere in between.) To derive an adaptive function, suppose that in a period of t generations, ct are spent in patch type 1 and $(1 - c)t$ in patch type 2. The mean fitness over t generations will then be $\bar{W}^t = W_1^{ct} W_2^{(1-c)t}$. Hence, $\bar{W} = W_1^c W_2^{(1-c)}$. The adaptive function for coarse-grain differences then becomes

$$W_1 = (\bar{W}/W_2^{1-c})^{1/c} \tag{12.38}$$

This expression yields a family of hyperbolic curves (Figure 12.19). Again we see that, for a convex set, the optimal strategy is a single intermediate phenotype. This is assuming, of course, that the population is unable to respond rapidly enough to selection to become adapted to both situations. If changes are sufficiently slow and predictable in time, the optimal phenotype may actually vary with relatively close genetic tracking of environmental conditions (Bryant, 1973). In the case of a concave fitness set with a coarse-grained environment, the optimum is a mixed strategy since the theoretically maximum fitness corresponds to a mixture of phenotypes rather than the phenotype of any one individual in the population. This could be achieved through a state of balanced polymorphism in which the specialized phenotypes occur in proportions that depend on the frequency of each patch type.

The fact that variation in fitness patterns over time or space can lead to a stable genetic polymorphism has been demonstrated by a variety of models. One that we shall consider is a spatial model developed by Levene (1953). Assume a population in which individuals spend their lives in randomly selected environments, and then mate at random with regard to patch type at the time of reproduction. This serves as an approximation to the behavior of several different species including a variety of marine invertebrates, which disperse their gametes randomly, and wind-pollinated plants. Levene referred to this situation as "the worst case," since individuals are not free to select the environment to which they are best suited and no barriers to mating exist between members of each patch type. If these restrictive conditions can lead to a stable polymorphism, then nonrandom selection of habitat and mate (at least when occurring in the proper direction) can obviously do so with an even greater chance of genetic divergence. Assuming two patch types occurring at proportions c and $1-c$, the population can be represented as follows:

	BB	Bb	bb
Patch type 1:	$W_{BB} = 1 - s_1$	$W_{Bb} = 1$	$W_{bb} = 1 - t_1$
Patch type 2:	$W_{BB} = 1 - s_2$	$W_{Bb} = 1$	$W_{bb} = 1 - t_2$

No restriction is placed on the values of the selection coefficients, s and t. They can be positive, negative, or zero. For example, one situation might be:

	BB	Bb	bb
Patch type 1:	0.5	1	0.5
Patch type 2:	3	1	3

in which the selection coefficients show both positive and negative values.

A suitable expression for Δq can now be derived. Recalling that $\bar{W} = \bar{W}_1^c \bar{W}_2^{1-c}$, we can write $d(\ln \bar{W})/dq = cd(\ln \bar{W}_1)/dq + (1-c)d(\ln \bar{W}_2)/dq$. Since the net change in gene frequency is $\Delta q = \frac{1}{2}pqd(\ln \bar{W})/dq$, we then have

$$\Delta q = \frac{1}{2}pq[cd(\ln \bar{W}_1)/dq + (1-c)d(\ln \bar{W}_2)/dq]$$
$$= pq[c(ps_1 - qt_1)/\bar{W}_1 + (1-c)(ps_2 - qt_2)/\bar{W}_2]$$

(12.39)

Thus, an equilibrium develops when

$$- c(ps_1 - qt_1)/\bar{W}_1 = (1-c)(ps_2 - qt_2)/\bar{W}_2$$

Several equilibrium situations are possible depending on the numerical values of the different variables. One example is shown in terms of a plot of Δq versus q in Figure 12.20 for $c = 0.5$, and using the specific numerical values for the selection coefficients which were given above. Note that more than one equilibrium point is possible, alternating with regard to stability.

Levene extended the model to include any number of patch types. For the general case, equilibrium occurs when

$$\Sigma c_i(ps_i - qt_i)/\bar{W}_i = 0$$

where c_i is the proportion of patch type i. More specifically, Levene demonstrated that a balanced polymorphism is possible if the weighted harmonic means of the fitness values for each of the homozygotes is less than the fitness of the heterozygote in all patch types (i.e., $1/\Sigma c_i/(1 - s_i) < 1$ and $1/\Sigma c_i/(1 - t_i) < 1$).

Another interesting feature of fitness set theory is its ability to account for the development of both gradual and abrupt character changes along an ecological gradient. Suppose there exists a gradient in the proportion c of a certain patch type throughout some region in space (as in the transition between, say, forest and prairie habitat types). Any change such as this will alter the slope of the adaptive function, causing the curve to rotate about the fitness set (Fig. 12.21). If the fitness set is convex, large alterations in slope will produce only

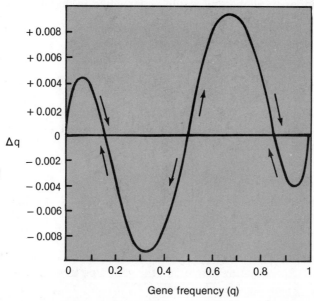

Figure 12.20.   Plot of equation (12.39) for $c = 0.5$, $s_1 = t_1 = 0.5$ and $s_2 = t_2 = -2$. Stable equilibrium points lie at $q = 0.15$ and $q = 0.85$, and an unstable equilibrium point lies at $q = 0.5$.

A.   B.

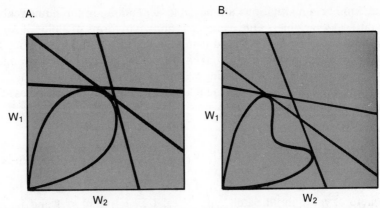

Figure 12.21.   The theoretical effects of a differing mixture of two environments on geographic variation. A gradual change is observed with a convex set, whereas, an abrupt change occurs with a concave set.

slight differences in the optimum phenotype. Under these conditions, we would expect to observe a regular form of geographic variation in which character changes occur in a gradual manner (e.g., a cline). On the other hand, a concave set would produce only slight character changes at either environmental extreme, but would have a sudden jump somewhere in between. In this case, abrupt transitions in phenotype would occur while in the midst of only slight changes in environmental conditions.

SOLVED EXAMPLE PROBLEMS

Measurement of Fitness

1. Consider a random-mating population with discrete nonoverlapping generations. Let the number of individuals of each genotype be as follows for two successive generations:

	BB	Bb	bb	Total
Mating adults at generation 0:	4,000	4,800	3,000	11,800
Mating adults at generation 1:	4,600	5,200	3,100	12,900

Estimate the relative fitness values for the three genotypes from the data. *solution*   Since mating is random, the genotype frequencies in generation 1 (P, H, Q) are expected to equal $(p^2 R_{0,1}/\bar{R}_0, 2pq R_{0,2}/\bar{R}_0, q^2 R_{0,3}/\bar{R}_0)$. The gene frequencies in these expressions can be computed as $p = (4{,}000 + \frac{1}{2}4{,}800)/11{,}800 = 0.543$ and $q = (3{,}000 + \frac{1}{2}4{,}800)/11{,}800 = 0.457$. Hence, $R_{0,1}/R_0 = P/p^2 = 0.357/0.295 = 1.21$; $R_{0,2}/R_0 = H/2pq = 0.403/0.495 = 0.811$; and $R_{0,3}/R_0 = Q/q^2 = 0.240/0.210 = 1.14$. The relative fitness values will then be given as $W_1 = 1.00$; $W_2 = 0.811/1.21 = 0.67$; and $W_3 = 1.14/1.21 = 0.94$.

General Selection Models: Constant Relative Fitness

2. A haploid population is composed of equal numbers of B and b genotypes at a locus. Calculate the genotype frequencies after 10 generations of selection against gene b, if the selection coefficient is 0.01.

    solution   Since $q_o = 0.50$ and $s = 0.01$, equation (12.1) gives $q_{10} = 0.50/0.50(1+ e^{0.1}) = 0.475$, a 5% reduction in the frequency of b.

3. Show how equation (12.2) can be derived directly from the relations of W_b and $\bar{W}$ to growth rates.

    solution   Let $n_{b,1}$ and $n_{b,0}$ be the number of b genes at generations 1 and 0, respectively, and n_1 and n_0 represent the corresponding total numbers of genes (both B and b) at the locus in question. Since W_b is proportional to $n_{b,1}/n_{b,0}$ and W is proportional to n_1/n_0, we then get

$$W_b/\bar{W} - 1 = \frac{n_{b,1}/n_{b,0}}{n_1/n_0} - 1 = \frac{n_{b,1}/n_1}{n_{b,0}/n_0} - 1 = \frac{q_1}{q} - 1 = \frac{\Delta q}{q}$$

which is the desired result.

4. Suppose that a recessive lethal disorder occurs in 1 out of 400 births. How many generations of selection are required to reduce the frequency of this trait to one-fourth its present value?

    solution   Let $q_0^2 = 1/400$. Thus, $q_o = 1/20$. Similarly, $q_t^2 = \frac{1}{4}(1/400)= 1/1,600$ so that $q_t = 1/40$. Substituting these values into the expression $t = (q_o - q_t)/q_o q_t$, we get $t = (1/20 - 1/40)/(1/20)(1/40) = 40 - 20 = 20$ generations.

Equilibria and Polymorphism

5. If heterozygosity is maintained in a population by mutation or as a result of selection favoring heterozygotes, an appreciable number of adaptively inferior genotypes will be produced in each generation. The cost to a population of producing inferior genotypes, in terms of the overall reduction in fitness, is referred to as its *genetic load, L*, and is usually expressed as

$$L = (W_{\max} - \bar{W})/ W_{\max}$$

where $W_{\max} - \bar{W}$ is the reduction in fitness from that of the optimum genotype (i.e., the genotype with the highest fitness value).

a. Show that the load incurred by the population from the mutational origin of a detrimental recessive gene is equal to the mutation rate, once an equilibrium has been established between mutation and selection.

b. Demonstrate that the load incurred from overdominance is determined strictly by the values of the selection coefficients.

solution   a. A population in which selection is against homozygous recessives has a mean fitness of $\bar{W} = 1 - sq^2$. Due to opposing mutation, however, an equilibrium is eventually established when $\hat{q}^2 = u/s$ [equation (12.8)]. Letting $W_{max} = 1$, the mutational load when mutation and selection are balanced becomes $L = 1 - \bar{W} = s(u/s) = u$.

b. The mean fitness, in the case of overdominance, is $\bar{W} = 1 - s_1 p^2 - s_2 q^2$. At equilibrium, however, $\hat{p} = s_2/(s_1 + s_2)$ and $\hat{q} = s_1/(s_1 + s_2)$ [equation (12.11)]. Therefore,

$$\bar{W} = 1 - s_1[s_2/(s_1 + s_2)]^2 - s_2[s_1/(s_1 + s_2)]^2$$

$$= 1 - s_1 s_2/(s_1 + s_2)$$

This component of the genetic load (i.e., the segregational load) can then be written

$$L = s_1 s_2/(s_1 + s_2)$$

Since selection coefficients are generally much larger than mutation rates, segregational loads will tend to have a significantly greater effect on populations than will mutational loads.

6. Employing equation (12.12), compute the relative fitnesses of homozygotes from the following data:

t	q_t	$x_t = p_t/q_t$	x_t/x_{t+1}
0	0.80	0.25	0.37
1	0.60	0.67	0.55
2	0.44	1.27	0.68
3	0.35	1.86	—

solution   Calculations of the quantities x_t^2/x_{t+1} and $x_t/x_{t+1} - x_t$ gives the following pairs of equations:

$t = 0{\rightarrow}1$ $W_3 = 0.0925\,W_1 + 0.12$ $W_1 = 0.870$, $W_3 = 0.200$

$\phantom{t = 0{\rightarrow}1}$ $W_3 = 0.3685\,W_1 - 0.12$

$t = 1{\rightarrow}2$ $W_3 = 0.3685\,W_1 - 0.12$ $W_1 = 0.943$, $W_3 = 0.227$

$\phantom{t = 1{\rightarrow}2}$ $W_3 = 0.8670\,W_1 - 0.59$

Taking the averages of these quantities, the estimates of fitness are $W_1 = 0.906$ and $W_3 = 0.214$. Since $W_2 = 1$, such values might be typical of a gene which has "semilethal" effects when in homozygous recessive condition, but confers a selective advantage on heterozygous carriers.

7. An example of selection against heterozygotes in humans concerns the Rh blood group system. In this case, however, only those heterozygotes conceived by Rh^- (genotype rr) mothers are selected against. Heterozygotes born to Rh^+ (genotype RR or Rr) females have no disadvantage. Show that if $1-s$ is the fitness of heterozygotes born to Rh^- mothers, the change in gene frequency expected per generation is $q = spq^2(q - \frac{1}{2})/(1 - spq^2)$.

solution   We first compute the frequencies of the heterozygous offspring from RR male $\times$ rr female and Rr male $\times$ rr female matings. They are

$p^2q^2(1-s)/\bar{W}$ and $pq^3(1-s)/\bar{W}$, respectively, where $\bar{W} = 1 - sp^2q^2 - spq^3 = 1 - spq^2$. The frequency of the r allele in the next generation is then $q_1 = (pq - \frac{1}{2}sp^2q^2 - \frac{1}{2}spq^3 + q^2)/(1 - spq^2) = (q - \frac{1}{2}spq^2)/(1 - spq^2)$, and $\Delta q = spq^2(q - \frac{1}{2})/(1 - spq^2)$.

Extensions of Basic Theory

8. Consider the case of selection against a sex-linked gene, occurring with a frequency q among both males and females. Show that, for $q < 1$, mean fitness values among males and females will only be equal when heterozygous females are exactly intermediate in phenotype between homozygous types.

   solution   Since females carry two doses of a sex-linked gene, while males carry only one, the general expressions for mean fitness are

   $$\bar{W}_f = 1 - 2hsq + (2h - 1)sq^2 \quad \text{and} \quad \bar{W}_m = 1 - sq$$

   where h is a measure of dominance. Equating the two expressions, we get

   $$sq(1 - 2h) - sq^2(1 - 2h) = (1 - 2h)(1 - q) = 0$$

   Thus, h must equal $\frac{1}{2}$.

Selection with Multiple Loci

9. A hypothetical population mates at random with respect to two loci, where $p_1 = q_1 = 0.5$ and $p_2 = 0.8$, $q_2 = 0.2$ prior to selection. Assume that each locus contributes to fitness in an independent and multiplicative fashion, such that $W_1 = W_2 = W_1' = W_2' = 1$, $W_3 = W_3' = 0.9$. Determine the gamete frequencies after one generation of selection.

   solution   Making the assumption of linkage equilibrium allows the use of equations (12.18) to determine gamete frequencies, where $h = j = 0.4$ and $i = k = 0.1$ and fitnesses are as follows: $W_{11} = W_{21} = W_{12} = W_{22} = 1$; $W_{31} = W_{32} = W_{13} = W_{23} = 0.9$; and $W_{33} = 0.81$. By equations (12.19), we obtain $\bar{W}_{AB} = 1$, $\bar{W}_{Ab} = 0.98$, $\bar{W}_{aB} = 0.95$, and $\bar{W}_{ab} = 0.93$. Since $\bar{W}_A = 0.975$ and $\bar{W}_B = 0.996$, then $\bar{W} = \bar{W}_A \cdot \bar{W}_B = 0.971$. Substitution into equations (12.18) then yields

   $$h_1 = (0.4)/0.971 = 0.412; \qquad i_1 = (0.1)(0.98)/0.971 = 0.101;$$

   $$j_1 = (0.4)(0.95)/0.971 = 0.391; \qquad k_1 = (0.1)(0.93)/0.971 = 0.093$$

10. Consider a randomly mating population where initial gamete frequencies at two unlinked loci are $h = k = 0.3$ and $i = j = 0.2$ and fitness values are $W_{13} = W_{31} = 0$, $W_{11} = W_{12} = W_{21} = W_{23} = W_{32} = W_{33} = 1$, and $W_{22} = 2$. Determine the gamete frequencies after one generation of selection.

    solution   In this case, there is functional interaction between loci. Thus, gamete frequencies can be calculated using equations (12.21), where $D = hk - ij = 0.05$, $R = 0.5$, and $\bar{W}_{AB} = \bar{W}_{ab} = 1.3$, $\bar{W}_{Ab} = \bar{W}_{aB} = 1.0$, $\bar{W} = 1.18$. Thus, $h_1 = (0.3)(1.3) - (0.5)(2)(0.05)/1.18 = 0.288$. Similarly, $i_1 = 0.212$, $j_1 = 0.212$, and $k_1 = 0.288$. The value of D is now 0.038.

Effects of Selection on Quantitative Traits

11. The monthly egg production of a poultry flock varies as a normal distribution with an average of 15 eggs per hen and a standard deviation of $\pm$ 2 eggs. If only the highest producing 16% of the flock is saved for breeding purposes, what is the selection differential used for improving egg production?

    solution Since selection only involves the upper tail of the distribution, a q value of 0.16 corresponds to a point of truncation of 1 standard deviation unit above the mean (i.e., $\bar{P} + \sigma_P = 15 + 2 = 17$ eggs). Inspection of a table of ordinates of the standard normal curve reveals that this point of truncation corresponds to an ordinate of 0.242. Thus, applying equation (12.30), we get $S = (0.242/0.16)\,2 = 3$ eggs.

Selection Models: Variable Relative Fitness

12. Employing equation (12.33), show that the model predicts that density-dependent selection can occur in the absence of frequency-dependent selection, while the reverse is not true.

    solution First observe that frequency dependence, but not density dependence, disappears if $\alpha = \beta = 1$. We get

    $$\Delta p = pq^2[(r_2 - r_1) - (r_2/K_2 - r_1/K_1)N]$$

    On the other hand, both density dependence and frequency dependence are lost when $r_2/K_2 - \alpha r_1/K_1 = \beta r_2/K_2 - r_1/K_1 = 0$.

13. In example problem 5, the segregational load of a population was computed for the classic case of heterozygote superiority and assumed a constancy of fitness values. If genetic variation is maintained, instead, by some form of frequency dependent selection, the segregational load can be considerably less. For a numerical example, consider a locus with two alleles showing incomplete dominance, and a scheme where each allele has a selective advantage when rare such that the fitnesses of the three genotypes are as follows:

Genotype:	BB	Bb	bb
Frequency:	p^2	$2pq$	q^2
Fitness	$W_1 = 1 + q$	$W_2 = 1.5$	$W_3 = 2 - q$

    Calculate the genetic load of the population at equilibrium.

    solution The expressions for $\bar{W}$ and W_b are $\bar{W} = 1 + 2q - 2q^2$ and $\bar{W}_b = 1.5 + 0.5q - q^2$. Using equation (12.2), we obtain $\Delta q = q(0.5 - 1.5q + q^2)/(1 + 2q - 2q^2)$, which is 0 when $q = \frac{1}{2}$. But, when $q = \hat{p} = \frac{1}{2}$, $W_1 = W_2 = W_3 = 1.5$. Since all genotypes have equal fitness in the balanced state, the segregational load will equal zero.

14. Show that the continuous analog to equation (12.2) is $dq/dt = (r_b - \bar{r})q$, where r_b is the intrinsic rate of increase for the b allele (i.e., the average

rate of increase of all genotypes containing this allele) and $\bar{r}$ is the average rate of increase for all genotypes within the population.

solution Assume that population size varies as $dN/dt = \bar{r}N$. Letting $n = 2N$ be the total number of genes at the b locus, we can also write $dn/dt = \bar{r}n$. Moreover, by comparison we see that $dn_b/dt = r_b n_b$. Since $n_b = nq$, differentiation yields $dn_b/dt = ndq/dt + qdn/dt$. Dividing by nq, we get $dn_b/n_b dt = dq/qdt + dn/ndt$. Hence, $dq/qdt = r_b - \bar{r}$, which is the desired result.

PROBLEM EXERCISES

1. Consider a population composed of three genotypes (BB, Bb, bb), with relative fitnesses (1, $1-hs$, $1-s$) and a gene frequency of $q = 0.25$. Calculate the change in gene frequency expected after one generation of selection ($s = 0.1$) if $h = 0$, $h = \frac{1}{2}$, and $h = 1$. Repeat your calculations for $q = 0.5$ and $q = 0.75$.

2. Find the number of generations required to reduce q from 0.4 to 0.04 in a diploid population in which dominance is completely lacking and the selection coefficient is 0.01.

3. Show that the rate of gene frequency change with selection against the recessive genotype is maximal when the recessive allele is twice as frequent as the dominant allele.

4. A particular gene is lethal in homozygous condition, but enhances the fitness of genotypes heterozygous for it, such that heterozygotes are twice as fit as homozygotes for the alternative allele. (a) If the present frequency of this gene is 0.4, what is its expected frequency in the next generation? (b) What will be the equilibrium gene frequency?

5. As explained in the text, gene interaction can result in a permanent linkage disequilibrium even if two loci are not linked. Show that this is the case in Example Problem 9.

6. In a crossing sequence involving bristle number in *Drosophila*, pure-bred parental stocks are found to give an F_1 having a variance of 6, which, in turn, yield an F_2 with a mean of 38 and a variance of 16. Predict the mean of the F_3, if parents selected from the F_2 have a mean of 45 bristles.

7. In a haploid population, there are 50% B and 50% b genotypes. How many generations of selection are required to reduce the frequency of gene b by half, if the value of the selection coefficient is 0.01?

8. Assume that in the haploid population of Problem 7, B and b occur at frequencies of p and q and have intrinsic rates of increase of r_B and r_b. Given that growth is continuous in time, show that the rate of change in

p will be given as $dp/dt = (r_B - r_b)pq$. What is the value of $r_B - r_b$ for this particular population?

9. One in 4,900 individuals are born with an abnormality caused by a recessive gene. What will be the frequency of the abnormality after 100 generations of complete selection against the trait? (Ignore mutation effects.)

10. For a diploid population experiencing selection against the recessive gene with a selection coefficient of 0.1, calculate the rate of change in gene frequency (Δq) when $q = 0.01, 0.10, 0.50, 0.90$. Repeat your calculations assuming no dominance.

11. The lethal genetic disease infantile amaurotic idiocy is caused by a recessive gene. If the mutation rate to this allele is 3×10^{-6} per generation, what fraction of the population is expected to be born with this disease at equilibrium? If the mutation rate is doubled due to exposure to radiation, what would be the new equilibrium value?

12. Consider again the experimental procedure of Dobzhansky and Pavlovsky involving selection in a population of *D. pseudoobscura*, this time using the third chromosome arrangements Chiricahua and Arrowhead. In this case, the relative fitness values are $0.75(AR/AR)$, $1.00(AR/CH)$, and $0.42(CH/CH)$. (a) If a population is started with 20% *AR* and 80% *CH* types, what are the expected frequencies in the next generation? (b) What are the expected equilibrium frequencies of the two chromosomes? (c) If selection acts through differential survival of larvae, what frequency of *AR/AR*, *AR/CH*, and *CH/CH* types would be expected at equilibrium among zygotes? Among adults?

13. *Drosophila* captured from the wild are often found to be heterozygous for recessive lethal genes. What explanation can you give for the persistence of such lethal genes in a population?

14. Consider the following symmetrical fitness sets:

$$\text{(a)} \quad \begin{Bmatrix} 0 & 0.5 & 0 \\ 0.5 & 1 & 0.5 \\ 0 & 0.5 & 0 \end{Bmatrix} \qquad \text{(b)} \quad \begin{Bmatrix} 0.5 & 0.2 & 0.5 \\ 0.3 & 1 & 0.3 \\ 0.5 & 0.2 & 0.5 \end{Bmatrix}$$

where $R = 0.2$. For each, determine the epistatic deviation, equilibrium frequencies for the gametes, and the linkage disequilibrium.

15. Referring to Problem 6, if instead of selecting F_2 parents of average bristle number 45, the top 20% of the F_2 distribution are used as parents for the F_3, predict the F_3 mean bristle number.

16. Show that the mutational load of a population (see Example Problem 5) from a detrimental gene showing complete or partial dominance is twice the mutation rate once mutation and selection are balanced.

13

Differentiation of
Populations and Speciation

Due to the discontinuous nature of suitable habitats, few species exist as single breeding units but are subdivided generally into local breeding populations called demes. This species structure permits the development of genetic variability in the form of interdemic differences. These differences arise as a result of the joint action of random and systematic evolutionary processes and, therefore, depend on the size of the breeding units, the nature of their local environments, and the amount of dispersal between them. When such variability develops in the absence of gene flow, through the establishment of barriers to gene exchange, local populations can diverge sufficiently to warrant the title of new species. Thus, long-term evolutionary changes such as speciation are ultimately a product of the dynamic processes involved in local adaptation.

GENETIC EFFECTS OF SUBDIVISION

When a large species population is subdivided into a series of smaller breeding units, the subpopulations will tend to differ in gene frequencies, either because of selection in different environments or simply due to chance variations. Whatever the cause, such differences in gene frequency will result in a reduction in the proportion of heterozygous individuals in the subdivided population as a whole.

Suppose, for example, that the subdivided population consists of n subgroups, each of size N, with gene frequencies $p_1, p_2, p_3, \ldots, p_n$. The mean and variance of the group gene frequencies will then be

$$\bar{p} = \sum_{i=1}^{n} p_i f_i$$

$$V_p = V_q = \sum_{i=1}^{n} (p_i - \bar{p})^2 f_i = \sum_{i=1}^{n} p_i^2 f_i - \bar{p}^2$$

where f_i is the proportion of subpopulations with gene frequency p_i. Now, if each subpopulation mates at random, the average genotype frequencies can be calculated as follows:

Genotype   Average frequency among subgroups

BB $$P = \sum_{i=1}^{n} p_i^2 f_i = \bar{p}^2 + V_p$$

Bb $$H = \sum_{i=1}^{n} 2p_i q_i f_i = 2\left[\sum_{i=1}^{n} p_i f_i - \sum_{i=1}^{n} p_i^2 f_i\right] = 2\bar{p}\bar{q} - 2V_p$$

bb $$Q = \sum_{i=1}^{n} q_i^2 f_i = \bar{q}^2 + V_p$$

In contrast to the frequencies given above, the values expected if all subgroups were to be consolidated again into one large random-mating population would be $\bar{p}^2$ (BB), $2\bar{p}\bar{q}$ (Bb), and $\bar{q}^2$ (bb). Thus, as a result of subdivision and gene frequency change, heterozygotes have decreased by an amount $2V_p$ and the homozygous types have increased correspondingly. Since V_p is a measure of genetic divergence, any further differentiation of local populations will be followed by an even greater reduction in the frequency of heterozygotes. This overall effect of subdivision was first deduced by Wahlund (1928) and has since been termed *Wahlund's principle*.

Subdivision and genetic variation. In addition to the differentiation between groups, subdivision, followed by a change in gene frequency, will also result in a reduction of genetic variation within local breeding populations. Individuals within each group will become more alike in genotype and thus in appearance. This can be readily shown by an analysis of genetic variance. Suppose, for example, that a gene locus in question contributes to a trait in an additive fashion. The genotypes, genotypic values, and genotype frequencies in the subdivided population can be represented as follows:

Genotype:	BB	Bb	bb
Genotypic value:	$2a$	a	0
Frequency:	$\bar{p}^2 + V_p$	$2\bar{p}\bar{q} - 2V_p$	$\bar{q}^2 + V_p$

The mean genotypic value is

$$\bar{G} = 2a(\bar{p}^2 + V_p) + a(2\bar{p}\bar{q} - 2V_p) = 2a\bar{p}$$

The genotypic variance, in turn, can be evaluated by writing it as the sum of the within-group and between-group variances. The within-group component of the genotypic variance (average genetic variance of all groups) will be

$$\overline{V}_G = \sum_{i=1}^{n} 2a^2 p_i q_i f_i = 2a^2 \left[\sum_{i=1}^{n} p_i f_i - \sum_{i=1}^{n} p_i^2 f_i \right]$$

where $2a^2 p_i q_i$ is the genetic variance of the ith group. Since $V_p = \Sigma p_i^2 f_i - \bar{p}^2$, we get

$$\overline{V}_G = 2a^2 [\bar{p}\bar{q} - V_p] \qquad (13.1)$$

On the other hand, the between-group variance (variance of group means) will be given by

$$V_{\overline{G}} = \sum_{i=1}^{n} (2ap_i - 2a\bar{p})^2 f_i = 4a^2 \left[\sum_{i=1}^{n} p_i^2 f_i - \bar{p}^2 \right]$$

or

$$V_{\overline{G}} = 4a^2 V_p \qquad (13.2)$$

Now, since $V_G = \overline{V}_G + V_{\overline{G}}$, the total genetic variance can be expressed as

$$V_G = 2a^2 \bar{p}\bar{q} - 2a^2 V_p + 4a^2 V_p$$
$$= 2a^2 [\bar{p}\bar{q} + V_p] \qquad (13.3)$$

Thus, we see that the genetic variance within groups will decrease as the subpopulations diverge in gene frequency. The opposite is true of the between-group component of variation. Due to a greater contribution of between-group variation, however, the overall effect is a net increase in the total genotypic variance.

SUBDIVISION AND GENETIC DRIFT

One evolutionary process which can be important in the continued divergence of local populations is genetic drift. This random process is particularly effective in small isolated populations. To demonstrate the effects of random drift, suppose that each of the n subgroups described in the preceding sections is completely isolated from all other such groups, and remains constant in size from one generation to the next. For present purposes, neglect the effects of mutation and assume that selection does not occur. Reproduction occurring in the subdivided population can then be represented as a series of n random samples, each consisting of $2N$ gametes derived from a parental generation of size N. This is pictured in the following diagram:

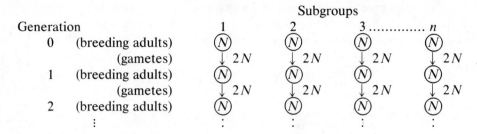

Subgroups

in which the labeling reads: Generation 0 (breeding adults), (gametes) $2N$ each, 1 (breeding adults), (gametes) $2N$ each, 2 (breeding adults), across Subgroups 1, 2, 3 .... n

As long as the sampling process is binomial, the variance in gene frequency for this subdivided population can be given, from Chapter 3, as

$$V_{p,t} = \bar{p}\bar{q}[1 - (1 - 1/2N)^t]$$
$$\simeq \bar{p}\bar{q}(1 - e^{-t/2N})$$

(13.4)

in which t is the number of generations over which the process has occurred. Since $H_t = 2\bar{p}\bar{q} - 2V_{p,t}$, the results of drift can also be summarized in terms of the reduction in heterozygotes. This gives

$$H_t = H_o e^{-t/2N}$$

(13.5)

where $H_o = 2\bar{p}\bar{q}$. Note that as t increases, $e^{-t/2N}$ approaches zero. Consequently, heterozygotes will eventually be eliminated from the subdivided population. When this happens, a proportion $\bar{p}$ of all subgroups will consist of only *BB* individuals and a proportion $\bar{q}$ will consist of all *bb* genotypes.

Effective population size.   In order to illustrate the effects of genetic drift on a subdivided population and still avoid mathematical complexity, a number of assumptions were made concerning the breeding structure of each population. Although these restrictive conditions are seldom, if ever, met in nature, we can still apply many of the formulae to real populations if N in each equation is replaced by a quantity known as the *effective population size* (N_e). The effective size of a population only equals the actual size when the breeding structure conforms to an idealized population; usually, it is smaller.

One simplification, which is rarely fulfilled under natural conditions, is the assumption that densities remain constant from one generation to the next. Instead, real populations often undergo seasonal changes as well as other types of fluctuation in size. When the size of a population varies from generation to generation, the reduction in heterozygotes can be predicted by substituting the appropriate effective size for N in equation (13.5). In this situation, then, ln $(H_t/H_o) = -t/2N_e$. The effective size can be computed as follows. Suppose that over a period of t generations, population sizes varied as $N_1, N_2, \ldots, N_t$. The proportion of heterozygotes after t generations can then be expressed in logarithmic form as

$$\ln(H_t/H_o) = -(1/2N_1 + 1/2N_2 + \ldots + 1/2N_t) = -t\sum_{i=1}^{t} (1/2N_i)/t$$

Thus, when population sizes vary, the effective size is approximately the harmonic mean given as

$$N_e = t/\sum_{i=1}^{t} (1/N_i) \tag{13.6}$$

Note that the generations with the lowest densities will have the greatest effect. For example, if there are three generations with numbers 100, 20, and 500, the effective size is $N_e = 3/(1/100 + 1/20 + 1/500) = 48$. This can be contrasted with the arithmetic mean which is 207. Thus, if a population undergoes periodic reductions in size, this bottleneck effect can markedly alter the genetic composition of a population even though its average size (arithmetic mean) is fairly large.

Another simplification, which is seldom realized in nature, is the assumption that gametes are sampled at random. This assumption implies that all individuals have an equal chance of contributing genes to the next generation. If the chance of survival is small, this also means that the family size of a stationary biparental population should correspond to a Poisson distribution with a mean and variance of 2. When gametes are not sampled at random because of selection, we define the effective size, for a monoecious population, as the reciprocal of the probability that two gametes chosen at random are from the same parent. To clarify the meaning of the effective size in this case, let k_i represent the variable number of gametes produced by the ith parent. This is equivalent to the family size in a biparental population. For a stationary population of size N, the number of gametes produced per parent will have a mean and variance of

$$\bar{k} = \Sigma k_i/N = 2$$

and

$$V_k = \Sigma k_i^2/N - \bar{k}^2 = \Sigma k_i^2/N - 4$$

Since there are $2N$ gametes which go to form the next generation, there are $2N!/2!(2N-2)! = 2N(2N-1)/2$ possible ways in which gametes can be chosen in pairs. Of which, $\Sigma k_i!/2!(k_i-2)! = \Sigma k_i(k_i-1)/2$ pairs are produced by the same parent. The proportion of all pairs that come from the same parent is then

$$\Sigma k_i(k_i-1)/2N(2N-1) = (\Sigma k_i^2 - \Sigma k_i)/2N(2N-1) = (V_k + 2)/(4N - 2)$$

Now, in the idealized population of effective size N_e, in which all parents are equally viable and fertile, the probability that two gametes chosen at random are derived from the same parent is $1/N_e$. Hence, the effective size can be written as (Wright, 1938)

$$N_e = (4N - 2)/(V_k + 2) \tag{13.7}$$

Kimura and Crow (1963) have extended this analysis to include the case of separate sexes. They find that, for a biparental population under stationary conditions, the corresponding effective size will be given as

$$N_e = (4N - 4)/(V_k + 2) \tag{13.8}$$

where V_k is now the variance of the family size in a stationary population. Note that, in both cases, when N is large and gametes are selected at random ($V_k = 2$), the effective size is essentially equal to N. With selection, however, reproductive inequalities among the parents tend to increase V_k above that expected for randomness and thereby reduce the effective size of the population.

Yet another simplification implicit in the ideal case is the assumption that there are equal numbers of both sexes. If their numbers differ, the effective size will be the harmonic mean (see equation 3.5):

$$N_e = 4N_m N_f/(N_m + N_f) \tag{13.9}$$

where N_m and N_f are the number of males and females, respectively. Note that unequal numbers of sexes further reduce the effective size of a population. For example, if $N_m = 5$ and $N_f = 95$, the actual size of the population is 100. Its effective size is $4(5)(95)/100 = 19$!

SUBDIVISION AND MIGRATION

Up to this point, we have excluded the effects of migration on a subdivided population by assuming that all subgroups are completely isolated and diverge in an independent fashion. Demes are open genetic systems, however, and there is always some potential for gene exchange. Even when lifetime dispersal is so small that individuals in remote populations have no chance to mate, the exchange of genes may still be possible by their gradual passage within occasional migrants through an intervening series of demes.

The effects of migration on genetic divergence can be illustrated in terms of an "island" model in which a species consists of an array of demes of effective size N with migration between them. It is assumed that migrants entering each deme at a rate M per generation constitute a random sample of the entire species population, so that the gene frequency among migrants can be taken as the average frequency in the population as a whole ($\bar{p}$). After one generation of migration, the gene frequency in the ith deme will then be $p_i + \Delta p_i$, where p_i is the frequency in the previous generation and $\Delta p_i = -M(p_i - \bar{p})$ (3.20). The variance in gene frequency can now be expressed in general as

$$V_{p,t} = \Sigma(p_i + \Delta p_i - \bar{p})^2 f_i$$
$$= (1-M)^2 \Sigma(p_i - \bar{p})^2 f_i \tag{13.10}$$
$$= (1-M)^2 V_{p,t-1}$$

Thus, if migration continues to occur unopposed by any other evolutionary process, the variance will decrease by a factor $(1-M)^2$ in each successive generation, resulting in a more homogeneous collection of subgroups.

This reduction in genetic variability can also be expressed in terms of an increase in the average frequency of heterozygotes. If the members of each deme mate at random, the average frequency of heterozygotes after migration will be

$$H_t = 2\bar{p}\bar{q} - 2V_{p,t} = 2\bar{p}\bar{q} - 2(1-M)^2 V_{p,t-1} \tag{13.11}$$

When written in this way, it can be seen that migration when acting alone will ultimately change the average genotype frequencies to the values expected if all demes were consolidated into one large random-mating population.

Migration and genetic drift.   The influence of migration on a subdivided population is rarely unopposed by the differential effects of other evolutionary forces. One process which can never be ruled out except in large local populations is genetic drift. The joint effects of drift and migration can be quantified by first recalling that as a consequence of sampling error the mean proportion of heterozygotes decreases by $(1 - 1/2N)$ in each generation. Therefore, when both processes are important, equation (13.11) can be expressed as

$$2\bar{p}\bar{q} - 2V_{p,t} = [2\bar{p}\bar{q} - 2(1-M)^2 V_{p,t-1}](1 - 1/2N)$$

Or, solving for $V_{p,t}$, we get

$$V_{p,t} = (1-M)^2 V_{p,t-1}(1 - 1/2N) + \bar{p}\bar{q}/2N \tag{13.12}$$

Since migration opposes the effects of drift by the introduction of new genes into each local population, eventually a steady-state will be reached when the rate of introduction of new genes equals their rate of loss due to drift. The conditions for the steady-state can be obtained by letting $V_{p,t} = V_{p,t-1} = V_p$ in equation (13.12). Solving for V_p, we obtain

$$V_p = \bar{p}\bar{q}/[2N - (1-M)^2(2N-1)] \tag{13.13}$$

When M is small, equation (13.13) reduces to

$$V_p = \bar{p}\bar{q}/(4NM + 1) \tag{13.14}$$

where NM is the effective number of migrants entering each deme per generation. Notice that only a small number of migrants need enter a deme to markedly reduce the effects of genetic drift. For example, if $NM = 1$, the variance is $\bar{p}\bar{q}/5$. If NM is increased to 10, however, the variance is reduced to $\bar{p}\bar{q}/41$. On the other hand, if major dispersal barriers exist so that $4NM \ll 1$, the variance is approximately $\bar{p}\bar{q}$ and essentially all demes have undergone fixation or loss of the gene in question.

Migration and selection.   Since conditions are rarely if ever uniform throughout a species range, different demes are expected to experience different selection pressures. For instance, in one deme a genotype may be favored, while in another the same genotype may be selected against. Such differential selection will tend to bring about divergence in the genetic structure of different demes and, as expected, the effects of migration will oppose such local differentiation.

To illustrate the joint effects of selection and migration, consider the case of selection against a gene lacking in dominance. In this instance, the change in the frequency of the favored gene due to selection occurring in the ith subgroup can be written as $\frac{1}{2}sp_i(1-p_i)$ when s is small. The net change in gene frequency in the ith deme (Δp_i) can now be written as the sum of the changes due to both selection and migration as follows:

$$\Delta p_i = \tfrac{1}{2}sp_i(1 - p_i) - M(p_i - \bar{p})$$

Equilibrium between selection and migration occurs when

$$\tfrac{1}{2}sp_i^2 - (\tfrac{1}{2}s - M)p_i - M\bar{p} = 0$$

Solving for the equilibrium gene frequency, we get

$$\hat{p} = [(\tfrac{1}{2}s - M) + \sqrt{(\tfrac{1}{2}s - M)^2 + 2sM\bar{p}}]/s \qquad (13.15)$$

Note that when $s = 2M$, the equilibrium frequency becomes $\hat{p} = \sqrt{\bar{p}}$. For example, when $\bar{p} = \frac{1}{4}$, $\hat{p} = \frac{1}{2}$. Thus, when M is small, a rather weak selection intensity can maintain considerable local differentiation.

BREEDING STRUCTURE OF POPULATIONS

In the preceding sections, we have assumed that all immigrants have an equal chance of originating from any deme in the subdivided population. In actual cases, however, dispersal patterns are such that the probability of immigration tends to decrease with the distance from source areas. Consequently, immigrants will come largely from neighboring demes and will differ little in gene frequency from the recipient population. One way to include the effects of differential gene flow into the preceding model is to define an effective migration rate given as

$$M_e = M(p_i - p_m)/(p_i - \bar{p})$$

where $p_i - p_m$ is the actual difference in gene frequency between the migrants and the deme in question. Since $p_i - p_m$ is generally less than $p_i - \bar{p}$, the overall influence of migration on genetic divergence will tend to be reduced from that predicted by the island model.

Isolation by distance.   The departure from the ideal case can be quite substantial in populations which are spread over large geographic areas. In instances such as these, widely separated individuals may be effectively isolated by distance. This is true for uniform as well as clumped spatial patterns. Even when discrete breeding clusters do not exist, the probability of mating will still fall off with distance between breeding adults. The population is then subdivided into neighborhoods, defined as the area in which the parents of individuals born near the center mate at random (Wright, 1943, 1946). The size of a neighborhood will depend on the dispersal facility of the organisms in question. For example, when lifetime dispersal is normally distributed, it is convenient to express the size of a neighborhood in terms of the variance, σ^2 (or standard deviation, σ), which, in turn, is a function of dispersal rate (see Chapter 7). If the population is dispersed along a linear range (as along a coastline or narrow valley), a one-dimensional neighborhood is defined as a strip of length 2σ, containing about 92.4% of the parents of centrally located individuals. The effective number of individuals making up the breeding unit is $N_e = 2\sigma N_d\sqrt{\pi} = 3.545\sigma N_d$, where N_d is the population density per unit length. On the other hand, if the population is continuous over an area, the size of a neighborhood can be taken as a circle of radius 2σ. The effective number of parents included in this area will then be $N_e = 4\pi\sigma^2 N_d = 12.566\sigma^2 N_d$ in which N_d is now the density defined on a per unit area basis. Wright has shown that a circle of this area will include 86.5% of the parents of central individuals under these conditions.

Steady-state models have been proposed which incorporate the concept of isolation by distance. Malecot (1955), for example, has derived one- and two-dimensional models for populations dispersed in a continuum that are valid for gamma as well as normally distributed dispersal patterns. If we let M, in this case, equal the rate of migration from the population as a whole, as in the island model, the steady-state value of V_p for a given neighborhood (i.e., the variance in gene frequency for a neighborhood once the introduction of new genes is balanced by their rate of loss due to drift) can be expressed as

$$V_p = \bar{p}\bar{q}/[1 + 2N_e\sqrt{2M/\pi}] \tag{13.16}$$

in one dimension, and as

$$V_p = \bar{p}\bar{q}/[1 + 2N_e(-1/\ln 2M)] \tag{13.17}$$

in two dimensions. In both equations, N_e is taken to be the effective number of parents within a neighborhood as defined earlier for a normal distribution pattern. It should be noted that for equal values of $\bar{p}$, N_e, and M, the magnitude of V_p will be smaller in the two-dimensional model than in the one-dimensional case. For instance, with $M = 0.1$, equations (13.16) and (13.17) become $V_p = \bar{p}\bar{q}/(1 + 0.504N_e)$ and $V_p = \bar{p}\bar{q}/(1 + 1.24N_e)$, respectively. It is, therefore, apparent that local differentiation along a linear range will tend to be greater than could be achieved if the population were able to disperse freely in two dimensions.

One may think of the island model and the model of uniform dispersion in a continuum as representing two limiting examples of population structure. The degree of subdivision in most populations, however, lies somewhere in between these extremes. Accounting for breeding structures of more intermediate character are the one- and two-dimensional stepping-stone models analyzed by Kimura and Weiss (1964). As shown in Figure 13.1, populations, in these models, are assumed to be subdivided into an array of discrete breeding clusters with migration occurring between adjacent clusters (short-range migration) at a rate M_1 and with the population as a whole (long-range migration) at a rate M. Note that by restricting short-range migration to adjacent colonies, the concept of isolation by distance is still retained, though in modified form. The one-dimensional stepping-stone model has been shown to yield an expression for V_p which is equivalent to equation (13.16) when $M_1 \gg M$. In this case, the variance of the migration distance per generation is $\sigma^2 = M_1$. Kimura and Weiss have also demonstrated that the correlation coefficient of gene frequencies between clusters, $r(x)$, decreases with distance x (number of steps between them) in an approximately exponential fashion. In the one-dimensional case, they find

$$r(x) \propto e^{-x\sqrt{2M/M_1}} \tag{13.18}$$

while, for two dimensions,

$$r(x) \propto (e^{-x\sqrt{4M/M_1}})/\sqrt{x} \tag{13.19}$$

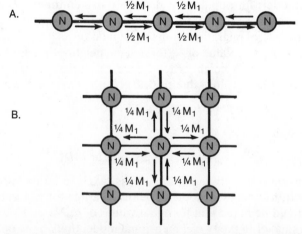

Figure 13.1. One-dimensional (A) and two-dimensional (B) stepping-stone models. Breeding clusters of size N are connected through migration at a total rate M_1.

The correlation between clusters will, therefore, decrease more rapidly with distance in two dimensions than along a linear range. Similar expressions were also derived by Malecot for the correlation between neighborhoods in a continuum. The equations are equivalent if M_1 in the stepping-stone model is taken as σ^2 in one dimension and as $2\sigma^2$ in the two-dimensional case.

The results of one study on the breeding structure in a human population is shown in Figure 13.2. The data in this example were obtained by pooling the frequencies of various blood-group alleles for inhabitants of the Parma Valley in northern Italy (Cavalli-Sforza, 1969). Values of V_p were estimated by first subdividing the area into units corresponding to administrative districts and computing the variance of gene frequencies between parishes within individual districts. The numerical results were then plotted according to the generalized theoretical expression $V_p/\bar{p}\bar{q} = 1/(1 + kN_d)$, in which N_d is the density (per square kilometer) and k is a constant. The agreement with theory was quite good despite the fact that the distribution, in this instance, did not conform precisely with either the one- or two-dimensional cases.

JOINT PRESSURES AND STATIONARY GENE DISTRIBUTIONS

In natural populations, all systematic and random evolutionary processes tend to act concurrently. A satisfactory mathematical description must, therefore, take the simultaneous action of all evolutionary forces into account. Although a completely satisfactory model has yet to be devised, simple one-locus models seem to approximate many natural situations and have proved quite useful in describing them. To illustrate, consider a large population subdivided into an array of demes (or neighborhoods), each of effective size N and experiencing

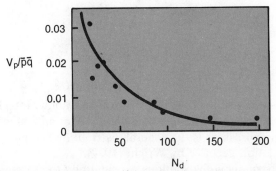

Figure 13.2. Relationship between the relative gene-frequency variance ($V_p/\bar{p}\bar{q}$) and population density (N_d) for inhabitants of the Parma Valley in northern Italy. (From L.L. Cavalli-Sforza. 1969. Proc. II Intern. Congr. Genet. 3: 405.)

the same systematic evolutionary pressures. Recall from previous sections that systematic forces, when acting alone or jointly, tend to result in stable equilibrium gene frequencies while random forces tend to scatter gene frequencies away from these equilibrium values. Thus, when acting jointly, systematic and dispersive pressures will oppose one another and will eventually give rise to a steady-state condition in which the dispersion of gene frequencies due to genetic drift (δp) is held in check by systematic processes (Δp). Once the steady-state condition is reached, there will be a certain amount of differentiation between demes, but the resulting distribution of gene frequencies remains the same as long as conditions are unchanged. This dynamic equilibrium condition can then be defined in terms of its *stationary gene distribution*, which gives the distribution of the gene frequency in question in an array of similar demes at any one time, or the distribution of the gene frequency in a single population when followed over several generations. Since the distribution is fixed, its variance and all higher moments about the mean value will remain the same during successive generations. Mathematically, such a stable distribution can be obtained by applying the Fokker-Planck equation (also termed the Kolmogorov forward equation) of physics:

$$\partial f(p,t)/\partial t = \tfrac{1}{2}\partial^2[V_{\delta p}f(p,t)]/\partial p^2 - \partial[\Delta pf(p,t)]/\partial p \qquad \textbf{(13.20)}$$

where $f(p,t)$ is the probability density function of p at time t. This expression has been used quite extensively by Kimura (1964) for the development of diffusion models which treat gene frequency changes as stochastic processes. Implicit in this expression is the assumption that such changes are, for all practical purposes, continuous in time. Once a steady-state is reached, $f(p,t)$ becomes independent of time. Under these conditions, the left-hand side of equation (13.20) is zero. Hence,

$$\tfrac{1}{2}d[V_{\delta p}f(p)]/dp - \Delta pf(p) = 0$$

which becomes

$$d\ln[V_{\delta p}f(p)]/dp = 2\Delta p/V_{\delta p}$$

Upon integration, we get

$$\begin{aligned} f(p) &= (C'/V_{\delta p})\exp[2\int (\Delta p/V_{\delta p})dp] \\ &= (C/pq)\exp[4N\int (\Delta p/pq)dp] \end{aligned} \qquad \textbf{(13.21)}$$

where C' and C are constants to make the total probability integrate to one and in which $V_{\delta p} = pq/2N$ and is the sampling variance for a population of effective size N. This final expression is the general distribution formula introduced into the field of population genetics by Wright (1937).

Some gene frequency distributions predicted by the formula are shown in Figure 13.3 for populations of different sizes under various systematic evolutionary pressures. Each distribution can be regarded as representing the prob-

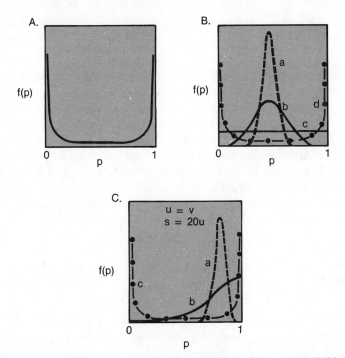

Figure 13.3. Steady-state gene distributions. (A) Plot of Equation 13.22. (B) Distributions under migration for $p_m = 0.5$; a. $4NM = 200$, b. $4NM = 20$, c. $4NM = 2$, d. $4NM = 0.2$. (C) Distributions under opposing mutation and selection against recessives; a. $4Ns = 200$, b. $4Ns = 20$, c. $4Ns = 2$.

ability that a population of size N will possess a specified frequency of a particular gene. The first, graph A, shows the distribution of p in very small populations in which systematic pressures are negligible. An approximate distribution function can be obtained by setting $\Delta p = 0$ in equation (13.21). We get

$$f(p) = C/pq = Cp^{-1}(1-p)^{-1} \qquad (13.22)$$

This represents one special case of the beta distribution function. The expression yields the U-shaped curve in which the probability is greatest for p near zero or one. Here we observe much differentiation since the majority of demes have the gene either fixed or lost.

Graph B illustrates the case when dispersion due to drift is balanced by migration. This was considered in some detail in an earlier section. To obtain the appropriate distribution function, in this case, express Δp in the general distribution formula as

$$\Delta p = -M(p - p_m) = (Mp_m)(1 - p) - (Mq_m)p$$

where $q_m = 1 - p_m$. Integration will then yield the beta distribution function

$$f(p) = Cp^{4NMp_m - 1}(1 - p)^{4NMq_m - 1} \qquad (13.23)$$

Observe when $4NMq_m = 4NMp_m = 1$, $f(p) = C$ and the distribution is flat. This means that all gene frequencies are equally probable. In contrast, large values of $4NM$ give rise to peaked distributions in which there is little variation in a single population from generation to generation; while, for very low values of $4NM$, distributions approach the U-shaped curve in the previous example. The variance of each distribution is given approximately by equation (13.14).

The final example is illustrated in graph C where selection, mutation, and drift are all assumed to act. In this instance, selection occurs against a detrimental recessive gene which is formed through recurrent mutation. The increase in the favored gene can then be expressed approximately as

$$\Delta p = v(1 - p) - up + sp(1 - p)^2$$

Making this substitution into equation (13.21) and integrating, we obtain

$$f(p) = Ce^{-2Ns(1-p)^2}p^{4Nv - 1}(1 - p)^{4Nu - 1} \qquad (13.24)$$

This equation was used to construct the curves in graph C for the conditions $u = v$ and $s = 20u$. Observe for an effective population size of $1/(40u)$, drift predominates and the distribution is U-shaped. With an effective size of $1/(0.4u)$, however, systematic forces are of prime importance resulting in a clustering of gene frequencies about an average value. In sufficiently large populations only one gene frequency would exist and this would correspond to the equilibrium value $\hat{p} = 1 - \sqrt{u/s}$, obtained from deterministic theory.

As the preceding examples serve to illustrate, the relative importance of dispersive and systematic forces on the nature of the steady-state depends not only on the effective breeding size (N) of populations but also on the magnitudes of M, s, and u. Thus when populations are exposed to joint pressures, a suitable measure of effective size can be made on the basis of $4NM$, $4Ns$, and $4Nu$. This is shown graphically in Figure 13.4 by means of three major types of stationary gene distributions. As pointed out by the first example plot, we would consider a population in which $4NM$, $4Ns$, and $4Nu$ are all significantly less than one as being "small" since drift predominates and a substantial amount of fixation and loss occurs. The population would then have the characteristic U-shaped gene distribution. Since drift is the dominant force, genetic changes are largely nonadaptive in character. Furthermore, little genetic variation remains within the group which would permit an adaptive response to any major environmental change. Hence, the eventual result is most likely extinction.

When $4NM$, $4Ns$, and $4Nu$, singly or in any combination, are significantly greater than unity, the population can be regarded as "large." The gene distribution is then I-shaped and gene frequencies will tend to remain in the vicinity

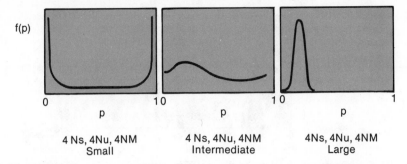

f(p)

| 0 | 10 | 1 0 | 1 |
| p | p | p |

4 Ns, 4Nu, 4NM
Small

4 Ns, 4Nu, 4NM
Intermediate

4Ns, 4Nu, 4NM
Large

Figure 13.4.   Three basic types of steady-state gene distributions.

of the average or equilibrium value. Since there is little tendency for gene frequency change, continued evolutionary progress is dependent on the rare occurrence of new advantageous mutations and on changes in environmental conditions. Such changes would alter the shape of the distribution and the population will move to a different equilibrium value during the approach to a new steady-state condition.

When $4NM$, $4Ns$, and $4Nu$ are intermediate in value, dispersive and systematic forces are both important in defining the steady-state condition. Although genes tend to remain in the vicinity of the equilibrium value, there is some appreciable scatter from one generation to the next. This situation would then permit a continued change in gene frequency even without a change in environmental conditions.

ADAPTIVE FIELDS

In the preceding analysis, an attempt was made to describe evolutionary change in terms of a single gene locus. Nevertheless, it should be apparent that continued evolutionary progress must involve changes at many loci, not just one. Although impossible to quantify, Wright has attempted to picture these changes by means of an adaptive field model. This is a model in which the average fitness of a population is represented by a series of peaks and valleys in a two-dimensional field of possible gene combinations. Its stepwise construction can be shown by first considering a single locus with two alleles. Assume that heterozygotes are selectively superior so that the mean fitness (12.10) can be given as

$$\bar{W} = 1 - s_1(1-q)^2 - s_2q^2$$

This expression is plotted in Figure 13.5 in which the arrows show how selection would change gene frequency. Since selection acts to maximize the average fitness of a population, q will change in such a way that the population moves

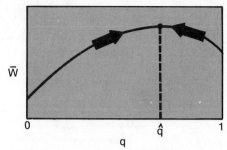

Figure 13.5. Improvement of mean fitness. Two-dimensional fitness plot for the case where heterozygotes are favored. The arrows indicate the direction a large population would move in response to selection to attain a gene frequency corresponding to the maximum value of $\bar{W}$.

up the "hill" to a point where $d\bar{W}/dq = 0$. We can determine the value of q that leads to the highest fitness by taking the derivative. We get

$$d\bar{W}/dq = 2s_1(1-q) - 2s_2q$$

Now letting $d\bar{W}/dq = 0$ and solving for q, we see that an equilibrium is established when

$$\hat{q} = s_1/(s_1 + s_2)$$

as shown before. An equilibrium at precisely this value will only happen when $4Ns_1$ and $4Ns_2$ are very large, since drift will tend to counteract the effects of selection and move the population down the slopes to q of one or zero.

Now, suppose that instead of just a single locus we consider two loci simultaneously. This is illustrated by a $\bar{W}$ versus q_1 and q_2 plot in Figure 13.6. We now obtain a three-dimensional surface which may contain more than a single peak. Although the peaks are not necessarily of equal height, a population

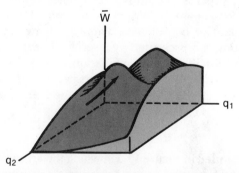

Figure 13.6. Improvement of mean fitness. Three-dimensional fitness plot with two fitness peaks. In this case, the population will move up the nearest peak in response to selection.

will find itself in the gradient of one of the peaks and will move accordingly in that direction. If there happens to be another peak with a higher value of $\bar{W}$, selection when acting alone cannot achieve the transition to the higher fitness value. A large population would then be stranded on a suboptimal peak until environmental changes drastically altered the adaptive topography. On the other hand, smaller populations might achieve this transition by chance variation in gene frequency brought about by genetic drift. Thus, nonadaptive changes could permit descent into the stronger gradient of a higher adaptive peak.

In order to show the contributions of additional loci to the mean fitness of a population, we would have to construct a multidimensional plot. For example, if we were to consider the effects of genes at 1,000 loci, a plot of this situation would require 1,001 dimensions with $\bar{W}$ representing one of them. To further complicate matters, such a plot is likely to include a vast number of adaptive gene combinations. To illustrate, take the case of two alleles at each of 1,000 loci. Here, there are $3^{1,000}$ possible genotypes. Even if only, say, 1% of these are favorable under present conditions, this would still result in an astronomical number of "peaks" on the 1,001-dimensional surface. Since such plots are impossible to visualize, Wright has done the next best thing by representing them as a contour map in which contour lines connect gene combinations of equal fitness. Some representative diagrams are shown in Figure 13.7. Parts (a) and (b) illustrate the effects of opposing mutation and selection pressures on the mean fitness of a large population. Being large, the population will tend to occupy a single peak, although the extent of the peak that it occupies will depend on the amount of genetic variability that it maintains. Thus, an

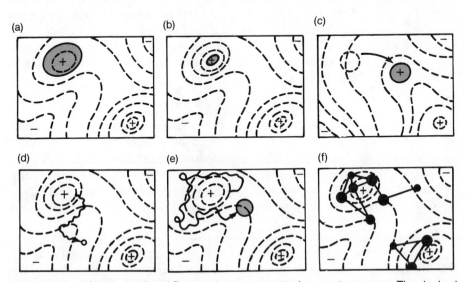

Figure 13.7.   Multidimensional fitness plots represented as contour maps. The dashed lines connect gene combinations of equal fitness. See text for details.

increase in mutation rates would cause the population to spread over a larger surface due to an increase in the number of ill-adapted genotypes. The opposite is true for an increase in selection intensity.

Part (c) illustrates the effects of environmental change. What was once a fitness peak may now be a valley. If the population contains sufficient genetic variability, it will respond to these selective changes and move up a neighboring peak. This is then the primary mode of evolutionary change in large populations.

In part (d), we observe the consequences of a small population size. In this case, nonselective changes in gene frequencies move the population down the slope into a neighboring valley. Although the population may enter the gradient of a higher adaptive peak, the random fixation and loss of genes has so depleted genetic variation that it is incapable of responding to new selective pressures. The end result is extinction.

Finally, parts (e) and (f) show an effective means of moving from peak to peak without the necessity of environmental change. In part (e), the population is intermediate in size so that both random and systematic forces are assumed to act. In this case, the population might wander down the slope through random changes in gene frequencies but still remain in the vicinity of an adaptive ridge due to relatively strong selective pressures. It could then accidentally encounter the gradient of a higher peak. Since progress is very slow, a more favorable condition is shown in part (f) where the population is assumed to be divided into numerous demes of intermediate size with migration between them. All evolutionary forces including migration are now acting on the subdivided population. Thus, progress is considerably more rapid with different demes now coming under the influence of different peaks. This increase in rate is also predicted by the fundamental theorem of natural selection. To illustrate, let $\bar{V}_{\text{II}}$ represent the average variance in fitness for all groups (demes), and V_{II} designate the variance of group means. Since the total variance in fitness is the sum of the within-group and between-group variances, the total increase in mean fitness, $\Delta\bar{W}$, is then, approximately,

$$\Delta\bar{W} = [\bar{V}_{\text{II}} + V_{\text{II}}]/\bar{W}$$

The increase in heterogeneity afforded by subdivision into local populations, as expressed in the $V_{\text{II}}/\bar{W}$ term in the above equation, thus enhances the overall rate of evolutionary change. When the environment is itself changing in time and space, the variability residing in the gene pools of the semi-isolated groups offers greater survival opportunity and provides a mechanism for rapid evolutionary progress, resulting in the occupancy of all available adaptive peaks.

The maximum principle with variable fitness.   The adaptive field model, as presented in the preceding section, is based on the proposition that selection will always act to maximize the mean fitness of the population. This concept is derived in part from the expression: $\Delta q = (pq/2\bar{W})d\bar{W}/dq$, which shows that, for a single locus with two alleles, Δq becomes zero when $d\bar{W}/dq = 0$; that is, when $\bar{W}$ is maximum. Although the expression is useful when applied to cases with constant relative fitness, it does not hold when fitness is a function of gene frequency, as in the event of frequency-dependent selection. This point of exception can be demonstrated by deriving a more general expression for Δq. To do so, first express the mean fitness in general terms as $\bar{W} = \Sigma W_i f_i$ where f_i is the frequency of the ith genotype and W_i is the genotype's adaptive value. Thus, in the more specific instance of two alleles (B,b), $\Sigma W_i f_i = W_1(1-q)^2 + 2W_2 q(1-q) + W_3 q^2 = W_B(1-q) + W_b q$, and $\Sigma W_i df_i/dq = 2[(W_2 p + W_3 q) - (W_1 p + W_2 q)] = 2(W_b - W_B)$. Since, with two alleles, the change in gene frequency can always be expressed as $\Delta q = q(W_b - \bar{W})/\bar{W} = pq(W_b - W_B)/\bar{W}$, regardless of fitness values, the general expression for Δq becomes

$$\Delta q = (pq/2\bar{W}) \Sigma \ W_i df_i/dq$$
$$= \tfrac{1}{2}pq\Sigma(W_i/\bar{W})df_i/dq \tag{13.25}$$

Note that Δq will be zero only when $\Sigma W_i df_i/dq = 0$. Its relationship to $d\bar{W}/dq$ is readily seen by expressing $\bar{W} = \Sigma W_i f_i$ in terms of its derivative. We get

$$d\bar{W}/dq = \Sigma W_i df_i/dq + \Sigma f_i dW_i/dq$$
$$= 2\bar{W}(\Delta q/pq) + \overline{dW/dq} \tag{13.26}$$

where $\overline{dW/dq}$ is the mean change in W at a particular value of q. Observe that $\overline{dW/dq} = 0$ when genotypic fitnesses are constant and independent of gene frequency. If we consider only selection effects, this means that the value of $\bar{W}$ is maximum when $\Delta q = 0$. This is in contrast to frequency-dependent selection in which $\Delta q = 0$ when $d\bar{W}/dq = \overline{dW/dq}$. Hence, a stationary point with regard to q will not correspond necessarily to a peak on the adaptive surface as defined by $\bar{W}$. To illustrate, consider the following example of a completely dominant trait showing frequency-dependent adaptive values:

Genotype	f_i	W_i	df_i/dq
$B-$	$1 - q^2$	$1 + s/(1 - q^2)$	$- 2q$
bb	q^2	$1 + s/q^2$	$+ 2q$

In this case,

$$\bar{W} = 1 + 2s$$

Hence, $\bar{W}$ is independent of gene frequency so that $d\bar{W}/dq = 0$ for all values of q. This means that $\overline{dW/dq}$ and $\Sigma W_i df_i/dq$ will have the same absolute value, differing only in sign. We can compute this value as follows:

$$W_i df_i/dq = 2q[1 + s/q^2] - 2q[1 + s/(1-q^2)]$$
$$= 2sq[1/q^2 - 1/(1-q^2)]$$

Whereupon,

$$\Delta q = spq^2[(1 - 2q^2)/q^2(1 - q^2)]/(1 + 2s)$$

It is, therefore, apparent that selection will move the population towards an equilibrium at $\hat{q} = \sqrt{1/2}$, even without a change in adaptive topography.

Given the preceding difficulties, the question arises as to how we might alter existing theory to accommodate frequency dependence and still retain the general usefulness and conceptual appeal of the adaptive field model. Wright has addressed the problem by expressing fitness in terms of a fitness function, $F(W/\bar{W})$, defined in such a way that

$$dF(W/\bar{W})/dq = \Sigma(W_i/\bar{W})df_i/dq$$

Hence, $\Delta q = \frac{1}{2}pqdF(W/\bar{W})/dq$ and is zero when $F(W/\bar{W})$ is at its maximum value. Also note that $dF(W/\bar{W})/dq = d(\ln \bar{W})/dq$ under conditions of constant relative fitness. The computation of $F(W/\bar{W})$ can be shown by means of the preceding example. In this case, $dF(W/\bar{W})/dq = 2sq[1/q^2 - 1/(1 - q^2)]$. The fitness function can then be obtained from the integral of this expression. We get

$$F(W/\bar{W}) = C + (s)\ln(q^2)(1-q^2)$$

where C is a constant. A plot of this expression and one of its counterpart, ln $\bar{W}$, are shown in Figure 13.8. Observe that an equilibrium develops when $F(W/\bar{W})$ is at its maximum value. It is also apparent from this example that $F(W/\bar{W})$ and ln $\bar{W}$ (or $\bar{W}$) can, at times, be extremely different.

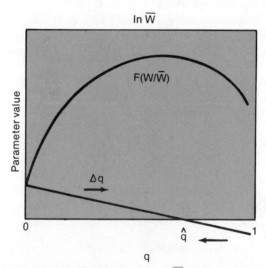

Figure 13.8.   Plot of the relationships between ln $\bar{W}$ and q and $F(W/\bar{W})$ and q for the model presented in the text.

GROUP SELECTION

All of our earlier discussions concerning evolutionary adaptation have dealt with selection operating on individual organisms. Selection is not restricted to individuals, however, but can also act on groups, such as families, demes, and even entire species, and is then referred to as group selection. This differential reproduction of whole groups, like that of individual genotypes, may either give rise to an equilibrium or otherwise lead to the replacement of one group by another as a result of the higher fitness of its members. It is this latter possibility that concerns us here.

One of the first attempts at providing a mechanism for group selection was that of Wright using his adaptive field model. He envisioned a form of *interdemic selection* in which selection would occur between demes for the highest adaptive peak. This is illustrated by way of the contour map in Figure 13.9. Note that once a deme encounters a high point on the adaptive surface, it will increase in numbers. Then, due to its larger size, it will tend to send out a disproportionate number of migrants, so altering the genetic composition of neighboring demes that the entire population is drawn into the field of influence of this higher adaptive peak. Thus, according to Wright, group selection plays a supplementary role to individual selection by increasing the rate at which adaptive gene combinations are spread throughout the entire population. Other concepts of group selection have since been proposed. One that has led to considerable controversy is the theory of Wynne-Edwards (1962) on the evolution of cooperative and interferential behavioral mechanisms which help to stabilize population growth and give rise to self-regulation (see Chapter 9). To Wynne-Edwards, individual selection must always lead to a maximization of fecundity and, since the mechanisms which he proposed entailed a self-curtailment of reproductive effort at optimal densities, the development of such mechanisms required that the short-term interests of individuals be overridden by the long-

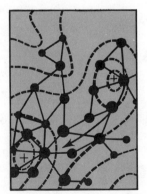

Figure 13.9.   Multidimensional fitness plot showing interdemic selection. See text for details.

term welfare of the group. This conflict between individual and group selection meant that genes for self-regulation can only be established through the success and failure of whole groups. Consider the following example. Suppose that without these regulatory mechanisms, a population will tend to fluctuate wildly about the equilibrium level set by food supply. Those demes which are characterized by high individual fertilities will contribute most to instability and have a large chance of going extinct. On the other hand, demes which possess genes for social mechanisms which can lower individual fertility, and thus lower the intrinsic growth rate, may persist and ultimately fix the genes in the population. Since Wynne-Edwards offered no genetic model to validate his views on group selection, it was left to others to analyze the evolutionary consequences of group extinction. The first major efforts along these lines were made by Levins (1970) and by Boorman and Levitt (1973). Both developed models which dealt with the evolution of genes responsible for so-called altruistic traits. These are characteristics that are beneficial to the group but individually disadvantageous, such as the self-sacrificing behavior of a worker bee in defense of its hive. The models differed in the assumed structure of the subdivided population. For instance, in Levin's model, a population of some opportunist species is assumed to occupy an area consisting of a number of habitable sites. At any moment, certain of these sites are colonized while others go extinct. The end result is a breeding structure maintained below the saturation level by a balance between extinction and migration. In contrast, Boorman and Levitt visualized a species structure consisting of a large, stable central population which serves as a continued source for numerous smaller, semi-isolated populations at the periphery of the range. Due to their small size and less favorable habitats, the marginal populations are characterized by comparatively high extinction rates. Despite differences in assumed breeding structure, both models confirm that group selection for altruistic characters is a highly improbable event. For it to occur requires numerous demes with very high extinction rates, comparable in magnitude to opposing individual selection rates. What is more, such selection is least likely in large, stable populations in which the social behavior cited by Wynne-Edwards as being responsible for population control is most highly developed.

      How, then, do truly altruistic traits evolve? One mode of selection generally believed responsible for these traits is *kin selection*. This is a form of group selection where the group, or unit of selection, is a kinship, not an entire deme as in the case of interdemic selection; and the favored individuals are close relatives (e.g., progeny, sibs, first cousins). Hamilton (1963, 1964) has shown that the effectiveness of kin selection depends directly on the degree of relatedness of individuals as measured by the coefficient of relationship, r_{IJ} (i.e., the relative proportion of genes identical by descent among relatives—see equation (6.9)). More specifically, if k is the ratio of the gain in fitness among the recipients of an altruistic act to the loss in fitness by the altruists, then an altruist gene will increase in frequency in the population if k exceeds the reciprocal of the average coefficient of relationship for all relatives involved. That is,

$$k > 1/\bar{r}_{IJ}$$

Suppose, for example, that an individual dies without leaving an offspring as a result of some altruistic act. Assume, however, that because of the act, the fitness of a sib is quadrupled. Since the advantage gained by the sib is more than twice the disadvantage incurred by the altruist ($k = 4$ in this case), and because, in the absence of inbreeding, sibs share half their genes in common ($\bar{r}_{IJ} = \frac{1}{2}$), the sib that dies actually increases its genetic contribution to the next generation by virtue of this altruistic act. It is then possible for the altruist gene to spread through the population. The model can be readily extended to effects on more distant relatives. It is easily shown, for example, that the advantage gained by half-sibs should be at least four times the disadvantage incurred by the altruist for the gene to spread, the advantage for cousins at least eight times, etc.

The extreme development of kin selection occurs among many social insects, particularly the Hymenoptera. In honey bees, for example, males are haploid and females are diploid. Consequently, any cross $B_1B_2 \times B_3$ can give rise to two kinds of female offspring, B_1B_3 and B_2B_3, with equal likelihood. Thus, a female parent and a daughter share half their genes in common ($r_{IJ} = \frac{1}{2}$). In contrast, the fraction of genes shared in common by sisters will be $r_{IJ} = (1)\text{Prob}(B_1B_3 \text{ and } B_1B_3) + (1)\text{Prob}(B_2B_3 \text{ and } B_2B_3) + (\frac{1}{2})\text{Prob}(B_1B_3$ and $B_2B_3) = (1)(\frac{1}{4}) + (1)(\frac{1}{4}) + (\frac{1}{2})(\frac{1}{2}) = 3/4$. A female bee can, therefore, make a greater genetic contribution to the next generation by becoming a worker and taking care of the queen's eggs (her sisters) than by producing offspring herself. Presumably, females will continue to develop into workers as long as the amount of time and energy spent in raising their sisters does not exceed four-thirds the cost of raising their own progeny.

SPECIATION

As pointed out in the foregoing discussions, the production of variation and the action of evolutionary forces within a population affect its relationship to neighboring demes. An important consequence of this interplay among local breeding populations is the evolutionary process of speciation.

There are three major modes of species formation. One is termed *phyletic evolution*, in which genetic changes can be visualized as occurring throughout the species range, eventually resulting in the development of a single new (successional) species. Since the entire collection of interbreeding groups is believed to evolve as a single unit, phyletic evolution does not increase the number of species in existence. A second important mode of species formation is the process of *primary speciation*. This is responsible for the splitting of one species into two or more contemporary species, and can occur when populations within a species diverge genetically in response to different environmental conditions. Finally, the third mode of species development is *secondary speciation*. This is an important evolutionary process in plants, which occurs through hybridization and fusion of two existing species to form a single interbreeding unit. In the discussion that follows, the term speciation, unless specified otherwise, is taken to mean primary speciation, or the proliferation of species, Moreover, the biological species concept is implied in which species are defined as population systems that are reproductively isolated from one another through genetic barriers to gene flow. This necessarily restricts application of the concepts to sexually reproducing organisms.

Races, semispecies, and species.   Species are usually composed of many demes having the potential for gene exchange. If the species habitat is at all heterogeneous, these local populations will diverge as each specifically adapts to its particular locale. This process of local differentiation can result in the development of geographic races. These are regional cohorts of local populations which differ in the frequencies of a number of genes. Since race formation is simply a result of genetic divergence under different geographic conditions, a discrete stage of differentiation where two populations are suddenly separated into distinct races does not exist. Instead, there occurs a gradual transition from local populations through microgeographic and macrogeographic races.

Just as the process of racial divergence is continuous with time, so is it usually continuous over a species range at any one moment. Since races are not genetically separated enough to severely restrict gene flow, local populations along a linear range can show progressive changes in gene frequency. The result can be a gradual change in the incidence of a given trait over the range. Such a character gradient is termed a *cline*. Where clinal variation exists, racial demarcation will be rather arbitrary and largely a matter of convenience in studying particular traits.

The so-called ecogeographic rules (e.g., Bergmann's rule, Chapter 7) pointing out the association of morphological traits with climate, suggest that geographic variation has an adaptive significance. However, blood groups in humans show wide geographic variation but appear to have no adaptive value. Different traits probably show racial divergence due to different combinations of the forces of natural selection and genetic drift. The importance of these evolutionary factors in determining variation patterns will be discussed in detail in Chapter 14.

A good example of racial variation involves the third chromosome gene arrangements in *Drosophila pseudoobscura* populations living at different elevations in the Sierra Nevada mountains at Yosemite. A continuous gradient in the relative proportions of the *ST*, *AR*, and *CH* chromosome arrangements with altitude has been discovered, as shown in Figure 13.10. Although it seems most probable that this gradient is due to selective pressures, the environmental

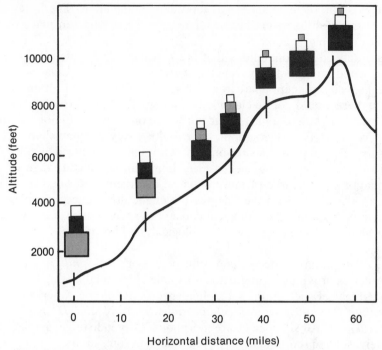

Figure 13.10. Altitudinal variation in the relative proportions of the *ST* (hatched), *AR* (solid), and *CH* (open) third chromosome arrangements in *Drosophila pseudoobscura* populations in Yosemite. The size of a square indicates the relative proportion of that chromosome. (From Th. Dobzhansky. 1948. Genetics 33: 158.)

variables remain obscure. Note that since localities differ only with respect to the proportion of the different arrangements, it would be impossible to categorize a single fly into any one racial group. Confusion over the use of the term *race* arises not because racial differences are not real—they are—but because categorization is necessarily an attempt to impose discontinuities, which are artificial in an evolutionary sense, on a naturally continuous scheme.

The fate of races is variable. Gene flow might keep them at racial status indefinitely, or they could merge back into a single population. Different parts of the species range may be occupied by various static or transitional forms. If divergence proceeds to the point where partial barriers develop to gene flow, semispecies are formed. Semispecies may then complete the development of reproductive isolation and become separate species.

Since the biological species concept involves dynamic systems which are constantly changing, difficulties arise in applying it in practice, especially in the identification of species by taxonomists. As a matter of convenience, the taxonomic species is a discrete category of classification, delineated by morphological features; whereas the biological species represents the final stage in the acquisition of mechanisms of reproductive isolation. The latter admits of, and in fact, fully expects intermediates; the former has no place for such forms. For example, much confusion has arisen over the term *sibling species*. These are defined as populations that are morphologically identical but completely isolated reproductively. Such species do not have a special place in the biological species concept apart from full species. On the basis of appearance, however, these would not be classified as separate species. Another term with special meaning to taxonomists, but not as it concerns the biological species concept, is *subspecies*. Geographic races with easily distinguishable characteristics that aid classification are sometimes formally recognized as subspecies, although this term does not necessarily imply an advanced stage of racial differentiation. The degree of morphological divergence between races is not necessarily correlated with their degree of genetic divergence as it pertains to reproductive isolation. The biological concept of species incorporates not only visible traits, but also physiological, ecological, and behavioral characteristics as well.

The distribution of species and semispecies of *Drosophila* in Central and South America provides an interesting example of the relationship between the final two stages of speciation. Six sibling species live in the American tropics: *D. willistoni, D. paulistorum, D. equinoxialis, D. tropicalis, D. insularis*, and *D. pavlovskiana*. All six species are morphologically indistinguishable, but are completely isolated reproductively, even though in some areas, as many as four of them exist within one another's dispersal range. Extensive studies of *D. paulistorum* show it to be a complex of six morphologically identical semispecies which exhibit incomplete reproductive isolation, occasionally interbreeding to form viable hybrids. The hybrid females are fertile, the males sterile. It is clear that the semispecies of *D. paulistorum* have diverged less extensively than the six sibling species of the *willistoni* group.

In nature three main species distributions are found. Sympatric species are those whose habitats overlap extensively, so that from purely spatial considerations, gene flow is possible. Sympatry is, therefore, the best criterion of true species status, as intrinsic reproductive isolating mechanisms must be fully developed to prevent interbreeding. Allopatric species are those whose ranges do not overlap, usually because of separation by some geographic barrier. Species status in this case is more difficult to ascertain, since the populations could be reproductively isolated by extrinsic barriers to gene flow, rather than through the acquisition of one or more intrinsic mechanisms. Finally, species can be distributed parapatrically in which case a partial, often quite narrow, zone of overlap characterizes their dispersal ranges.

Reproductive isolating mechanisms.   With respect to the stage at which they operate, there are two broad classes of reproductive isolating mechanisms, postzygotic and prezygotic. Postzygotic mechanisms develop as accidental byproducts of the genetic divergence that occurs when populations adapt to differing habitats. As the populations become more dissimilar, it becomes less likely that their genes can act harmoniously in a hybrid. Since the formation of an unfit hybrid is wasteful, however, the speciating populations should begin to undergo selection directed against interpopulation matings. Prezygotic isolating mechanisms will then evolve. Selection for prezygotic reproductive isolation requires sympatry of the differentiating populations; the degree to which reproductive isolation develops and spreads over the species range depends on the degree of contact between the populations. This form of character displacement is not expected to be achieved to the same degree in various speciating populations.

Little is known of the exact genetic events that occur during the acquisition of reproductive isolating mechanisms. Since their development is not always correlated with morphological change, mating tests often have to be performed to detect such isolation. However, many populations that are reproductively isolated in nature interbreed quite well in the laboratory, complicating efforts to study the speciation process. It is known that speciation usually requires the acquisition of at least two different isolating mechanisms, since operation of each is a matter of degree.

There are five main prezygotic mechanisms, each of which acts to impede the formation of interspecific hybrids:

1. *Ecological (habitat) isolation* can occur if species occupy different habitats to which they have become specifically adapted for survival and reproduction. For example, in the Eastern United States sympatric species of oak are adapted to different soil types. The scarlet oak (*Quercus coccinea*) prefers wet, poorly drained areas, whereas the black oak (*Q. velutina*) lives on drier, well-drained soils. In certain man-made intermediate habitats, hybridization between the two oak species is observed, so that ecological isolation is apparently the major factor keeping these species separate in nature.

2. *Temporal isolation* results when the members of different populations become sexually active at different seasons or times of the day. A case in point is the partial seasonal isolation that separates the toads *Bufo americanus* and *B. fowleri*. The former breeds earlier in the spring than the latter, although there is some overlap in breeding times. Isolation is reinforced by habitat preference, *B. americanus* favoring forested areas, *B. fowleri* grasslands. Only in man-made habitats does hybridization occur.

3. *Ethological or sexual isolation* is the weakening of sexual attraction between females and males of different species, through disturbances of the search-court-mate ritual. It is thought to be the most efficient mechanism for reproductive isolation in sympatric animal species. Behavioral isolation can operate in a variety of ways, including species-specific sex pheromones, specific courtship displays, and auditory signals (calls), all of which function in mate recognition.

4. *Mechanical isolation* involves differences among animal species in genitalia size and shape, which can impede interspecific copulation and sperm transfer, and the specificity of flower structure for a particular pollination vector.

A striking example of a vector-specific flower is found in the beard tongues of the Western United States. The scarlet bugler (*Penstemon centranthifolius*) has bright red flowers with tubular corollas. In contrast, the mountain *Penstemon* (*P. grinnellii*) has blue flowers with large, widely gaping corollas. Since hummingbirds perceive red and infrared wavelengths best, whereas bees see best in the blue and ultraviolet ranges, the combination of floral structure and color adapts the species to quite different pollinators. Large carpenter bees serve *grinnellii*, while the long, slender beaks of hummingbirds pollinate *centranthifolius*, maintaining reproductive isolation between these species in nature.

5. *Gametic isolation* refers to a gametic incompatibility between species. The spermatozoa or pollen of one species might be inviable in the sexual ducts of another, as occurs in one *Drosophila* species, or female and male gametes may simply fail to attract one another. The latter may be important in some marine animals (e.g., sea urchins) where gametes are discharged separately into the water. Fertilization then depends on chemical recognition between gametes of the same species.

Postzygotic reproductive isolating mechanisms reduce the fitness of hybrids:

1. *Hybrid inviability* is simply death of the hybrid before sexual maturity, usually at an early stage of development. It appears to involve abnormalities in the nuclear-cytoplasmic interactions that occur following gastrulation, when nuclear gene activity begins to be expressed.

2. *Hybrid sterility* is the failure of hybrids to produce functional gametes. The term *segregational sterility* is used to include any abnormalities in meiotic synapsis or segregation, or genic imbalance in the gametes. This form of hybrid sterility is more common in plants, and can be readily detected when spores fail to vegetate into gametophytes. The other form of hybrid sterility, *developmental sterility,* is more common in animals and involves genic imbalance adversely affecting development of the gonads of the hybrid. In plants, application of a spindle poison (e.g., colchicine) distinguishes between the two forms of sterility, since doubling of the hybrid's chromosome number will increase its fertility only if the sterility is segregational. Developmental hybrid sterility and hybrid inviability are thought to be the consequence of selection for different developmental sequences, metabolic rates, and temperature optima during the course of adaptation to different environmental regimes. Segregational sterility is the indirect result of the establishment of a succession of new chromosome arrangements during speciation.

3. *Hybrid breakdown* refers to lowered viability or fertility among the descendants of a hybrid. The recombination of parental genes that occurs during meiosis in a hybrid can give rise to genotypes of reduced fitness. *Drosophila pseudoobscura* and *D. persimilis,* for example, can be made to

hybridize in the laboratory. The F_1 are fully vigorous, the females being completely fertile and the males sterile. Backcrosses of the hybrid females to males of either parental species give offspring whose general viability and fertility are low.

The reproductive isolation of natural populations of *D. pseudoobscura* and *D. persimilis* provides an excellent example of the combination of mechanisms often required to insure a block to gene flow between the species. Two pre-zygotic and two postzygotic mechanisms separate these species (Dobzhansky, 1951). Ecological isolation, with respect to temperature and humidity; temporal isolation, with respect to the time of day when mating occurs; sterility of hybrid males (developmental); and hybrid breakdown all act together to completely isolate the gene pools of these sibling species in nature.

Modes of speciation.   The overall process of speciation can be divided into three successive steps: (1) the production of genetic variation within a popu-lation (gene or chromosome mutation, recombination), (2) the establishment of a variant gene combination in a derivative population, and (3) the maintenance of genetic differences between the populations by reproductive isolation. Of present concern is the establishment of the last step, namely the various means by which reproductive isolating mechanisms can be acquired. Although much has been written on the subject, the models that have been developed are still rather crude and incomplete in the sense that the genetic and environmental factors that determine the mode of speciation employed have not been defined well enough to allow prediction of the speciation course of any population.

The most widely accepted model is allopatric or geographic speciation. In this case, populations become separated spatially, so that their respective mem-bers are beyond one another's dispersal ranges. Most commonly, a geographic barrier to migration is envisioned. The divergence of the geographically sep-arated populations cannot then be countered by gene flow between them. As a result of the differing selection pressures characterizing their environments, the populations diverge genetically. Races acquire postzygotic isolating mech-anisms and evolve into allopatrically distributed semispecies. If ever-changing environmental pressures allow migration of the semispecies back into the range of the ancestral species, some hybridization will take place, and the hybrids, being less fit than their parents, will be selected against. Prezygotic isolating mechanisms will, therefore, evolve, to prevent hybrid formation. The allopatric scheme of speciation is diagrammed in Figure 13.11A.

Allopatric speciation involves a gradual succession of small changes, re-quiring a relatively long period of time and the deterministic force of natural selection. No special genetic differences (such as species-specific mutations) are required. Cummulative adaptive changes at structural and regulatory gene loci occur, without extensive reorganization of gene pools. Allopatric speciation

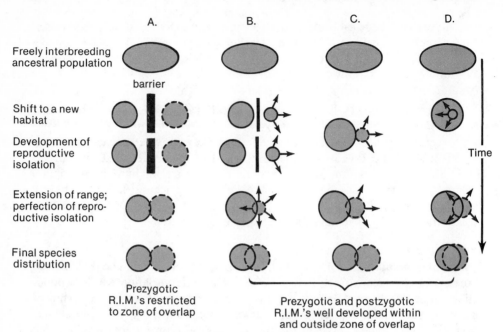

Figure 13.11. Diagrammatic representation of basic speciation modes. The models are distinguished by the stage at which reproductive isolation is first acquired. In allopatric speciation (A and B), reproductive isolating mechanisms are acquired after the shift to a new habitat. In parapatric speciation (C), they are acquired during the adaptation to a new habitat, and in sympatric speciation (D), they must be acquired prior to the habitat shift. (Adpated from Bush, 1975.)

appears to have been the most common method of speciation, applying to many mammalian species and birds, certain reptiles and amphibians, and many fish.

A variation of the allopatric scheme, involving marginal isolates and a combination of selection and genetic drift in a "founder effect" has been proposed by Simpson (1944) and discussed by Grant (1963). In quantum speciation (Fig. 13.11B), a small group of individuals from the margin of the ancestral species range migrates into a new habitat, becoming spatially separated from the main population so that gene flow cannot occur. A marginal isolate is thought to be more likely to have a flexible gene combination that could successfully invade a new habitat, being less strongly adapted to the ancestral species range than individuals at its center. Genetic drift will also influence the genetic composition of the founder population. The result is a group of migrants with a genetic composition somewhat different from that of the main species population. Inbreeding within this small group of migrants further enhances divergence from the ancestral group and permits selection for favorable homozygous genotypes that are precisely adapted to the new habitat. The major distinguishing feature of this form of allopatric speciation is that it occurs rapidly, major genic divergence coming about through the very composition of the founder population. For this reason, Mayr has termed this process a "genetic revolution." Genetic revolution offers an explanation for the absence from the fossil record of common ancestral species for higher taxonomic groups, since major evolutionary changes would occur too rapidly to be distributed on a widespread geographical basis.

Quantum speciation involving population flush-crash cycles has been proposed by Carson (1975) to explain the origins of the diverse species of *Drosophila* on the Hawaiian Islands. These species have evolved in the relatively short period of time since the formation of the islands, and exhibit few intermediate semispecies. Carson proposes that there exist two kinds of genetic variation— a recombinationally open form, which freely recombines in meiosis and is directly subject to change by selection, and a recombinationally closed form, the elements of which cannot be segregated into a viable, fit organism under the normal constraints of selection pressures for a highly adapted, genetically buffered population. The closed form of variability would be composed of coadapted linked gene complexes (supergenes), whose elements interact to determine fitness, so that only a genetic revolution could alter the genetic composition and fitness of a group. Such a revolution could occur if a small group of individuals (perhaps only one fertile female) enters a habitat unoccupied by potential competitors, and rapidly increases its population size and genetic diversity under the relaxation of natural selection (flush part of cycle). Novel epistatic gene combinations could arise during this period. Eventually, the population would probably crash, and if selection is then resumed, a new coadapted gene complex could be selected for. This mode of speciation appears especially well suited to explain the development of species in unoccupied areas, such as islands.

A second model for speciation is *parapatric speciation*, where species evolve even as populations overlap in continuous clines. This model is similar to quantum speciation in that a founder effect is involved, but the small group adapting to a new habitat remains in constant contact with the ancestral population (Fig. 13.11C).

Parapatric speciation is postulated to occur when chromosome rearrangements have a selective advantage in a certain portion, for example a margin, of a species range. Since no spatial isolation separates the variant group, its differentiation proceeds through a delicate balance between a high degree of inbreeding and local selection for the aberration, and selection against the chromosomally heterozygous hybrids in the region of overlap. Divergence to the species stage can probably only occur if the founders are from the periphery of the ancestral range, so that the new genotypes will not be totally swamped by the low fitness of the hybrids. For this same reason, the model may apply only to organisms with low vagility. It is important to note that the parapatric model requires that mechanisms of reproductive isolation arise simultaneously with, rather than as a by-product of, adaptation to a new habitat.

Parapatric speciation has been postulated to have occurred in some snails, fossorial rodents, flightless insects, and some plants. White (1968) has extensively studied speciation in the Australian morabine grasshoppers and has found a chromosomally differentiated complex of species distributed parapatrically, with some hybridization occurring in the extremely narrow zones of overlap. He has postulated a stasipatric mode of speciation for these grasshoppers, in which a reproductively isolated chromosome rearrangement spreads along an advancing front through the existing range of a species. According to this model, the new species gradually takes over whatever area it can from the parental species, the displacement continuing until a population is encountered that is better adapted to local conditions. This stops the spread and gives a parapatric distribution of species. Although stasipatric speciation might be possible if an ancestral species inhabits a patchy environment, for reasons noted previously, it would still seem necessary to initiate the process with a marginal group. Once that group establishes itself on the periphery of the parental species range, it might then be able to spread inward, displacing the old species in places.

Factors such as chromosome rearrangements, that can simultaneously confer both a selective advantage and a degree of reproductive isolation, are essential to parapatric speciation. Darlington (1940) and Stebbins (1950) have proposed that extensive chromosome reorganization is based largely on divergent selection for supergenes favored when populations enter new habitats. Although there is some question as to whether enough chromosomal divergence can be expected within a single species range to bring about hybrid sterility, effective barriers to gene flow could arise as the product of a succession of environmental shifts accompanied by rapid genetic reorganization. In this vein, several modes of hybrid speciation, common in plants but rare in animals, have been discussed by Grant (1971). Hybrid speciation refers to the production among the offspring of a hybrid of true-breeding genotypes that are reproductively isolated from the parental species, the hybrid, and other progeny from the hybrid. Two such means of speciation are recombinational speciation and allopolyploidy. Recombinational speciation has been observed among the progeny of experimental plant hybrids, but its frequency in nature is not clear. The process can be illustrated by means of a hybrid of genetic constitution $T_1t_1T_2t_2$, where the subscripts refer to independently assorting chromosome translocations, in heterozygous condition. Of those structurally homozygous offspring classes that result from selfing the translocation heterozygote, two ($T_1T_1T_2T_2$ and $t_1t_1t_2t_2$) are like the parents of the hybrid, but the other two ($T_1T_1t_2t_2$ and $t_1t_1T_2T_2$) represent new, fertile gene complexes, separated from one another and from the parent by a weak segregational barrier. If several such translocations occurred, the barrier to gene flow could be quite strong. In theory, recombination of any factors (chromosomal aberrations or genic sterility factors) responsible for postzygotic isolation could lead to speciation.

Union of unreduced gametes following complete nondisjunction in meiosis in an interspecific hybrid yields allotetraploid offspring. These types, being double diploids, can be fertile. Due to a chromosome sterility barrier (formation of sterile triploids), the allotetraploid will be genetically isolated from the hybrid. Particularly in the case of segmental alloploids (those having partial homology between diploid genome complements), polyploidy can be expected to enhance a population's ability to exploit diverse habitats. Production of new gene combinations by intergenomic crossing over and tetrasomic segregation, diversification of enzyme function through an increased variety of multimeric protein subunit associations, and the ability of some polyploids to differentially regulate their genomes with respect to diploid versus tetraploid gene expression, are several means by which polyploids can generate additional variability not possessed by their diploid progenitors. Allopolyploidy is the most widespread cytogenetic process of speciation in higher plants, where as many as 47% of angiosperm species and 95% of pteridophyte species (ferns) are polyploids (Grant, 1971).

The third major model of speciation is similar to the parapatric one in that no geographic isolation is involved, and is termed *sympatric speciation*. In this case, reproductive isolating mechanisms arise prior to differentiation through habitat selection, and chromosome rearrangements are rarely involved. Radical differences in habitat preference between populations are envisioned, so that their final distribution can be broadly overlapping (Fig. 13.11D).

Sympatric speciation is a definite possibility from a theoretical standpoint. Mathematical models based on selection in a heterogeneous environment (Basykin, 1965; Maynard-Smith, 1966) show that in the presence of sufficiently intense selection coefficients for different niches, some degree of assortative mating, and an absence of heterozygote advantage, reproductive isolation can be achieved. However, verification of the theory has been difficult, since it is virtually impossible to distinguish sympatric speciation as the primary agent of divergence from secondary sympatry following an allopatric divergence.

Sympatric speciation has possibly occurred in the species *Drosophila pachea*, which inhabits the Sonoran Desert of North America. This fly is completely dependent on a sterol found only in the cactus *Lophocereus schottii* for its reproduction. Interestingly, this sterol is toxic to the larvae of other *Drosophila* species. No chromosomal structural changes distinguish *D. pachea*; this species has achieved complete ecologically based reproductive isolation by only the few gene changes needed to detoxify and metabolize this chemical.

Sympatric speciation may have occurred in the most abundant of all eukaryotes, namely the phytophagous and zoophagous parasites and parasitoids. Most parasites are monophagous, and selection of a host and mate are coupled, accomplished by chemical means, and under the control of just a few genes. Hence, variation arising in a population can yield quick adaptation to a new host. It seems reasonable to assume that shifts in host specificity will most likely occur if the old and new hosts are together within the normal dispersal range of the parasites.

SOLVED EXAMPLE PROBLEMS

Genetic Effects of Subdivision

1. Consider a species population subdivided into two demes of equal size in which the frequencies of the genotypes (*BB*, *Bb*, *bb*) are (0.04, 0.32, 0.64) in deme 1 and (0.64, 0.32, 0.04) in deme 2. (a) Determine the average genotype frequencies for the demes and compare them with the frequencies expected if both groups were consolidated into one random-mating population. (b) Compute the variance of gene frequency in the subdivided population.

   solution   The average genotype frequencies are 0.34(*BB*), 0.32(*Bb*), and 0.34(*bb*). The frequencies expected in a random-mating population consisting of both groups would be $\bar{p}^2 = 0.25$, $2\bar{p}\bar{q} = 0.50$, and $\bar{q}^2 = 0.25$. Since the frequency of heterozygotes in the subdivided population is $H = 0.32 = 0.50 - 2V_p$, the variance of p will be $V_p = (0.50 - 0.32)/2 = 0.09$.

Subdivision and Genetic Drift

2. Assume a population that is subdivided into a large number of demes, all of size N. How would the frequency of heterozygotes change in the subdivided population if all of the demes were to undergo exponential growth?

   solution   Let $N = N_o e^{rt}$ represent the time-dependent change in N within each of the many demes. We know from equation (13.5) that $dH/Hdt = -1/2N$. Therefore, substituting for N and rearranging the resulting expression yields $d(\ln H) = -(1/2N_o)e^{-rt}dt$. Upon integration, we get $H_t = H_o \exp\left[-\dfrac{1}{2rN_o}(1 - e^{-rt})\right]$. Note that H_t will initially decrease as $(1 - e^{-rt})$ increases. However, an equilibrium is eventually established with $H = H_o e^{-1/2rN_o}$.

Subdivision and Migration

3. A population with gene frequencies of $p = q = \frac{1}{2}$ is subdivided into a large number of demes, each of size 100. If migration occurs between demes at a rate of $M = 0.01$, what will be the variance in gene frequency at equilibrium? Between what two values will approximately 68% of the gene frequencies be found?

   solution   Using equation (13.14), $V_p = (\frac{1}{2})(\frac{1}{2})/[4(100)(0.01) + 1] = 0.05$. Assuming an approximately normal distribution of gene frequencies, 68% correspond to the values within the range of $\bar{p} \pm \sqrt{V_p} = 0.500 \pm 0.224$. Thus, the desired range is from 0.276 to 0.724.

Breeding Structure of Populations

4. Using equations (13.16) and (13.17), compare the degree of local differentiation expected for populations dispersed in a continuum along a linear range and in two dimensions for $\bar{p} = \bar{q} = 0.5$, $N_e = 50$, and $M = 0.1$.

solution In one dimension, $V_p = (\frac{1}{2})(\frac{1}{2})/[1 + (0.504)(50)] = 0.0095$, while for two dimensions, $V_p = (\frac{1}{2})(\frac{1}{2})/[1 + (1.24)(50)] = 0.0040$. Thus, the value of V_p is some 2.4 times greater for populations dispersed along a one-dimensional range.

Joint Pressures and Stationary Gene Distributions

5. Derive the stationary gene frequency distribution for a subdivided population where dispersion due to drift is balanced by selection against a gene lacking in dominance.

   solution In this case, $\overline{W} = 1 - 2s(1-p)$, so that $\Delta p \simeq sp(1-p)$ when $2sq$ is small. Substitution into equation (13.21) and integration gives

$$f(p) = Ce^{4Ns(1-p)}p^{-1}(1 - p)^{-1}$$

6. Show that when all offspring have a small but equal chance of surviving to the reproductive age, family size in a stationary biparental population will correspond, approximately, to a Poisson distribution with a mean and variance of 2.

   solution Assume, for present purposes, that each female produces $2m$ offspring during the reproductive season, and that a fraction p of the progeny survive to sexual maturity. If survival is random, the probability that k of the $2m$ offspring survive is then

$$p(k) = \frac{(2m)!}{k!(2m-k)!} p^k(1 - p)^{2m-k}$$

   which, for small values of p, becomes

$$p(k) = \frac{(\bar{k})^k}{k!} e^{-\bar{k}}$$

   where $\bar{k} = 2mp$. In a stationary population, $mp = 1$. Thus, $p(k) = \frac{2^k}{k!} e^{-2}$. Under these conditions, as many as e^{-2} or 13.5% of all females fail to produce any surviving offspring. Only 27% of the matings actually produce exactly two offspring that survive to reach the reproductive age.

PROBLEM EXERCISES

1. Continued sib mating subdivides a population into isolates of size $N = 2$. Determine the mean and variance of the gene frequency after 1, 2, and 3 generations of sib mating in a population composed initially only of heterozygotes.

2. What is the variance of family size in a population of size N, which is subject to selection to the extent that matings involving BB females

produce 5 times as many offspring as those with Bb or bb types? (Let $p = q = \frac{1}{2}$.)

3. A population having $\bar{p} = \bar{q} = 0.5$ has been subdivided into a number of large, local populations for a very long period of time, with no migration between demes. If migration were to start with a rate $M = 0.05$, what would be the variance in gene frequency after 5 generations? How many generations of migration will it take to reduce the variance to half its maximum value?

4. Suppose that the size of each local group in Problem 3 is not large but only $N = 10$. What will be the variance in gene frequency after 5 generations? Assume that M still has the value 0.05 and that deme size remains constant.

5. Calculate the equilibrium gene frequency expected in the ith deme of a subdivided population where migration, at a rate of 0.05, is countered by selection against a gene lacking in dominance, if (a) $s = 0.005$, (b) $s = 0.05$, (c) $s = 0.5$. Let $\bar{p} = \bar{q} = 0.5$.

6. Consider a population which is subdivided into 5 local breeding groups of equal size, where $p_1 = 0.7$, $p_2 = 0.5$, $p_3 = 0.4$, $p_4 = 0.3$, and $p_5 = 0.1$. Determine the mean and variance of the group gene frequencies, the average genotype freqencies among subgroups, and the within-group, between-group, and total genetic variances. For the latter, assume a metric trait where each contributing gene adds a value of 2 to the phenotype.

7. A large, randomly mating population, with allele frequencies $p = q = 0.5$, is subdivided into 1,000 demes, each of size 10. (a) What is the frequency of heterozygotes in the base population? (b) What is the frequency of heterozygotes immediately after subdivision at generation 1? (c) Assuming that the size of each deme remains constant, what is the average number of heterozygous loci that reach fixation or loss after 5 generations? (d) What is the mean and variance of the frequency of the recessive allele after 5 generations? (e) How many generations are required for the variance to increase from zero to half its maximum value?

8. Assume that in Problem 7, the alleles at this locus contribute to a quantitative trait in an additive fashion. In the base population, this locus contributed a mean phenotypic value of 2 cm to the overall trait and a genetic variance of 2 cm². (a) What is the within-group variance for the isolated demes after 5 generations? (b) What is the between-group variance after 5 generations? (c) What is the total genetic variance after 5 generations?

9. Over a period of 4 generations of growth, the size of a certain population first decreases from 500 to 50, and then increases to 400 in the third generation and, in the fourth generation, to 600. (a) What is the effective

size of this population during the 4 generations? (b) What proportion of the initial heterozygosity will remain after the 4 generations?

10.   A subdivided population experiences differential selection pressures over its range, with selection against an unfavorable allele which occurs at a mean frequency within the population of 0.4. There is no dominance. (a) Employing the island model, what will be the equilibrium frequency of the gene in a deme with $M = 0.01$ and $s = 0.1$? (b) What will be the equilibrium frequency in another deme where $M = 0.1$ and $s = 0.01$?

11.   Compare the variances in gene frequency for the one- and two-dimensional cases of isolation by distance with that predicted by the island model. Let $M = 0.1$ and $N_e = 10$ in all cases. Comment on your findings.

12.   Derive the stationary gene frequency distribution under the joint pressures of mutation and selection against a rare gene lacking in dominance. Graph the result for $4Nu = 4Nv = 0.2, 2,$ and 20, and for $s = u/20$, $s = u$, and $s = 20u$.

14

Patterns of Variation

The previous chapters have dealt mainly with the theoretical aspects of population biology. We take a somewhat different approach in this final chapter, to relate how experimental work on the nature of genetic variability in populations has given insight into the patterns of variation associated with evolutionary change. Over the past decade, the measurement and characterization of genetic variability in natural populations has been central to the study of evolution. The question of how much variation exists in populations has now been resolved. However, the fraction of this variability that is relevant to evolutionary processes is still undetermined. In this chapter, we will discuss the techniques used to measure variation, the theories on how this variation is maintained within populations, applications of the techniques to the study of speciation and phylogeny, and, finally, the conflicting theories on the nature of molecular evolution.

DETECTION OF VARIABILITY IN NATURAL POPULATIONS

Both the amount of allelic variation per locus, and the distribution of that variation among genotypes, must be known in order to characterize the genetic structure of a population. There are different techniques used to detect variability in natural populations, which necessarily give different estimates of the kinds and amounts of variation present. Based on methods of analysis employed prior to 1960, it was thought that very little genic diversity existed in populations. This so-called classical view of population structure was defended principally by H.J. Muller and his colleagues. However, with the application of methods from molecular biology, large stores of variability have been detected in nearly all populations. The magnitude of this variation has forced at least a reexamination of theories concerning maintenance of genetic variation.

Morphological variation.   Genetic analysis for morphological variation, mainly color and pattern polymorphisms, has been carried out in mammals, birds, snails, insects, and plants. Visible variants have been noted in frequencies of approximately 2%. Since recessive mutant genes are often carried hidden in a heterozygous condition, crosses promoting inbreeding have been used to detect concealed variability. Extensive inbreeding with *Drosophila* gives estimates of 2 to 5 visible or lethal mutant genes per wild-type fly, carried in heterozygous condition. Traditional genetic analysis is based on gene loci for which a single mutation makes an obvious phenotypic change. This is because elucidation of the mechanisms of heredity requires an unambiguous association of phenotype with genotype. In contrast, most of the genetic variation relevant to evolution has subtle effects on fitness, involving polygenic traits, where a single gene substitution does not make an obvious change in phenotype. The low estimates of genetic variability levels provided by studies of morphological mutants therefore are, as we shall see, not typical of gene loci as a whole.

   That there exists much concealed genetic variation segregating in natural populations is shown by the high frequency of success of artifical selection practiced on a wide variety of traits in many different organisms. Successful selection programs have drastically improved commercially desirable traits in cattle, poultry, corn, and wheat, to name a few. Even after many generations of selection, genetic variation is still often present, For example, Robertson (1955) noted that selection for thorax length in *Drosophila melanogaster* could be reversed even after 17 generations of selection (Fig. 14.1).

Variation affecting fitness.   Techniques to study concealed variation affecting fitness traits such as viability, fecundity, and developmental rate, have been developed using *Drosophila*. One such procedure involves the replication of a chromosome obtained from a wild population into homozygous condition, so that recessive fitness alleles will be expressed. The crossing sequences utilized are diagrammed in Figure 14.2. Consider first the experimental sequence. The initial cross is made between a male from a wild population and a female from a laboratory "balancer" stock. The male carries two wild chromosomes, either of which can be tested for recessive variation affecting fitness; in this case, chromosome "$+_1$" will be tested. The balancer stock female is homozygous for a recessive marker gene, r, and heterozygous for gene D, which has a dominant visible phenotypic effect in heterozygous condition, but is lethal in homozygous condition. The r-D chromosome has multiple inversions to prevent crossing over in the female; no crossing over occurs in male *Drosophila*.

   Of the two offspring phenotypic classes in the F_1, a single D-phenotype male is selected and it is crossed to a balancer female. From the three F_2

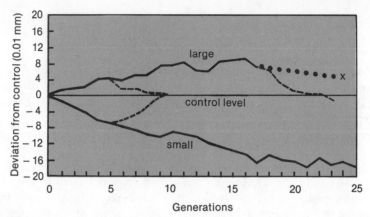

Figure 14.1. Mass selection for large and small thorax size in a *Drosophila melanogaster* population captured from the wild. Selection was reversed in both lines after five generations and in the large line after 17 generations (dashed lines). The dotted line represents relaxation of selection. (After F.W. Robertson. 1955. Cold Spring Harbor Sympos. Quant. Biol. 20: 166.)

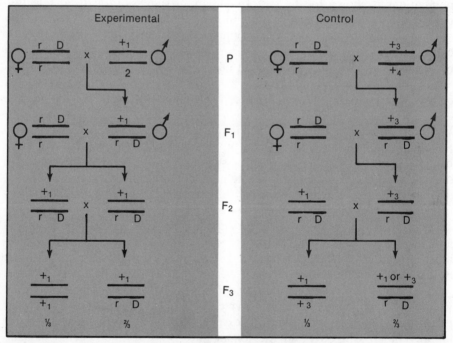

Figure 14.2. Chromosome replication technique for testing chromosomes from natural populations for concealed variablity affecting fitness. The 1:2 expected phenotypic ratios are for chromosomes having no affect on fitness.

phenotypic classes so produced, $+_1/r$-D males and females are chosen and these are intercrossed. If the wild chromosome being tested ($+_1$) carries no mutations affecting viability, then a 1:2 phenotypic ratio is expected in the F_3. Any alteration from this ratio indicates the presence of concealed variation affecting viability on the tested chromosome. Developmental rates can also be checked by timing the appearance of phenotypically wild offspring, and fecundity can be scored by appropriate matings of F_3 flies.

Dominant visible, recessive lethal genes, such as D, often affect the viability of their heterozygous carriers, which in itself would alter the expected F_3 ratio. Therefore, a control crossing sequence is usually run, using a different $+$ chromosome (say $+_3$ or $+_4$) from the wild population. Starting with a $+_3/+_4$ male, an F_2 is secured following the previously outlined crossing sequence. $+_3/r$-D F_2 flies are selected and crossed to $+_1/r$-D types from the experimental crossing sequence. Since $+_1$ and $+_3$ are not the same wild chromosome, recessive fitness mutants remain in heterozygous condition, and there should be no depression in the yield of phenotypically wild flies in the F_3. A control ratio different from 1:2 then reflects a lack of normal viability associated with the balancer chromosome. This effect can be eliminated by expressing the experimental F_3 phenotypic ratio relative to that of the control.

Using this chromosome replication technique, Dobzhansky and Spassky (1963) tested the viability of 1,063 second chromosomes from a natural population of *D. pseudoobscura*, with the results shown in Figure 14.3. The data are plotted as the distribution of homozygous viabilities, and that of the control heterozygotes is shown for comparison. The mean of the heterozygote distribution is 32.3%, indicating that the marker gene had little effect on viability. The standard deviation of the heterozygote distribution is 4%, so that the homozygous viabilities can be classed according to their distance from the mean as shown in the figure. Viabilities within $\pm 2\sigma$ units of the heterozygote mean are designated *quasinormals*, while those greater than 2σ units above the mean are termed *supervitals*, and those between 2σ and 3σ units below the mean are called *subvitals*. Viabilities less than 3σ units below the mean are termed *semilethals* and *lethals;* 28% of the chromosomes tested fell into this category. Similar results were obtained for the third and fourth chromosomes. Studies on five other *Drosophila* species (where appropriate balancer stocks are available) show a frequency of lethal or semilethal chromosomes in the range of 10 to 60%. Investigations with *D. pseudoobscura* and *D. melanogaster* indicate that the extent of concealed variability affecting fecundity is at least as great as that affecting viability, and that developmental times are slightly increased in homozygous flies.

The chromosome replication technique treats a chromosome as one genetic unit, so that it is the joint effect of all mutations contained on a chromosome that is measured. Hence, even those chromosomes that appear normal may not be "wild" at every locus. Parts of ostensibly normal chromosomes can be made homozygous by first allowing recombination in females heterozygous for pairs

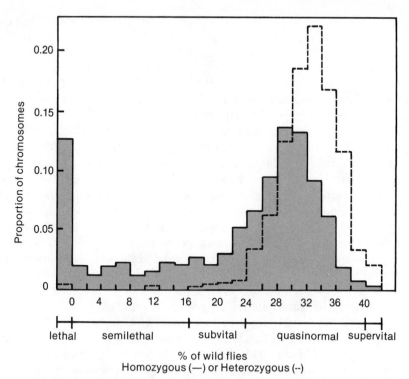

Figure 14.3. Distribution of homozygous (solid line) and heterozygous (dashed line) viabilities for second chromosomes of *D. pseudoobscura* sampled from a natural population. The heterozygotes represent random combinations of wild chromosomes. (Data from Th. Dobzhansky and B. Spassky. 1963. Genetics 48: 146.)

of quasinormal chromosomes obtained from nature. Subjecting these recombinant chromosomes to the chromosome replication technique, Dobzhansky *et al.* (1959) found that the distribution of homozygous viabilities spanned the same range as that of the original chromosomes tested, with recombinant chromosomes from *D. prosaltans* and *D. pseudoobscura* yielding 5.7% and 4.1% lethal chromosomes, respectively. The variability among recombinant chromosomes is 25 to 43% as large as that of the original chromosomes (Table 14.1). These results suggest that seemingly normal chromosomes actually constitute a heterogeneous group that carries considerable variability which is masked by epistasis.

We conclude that chromosomes carry significant amounts of variation affecting fitness. Fitness variability is underestimated by the above studies, however, since viability, fecundity, and developmental time are but three components of total fitness. This means that actual variation levels may be even higher. To measure the extent of concealed variability affecting total fitness in *D. pseudoobscura*, Sved and Ayala (1970) allowed the two classes produced

TABLE 14.1 Effect of recombination in generating variability from quasinormal chromosomes.*

Species	Mean viability	Variance of viability
D. prosaltans		
natural:	21.17%	200
recombinant:	28.14%	50
D. pseudoobscura		
natural:	20.29%	140
recombinant:	22.92%	60

*Data from Dobzhansky *et al.,* (1959)

in the F_3 of a chromosome replication procedure to establish experimental populations, in order that the course of selection could be followed over many generations. A stable equilibrium between the two phenotypes eventually occurred, showing that the wild chromosome had the lower fitness. The relative fitness of the homozygous flies was calculated from the equilibrium frequency of the wild-type phenotype, and is shown in Table 14.2, along with similar data obtained from *D. melanogaster* and *D. willistoni.* In all three cases, chromosomes became either lethal or semilethal with respect to overall fitness, even when chromosomes that are quasinormal with respect to viability alone were used to initiate the populations. The small variance in fitness suggests that a large number of polymorphic loci affecting fitness are maintained in *Drosophila* populations.

That a large amount of genetic variability exists in natural populations clearly supports the balance model of population structure, where the gene pool of a population is envisioned to consist of an array of alleles at each locus, most alleles in moderate frequency. According to this view, the typical individual is heterozygous at nearly all loci, and different individuals are usually heterozygous for different alleles. Hence, the population consists of an array of genotypes satisfactorily adapted to the environment, rather than just one

TABLE 14.2 Overall fitness of *Drosophila* homozygous for chromosomes conferring quasinormal viability.*

Species	Chromosome	Mean fitness	Standard deviation
D. pseudoobscura	II	0.366	0.030
D. melanogaster	II	0.192	0.029
	III	0.318	0.037
D. willistoni	II	0.339	0.023

*Data from Sved and Ayala (1970), Tracey and Ayala (1974), Sved (1971), and Mourão, Ayala, and Anderson (1972).

ideal genotype with variation about it. Fitness would depend on interactions among many loci and on gene-environment interactions.

In contrast to the balance concept, the classical model of population structure says that there is a single most fit genotype, which is homozygous for wild-type alleles at nearly all loci, and that only an occasional variant allele exists in the population, having recently arisen by mutation. Except in the rare case where this allele is advantageous, it will be quickly eliminated by selection. While the classical view does hold for those genes having singular effects on fitness, most loci do not act in such a manner. Still, the balance concept was not definitely established until techniques were developed to determine the proportion of individual loci having variant alleles.

Protein variability.   The question of what proportion of gene loci are polymorphic can be answered only if the loci studied represent a random sample of all gene loci with respect to both degree of phenotypic expression and amount of variation. Developments in molecular genetics have made it possible to study a locus whether or not it exhibits allelic variation.

All genetic variation is ultimately due to change in the nucleotide sequence of a gene. Determination of the complete nucleotide sequence at a random sample of loci from the gene pool would, therefore, give an unbiased measure of the degree of genetic variation in a population. Unfortunately, large-scale nucleotide sequencing is not technically feasible at the present time.

The next best technique for studying the proportion of gene loci that are polymorphic is to determine the amino acid sequence for a wide variety of proteins. The sequence of code words composing a structural gene linearly determines the sequence of amino acids in the peptide for which it codes, so that amino acid substitutions do reflect nucleotide substitutions. If a sample of proteins is random with respect to function and amount of observed phenotypic variation, then the genes which code for these proteins will represent a random sample of the genome, and accurate estimates of the proportions of variant and invariant loci can be made. While amino acid sequencing has contributed to the study of molecular evolution, it is too time-consuming and costly to be applied on a wide enough scale to study intrapopulation variability. It is, however, possible to detect many amino acid substitutions in proteins using the physiochemical technique, gel electrophoresis. Figure 14.4 illustrates the procedure. A sample of tissue homogenate is centrifuged and the soluble protein fraction is collected and placed on a supportative gel matrix composed of starch, polyacrylamide, cellulose, or agar. Each variant protein species in the sample, being composed of a different amino acid sequence, will have a different net charge. Based on its charge, and molecular size and shape, a protein will migrate in an electric field in a particular direction and at a particular rate. After electrophoresis has proceeded for a given period of time, the gel can be specifically stained to visualize the positions of the various proteins. The technique is limited mainly by the availability of suitable stains to differentiate the protein species.

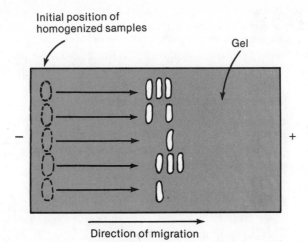

Figure 14.4. Diagram of a gel electrophoresis aparatus. The pH has been adjusted so that all proteins carry a net negative charge. The distance traversed from the origin by any protein in a fixed amount of time depends on its charge and molecular size and shape, so that variant protein species are detected as discrete bands.

Figure 14.5 shows the result of analysis of a wild population of *D. pseudoobscura* for electrophoretic variation at the esterase-5 locus. Samples 1, 2, 3, 5, and 6 represent homozygous genotypes: sample 1 contains the standard allele (est-$5^{1.00}$), samples 2, 3, and 6 a variant allele denoted est-$5^{0.95}$, and sample 5 another variant allele, est-$5^{1.12}$. Sample 4 contains protein from a genotype

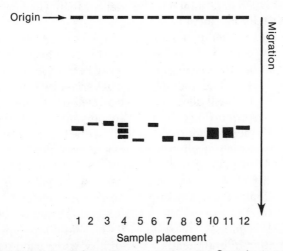

Figure 14.5. Adult esterases from *D. pseudoobscura*. Sample 1: est$-5^{1.00}$/est$-5^{1.00}$ (standard strain); samples 2 and 3: est$-5^{0.95}$/est$-5^{0.95}$; sample 4: est$-5^{0.95}$/est$-5^{1.12}$; sample 5: est$-5^{1.12}$/est$-5^{1.12}$; sample 6: est$-5^{0.95}$/est$-5^{0.95}$. (From Hubby, J.L. and R.C. Lewontin, 1966. *Genetics* 54: 577.)

heterozygous for the alleles 0.95 and 1.12. The three bands in sample 4 indicate that esterase-5 is a dimer, so that three subunit associations are possible in a heterozygote—0.95-0.95, 1.12-1.12, and 0.95-1.12—the latter having an electrophoretic mobility midway between the two homozygous forms. (In cases of monomeric proteins, heterozygotes give two bands.) Note that there is no dominance at the molecular level; each allele yields its protein product. Samples 10 and 11 may also represent heterozygous genotypes, since when mobilities of protein variants from the same locus are not too different, the bands from a heterozygote will not be distinct but instead appear as a single thick band. Genetic crosses are often performed concurrently with electrophoresis, to make certain that electrophoretic differences are the result of genic variation at a single locus.

The most commonly used quantitative measures of electrophoretic variability are the average frequency of heterozygous genotypes per locus, $\bar{H}$, and the proportion of loci in a population that are polymorphic, $\bar{P}$. $\bar{H}$ is the average of H_k, the heterozygosity at the kth locus, and it can be calculated once the allele frequencies are known, assuming random mating. If a locus has n alleles, at frequencies of $q_1, q_2, q_3, \ldots, q_n$, then the expected frequency of homozygotes at this locus is $\sum_{i=1}^{n} q_i^2$. Hence,

$$H = 1 - \sum_{i=1}^{n} q_i^2 \quad \text{and} \quad \bar{H} = \sum_{k=1}^{m} H_k / m \tag{14.1}$$

where m is the total number of loci studied. $\bar{H}$ can also be defined as the average frequency of heterozygous loci per individual, although the variance of $\bar{H}$ will usually be smaller when determined in this manner than when calculated as the average heterozygosity per locus.

Nei (1973) has suggested that a more general term, *gene diversity*, be used in place of heterozygosity, in referring to $\bar{H}$. This is to allow $\bar{H}$ to be used as a measure of variation for any organism, regardless of its mating system or ploidy. Since this does facilitate comparisons of variability levels among a wide variety of organisms, we will adopt Nei's suggested terminology.

To determine the proportion of loci that are polymorphic, it must be decided what criterion establishes polymorphism. No universal agreement exists on this point, the two most widely used criteria being a maximum frequency of the most common allele of 0.95 or 0.99. Another reason why $\bar{P}$ is not a precise estimate of variability is that it does not measure the degree of polymorphism at a locus. For example, a locus with two alleles at frequencies of 0.9 and 0.1 would contribute to $\bar{P}$ to exactly the same extent as another locus with five alleles all at equal frequency. In spite of its lack of precision, however, $\bar{P}$ is useful in estimating overall genome variability when used in conjunction with $\bar{H}$.

Human and *Drosophila* proteins were the first to be analyzed electrophoretically (Harris, 1966; Lewontin and Hubby, 1966; Johnson *et al.*, 1966).

Harris found that of the enzyme products of 10 randomly chosen gene loci in humans, 7 were monomorphic. The 3 polymorphic loci included red-cell phosphatase, with 3 alleles at frequencies of 0.36, 0.60, and 0.04; phosphoglucomutase, with two alleles at frequencies of 0.74 and 0.26; and adenylate kinase, with two alleles at frequencies of 0.95 and 0.05. Using equation (14.1), this gives gene diversity values of 0.509, 0.385, and 0.095, respectively, with $\bar{H} = 0.099$.

Lewontin and Hubby studied 43 strains of *D. pseudoobscura* maintained in the laboratory for varying numbers of generations after being trapped from 5 natural populations. Of the 18 loci represented in the sample, 7 had electrophoretic variants, and 5 of these 7 had at least 3 alleles each. The average proportion of polymorphic loci for the 5 populations was 0.30, and the average frequency of heterozygous loci per individual was 0.115.

Considering that electrophoresis detects at most only one-third of all protein variability, both of these pioneering studies indicated that very high levels of variability exist in natural populations. This conclusion has since been consistently reinforced as other species have been studied. Gene diversity and polymorphism values are given in Table 14.3 for various species of plants and animals divided into 9 taxonomic groups and 3 major taxa. Estimates of $\bar{P}$ generally range from 0.10 to 0.40, with an overall mean of 0.263. Gene diversity values typically range from 0.025 to 0.15, with an overall mean of 0.074. Recent techniques designed to measure protein variation hidden from routine electro-

TABLE 14.3   Average levels of gene diversity and polymorphism in animals and plants.*

	Number of species	$\bar{H}$ Mean	S.D.	$\bar{P}$ Mean	S.D.
Taxonomic group:					
Plants	15	0.0706	0.0706	0.259	0.166
Invertebrata (excluding Insecta)	27	0.1001	0.0740	0.399	0.275
Insecta (excluding *Drosophila*)	23	0.0743	0.0810	0.329	0.203
Drosophila	43	0.1402	0.0534	0.431	0.130
Osteichthyes	51	0.0513	0.0338	0.152	0.098
Amphibia	13	0.0788	0.0420	0.269	0.134
Reptilia	17	0.0471	0.0228	0.219	0.129
Aves	7	0.0473	0.0360	0.150	0.111
Mammalia	46	0.0359	0.0245	0.147	0.098
Total	242	0.0741	0.0510	0.263	0.153
Major taxon:					
Plants	15	0.0706	0.0706	0.259	0.166
Invertebrates	93	0.1123	0.0720	0.397	0.201
Vertebrates	135	0.0494	0.0365	0.173	0.119

*Data from Nevo (1978), where specific references are given.

phoresis give even higher estimates. For example, proteins with different amino acid compositions but identical electrophoretic mobilities are often separable if electrophoresis is preceded by heat denaturation, revealing in some cases a two- to three-fold increase in the number of alleles detected (Singh *et al.*, 1976).

Since electrophoresis detects only variation at loci coding for soluble proteins, it is possible that a truly random sample of the genome still is not being studied. It is known, for example, that a large fraction of the DNA in various organisms (90% in *Drosophila*) does not code for enzymes. If a significant proportion of this DNA codes for nonsoluble proteins (e.g., structural proteins) or serves a function in the control of gene activity, then the estimates of variability gained from electrophoresis, and its relevance to evolutionary processes, may not represent the genome as a whole. We will return to this point later.

MAINTENANCE OF VARIABILITY

The large stores of genetic variability existing in natural populations must be maintained by one or more of the evolutionary forces of mutation, migration, selection, and genetic drift. There is far too much variation to be accounted for by mutation and migration alone. A major concern among population biologists at the present time is the relative importance of selection and genetic drift in maintaining genetic polymorphisms. As is the case with most controversies, it is not likely that simplistic models which depend entirely on random processes, or exclusively on a particular form of selection, will explain the majority of such polymorphisms. The genetic structure of a population requires a more complex explanation, integrating various types of evolutionary pressures. Some of the mechanisms thought to play significant roles in maintaining genetic variation in populations are discussed below.

Selection. Stable polymorphisms can be maintained indefinitely by *balancing selection*, a term which includes any form of selection which keeps two or more genetic variants in a population at stable equilibrium frequencies. Overdominance, frequency-dependent selection, and variable selection coefficients are forms of balancing selection discussed in Chapter 12. There are scattered reports of each of these forms of selection having been demonstrated in natural populations. For example, Koehn (1969) found a correlation between an altitudinal cline with respect to gene frequency and temperature-dependent esterase activity in a freshwater fish, with the enzyme from heterozygotes having higher activity than that from homozygotes at intermediate temperatures. Kojima (1971) has reported results indicating frequency-dependent selection affecting enzyme polymorphisms in *Drosophila*, although subsequent studies by other investigators have failed to confirm these results (Yoshimaru and Mukai, 1979). Selection in heterogeneous environments may be a means of maintaining polymorphisms, as recently discussed by Hedrick, Ginevan, and Ewing (1976). Correlations of allele frequencies with environmental parameters such as season, temperature, and rainfall have often been reported. Johnson (1971) found that one of three alleles at the lactate dehydrogenase locus in the crested blenny (*Anplorchus purpurescens*) changed in frequency from 0.021 to 0.305 over 3° of latitude around Puget Sound. Allele frequency was correlated with surface temperature, O_2 concentration, and the frequency of another species. McDonald and Ayala (1974) have demonstrated that laboratory populations of *Drosophila* living in a heterogeneous environment are more polymorphic than populations in more homogeneous environments. One way in which populations could cope with a spatially heterogeneous environment would be diversifying selection favoring different genotypes in different regions of the range (Levins, 1968). Gillespie (1974) has shown that it is also theoretically possible to maintain a stable polymorphism in a fine-grained environment, through temporal fluctuations in environmental conditions.

In a recent review of electrophoretically-detectable variation in natural populations, Nevo (1978) concludes that genic variability is correlated with ecological heterogeneity. Defining habitat generalists as those species that are common, widespread, vagile, and broad-niched, and habitat specialists as those which are rare, geographically restricted, local, and narrow-niched, Nevo gives genic diversity and polymorphism values for 117 generalists and 120 specialists (Table 14.4). Generalists appear to have approximately twice the amount of genic variability as specialists, as expected if some form of natural selection is the major determinant of variability patterns.

Another manner in which selection could be involved in the maintenance of polymorphisms concerns the transient nature of allele variability associated with selective fixation of a favorable gene. However, Maruyama (1972) has shown that the proportion of heterozygosity due to selection for advantageous genes is $\alpha_s/(2N_e s \alpha_n + \alpha_s)$, where α_s and α_n are the proportions of selective and neutral gene substitutions, respectively. Note that even if α_n is small, most heterozygosity will be due to neutral rather than selective substitutions, as long as $2N_e s$ is fairly large ($\gg 1/\alpha_n$). Hence, Maruyama concluded that selective transient polymorphism cannot explain most of the variation existing in natural populations.

TABLE 14.4   Genic variability levels for habitat generalists and specialists.*

	Plants		Invertebrates		Vertebrates		All species	
	$\bar{H}$	$\bar{P}$	$\bar{H}$	$\bar{P}$	$\bar{H}$	$\bar{P}$	$\bar{H}$	$\bar{P}$
generalists	0.082	0.267	0.149	0.488	0.071	0.248	0.106	0.348
specialists	0.040	0.385	0.064	0.282	0.037	0.142	0.046	0.189

*From Nevo (1978).

Genetic drift.   In Chapter 3 we stated that the apparent uniformity of the rate of amino acid substitution in homologous proteins over diverse evolutionary lines has led to the theory that molecular evolution is in large part due to the substitution of selectively neutral mutations. As an extension of this theory, Kimura (1971b) has proposed that random genetic drift of neutral mutations in finite populations can also account for observed protein polymorphisms. Under such a view, protein polymorphism is simply a phase of molecular evolution. The neutral theory does not preclude the existence of deleterious or advantageous genes. In fact, most newly arising mutations probably do have deleterious effects. The theory simply states that no matter what fraction of new mutants are harmful, they will quickly be eliminated by selection, thus contributing little to the pool of genetic variability in a population.

No unambiguous correlation has been shown between heterozygosity levels and population size or age, extent of species range, reproductive strategy, or environmental stability, so that the relative significance of selection and drift in maintaining polymorphisms remains unclear. Existence of a gene frequency cline associated with environmental factors is not strong evidence against neutrality, as would be the existence of clines in different directions for different loci, each correlated with an environmental variable relevant to that locus. While the data given in Table 14.4 appear to support a major role for selection as a determinant of variation patterns, possible effects of uncontrolled variables such as population size and evolutionary age complicate the issue. Data purporting to show selection are often ambiguous because genic fitness values in natural populations are often too small to be reliably detected. Perhaps the strongest evidence for selection would be the finding of a relationship between the degree of polymorphism at a locus and the physiological function of its protein. Although Johnson (1974) has reported finding differential enzyme variability related to substrate diversity, and a difference in the level of polymorphism between regulatory and nonregulatory genes, there is as yet no evidence that these are general phenomena. Ohta and Kimura (1975) have recently suggested that both selection and mutation might be involved in polymorphisms if many alleles, rather than being strictly neutral, have very small selective values. The maintenance of such alleles through an equilibrium between mutation and selection might then contribute significantly to the observed variability levels in populations. Note that in this case directional selection, against an allele, rather than balancing selection acting to maintain the allele, is involved.

It should be obvious at this point that little is known of the precise mechanisms acting to maintain variability in populations. Different gene loci can be expected to be subject to different evolutionary pressures, and even with respect to a single locus, different alleles may exhibit a spectrum of selective values. In addition, any gene exists linked with others. Recall that if there is linkage disequilibrium in a population, the allele frequencies at a neutral locus can be controlled largely by a closely linked selected locus. It is not known how frequently linkage disequilibrium occurs in nature. Because of linkage, and epistatic and regulatory gene interactions, single locus analysis may not be appropriate to the study of evolutionary forces acting on genes. Even in the most extensively studied populations, explanations for the large amounts of variability are far from complete. The complexity of the situation is illustrated by morphological polymorphism in populations of *Cepaea*, a land snail which has been the subject of a recent review by Jones, Leith, and Rawlings (1977).

Populations of *Cepaea* are highly polymorphic with respect to shell, body, and lip colors, and the shell banding pattern. Shell colors range from yellow through pink and brown; superimposed on this color may be from zero to five bands. Genetic variation has been found for shell shape and size, and for fitness characters as well. More than one million specimens from ten thousand populations have been studied.

For many years shell color and banding pattern were thought to be completely caused by genetic drift. The snails often exist in small populations, isolated in patchy environments, and frequently a year-class will fail to reproduce, so that drift through founder effects seemed likely. Founder effects have been documented following introductions of the snail into North America. It is now known that drift is not the only evolutionary force affecting the polymorphisms; selection plays an important role. Genes for shell color, presence versus absence of bands, and band and lip color are tightly linked in a supergene complex. An association between shell color and climate has been discovered, with lighter colored shells more frequent in the warmer parts of the species range. Frequency-dependent selection with predators hunting by sight is at least partly responsible for maintaining the shell color and banding polymorphisms. Linkage disequilibrium extends the effects of selection to other loci. In addition, polymorphism is influenced by extensive gene flow between populations. Many types of evolutionary forces are thus seen to act on *Cepaea* polymorphisms.

GENETIC DIFFERENTIATION BETWEEN POPULATIONS

Quantitative measures of the extent of genetic differentiation accompanying the divergence of populations are based on comparisons of their nucleic acids and proteins. Those comparative methods employed on a widespread basis include nucleic acid hybridization, immunological techniques, and protein electrophoresis.

Nucleic acid hybridization estimates the proportion of nucleotide pairs that are different in the two populations being compared. This technique has the advantage that all genetic material, regardless of whether or not it codes for a protein, is measured. DNA from one kind of organism, say species *A*, is denatured into single strands. The strands are then sheared into short-length fragments and trapped on a supportative matrix, such as an agar or nitrocellulose filter. The filter-bound fragments are then incubated at 60°C with a constant concentration of complementary single-stranded fragments from species A and varying amounts of single-stranded fragments isolated from a second species, species B. Since the species A DNA in solution is labeled (e.g., with ^3H or ^{32}P), one can follow the extent of its renaturation with complementary filter-bound DNA. The degree to which species B DNA is homologous (complementary) to that of species A is measured by the extent to which species B DNA competes with labeled type A DNA for the filter-bound fragments. The results of competition between labeled human DNA and the DNAs from 11 different species for filter-bound human DNA are shown in Table 14.5. Note that by the nucleic acid hybridization criteria, chimpanzee DNA is identical to human DNA.

Competitor DNA will undergo hybridization even if a few of its nucleotides are not complementary to those of the filter-bound DNA. The hybridization technique does not have sufficient resolution to detect short regions of nucleotide pair mismatch. However, the extent of mismatch can be determined from knowledge of the melting temperature of the hybrid molecule. Gradual heating of nucleic acid duplexes disrupts the hydrogen bonds in such a fashion that the precise melting (denaturation) temperature characterizing the molecule can be determined. The melting temperature is defined as that temperature at which 50% of the hydrogen bonds holding a duplex together have dissociated. An imperfectly formed hybrid duplex, having fewer hydrogen bonds than native DNA, will exhibit a lowered melting temperature. The change in melting temperature has been found to be directly proportional to the frequency of unpaired nucleotides, with a 1° change in melting temperature equivalent to 1.0 to 1.5% mismatch in base pairs. When the melting temperature technique is

TABLE 14.5   Degree of similarity between human DNA and DNA from 11 other species, expressed as the degree of inhibition of human-human DNA binding.*

Organism	Degree of taxonomic differentiation	Percent inhibition of human-human DNA binding
man	—	100
chimpanzee	family	100
gibbon	family	94
rhesus monkey	superfamily	88
capuchin monkey	superfamily	83
tarsier	suborder	65
slow loris	suborder	58
lemur	suborder	47
tree shrew	suborder	28
mouse	order	21
hedgehog	order	19
chicken	class	10

*Data from Hoyer and Roberts (1967).

applied to human-chimpanzee DNA hybrids, it is found that their DNAs differ at about 2 to 2.5% of the nucleotides.

Although the nucleic acid hybridization-melting technique does have the resolution to detect relatively small changes in genes, it is extremely sensitive to environmental conditions. It is, therefore, difficult to obtain consistent results. Thus, other methods have been employed to measure genetic differentiation, one of which is immunological distance. The immunological technique most widely used is *microcomplement fixation*. Complement is a blood component that becomes fixed to antigen-antibody complexes. However, when unbound and circulating freely in the blood, it lysis red blood cells. Hence, the extent of lysis is inversely proportional to the degree of antigen-antibody reaction and can be used as a measure of immunological recognition. Purified protein, commonly serum albumin, from an organism, say man, is injected into a rabbit, and the antiserum to the protein is collected. Albumin from other sources can then be tested for its extent of reaction with the human antiserum. The index of dissimilarity, *I.D.*, is the factor by which the antiserum concentration must be raised to promote the same extent of reaction as occurs with human albumin. The log *I.D.*, termed the *immunological distance*, has been demonstrated empirically to be approximately proportional to the number of amino acid differences between two proteins.

One drawback to using immunological distance to measure genetic relatedness among species is that different species often exhibit quite different log *I.D.* values when different antigenic proteins are used. For example, Table 14.6 gives the immunological distances between humans and various primates, based on albumin and on lysozyme. Note that human albumin differs somewhat from chimpanzee albumin, but with respect to their lysozymes, the two are the same. Also note that the degree of similarity between humans and gorillas is greater than between humans and organgutans by the albumin immunological criteria, but that this is reversed using lysozyme as the antigen.

Detection of amino acid differences through electrophoresis has been extensively used to measure interpopulational genic differentiation. Generally, the same loci are used for electrophoretic studies of all organisms. Thus, even

TABLE 14.6   Immunological distances between human and primate albumins and lysozymes.*

Species tested against human	Immunological distance between	
	Albumins	Lysozymes
human	0	0
chimpanzee	5.7	0
gorilla	3.7	32
orangutan	8.6	1
Old World monkeys	38.6	120

*Data from Sarich and Wilson (1967) and Wilson and Prager (1974).

if such proteins are not representative of the overall genome, they are useful in making comparisons within and between species. Using electrophoresis, the amount of genetic divergence between two populations can be expressed as a function of gene frequencies. Nei (1973) has developed a statistical technique by which the average number of codon differences per locus, termed the *genetic distance*, can be estimated from gene frequency data. Actually, there are several related measures of the number of codon differences that can be used. The simplest is the gene diversity, $\bar{H}$, which represents the minimum number of codon differences per locus between two randomly chosen genomes, since it assumes that each amino acid substitution is the result of a single change in one codon of a gene. $\bar{H}_{XY} = 1 - \bar{J}_{XY}$, where $\bar{J}_{XY}$ is the average probability of identity between two genes chosen at random, one from population X and the other from population Y. $\bar{J}_{XY}$ is calculated from the data by first obtaining the probability of electrophoretic identity for each locus, which is $\Sigma q_{X,i} q_{Y,i}$ over all i alleles, and then averaging this quantity over all loci. Correcting for intrapopulation gene diversity, the expression for the minimum genetic distance between populations X and Y becomes

$$D_m = \bar{H}_{XY} - (\bar{H}_X + \bar{H}_Y)/2 \qquad (14.2)$$

Another measure of genetic distance is I, the genetic identity. This is defined as $I = J_{XY}/\sqrt{J_X J_Y}$, which is the normalized mean identity of genes between X and Y. Although data are sometimes analyzed in terms of genetic identity, I is more often used to calculate D, the standard genetic distance. Assuming a random distribution of nucleotide substitutions with a mean number D per locus, the number of substitutions per locus can be treated as a Poisson variable. The probability of identity is, therefore, given as e^{-D}, and $D = - \ln I$. This is Nei's standard genetic distance, defined as the average number of codon substitutions per locus accumulated in two populations since their divergence from a common ancestor. Note that the expression for D can also be given as

$$D = D_{XY} - (D_X + D_Y)/2 \qquad (14.3)$$

where $D_{XY} = - \ln J_{XY}$, $D_X = - \ln J_X$, and $D_Y = - \ln J_Y$.

D is usually a more accurate measure of genetic distance than D_m, because it makes no assumption about the number of nucleotide changes per change in amino acid. However, D may still underestimate the number of codon differences if the rate of codon substitution is not constant from one locus to the next. In this case, the mean number of net codon differences may be estimated by

$$D' = - \ln I' \qquad (14.4)$$

where $I' = J'_{XY}/\sqrt{J'_X J'_Y}$ and J'_{XY}, J'_X, and J'_Y are the geometric mean gene diversities. D' is termed the maximum genetic distance. It is, however, heavily influenced by small gene frequency values, and often overestimates the mean number of codon differences. It is, therefore, seldom used.

Genetic differentiation during speciation.   Table 14.7 gives the genetic distances between taxa of various rank for a wide variety of organisms. Genetic distances are, on the whole, smaller between races than between subspecies, which, in turn, show less genetic divergence than species. No sharp discontinuities appear, however.

At the racial level, Table 14.7 shows that there is little genetic differentiation between populations. Nei and Roychoudhury (1974) have compared intraracial and interracial genic variation for American Negroid and Caucasoid populations, finding that $D_C = 0.110$, $D_N = 0.097$, and $D_{CN} = 0.114$, giving a value for D of 0.011. Net codon differences between the races detected by electrophoresis are only about 0.01 per locus, and interracial genic variation is small relative to intraracial variation.

TABLE 14.7   Estimates of genetic distance between taxa of various rank.*

Taxa	Number of taxa	Number of loci	$D = -\ln I$
races			
man	3	35	0.011–0.019
mice	4	41	0.010–0.024
kangaroo rats	9	18	0.000–0.058
lizards	3	23	0.001–0.017
Astyanax			
surface fish	6	17	0.002–0.013
horshoe crab	4	25	0.001–0.013
Drosophila			
pseudoobscura	3	24	0.003–0.010
subspecies			
mice	2	41	0.194
gophers	4	27	0.009–0.054
lizards	4	23	0.335–0.351
newts	2	18	0.164
Astyanax	9	17	0.062–0.218
Drosophila			
pseudoobscura	5	24	0.083–0.126
species			
kangaroo rats	2	18	0.049
gophers	2	27	0.12
lizards	4	23	1.32–1.75
newts	3	18	0.27–0.57
Drosophila			
sibling	18	13–23	0.18–1.54
nonsibling	27	13–23	1.3–2.54
families			
man-chimpanzee	2	42	0.62
orders			
man-horse	2	—	19**

*Calculations by Nei (1975), where specific references are given.
**Based on amino acid sequence data

To determine the amount of genic differentiation accompanying the acquisition of reproductive isolation, data on races (subspecies) and semispecies must be compared. The most extensive study of this sort has been carried out using the *Drosophila willistoni* group (see Ayala *et al.*, 1974). A graded series of genic similarities has been found. Local populations are 97% identical in their genes, subspecies and semispecies are 80% identical, sibling species 56% identical, and nonsibling species are identical in only 35% of their genes. These values are mean genetic identities (I), and are based on electrophoretically detected proteins. Figure 14.6 shows that, in some cases, large variability in the data was obtained. However, subspecies and semispecies show quite similar distributions. The subspecies category in these studies included populations showing no prezygotic isolation in the laboratory. Semispecies were those populations, some existing sympatrically, that were advanced with respect to the development of reproductive isolation. The extent of genic divergence being the same in the two groups strongly suggests that speciation (acquisition of reproductive isolation) requires very little reorganization of the gene pool. That geographic races have diverged very little, whereas considerable genic differentiation, on the average, exists between subspecies, indicates that most gene substitution accompanying speciation takes place early, prior to the acquisition of mechanisms of reproductive isolation. However, it may be necessary to distinguish between divergence necessary for speciation, and that involved in evolution independent of speciation (Throckmorton, 1977). In this case, comparisons of minimum divergence values rather than averages might be appropriate. The minimum subspecies distance observed in the *willistoni* study was approximately 20%, and the minimum divergence for semispecies was 5%. On this basis the conclusion of major genic differentiation early in the speciation process is not warranted. Larger sample sizes and the study of a wider variety of organisms may resolve this matter.

A great deal of genic divergence seems to occur following the development of reproductive isolation, as noted from the finding that sibling species of the *willistoni* group are markedly more similar electrophoretically than nonsibling species. This has been confirmed in other *Drosophila* groups as well, and suggests that sibling species are genetically more similar than nonsibling species. This result would be expected if speciation is simply part of an overall process of gradual, continual genic differentiation between populations.

It appears, then, that evolution to the species level and beyond is associated with ever-increasing amounts of electrophoretically detectable genic differentiation. However, the extent to which such variation is relevant to the development of reproductive isolation and fitness differences is not known. The finding by King and Wilson (1975) of a genetic distance of 0.62 between man and chimpanzee (Table 14.7) is germane to the general question of the degree to which electrophoretic variation randomly represents the gene pool. This value is no greater than some interspecies distances in other organisms, even though man and chimpanzee are in different families. King and Wilson suggest

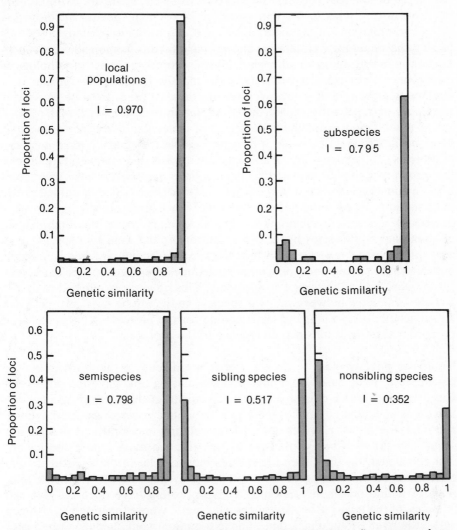

Figure 14.6. Distribution of loci with respect to genetic identity at five stages of evolutionary divergence in the *Drosophila willistoni* group of populations. Local populations exhibit little genetic differentiation. Considerably more genetic divergence exists between subspecies, which represent the first stage of geographic speciation. Semispecies, characterized by advanced reproductive isolating mechanisms, exhibit no more differentiation than subspecies. Sibling and nonsibling species are extensively differentiated, reflecting continued genetic divergence after adquisition of reproductive isolation. (From F.J. Ayala et al., 1974. Evolution 28: 576.)

that major differences between the two organisms are the result of differences in regulatory systems rather than in enzyme-producing genes. According to this view, mutations in regulatory genes and chromosome rearrangements affecting the regulatory system are the primary factors responsible for reproductive incompatibilities and morphological evolution. Thus, morphological divergence is not expected to necessarily parallel protein divergence. It is obvious that the role of regulatory versus structural genes must be clarified if the nature of genetic divergence during evolution is to be understood.

A much better estimate of the degree of molecular divergence associated with speciation could be made if it were possible to sequence large numbers of proteins. This promises to be an important area of study in the future. Those few proteins whose amino acid sequences have been determined have been used to construct molecular phylogenetic relationships, to be discussed in the next section. Two methods have been used in expressing divergence as a function of amino acid substitutions. The first simply counts the total number of amino acid differences in the same kind of protein from two species, and uses this total as a measure of genetic distance. A second, and better, method is to determine the minimum number of nucleotide differences needed to account for the observed amino acid replacements. This quantity is referred to as the *mutation distance* between the two species, and it can be used as a measure of the genetic distance at the locus coding for the proteins. This distance is proportional to the time since divergence of the proteins.

Molecular phylogenies.   In Chapter 3, we discussed the construction of phylogenetic trees based on amino acid sequencing, and gave the phylogeny based on cytochrome c as an example. To construct this tree, mutational distances were computed, and a numerical taxonomic scheme was employed to minimize the number of genetic changes relating ancestral and descendant sequences. At its simplest, this means that the two most similar species are first connected together, then the species most similar to the previous two is added, and so on. Interpretation as a phylogeny depends on whether similar rates of amino acid substitution in a given protein have occurred over all branches of the tree. In the case of cytochrome c, whose function has changed very little over evolutionary time, this assumption would appear to be valid. This appears not to be the case for many other proteins, however.

For a small number of protein sequences, the appropriate order of addition to the phylogenetic tree can often be determined by inspection. As the number of sequences increases, however, the order in which they should be added to the tree becomes less clear. Addition of sequences in different orders generates trees with distinct topologies, so that the problem becomes how to pick that topology which minimizes the number of mutations over the tree as a whole. Maximum parsimony or maximum homology procedures use a computer to accomplish this minimization. Parsimony techniques have the advantage that similar rates of codon substitutions over all codons and all branches of the tree are not required. As we shall see, variation in molecular evolutionary rates among lineages of parsimonious phylogenies has been used as evidence of a role for natural selection in protein evolution.

Molecular phylogenies can also be constructed based on hybrid DNA thermal stability, immunological distance, and electrophoretically detectable protein differences. All of these methods are relatively new, and their full potential has not as yet been realized. Their use in conjunction with anatomical, embryological, ethological, ecological, paleontological, and biogeographical knowledge promises to aid significantly in deciphering evolutionary relatedness among organisms.

Chromosome phylogenies.   Another method that has been used to determine phylogeny in certain *Diptera* is based on the linear arrangement of genes on chromosomes. Organisms such as flies, mosquitos, and midges have in their salivary glands the large polytene chromosomes. These chromosomes contain specific patterns of banding delineating the arrangement of gene loci. It has, therefore, been possible in these organisms to detect chromosome rearrangements, such as inversions, translocations, and centric fusions, by noting changes in the polytene chromosome banding pattern, and to use this information comparatively to deduce evolutionary relatedness (see Example Problem 3.9). The 22 third-chromosome arrangements found in populations of *Drosophila pseudoobscura* and *D. persimilis* have been used to construct the phylogeny shown in Figure 14.7. Only the Standard arrangement is found in both species. The Hypothetical arrangement has never been found, but is postulated as being necessary to connect Standard and Santa Cruz. The pattern suggests that the ancestral arrangement is either Standard, Hypothetical, Santa Cruz, or Tree Line.

Carson has applied the comparative study of polytene chromosome gene arrangements to 101 of the estimated 800 endemic Hawaiian *Drosophila* species (Carson and Kaneshiro, 1976). The resulting phylogeny suggests certain patterns of colonization of the islands and particular modes of speciation, thereby contributing significantly to the study of speciation and island evolutionary ecology.

THEORIES OF MOLECULAR EVOLUTION

It is possible that evolution of macromolecules proceeds through mutation pressure and genetic drift, or natural selection. The question as to the relative contributions of each of these forces to molecular evolutionary change is far from settled, even though volumes of data have been collected and a multitude of interpretations offered. The purpose of this final section is to summarize the major features characterizing the neutralist-selectionist controversy, as it pertains to molecular evolution.

According to the neutral theory, the majority of amino acid substitutions that occur in proteins are the result of fixation of selectively neutral alleles.

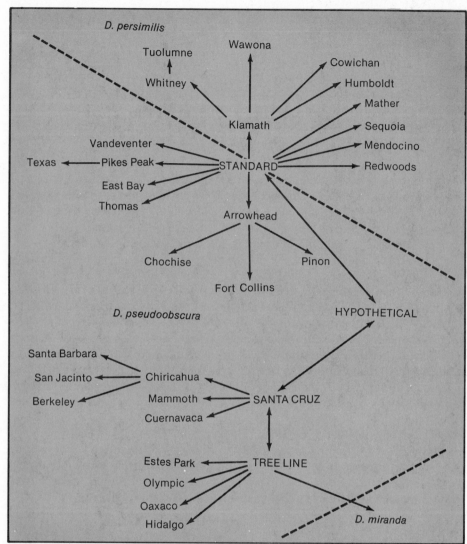

Figure 14.7. Phylogeny based on gene arrangements on third chromosomes of *Drosophila persimilis*, *D. pseudoobscura*, and *D. miranda*. The Standard arrangement is found in both *D. persimilis* and *D. pseudoobscura*. Any two arrangements connected by an arrow can be derived from one another by a single inversion. (From Th. Dobzhansky et al., 1975. J. Hered. 66: 203. Copyright 1975 by the American Genetic Association.)

Adaptive gene substitutions do occur, but they are a minority of all replacements since mutation to a better adapted allele is a very rare event. Considering the large stores of variability in natural populations, this still leaves ample opportunity for adaptive gene substitution. In the view of the neutralists, the main role of natural selection, at the molecular level, is to conserve the established function of a molecule, protecting it from deleterious mutations. To be sure, during the initial period of evolution of a new gene, selection for advantageous alleles operates to establish and perfect its function. However, once that function is well-established, further evolution is postulated to occur through the fixation of neutral alleles. Regardless of the stage of evolution of the molecule, most newly arising mutations are deleterious. These are quickly weeded out, so that only selectively neutral and rare advantageous genes will be fixed.

Since the neutral theory states that the amino acid substitution rate is dependent only on the rate of mutation (3.21), a comparison of these rates should provide an estimate of the fraction of new mutants that are neutral for a given protein family. Taking an average rate from a variety of different proteins of $k_s = 1.6 \times 10^{-9}$ amino acid substitutions per residue site per year, and an average protein size of 300 amino acids, the total number of substitutions in a protein per year would be about 4.8×10^{-7}. Conversion to a rate per generation, of course, depends on the organism. If we consider a generation time of 5 years, for example, the amino acid substitution rate per protein per generation would be approximately 2.4×10^{-6}. Since the standard gene mutation rate is about 10^{-5} per generation, this suggests that neutral mutants constitute a small fraction of all mutants at a locus.

The neutral theory forces one to distinguish between adaptive and nonadaptive evolution. Neutralists agree with selectionists that major morphological, behavioral, and physiological traits evolve under the direction of natural selection, particularly when controlled by a series of interacting gene loci. However, on the molecular level, many of the changes that occur are postulated to be nonadaptive, especially those that involve parts of molecules not critical to function. Thoday (1975) postulates that some so-called neutral alleles are actually "conditionally neutral." These are alleles that were neutral in the past, but may be nonneutral in future genetic or environmental circumstances. Neutral evolution can then be progressive in the sense that neutral alleles can be stored as potential variation for selection in the future. All "strictly neutral" mutations are irrelevant to evolution in the classical sense, which is strictly adaptive.

The neutral theory is supported by, and is heavily dependent on, the observed uniformity in the rates of amino acid substitution over the course of evolution. (This constancy is for the total number of changes, and not necessarily for the individual sites involved or the type of substitution.) For example, when the human β hemoglobin polypeptide is compared to the α chain from human, mouse, rabbit, horse, cow, or even carp, 75 to 79 amino acid differences are found. The amount of divergence is the same whether the compared peptides are from the same organism (but different genes) or from two different organisms, which, in the case of man and carp, have evolved independently for over 350 million years (Kimura and Ohta, 1971). Figure 14.8 shows the constancy of the average rate of evolution for hemoglobin and three other protein families. In each family, the difference between any two organisms depends almost entirely on their time of divergence. A constant rate of amino acid substitution

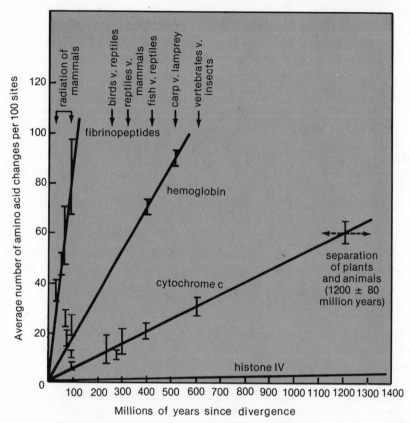

Figure 14.8. Relationship between the accumulated number of amino acid substitutions and the divergence time in fibrinopeptides, hemoglobin, cytochrome c, and histone IV. The number of amino acid substitutions has been corrected for the occurrence of multiple mutations at any given site. Times since divergence of two lines of organisms have been obtained from the geological record. (After R.E. Dickerson. 1972. Scientific American 226: 58.)

throughout diverse lines of evolution suggests that amino acid changes have not been subject to selection pressure. It is difficult to imagine how three unrelated parameters (N, s, and k; (3.24)) could have varied over all of evolutionary time to keep their product constant.

If the rate of molecular evolution is constant through time, then evolutionary events can be dated. Once the actual geological time of one of the events in a molecular phylogenetic tree is known (from the paleontological record, for example), the time of occurrence of all other events in the phylogeny could be determined. Obviously, there would be some variation, since the number of amino acid substitutions per residue site is postulated to be a random variable. However, over long periods of time, the clock should be fairly accurate. Because of the implication such a clock would have to the study of evolutionary biology, it is of critical importance to determine whether or not the neutral theory is correct.

Although Figure 14.8 demonstrates that the rate of evolution of certain proteins is roughly constant over long periods of time, as a greater variety of proteins is studied over shorter evolutionary spans, the rate-constancy feature is no longer so striking. The per codon substitution rate and the rate of change for the whole molecule are often not constant for any one particular protein. This could simply mean that those amino acid positions that are variable change from time to time, perhaps due to restrictions on amino acid substitutions imposed by intramolecular interactions (Fitch and Markowitz, 1970). However, it could also mean that molecular evolution does not proceed by fixation of neutral alleles. Assuming that the number of substitutions along any arm of a phylogenetic tree is a Poisson random variable, and using codon substitution data for several proteins simultaneously, Langley and Fitch (1974) constructed a parsimonious phylogenetic tree and statistically tested the hypothesis of constant, uniform molecular change over all branches. They found a highly significant test statistic. This result does not favor the neutral theory, although the proportion of the phylogeny contributing to the statistical significance is not known. Nevertheless, the average amount of molecular change over many proteins evolving over long periods of time does appear to be sufficiently constant to be used as an approximate clock of evolutionary events (Fig. 14.9).

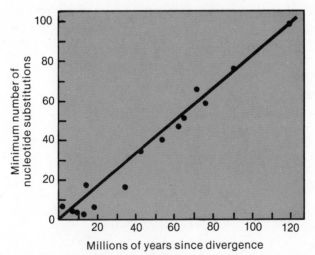

Figure 14.9. Nucleotide substitutions between various pairs of species versus paleontological time. The total number of nucleotide substitutions for seven proteins (cytochrome c, fibrinopeptides A and B, hemoglobin alpha and beta, insulin C-peptide, and myoglobin) is plotted as a function of the time since the ancestors of the species diverged. The line has been drawn to the outermost point, which represents the marsupial-placental divergence. With the exception of primates (points below the line at lower left), the overall correlation is fairly good. (After W.M. Fitch. 1976. In *Molecular Evolution.* F.J. Ayala, ed. Sinauer Associates, Sunderland, Massachusetts.)

From the slope of the line, the rate of molecular evolution is calculated to be 1.5×10^{-9} amino acid substitutions per codon per year.

Present arguments are not sufficiently powerful or precise to determine whether or not the neutral theory is correct. As Ewens (1977) has pointed out, the matter will be resolved not by the accumulation of more and more data, but by advances in population genetics theory.

Appendix I

Differentiation

Let the slope of a graph of the continuous function $y = f(x)$ be denoted as $\Delta y/\Delta x = (x_1 - x_o)/(y_1 - y_o)$, where the coordinates (x_1, y_1), (x_o, y_o) mark off the interval over which the slope is evaluated. For the linear function $y = mx + b$, the value of the slope is the same for all intervals. To illustrate, take the value $x_1 = x_o + \Delta x$. The corresponding value of y is $y_1 = m(x_o + \Delta x) + b$, and that of $\Delta y = y_1 - y_o$ is $m(x_o + \Delta x) + b - (mx_o + b) = m\Delta x$. Hence the slope $= \Delta y/\Delta x = m$, a constant.

This is in contrast to a nonlinear function for which the value of the slope depends on the interval over which it is measured; that is, the slope of a nonlinear function depends on x. For example, consider the function $y = 3x^2 + 2$. Let x change to $x + \Delta x$. Then the corresponding value of y is $3(x + \Delta x)^2 + 2 = 3x^2 + 5x \Delta x + 3\Delta x^2 + 2$, and $\Delta y = 3x^2 + 6x \Delta x + 3\Delta x^2 + 2 - (3x^2 + 2) = 6x \Delta x + 3\Delta x^2$. The slope is thus, $\Delta y/\Delta x = 6x + 3\Delta x$, dependent on both x and Δx. To find the value of the slope at some particular value x, we make the interval $x_1 - x_o$ infinitesimally small, and find the limiting value of the ratio $\Delta y/\Delta x$ as Δx approaches zero. The result is the slope at x, which is given by $\lim_{\Delta x \to 0} (\Delta y/\Delta x) = \lim_{\Delta x \to 0} (6x + 3\Delta x) = 6x$.

Letting dy and dx represent the infinitesimally small values of Δy and Δx, the generalized result for any function $f(x)$ is the derivative with respect to x:

$$\lim_{\Delta x \to 0} (\Delta y/\Delta x) = \lim_{\Delta x \to 0} \frac{f(x + \Delta x) - f(x)}{\Delta x} = \frac{f(x + dx) - f(x)}{dx} = dy/dx$$

dy/dx is also symbolized $f'(x)$, y', or $D_x y$. This limit is often termed the instantaneous rate of change of y with respect to x. In differential form, $dy = f'(x)\, dx$.

Some commonly used derivatives are listed below:

1. $dx/dx = 1$
2. $dc/dx = 0$, where c is a constant
3. $d[cf(x)]/dx = c[d(f(x))/dx]$

Letting u and v represent functions of x,

4. $d(u + v)/dx = du/dx + dv/dx$
5. $d(uv)/dx = u(dv/dx) + v(du/dx)$
6. $d(u/v)/dx = [v(du/dx) - u(dv/dx)]/v^2$ Thus, if $u = 1$, we obtain $d(1/v)/dx = -(1/v^2)(dv/dx)$.
7. $d(u^m)/dx = mu^{m-1}(du/dx)$ Thus if $u = x$, we obtain $d(x^m)/dx = mx^{m-1}$.
8. $d(a^u)/dx = a^u(\ln a)(du/dx)$ Thus, if $a = e$, we obtain $d(e^u)/dx = e^u(du/dx)$.
9. $d(\log_n u)/dx = (1/u)(\log_n e)(du/dx)$ Thus, if $a = e$, we obtain $d(\ln u)/dx = (1/u)(du/dx)$.
10. Chain rule. If $y = f(u)$, where $u = g(x)$, then $y = f\{g(x)\}$ and $dy/dx = (dy/du)(du/dx)$

11. $dy/dx = \dfrac{1}{(dx/dy)}$

Consider some function, z, of two independent variables, x and y, so that $z = f(x, y)$. Then the partial derivative of z with respect to x (holding y constant) is denoted $\partial z/\partial x$ or $(\partial f/\partial x)_y$, and is equal to $\lim\limits_{\Delta x \to 0} \dfrac{f(x + \Delta x, y) - f(x, y)}{\Delta x}$. Similarly, the partial derivative of z with respect to y (holding x constant) is denoted $\partial z/\partial y$ or $(\partial f/\partial y)_x$, and is equal to $\lim\limits_{\Delta y \to 0} \dfrac{f(x, y + \Delta y) - f(x, y)}{\Delta y}$. The total differential, dz, is then the sum of the partial differentials: $dz = (\partial z/\partial x)dx + (\partial z/\partial y)dy$. For example, let $z = 3x^2 y^3 + 4xy^2 + 2y$. Then $\partial z/\partial x = 6xy^3 + 4y^2$, and $\partial z/\partial y = 9x^2y^2 + 8xy + 2$. Hence, $dz = (6xy^3 + 4y^2)dx + (9x^2y^2 + 8xy + 2)dy$.

The chain rule for two variables, x and y, both functions of a third variable, t, becomes $dz/dt = (\partial z/\partial x)(dx/dt) + (\partial z/\partial y)(dy/dt)$. As an example, let $z = x^2y^3$, $x = 2t^3$, and $y = 3t^2$. Then $\partial z/\partial x = 2xy^3$, $\partial z/\partial y = 3x^2y^2$, $dx/dt = 6t^2$, $dy/dt = 6t$, and so $dz = 2xy^3(6t^2) + 3x^2y^2(6t) = 6xy^2t(2yt + 3x)$.

Finally, we remind the reader that if the function $f(x)$ has a maximum or minimum value, this occurs at the value of x satisfying the relationship $d(f(x))/dx = 0$. Evaluation of the second derivative yields the inflection point, that x value satisfying the equation $d^2(f(x))/dx^2 = 0$. As an example, find the values of x where the function $y = ax(1 - x)^2$ has its maximum value and point of inflection. Differentiating, we obtain $dy/dx = -2ax(1 - x) + a(1 - x)^2 = a(3x^2 - 4x + 1)$. Setting this expression equal to zero and solving for x gives $3x^2 - 4x + 1 = 0$, and $x = 1$ or $x = 1/3$. When $x < 1/3$, dy/dx is positive, and when $x > 1/3$, dy/dx is negative. Hence, $x = 1/3$ gives the maximum value of y. To locate the inflection point, solve for x in the expression $d^2y/dx^2 = 6ax - 4a = 0$, giving $x = 2/3$.

Appendix II

Integration

If $F(x)$ is a function whose derivative is $f(x)$, then $F(x)$ is termed the anti-derivative or integral of $f(x)$. Some fundamental integration formulas are listed below. Others can be found in any mathematics handbook.

1. $\int au\,dx = a \int u\,dx$, where a is a constant
2. $\int (u + v)\,dx = \int u\,dx + \int v\,dx$
3. $\int u^m du = u^{m+1}/(m+1) + C$, where C is the integration constant
4. $\int du/u = \ln|u| + C$
5. $\int a^u du = a^u/\ln a + C$ If $a = e$, we obtain
   $\int e^u du = e^u + C$

Integration by parts is a useful method in finding some integrals. Since $d(uv) = u\,dv + v\,du$, then $u\,dv = d(uv) - v\,du$, and $\int u\,dv = uv - \int v\,du$. For example, $\int xe^x dx$ can be found by letting $u = x$ and $dv = e^x dx$. Then $du = dx$ and $v = e^x$, and $\int xe^x dx = xe^x - \int e^x dx = xe^x - e^x + C$.

Integrals of the form $\int f(x)\,dx/g(x)$ can often be solved through the method of partial fractions. The denominator is factored, and the quotient $f(x)/g(x)$ is expressed as the sum of the partial fractions. As an example, the integral of $(x + 1)\,dx/(x^3 + x^2 - 6x)$ can be found by noting that the denominator can be factored as $x^3 + x^2 - 6x = x(x - 2)(x + 3)$. Hence, $(x + 1)/(x^3 + x^2 - 6x)$ can be set equal to $A/x + B/(x - 2) + C/(x + 3)$, where A, B, and C are constants whose values must be determined. Clearing of fractions, we obtain $x + 1 = A(x - 2)(x + 3) + Bx(x + 3) + Cx(x - 2)$, or $x + 1 = (A + B + C)x^2 + (A + 3B - 2C)x - 6A$. Since like powers of x on the two sides of this equation have equal coefficients, the result is $A + B + C = 0$, $A + 3B - 2C = 1$, and $-6A = 1$. Solving these equations simultaneously gives $A = -1/6$, $B = 3/10$, and $C = -2/15$. Thus, $\int (x + 1)\,dx/(x^3 + x^2 - 6x) = -1/6 \int dx/x + 3/10 \int dx/(x-2) - 2/15 \int dx/(x+3) = -1/6 \ln|x| + 3/10 \ln|x-2| - 2/15 \ln|x+3| + C = \ln[(x-2)^{3/10}/x^{1/6}(x+3)^{2/15}] + C$.

The definite integral $\int_a^b f(x)dx$ can be interpreted geometrically as the area under the graph of $f(x)$ versus x over the interval defined by $a \leq x \leq b$. Subdividing this interval into n infinitesimally small subintervals, the ith subinterval of length $\Delta_i x$, we let the largest such subinterval length approach zero. Then, letting $f(x_i)$ be the value of the function at a point on the ith subinterval, it can be shown that $\int_a^b f(x)dx = \lim_{n \to \infty} \sum_{i=1}^{n} f(x_i)\Delta_i x$.

The fundamental theorem of integral calculus states that $\int_a^b f(x)dx = F(x)]_a^b = F(b) - F(a)$. For example, $\int_2^6 dx/x = \ln|x| \,]_2^6 = \ln 6 - \ln 2 = \ln 3$.

Appendix III

Second Order Linear Equations

Solutions to the second order linear difference equation $x_{t+2} - Bx_{t+1} + Cx_t = 0$ can be found by assuming solutions to be of the form $x_t = k\lambda^t$. This gives the quadratic auxiliary equation $\lambda^2 - B\lambda + C = 0$, having roots λ_1 and λ_2. There are three possibilities that may arise in solving this auxiliary equation.

Case 1: $B^2 - 4C > 0$

In this case, both roots are real and the general solution can be expressed as a linear combination of the two basic solutions:

$$x_t = k_1\lambda_1^t + k_2\lambda_2^t \qquad \text{(A.III.1)}$$

To verify that this is a general solution to the difference equation, merely substitute it into our recurrence relation. Since $x_{t+2} - Bx_{t+1} + Cx_t$ is equal to zero, then if $k_1\lambda_1^t + k_2\lambda_2^t$ is a solution, $(k_1\lambda_1^{t+2} + k_2\lambda_2^{t+2}) - B(k_1\lambda_1^{t+1} + k_2\lambda_2^{t+1}) + C(k_1\lambda_1^t + k_2\lambda_2^t)$ must also equal zero. This is easily seen if we collect like terms and express the latter equation as $k_1\lambda_1^t(\lambda_1^2 - B\lambda_1 + C) + k_2\lambda_2^t(\lambda_2^2 - B\lambda_2 + C)$. Recalling that λ_1 and λ_2 are both roots of the quadratic equation $\lambda^2 - B\lambda + C = 0$, it should be apparent that both $\lambda_1^2 - B\lambda_1 + C$ and $\lambda_2^2 - B\lambda_2 + C$, and therefore the complete equation, must equal zero. Hence, (A.III.1) is a solution.

Case 2: $B^2 - 4C < 0$

In this case both roots are complex. In order to understand the development of solutions, we must first review complex numbers and their conversion to trigonometric form. A complex number can be represented as the quantity $(x + iy)$, where x denotes the real part, and iy the imaginary part, i being $\sqrt{-1}$. The quantity $(x + iy)$ is the most

575

general way of representing any number. If $y = 0$, the number is simply x, and is real, whereas if $x = 0$, the number is iy, and is a pure imaginary number.

Complex numbers often arise in finding solutions to quadratic equations. For example, the equation $x^2 + 4x + 5 = 0$ has solutions of the form $-2 \pm \frac{1}{2} \sqrt{-4} = -2 \pm \frac{1}{2} i \sqrt{4}$, giving $x_1 = -2 + i$ and $x_2 = -2 - i$.

The meaning of i can perhaps be clarified by representing a complex number graphically. Any real positive number x can be expressed as a vector lying along the horizontal axis (real number line) in a positive direction. The vector $-x$ can be obtained from x by rotation counterclockwise through 180°:

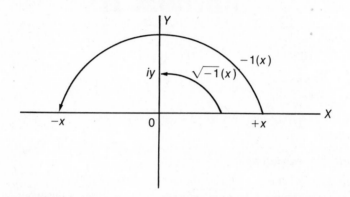

Hence, we see that rotation of a vector through 180° is equivalent to multiplication of x by the quantity (-1). But rotation by 180° is the same as applying two consecutive 90° rotations, and, therefore, two successive multiplications by the quantity $\sqrt{-1}$. Thus, multiplication by $\sqrt{-1}$ or i is equivalent to rotation by 90°. This means that while all real numbers are represented by points on the horizontal axis of our graph, all pure imaginary numbers can be represented by points along the vertical axis. The complex number $(x + iy)$ can, therefore, be represented in the coordinate plane by the point P:

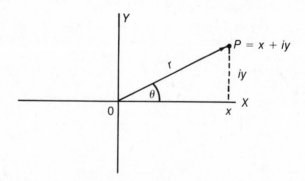

Using all four quadrants, we see that all complex numbers can be represented in this fashion:

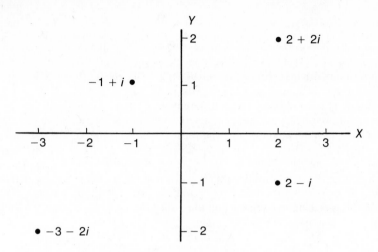

Since $(x + iy)$ can also be represented by the vector $\overrightarrow{OP}$, arithmetic manipulation of complex numbers follows the laws of vector addition.

The equivalent trigonometric (polar) representation can be obtained as follows. Let r equal the length of $\overrightarrow{OP}$, and recall that $x = r\cos(\theta)$ and $y = r\sin(\theta)$, where θ is the angle XOP. Then $(x + iy) = r(\cos(\theta) + i\sin(\theta))$. For example, find the trigonometric form of the number $(-5 + 6i)$. First, since $r = \sqrt{x^2 + y^2}$, where $x = -5$ and $y = 6$, we have $r = \sqrt{61}$. The point $(-5 + 6i)$ lies in the second quadrant, and $\tan(\theta) = y/x = -6/5 = -1.200$. Hence $\theta = 129.8°$, and $(-5 + 6i) = \sqrt{61}[\cos(129.8) + i\sin(129.8)]$ in polar coordinates.

Finally, from the addition rules of trigonometry, it can easily be demonstrated that $[r_1(\cos(\theta_1) + i\sin(\theta_1))] [r_2(\cos(\theta_2) + i\sin(\theta_2))] = r_1 r_2[\cos(\theta_1 + \theta_2) + i\sin(\theta_1 + \theta_2)]$. Generalizing gives DeMoivre's theorem: $[r(\cos(\theta) + i\sin(\theta))]^n = r^n[\cos(n\theta) + i\sin(n\theta)]$, where n is any positive integer.

We are now prepared to consider solutions to our second order difference equation. Since $B^2 - 4C < 0$, solutions are of the form $\lambda_1 = \frac{1}{2}B + \frac{1}{2}i\sqrt{4C - B^2}$; and $\lambda_2 = \frac{1}{2}B - \frac{1}{2}i\sqrt{4C - B^2}$. Changing to trigonometric form, where $x = B/2$, and $y = \sqrt{4C - B^2}/2$, we obtain $\lambda_1 = r(\cos(\theta) + i\sin(\theta))$ and $\lambda_2 = r(\cos(\theta) - i\sin(\theta))$, where θ is the angle whose cosine is $B/2r$, and $r = \sqrt{C}$. Since any linear combination of λ_1^t and λ_2^t will yield a general solution, we will express the solution in this case as $x_t = k_1(\lambda_1^t + \lambda_2^t)/2 + k_2(\lambda_1^t - \lambda_2^t)/2i$. But $\lambda_1^t = [r(\cos(\theta) + i\sin(\theta))]^t = r^t[\cos(\theta t) + i\sin(\theta t)]$, and $\lambda_2^t = [r(\cos(\theta) - i\sin(\theta))]^t = r^t[\cos(\theta t) - i\sin(\theta t)]$. Substituting these into our expression for x_t, we then get as a general solution $x_t = k_1 r^t\cos(\theta t) + k_2 r^t\sin(\theta t)$. Substituting $r = \sqrt{C}$ gives

$$x_t = (C)^{\frac{1}{2}t}[k_1\cos(\theta t) + k_2\sin(\theta t)] \tag{A.III.2}$$

As in case 1, the values of k_1 and k_2 can be evaluated from knowledge of x_0 and x_1. Note that when $t = 0$, $x_0 = k_1$, since $\sin(\theta) = 0$ and $\cos(\theta) = 1$, and when $t = 1$, $x_1 = (C)^{\frac{1}{2}}[k_1\cos(\theta) + k_2\sin(\theta)]$. Solving for k_1 and k_2, we obtain the following pair of relations

$$k_1 = x_0 \text{ and } k_2 = [x_1 - x_0\cos(\theta)]/(C)^{\frac{1}{2}}\sin(\theta)$$

Case 3: $B^2 - 4C = 0$

Here there is one real root, since $\lambda_1 = \lambda_2 = -B/2$. The general solution can be expressed as $x_t = k_1\lambda_1^t + k_2 t\lambda_1^{t-1}$. The reader can verify that this is a solution by substitution into our original recurrence relationship. The constants k_1 and k_2 can be determined in terms of x_0 and x_1, giving $k_1 = x_0$ and $k_2 = x_1 - k_1\lambda_1$.

Solutions of second order linear differential equations of the form $d^2x/dt^2 - adx/dt + bx = 0$ are found in a manner completely analogous to that employed for difference equations. We assume a solution of the form $x = ke^{\lambda t}$, giving as the general solution $x_t = k_1e^{\lambda_1 t} + k_2e^{\lambda_2 t}$. If $a^2 - 4b < 0$, the roots are complex, of the form $\frac{1}{2}a \pm \frac{1}{2}i \sqrt{4b - a^2}$, giving $e^{\lambda_1 t} = e^{\frac{1}{2}at} e^{\frac{1}{2}i \sqrt{4b-a^2}t}$ and $e^{\lambda_2 t} = e^{\frac{1}{2}at} e^{-\frac{1}{2}i \sqrt{4b-a^2}t}$. To change to polar form, we employ Euler's formula, which states that $e^{ix} = \cos(x) + i\sin(x)$. Therefore, $e^{\lambda_1 t} = e^{\frac{1}{2}at}[\cos(\frac{1}{2} \sqrt{4b-a^2}t) + i\sin(\frac{1}{2} \sqrt{4b-a^2}t)]$ and $e^{\lambda_2 t} = e^{\frac{1}{2}at} [\cos(\frac{1}{2} \sqrt{4b-a^2}t) - i\sin(\frac{1}{2} \sqrt{4b-a^2}t)]$. Expressing the general solution as $k_1(e^{\lambda_1 t} + e^{\lambda_2 t})/2 + k_2(e^{\lambda_1 t} - e^{\lambda_2 t})/2i$, we obtain $x_t = e^{\frac{1}{2}at}[k_1\cos(\frac{1}{2} \sqrt{4b-a^2}t) + k_2\sin(\frac{1}{2} \sqrt{4b-a^2}t)]$.

Appendix IV

Matrix Algebra

The $m \times n$ matrix A has m rows and n columns, a_{ij} being the ijth component:

$$A = \begin{bmatrix} a_{11} & a_{12} & \ldots & a_{1j} & \ldots & a_{1n} \\ a_{21} & a_{22} & \ldots & a_{2j} & \ldots & a_{2n} \\ \vdots & \vdots & & \vdots & & \vdots \\ a_{i1} & a_{i2} & \ldots & a_{ij} & \ldots & a_{in} \\ \vdots & \vdots & & \vdots & & \vdots \\ a_{m1} & a_{m2} & \ldots & a_{mj} & \ldots & a_{mn} \end{bmatrix}$$

Vectors are simply special cases of matrices, having just one row or column. For example, the column vector B is the $m \times 1$ matrix

$$B = \begin{bmatrix} b_1 \\ \vdots \\ b_i \\ \vdots \\ b_m \end{bmatrix}$$

If two matrices A and B both have the same number of rows and columns, their sum is defined and is obtained by adding corresponding components, i.e., $C = A + B$, where $c_{ij} = a_{ij} + b_{ij}$:

$$A + B = \begin{bmatrix} a_{11} + b_{11} & \ldots & a_{1j} + b_{1j} & \ldots & a_{1n} + b_{1n} \\ \vdots & & \vdots & & \vdots \\ a_{i1} + b_{i1} & \ldots & a_{ij} + b_{ij} & \ldots & a_{in} + b_{in} \\ \vdots & & \vdots & & \vdots \\ a_{m1} + b_{m1} & \ldots & a_{mj} + b_{mj} & \ldots & a_{mn} + b_{mn} \end{bmatrix}$$

For example, if $A = \begin{bmatrix} 1 & 2 & 3 \\ -2 & 1 & 3 \end{bmatrix}$ and $B = \begin{bmatrix} 5 & 4 & 3 \\ 4 & -2 & 1 \end{bmatrix}$, then $A + B = \begin{bmatrix} 6 & 6 & 6 \\ 2 & -1 & 4 \end{bmatrix}$.

If A and B do not have the same dimensions, their sum is not defined.

To multiply a matrix by a scalar quantity, k, each entry is simply multiplied by k:

$$kA = \begin{bmatrix} ka_{11} & \cdots & ka_{1j} & \cdots & ka_{1n} \\ \vdots & & \vdots & & \vdots \\ ka_{i1} & \cdots & ka_{ij} & \cdots & ka_{in} \\ \vdots & & \vdots & & \vdots \\ ka_{m1} & \cdots & ka_{mj} & \cdots & ka_{mn} \end{bmatrix}$$

The product of two matrices, $C = AB$, is defined if the number of columns of A is equal to the number of rows of B. For example, let A be a $m \times p$ matrix and B a $p \times n$ matrix. Then $C = AB$ is the $m \times n$ matrix having component c_{ij} obtained by multiplying the ith row of A by the jth column of B:

$$\begin{bmatrix} a_{11} & \cdots & a_{1h} & \cdots & a_{1p} \\ \vdots & & \vdots & & \vdots \\ a_{i1} & \cdots & a_{ih} & \cdots & a_{ip} \\ \vdots & & \vdots & & \vdots \\ a_{m1} & \cdots & a_{mh} & \cdots & a_{mp} \end{bmatrix} \cdot \begin{bmatrix} b_{11} & \cdots & b_{1j} & \cdots & b_{1n} \\ \vdots & & \vdots & & \vdots \\ b_{h1} & \cdots & b_{hj} & \cdots & b_{hn} \\ \vdots & & \vdots & & \vdots \\ b_{p1} & \cdots & b_{pj} & \cdots & b_{pn} \end{bmatrix} = \begin{bmatrix} c_{11} & \cdots & c_{1j} & \cdots & c_{1n} \\ \vdots & & \vdots & & \vdots \\ c_{i1} & \cdots & c_{ij} & \cdots & c_{in} \\ \vdots & & \vdots & & \vdots \\ c_{m1} & \cdots & c_{mj} & \cdots & c_{mn} \end{bmatrix}$$

where $c_{ij} = \sum\limits_{h=1}^{p} a_{ih}b_{hj} = a_{i1}b_{1j} + a_{i2}b_{2j} + \ldots + a_{ih}b_{hj} + \ldots + a_{ip}b_{pj}$.

As an example, let the matrices A and B be, respectively,

$$\begin{bmatrix} 3 & 2 & 1 \\ 2 & 1 & 1 \end{bmatrix} \text{ and } \begin{bmatrix} 2 & 1 \\ 3 & 2 \\ 1 & 3 \end{bmatrix}. \text{ Then } AB \text{ is } \begin{bmatrix} 6+6+1 & 3+4+3 \\ 4+3+1 & 2+2+3 \\ 2+6+3 & 1+4+9 \end{bmatrix} = \begin{bmatrix} 13 & 10 \\ 8 & 7 \\ 11 & 14 \end{bmatrix}$$

Note that the product AB does not necessarily equal the product BA. (In fact, in this case, BA is undefined.) However, the multiplication is associative; i.e., $(AB)C = A(BC)$, and $k(AB) = (kA)B = A(kB)$.

If $m = n$, a matrix is referred to as a square matrix. A diagonal matrix is a square matrix having all nondiagonal components equal to 0. If all a_{ij} of a diagonal matrix are equal to 1, the matrix is termed the identity matrix, I. I plays the same role in matrix algebra as the number one does in ordinary algebra.

The $n \times n$ (square) matrix A is said to be invertible if there exists a $n \times n$ matrix A^{-1} such that $AA^{-1} = A^{-1}A = I$. A^{-1} is the inverse of A and is analogous to the reciprocal of a number. A textbook on matrix algebra should be consulted if the reader desires to learn or review the somewhat complex procedures involved in finding the inverse of a matrix.

Matrices are often used as a convenient means of solving systems of linear equations. In such cases, the determinant of the square matrix A is calculated, where det A, symbolized as $|A|$, is defined as $|A| = \sum\limits_{i \text{ or } j} (-1)^{i+j}a_{ij} |A_{ij}|$. $|A_{ij}|$ is the determinant of the matrix obtained from A by deleting the ith row and jth column. Any row or column of A can be used as the basis for the expansion. For example, using the first row, we find the determinant of the matrix

$$\begin{bmatrix} a_{11} & a_{12} \\ a_{21} & a_{22} \end{bmatrix}$$

to be $(-1)^{1+1}a_{11} |A_{11}| + (-1)^{1+2}a_{12} |A_{12}| = a_{11}a_{22} - a_{12}a_{21}$. A 3×3 matrix is a bit more complex, but the same procedure can be employed:

$$\begin{bmatrix} a_{11} & a_{12} & a_{13} \\ a_{21} & a_{22} & a_{23} \\ a_{31} & a_{32} & a_{33} \end{bmatrix} = (-1)^{1+1}a_{11}\left|A_{11}\right| + (-1)^{1+2}a_{12}\left|A_{12}\right| + (-1)^{1+3}a_{13}\left|A_{13}\right|.$$

Since $\left|A_{11}\right| = a_{22}a_{33} - a_{23}a_{32}$, and $\left|A_{12}\right| = a_{21}a_{33} - a_{23}a_{31}$, and $\left|A_{13}\right| = a_{21}a_{32} - a_{22}a_{31}$, the result is $\left|A\right| = a_{11}a_{22}a_{33} + a_{12}a_{23}a_{31} + a_{13}a_{21}a_{32} - (a_{31}a_{22}a_{13} + a_{32}a_{23}a_{11} + a_{33}a_{21}a_{12})$.

As an example, the determinant of the matrix

$$\begin{bmatrix} 2 & 1 & 2 \\ 1 & 2 & 1 \\ 2 & -3 & 4 \end{bmatrix}$$

is calculated as $2\begin{vmatrix} 2 & 1 \\ -3 & 4 \end{vmatrix} - \begin{vmatrix} 1 & 1 \\ 2 & 4 \end{vmatrix} + 2\begin{vmatrix} 1 & 2 \\ 2 & -3 \end{vmatrix} = 2\,(8 + 3) - (4 - 2) + 2(-3 - 4) = 22 - 2 - 14 = 6$.

Appendix V

Chi-square Test

In population biology, as in other branches of science, experimental tests are often performed by comparing observed numerical results with those predicted on the basis of some hypothesis. For example, suppose we cross fruit-flies heterozygous for two pairs of genes, $AaBb$, and obtain, among 240 total offspring, 143 $A-B-$, 36 $A-bb$, 49 $aaB-$, and 12 $aabb$ phenotypes. We hypothesize that the two gene loci are assorting independently. This predicts a 9:3:3:1 ratio among these four phenotypic classes. Thus, the expected values are $\frac{9}{16}(240) = 135$, $\frac{3}{16}(240) = 45$, and $\frac{1}{16}(240) = 15$. In each of the four classes there is some deviation of the observed number from that expected. We must, therefore, decide whether these deviations are significant—reflect a real difference between observation and theory, or insignificant—reflect random sampling error. If the deviations are significant, then we must conclude that the hypothesis of independent assortment is not the correct one to explain these data. In statistical terms we ask, if the proposed genetic mechanism is correct (if expected values are correct), what is the probability of obtaining observed results that differ this much or more from their expected values?

One way to approach this problem would be to calculate the probability of the observed outcome using the multinomial distribution. Obviously this would be an extremely tedious procedure if the numbers are at all large. Fortunately, a good approximation to this probability can be obtained by employing the statistical procedure known as the chi-square test. The first step in using this method is to calculate the value of the statistic χ^2, using the following formula:

$$\chi^2 = \sum_i (O_i - E_i)^2/E_i$$

where O_i = observed number in class i and E_i = expected number in class i. For the preceding data, $\chi^2 = (143 - 135)^2/135 + (36 - 45)^2/45 + (49 - 45)^2/45 + (12 - 15)^2/15 = 3.23$.

Consultation with a table of χ^2 values will determine the probability of obtaining deviations this large or larger, if the hypothesized ratio is indeed correct. To use the table (found at the end of this appendix), the number of degrees of freedom (d.f.) must be determined. In general, the number of degrees of freedom in a chi-square test equals the number of classes minus one, minus one for each parameter that has to be estimated from the data in order to calculate expected values. In the present example, no parameter had to be estimated from the data, so d.f. = number of classes − 1 = 4 − 1 = 3. From the table we obtain a probability value of approximately 30%. Hence, if the hypothesis is correct, the chance of obtaining deviations of at least the magnitude observed is given by the probability of obtaining a χ^2 value equal to or greater than that observed, and is, in this case, approximately 30%.

To make the final decision as to whether or not the observed results can be explained by the hypothesis, one must decide on the level of significance to be used. The most widely used level is 0.05. Thus, if the probability value associated with χ^2 is less than 0.05, the deviations of observed from expected are significant, and the hypothesis proposed to account for the data is rejected. In our example, $P > 0.05$, and we conclude that the genes are assorting independently. There is no significant difference between the observed results and those expected on the basis of independent assortment.

Probabilities of different chi-square values for degrees of freedom from 1 to 50.

d.f.	PROBABILITIES									
	0.95	0.90	0.70	0.50	0.30	0.20	0.10	0.05	0.01	0.001
1	0.004	0.016	0.15	0.46	1.07	1.64	2.71	3.84	6.64	10.83
2	0.10	0.21	0.71	1.39	2.41	3.22	4.61	5.99	9.21	13.82
3	0.35	0.58	1.42	2.37	3.67	4.64	6.25	7.82	11.35	16.27
4	0.71	1.06	2.20	3.36	4.88	5.99	7.78	9.49	13.28	18.47
5	1.15	1.61	3.00	4.35	6.06	7.29	9.24	11.07	15.09	20.52
6	1.64	2.20	3.83	5.35	7.23	8.56	10.65	12.59	16.81	22.46
7	2.17	2.83	4.67	6.35	8.38	9.80	12.02	14.07	18.48	24.32
8	2.73	3.49	5.53	7.34	9.52	11.03	13.36	15.51	20.09	26.13
9	3.33	4.17	6.39	8.34	10.66	12.24	14.68	16.92	21.67	27.88
10	3.94	4.87	7.27	9.34	11.78	13.44	15.99	18.31	23.21	29.59
11	4.58	5.58	8.15	10.34	12.90	14.63	17.28	19.68	24.73	31.26
12	5.23	6.30	9.03	11.34	14.01	15.81	18.55	21.03	26.22	32.91
13	5.89	7.04	9.93	12.34	15.12	16.99	19.81	22.36	27.69	34.53
14	6.57	7.79	10.82	13.34	16.22	18.15	21.06	23.69	29.14	36.12
15	7.26	8.55	11.72	14.34	17.32	19.31	22.31	25.00	30.58	37.70
20	10.85	12.44	16.27	19.34	22.78	25.04	28.41	31.41	37.57	45.32
25	14.61	16.47	20.87	24.34	28.17	30.68	34.38	37.65	44.31	52.62
30	18.49	20.60	25.51	29.34	33.53	36.25	40.26	43.77	50.89	59.70
50	34.76	37.69	44.31	49.34	54.72	58.16	63.17	67.51	76.15	86.66

Bibliography

Abrams, P.A. 1977. Density independent mortality and interspecific competition: A test of Pianka's niche overlap hypothesis. Amer. Natur. 111: 539–552.

Anderson, F.S. 1965. Simple population models and their application to the formation of complex models. Proc. XII Int. Congr. Entomol., London, 620–622.

Anderson, W.W. 1969. Polymorphism resulting from the mating advantage of rare male genotypes. Proc. Nat. Acad. Sci. U.S.A., 64: 190–197.

Andrewartha, H.C. 1944. The distribution of plagues of *Austroicetes cruciata* Sauss (Acrididae) in Australia in relation to climate, vegetation, and soil. Trans. Roy. Soc. South Australia 68: 315–326.

Andrewartha, H.C. and L.C. Birch. 1954. *The Distribution and Abundance of Animals*. University of Chicago Press, Chicago.

Asmussen, M.A. and Feldman, M.W. 1977. Density dependent selection 1: a stable feasible equilibrium may not be attainable. J. Theor. Biol. 64: 603–618.

Ayala, F.J. 1969. Experimental invalidation of the principle of competitive exclusion. Nature 224: 1076–1079.

Ayala, F.J., Tracey, M.L., Hedgecock, D., and Richmond, R.C. 1974. Genetic differentiation during the speciation process in *Drosophila*. Evolution 28: 576–592.

Bachman, K., Goin, O.B., and Goin, C.J. 1974. Nuclear DNA amounts in vertebrates. In *Evolution of Genetic Systems*, H.H. Smith, ed. Brookhaven Symp. Biol. No. 23, 419–450.

Bailey, N.T. 1951. On estimating the size of mobile populations from recapture data. Biometrika 38: 293–306.

Bailey, N.T. 1952. Improvements in the interpretation of recapture data. J. Anim. Ecol. 21: 120–127.

Bartlett, M.S. 1960. *Stochastic Population Models in Ecology and Epidemiology*. Methuen and Company Ltd., London.

Basykin, A.D. 1965. On the possibility of sympatric species formation. Byull. Mosk. Obshchest. Ispyt. Prir. Otd. Biol. 70: 161–165.

Bazzaz, F.A. 1975. Plant species diversity in old-field successional ecosystems in southern Illinois. Ecology 56: 485–488.

Beddington, J.R., Free, C.A., and Lawton, J.H. 1976. Concepts of stability and resilience in predator-prey models. J. Anim. Ecol. 45: 791–813.

Benzer, S. 1955. Fine structure of a genetic region in bacteriophage. Proc. Nat. Acad. Sci. U.S.A., 41: 344–354.

Beyer, W.H. 1968. *Handbook of Tables for Probability and Statistics*. Chemical Rubber Company, Cleveland.

Birch, L.C. 1948. The intrinsic rate of natural increase of an insect population. J. Anim. Ecol. 17: 15–26.

Birch, L.C. 1953. Experimental background to the study of the distribution and abundance of insects. I. The influence of temperature, moisture, and food on the innate capacity for increase of three grain beetles. Ecology 34: 698–711.

Blackman, F.F. 1905. Optima and limiting factors. Ann. Botany 19: 281–298.

Bliss, C.I. and Fisher, R.A. 1953. Fitting the negative binomial distribution to biological data and a note on the efficient fitting of the negative binomial. Biometrics 9: 176–200.

Bodmer, W.F. and Edwards, A.W.F. 1960. Natural selection and the sex ratio. Ann. Hum. Genet. 24: 239–244.

Boorman, S.A. and Levitt, P.R. 1973. Group selection on the boundary of a stable population. Theor. Pop. Biol. 4: 85–128.

Boughey, A.S. 1975. *Man and the Environment. An Introduction to Human Ecology and Evolution*. MacMillan, New York.

Boyce, J.B. 1946. The influence of fecundity and egg mortality on the population growth of *Tribolium confusum* Duval. Ecology 27: 290–302.

Boyd, W.C. 1950. *Genetics and the Races of Man*. Little, Brown and Company, Boston.

Britten, R. J. and Kohne, D.E. 1968. Repeated sequences in DNA. Science 161: 529–540.

Brower, J. Van Z. 1958. Experimental studies of mimicry in some North American butterflies. Part I. The Monarch, *Danus plexippus*, and Viceroy, *Limenitis archippus archippus*. Evolution 12: 32–47.

Brown, J. 1969. Territorial behavior and population regulation in birds. Wilson Bull. 81: 293–329.

Brown, J.L. 1975. *The Evolution of Behavior*. W.W. Norton and Company, New York.

Bryant, E.H. 1973. Habitat selection in a variable environment. J. Theor. Biol. 41: 421–429.

Burnett, T. 1951. Effects of temperature and host density on the rate of increase of an insect parasite. Amer. Natur. 85: 337–352.

Burt, E. and Howard, M. 1956. The multifactorial theory of inheritance and its application to intelligence. Brit. J. Statist. Psychol. 8(2): 95–131.

Bush, G.L. 1975. Modes of animal speciation. Annu. Rev. Ecol. Syst. 6: 339–364.

Carson, H.L. 1975. The genetics of speciation at the diploid level. Amer. Natur. 109: 83–92.

Carson, H.L. and Kaneshiro, K.Y. 1976. *Drosophila* of Hawaii: Systematics and ecological genetics. Annu. Rev. Ecol. Syst. 7: 311–346.

Caughley, G. 1976. Wildlife management and the dynamics of ungulate populations. In *Advances in Applied Biology*, T.H. Coaker, ed. Vol. I.

Cavalli-Sforza, L.L. 1959. Some data on the genetic structure of human populations. Proc. 10th Intern. Congr. Genet. 1: 389–407.

Cavalli-Sforza, L.L. 1969. Human diversity. Proc. II. Intern. Congr. Genet. 3: 405–416.

Charlesworth, B. 1971. Selection in density-regulated populations. Ecology 52: 469–474.

Charnov, E.L. and Schaffer, W.M. 1973. Life history consequences of natural selection: Cole's result revisited. Amer. Natur. 107: 791–793.

Chetverikov, S.S. 1926. On certain features of the evolutionary process from the viewpoint of modern genetics. J. Exptl. Biol. (Russian) 2: 3–54. Translated into English and reprinted 1961 in Proc. Amer. Phil. Soc. 105: 167–195.

Chitty, D. 1960. Population processes in the vole and their relevance to general theory. Can J. Zool. 38: 99–113.

Christian, J.J. 1950. The adreno-pituitary system and population cycles in mammals. J. Mammal. 31: 247–259.

Christian, J.J. and Davis, D.E. 1964. Endocrines, behavior and population. Science 146: 1550–1560.

Clarke, B. 1962. Balanced polymorphism and the diversity of sympatric species. Taxonomy and geography. D. Nichols, ed. Systematics Assoc. Publ. No. 4.

Clarke, B. 1969. The evidence for apostatic selection. Heredity 24: 347–352.

Clough, G.C. 1965. Variability of wild meadow voles under various conditions of population, density, season, and reproductive activity. Ecology 46: 119–134.

Clayton, G.A., Morris, J.A., and Robertson, A. 1957. An experimental check on quantitative genetical theory. I. Short-term responses to selection. J. Genet. 55: 131–151.

Cody, M.L. 1966. A general theory of clutch size. Evolution 20: 174–184.

Cody, M.L. 1968. On the methods of resource division in grassland bird communities. Amer. Natur. 102: 107–148.

Cody, M.L. 1971. Ecological aspects of reproduction. In *Avian Biology,* Farner and King, eds. Academic Press, New York.

Cole, L.C. 1951. Population cycles and random oscillations. J. Wildl. Mgt. 15: 233–252.

Cole, L.C. 1954a. Some features of random population cycles. J. Wildl. Mgt. 18: 2–24.

Cole, L.C. 1954b. The population consequences of life history phenomena. Quart. Rev. Biol. 29: 103–137.

Collier, B.D., Cox, G.W., Johnson, A.W., and Miller, P.C. 1973. *Dynamic Ecology.* Prentice-Hall, Englewood Cliffs, New Jersey.

Connell, J.H. 1961. The influence of interspecific competition and other factors on the distribution of the barnacle *Chthamalus stellatus.* Ecology 42: 710–723.

Connell, J.H. 1970. A predator-prey system in the marine intertidal region. I. *Balanus glandula* and several predatory species of *Thais.* Ecol. Monogr. 40: 49–78.

Covich, A.P. 1976. Analyzing shapes of foraging areas: some ecological and economic theories. Annu. Rev. Ecol. Syst. 7: 235–257.

Cox, E.C. 1976. Bacterial mutator genes and the control of spontaneous mutation. Annu. Rev. Genet. 10: 135–156.

Critchfield, H.J. 1974. *General Climatology.* Prentice-Hall, Englewood Cliffs, New Jersey.

Crombie, A.C. 1944. On intraspecific and interspecific competition in larvae of graminivorous insects. J. Expt. Biol. 20: 135–166.

Crow, J.F. 1958. Some possibilities for measuring selection intensities in man. Human Biol. 30: 1–13.

Crow, J.F. 1969. Molecular genetics and population genetics. Proc. XII Intern. Congr. Genet. 3: 105–113.

Crow, J.F. and Kimura, M. 1965. Evolution in sexual and asexual populations. Amer. Natur. 99: 439–450.

Crow, J.F. and Kimura, M. 1970. *An Introduction to Population Genetics Theory*. Harper and Row, New York.

Crow, J.F. and Mange, A.P. 1965. Measurement of inbreeding from the frequency of marriages between persons of the same surname. Eugen. Quart. 12: 199–203.

Darlington, C.D. 1940. Taxonomic species and genetic systems. In *The New Systematics*, J. Huxley, ed. Clarendon Press, Oxford.

Darwin, C. 1859. *On the Origin of Species*. Murray, London.

Darwin, C. 1871. *The Descent of Man and Selection in Relation to Sex*. Murray, London.

Daubenmire, R.F. 1943. Soil temperature versus drought as a factor determining lower altitudinal limits of trees in the Rocky Mountains. Bot. Gaz. 105: 1–13.

Davidson, J. and Andrewartha, H.G. 1948. Annual trends in a natural population of *Thrips imaginis* (Thysanoptera). J. Anim. Ecol. 17: 193–199.

DeBach, P. and Smith, H.S. 1941. Are population oscillations inherent in the host-parasite relation? Ecology 22: 363–369.

Dempster, J.P. 1963. The population dynamics of grasshoppers and locusts. Biol. Rev. 38: 490–529.

Dempster, J.P. 1975. *Animal Population Ecology*. Academic Press, New York.

Dickerson, R.E. 1971. The structure of cytochrome c and the rates of molecular evolution. J. Mol. Biol. 1: 26–45.

Dickerson, R.E. 1972. The structure and history of an ancient protein. Scientific American 226: 58–72.

Dickerson, R.E. and Geis, I. 1969. *The Structure and Action of Proteins*. Harper and Row, New York.

Dobzhansky, Th. 1948. Genetics of natural populations. XVI. Altitudinal and seasonal changes produced by natural selection in certain populations of *Drosophila pseudoobscura* and *Drosophila persimilis*. Genetics 33:158–176.

Dobzhansky, Th. 1951. *Genetics and the Origin of Species*. Columbia University Press, New York.

Dobzhansky, Th. and Levene, H. 1951. Development of heterosis through natural selection in experimental populations of *Drosophila pseudoobscura*. Amer. Natur. 85: 247–264.

Dobzhansky, Th. and Pavlovsky, O. 1953. Indeterminate outcome of certain experiments on *Drosophila* populations. Evolution 7: 198–210.

Dobzhansky, Th. and Spassky, B. 1963. Genetics of natural populations. XXXIV. Adaptive norm, genetic load and genetic elite in *Drosophila pseudoobscura*. Genetics 48: 1467–1485.

Dobzhansky, Th. and Wright, S. 1943. Genetics of natural populations. X. Dispersion rates of *Drosophila pseudoobscura*. Genetics 28: 304–340.

Dobzhansky, Th., Levene, H., Spassky, B., and Spassky, N. 1959. Release of genetic variability through recombination. III *Drosophila prosaltans*. Genetics 44: 75–92.

Dobzhansky, Th., Felix, R., Guzman, J., Levine, L., Olivera, O., Powell, J.R., de la Rosa, M.E., and Salceda, V.M. 1975. Genetics of Mexican *Drosophila*. J. Heredity 66: 203–206.

Ehrman, L. 1967. Further studies on genotype frequency and mating success in *Drosophila*. Amer. Natur. 101: 415–424.

Einarsen, A.S. 1945. Some factors affecting ring-necked pheasant population density. Murrelet 26: 39–44.

Elton, C. 1924. Periodic fluctuations in the numbers of animals: their causes and effects. Br. J. Exp. Biol. 2(1): 119–163.

Elton, C. 1927. *Animal Ecology*. Sidwick and Jackson, London.

Emerson, S. and East, E.M. 1913. The inheritance of quantitative characters in maize. Nebraska Agric. Exp. Res. Bull.

Emlen, J.M. 1973. *Ecology: An Evolutionary Approach*. Addison-Wesley, Reading, Mass.

Errington, D.L. 1963. *Muskrat Populations*. Iowa State University Press, Ames, Iowa.

Ewens, W.J. 1969. *Population Genetics*. Methuen, London.

Ewens, W.J. 1977. Population genetics theory in relation to the neutralist-selectionist controversy. Adv. Human Genetics 8: 67–134.

Falconer, D.S. 1953. Selection for large and small size in mice. J. Genet. 51: 470–501.

Falconer, D.S. 1954. Validity of the theory of genetic correlation. An experimental test with mice. J. Heredity 45: 42–44.

Falconer, D.S. 1955. Patterns of response in selection experiments with mice. Cold Spring Harbor Symp. Quant. Biol. 20: 178–196.

Falconer, D.S. 1960. *Introduction to Quantitative Genetics*. Ronald Press, New York.

Feeny, P. 1970. Seasonal changes in oak leaf tannins and nutrients as a cause of spring feeding by winter moth caterpillars. Ecology 51: 565–581.

Fenchel, T. 1974. Intrinsic rate of natural increase: the relationship with body size. Oecologia 14: 317–326.

Fenchel, T. 1975. Character displacement and coexistence in mud snails (*Hydrobiidae*). Oecologia 20: 19–32.

Finney, D.J. 1947. *Probit Analysis; A Statistical Treatment of the Sigmoid Response Curve*. Cambridge University Press. 91: 229–234.

Fisher, R.A. 1918. The correlation between relatives on the supposition of Mendelian inheritance. Trans. Roy. Soc. Edinb. 52: 399–433.

Fisher, R.A. 1922. On the dominance ratio. Proc. Roy. Soc. Edinb. 52: 321–341.

Fisher, R.A. 1930. *Genetical Theory of Natural Selection*. Clarendon Press, Oxford.

Fisher, R.A. 1956. *Statistical Methods and Scientific Inference*. Oliver and Boyd, London.

Fisher, R.A. 1958. *The Genetical Theory of Natural Selection*. Dover Press, New York.

Fisher, R.A., Corbet, A.S., and Williams, C.B. 1943. The relation between the number of species and the number of individuals in a random sample of an animal population. J. Anim. Ecol. 12: 42–58.

Fitch, W.M. 1976. Molecular evolutionary clocks. In *Molecular Evolution*, F.J. Ayala, ed. Sinauer Associates, Sunderland, Mass.

Fitch, W.M. and Margoliash, E. 1967. Construction of phylogenetic trees. Science 155: 279–284.

Fitch, W.M. and Markowitz, E. 1970. An improved method for determining codon variability in a gene and its application to the rate of fixation of mutations in evolution. Biochemical Genetics 4: 579–593.

Frank, P.W., Boll, C.D., and Kelly, R.W. 1957. Vital statistics of laboratory cultures of *Daphnia pulex* (DeGeer), as related to density. Physiol. Zool. 30: 287–305.

Gaastra, P. 1958. Light energy conversion in field crops in comparison with photosynthetic efficiency under laboratory conditions. Medeleel. Landbouwhogeschool Wageningin 58(4): 1–12.

Gadgil, M. and Solbrig, O.T. 1972. The concept of r- and K- selection: evidence from wild flowers and some theoretical considerations. Amer. Natur. 106: 14–31.

Gaines, M.S. and Krebs, C.J. 1971. Genetic changes in fluctuating vole populations. Evolution 25: 702–723.

Gause, G.F. 1934. *The Struggle for Existence*. Williams and Wilkins, Baltimore.

Gause, G.F. 1935. Experimental demonstration of Volterra's periodic oscillation in the numbers of animals. J. Exp. Biol. 12: 44–48.

Gill, D.E. 1974. Intrinsic rate of increase, saturation density, and competitive ability. II. The evolution of competitive ability. Amer. Natur. 108: 103–116.

Gillespie, J.H. 1974. The role of environmental grain in the maintenance of genetic variation. Amer. Natur. 108: 831–836.

Gillespie, J.H. and Langley, C.H. 1974. A general model to account for enzyme variation in natural populations. Genetics 76: 837–848.

Gilpin, M.E. 1975. *Group Selection in Predator-Prey Communities*. Princeton University Press, Princeton.

Glass, B. and Ritterhoff, R.K. 1956. Spontaneous mutation rates at specific loci in *Drosophila* males and females. Science 124: 314–315.

Gompertz, B. 1825. On the nature of the function expressive of the law of human mortality. Phil. Trans. Roy. Soc. London. 36: 513–585.

Grant, V. 1963. *The Origin of Adaptations*. Columbia University Press, New York.

Grant, V. 1971. *Plant Speciation*. Columbia University Press, New York.

Green, M.M. 1973. Some observations and comments on mutable and mutator genes in *Drosophila*. Genetics (suppl.), 73: 187–194.

Grinnell, J. 1917. The niche-relationships of the California thrasher. Auk 34: 427–433.

Haldane, J.B.S. 1919. The combination of linkage values, and the calculation of distance between loci of linked factors. J. Genet. 8: 299–309.

Haldane, J.B.S. 1946. The interaction of nature and nurture. Ann. Eugen. 13(3): 197–205.

Haldane, J.B.S. 1957. The cost of natural selection. J. Genet. 55: 511–524.

Hamilton, W.D. 1963. The evolution of altruistic behavior. Amer. Natur. 97: 354–356.

Hamilton, W.D. 1964. The genetical evolution of social behavior. I. II. J. Theor. Biol. 7: 1–52.

Hamilton, W.J. 1937. Activity and home range of the field mouse (*Microtus pennsylvanicus*). Ecology 18: 255–263.

Hardy, G.H. 1908. Mendelian proportions in a mixed population. Science 28: 49–50.

Harper, J.L. 1967. A Darwinian approach to plant ecology. J. Ecology 55: 247–270.

Harris, H. 1966. Enzyme polymorphisms in man. Proc. Roy. Soc. London, Ser. B, 164: 298–310.

Harris, H. and Hopkinson, D.A. 1972. Average heterozygosity per locus in man: an estimate based on the incidence of enzyme polymorphism. Ann. Human Genet. 36: 9–20.

Hassell, M.P. 1970. Parasite behavior as a factor contributing to the stability of insect host parasite interactions. In Proc. Adv. Study Inst. Dynamics Popul. (Oosterbeck), P.J. den Boer and G.R. Gradwell, eds. pp. 366–379.

Hassell, M.P. 1975. Density-dependence in single-species populations. J. Anim. Ecol. 44: 283–295.

Hassell, M.P., Lawton, J.H., and May, R.M. 1976. Patterns of dynamical behavior in single-species populations. J. Anim. Ecol. 45: 471–486.

Hedrick, P.W., Ginevan, M.E., and Ewing, E.P. 1976. Genetic polymorphism in heterogeneous environments. Annu. Rev. Ecol. Syst. 7: 1–32.

Herbert, D., Elsworth, R., and Telling, R.C. 1956. The continuous culture of bacteria: a theoretical and experimental study. J. Gen. Microbiol. 14: 601–622.

Heron, A.C. 1972. Population ecology of a colonizing species: the pelagic tunicate *Thalia democratica*. II. Population growth rate. Oecologia 10: 294–312.

Hinegardner, R. 1976. Evolution of genome size. In *Molecular Evolution,* F.J. Ayala, ed. Sinauer Associates, Sunderland, Mass.

Holling, C.S. 1959a. The components of predation as revealed by a study of small-mammal predation of the European pine sawfly. Can. Entomol. 91: 293–320.

Holling, C.S. 1959b. Some characteristics of simple types of predation and parasitism. Can. Entomol. 91: 385–398.

Holling, C.S. 1965. The functional response of predators to prey density and its role in mimicry and population regulation. Mem. Entomol. Soc. Can. No. 45.

Holt, R.D. 1977. Predation, apparent competition, and the structure of prey communities. Theor. Pop. Biol. 12: 197–229.

Horn, H.S. 1968. Regulation of animal numbers: a model counter example. Ecology 49: 776–778.

Hoyer, B.H. and Roberts, R.B. 1967. Studies of DNA homology by the DNA-agar technique. In *Molecular Genetics,* pp. 425–479. Academic Press, New York.

Hubby, J.L. and Lewontin, R.C. 1966. A molecular approach to the study of genic heterozygosity in natural populations. I. The number of alleles at different loci in *Drosophila pseudoobscura*. Genetics 54: 577–594.

Huffaker, C.B. 1958. Experimental studies on predation dispersion factors and predator-prey oscillations. Hilgardia 27: 343–383.

Huffaker, C.B., Shea, K.P., and Herman, S.G. 1963. Experimental studies on predation: complex dispersion and levels of food in an acarine predator-prey interaction. Hilgardia 34: 305–330.

Hutchinson, G.E. 1948. Circular causal systems in ecology. Ann. N.Y. Acad. Sci. 50: 221–246.

Hutchinson, G.E. 1958. Concluding remarks. Cold Spring Harbor Symp. Quant. Biol. 22: 415–427.

Ivlev, V.S. 1961. *Experimental Ecology of the Feeding of Fish*. Yale University Press, New Haven.

Janzen, D.H. 1970. Herbivores and the number of tree species in tropical forests. Amer. Natur. 104: 501–528.

Jewell, P.A. 1966. The concept of home range in mammals. Symp. Zool. Soc. London 18: 85–109.

Johnson, F.M., Kanapi, C.G., Richardson, R.H., Wheeler, M.R., and Stone, W.S. 1966. An analysis of polymorphisms among isozyme loci in dark and light *Drosophila ananassae* strains from American and Western Samoa. Proc. Nat. acad. Sci. U.S.A. 56: 119–125.

Johnson, G.B. 1974. Enzyme polymorphism and metabolism. Science 184: 28–37.

Johnson, G.B. 1976. Genetic polymorphism and enzyme function. In *Molecular Evolution*, F.J. Ayala, ed. Sinauer Associates, Sunderland, Mass.

Johnson, M.S. 1971. Adaptive lactate dehydrogenase variation in the crested blenny, *Anoplorchus*. Heredity 27: 205–226.

Jolly, G.M. 1965. Explicit estimates from capture-recapture data with both death and immigration: stochastic model. Biometrika 52: 225–247.

Jones, J.S., Leith, B.H., and Rawlings, P. 1977. Polymorphism in *Cepaea*. Annu. Rev. Ecol. Syst. 8: 109–144.

Karlin, S. and Feldman, M.W. 1970. Linkage and selection: two-locus symmetric viability model. Thor. Pop. Biol. 1: 39–71.

Karn, M.N. and Penrose, L.S. 1951. Birth weight and gestation time in relation to maternal age, parity, and infant survival. Ann. Eugen. 16(1) 147–164.

Keith, L.B. 1963. *Wildlife's Ten-year Cycle*. University of Wisconsin Press, Madison.

Kermack, W.O. and McKendrick, A.G. 1939. Contributions to the mathematical theory of epidemics. V. Analysis of experimental epidemics of mouse typhoid, a bacterial disease conferring incomplete immunity. J. Hyg. 39: 271–288.

Kettlewell, H.B.D. 1958. Industrial melanism in the Lepidoptera and its contribution to our knowledge of evolution. Proc. Tenth Intern. Congr. Entomol. 2: 831–841.

Kimura, M. 1964. Diffusion models in population genetics. J. Appl. Probab. 1: 177–232.

Kimura, M. 1968. Evolutionary rate at the molecular level. Nature 217: 624–626.

Kimura, M. 1979. The neutral theory of molecular evolution. Scientific American 241: 98–129.

Kimura, M. and Crow, J.F. 1963. The measurement of effective population number. Evolution 17: 279–288.

Kimura, M. and Ohta, T. 1971a. *Theoretical Aspects of Population Genetics*. Princeton University Press, Princeton.

Kimura, M. and Ohta, T. 1971b. Protein polymorphism as a phase of molecular evolution. Nature 229: 467–469.

Kimura, M. and Ohta, T. 1973. Mutation and evolution at the molecular level. Genetics (suppl.), 73: 19–35.

Kimura, M. and Weiss, G.H. 1964. The stepping stone model of population structure and the decrease of genetic correlation with distance. Genetics 49: 561–576.

King, M. and Wilson, A.C. 1975. Evolution at two levels: molecular similarities and biological differences between humans and chimpanzees. Science 188: 107–116.

Koehn, R.K. 1969. Esterase heterogeneity: Dynamics of a polymorphism. Science 163: 943–944.

Kojima, K. 1971. Is there a constant fitness value for a given genotype? No! Evolution 25: 281–285.

Kojima, K. and Kelleher, T.M. 1961. Changes of mean fitness in random mating populations when epistasis and linkage are present. Genetics 46: 527–540.

Krebs, C.J. 1978. *Ecology*. Harper and Row, New York.

Krebs, C.J. and Myers, J.H. 1974. Population cycles in small mammals. Adv. Ecol. Res. 8: 268–399.

Krebs, C.J., Halpin, Z.T., and Smith, J.N.M. 1977. Agression, testosterone, and the spring decline in populations of the *Microtus townsendii*. Can. J. Zool. 55: 430–437.

Lack, D.L. 1947. *Darwin's Finches*. Cambridge University Press, Cambridge.

Lack, D.L. 1953. Darwin's finches. Scientific American 188: 66–72.

Lack, D.L. 1954. *The Natural Regulation of Animal Numbers*. Clarendon Press, Oxford.

Lack, D.L. 1966. *Population Studies of Birds*. Oxford University Press, New York.

Lack, D.L. 1968. *Ecological Adaptations for Breeding in Birds*. Methuen, London.

Langley, C.H. and Fitch, W.M. 1974. An examination of the constancy of the rate of molecular evolution. J. Mol. Evol. 3: 161–177.

Lawlor, L.P. and Maynard Smith, J. 1976. The coevolution and stability of competing species. Amer. Natur. 110: 79–99.

Leigh, E.G. Jr. 1973. The evolution of mutation rates. Genetics (suppl.), 73: 1–18.

Leslie, P.H. 1945. On the use of matrices in certain population mathematics. Biometrika 33: 183–212.

Leslie, P.H. 1948. Some further notes on the use of matrices in population mathematics. Biometrika 35: 213–245.

Leslie, P.H. 1958. A stochastic model for studying the properties of certain biological systems by numerical methods. Biometrika 45: 16–31.

Leslie, P.H. 1959. The properties of a certain lag type of population growth and the influence of an extreme random factor on a number of such species. Physiol. Zool. 32: 151–159.

Leslie, P.H. and Gower, J.C. 1960. The properties of a stochastic model for the predator-prey type of interaction between two species. Biometrika 47: 219–234.

Leslie, P.H. and Park, T. 1949. The intrinsic rate of natural increase of *Tribolium castaneum* Herbst. Ecology 30: 469–477.

Leslie, P.H., Park, T., and Mertz, D.B. 1968. The effect of varying the initial numbers on the outcome of competition between two *Tribolium* species. J. Anim. Ecol. 37: 9–23.

Levene, H. 1953. Genetic equilibrium when more than one ecological niche is available. Amer. Natur. 87: 331–333.

Levin, D.A. 1976. The chemical defenses of plants to pathogens and herbivores. Annu. Rev. Ecol. Syst. 7: 121–159.

Levins, R. 1968. *Evolution in Changing Environments*. Princeton University Press, Princeton.

Levins, R. 1970. Extinction. In Some Mathematical Questions in Biology. Lectures on Mathematics in the Life Sciences, American Mathematical Society 2: 77–107.

Lewontin, R.C. 1965. Selection for colonizing ability. In *The Genetics of Colonizing Species*, H.G. Baker and G.L. Stebbins, eds. Academic Press, New York.

Lewontin, R.C. 1974. *The Genetic Basis of Evolutionary Change*. Columbia University Press, New York.

Lewontin, R.C. and Hubby, J.L. 1966. A molecular approach to the study of genic heterozygosity in natural populations. II. Amount of variation and degree of heterozygosity in natural populations of *Drosophila pseudoobscura*. Genetics 54: 595–609.

Lewontin, R.C. and Kojima, K. 1960. The evolutionary dynamics of complex polymorphisms. Evolution 14: 458–472.

Li, C.C. 1953. Some general properties of recessive inheritance. Amer. J. Human Genet. 5: 269–279.

Li, C.C. 1963. Genetic aspects of consanguinity. Amer. J. Med. 34: 702–714.

Li, C.C. 1967. Genetic equilibrium under selection. Biometrics 23: 397–484.

Li, C.C. 1976. *First Course in Population Genetics*. The Boxwood Press, Pacific Grove, California.

Li, W.H. and Nei, M. 1974. Stable linkage disequilibrium without epistasis in subdivided populations. Theor. Pop. Biol. 6: 173–183.

Liebig, J. von. 1840. Organic chemistry and its applications to agriculture and physiology. Taylor and Walton, London.

Lloyd, M. 1967. 'Mean crowding.' J. Anim. Ecol. 36: 1–30.

Loschiaro, S.R. 1968. Effect of oviposition on egg production and longevity in *Trogoderman parabile* (Coleoptera: Dermestidae). Can. Entomol. 100: 86–89.

Lotka, A.J. 1925. *Elements of Physical Biology*. Reprinted 1956 by Dover Publications, New York.

Lowe, V.P.W. 1969. Population dynamics of the red deer (*Cervus elaphus* L.) on Rhum. J. Anim. Ecol. 38: 425–457.

MacArthur, R.H. 1958. Population ecology of some warblers of north-eastern coniferous forests. Ecology 39: 599–619.

MacArthur, R.H. 1968. The theory of the niche. In *Population Biology and Evolution*, R.C. Lewontin, ed. Syracuse University Press, Syracuse.

MacArthur, R.H. 1969. Patterns of communities in the tropics. Biol. J. Linn. Soc. 1: 19–30.

MacArthur, R.H. and MacArthur, J.W. 1961. On bird species diversity. Ecology 42: 594–598.

MacArthur, R.H. and Wilson, E.O. 1967. *The Theory of Island Biogeography*. Princeton University Press, Princeton.

Major, J. 1963. A climatic index to vascular plant activity. Ecology 44: 485–498.

Malecot, G. 1948. *The Mathematics of Heredity*. Masson, Paris.

Malecot, G. 1955. Decrease of relationship with distance. Cold Spring Harbor Symp. Quant. Biol. 20: 52–53.

Maly, E.J. 1969. A laboratory study of the interaction between the predator rotifer *Asplanchna* and *Paramecium*. Ecology 50: 59–73.

Maruyama, T. 1972. A note on the hypothesis: protein polymorphism as a phase of molecular evolution. J. Mol. Evol. 1: 368–370.

Mather, K. 1941. Variation and selection of polygenic characters. J. Genet. 41: 159–193.

Mather, K. and Jinks, J.L. 1971. *Biometrical Genetics*. Chapman and Hall, London.

May, R.M. 1971. Stability in multi-species community models. Math. Biosci. 12: 59–79.

May, R.M. 1973a. Time-delay versus stability in population models with two and three trophic levels. Ecology 54: 315–325.

May, R.M. 1973b. Qualitative stability in model ecosystems. Ecology 54: 638–641.

May, R.M. 1973c. Stability in randomly fluctuating versus deterministic environments. Amer. Natur. 107: 621–650.

May, R.M. 1974a. Ecosystem patterns in randomly fluctuating environments. In *Progress in Theoretical Biology,* R. Rosen and F. Snell, eds. Academic Press, New York.

May, R.M. 1974b. On the theory of niche overlap. Theor. Pop. Biol. 5: 297–332.

May, R.M. 1975a. *Stability and Complexity in Model Ecosystems.* Princeton University Press, Princeton.

May, R.M. 1975b. Biological populations obeying difference equations: stable points, stable cycles, and chaos. J. Theor. Biol. 49: 511–524.

May, R.M. 1975c. Patterns of species abundance and diversity. In *Ecology and Evolution of Communities,* M.L. Cody and J.M. Diamond, eds. The Belknap Press of Harvard University Press, Cambridge.

May, R.M. 1976. *Theoretical Ecology: Principles and Applications.* Saunders, Philadelphia.

May, R.M. and MacArthur, R.H. 1972. Niche overlap as a function of environmental variability. Proc. Nat. Acad. Sci. U.S.A. 69: 1109–1113.

May, R.M. and Oster, G.F. 1976. Bifurcations and dynamic complexity in simple ecological models. Amer. Natur. 110: 573–599.

May, R.M., Conway, G.R., Hassell, M.P., and Southwood, T.R.E. 1974. Time delays, density-dependence, and single-species oscillations. J. Anim. Ecol. 43: 747–770.

Maynard Smith, J. 1966. Sympatric speciation. Amer. Natur. 100: 637–650.

Maynard Smith, J. 1968. Evolution in sexual and asexual populations. Amer. Natur. 102: 469–473.

Maynard Smith, J. 1968. *Mathematical Ideas in Biology.* Cambridge University Press, Cambridge.

Maynard Smith, J. 1974. *Models in Ecology.* Cambridge University Press, Cambridge.

Mayr, E. 1963. *Animal Species and Evolution.* Harvard University Press, Cambridge.

McDonald, J.F. and Ayala, F.J. 1974. Genetic response to environmental heterogeneity. Nature 250: 572–574.

Mettler, L.E., Moyer, S.E., and Kojima, K. 1966. Genetic loads in cage populations of *Drosophila*. Genetics 54: 887–898.

Milkman, R.D. 1967. Heterosis as a major cause of heterozygosity in nature. Genetics 55: 493–495.

Mitscherlich, E.A. 1909. Das gesetz des minimums und das gesetz des abnehmenden bodenertrags. Landwirtsch Jahrb. 38: 537–552.

Monod, J. 1942. The growth of bacterial cultures. Annu. Rev. Microbiol. 3: 371–394.

Moran, P.A.P. 1962. *The Statistical Processes of Evolutionary Theory*. Clarendon Press, Oxford.

Mourão, C.A., Ayala, F.J., and Anderson, W.W. 1972. Darwinian fitness and adaptedness in experimental populations of *Drosophila willistoni*. Genetics 43:.552–574.

Muller, H.J. 1950. Our load of mutations. Amer. J. Human Genet. 2: 111–176.

Murdie, G. and Hassell, M.P. 1973. Food distribution, searching success, and predator-prey models. In *The Mathematical Theory of the Dynamics of Biological Populations,* M.S. Bartlett and R.W. Hiorns, eds. Academic Press, London.

Neel, J.V. 1962. Mutations in the human population. In *Methodology in Human Genetics,* W.J. Burdette, ed. Holden-Day, San Francisco.

Neel, J.V., Kodanis, M., Brewer, R., and Anderson, R.C. 1949. The incidence of consanguineous matings in Japan. Amer. J. Human Genet. 1: 156–178.

Nei, M. 1973. The theory and estimation of genetic distance. In *Genetic Structure of Populations,* N.E. Morton, ed. University of Hawaii Press, Honolulu.

Nei, M. 1975. *Molecular Population Genetics and Evolution.* Elsevier/North-Holland, Amsterdam.

Nei, M. and Chakraborty, R. 1973. Genetic distance and electrophoretic identity of proteins between taxa. J. Mol. Evol. 2: 323–328.

Nei, M. and Roychoudhury, A.K. 1974. Genic variation within and between the three major races of man, Caucasoids, Negroids, and Mongoloids. Amer. J. Human Genet. 26: 421–443.

Nevo, E. 1978. Genetic variation in natural populations: patterns and theory. Theor. Pop. Biol. 13: 121–177.

Nicholson, A.J. 1933. The balance of animal populations. J. Anim. Ecol. 2: 132–178.

Nicholson, A.J. 1948. Competition for food among *Lucilia cuprina* larvae. Proc. 8th Intern. Congr. Entomol., 277–281.

Nicholson, A.J. 1954. An outline of the dynamics of animal populations. Aust. J. Zool. 2: 9–65.

Nicholson, A.J. 1957. The self-adjustment of populations to change. Cold Spring Harbor Symp. Quant. Biol. 22: 153–173.

Nicholson, A.J. and Bailey, V.P. 1935. The balance of animal populations. Proc. Roy. Soc. London 3: 551–598.

Nisbet, R.M., Gurney, W.S.C., and Pettipher, M.A. 1977. An evaluation of linear models of population fluctuations. J. Theor. Biol. 68: 143–160.

Obeid, M. 1965. Experimental models in the study of plant competition. Ph.D. thesis, University of Wales.

O'Donald, P. 1962. The theory of sexual selection. Heredity 17: 541–552.

O'Donald, P. 1967. A general model of sexual and natural selection. Heredity 22: 499–518.

Odum, E.P. 1971. *Fundamentals of Ecology*. Saunders, Philadelphia.

Ohta, T. and Kimura, M. 1975. The effect of selected linked locus on heterozygosity of neutral alleles (the hitch-hiking effect). Genet. Res. Camb. 25: 313–325.

Orians, G.H. 1969. On the evolution of mating systems in birds and mammals. Amer. Natur. 103: 589–603.

Orians, G.H. and Solbrig, O.T. 1977. A cost-income model of leaves and roots with special reference to arid and semiarid areas. Amer. Natur. 111: 677–690.

Osborne, R.H. and DeGeorge, F.V. 1959. *Genetic Basis of Morphological Variation*. Harvard University Press, Cambridge.

Oster, G.F., Auslander, D., and Allen, J. 1976. Deterministic and stochastic effects of population dynamics. J. Dynamic Systems, Measurement, and Control, 44–48.

Paine, R.T. 1966. Food web complexity and species diversity. Amer. Natur. 100: 65–75.

Park, T. 1962. Beetles, competition, and populations. Science 138: 1369–1375.

Pearl, R. 1927. The growth of populations. Quart. Rev. Biol. 2: 532–548.

Pearson, O.P. 1966. The prey of carnivores during one cycle of mouse abundance. J. Anim. Ecol. 35: 217–233.

Penrose, L.S. 1954. Some recent trends in human genetics. Proc. 9th Intern. Congr. Genet. [Bellagio (como)], 1953, Pt. 1 (suppl. to Caryologia 6): 521–530.

Pianka, E.R. 1966. Convexity, desert lizards, and spatial heterogeneity. Ecology 47: 1055–1059.

Pianka, E.R. 1967. On lizard species diversity: North American flatland deserts. Ecology 48: 333–351.

Pianka, E.R. 1970. On r- and K- selection. Amer. Natur. 104: 592–597.

Pielou, E.C. 1977. *Mathematical Ecology.* Wiley-Interscience, New York.

Pimental, D. 1968. Population regulation and genetic feedback. Science 159: 1432–1437.

Pimental, D., Feinberg, E.H., Wood, P.W., and Hayes, J.T. 1965. Selection, spatial distribution, and the coexistence of competing fly species. Amer. Natur. 99: 97–109.

Pitelka, F.A. 1964. The nutrient-recovery hypothesis for artic microtine cycles: Introduction. In *Grazing in Terrestrial and Marine Environments,* a symposium of the British Ecological Society, D.T. Crisp, ed. Blackwell Scientific Publications, Oxford.

Powers, L. 1951. Gene analysis by the partitioning method when interactions of genes are involved. Bot. Gaz. 113: 1–23.

Pratt, D.M. 1943. Analysis of population development in *Daphnia* at different temperatures. Biol. Bull. 85: 116–140.

Preston, F.W. 1948. The commonness and rarity of species. Ecology 29: 254–283.

Pruzan, A. and Ehrman, L. 1974. Age, experience, and rare male mating advantage in *Drosophila pseudoobscura.* Beh. Genet. 4: 159–164.

Rendel, J.M. 1959. Canalization of the scute phenotype of *Drosophila.* Evolution 13: 425–439.

Rendel, J.M. and Sheldon, B.L. 1960. Selection for canalization of the scute phenotype in *Drosophila melanogaster.* Aust. J. Biol. Sci. 13: 36–47.

Richards, O.W. and Waloff, N. 1961. A study of a natural population of *Phytodecta olivacea* (Forster) (Coleoptera, Chrysomeloided). Phil. Trans. Roy. Soc., Ser. B. 244: 205–257.

Richardson, J.L. 1977. *Dimensions of Ecology.* Williams and Wilkins, Baltimore.

Ricker, W.E. 1954. Stock and recruitment. J. Fisheries Res. Board Can. 11: 559–623.

Ricklefs, E.E. 1977. On the evolution of reproductive strategies in birds: reproductive effort. Amer. Natur. 111: 453–478.

Robertson, F.W. 1955. Selection response and the properties of genetic variation. Cold Spring Harbor Symp. Quant. Biol. 20: 166–177.

Robertson, F.W. 1957. Studies in quantitative inheritance. XI. Genetic and environmental correlation between body size and egg production in *Drosophila melanogaster.* J. Genet. 55: 428–443.

Rosenzweig, M.L. 1969. Why the prey curve has a hump. Amer. Natur. 103: 81–87.

Rosenzweig, M.L. 1975. On continental steady states of species diversity. In *Ecology and Evolution of Communities,* M.L. Cody and J.M. Diamond, eds. The Belknap Press of Harvard University Press, Cambridge.

Rosenzweig, M.L. and MacArthur, R.H. 1963. Graphical representation and stability conditions of predator-prey interactions. Amer. Natur. 97: 209–223.

Roughgarden, J. 1971. Density-dependent natural selection. Ecology 52: 453–468.

Roughgarden, J. 1972. Evolution of niche width. Amer. Natur. 106: 683–718.

Roughgarden, J. 1976. Resource partitioning among competing species—a coevolutionary approach. Theor. Pop. Biol. 9: 388–424.

Russell, E.S. 1949. A quantitative histological study of the pigment found in the coat-color mutants of the house mouse. IV. The nature of the effects of genic substitution in five major allelic series. Genetics 34: 146–166.

Sandler, L. and Novitsky, E. 1957. Meiotic drive as an evolutionary force. Amer. Natur. 91: 105–110.

Sarich, V.M. and Wilson, A.C. 1967. Immunological time scale for hominid evolution. Science 158: 1200–1203.

Schaeffer, H.E. and Johnson, F.M. 1974. Isozyme allelic frequencies related to selection and gene-flow hypothesis. Genetics 77: 163–168.

Schaffer, W.M. 1974. The evolution of optimal reproductive strategies: the effects of age structure. Ecology 55: 291–303.

Schaffer, W.M. and Gadgil, M.D. 1975. Selection for optimal life histories in plants. In *Ecology and Evolution of Communities,* M.L. Cody and J.M. Diamond, eds. The Belknap Press of Harvard University Press, Cambridge.

Schlager, G. and Dickie, M.M. 1967. Spontaneous mutations and mutation rates in the house mouse. Genetics 57: 319–330.

Schoener, T.W. 1968. Sizes of feeding territories among birds. Ecology 49: 123–141.

Schoener, T.W. 1974. Resource partitioning in ecological communities. Science 185: 27–39.

Schroeder, L. 1969. Population growth efficiencies of laboratory *Hydra pseudoligactis* Hyman populations. Ecology 50: 81–86.

Shaw, R.F. and Mohler, J.D. 1953. The selective significance of the sex ratio. Amer. Natur. 87: 337–342.

Shinozaki, K. and Kira, T. 1956. Intraspecific competition among higher plants. VII. Logistic theory of the C-D effect. J. Inst. Polytech. Osaka City University D7: 35–72.

Shinozaki, K. and Kira, T. 1961. The C-D rule, its theory and practical uses. J. Biol, Osaka City University 12: 69–82.

Simberloff, D.S. and Wilson, E.O. 1970. Experimental zoogeography of islands. A two-year record of colonization. Ecology 51: 934–937.

Simpson, G.G. 1944. *Tempo and Mode in Evolution*. Columbia University Press, New York.

Singh, R.S., Lewontin, R.C., and Felton, A.A. 1976. Genetic heterogeneity within electrophoretic "alleles" of xanthine dehydrogenase in *Drosophila pseudoobscura*. Genetics 85: 609–629.

Skellam, J.G. 1951. Random dispersal in theoretical populations. Biometrika 38: 196–218.

Slobodkin, L.B. 1962. *Growth and Regulation of Animal Populations*. Holt, Rinehart, and Winston, New York.

Smith, F.E. 1961. Density dependence in the Australian thrips. Ecology 42: 403–407.

Smith, F.E. 1963. Population dynamics in *Daphnia magna* and a new model for population growth. Ecology 44: 651–663.

Smith, H.H. 1937. The relations between genes affecting size and color in certain species of *Nicotiana*. Genetics 22: 361–375.

Smouse, P.E. 1976. The implications of density-dependent population growth for frequency- and density-dependent selection. Amer. Natur. 110: 849–860.

Sokal, R.R. 1967. A comparison of fitness characters and their responses to density in stock and selected cultures of wild type and black *Tribolium castaneum*. Tribolium Inf. Bull. 10: 142–147.

Solomon, M.E. 1949. The natural control of animal populations. J. Anim. Ecol. 18: 1–35.

Southwood, T.R.E. 1966. *Ecological Methods*. Methuen, London.

Southwood, T.R.E., May, R.M., Hassell, M.P., and Conway, G.R. 1974. Ecological strategies and population parameters. Amer. Natur. 108: 791–804.

Stadler, L.J. 1942. Some observations on gene variation and spontaneous mutation. The Spragg memorial Lectures (Third Series), Mich. State College.

Stearns, S.C. 1976. Life-history tactics: a review of the ideas. Quart. Rev. Biol. 51: 3–47.

Stebbins, G.L. 1950. *Variation and Evolution in Plants*. Columbia University Press, New York.

Strobeck, C. 1973. N species competition. Ecology 54: 650–654.

Sturtevant, A.H. and Novitski, E. 1941. The homologies of the chromosome elements in the genus *Drosophila*. Genetics 26: 517–541.

Sved, J.A. 1971. An estimate of heterosis in *Drosophila melanogaster*. Genet. Res. 18: 97–105.

Sved, J.A. and Ayala, F.J. 1970. A population cage test for heterosis in *Drosophila pseudoobscura*. Genetics 66: 97–113.

Talbot, L.M. and Talbot, M.H. 1963. The wildebeest in Western Masailand, East Africa. Wildlife Monographs No. 12, 88.

Thoday, J.M. 1975. Non-Darwinian "evolution" and biological progress. Nature 255: 675–677.

Thoday, J.M. and Gibson, J.B. 1962. Isolation by disruptive selection. Nature 193: 1164–1166.

Thornthwaite, C.W. 1948. An approach toward a rational classification of climate. Geogr. Rev. 38: 55–94.

Throckmorton, L.H. 1977. *Drosophila* systematics and biochemical evolution Annu. Rev. Ecol. Syst. 8: 235–254.

Tracey, M.L. and Ayala, F.J. 1974. Genetic load in natural populations: Is it compatible with the hypothesis that many polymorphisms are maintained by natural selection? Genetics 77: 569–589.

Twomey, A.C. 1936. Climographic studies of certain introduced and migratory birds. Ecology 17: 122–132.

Ullyett, G.C. 1945. Oviposition by *Ephestia kuhniella* Zeller. J. Entomol. Soc. S. Afr. 8: 53–59.

Utida, S. 1953. Interspecific competition between two species of bean weevils. Ecology 34: 301–307.

Utida, S. 1957. Population fluctuation, an experimental and theoretical approach. Cold Spring Harbor Symp. Quant. Biol. 22: 139–151.

Uvarov, B.P. 1966. *Grasshoppers and Locusts. A Handbook of General Acridology,* Vol. 1. Cambridge University Press, London.

Vandermeer, J.H. 1969. The competitive structure of communities: an experimental appraoch with protozoa. Ecology 50: 362–371.

Varley, G.C. 1949. Population changes in German forest pests. J. Anim. Ecol. 18: 117–122.

Varley, G.C. and Gradwell, G.R. 1960. Key factors in population studies. J. Anim. Ecol. 29: 399–401.

Verhulst, P.F. 1838. Notice sur la loi que la population suit dans son accroissement. Corresp. Math. et Phys. 10: 113–121.

Vogel, F. and Chakravartti, M. 1966. ABO blood groups and smallpox in a rural population of West Bengal and Bihar (India). Humangenetik 3: 166–180.

Volterra, V. 1926. Fluctuations in the abundance of a species considered mathematically. Nature 118: 558–560.

Waaler, G.H.M. 1927. Uber die Erblichkeitsverhaltnisse der verschiedenen Arten von angeborener Rotgrunblindheit. Zeitschr. Abstgs. u. Vererbgsl. 45: 279–333.

Waddington, C.H. 1962. *New Patterns in Genetics and Development*. Columbia University Press, New York.

Wahlund, S. 1928. Zusammensetzung von population and korrelation-serscheinungen von standpunkt der vererbungslehre ans betrachtet. Hereditas 11: 65–106.

Wallace, B. 1963. The elimination of an autosomal lethal from a experimental population of *Drosophila melanogaster*. Amer. Natur. 97: 65–66.

Wallace, B. 1966. On the dispersal of *Drosophila*. Amer. Natur. 100: 551–563.

Wallace, B. and A.M. Srb. 1964. *Adaptation*. Prentice-Hall, Englewood Cliffs, New Jersey.

Weinberg, W. 1910. Weiteres Beitrage zur Theorie der Vererbung. Arch. Rass. Ges. Biol. 7: 35–49, 169–173.

Weiner, W. 1943. *Blood Groups and Transfusion*. Thomas.

Wellington, W.G. 1964. Qualitative changes in populations in unstable environments. Can. Entomol. 96: 436–451.

White, M.J.D. 1968. Models of speciation. Science 159: 1065–1070.

White, M.J.D. 1977. *Modes of Speciation*. Freeman, San Francisco.

Williams, C.B. 1964. *Patterns in the Balance of Nature*. Academic Press, London.

Williamson, M. 1972. *The Analysis of Biological Populations*. Edward Arnold, London.

Wilson, D.S. 1977. Structured demes and the evolution of group-advantageous traits. Amer. Natur. 111: 157–185.

Wilson, E.O. 1961. The nature of the taxon cycle in the Melanesian ant fauna. Amer. Natur. 95: 169–193.

Wilson, A.C. and Prager, E.M. 1974. Antigenic comparison of animal lysozymes. In *Lysozyme,* E.S.O. Osserman, R.E. Canfield and S. Beychok, eds. Academic Press, New York.

Wright, S. 1921a. Correlation and causation. J. Agric. Res. 20: 557–585.

Wright, S. 1921b. Systems of mating, I-V. Genetics 6: 111–178.

Wright, S. 1922. Coefficients of inbreeding and relationship. Amer. Natur. 56: 330–338.

Wright, S. 1931. Evolution in Mendelian populations. Genetics 16: 97–159.

Wright, S. 1937. The distribution of gene frequencies in populations. Proc. Nat. Acad. Sci. U.S.A. 23: 307–320.

Wright, S. 1938. Size of population and breeding structure in relation to evolution. Science 87: 430–431.

Wright, S. 1942. Statistical genetics and evolution. Bull Amer. Math. Soc. 48: 223–246.

Wright, S. 1943. Isolation by distance. Genetics 28: 114–138.

Wright, S. 1945. Tempo and mode in evolution: a critical review. Ecology 26: 415–419.

Wright, S. 1946. Isolation by distance under diverse systems of mating. Genetics 31: 39–59.

Wright, S. 1968, 1969, 1976. *Evolution and the Genetics of Populations*. Volumes I, II, and III. University of Chicago Press, Chicago.

Wynne-Edwards, V.C. 1962. *Animal Dispersion in Relation to Social Behavior*. Oliver and Boyd, Edinburgh and London.

Yoshimaru, H. and Mukai, T. 1979. Lack of experimental evidence for frequency-dependent selection at the alcohol dehydrogenase locus in *Drosophila melanogaster*. Proc. Nat. Acad. Sci. 76: 876–878.

Zuckerkandl, E. 1965. The evolution of hemoglobin. Scientific American 212(5): 110–118.

Answers to Problems

Chapter 1

1. (a) 0.035   (b) 20.06   2. 1/16
3. (a) 2/3   (b) $(1.10)^n \times$ weight difference at time 0
4. $dx/dt = a(B-x)$, and $x_t = B - (B - x_o)e^{-at}$ 5. $dx/dt = ax(B-x)$
6. $x_t = k_1 + k_2 e^{-2t}$ 7. (a) 64   (b) 16 hours   8. 46.4%
9. 12.5%   10. 274.4   11. 3 days
12. $dc/dt = k(a_o - c)(b_o - c)$, giving $c_t = a + (b-a)/(1 + k'e^{k(b-a)t})$
13. $y/y_o = (x/x_o)^k$ 14. (a) $x_t = (-1)^t(x_o - 2) + 2$ (b) $x_t = k_1 + k_2(-2)^t$
    (c) $x_t = k_2\cos(2\pi t/3) + k_2\sin(2\pi t/3)$
    (d) $x_t = (3)^{t/2}[k_1\cos(0.593\pi t) + k_2\sin(0.593\pi t)]$
    (e) $x_t = e^{-2t}(x_o - 2) + 2$ (f) $x_t = k_1 + k_2 e^{-3t}$
    (g) $x_t = e^{3t/2}[k_1\cos(\sqrt{3}t/2) + k_2\sin(\sqrt{3}t/2)]$
    (h) $x_t = e^{3t/2}[k_1\cos(\sqrt{11}t/2) + k_2\sin(\sqrt{11}t/2)]$
15. (a) $x_t = k_1 + k_2(-4)^t$, unstable, divergent oscillations
    (b) $x_t = k_1(6)^t + k_2$, unstable   (c) $x_t = k_1 + k_2 e^{-5t}$, stable
    (d) $x_t = k_2 e^{5t/4} + k_2$, unstable

Chapter 2

1. (a) 90   (b) 111   2. (a) 0.60   (b) 3.5
3. (a) $f(t) = ae^{-at}$ (b) 0.25   (c) 1442.8 time units
4. (a) 95.45%   (b) 2.27%   5. modes are $x = m$ and $x = m-1$
7. 1/2   8. 0.411   9. 0.423   10. 0.84.
11. (a) $P(n=4) = 1/16$; $P(n=5) = 1/8$; $P(n=6) = 5/32$; $P(n=7) = 5/32$
    (b) $P(n=4) = 16/81$; $P(n=5) = 64/243$; $P(n=6) = 160/729$; $P(n=7) = 320/2187$
12. (a) 4   (b) 9   13. 0.98
14. (a) yes   (b) 15.9 minutes
15. $b_{xy} = 0.063$, giving $\ln y = \ln y_o - (0.063)x$

Chapter 3

1. 0.225, 0.775; 0.40, 0.60; 0.60, 0.40
2. (a) 0.65 ± 0.12 (b) 0.65 ± 0.09 (c) ~ 0; 650 will undergo fixation for one allele and 350 for the other
3. 0.368   4. (a) 20   (b) 20 ± 4.5
5. (a) 0.091, 0.909   (b) no, selection against the recessive
6. (a) 0.1, 0.11, 0.19   (b) 5.9×10^4 generations
7. (a) $\hat{p} = \hat{q} = 0.5$ (b) 3.5×10^5 generations
8. no, true back mutation is just one of many mutational events that could occur among these 500 codons
9. (a) 0.16   (b) 0.07, 0.93
10. man-horse, $k_s = 8.6 \times 10^{-10}$ per year
     man-rabbit, $k_s = 12.2 \times 10^{-10}$ per year
     man-mouse, $k_s = 8.1 \times 10^{-10}$ per year
     man-carp, $k_s = 11.6 \times 10^{-10}$ per year

Chapter 4

1. (a) populations 1, 2, 5, 6   (b) pop. 1: $(\frac{1}{4}, \frac{1}{2}, \frac{1}{4})$; pop. 2: (0.14, 0.47, 0.39); pop. 5: $(\frac{1}{4}, \frac{1}{2}, \frac{1}{4})$; pop. 6: (0.55, 0.38, 0.07)   (c) one generation
2. no!   3. (a) 0.6, 0.4   (b) 0.57   (c) 0.08
4. (a) pop. 1: $p_m = 0.3$, $p_f = 0.6$, and pop. 2: $p_m = p_f = 0.5$ (b) no (c) $p_{m,1} = 0.6$, $p_{m,2} = 0.45$, $p_{m,3} = 0.525$, $p_{m,4} = 0.4875$, $p_{m,5} = 0.506$; $p_{f,t} = p_{m,t+1}$
     (d) males $(\frac{1}{2}, \frac{1}{2})$; females $(\frac{1}{4}, \frac{1}{2}, \frac{1}{4})$
5. (a) $p = q = r = 1/3$; $p^2 = q^2 = r^2 = 1/9$, $2pq = 2pr = 2qr = 2/9$ (b) $r = 0.5$, $q = 0.3$, $p = 1-q-r = 0.2$
7. $q = 1/3$ 8. $2pq \simeq 2q$ if $p \simeq 1$
10. (a) males $(\frac{1}{2}, \frac{1}{2})$, females $(\frac{1}{4}, \frac{1}{2}, \frac{1}{4})$ (b) $q/q^2 > 1$; no, $p/(p^2 + 2pq) \leqslant 1$
     (c) $q = 0.1$
12. after one generation, $f(BB) = 2/9$, $f(Bb) = 5/9$, $f(bb) = 2/9$, and $f(B_4) = 1/36$, $f(B_3b) = 8/36$, $f(B_2b_2) = 18/36$, $f(Bb_3) = 1/36$, $f(b_4) = 8/36$. At equilibrium, $f(BB) = 1/4$, $f(Bb) = 2/4$, $f(bb) = 1/4$ and $f(B_4) = 1/16$, $f(B_3b) = 4/16$, $f(B_2b_2) = 6/16$, $f(Bb_3) = 4/16$, $f(b_4) = 1/16$
13. (a) $p_1 = 0.49$; $p_2 = 0.78$ (b) expected equilibrium proportions are:
     $p_1^2 p_2^2 = 0.146$ $2p_1^2 p_2 q_2 = 0.082$ $p_1^2 q_2^2 = 0.012$ $\chi^2 = 78.1$
     $2p_1 q_1 p_2^2 = 0.304$ $4p_1 q_1 p_2 q_2 = 0.172$ $2p_1 q_1 q_2^2 = 0.024$
     $q_1^2 p_2^2 = 0.158$ $2q_1^2 p_2 q_2 = 0.089$ $q_1^2 q_2^2 = 0.013$
     (c) $h = 0.4$, $i = 0.09$, $j = 0.38$, $k = 0.13$ (d) 0.0178   (e) 3.3
14. (a) $h = 0.3875$, $i = j = 0.0625$, $k = 0.4875$
     (b) $h = 0.2025$, $i = j = 0.2475$, $k = 0.3025$
     (c) f (any zygote) = product of chromosome frequencies determined in (a)
     (d) 2.4 generations
15. (a) 0.015   (b) 0.124   (c) 0.062   16. $S_1 = 0.356$ and $S_2 = 0.127$

Chapter 5

1. $n \simeq 7$, $\bar{a} = 0.84$ 2. $n = 10.76$, $V_A = 0.030735$, $V_D \simeq 0$
3. $A_{BB} = 2aq = 6.24$; $A_{Bb} = a(q - p) = 1.04$; $A_{bb} = -2ap = -4.16$.

5. 48 to 62   6. (a) 0.59   (b) 0.65
7. genotype: *BB*   *Bb*   *bb*   *CC*   *Cc*   *cc*
   A value: 0.455   0.095   −0.265   0.120   −0.014   0.148
   D value: −0.228   0.132   0.077   −0.060   0.074   0.092
   I values: $I_{BC} = 0.040$, $I_{Bc} = 0.160$, $I_{bC} = 0.060$, $I_{bc} = 0.240$, $V_A = 0.0648$, $V_D =$
   0.0308, $V_I = 0.0096$
8. before − group 1: $\bar{x} = 3.28$, $s = 0.286$, $\bar{x}/s = 11.47$
            group 2: $\bar{x} = 6.94$, $s = 0.602$, $\bar{x}/s = 11.53$
   after − group 1: $\bar{x} = 0.5145$, $s = 0.038$
            group 2: $\bar{x} = 0.8400$, $s = 0.038$
   multiplicative

Chapter 6

1. (a) (0.489, 0.021, 0.489)   (b) ~ 5
2. (a) 1/16   (b) 0.165   (c) 0.77   3. 0.4   4. 0.045
5. (a) 0.96   (b) 0.94   (c) 0.95   (d) 0.36
7. (a) ~ 7   (b) 0.5, 0.5   8. (a) 1/32   (b) 1/64   (c) 1/8
9. (0.2513, 0.4973, 0.2513)   10. (a) (0.432, 0.336, 0.232)   (b) 0.4
11. 3.5%   12. (a) $P = 0.4677$, $Q = 0.1677$ (b) $\hat{H} = 0.364$, $\hat{F} = 0.2$
13. (a) 0.01   (b) 0.095   (c) 0; same as (b) approximately
14. $F = 0.11$ 17. (a) (9/21, 3/21, 9/21)   (b) 6
18. 10.5%, 10.8%, 11%

Chapter 7

1. (b) rectangular hyperbola   (c) $Y = 1.3$ div/hr; $u \simeq 0.2$ (d) one of the
   other (inorganic) components of the medium, secretion of toxic (perhaps acidic)
   end products of metabolism by the cells into the medium
4. (b) $E_a \simeq 10{,}114$ cal/mole   6. (a) 0.2   (b) 0.2
7. (a) 0.45   (b) 0.27   (c) 0.64   (d) 0.28   (e) 0.45
8. (a) $\bar{x} = 1.147$, $s^2 = 2.274$, $k = 1.167$ (b) 69.5, 37.6, 20.1, 10.7, 5.7, 3.0, 1.6,
   0.8, 1.0
9. (a) $D = 0.225$ (b) 1.1×10^4

Chapter 8

1. $N_2 = 1960$, $N_6 = 7530$ 2. 7.35×10^{10}
3. (a) 1.045   (b) 15.8   4. $(\lambda_p - \lambda_a)/\lambda_a = 1.24$ 5. 933
6. (a) 14.67   (b) 9256
7. (a) 6348   (b) 47.6 per year   (c) 192 years   (d) 146 years
8. $r = 0.031$, $K = 201 \times 10^6$
9.

t:	5	10	15	20	30	40	50	75	100
N_t:	275	582.5	1362.5	1506	2558.5	3453.5	4053	4804	4950

11. (a) 0.9537   (b) $e_{20} = 5.184$ age intervals; $e_{40} = 3.318$, $e_{60} = 1.694$
12. (a) 1.5   (b) 1.2 years   (c) $N_1/N_o = 1.253$, $N_2/N_1 = 1.551$, $N_3/N_2 = 1.406$,
    $N_4/N_3 = 1.413$, $N_5/N_4 = 1.412$, $N_6/N_5 = 1.412$ (d) 0.345   (e) ~5 years
13. (b) $v_o = v_1 = 2.98$, $v_2 = 1$

14. R_o = 1.2829, r = 0.085, λ = 1.08871, b = 0.00820829, d = 0.07679171, c_o = 0.99987467, c_1 = 0.00005693, c_2 = 0.00002867, c_3 = 0.00001549, c_4 = 0.00001102, c_5 = 0.00000718, c_6 = 0.00000389, c_7 = 0.00000109, c_8, = 0.00000101.

15.

time	0	1	age 2	3	4	N_t
0	200	100	0	0	0	300
1	517	188	47	0	0	752
2	1165.4	449.8	81.8	10.2	0	1707.2
3	2284.8	874	168.7	15.4	0.8	3343.7
4	3579	1370.9	262.2	25.3	0.9	5238.3
5	4672.7	1789.5	342.7	32.8	1.3	6839
6	5124.4	1962.5	375.8	36	1.4	7500.1
7	5314.7	2049.8	392.5	37.8	1.4	7769
8	5421.1	2072.7	399.7	38.3	1.5	7933.3
9	5462.4	2092.5	400	38.6	1.5	7995

16. (a) no   (b) less than 100% of the infants survive to sexual maturity

Chapter 9

5. 0.05
6. letting $b = b_o/(1 + cN)$, and $d = d_o$, then $d(\ln N)/dt = b_o/(1 + cN) - d_o$
8. $E(N \backslash 6) = 49,402$; $V(N \backslash 6) = 275,902.5$
10. upper point stable, lower point unstable
11.

	1954	1955	1956	1957	1958
k_o	0.4834	0.5398	0.4820	0.6645	0.8828
k_1	0.8572	0.6806	1.9924	0.6533	1.0778
k_2	0.2736	0.5506	0.1297	0.7856	0.2904
k_3	0.3913	0.4971	0.2609	0.1780	0.2908
K	2.0055	2.2681	2.8650	2.2814	2.5418

Chapter 10

1. would double   2. $N_1 > N_2$, meaning that $r/a > q/u$
3. $D_{max} = u\,[\,1 - \sqrt{K_s/(K_s + S)}\,]$
4. $Y_c/Y = 1 - DK_s/S\,(u-D)$, therefore $Y_c/Y \to 1$ as $D/S \to 0$
6. Consider hypothetical organism shaped like sphere with radius r. The surface area $(S) = 4\pi r^2$ and volume $(V) = (4/3)\,\pi r^3$, giving $S \propto V^{2/3}$
7. $N = K/2$
8. eq. (10.17): $1/n_a = 1/aN + t_h$
    eq. (10.18): $1/n_a = 1/a'N^2 + t_h$
9. (a) lower is stable, upper is unstable   10. $q = 0.219$
15. $a = 0.045$

Chapter 11

1. species 2 wins
2. One species or the other will ultimately become extinct as a result of chance; if $\alpha = \beta$, species inhibit each other to same extent; if $\alpha = 1/\beta$, species have identical resource preferences

3. species 1 wins
5. community A: $C = 0.814$, $H' = 1.946$
   community B: $C = 0.855$, $H' = 1.938$
6. $\Delta S_t = m_o (P - S_t)^2 - u_o S_t^2$ 7. 3.4 generations

Chapter 12

1. for $q = \frac{1}{4}$, $h = 0$, $\Delta q = -0.047$; $h = \frac{1}{2}$, $\Delta q = -0.010$; $h = 1$, $\Delta q = -0.015$
   for $q = \frac{1}{2}$, $h = 0$, $\Delta q = -0.013$; $h = \frac{1}{2}$, $\Delta q = -0.013$; $h = 1$, $\Delta q = -0.014$
   for $q = \frac{3}{4}$, $h = 0$, $\Delta q = -0.015$; $h = \frac{1}{2}$, $\Delta q = -0.010$; $h = 1$, $\Delta q = -0.005$
2. ~ 554 generations   4. (a) 0.36   (b) $\hat{q} = 1/3$ 6. 42.4
7. ~ 109 generations   8. 0.01   9. 3.5×10^{-5}

10. selection against recessive
$q = 0.01$	$\Delta q = -0.0000099$
$q = 0.10$	$\Delta q = -0.0009009$
$q = 0.50$	$\Delta q = -0.0128205$
$q = 0.90$	$\Delta q = -0.0088139$

   selection with no dominance
$q = 0.01$	$\Delta q = -0.0004954$
$q = 0.10$	$\Delta q = -0.0045454$
$q = 0.50$	$\Delta q = -0.0131578$
$q = 0.90$	$\Delta q = -0.0049450$

11. 3×10^{-6}; 6×10^{-6}
12. (a) $p_1 (AR) = 0.31$, $q_1 (CH) = 0.69$ (b) $\hat{p} = 0.7$, $\hat{q} = 0.3$
    (c) eggs: $AR/AR = 0.49$, $AR/CH = 0.42$, $CH/CH = 0.09$
    adults: $AR/AR = 0.45$, $AR/CH = 0.50$, $CH/CH = 0.05$
14. (a) $E = 0$, $\hat{x} = \frac{1}{4}$, $D = 0$ (b) $E = 1$, $\hat{x} = 0.14$ or 0.36, $D = \pm 0.11$
15. 54.8

Chapter 13

1. $\bar{p} = 0.5$, $V_p = 0.0625$ after 1 generation
   $\bar{p} = 0.5$, $V_p = 0.1094$ after 2 generations
   $\bar{p} = 0.5$, $V_p = 0.1445$ after 3 generations
2. $V_k = 3$ 3. $V_{p,5} = 0.15$, ~ 7 generations   4. $V_{p,5} = 0.155$
5. (a) $\hat{p} = 0.52$ (b) $\hat{p} = 0.62$ (c) $\hat{p} = 0.91$
6. $\hat{p} = 0.4$, $V_p = 0.04$, $P = 0.2$, $H = 0.4$, $Q = 0.4$, $\bar{V}_G = 1.6$, $V_{\bar{G}} = 0.64$, $V_G = 2.24$
7. (a) 0.5   (b) 0.4756   (c) 1   (d) 0.5, 0.055   (e) ~ 14
8. (a) 1.56   (b) 0.88   (c) 2.44   9. (a) ~ 153 (b) 0.986
10. (a) 0.89   (b) 0.41
11. one-dimensional case, $V_p = 0.0414$
    two-dimensional case, $V_p = 0.0186$
    island model, $V_p = 0.05$
12. $f(p) = Ce^{-4Ns(1-p)}p^{4Nv-1}(1-p)^{4Nu-1}$

Author Index

Subject Index